OBSERVER'S HANDBOOK 2022

USA EDITION

The Royal Astronomical Society of Canada is dedicated to the advancement of astronomy and its related sciences; this Handbook espouses the scientific method, and supports dissemination of information, discoveries, and theories based on that well-tested method.

EDITOR
JAMES S. EDGAR

ONE-HUNDRED-AND-FOURTEENTH YEAR OF PUBLICATION

ISSN 0080-4193
ISBN 978-1-927879-25-2

MIX
Paper from responsible sources
FSC www.fsc.org FSC® C103567

PRINTED IN CANADA
BY MARQUIS BOOK PRINTING INC.

TABLE OF CONTENTS

N New content   R Revised significantly

Key to Marginal Chapter Symbols

Basic Data

Time

Optics and Observing

The Sky Month by Month

Eclipses

The Moon

The Sun

Planets and Satellites

Dwarf and Minor Planets

Meteors, Comets, and Dust

Stars

The Deep Sky

LIST OF CONTRIBUTORS

JAY ANDERSON, Prairie Storm Prediction Centre, Winnipeg, Manitoba................................ (Eclipse Weather, Frequency of Nighttime Cloud Cover)

J. RANDY ATTWOOD, Mississauga, Ontario ....(Voyages in the Solar System)

CHRIS BECKETT, Regina, Saskatchewan ....(Feature Star Field, Wide-Field Wonders)

ROY BISHOP, Avonport, Nova Scotia.............................(Astronomical Precession, Binoculars, Eclipse Patterns, Electromagnetic Spectrum, Expired Stars, Filters, Interplanetary Dust, Map of the Moon, Maps of the Night Sky, Oppositions of Mars diagram, Orbital Motion, Rainbows, Saturn Ring Diagram, Sky Brightness at Midnight, Some Astronomical and Physical Data, Telescope Exit Pupils, Telescope Parameters, Tides and the Earth–Moon System, Time and Time Scales, Viewing a Solar Eclipse–A Warning)

LARRY D. BOGAN, Brooklyn Corner, Nova Scotia.........(Configurations of Jupiter's Galilean Satellites, Configurations of Saturn's Brightest Satellites)

JULIE BOLDUC-DUVAL, Thetford Mines, Québec ..(Teaching and the *Observer's Handbook*)

DEREK BREIT (IOTA*), Morgan Hill, California................................(Planetary Occultations)

RANDALL BROOKS, Halifax, Nova Scotia ....(Astronomical Twilight and Sidereal Time)

PETER BROWN, Western University, London, Ontario ....(Meteors)

IAN CAMERON, University of Manitoba, Winnipeg, Manitoba ....(Finder Charts)

MARGARET CAMPBELL–BROWN, Western University, London, Ontario............(Meteors)

DAVID M.F. CHAPMAN, Dartmouth, Nova Scotia...(Night Vision, Eyeglasses, and Observing, Some Easily Observable Nearby Stars)

AARON CLEVENSON, Humble, Texas ....(Astronomical League Observing Programs)

CHRIS CORBALLY, Vatican Observatory, Vatican City State ....(The Brightest Stars, Spectroscopy of Stars)

ROBERT DICK, Carleton University & University of Ottawa, Ottawa, Ontario........................ (Light Pollution)

DAVID W. DUNHAM (IOTA*), Greenbelt, Maryland ....(Lunar Occultations, Planetary Occultations)

MICHEL DUVAL, Montréal, Québec ....(Colored Double Stars)

ALAN DYER, Strathmore, Alberta (Deep-Sky Challenge Objects, Deep-Sky Observing Hints, The Finest NGC Objects, The Messier Catalogue)

LOUISE EDWARDS, California Polytechnic State University, San Luis Obispo, California. .... (The Deep Sky—From Near to Far)

FRED ESPENAK, Portal, Arizona...(Eclipses in 2022)

PAUL GRAY, South Greenwood, Nova Scotia...(Dark Nebulae)

RICHARD GRAY, Appalachian State University, Boone, North Carolina.(The Brightest Stars, Spectroscopy of Stars)

DANIEL W.E. GREEN, Harvard University, Cambridge, Massachusetts.................................. (Minor Planet Ephemerides, Comets in 2022)

KIM HAY, Yarker, Ontario..(Solar Observing)

TODD J. HENRY, Georgia State University, Atlanta, Georgia ....(The Nearest Stars)

DAVID HERALD (IOTA*), Murrumbateman, Australia.............................(Lunar Occultations, Planetary Occultations)

CHRISTOPHER D.K. HERD, Univ. of Alberta, Edmonton, Alberta........(Meteorite Identification)

RICHARD K. HERD, Curator (Retired) National Meteorite Collection, Ottawa, Ontario................. (Meteorite Identification)

KATHLEEN E. HOUSTON, Saskatoon, Saskatchewan.................................. (AstroSketching)

---

*International Occultation Timing Association   †American Association of Variable Star Observers

RICHARD HUZIAK, Saskatoon, Saskatchewan..(Carbon Stars)
PRANVERA HYSENI, San Jose, California ....(Guest Editorial)
PETER JEDICKE, London, Ontario ....(Star Clusters)
LEE JOHNSON, Vancouver, B.C. .... (Magnification and Contrast in Deep-Sky Observing)
STELLA KAFKA (AAVSO†), Cambridge, Massachusetts...................................(Variable Stars)
TOOMAS KARMO, Töravere, Estonia................... (The Brightest Stars, Spectroscopy of Stars)
PATRICK KELLY, Falmouth, Nova Scotia ....(Ephemeris of the Sun, Magnitudes of Naked-eye Planets, Phenomena of Jupiter's Satellites, RAs of the Sun and Planets, The Sky Month by Month (events))
DAVE LANE, Saint Mary's University, Halifax, Nova Scotia .... (Nebular Filter Transmission Chart, The Sky Month by Month (tables))
DAVID H. LEVY, Vail, Arizona ....(Deep-Sky Gems, Observing Comets)
ALISTER LING, Edmonton, Alberta .... (Deep-Sky Challenge Objects, The Sky Month by Month (lunar graphics))
BLAIR MACDONALD, Bedford, Nova Scotia ....(Polar Alignment)
BARRY F. MADORE, Carnegie Institution for Science, Pasadena, California .... (Galaxies: Brightest and Nearest, Galaxies with Proper Names)
PAUL D. MALEY, Carefree, Arizona .... (Observing Artificial Satellites)
PAUL MARKOV, Toronto, Ontario .... (The Observing Logbook)
BRIAN D. MASON, U.S. Naval Observatory, Washington, D.C......(Double and Multiple Stars)
RACHEL MATSON, U.S. Naval Observatory, Washington, D.C.....(Double and Multiple Stars)
PHILIP MCCAUSLAND, Western University, London, Ontario .... (Fireballs)
BRUCE MCCURDY, Edmonton, Alberta......(Lunar Observing, The Sky Month by Month text)
ANTHONY MOFFAT, Université de Montréal, Montréal, Québec........................(Star Clusters)
JOHN E. MOORES, York University, Toronto, Ontario.............. (Natural Satellites of the Planets)
SYUICHI NAKANO, Sumoto, Japan .... (Comets in 2022)
RON OSTROMECKI, Erie, Pennsylvania..(Carbon Stars)
MURRAY PAULSON, St. Albert, Alberta.. (The Planets in 2022)
HUGH PETT, Kelowna, British Columbia ....(Radio Astronomy and Radio Sources)
DOUGLAS PITCAIRN, Dartmouth, Nova Scotia ....(Limiting Magnitudes)
STEVE PRESTON (IOTA*), Medina, Washington .... (Planetary Occultations)
ALLAN RAHILL, Canadian Meteorological Centre, Dorval, Québec .... (Weather Resources on the Internet)
EBERHARD RIEDEL (IOTA*), München, Germany..............(Grazing Occultation Predictions)
RICHARD ROBERTS (AAVSO†), Carrollton, Virginia.......................................(Variable Stars)
WILLIAM ROBERTS, Vancouver, B.C. . (Magnification and Contrast in Deep-Sky Observing)
RANDALL ROSENFELD, Toronto, Ontario .... (Feature Star Field)
JOHN SPRAY, University of New Brunswick, Fredericton, New Brunswick.............................. (Meteorite Impact Craters of North America)
IAN STEER, Toronto, Ontario ....(Galaxies: Brightest and Nearest)
KEN TAPPING, Dominion Radio Astrophysical Observatory, Penticton, British Columbia ...... (Radio Astronomy and Radio Sources, Solar Activity)
TENHO TUOMI, Lucky Lake, Saskatchewan .... (Digital Astrophotography)
DAVID TURNER, Dartmouth, Nova Scotia ....(Astronomical Precession)
ELIZABETH O. WAAGEN (AAVSO†), Cambridge, Massachusetts ....(Variable Stars)
ALAN WHITMAN, Penticton, British Columbia....................(Southern Hemisphere Splendors)

*International Occultation Timing Association ....†American Association of Variable Star Observers

THE *OBSERVER'S HANDBOOK*

The *Observer's Handbook* is one of Canada's oldest scientific publications. Created by C.A. Chant, Professor of Astronomy at the University of Toronto, it first appeared as *The Canadian Astronomical Handbook for 1907*, a small (13 × 17 cm), 108-page publication. A second edition covered the year 1908, but for the following two years most of the information that would have appeared was published instead in installments in the *Journal of the RASC*. The Council of the Society decided to return to a separate publication for 1911 with a new name—the *Observer's Handbook*—and it has been published annually ever since.

Each year, some 11 000 copies of the Handbook are distributed to many countries throughout the world, to amateur and professional astronomers, to educators at schools and universities, and to many observatories, planetaria, and libraries. The Handbook is the main source of income for The Royal Astronomical Society of Canada. Since the first edition in 1907, the editorial team (see p. 8) and contributors (see p. 4) have voluntarily given their time and expertise every year to produce this unique book.

EDITORS OF THE *OBSERVER'S HANDBOOK*

		Position	**Editions**	**RASC President**
C.A. Chant	(1865–1956)	Editor	1907–1957	1903–1907
Frank S. Hogg	(1904–1951)	*Ass't Editor*	1939–1951	1940–1942
Ruth J. Northcott	(1913–1969)	*Ass't Editor*	1952–1957	1962–1964
		Editor	1958–1970	
John R. Percy	(1941–	Editor	1971–1981	1978–1980
Roy L. Bishop	(1939–	Editor	1982–2000	1984–1986
Rajiv Gupta	(1958–	Editor	2001–2006	2002–2004
Patrick Kelly	(1958–	Editor	2007–2011	
David M.F. Chapman	(1953–	Editor	2012–2016	
James S. Edgar	(1946–	*Ass't Editor*	2012–2016	2014–2016
		Editor	2017–	
Chris Malicki	(1949–	*Ass't Editor*	2018–	

The *Observer's Handbook* is intended to be "a companion which the observer would wish always to have in his pocket or on the table before him."

C.A. Chant, Toronto, 1906

"We believe that the *Observer's Handbook* is a truly significant contribution that Canadian astronomy in general and our Society in particular has been making to the dissemination of astronomical knowledge for half a century. I trust that it will still occupy the same position of respect after the first hundred years."

Ruth Northcott, Ottawa, 1964

"The more one knows, the more one can benefit from the Handbook. It inspires all who leaf through its pages to learn and question what the tables, graphs and data mean, perhaps to speculate on the mysteries of the Universe, and above all, to get out and look beyond our world. You have in your hands a key to the Universe—a key which will fit many doors. Please use it well and treasure it."

Peter Broughton, Toronto, 1992
Author of *Looking Up, A History of the RASC*

"The *Observer's Handbook* is the single most useful publication for the observational astronomer. Its combination of authoritative data, informative diagrams, and concise text is unique. Anyone interested in astronomy, beginner or expert, amateur or professional, student or teacher, will find the *Observer's Handbook* indispensable. Its international reputation for quality is a credit both to its many contributors and to Canadian astronomy."

Roy Bishop, Halifax, 2000

THE ROYAL ASTRONOMICAL SOCIETY OF CANADA

The beginnings of The Royal Astronomical Society of Canada go back to 1868. Then, in 1890, the Society was incorporated within the province of Ontario, received its Royal appellation from King Edward VII in 1903, and was federally incorporated in 1968. The Society Office (containing the business office and historical archives) is located at 203–4920 Dundas Street West, Toronto ON M9A 1B7; telephone: 416-924-7973 or 888-924-7272 from within Canada; email: nationaloffice@rasc.ca; website: rasc.ca.

The RASC has over 5200 members, who are from many countries and all walks of life. Members receive this *Observer's Handbook* (published every fall for the next calendar year) and electronic access to the bimonthly *Journal of the RASC*, which contains review articles, research papers on historical and contemporary topics, education notes, general notes of astronomical interest, book reviews, news items concerning the Society and its Centres, informal articles, and letters. (A print version of the *Journal* is available at a modest extra cost.) Also included in membership is *SkyNews*, Canada's popular bimonthly astronomy magazine, published by the RASC.

Membership fees are $86 per year, with a reduced rate for persons under 21 years of age (under 25, if enrolled in postsecondary education). Family memberships are also available. For members outside of Canada, dollar figures are to be read as U.S. funds, and there is an additional fee ($18 for U.S. addresses; $48 for international addresses) to cover higher mailing costs. An applicant may affiliate with one of the Centres of the Society across Canada or join the Society directly as a National Member. Membership in some Centres may require a higher fee.

The Society currently has 30 Centres located in Canada's major cities. Most Centres hold monthly meetings at which prospective members are welcome. For contact information and details on activities, visit rasc.ca/centres for the appropriate Centre website URL.

REPORTING OF ASTRONOMICAL DISCOVERIES

Historically, the worldwide center for reporting transient astronomical discoveries (including new comets, novae, unusual variable stars, interesting meteor activity, interesting planetary features, new planetary satellites, etc.) has been the Central Bureau for Astronomical Telegrams; since 1965, it has been located on the Harvard University campus. You can email discovery reports to the CBAT at cbatiau@eps.harvard.edu or cbat@iau.org, and the CBAT's Transient Objects Confirmation Page is where observers can post observations of non–Solar System transient variables and get preliminary designations (see cbat.eps.harvard.edu/unconf/tocp.html). Starting in early 2016, supernovae discoveries were moved to the "Transient Name Server" (see wis-tns.weizmann.ac.il//user/register).

All discovery reports should include your name, contact details, observation method (visual, CCD, etc.), a description of the instruments used, exposure details (if nonvisual), and the observation site. If new to reporting discoveries, you should provide background information on your observing experience. Inexperienced observers should have their observation checked before contacting CBAT.

Regarding the object itself, report the date and time (UT) of observation, RA and Dec (with equinox) of the object, its estimated magnitude (with bandpass noted), and details of its physical appearance, depending on the type of object. Incomplete discovery reports may be ignored as not being truly serious. Please review the detailed instructions at cbat.eps.harvard.edu/DiscoveryInfo.html.

To avoid false alarms, before emailing CBAT, it is highly recommended to make one or more additional observations of the object over a time period of hours or a day. Such observations may be contributed by a privately notified independent observer.

Possible new **minor planets** should be reported to the IAU Minor Planet Center (minorplanetcenter.net/iau/info/TechInfo.html), as well as astrometry on new comets.

To report a **fireball** (a meteor brighter than magnitude –5), see p. 256.

EDITOR'S COMMENTS

The Handbook is a fluid thing, changing with each issue, and this issue is no different, with the deletion of pages at the end of LUNAR OCCULTATIONS (p. 162) and an addition of pages at the end of PLANETARY OCCULTATIONS (p. 243), keeping the total at 352, but re-numbering the pages in between. Important and interesting occultation data is contained in those new pages.

Another thing that's fluid is people, and after many, many years, Dr. Brian Mason of the United States Naval Observatory is handing over the reins to his colleague, Dr. Rachel Matson, also of the USNO. Welcome aboard, Rachel! (Is that a mixed metaphor? Do ships have reins?) Brian and Rachel share the credits for this one issue. Also "Welcome aboard!" to Blake Nancarrow, who joins the Editorial Team as a Proofreader. There can never be too many eyes looking over this complicated book.

A big "Thank you!" goes out to all who contribute to the *Observer's Handbook.* This is the 114th year of publication and we couldn't do it without you!

Be sure to read ASTRONOMICAL LEAGUE OBSERVING PROGRAMS, available to all as a PDF extract from the USA Edition on the Handbook site at rasc.ca/handbook.

Clear skies!

James S. Edgar
handbookeditor@rasc.ca
Melville, Saskatchewan
2021 Sep. 14

Several other individuals and organizations played a role in the production of this Handbook. Some of the data come from the publications *Astronomical Phenomena for the Year 2022* and *The Astronomical Almanac 2022*, both prepared jointly by the U.S. Naval Observatory's Nautical Almanac Office and Her Majesty's Nautical Almanac Office.

Front cover: M20, the Trifid Nebula, and Barnard 85, the dark nebulae that cause the three lobed appearance of this unusual object, also contains a star cluster and reflection nebulae. Image acquisition and processing by Paul Gray in Pixinsight and Images Plus. Imaged data was captured with Canon T3 on a Sky-Watcher MN190 on a Sky-Watcher EQ6 mount. A total of 12 x 5-min sub frames at ISO 800 were captured on two nights, 2020 May 16 and 2021 May 14 through a small gap in the trees to the south.

Back cover: Dan Falk writes: As a Knight Science Journalism Fellow, I visited the Big Island of Hawaii in January 2012. We arranged to tour some of the telescopes at the summit of Mauna Kea. After our tours, we remained at the summit for the sunset and some night photography. Though I also had a digital camera with me, this shot is scanned from slide film (Fuji Provia 400). In this north-facing image, with an exposure time of about 40 minutes, we see stars trailing around Polaris, which stands low above the mountain (the site is a bit less than 20 degrees north of the Equator). At right are the twin domes of the W.M. Keck Observatory, and to the left is the dome of Japan's Subaru telescope.

GUEST EDITORIAL
BY PRANVERA HYSENI

The impact of science-outreach activities on future generations

Science is not just an important discipline; it touches everything in our lives and is the basis for the technology that we encounter daily. Unfortunately, many young students are turned off by STEM subjects. There are many school systems that neither prioritize science nor make it exciting, which is the reason a lot of students do not pursue STEM subjects in their career. Clearly, getting the younger generation excited about science is important for the future. The goal of science outreach is to do exactly that.

Astronomy encompasses many science disciplines, including physics (optics, the electromagnetic spectrum, the fundamental nature of matter, etc.), chemistry, engineering, and even biology as we search for extraterrestrial life. Many people don't realize the breadth of topics included in astronomy and planetary science. I believe that astronomy outreach is an ideal platform for reaching young minds. Astronomy can appeal to all ages, a fact that is obvious from the look on children's faces when they first gaze through a telescope, even if they are looking at common objects such as the Moon, Jupiter, or Saturn.

I personally have been involved with public astronomy outreach activities for the last decade. Coming from a war-torn country, Kosovo, where no advanced facilities or even basic equipment was available, I felt it was necessary to make changes. My outreach activities were mainly focused on schools and rural communities. I was surprised at the degree of interest and enthusiasm even a few small telescopes could provoke. Many of the people that were involved in our astronomy outreach activities are now either pursuing STEM-related careers or have completed advanced degrees in STEM subjects.

My Astronomy Outreach of Kosovo program has been recognized and supported by a variety of individuals and international organizations. Their contributions and donations have greatly improved our ability to provide outreach activities to our community. This demonstrates that supporting science outreach programs has major benefits, even in underdeveloped countries. I believe governments and institutions should always partner with science-outreach organizations to help provide the resources required to reach the public. This includes equipment, facilities, educational programs, and joint funding.

We, as leaders in outreach, need to find fledgling organizations around the world and help them acquire resources that will enable them to further their own outreach activities in their local communities. These resources need not be expensive. A simple telescope gifted to me ten years ago led me to develop the first astronomy organization in my country. Similar efforts can inspire millions, and can lead to STEM-related careers that will have a direct impact on their countries and on the world.

Pranvera Hyseni is a vibrant, interesting, and interested student of the world. She has travelled to numerous countries, acting as an outreach ambassador to all she encounters. She is currently pursuing her Master's degree in the Department of Earth and Planetary Sciences at the University of California, Santa Cruz.

RECOMMENDED READING, ATLASES, AND SOFTWARE

Annals of the Deep Sky, Vols. 1–6 by Jeff Kanipe and Dennis Webb, subsequent volumes (currently to No. 10) by Jeff Kanipe, hailed as successor to Burnham's Celestial Handbook; they cover constellations alphabetically. ShopAtSky.com

Astronomy, a non-technical monthly magazine for amateur astronomers (Canada and U.S.: 877-246-4835; astronomy.com).

The Backyard Astronomer's Guide (4th ed.; completely revised and expanded in 2021), by Terence Dickinson and Alan Dyer; **Nightwatch** (Revised 4th edition); **Exploring the Night Sky** (recommended for beginners), both by Terence Dickinson. Firefly Books (Canada: 800-387-6192, U.S.: 800-387-5085; fireflybooks.com).

Cambridge Double Star Atlas (2nd ed.), by Bruce MacEvoy and Wil Tirion. This spiral-bound atlas covers 2500 double and multiple stars for amateur instruments.

Catalog of the Astronomical Society of the Pacific, an excellent source of astronomical educational resources (415-337-1100; astrosociety.org).

A Field Guide to the Stars and Planets, by Jay M. Pasachoff. Houghton Mifflin Harcourt Publishing, Boston, 2016. In the Peterson Field Guides series, this classic work (also as an e-book) is packed with star maps and accessible information.

50 Things to See... by John A. Read. Eleven titles include the Moon, Small Telescopes, Medium-Sized Scopes, other languages, and the Southern Hemisphere—there's even a well-done book for kids. Available at Amazon.com and chapters.indigo.ca.

Institute of Physics, an online service for journal content. iopscience.iop.org

interstellarum Deep Sky Atlas, by Ronald Stoyan and Stephan Schurig, 2015. Full-sky atlas with a limiting magnitude of 9.5, has 15 000 deep-sky objects. **interstellarum Deep Sky Guide** by Ronald Stoyan and Uwe Glahn. This entry is designed as a companion to the Interstellarum Deep Sky Atlas, and is a rich source of deep-sky sketches for the serious observer. deep-sky-atlas.com

Sky Atlas 2000.0 (2nd ed.), by Wil Tirion and Roger Sinnott, 2000. Large format and well done. Contains 81 000 stars to mag. 8.5 and 2700 clusters, nebulae, and galaxies on 26 charts; laminated version available.

Sky & Telescope, a monthly magazine widely read by both amateur and professional astronomers (617-864-7360; skyandtelescope.org); **Pocket Sky Atlas Jumbo Edition**, by Roger W. Sinnott, 2015. Introductory atlas in large format containing 30 796 stars to mag. 7.6, many double stars, and the brighter deep-sky objects, on 80 charts. Spiral-bound, folds flat. **Binocular Highlights** by Gary Seronik, considered by many as the best binocular guide around. (888-253-0230; shopatsky.com)

SkyNews, the Canadian magazine of astronomy and stargazing, published bimonthly by the RASC—"Where Earth Meets Sky" (866-759-0005; skynews.ca)

Turn Left at Orion by Guy Consolmagno and Dan M. Davis, Cambridge University Press, 2018. "A hundred night-sky objects to see in a small telescope and how to find them." Spiral bound, it's about observing the Moon, planets, seasonal skies, and more.

2022 Night Sky Almanac, published annually by the RASC and Firefly Books and edited by Nicole Mortillaro; the ideal resource for entry-level North American sky watchers. (secure.rasc.ca/store/product/2022-night-sky-almanac)

Computer-based Planetarium Programs: Available for a variety of platforms, e.g. *Coelix*, *ECU V6.1 (Earth Centered Universe)*, *Redshift*, *Starry Night*, *TheSkyX*, *Stellarium* (freeware, except for mobile apps), and *SkySafari*.

Applications for Mobile Devices: Convenient apps for smart phones and tablets cover star charting, lunar phases, observing logs, telescope controllers, eclipse guides, aurora predictors, and much more. See iTunes (apple.com/itunes); Windows Store (microsoft.com/en-us/store/apps/windows); and Android Market (market.android.com). Also see Andrew Fraknoi's article at tinyurl.com/ybg2mzvj.

SELECTED OBSERVATORIES, *STAR PARTIES*, AND PLANETARIA

Observatories and *star parties* are ordered by longitude; planetaria are ordered alphabetically by city. Some *star party* dates are listed on p. 352.

Location	Lat.	Long.	Alt. (m/ft.)
Dark Sky Project—Lake Tekapo, New Zealand darkskyproject.co.nz	43°59′S	170°28′E	1029/3376
Australian Astronomical Observatory—Siding Spring, Australia sidingspring.com.au	31°17′S	149°04′E	1164/3819
Mount Stromlo Observatory—Canberra, Australia rsaa.anu.edu.au/observatories/mount-stromlo-observatory	35°19′S	149°00′E	767/2516
Perth Observatory—Bickley, Australia perthobservatory.com.au	32°00′S	116°08′E	380/1247
MeerKAT Radio Observatory—Carnarvon, South Africa sarao.ac.za	30°43′S	21°27′E	1051/3448
Effelsberg Radio Telescope—Effelsberg, Germany mpifr-bonn.mpg.de/effelsberg	50°31′N	6°53′E	319/1046
Greenwich Observatory—Greenwich, England rmg.co.uk/royal-observatory	51°29′N	0°00′	31/102
Lovell Radio Telescope—Jodrell Bank, England jodrellbank.net	53°14′N	2°18′W	89/292
Armagh Observatory—Armagh, Northern Ireland armagh.space	54°21′N	6°39′W	43/144
"Leviathan" Great Telescope—Birr, Ireland birrcastle.com/telescope-astronomy	53°05′N	7°54′W	59/194
Isaac Newton Group of Telescopes—La Palma, Canary Islands ing.iac.es	28°45′N	17°53′W	2336/7664
Butterpot Star Party—Butter Pot Prov. Park, Newfoundland stjohnsrasc.ca/bpsp/star-party.shtml	47°23′N	53°04′W	164/538
Burke-Gaffney Observatory—SMU, Halifax, Nova Scotia ap.smu.ca/pr/bgo	44°38′N	63°35′W	93/300
Nova East—Smileys Provincial Park, Nova Scotia halifax.rasc.ca/index.php/activities/43-nova-easr-star-party	45°01′N	63°58′W	150/492
St. Croix Observatory—St. Croix, Nova Scotia halifax.rasc.ca/index.php/observing/14-st-croix-observatory	44°57′N	64°02′W	65/213
Acadia Night Sky Festival—Bar Harbor, Maine acadianightskyfestival.org	44°23′N	68°12′W	30/96
Paranal Observatory (ESO)—Cerro Paranal, Chile eso.org/public/teles-instr/paranal-observatory	24°38′S	70°24′W	2635/8645
Las Campanas Observatory—Cerro Las Campanas, Chile lco.cl	29°00′S	70°42′W	2282/7486
La Silla Observatory (ESO)—Cerro La Silla, Chile eso.org/sci/facilities/lasilla.html	29°15′S	70°44′W	2400/7980
Gemini South Observatory—Cerro Pachon, Chile gemini.edu	30°14′S	70°44′W	2722/8930
Cerro Tololo Inter-American Observatory—Cerro Tololo, Chile ctio.noao.edu/noao	30°10′S	70°49′W	2200/7220
Mont Mégantic Observatory—Mont Mégantic, Québec omm.craq-astro.ca	45°27′N	71°09′W	1114/3654
Stellafane—Springfield, Vermont stellafane.com	43°16′N	72°31′W	393/1290
Franklin Institute Bloom Observatory—Philadelphia, Pennsylvania fi.edu/exhibit/observatory	39°58′N	75°10′W	76/250

Location	Lat.	Long.	Alt. (m/ft.)
Harrisburg Star Party—Harrisburg, Pennsylvania astrohbg.org/public-observing	40°09′N	76°54′W	165/541
Cherry Springs Star Party—Cherry Springs S.P., Coudersport, PA cherrysprings.org	41°40′N	77°49′W	704/2310
Staunton River Star Party—Halifax County, Virginia chaosastro.org/starparty	36°42′N	78°41′W	107/350
Almost Heaven Star Party—Spruce Knob, West Virginia ahsp.org	38°40′N	79°34′W	1201/3942
Green Bank Star Quest—Green Bank, West Virginia greenbankstarquest.org	38°26′N	79°50′W	803/2634
Green Bank Telescope—Green Bank, West Virginia greenbankobservatory.org	38°26′N	79°50′W	803/2634
Allegheny Observatory—Pittsburgh, Pennsylvania pitt.edu/~aobsvtry	40°29′N	80°01′W	380/1247
Winter Star Party—Camp Wesumkee, Florida scas.org/winter-star-party	24°39′N	81°19′W	1/4
Apollo Rendezvous—John Bryan State Park, Ohio mvas.org	39°48′N	83°51′W	319/1049
Great Lakes Star Gaze—Gladwin, Michigan greatlakesstargaze.com	43°58′N	84°39′W	250/820
Midsouth Star Gaze—French Camp, Mississippi rainwaterobservatory.org/events	33°17′N	89°23′W	146/479
Illinois Dark Sky Star Party—Jim Edgar Panther Creek FWA sas-sky.org	39°59′N	90°04′W	187/615
Heart of America Star Party—Butler, Missouri askc.org/events/hoasp	38°15′N	94°19′W	252/828
Nebraska Star Party—Valentine, Nebraska nebraskastarparty.org	42°36′N	100°53′W	909/2982
Okie-Tex Star Party—Camp Billy Joe, Oklahoma okie-tex.com	36°54′N	102°57′W	353/4439
Texas Star Party—Fort Davis, Texas texasstarparty.org	30°36′N	103°57′W	1542/5057
McDonald Observatory—Fort Davis, Texas mcdonaldobservatory.org	30°40′N	104°01′W	2065/6773
Rocky Mountain Star Stare—Gardner, Colorado rmss.org	37°50′N	105°11′W	2320/7612
Enchanted Skies Star Party—Magdalena, New Mexico enchantedskies.org/essp/index.html	34°05′N	107°18′W	2123/6965
Very Large Array—Socorro, New Mexico public.nrao.edu/telescopes/vla	34°05′N	107°37′W	2123/6965
Steward Observatory—Tucson, Arizona skycenter.arizona.edu	32°26′N	110°47′W	2510/8230
Fred Lawrence Whipple Observatory—Amado, Arizona www.sao.arizona.edu/FLWO/whipple.html	31°41′N	110°53′W	2554/8379
Kitt Peak National Observatory—Tucson, Arizona noao.edu/kpno	31°57′N	111°36′W	2078/6816
Alberta Star Party—Starland Recreation Campground, Alta. calgary.rasc.ca/asp.htm	51°40′N	112°54′W	698/2289

Location	Lat.	Long.	Alt. (m/ft.)
Craters of the Moon Star Party—Craters of the Moon NM nps.gov/crmo/learn/news/star-party.htm	43°27′N	113°32′W	1755/5759
Logan Pass Star Party—West Glacier, Montana bigskyastroclub.org	48°42′N	113°43′W	1963/6440
Idaho Star Party—Bruneau Dunes State Park, Idaho boiseastro.org/isp.html	42°53′N	115°43′W	771/2530
Death Valley Dark Sky Festival—Death Valley, California www.oasisatdeathvalley.com/plan/stargazing	36°27′N	116°51′W	9/28
Palomar Observatory—San Diego, California astro.caltech.edu/palomar/homepage.html	33°21′N	116°52′W	1706/5597
Jasper Dark-Sky Festival—Jasper, Alberta jasperdarksky.travel	52°54′N	118°03′W	1060/3478
Mt. Wilson Observatory—Pasadena, California mtwilson.edu	34°13′N	118°03′W	1740/5700
Table Mountain Star Party—Eden Valley, Oroville, Wash. tmspa.com	48°54′N	119°15′W	996/3268
Dominion Radio Astrophysical Observatory—Penticton, B.C. tinyurl.com/yyzaal67	49°19′N	119°37′W	545/1788
Mount Kobau Star Party—Osoyoos, British Columbia mksp.ca	49°07′N	119°40′W	1860/6102
Oregon Star Party—Ochoco National Forest, Oregon oregonstarparty.org	44°18′N	120°08′W	1499/4918
Goldendale Observatory—Goldendale, Washington parks.state.wa.us/512/Goldendale-Observatory	45°51′N	120°47′W	640/2100
Pine Mountain Observatory—Pine Mountain, Oregon pmo.uoregon.edu	43°47′N	120°57′W	1905/6250
Lick Observatory—San Jose, California mthamilton.ucolick.org	37°20′N	121°39′W	1290/4232
Golden State Star Party—Bieber, California goldenstatestarparty.org	40°08′N	120°59′W	1315/4314
Gordon Southam Observatory—Vancouver, B.C. spacecentre.ca/gordon-southam-observatory	49°16′N	123°09′W	6/21
Cowichan Valley Star Party—Bright Angel Regional Park, B.C. starfinders.ca/island-star-party	48°44′N	123°41′W	30/97
James Clerk Maxwell Telescope—Mauna Kea, Hawaii eaobservatory.org/jcmt	19°49′N	155°28′W	4092/13 426
Canada-France-Hawaii Telescope—Mauna Kea, Hawaii cfht.hawaii.edu	19°49′N	155°28′W	4204/13 793
Gemini North—Mauna Kea, Hawaii gemini.edu/pio	19°49′N	155°28′W	4213/13 824

Planetarium	Notes
Fiske Planetarium—Boulder colorado.edu/fiske 303-492-5002	Evening shows and weekend matinees; observatory available following shows for stargazing; school groups welcome
Morehead Planetarium—Chapel Hill moreheadplanetarium.org 919-962-1236	Regular programming and special events for youth, teens, and adults; science summer camps, skywatching, and starry nights
Adler Planetarium—Chicago adlerplanetarium.org 312-322-0323	Historic, first in Western Hemisphere; large collection of historic instruments; Doane Observatory on-site

Planetarium	Notes
McAuliffe-Shepard Discovery Center—Concord starhop.com 603-271-7827	Dedicated to first "Teacher In Space" who tragically died in shuttle *Challenger* disaster 1986 Jan. 28
Denver Museum of Nature and Science—Denver dmns.org 303-370-6000	Planetarium; IMAX theater; exhibit galleries; event planning and venue for large groups; programs for kids of all ages
Halifax Planetarium—Halifax astronomynovascotia.ca/index.php/planetarium 902-494-2314	Features a historic Spitz Model A-1 projector; great venue for small groups; teachers, group leaders, and individuals welcome
W.J. McCallion Planetarium—Hamilton, Ontario physics.mcmaster.ca/planetarium 905-525-9140, ext. 27777	Shows are especially geared toward a younger audience and their family members; programs include solar and nighttime viewing
Burke Baker Planetarium—Houston hmns.org/planetarium 713-639-4629	One of the Challenger Centers; dome is used for training astronauts to identify star fields; SkyScan digital stars; theatre seats 232
Samuel Oschin Planetarium—Los Angeles griffithobservatory.org/programs/soplanetarium.html 213-473-0800	Completely renovated with state-of-the-art technology; 300-seat theatre; Zeiss Mark IX star projector; and Digistar 3-laser system
Frost Museum of Science—Miami frostscience.org 305-434-9600	Frost Planetarium, with 250 seats, uses 16-million-color 8K projection; on-site food; retail store; easy access from city center
Planétarium de Montréal—Montréal espacepourlavie.ca/en/access/rio-tinto-alcan-planetarium 514-868-3000	The Rio Tinto Alcan Planetarium offers an original and innovative approach to astronomy, with two theaters resembling telescopes
Treworgy Planetarium—Mystic mysticseaport.org/explore/planetarium 860-572-0711	Celestial navigation workshops; 30-foot dome; specialized group programs; history of navigation exhibit; GPS workshop
Hayden Planetarium—New York amnh.org/our-research/hayden-planetarium 212-769-5100	At American Museum of Natural History; programs, courses, and lectures; Zeiss Mark IX Universarium Star Projector
Harry C. Kendall Planetarium—Portland omsi.edu/planetarium 503-797-4610	Fifty-two-foot domed theater with Digistar 3 projection; presentations on astronomy, space science, and lasers; school programs
James S. McDonnell Planetarium—St. Louis slsc.org 314-289-4400	The 80-foot dome houses a Zeiss Model IX; includes exhibits about living and working in space; camp-ins for the whole family
Clark Planetarium—Salt Lake City slco.org/clark-planetarium 385-468-7827	Salt Lake City's go-to destination for visitors of all ages who want to discover and learn about space and science.
Ontario Science Centre—Toronto ontariosciencecentre.ca/what-s-on 416-696-1000	Near central Toronto; OMNIMax theater; kids' sleepovers; summer day camps; home of the RASC Toronto Centre
MacMillan Planetarium—Vancouver spacecentre.ca 604-738-7827	Close to downtown Vancouver; special laser shows in summer; numerous programs for school groups of all ages; teacher packages
Albert Einstein Planetarium—Washington si.edu/theaters/planetarium 202-633-1000	At National Air and Space Museum; café; Lockheed Martin IMAX Theater; refurbished planetarium opening in 2022
Northern Lights—Watson Lake, Yukon northernlightscentre.ca 867-536-7827	All-dome video planetarium; daily shows; programs concentrate on aurora borealis and northern experience
Aldrin Planetarium—West Palm Beach sfsciencecenter.org/planetarium-shows 561-832-1988	Laser shows; telescopes; exhibits; science camps; teachers' programs; birthday party programs
Manitoba Planetarium—Winnipeg manitobamuseum.ca/main/visit/planetarium/ 204-956-2830	In central Winnipeg; science center, museum, and planetarium in one site; school programs; new Digistar 5 All-Dome projector

SELECTED INTERNET RESOURCES

The internet is an important source of astronomical information. A selection of websites together with a reference to a page number in this Handbook (if any) is given below. A listing of all websites mentioned in this Handbook, with URL links to the various sites, is available at rasc.ca/web-links.

URL	Description
aavso.org	American Association of Variable Star Observers (p. 298)
alpo-astronomy.org	Association of Lunar and Planetary Observers (p. 221)
asc-csa.gc.ca	Canadian Space Agency
astronomerswithoutborders.org	Astronomers Without Borders
astronomy.com	*Astronomy* magazine (p. 10)
astrosociety.org	Astronomical Society of the Pacific (p. 18)
cbat.eps.harvard.edu/index.html	International Astronomical Union Central Bureau for Astronomical Telegrams (p. 7)
cleardarksky.com/csk	Clear Sky Chart, by Attilla Danko (p. 78)
darksky.org	International Dark-Sky Association (p. 80)
fireball.amsmeteors.org/members/imo/report_intro	Meteorite and fireball reporting, American Meteor Society (p. 256)
heavens-above.com	Satellite tracking information, including the *International Space Station* (p. 38)
heritage.stsci.edu	Hubble Heritage Site, access to HST images
imo.net	International Meteor Organization (p. 254)
jpl.nasa.gov	Jet Propulsion Laboratory, activities for adults and kids
MrEclipse.com	Eclipse photography and safety (p. 143)
ned.ipac.caltech.edu	NASA/IPAC Extragalactic Database (p. 334)
occultations.org	International Occultation Timing Association (p. 162)
planetary.org	Planetary Society—contains over 2000 pages of information about space exploration
rasc.ca	The Royal Astronomical Society of Canada (p. 7)
rasc.ca/handbook	*Observer's Handbook* website (inside front cover)
saguaroastro.org	Saguaro Astronomy Club, includes observing list database (p. 87)
seds.org	Students for the Exploration and Development of Space
simbad.u-strasbg.fr/simbad	SIMBAD astronomical database
skyandtelescope.com	*Sky & Telescope* and Sky Publishing (p. 10)
skynews.ca	*SkyNews*—Canada's astronomy magazine, published by the RASC (p. 10)
spaceflight.nasa.gov	NASA space-flight site giving current information on ISS activities and human space flight
stsci.edu	Space Telescope Science Institute; access to Digitized Sky Survey
syfy.com/tags/bad-astronomy	Phil Plait's "Bad Astronomy" site
ui.adsabs.harvard.edu	NASA Astrophysics Data System (ADS); bibliographic database, access to millions of articles
vizier.hia.nrc.ca/viz-bin/VizieR	VizieR service; access to most astronomical catalogs

TEACHING AND THE *OBSERVER'S HANDBOOK*

BY JULIE BOLDUC-DUVAL

If you're an educator with a copy of the *Observer's Handbook*, we've got some helpful tips on how you can make use of this resource in your classroom!

This Handbook is developed to assist in observing the sky. While observing the sky with your students might not seem like an obvious activity to do during the day, there are actually many ways you can incorporate it in your teaching.

Look Up!

Astronomy is an observational science. Almost everything we know about the Universe was learned by pointing instruments at celestial objects. Your students can learn a lot by simply looking at the sky. Interesting activities and discoveries are easily designed around the many objects and phenomena that are visible just about anywhere.

You don't need a telescope or fancy equipment to make your observations. The naked eye is all you need to get started! If your students have observing equipment at home, like binoculars or telescopes, they can make use of them but there's certainly no need to buy anything new.

Plan your observations using the section THE SKY MONTH BY MONTH (p. 94). From here you can see what will be visible in the sky during any given month. Start by paying attention to when a planet or a bright star will be visible next to the Moon. When this happens, it can make identifying planets and stars an easy task, which should be fascinating to students since most them have never seen planets in the sky. With this section, you can also plan for meteor showers, learn when eclipses will take place and see the cycle of the Moon phases. It's a great way to encourage your students to start looking up more often.

Observe the Moon

Starting a few days after a new Moon, invite your students to take notice of the Moon in the evenings over the course of a few nights. They will begin to notice different lunar phases and how much they change every day. The Moon is not only visible at night—it can sometimes be observed in daylight. Invite your students to try to spot the Moon in the sky as often as possible, day or night. Have your students create a journal to help them keep track of their discoveries (see the educational resource *Looking Up!* mentioned at the end of this section).

Using the MAP OF THE MOON (p. 148), your students can identify the main maria of the Moon (the dark plains on the Moon, made from ancient lava flows) and some of the more obvious craters (the light spots, made from impacting space rocks), such as Copernicus and Tycho. Why not have them look for the *Apollo 11* landing site?

Eclipses

Solar and lunar eclipses happen as often as every six months. While it's not possible to see them all from your location, they are excellent teaching opportunities. The section ECLIPSES IN 2022 (p. 126) will provide details on all eclipses happening this year. Make sure to check each map to know which ones will be visible in your area. For a hands-on demonstration, use balls of different sizes for the Earth and the Moon, as well as a light source for the Sun, and invite your students to create eclipses, both lunar and solar.

Observing the Stars

When we think about astronomy, most people imagine observing the night sky. Unfortunately, with the light pollution in cities, not everyone can easily see stars. Whether you have access to a dark open space or not, you can use the MAPS OF THE NIGHT SKY (p. 339) to identify primary constellations, and where they are relative to one another. You can also use these maps to see differences in the sky month after month, or how different the southern sky is from the northern sky (p. 346).

This Handbook has a lot of information about stars and constellations. Here are a few interesting sections:

- List of CONSTELLATIONS—quick reference to find the names of all constellations and what they represent (p. 270)
- A table of THE BRIGHTEST STARS in our sky (pp. 275–283)
- THE NEAREST STARS—look for the distance D in light-years in the table (p. 289–290).

Did you know that the majority of nearby stars are not even visible to the naked eye? They are small, faint stars called red dwarfs. Red dwarfs are the most common type of stars in our galaxy.

Solar System

If you're looking for quick information on the planets or other celestial bodies, the section PRINCIPAL ELEMENTS OF THE SOLAR SYSTEM (p. 22) is a great place to start. For example, the table there provides the size of each planet. You can use the information to figure out how many times heavier or lighter you would be on each world, e.g. using the column Gravity, you can see that you would be almost 28 times heavier if you could stand on the Sun!

If you're interested in the history of exploring the Solar System, check out VOYAGES IN THE SOLAR SYSTEM on p. 36. You will see a list of selected space missions, both human (to the Moon and the low-Earth orbit) and probes to other planets.

The section THE PLANETS AND SATELLITES (p. 207), updated every year, offers detailed information about observing the planets. An interesting project for students with access to a telescope would be to regularly observe the four main moons of Jupiter, called the Galilean moons. Galileo was first to notice the movement of these moons in 1610, showing that not everything in the Universe revolved around the Earth. The section THE SKY MONTH BY MONTH (p. 94) has diagrams of the various positions of the Galilean satellites around Jupiter night after night.

Interesting Facts

Many lists and tables in the Handbook can be useful as references. Here we highlight a few ideas on how to use them:

- What types of objects are visible with a telescope? Get your students to explore the MESSIER CATALOGUE (p. 314) or other lists in THE DEEP SKY (p. 307). These are great places to start learning about celestial objects such as galaxies, nebulae, and star clusters.
- Did you know that many comets visit the inner Solar System every year? The list on page 264 will show you all comets expected to return in 2022. In addition to those, there are always new comets being discovered and added to the list. Unfortunately, the vast majority of these comets are not visible to the naked eye or with binoculars, and require a telescope (and a lot of patience!) to observe.

However, it is interesting to know that these celestial visitors are nearby. You could share the list with your students when discussing comets.

– Students are usually fascinated by METEORITE IMPACTS AND CRATERS. The section on this subject (p. 260) includes a list and a map of North American craters. Your students could research the one nearest them, or another of their choice, to learn about the geology of the area. Some interesting facts can be seen in the table provided, such as the age of the craters (in millions of years) and their sizes.

Be Curious

If you don't understand everything in this Handbook, don't worry and don't let it intimidate you! Astronomy is a very vast subject and there's always more to learn. Browse through each section to get a glimpse of what information is available. If something catches your attention, but seems too advanced, find more information online or in other resources mentioned in this Handbook. You can also ask your students to help you with this research—learn together!

Use your Local Experts

The Royal Astronomical Society of Canada (p. 7) has members across the country. Many of them visit classrooms regularly to talk about space or to offer demonstrations with telescopes. Local Centres also organize evening viewing activities where youth are always welcome. Don't hesitate to contact your local Centre or even the National Office to see if they can recommend someone in your area.

You should also check the list of SELECTED OBSERVATORIES, *STAR PARTIES*, AND PLANETARIA (pp. 11–14) to know the resources available in your region. Many of them offer educational activities and are happy to help kids learn about the Universe. Don't forget to check if your local college or university has an astronomy department; they might also offer outreach activities.

Educational Resources

Discover the Universe—Canadian astronomy training program for educators. Free resources and online training: discovertheuniverse.ca. We specifically recommend the educational module *Looking Up* found in the Resources section to discover educational activities related to observing the sky. All training and resources are also available in French at www.decouvertedelunivers.ca.

The Royal Astronomical Society of Canada—The RASC has compiled a list of resources for teachers rasc.ca/classroom-help. It also publishes *Skyways, Astronomy Handbook for Teachers,* rasc.ca/skyways-explorons-lastronomie.

Astronomical Society of the Pacific—An international reference for astronomy education. Lots of educational information, newsletters and activities, astrosociety.org.

AstroEDU – Educational site from the International Astronomical Union with peer-reviewed activities, astroedu.iau.org.

SkyNews – Canadian magazine of astronomy, published bimonthly by the RASC and included as a membership benefit,skynews.ca.

Canadian Space Agency – Page for educators, with resources and activities, asc-csa.gc.ca/eng/resources-young.

BASIC DATA

TERMINOLOGY AND SYMBOLS

COORDINATE SYSTEMS

Astronomical positions are usually measured in a system based on the *celestial poles* and *celestial equator*, the intersections of Earth's rotation axis and equatorial plane, respectively, and the infinite sphere of the sky. *Right ascension* (RA or α) is measured in hours (h), minutes (m), and seconds (s) of time, eastward along the celestial equator from the vernal equinox (see below). *Declination* (Dec or δ) is measured in degrees (°), minutes (′), and seconds (″) of arc, northward (N or +) or southward (S or −) from the celestial equator toward the north or south celestial pole.

Positions can also be measured in a system based on the *ecliptic*, the intersection of Earth's orbital plane and the infinite sphere of the sky. The Sun appears to move eastward along the ecliptic during the year. *Longitude* is measured eastward along the ecliptic from the vernal equinox; *latitude* is measured at right angles to the ecliptic, northward or southward toward the north or south ecliptic pole. The *vernal equinox* is one of the two intersections of the ecliptic and the celestial equator; it is the one at which the Sun crosses the celestial equator moving from south to north.

An object is *in conjunction with the Sun* if it has the same longitude as the Sun and *at opposition* if its longitude differs from that of the Sun by 180°. Mercury and Venus are in *superior* conjunction when they are more distant than the Sun and in *inferior* conjunction when they are nearer than the Sun (see the diagram on the next page). An object is *stationary* when it reaches an extreme longitude.

Two *nonsolar* objects are in conjunction if they have the same RA. Generally, but not always, close mutual approaches correspond to conjunctions; following Jean Meeus, we use the term *quasi-conjunction* to denote close (< 5°) nonconjunctional approaches.

If an object crosses the ecliptic moving northward, it is at the *ascending node* of its orbit; if it crosses the ecliptic moving southward, it is at the *descending node*.

Elongation is the geocentric angle between an object and the Sun, or between a satellite and its primary, measured in the plane formed by Earth and the other two bodies.

SYMBOLS

Solar System Objects

☉ Sun	♀ Venus	♃ Jupiter	♆ Neptune
☾ Moon	⊕ Earth	♄ Saturn	♇ Pluto
☿ Mercury	♂ Mars	⛢ Uranus	

Signs of the Zodiac

♈ Aries ..... 0°	♌ Leo ..... 120°	♐ Sagittarius ..... 240°
♉ Taurus ..... 30°	♍ Virgo ..... 150°	♑ Capricornus ..... 270°
♊ Gemini ..... 60°	♎ Libra ..... 180°	♒ Aquarius ..... 300°
♋ Cancer ..... 90°	♏ Scorpius ..... 210°	♓ Pisces ..... 330°

The Greek Alphabet

Α, α ..... alpha *(alfa)**	Η, η ..... eta	Ν, ν ..... nu *(niu)*	Τ, τ ..... tau
Β, β ..... beta	Θ, θ, ϑ ..... theta *(teta)*	Ξ, ξ ..... xi *(ksi)*	Υ, υ ..... upsilon
Γ, γ ..... gamma	Ι, ι ..... iota	Ο, ο ..... omicron	Φ, φ ..... phi
Δ, δ ..... delta	Κ, κ ..... kappa	Π, π ..... pi	Χ, χ ..... chi *(khi)*
Ε, ε ..... epsilon *(eps)*	Λ, λ ..... lambda	Ρ, ρ ..... rho	Ψ, ψ ..... psi
Ζ, ζ ..... zeta	Μ, μ ..... mu *(miu)*	Σ, σ ..... sigma	Ω, ω ..... omega

* *Variant spellings are used in some online search databases* (see aavso.org/greek-letters).

SOLAR SYSTEM GEOMETRY

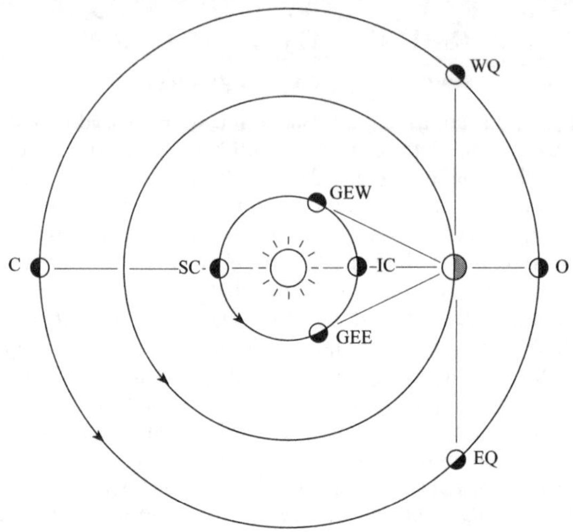

This diagram is a simplified view of the Solar System, from the north side. Earth is shown (middle orbit) together with an inferior planet (i.e. Mercury or Venus) and a superior planet (e.g. Mars). Four special geometrical configurations of the inferior planet relative to Earth are shown; in counterclockwise chronological sequence they are inferior conjunction (IC), greatest elongation west (GEW), superior conjunction (SC), and greatest elongation east (GEE). Four special configurations of the superior planet relative to Earth are also shown; in clockwise chronological sequence they are opposition (O), eastern quadrature (EQ), conjunction with the Sun (C), and western quadrature (WQ).

HANDY SKY MEASURES

Angular measure in the sky can be quickly estimated using the fingers of an outstretched arm, or by comparing with the star separations in the Big Dipper.

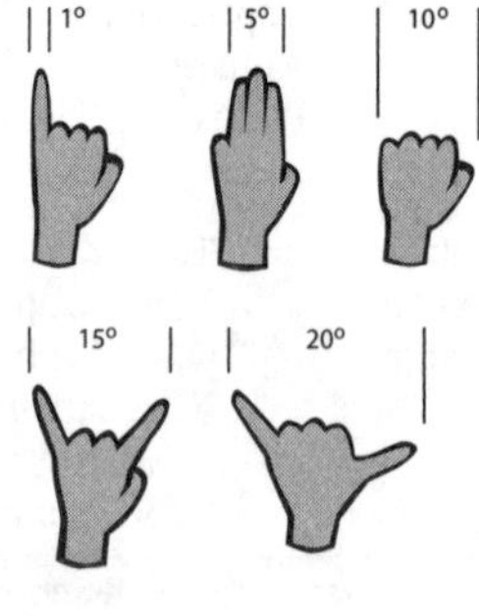

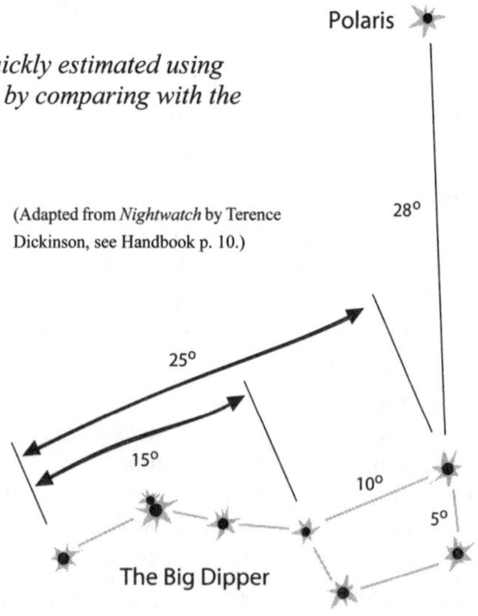

ASTRONOMICAL PRECESSION

BY DAVID TURNER AND ROY BISHOP

Physical causes of precession: The Moon, and to a lesser extent the Sun, and to a much lesser extent the other seven planets exert tidal torques on Earth's equatorial bulge, tending to align Earth's equatorial plane with those other bodies. The axis of the spinning Earth responds, not by tilting to achieve that alignment, but by slowly moving in a conical path, a motion called *precession.* The precession of a rotating body, be it a toy top or planet Earth, appears strange or counterintuitive only because we naively tend to assume that the body should behave in the same way that it would if it were not spinning. Once the spin is acknowledged, it becomes apparent that the various parts of the body are moving as expected, according to Newton's second law of motion. The off-center support force on a tilted, spinning, toy top on a table applies a torque tending to increase the tilt, and the resulting precession is in the same rotational sense as the spin. The tidal torque on Earth tends to decrease the tilt, so Earth's precession is opposite to its spin. The other planets also cause the plane of Earth's orbit, the ecliptic, to wobble a very small amount (see **Earth's rotation relative to the equinox**, p. 40). As a result of the combined precession of the equator and precession of the ecliptic, the equinoxes (the intersection points of the celestial equator and the ecliptic) drift westward (retrograde) about 50.29″ per year (a period of approximately 25 800 years).

Coordinates of celestial objects: As a consequence of precession, the locations of the celestial poles continually move along circles of radius 23.4° around the north and south ecliptic poles; consequently, the RA and Dec coordinates of even a "fixed" celestial body continually change, and must be referred to the *epoch* (i.e. Julian year date) of the equatorial grid used. Most of the positions in this Handbook are referred to J2000.0 for compatability with current star charts and atlases. In the event that a conversion of coordinates is required from one epoch to another, use the precession formulae found in ANGULAR RELATIONS, p. 32. To the accuracy that amateur computer-controlled or Go To telescopes are capable of pointing, precession may not be a significant factor, although it is always advisable to keep software and firmware up to date.

Precession and the constellations: The vernal equinox was located in the constellation Gemini 7500 years ago, in Taurus 4500 years ago, and in Aries 3000 years ago. It moved into Pisces from the "first point of Aries" around the beginning of the Christian era 2000 years ago, at roughly the same time as Hipparchus discovered precession of the equinoxes.

Precession causes stars to apparently move almost parallel to the ecliptic, relative to the vernal equinox, but our civil calendar (since the inception of the Gregorian calendar) is regularly adjusted so that the annual seasons are synchronized with the months. Consequently, *where* and *when* the constellations appear in the sky slowly change over the years. The faint stars in the 105-degree-long constellation of Hydra, the Water Snake, lay along the celestial equator 4600 years ago, but are inclined more than 30° away from the celestial equator today. With so few stars of any significance, it could only have originated as a navigational aid, helping ancient sailors steer an east-west course. In 12 000 years, the "summer" constellation Sagittarius will appear high in Northern Hemisphere winter skies, while Orion will barely rise in the summer sky.

The *shape* of a constellation is affected mainly by the relative proper motions of its member stars in the sky, and this effect on sky lore can be more interesting. The bright stars of Ursa Major, for example, bore a resemblance to the outline of a bear's head 125 000 years ago; and 4000 years ago, the bright star Arcturus was located near the center of Boötes rather than at its southern tip.

PRINCIPAL ELEMENTS OF THE SOLAR SYSTEM

PHYSICAL ELEMENTS

Object (Pronun.†‡)	Equatorial Diameter km	Oblateness	Mass Earth=1*	Density t/m³	Gravity† Earth=1	Escape Speed† km/s	Rotation Period d	Inclination‡ °	Albedo
Sun	1 392 530	0	332 946.0	1.41	27.9	617.5	25–35††		
Mercury (mûr′kū-rē)	4 879	0	0.055 274	5.43	0.38	4.2	58.6462	0.0	0.11
Venus (vē′nŭs)	12 104	0	0.815 01	5.24	0.90	10.4	–243.0185	2.6	0.65
Earth (ûrth)	12 756	1/298	1	5.513	1.00	11.2	0.997 27	23.4	0.37
Moon	3 475	0	0.012 300	3.34	0.17	2.4	27.321 66	6.7	0.12
Mars (märz)	6 792	1/170	0.107 45	3.93	0.38	5.0	1.025 96	25.2	0.15
Ceres[A] (cē′rēz)	952	1/15	0.000 157	2.08	0.028	0.5	0.3781	10.6	0.07
Jupiter (jo͞o′pĭ-tĕr)	142 984 ‡‡	1/15	317.83	1.33	2.53	59.5	0.4135†††	3.1	0.52
Saturn (săt′ûrn)	120 536 ‡‡	1/10	95.161	0.69	1.06	35.5	0.444 01	26.7	0.47
Uranus[B] (yûr′à-nŭs)	51 118 ‡‡	1/49	14.536	1.27	0.90	21.3	–0.718 33	82.2	0.51
Neptune[C] (nĕp′tyo͞on)	49 528 ‡‡	1/59	17.148	1.64	1.14	23.5	0.671 25	28.3	0.41
Pluto[A] (plo͞o′tō)	2 377	0?	0.002 184	1.82	0.067	1.3	–6.3872	60.4	0.30
Eris[A] (ĕr′ĭs)	2 400	0?	0.002 795	2.52	0.08	1.4	1.0800	44.0	0.86

†‡ Refer to p. 271 for a comprehensive pronunciation guide.
*5.972×10^{24} kg †At the equator ‡Inclination of equator to orbital plane †† Depending on latitude
‡‡At 1 atmosphere (101.325 kPa) †††For the most rapidly rotating part, the equatorial region

[A]*Dwarf planet* (see 2006 IAU Resolution B5). *Ceres* discovered by Giuseppe Piazzi, 1801 Jan. 1; *Pluto* discovered by Clyde Tombaugh, 1930 Feb. 18; *Eris* discovered by M. Brown et al., 2005 Jan. 5
[B]Discovered by William Herschel, 1781 Mar. 13
[C]Position predicted by Le Verrier (independently by Adams) and located by Johann G. Galle, 1846 Sep. 23

OSCULATING ORBITAL ELEMENTS FOR 2022

The tables at the right give the orbital elements of the planets and the 28 brightest minor planets, from the *Astronomical Almanac*. At any given time or "epoch," six basic quantities determine each body's elliptical orbit, for example:

(1) the mean distance from the Sun, a, equal to the semi-major axis of the ellipse;
(2) the eccentricity e of the ellipse;
(3) the inclination i of the orbital plane to the ecliptic;
(4) the longitude Ω of the ascending node of the orbital plane on the ecliptic;
(5) the longitude $\tilde{\omega}$ of perihelion;
(6) the body's mean longitude L at the given epoch.

The date of the ecliptic and equinox used to measure the last four quantities must also be specified, and may be different from the given epoch. Other, equivalent, parameters may be substituted: the distance q of perihelion in place of a; the argument of perihelion, $\omega = \tilde{\omega} - \Omega$, in place of $\tilde{\omega}$; or the mean anomaly, $M = L - \tilde{\omega}$, or time T of perihelion in place of L. Once six fundamental quantities are known, all other attributes of the orbit of the body, such as the sidereal period P and synodic period S, can be derived.

If the body followed a perfectly elliptical orbit as predicted by classical orbital mechanics, then for a fixed ecliptic and equinox the first five quantities above would be constant over time. However, because of perturbations caused by the gravitational influence of other bodies, the orbits are not perfectly elliptical; hence the orbital elements depend on the epoch. The given *osculating* elements can be used to determine an elliptical orbit that is a close approximation to the actual path of the body for times near the given epoch. Elements for two epochs are provided for the inner planets, 200 days apart, except that Uranus and Neptune have one date—2022 Jan. 21; the elements can be linearly interpolated to other epochs in 2022 for precision of a few arcseconds (typically 1″ or 2″), noting that multiples of 360° must be added to the second value of L if the planet completes one (or more) orbits between those dates. For selected *dwarf planets* and minor planets, elements for epoch 2022 Jan. 21 and May 1 are given as noted, with resulting precision of about 1′ (for more information, see **ssd.jpl.nasa.gov**).

HELIOCENTRIC OSCULATING ORBITAL ELEMENTS FOR 2022 REFERRED TO THE MEAN ECLIPTIC AND EQUINOX OF J2000.0

Planet	Epoch Julian Date 245...	Mean Distance* a au	Eccen-tricity e	Incli-nation i °	Long. of Asc. Node Ω °	Long. of Perihelion $\tilde{\omega}$ °	Long. at Epoch L °	Sidereal Period P y	Synodic Period† S d
For Julian Date 245 9600.5 (2022 Jan. 21.0) and JD 245 9800.5 (2022 Aug. 9.0); single dates for Uranus and Neptune.									
Mercury	9600	0.387 099	0.205 623	7.003 6	48.302 7	77.493 7	98.086 7	0.240 9	115.9
	9800	0.387 099	0.205 625	7.003 6	48.302 0	77.490 3	196.554 6	—	—
Venus	9600	0.723 345	0.006 776	3.394 4	76.619 8	131.543	127.942 3	0.615 2	583.9
	9800	0.723 326	0.006 748	3.394 4	76.617 6	131.396	88.368 3	—	—
Earth‡	9600	0.999 997	0.016 687	0.002 8	174.5	103.167 1	120.040 3	1.000 0	—
	9800	1.000 001	0.016 709	0.002 9	173.9	103.167 5	317.163 0	—	—
Mars	9600	1.523 580	0.093 391	1.847 9	49.490 2	336.241 8	256.788 5	1.880 9	779.9
	9800	1.523 770	0.093 503	1.847 9	49.489 2	336.190 1	1.594 7	—	—
Jupiter	9600	5.202 965	0.048 432	1.303 6	100.516 2	13.964 6	343.691 5	11.862 9	398.9
	9800	5.202 770	0.048 389	1.303 6	100.516 8	13.960 9	0.307 3	—	—
Saturn	9600	9.572 505	0.053 263	2.486 3	113.595 6	89.721 0	319.678 3	29.448 1	378.1
	9800	9.571 363	0.053 732	2.486 4	113.597 0	89.519 2	326.396 0	—	—
Uranus	9600	19.229 82	0.044 704	0.770 5	74.087 7	170.168 9	47.514 9	84.018 6	369.7
Neptune	9600	30.227 84	0.012 845	1.768 8	131.740 2	21.889 0	352.996 4	164.794 8	367.5

*1 au ≡ 1.495 978 707 × 10^{11} m;
† Synodic period = (product of *P*s of two planets) ÷ (difference of the *P*s)
Tabular values are relative to Earth. The periods in both columns are long-term averages, not osculating values.
‡ Values are actually for the Earth–Moon barycenter

Dwarf Planet or Minor Planet	Absolute Mag. *	Diam. km	Semi-major Axis a au	Eccen-tricity e	Incli-nation i °	Long. of Asc. Node Ω °	Long. of Perihelion $\tilde{\omega}$ °	Long. at Epoch L °	Sidereal Period P y
For Julian Date 245 9600.5 (2022 Jan. 21.0); 245 9700.5 for Eris, Pluto, and Ceres (2022 May 1).									
136199 Eris	−1.10	2400	68.054	0.433	43.820	36.046	187.312	359.003	559.6
134340 Pluto	−0.45	2377	39.639	0.248	17.115	110.302	225.121	271.611	248.5
4 Vesta	**3.20**	**525**	**2.3613**	**0.0882**	**7.142**	**103.804**	**254.895**	**261.926**	**3.6298**
1 Ceres	3.40	939	2.766	0.078	10.587	80.268	153.864	106.706	4.603
2 Pallas	4.06	502	2.7711	0.2300	34.925	172.917	123.614	36.094	4.6179
15 Eunomia	**5.28**	**248**	**2.6441**	**0.1866**	**11.752**	**292.926**	**31.558**	**184.058**	**4.2979**
3 Juno	**5.33**	**250**	**2.6688**	**0.2569**	**12.992**	**169.848**	**57.790**	**319.089**	**4.3597**
10 Hygiea	**5.43**	**434**	**3.1419**	**0.1116**	**3.831**	**283.184**	**235.677**	**204.574**	**5.5699**
7 Iris	**5.51**	**214**	**2.3866**	**0.2295**	**5.518**	**259.526**	**44.869**	**128.511**	**3.6858**
6 Hebe	**5.71**	**193**	**2.4257**	**0.2031**	**14.739**	**138.641**	**18.147**	**56.460**	**3.7760**
532 Herculina	5.81	198	2.7708	0.1788	16.296	107.448	184.074	21.244	4.6200
29 Amphitrite	**5.85**	**204**	**2.5542**	**0.0734**	**6.083**	**356.329**	**59.418**	**225.300**	**4.0841**
16 Psyche	5.90	226	2.9245	0.1339	3.097	150.032	19.252	144.380	4.9969
349 Dembowska	**5.93**	**156**	**2.9263**	**0.0905**	**8.247**	**32.200**	**16.675**	**359.633**	**4.9999**
704 Interamnia	**5.94**	**332**	**3.0563**	**0.1555**	**17.310**	**280.283**	**15.081**	**300.349**	**5.3431**
39 Laetitia	6.10	164	2.7701	0.1117	10.371	156.940	6.482	158.487	4.6090
511 Davida	6.22	289	3.1625	0.1884	15.940	107.585	84.744	126.541	5.6281
9 Metis	**6.28**	**201**	**2.3853**	**0.1236**	**5.577**	**68.900**	**75.064**	**259.627**	**3.6856**
14 Irene	**6.30**	**148**	**2.5859**	**0.1659**	**9.121**	**86.116**	**183.830**	**225.865**	**4.1587**
52 Europa	6.31	315	3.0953	0.1108	7.478	128.597	111.741	170.403	5.4430
8 Flora	**6.35**	**140**	**2.2017**	**0.1561**	**5.889**	**110.872**	**36.422**	**172.681**	**3.2683**
354 Eleonora	6.44	165	2.8034	0.1121	18.396	140.348	146.736	330.567	4.6801
22 Kalliope	6.45	166	2.9102	0.0984	13.701	65.993	63.594	97.078	4.9715
20 Massalia	**6.50**	**141**	**2.4088**	**0.1431**	**0.709**	**205.974**	**103.553**	**123.907**	**3.7429**
18 Melpomene	6.51	162	2.2958	0.2179	10.132	150.362	18.481	208.855	3.4787
451 Patientia	6.52	250	3.0674	0.0717	15.200	89.110	64.968	353.365	5.3599
196 Philomela	6.54	145	3.1150	0.0154	7.261	72.306	274.760	183.140	5.4999
89 Julia	6.60	142	2.5502	0.1847	16.128	311.547	356.592	16.401	4.0699

*Ordered by absolute magnitude, which is the hypothetical magnitude at zero phase angle with both Earth and Sun at 1 au distance. At opposition, the body will appear dimmer than this value by 2–20 mag., depending on the actual distance. Note that the largest are not always the brightest. **Bold** = opposition in or near 2022 at mag. 10 or brighter (see p. 245 for the ephemerides of these and some others).

NATURAL SATELLITES OF THE PLANETS

BY JOHN E. MOORES

Of the 205 known natural satellites of the 8 Solar System planets, all but 3 orbit the giant planets. At latest count, Jupiter has 79, Saturn has 82, Uranus has 27, and Neptune has 14. With a few exceptions, these moons may be divided into three groups, which presumably reflect their different origins. Closest to the planets are small ring moons, less than 200 km in diameter and with strong evolutionary and dynamical connections to the planetary ring systems. Many of these objects were discovered during the Voyager flybys of 1979–1989, and all are very difficult to observe from Earth. They include the Saturnian shepherd satellites Prometheus and Pandora, and the co-orbital satellites Janus and Epimetheus, all of which have been photographed from Earth (or by the *Hubble Space Telescope*) when the rings turn edge-on.

Next come the larger "regular" satellites in near-circular orbits in or near their planets' equatorial planes, thought to have been formed in situ via accretion in circumplanetary disks at the dawn of the Solar System. This group extends out to Callisto, Iapetus, Oberon, and Proteus, but does not include Triton, which is now thought to have been captured. There are numerous orbital resonances among the regular satellites, for example, Io:Europa:Ganymede (1:2:4), Mimas:Tethys (1:2), Enceladus:Dione (1:2), and Titan:Hyperion (3:4); the origin of these resonances is generally ascribed to orbital expansion driven by tidal interactions with Jupiter or Saturn. Temporary capture in similar resonances in the past may have been responsible for the anomalously large inclinations of Miranda and (perhaps) Naiad. Tidal-energy dissipation within Io is responsible for this moon's spectacular volcanic activity, and similar heating at a lower level may still occur within Europa and Enceladus.

The third and outermost group—and the group whose numbers have increased so much in recent years—comprises the "irregular"satellites. These generally small bodies (2–200 km in diameter, except for 340-km Nereid) move in quite eccentric orbits at large inclinations. Their orbits are not random; rather, they fall into several more-or-less tight clusters in semi-major axis and inclination: three or four at Jupiter (all but one retrograde), and three at Saturn (one retrograde). These clusters are believed to be due to collisional disruptions of a smaller number of original objects captured from heliocentric orbits. The situation at Uranus and Neptune remains unclear, although there are now nine Uranian irregulars (all but one retrograde) and six Neptunians (three retrograde). The orbits of the irregular satellites, along with that of Earth's Moon, are subject to strong solar gravitational perturbations, and thus maintain approximately fixed inclinations to their respective planet's orbital planes rather than to their equators.

Of the five officially recognized dwarf planets, three have satellites, for a total of eight: 134340 Pluto has five, 136108 Haumea has two, and 136199 Eris has one.

The *New Horizons* spacecraft flew by the Pluto system in July 2015 and continues to transmit data. The current diameter estimates of 134340 Pluto (2377 ±2 km) and its satellites are Charon (1210 km), Hydra and Nix (55 & 50 km in longest direction, respectively), Kerberos and Styx (19 & 16 km in longest direction, respectively). On 2019 Jan. 1, *New Horizons* flew by Kuiper belt object 2014 MU69, named "Arrokoth."

The table OBSERVABLE SATELLITES OF THE PLANETS (opposite and on p. 26) contains those satellites considered to be visually observable using typical amateur telescopes. The level of difficulty ranges from "easy" to "very challenging." For up-to-date orbital and physical elements of all the planetary satellites, see ssd.jpl.nasa.gov/?satellites.

OBSERVABLE SATELLITES OF THE PLANETS

Name (pronunciation)[1]	Mean Diameter km	GM^2 km^3/s^2	Density gm/cm^3	Visual Mag.[3]	Albedo	Mean Dist. from Planet 10^3 km	Orbital Period d	Eccentricity	Orbital Incl.[4] °	Discovery
Satellite of Earth										
Moon (mo͞on)	3475	4902.801 (1)	3.34	−12.7	0.12	384.4	27.322	0.055	5.16	—
Satellites of Mars[5]										
I Phobos (fō′bŏs)	22	0.000 711 (1)	1.9	11.4	0.07	9.38	0.319	0.015 1	1.08	A. Hall, 1877
II Deimos (dī′mŏs)	12	0.000 099 (2)	1.5	12.5	0.07	23.46	1.262	0.000 2	1.79	A. Hall, 1877
Satellites of Jupiter										
V Amalthea[6] (ăm″l–thē′ȧ)	167	0.14 (3)	0.85	14.1	0.09	181.4	0.498	0.003 2	0.38	E. Barnard, 1892
I Io[7] (ī′ō)	3643	5959.92 (1)	3.53	5.0	0.63	421.8	1.769	0.004 1	0.04	Galileo, 1610
II Europa[7] (ū–rō′pȧ)	3122	3202.74 (1)	3.01	5.3	0.67	671.1	3.551	0.009 4	0.47	Galileo, 1610
III Ganymede[7] (găn′ĕ–mēd′)	5262	9887.83 (2)	1.94	4.6	0.43	1070.4	7.155	0.001 3	0.18	Galileo, 1610
IV Callisto (kȧ–lĭs′tō)	4821	7179.29 (1)	1.83	5.7	0.17	1882.7	16.689	0.007 4	0.19	Galileo, 1610
VI Himalia[8] (hĭm′ȧ–lĭ–ȧ)	170	0.45	2.6	14.2	0.04	11 460.0	250.6	0.159	28.6	C. Perrine, 1904

[1] See pronunciation guide on p. 271
For some background on the names of the satellites, visit planetarynames.wr.usgs.gov/Page/Planets.
[2] The satellite's *standard gravitational constant*. Divide by G for mass in kg, where $G = 6.674 \times 10^{-20}$ $km^3/kg\ s^2$. The numbers in parentheses are uncertainties in the last digit.
[3] Visual magnitude at mean opposition distance.
[4] Inclinations are relative to the *Laplace Plane*, which for inner satellites (those closer than 100 planetary radii) is close to the planet's *equator*, but for most outer satellites (such as Himalia) is close to the planet's *orbital plane*. For our Moon, the inclination relative to Earth's orbital plane is 5°; relative to Earth's equator it varies between 18° and 29° in an 18.61-year cycle.
[5] The Martian satellites are so close to the primary, the use of an *occulting bar eyepiece* is recommended. For instructions on how to modify an eyepiece in this way, see skyandtelescope.com/observing/the-martian-moons-in-200708.
[6] Amalthea, the last satellite to be discovered visually, is but one example of a *very challenging* visual object, owing to its proximity to Jupiter. Amateurs using large professional telescopes have observed Amalthea and other challenging natural satellites not shown in this table.
[7] The revolutions of this trio of Jovian satellites form a *Laplace resonance*; longitudes satisfy L(Io) − 3L(Europa) + 2L(Ganymede) ≈ 180°. Also, the mean motions are such that the three periods are nearly 1:2:4.
[8] Himalia is an *irregular satellite* with a highly inclined and highly eccentric orbit that carries it well out of Jupiter's equatorial plane.

OBSERVABLE SATELLITES OF THE PLANETS (continued)

Name (pronunciation)	Mean Diameter km	*GM* km^3/s^2	Density gm/cm^3	Visual Mag.	Albedo	Mean Dist. from Planet 10^3 km	Orbital Period d	Eccen- tricity	Orbital Incl. °	Discovery
Satellites of Saturn										
I Mimas[9, 10] (mī′măs)	396	2.5026 (6)	1.15	12.8	0.6	185.5	0.942	0.0196	1.57	W. Herschel, 1789
II Enceladus[10] (ĕn–sĕl′ȧ–dŭs)	504	7.20 (1)	1.61	11.8	1.0	238.0	1.370	0.0000	0.00	W. Herschel, 1789
III Tethys[10] (tē′thĭs)	1066	41.207 (4)	0.97	10.3	0.8	294.7	1.888	0.0001	1.09	J. Cassini, 1684
IV Dione[10] (dī–ŏ′nē)	1123	73.115 (2)	1.48	10.4	0.6	377.4	2.737	0.0022	0.03	J. Cassini, 1684
V Rhea (rē′ȧ)	1529	153.943 (4)	1.23	9.7	0.6	527.1	4.518	0.0002	0.33	J. Cassini, 1672
VI Titan (ti′t’n)	5149[11]	8978.138 (2)	1.88	8.4	0.2	1221.8	15.945	0.0288	0.31	C. Huygens, 1655
VII Hyperion (hī–pēr′ĭ–ŏn)	270	0.373 (1)	0.54	14.4	0.3	1500.9	21.277	0.0232	0.62	Bond et al.[12], 1848
VIII Iapetus[13] (ī–ăp′ĕ–tŭs)	1471	120.504 (8)	1.08	11.0v	0.05–0.5	3560.9	79.330	0.0293	8.30	J. Cassini, 1671
Satellites of Uranus[14]										
V Miranda (mĭr–ănd′ă)	472	4.4 (4)	1.21	15.8	0.32	129.9	1.413	0.0013	4.34	G. Kuiper, 1948
I Ariel (âr′ē–ĕl)	1158	86. (5)	1.59	13.7	0.39	190.9	2.520	0.0012	0.04	W. Lassell, 1851
II Umbriel (ŭm′brē–ĕl′)	1169	82. (5)	1.46	14.5	0.21	266.0	4.144	0.0039	0.13	W. Lassell, 1851
III Titania (tī′tā′nē–ȧ)	1578	228. (5)	1.66	13.5	0.27	436.3	8.706	0.0011	0.08	W. Herschel, 1787
IV Oberon (ō′bȧ–rŏn)	1523	192. (7)	1.56	13.7	0.23	583.5	13.463	0.0014	0.07	W. Herschel, 1787
Satellites of Neptune										
I Triton (trī′t’n)	2707	1428. (2)	2.06	13.5	0.72	354.8	5.877	0.0000	156.9	W. Lassell, 1846

9 Mimas is another *very challenging* object, best observed when Saturn's rings are edge-on, so their glare is reduced.

10 The orbital periods of the pair Mimas:Tethys show a near-1:2 resonance, as do Enceladus:Dione.

11 As seen in the eyepiece, Titan's cloud-top diameter is 5550 km.

12 W. Bond, G. Bond, and W. Lassell

13 The highly variable magnitude of Iapatus is due to its dark and bright hemispheres, tidally locked to Saturn (see p. 233).

14 Best within 6 weeks of opposition. An occulting-bar eyepiece is recommended for Ariel and Umbriel.

ORBITAL MOTION

BY ROY BISHOP

Whether you are observing a distant galaxy, the stars in a globular cluster, the waltz of Jupiter's Galilean satellites, the drift of the Moon during an occultation, or merely uttering an expletive as an artificial satellite passes through the field of your camera, an understanding of orbital motion is central to an appreciation of the heavens.

Among early cosmologies were those of **Aristotle** (340 BC) and **Ptolemy** (published as the *Almagest*, c. 150 CE), and the superior heliocentric model proposed by **Copernicus** (*De revolutionibus*, 1543). These attempts at modeling the heavens used complex systems of circles upon circles, of eccentric deferents and epicycles. John Milton, a contemporary of Galileo, wrote the following lines in his epic poem "Paradise Lost" (1674), possibly expressing his discontent with the Ptolemaic and Copernican systems of compounded circles:

From Man or Angel the great Architect
Did wisely to conceal, and not divulge
His secrets to be scann'd by them who ought
Rather admire; or if they list to try
Conjecture, he his Fabric of the Heav'ns
Hath left to thir disputes, perhaps to move
His laughter at thir quaint Opinions wide
Hereafter, when they come to model Heav'n
And calculate the Stars, how they will wield
The mighty frame, how build, unbuild, contrive
To save appearances, how gird the Sphere
With Centric and Eccentric scribbl'd o'er,
Cycle and Epicycle, Orb in Orb.

Kepler, using observations accumulated by Tycho Brahe, broke with the 2000-year preoccupation with circles when he discovered that the planets move in an elegantly simple way along elliptical paths (*Astronomia nova*, 1609). Although he had discovered *how* the planets move, Kepler was unable to explain quantitatively *why* they move in this way.

Galileo strongly supported the Copernican heliocentric Universe (*Dialogue on the Two Chief World Systems*, 1632) and achieved brilliant insights concerning the motion of objects (*Two New Sciences*, 1638); however, he ignored Kepler's ellipses and did not apply his mechanics to the sky.

Newton united the heavens and Earth by showing that the laws governing motions on Earth also apply to the heavens. In his *Principia* (1687), the greatest book in the physical sciences, Newton presented his three laws of motion and the first ever physical force law, his law of gravitation. He used these to explain the motions not only of bodies on Earth, but also of the planets, comets, stars, equinoxes, tides, etc. Newton was the first to realize that the Moon is falling toward Earth just as freely as does an apple, and that the elliptical orbit of the center of mass of the Earth–Moon system is the path that results (as he described it) as these two bodies free-fall under the action of the Sun's gravitational force.

In popular-level explanations of phenomena involving rotary motion, such as spinning wheels, automobiles on corners, tides, and orbital motion, "centrifugal force" is usually invoked. That is unfortunate because centrifugal force is a fiction, and its use in a popular description of motion obscures understanding.[*]

[*]Brief descriptions of tides in the Newtonian context (without invoking the obfuscating centrifugal force!) and in the context of the general theory of relativity appear on p. 179 and p. 183, respectively.

In the case of orbits, the common misconception is that the inward gravitational force is balanced by an outward "centrifugal force." Newton's view is simpler: There is only one force, the inward pull of gravity. There is *no physical agent* to cause an outward force. (Note that forces cause accelerations, not vice versa.) Also, if there *were* an outward supporting force, the two forces would cancel and, as Galileo realized, the body would then move along a straight line. If you choose a rotating reference frame and then ignore the rotation (mistake no. 1), you have to pretend there is a "centrifugal force" (mistake no. 2) in order to make sense of motions occurring within that frame. The two mistakes effectively cancel, but the description has been made needlessly complicated, and if you do not realize what you have done, you do not understand the motion.

Einstein's general theory of relativity (GTR) of 1915 superseded Newton's description of gravity. The arbiter of which is a good theory and which theory is wrong is nature. Newton's laws are accurate enough for most of NASA's calculations, but they do not work exactly. For example, if the computer programs used in the Global Positioning System (GPS) were based on Newton's gravitation, the system would be a multibillion-dollar boondoggle. Einstein's conception of gravitation is essential to the operation of this satellite-based navigation system. In the case of strong gravitation and/or speeds approaching the speed of light, Newton's laws fail dramatically. The GTR may be wrong too, but so far it has passed all experimental tests. Science does not hie after ultimate explanations or "truth"; its goal is a rational, coherent description of the measurable physical world, a description that has beauty in its simplicity, a description that makes sense. In the courtroom of nature, any aspect of science is falsifiable. Modern technology is making possible increasingly precise tests of general relativity (for instance, see einstein.stanford.edu, and also *Phys. Rev. Lett. 116*, 061102, 2016 and *ApJ 848*:L12, 2017).

According to Einstein's GTR, gravitation is not a mysterious force that one mass exerts upon a distant mass; gravitation is the geometry (non-Euclidean) of the 4-dimensional spacetime within which we and the stars exist. Golf balls (if air friction is ignored), satellites, planets, stars, and light follow *geodesics*, the straightest possible, force-free paths through a spacetime whose geometry is shaped by mass–energy. The difficulty in intellectually grasping a non-Euclidean spacetime originates with us. Common sense is inadequate. That is not surprising, given that our common sense is based on the Euclidean, three-dimensional geometry of straight lines, rectangles, and spheres we learned in the crib by age two. The underlying cause of our delusion is that our senses and thought processes are constrained by the speed of neuron signals. Compared to light, neuron signals ooze along at a very slow rate, about one ten-millionth the speed of light. Consequently, to us a second of time is brief, light looks instantaneous, relativistic effects seem foreign, and time appears to be independent of space.

Gravitation is geometry. That is why no one has ever felt a force of gravity. Like the centrifugal force, it never did exist. A force of gravity was the glue Newton invented to make his naïve, Euclidean, space-plus-time model of the Universe approximate reality. Newton himself was well aware of the unsatisfactory nature of several of his assumptions, far more so than most people who came after him.

When you release a coin from your hand, you see the coin "fall" because the contact force of the ground on your feet (the *only* force you feel) accelerates you the other way. An orbiting astronaut experiences no such force, so he or she remains beside a released coin. Orbital motion could not be simpler—*no* forces are involved.

What would Milton have written had he been familiar with the conjectures of Newton and Einstein?

SOME ASTRONOMICAL AND PHYSICAL DATA

BY ROY BISHOP

Many of the numbers listed below are based on measurement. Exceptions include defined quantities (indicated by ≡), quantities calculated from defined quantities (e.g. m/ly, au/pc), and numbers of mathematical origin such as π and conversion factors in angular measure. Of those based on measurement, some are known to only approximate precision and the equal sign is reduced to ≈. Many others are known to quite high precision (the uncertainties occur after the last digit given), and several are from "the 2018 CODATA recommended values of the fundamental physical constants" (see physics.nist.gov/cuu/Constants). The units (Système International, SI, where possible) symbols, and nomenclature are based on recommendations of the International Astronomical Union and the International Union of Pure and Applied Physics.

LENGTH

1 metre (m) ≡ the distance traveled by light in a vacuum in $(299\,792\,458)^{-1}$ s

1 astronomical unit (au)	≡ $1.495\,978\,707 \times 10^{11}$ m = 499.0047... light-s
1 light-year (ly)	= $9.4607... \times 10^{15}$ m (based on average Julian year)
	= 63 241 au (63 360 inches = 1 mile)
1 parsec (pc)	= $3.085\,678 \times 10^{16}$ m = 206 264.8 au = 3.261 564 ly
1 mile*	≡ 1.609 344 km
1 micron*	≡ 1 μm
1 angstrom*	≡ 0.1 nm

*Indicates deprecated unit; unit on right is preferred

TIME

1 second (s) ≡ 9 192 631 770 periods of the radiation involved in the unperturbed transition between the two hyperfine levels of the ground state of the ^{133}Cs atom

Day:	Mean sidereal (equinox to equinox)	= 86 164.0904 s
	Mean rotation (fixed star to fixed star)	= 86 164.0988 s
	Day (d)	≡ 86 400. s
	Mean solar	= 86 399.9999 s
Month:	Draconic (node to node)	= 27.212 221 d
	Tropical (equinox to equinox)	= 27.321 582 d
	Sidereal (fixed star to fixed star)	= 27.321 662 d
	Anomalistic (perigee to perigee)	= 27.554 550 d
	Synodic (new Moon to new Moon)	= 29.530 589 d
Year:	Eclipse (lunar node to lunar node)	= 346.620 082 d
	Tropical (equinox to equinox) (y)	= 365.242 189 d
	Average Gregorian	≡ 365.242 5 d
	Average Julian	≡ 365.25 d
	Sidereal (fixed star to fixed star)	= 365.256 363 d
	Anomalistic (perihelion to perihelion)	= 365.259 636 d

EARTH

Mass, $M_E = 5.972 \times 10^{24}$ kg   Age ≈ 4.6 Gy   Central T ≈ 5000 K to 6000 K

Geocentric gravitational constant, $GM_E = 3.986\,004\,42 \times 10^{14}$ m³/s²

Radius: Equatorial, a = 6378.14 km   Polar, b = 6356.75 km

Mean = $(a^2b)^{1/3}$ = 6371.00 km   Of metallic core = 3475 km

Solar parallax = 8.794 15″ (Earth equatorial radius ÷ 1 au)

1° of latitude = 111.132 95 − 0.559 82 cos 2ϕ + 0.001 17 cos 4ϕ km (at latitude ϕ)

1° of longitude = 111.412 88 cos ϕ − 0.093 50 cos 3ϕ + 0.000 12 cos 5ϕ km

1 knot = 1 nautical mile (≈ 1′ of latitude) per hour ≡ 1.852 km/h = 0.51444 m/s

Distance of sea horizon for eye h metres above sea level
(allowing for refraction) ≈ $3.9h^{1/2}$ km ≈ $2.1h^{1/2}$ nautical miles
Oceanographic unit of volumetric flow: 1 sverdrup ≡ 10^6 m³/s
Atmospheric pressure: 1 atm ≡ 101.325 kPa (There is ≈ 1 kg of air above 1 cm².)
Density of air at sea level (1 atm, 20 °C) = 1.2 kg/m³
Values of atmospheric refraction for various elevations (assuming 1 atm, 10 °C):
90°: 0′; 44°: 1′; 26°: 2′; 18°: 3′; 11°: 5′; 6°: 8′; 4°: 12′; 2°: 18′; 0°: 34′
Speed of sound in standard atmosphere = 331 m/s ≈ 1 km/3 s ≈ 10^{-6} c
Magnetic field at surface ≈ 5×10^{-5} T (**B** field comes out of a N-seeking pole)
Magnetic dip poles: 86°N, 151°E; 64°S, 136°E (as of 2022)
Standard acceleration of gravity ≡ 9.806 65 m/s²
Meteoritic flux ≈ 1×10^{-15} kg/(m²s) ≈ 10^4 t/y over entire Earth
Obliquity of ecliptic = 23.4364° (2021.0)   Constant of aberration = 20.495 52″
Annual general precession = −50.29″ (2000.0); Precession period ≈ 25 800 y
Escape speed from Earth = 11.2 km/s   Mean orbital speed = 29.786 km/s
Escape speed at 1 au from Sun = 42.1 km/s (= √2 × orbital speed)

SUN

Mass = 1.9891×10^{30} kg   Radius = 695 660 km   Eff. temp. ≈ 5770 K
Output: Power = 3.83×10^{26} W, M_{bol} = 4.74
Luminous intensity = 2.84×10^{27} cd, M_V = 4.82
At 1 au outside Earth's atmosphere:
Energy flux = 1.36 kW/m², m_{bol} = −26.83
Illuminance = 1.27×10^5 lx, m_V = −26.75
Inclination of the solar equator on the ecliptic of date = 7.25°
Longitude of ascending node of the solar equator on the ecliptic of date = 76°
Period of rotation at equator ≡ 25.38 d (sidereal), 27.2753 d (mean synodic)
Solar wind speed near Earth ≈ 450 km/s (travel time, Sun to Earth ≈ 4 d)
Solar velocity = 19.4 km/s toward α = 18.07h, δ = +30° (solar apex)
Location in Milky Way Galaxy: ≈ 26 kly from center, ≈ 50 ly N of galactic
plane, on the inner edge of the Orion arm

MILKY WAY GALAXY

Mass ≈ 10^{12} solar masses   Diameter ≈ 300 kly (including the galactic halo)
Center: α = 17h 45.7m, δ = −29°00′; N pole: α = 12h 51m, δ = 27°08′ (2000.0)
Rotation speed at Sun ≈ 230 km/s, period ≈ 210 My
Velocity relative to 3 K background radiation ≈ 400 km/s toward α ≈ 14h, δ ≈ −30°

CONSTANTS

Speed of light in vacuum, c ≡ 299 792 458 m/s
Planck's constant, h ≡ $6.626\,070\,15 \times 10^{-34}$ J·s = $4.1356... \times 10^{-15}$ eV·s
Gravitational constant, G = 6.674×10^{-11} N·m²/kg²
Elementary charge, e ≡ $1.602\,176\,634 \times 10^{-19}$ C
Constant in Coulomb's law = 10^{-7} c^2 (Not exact, but very accurate.)
Avogadro constant, N_A ≡ $6.022\,140\,76 \times 10^{26}$ kmol^{-1}
Boltzmann constant, k ≡ $1.380\,649 \times 10^{-23}$ J/K = $8.61... \times 10^{-5}$ eV/K ≈ 1 eV/10^4 K
Stefan–Boltzmann constant, σ = $5.6703... \times 10^{-8}$ W/(m²K⁴)
Wien's Law: $\lambda_m T$ = $2.897\,77 \times 10^{-3}$ m·K (per dλ)
Hubble constant, H = 70 ± 2 km/(s·Mpc)   Age of Universe = 13.80 ± 0.04 Gy
−273.15 °C (degree Celsius) = 0 K (kelvin) (lowest thermodynamic temperature)
Volume of ideal gas at 0 °C, 101.325 kPa = 22.4140 m³/kmol
Water: fusion at 0 °C: 0.333 MJ/kg   vaporization at 100 °C: 2.26 MJ/kg
thermal capacity and density (near 20 °C): 4.18 kJ/(kg·C°) and 1.00 t/m³
surface tension (near 20 °C): 0.073 N/m

MASS AND ENERGY

Mass is a measure of sluggishness of response to a net force. (SI unit: kg)
Weight ($\neq$ mass) is the magnitude of the force required to support a body. (SI unit: N)
(1 pound-mass* = 0.453 59 kg) (1 pound-force* = 4.4482 N)

1 kilogram (kg) is defined via the exact values of Planck's constant, the second of time, and the speed of light.

1 atomic mass unit (u) $\equiv$ 1/12 of the mass of an atom of ^{12}C = 1 dalton (da)
= $1.660\,539\,06 \times 10^{-27}$ kg = 931.494 10 MeV

1 joule (J) $\equiv$ work done by a force of 1 N acting through a distance of 1 m
$\approx$ the kinetic energy gained by this Handbook in falling freely 0.3 m

1 electron-volt (eV) $\equiv$ the kinetic energy gained by a particle carrying one unit of elementary electrical charge *(e)* in falling through an electrical potential difference of one volt (V) in vacuum
$\equiv 1.602\,176\,634 \times 10^{-19}$ J

Electron mass = $9.109\,383 \times 10^{-31}$ kg = 548.579 909 μu = 0.510 998 950 MeV
Proton mass = $1.672\,622 \times 10^{-27}$ kg = 1.007 276 467 u = 938.272 088 MeV
Neutron mass = $1.674\,927 \times 10^{-27}$ kg = 1.008 664 91 u = 939.565 42 MeV

Some atomic masses: ^1H (1.007 825 u) ^2H (2.014 102 u) ^4He (4.002 603 u)

Thermochemical calorie* (cal) = 4.184 J
1 erg*/s = 10^{-7} J/s = 10^{-7} W
1 BTU*/h = 1054.35 J/h = 0.292 88 W
1 horsepower* = 745.7 W

*Indicates deprecated unit; unit on right is preferred.

$C + O_2 \rightarrow CO_2$ + 4.1 eV $4\,^1H \rightarrow {}^4He$ + 26.73 MeV

Highest cosmic-ray energy (carried by protons) $\approx 10^{20}$ eV
Power output (average) of an adult human $\approx$ 100 W
1 kg of TNT or milkshake releases 4.2 MJ $\approx$ 1000 kcal $\approx$ 1 kWh
Fuel oil: 6.36 GJ/barrel (1 barrel $\equiv$ 42 U.S. gallons = 35.0 Imp. gallons = 159 L)

Relation between rest mass *(m)*, linear momentum *(p)*, total energy *(E)*, kinetic energy *(KE)*, and $\gamma \equiv (1 - v^2/c^2)^{-0.5}$, where c is the speed of light and v is the speed of the object: $E = \gamma mc^2 = mc^2 + KE = [(mc^2)^2 + (pc)^2]^{0.5}$

MAGNITUDE RELATIONS (See also p. 49 and p. 54.)

Log of light intensity ratio $\equiv$ 0.4 times magnitude difference
Distance modulus *(D)* $\equiv$ apparent magnitude *(m)* − absolute magnitude *(M)*
Log of distance in ly = $0.2D + 1.513\,435$ (neglecting absorption)
Magnitude of sum of magnitudes m_i is equal to $-2.5 \log \Sigma_i\, 10^{-0.4 m_i}$

Moon's apparent visual magnitude at phase angle P degrees (0° = full Moon) when at its average distance from Earth: $-12.7 + 0.026\,|P| + (4 \times 10^{-9})P^4$

A light source of apparent visual magnitude m provides an illuminance E (lux) where $E = 10^{-0.4\,(m + 13.99)}$ or $m = -13.99 - 2.5 \log E$

A diffuse (matte) surface with albedo A subject to illuminance E (lux) will have luminance L (visual surface brightness): $L = AE \div \pi$ (cd/m^2)

To convert luminance S (magnitude/arcsecond^2) to luminance L (cd/m^2):
$L = 10^{0.4(12.59 - S)}$ or $S = 12.59 - 2.5 \log L$

DOPPLER RELATIONS FOR LIGHT

$\alpha \equiv$ angle between velocity of source and line from source to observer
$\beta \equiv v/c$ $\gamma \equiv (1 - \beta^2)^{-0.5}$
Frequency: $f = f_0\, \gamma^{-1}(1 - \beta \cos \alpha)^{-1}$ $z \equiv (\lambda - \lambda_0)/\lambda_0 = \gamma\,(1 - \beta \cos \alpha) - 1$
For $\alpha = \pi$ radians: $z = (1 + \beta)^{0.5}(1 - \beta)^{-0.5} - 1$ ($\approx \beta$ if $\beta << 1$)
$\beta = [(1 + z)^2 - 1][(1 + z)^2 + 1]^{-1}$

VISIBLE WAVELENGTH DATA

Bright-adapted (photopic) visible range ≈ 400 – 750 nm ($L \approx 0.005 - 10^5$ cd/m^2)
Dark-adapted (scotopic) visible range ≈ 400 – 620 nm ($L \approx 1 - 5000$ μcd/m^2)
Wavelength of peak sensitivity of eye: ≈ 555 nm (photopic), 507 nm (scotopic)
Luminous efficacy at 540 THz (λ ≈ 555 nm) ≡ 683 lm/W

e.g. A 60 W incandescent light bulb emits about 800 lm. Compared to an optimum photopic light source that delivers all of its energy as light at 540 THz, its efficiency is about (800/60)/(683) = 2.0%.

Colors (representative wavelength, nm):
violet (420), blue (470), green (530), yellow (580), orange (610), red (660)

Some useful wavelengths (element, spectral designation or color and/or (Fraunhofer line)):

H Lyman α	121.6 nm	N_2^+ blue†	465.2	Hg yellow	577.0
Ca (K solar)	393.4	Hβ (F solar)*	486.1	Hg yellow	579.1
Ca (H solar)	396.8	O^{++} green*	495.9	Na (D_2 solar)	589.0
Hg violet	404.7	O^{++} green*	500.7	Na (D_1 solar)	589.6
Hδ (h solar)	410.2	Green laser	532.	O red†	630.0
Hγ (g solar)	434.0	Hg green	546.1	O red†	636.4
Hg deep blue	435.8	O yel.-green†	557.7	Hα (C solar)	656.3

* Strong contributor to the visual light of gaseous nebulae † Strong auroral lines

ANGULAR RELATIONS

2π radians = 360° $\pi = 3.141\,592\,653\,589\,793\,2\ldots \approx (113 \div 355)^{-1}$
Number of square degrees on a sphere = 41 253

For 360° = 24 h, 15° = 1 h, 15′ = 1 min, 15″ = 1 s (Earth turns 360° in 86 164.1 s)

Relations between sidereal time t, right ascension α, hour angle h, declination δ, azimuth A (measured east of north), altitude a, and latitude ϕ:

$$h = t - \alpha$$
$$\sin a = \sin\delta \sin\phi + \cos h \cos\delta \cos\phi$$
$$\cos\delta \sin h = -\cos a \sin A$$
$$\sin\delta = \sin a \sin\phi + \cos a \cos A \cos\phi$$

Annual precession in α (in seconds) ≈ 3.0748 + 1.3361 sin α tan δ
Annual precession in δ (in seconds of arc) ≈ 20.042 cos α
(Convert α to degrees for the trigonometric functions above.)
e.g. for RA 4h 20m, Dec +40°, the annual change is Δα = 4.091 s and Δδ = 8.470″

SOME SI ABBREVIATIONS AND PREFIXES

m	metre	N	newton (kg·m/s^2)	a	atto	10^{-18}
kg	kilogram	J	joule (N·m)	f	femto	10^{-15}
t	tonne (10^3 kg)	W	watt (J/s)	p	pico	10^{-12}
s	second	Pa	pascal (N/m^2)	n	nano	10^{-9}
min	minute	A	ampere	μ	micro	10^{-6}
h	hour	C	coulomb (A·s)	m	milli	10^{-3}
d	day	V	volt (J/C)	c	centi	10^{-2}
y	year (tropical) (*not SI*)	Ω	ohm (V/A)	h	hecto	10^2
Hz	hertz (s^{-1})	F	farad (C/V)	k	kilo	10^3
rad	radian	Wb	weber (V·s)	M	mega	10^6
sr	steradian	T	tesla (Wb/m^2)	G	giga	10^9
K	kelvin (temperature)	lm	lumen	T	tera	10^{12}
L	litre (10^{-3} m^3)	cd	candela (lm/sr)	P	peta	10^{15}
ha	hectare (10^4 m^2)	lx	lux (lm/m^2)	E	exa	10^{18}

THE ELECTROMAGNETIC SPECTRUM

BY ROY BISHOP

The Scottish physicist James Clerk Maxwell (1831–1879) was the first to understand the nature of light. In 1865, with elegant mathematics, Maxwell predicted that light is a self-sustaining electromagnetic wave, a quivering linkage of electric and magnetic fields in which a changing electric field generates a magnetic field, and vice versa, sustaining each other as they travel at a prodigious speed.

Four decades later Albert Einstein (1879–1955) revealed three more remarkable properties of light: (1) unlike water waves and sound waves, electromagnetic waves require no medium whatsoever in which to travel; (2) the speed of electromagnetic waves is the same for all observers, irrespective of any motion of the source of the waves; (3) when electromagnetic waves interact with matter, they do so as if composed of discrete particles, photons, whose individual energy E is proportional to the frequency f of the wave: $E = hf$, where h is Planck's constant (see p. 30).

The product of wavelength λ and wave frequency is the speed of a wave: $\lambda f = c$, where c is the usual symbol for the speed of an electromagnetic wave. The frequency (or photon energy, or wavelength) range of electromagnetic waves is unlimited, but our eyes see only a very narrow slice of this spectrum. Vision has a range of less than an octave, $\lambda \sim 400$ to 750 nm (see p. 32). We are almost blind! Nevertheless, once the physics was understood, the technologies to generate and detect all parts of the electromagnetic spectrum were soon developed. The first step in this direction occurred prior to Maxwell's work, in 1800 when astronomer William Herschel (1738–1822) discovered *infrared* radiation beyond the red end of the visible spectrum.

The diagram at the end of this article summarizes the electromagnetic spectrum. The various named parts of the spectrum overlap to some extent. Historically, one part was defined by the source of the radiation rather than by wavelength or photon energy: *gamma rays* referred to electromagnetic radiation emitted by radioactive atomic nuclei. *X-rays* overlap with gamma rays but are produced by sources other than atomic nuclei—an arbitrary distinction based on the historical origins of these two terms. A detector defines another part of the spectrum: *light* is usually restricted to human vision, although occasionally this term is extended to include the adjacent *ultraviolet* portion of the spectrum.

The importance of the particle aspect at high frequencies and of the wave aspect at low frequencies is implied by the names; for instance, gamma **rays** and radio **waves**. Photon energy, not wavelength, dominates the behavior of gamma rays. At the other end of the spectrum, the energy of individual photons is very small, obscuring the granular nature of the radiation, and frequency is usually the measured characteristic of the radiation. Vision operates between these two extremes where *both* particle and wave properties play significant roles. Events in the retina are triggered by individual photons, and wave diffraction is relevant for minimum eye pupil size and the spacing of retinal photoreceptors. For the infrared and microwave regions, wavelength has a convenient range and is usually cited. The transition across the spectrum from photon through wavelength to frequency domination is indicated in the diagram by the range of the units on the left side of each of the three scales.

Photon energy determines how electromagnetic radiation interacts with matter. Chemistry and biology involve changes in atomic and molecular structure, the energies involved being typically a few *electron-volts* (eV) per reaction (see p. 31). Retinal photochemistry operates over a very limited energy range, and thereby determines the narrow visual window on the electromagnetic spectrum. For $\lambda > 750$ nm, the photon energy is insufficient (<1.6 eV) to alter the structure of light-sensing protein molecules in the retina, so we cannot see the infrared. For $\lambda < 400$ nm, the photon energy is high enough (>3.1 eV) to damage these delicate molecules; however, the cornea and lens of the eye absorb that radiation before it can reach the retina. Thus, we cannot see the ultraviolet.

Although the energy of an infrared photon is too weak to stimulate vision, infrared photons are readily absorbed by many types of molecules, such as water, causing the molecules to move more rapidly, thereby increasing the temperature of the substance. In this manner, infrared radiation from the Sun, a fire, or a hot stove warms us. Hence infrared is often called heat radiation, although it is *not* heat that is being radiated. The heating is a secondary effect, generated in our bodies subsequent to the absorption of the photons.

Confusion of sensation with electromagnetic radiation also occurs with visible light. For instance, almost invariably we speak of colors as if they were a property of light, or of the bodies emitting the light, rather than being indescribable hue sensations arising in the brain. As Sir Isaac Newton cautioned us three centuries ago: "The rays, to speak properly, are not colored." The light reflected by a leaf is not green, and neither is the leaf; green exists only in the neuron-based representation of the leaf in the observer's consciousness, and then only if the light is not too dim. The electromagnetic radiation from a leaf is characterized by a particular spatial and spectral distribution of radiant power. A CCD or CMOS chip finds only photons. It is we who create the color and the brightness. The distinction between our internal visual world and the external physical world is profound but rarely appreciated. It is the distinction between how the world *looks* to us, and how it *is*.

Visual perception aside, what *is* light, a wave or a particle? Light travels like a wave (Maxwell was right) and interacts like a particle (Einstein was right). A detector finds photons, but *where* the detector finds photons is determined by a wave. When a typical backyard telescope is aimed at an average star in the night sky, at any instant there is seldom more than one photon from that star in transit through the telescope. Yet the distribution of light in the star's image at the focal plane is determined by an aperture-filling wave. In the case of a Newtonian telescope with a four-vane spider support for the secondary mirror, in some real sense, each photon passes through all four quadrants of the spider. But it is not that the spider quarters the hapless photon like a cleaver quarters a steak in a butcher shop; whole photons, not quartered photons arrive at the detector. The message of physics revealed during the first half of the last century is that it is simply *wrong* to speak of the path of a photon while in transit to a detector. Light is queerer than we can imagine. Matter is equally queer, for it too displays a wave-particle duality, a duality that is particularly obvious on the subatomic scale. Just as it is wrong to speak of the path of a photon, it is wrong to speak of the path of an electron in an atom—as if, for example, it were in orbit about the nucleus. The wave-particle puzzle is of our own making, for we try to apply naïve concepts abstracted from crude sensory experiences on the macroscopic scale of everyday life to the subatomic world. Pure waves or pure particles never did exist. Reality is more subtle.

Despite the strange behavior of electromagnetic radiation, we know how to describe its interaction with matter quantitatively and with astounding accuracy. The theory encompasses the work of Maxwell and Einstein, and was completed in the mid-20th century by Richard Feynman (1918–1988) and Julian Schwinger (1918–1994) of the United States, and Sin-Itiro Tomonaga (1906–1979) of Japan, for which they shared the Nobel Prize in Physics in 1965. The theory is called quantum electrodynamics. With the exception of gravitation and things that go on inside atomic nuclei, quantum electrodynamics appears to describe all phenomena in the physical world—in principle, if not in actuality, in the case of complex systems because of the complexity.

THE ELECTROMAGNETIC SPECTRUM

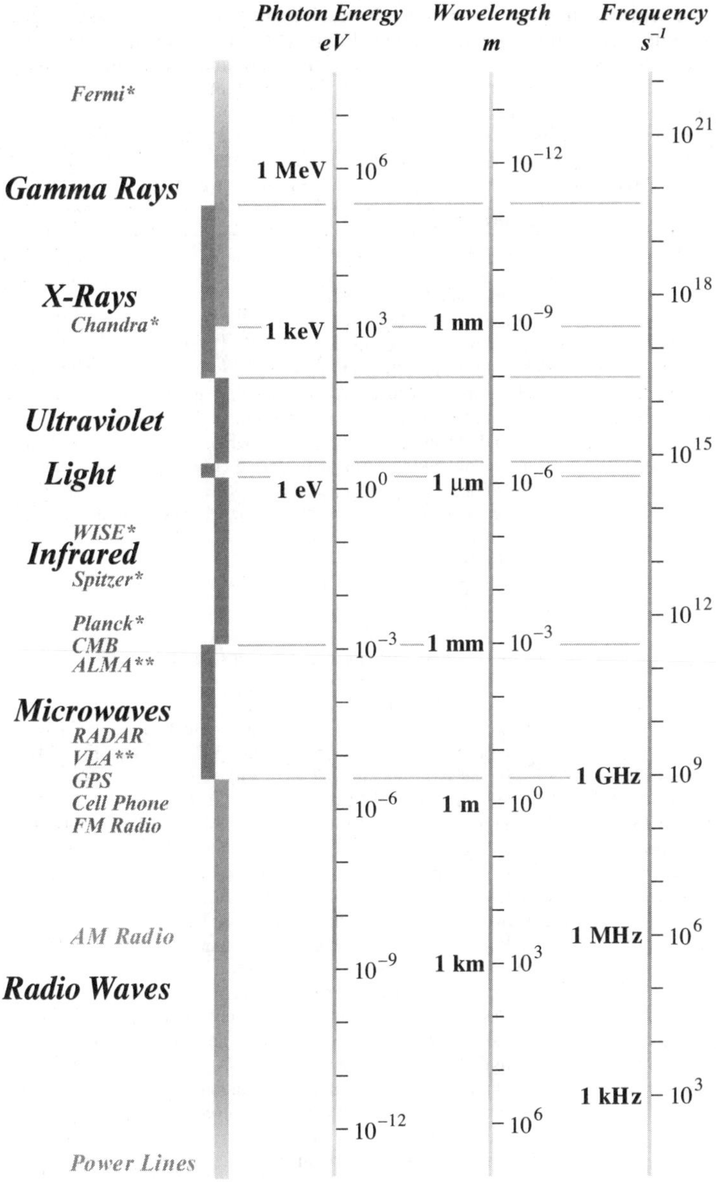

* space observatory ** ground observatory Diagram by Roy Bishop

VOYAGES IN THE SOLAR SYSTEM

BY J. RANDY ATTWOOD

During the second half of the 20th century, humankind began its reconnaissance of the Solar System. Although people have traveled only as far as the Moon, robotic space probes have been sent to all the major planets plus a few minor planets and comets. Our understanding of the solar neighborhood is increasing at a tremendous pace as a result of the improving sophistication of these spacecraft.

The following is a list of some of the important firsts in the short history of the exploration of the Solar System. Note that all space missions are not recorded, not even all the space firsts. A short list of upcoming missions to watch for is also included.

Year	Name	Significance
1957	*Sputnik 1*	First artificial satellite of Earth (Oct. 4); USSR
1957	*Sputnik 2*	First living being in Earth orbit (a dog named Laika); USSR
1959	*Luna 1*	First to escape Earth's gravity; USSR
1959	*Luna 2*	First to impact on the Moon; USSR
1959	*Luna 3*	First to image the far side of the Moon; USSR
1961	*Vostok 1*	First human in Earth orbit (Yuri Gagarin, Apr. 12); USSR
1961	*Freedom 7*	First American in space (Alan Shepard, May 5); USA
1962	*Friendship 7*	First American in Earth orbit (John Glenn, Feb. 20); USA
1962	*Mariner 2*	First to fly by another planet, Venus; USA
1962	*Alouette 1*	First Canadian satellite placed in Earth orbit
1963	*Vostok 6*	First woman to fly in space (Valentina Tereshkova, Jun. 16); USSR
1965	*Voshkod 2*	First astronaut to take a spacewalk (Alexei Leonov, Mar. 18); USSR
1965	*Mariner 4*	First to fly by Mars and take pictures; USA
1966	*Luna 9*	First soft landing on the Moon; USSR
1966	*Venera 3*	First to impact on another planet, Venus; USSR
1966	*Luna 10*	First to orbit the Moon; USSR
1967	*Apollo 1*	Astronauts perish in a fire during a launch-pad test (Gus Grissom, Ed White, and Roger Chaffee, Jan. 27); USA
1967	*Soyuz 1*	First astronaut to die during spaceflight (Vladimir Komarov, Apr. 24); USSR
1968	*Apollo 8*	First human voyage to the Moon (orbit without landing); USA (Frank Borman, James Lovell, and William Anders, Dec. 24)
1969	*Apollo 11*	First humans to land and walk on the Moon; USA (Neil Armstrong and Edwin Aldrin, Jul. 20)
1970	*Apollo 13*	Moon mission canceled after onboard explosion (Apr. 14); USA
1970	*Venera 7*	First soft landing on another planet, Venus; USSR
1971	*Mariner 9*	First to orbit another planet, Mars; USA
1972	*Anik A1*	First Canadian communications satellite placed in Earth orbit
1972	*Apollo 17*	Last two of 12 men to walk on the Moon; USA
1973	*Pioneer 10*	First to fly by Jupiter, reach solar escape speed; USA
1974	*Mariner 10*	First to fly by and study Mercury; USA
1975	*Venera 9*	First to return surface pictures of Venus; USSR
1976	*Viking 1*	First to softly land on Mars, return pictures; USA
1979	*Voyager 1*	First close-up study of Jupiter and its moons; USA
1979	*Pioneer 11*	First to fly by Saturn; USA
1980	*Voyager 1*	First close-up study of Saturn and its moons; USA
1981	STS 1	First launch of the reuseable *Space Transportation System* (Space Shuttle); USA
1983	STS 7	First American woman to fly in space (Sally Ride, Jun. 18); USA
1984	*Soyuz T–7*	First woman to walk in space (Svetlana Savitskaya, Jul. 25); USSR
1984	STS 41G	First Canadian to fly in space (Marc Garneau, Oct. 5); Canada
	"	First American woman to walk in space (Kathy Sullivan); USA
	"	First time two women in space at the same time (Kathy Sullivan, Sally Ride); USA
1985	ICE	*(International Cometary Explorer)* First to study a comet; USA

Year	Name	Significance
1986	*Voyager 2*	First close-up study of Uranus and its moons; USA
1986	*Challenger*	First American astronauts to die during spaceflight (Jan. 28); USA
1986	*Giotto*	First images taken of a comet nucleus, Halley; ESA
1989	*Voyager 2*	First close-up study of Neptune and its moons; USA
1989	*Magellan*	First radar maps made of Venus from orbit; USA
1989	COBE	First precise data on cosmic microwave background radiation; USA
1990	*Hubble*	Launch of the *Hubble Space Telescope*
1991	*Galileo*	First flyby, closeup photos of a minor planet, 951 Gaspra; USA
1992	STS 42	First Canadian woman in space (Roberta Bondar, Jan. 22); Canada
1994	*Clementine*	First images of perma-shadowed areas at the Moon's south pole; USA
1994–5	*Mir*	Longest single spaceflight: 437 days in Earth orbit (V. Polyakov); USSR
1995	*Ulysses*	First flyby above the Sun's south/north poles; ESA
1995	*Galileo*	First to orbit Jupiter and 1st to send probe into Jupiter's atmosphere; USA
1996	*Pathfinder*	First rover on Mars (Sojourner); USA
1998	*Deep Space 1*	First test of ion propulsion; navigates to Comet Borelly (2001); USA
1999	*Chandra*	Launch of the *Chandra X-Ray Observatory*; USA
2001	*Soyuz TM-32*	First private citizen to pay for a spaceflight (Dennis Tito)
2001	NEAR *Shoemaker*	First to orbit and land softly on a minor planet, 433 Eros; USA
2001	*Genesis*	First solar-wind sample return; USA
2003	*Columbia*	Second Space Shuttle disaster; crew of seven lost (Feb. 1)
2003	MOST	First Canadian space telescope launched into Earth orbit
2003	*Shenzhou V*	First Chinese taikonaut to orbit Earth (Yang Liwei)
2004	*Mars Rovers*	First long-range surface exploration of Mars; USA
2004	*Stardust*	First collection and return of cometary material, Wild 2; USA
2004	*Cassini*	First to orbit Saturn; USA
2004	*Gravity Probe B*	First test of Einstein's general theory of relativity in space; USA
2005	*Huygens*	First to land on Titan; USA/ESA
2005	*Deep Impact*	First to impact on and study the interior of a comet, Tempel 1; USA
2008	*Mars Phoenix*	First to examine Martian arctic soil; discovered water ice; USA
2009	ISS	Most people (13) together in one spacecraft: (Expedition 20/21 and STS 127), including two Canadians (Robert Thirsk, Julie Payette)
2009	*Kepler*	First to verify Earth-sized planets at nearby stars; USA
2010	*Hayabusa*	First minor-planet-sample return mission(rendezvous in 2005); Japan
2010	ISS	Four women in space at one time: Expedition 23, STS 131
2011	*Messenger*	First spacecraft to orbit and study Mercury; USA
2011	*Atlantis*	135th and last Space Shuttle flight
2011	*Dawn*	First to orbit a minor planet (4 Vesta) and a dwarf planet (1 Ceres), in 2015; USA
2011	*Juno*	First mission to study Jupiter from a polar orbit (July 2016); USA
2012	*Mars Science Lab*	Carrying Curiosity, the first nuclear-powered rover on Mars; USA
2012	*NEOSSat*	First to look for objects on a potential Earth-collision course; Canada
2014	*Rosetta/Philae*	First to soft land on a comet (67P/Churyumov–Gerasimenko); ESA
2015	*New Horizons*	First to fly by and closely image the Pluto system; USA
2016	OSIRIS-*Rex*	First NASA/CSA mission to sample an asteroid (101955 Bennu)
2018	*Parker Solar Probe*	NASA mission to fly through the edges of the Sun's corona
2019+	*New Horizons*	First to fly by Kuiper Belt Object (2014 MU69, Arrokoth); USA
2021		First commercial space tourists on sub-orbital trips began
2021	Ingenuity	First helicopter to fly on another planet; USA

As of August 2021, a total of 587 people have traveled into space.

Upcoming Missions

2021	JWST*	Launch of the *James Webb Space Telescope*; NASA/ESA/CSA
2022	*Euclid*	First mission to map the Dark Universe; ESA
2022	JUICE	First mission to primarily study JUpiter's ICEy moons; ESA
2024	*Europa Clipper*	First to study the Jovian moon Europa in depth; USA.
2031	*Mars Sample Return*	Mission to return Martian rock samples to Earth; NASA

* Mission not yet launched

OBSERVING ARTIFICIAL SATELLITES

BY PAUL D. MALEY

Considering taking up watching Earth-orbiting satellites as a hobby in 2022? The hobbyist activity of satellite observers extends from the casual observer who will consult a commonly available webpage for localized viewing predictions of a bright spacecraft like the *International Space Station* to the most serious of satellite trackers. This latter category tracks a wide range of Earth space activities that range from launches of satellites primarily from the Kennedy Space Center, to explosions in near-Earth orbit, and even onto spacecraft on their way out of the Solar System. Such interests can be demonstrated by optical measurements carried out by naked eye, binoculars, and small and large telescopes. The cost of instrumentation ranges from zero dollars to many thousands of dollars, depending upon how far one wants to go. The scope of what can be seen extends from viewing satellites as star-like dots, to imaging the actual shape of orbiting spacecraft, and to recording reentries of space junk with smart phones. Of course, the final images of what can be revealed with shape-defining equipment is limited by the Earth's atmosphere but still, some recent images can best be described as no less than incredible.

Tracking satellites is done not only in the visual spectrum but also with radio monitoring of known or discoverable frequencies on which these objects transmit. Satellites are only visible for the most part in the narrow interval of dawn (before) and dusk (after), but at high latitudes many spacecraft are illuminated through much of the night as compared to those at lower latitudes or near the equator. Receiving signals from an active orbiting object can be uniquely interesting if this object's orbital data is unannounced and presents a mystery to the public; an example of this might be satellites launched from Iran or North Korea.

Others who have an interest in the topic of satellite observation may be mobility limited, visually impaired, or otherwise unable or unwilling to observe optically. Most observations can be done in situ and do not require travel. As an alternative, observers may choose to study the published orbital elements of certain spacecraft with the goal of understanding maneuvers, close approaches of satellites, unannounced orbit changes, results of an explosion or collision, or effects on orbits from solar radiation or other impactors. This requires access to certain databases, some of which are easily found online, while others are more difficult to acquire. Still, the mathematical study of on-orbit behavior can be used as an educational tool to train students in orbital mechanics inside the classroom and then following up with real-life laboratory proof of concept by going out at night and watching/confirming what has been predicted.

On a personal note, in 1965 when I entered undergraduate school in Texas, I was able to upload a satellite-tracking program and predict an overflight the very first night of my college life. Seeing it fly over within an hour of getting the software to work was a truly exciting confirmation that the program executed properly and that I could depend on making predictions for the rest of the semester.

Other modern-day satellite trackers engage in predicting the re-entries of certain satellites and rocket bodies. Even in 2022, forecasting the exact time and location of a satellite burning up in the atmosphere is extremely difficult to predict with certainty, even several orbits ahead.

Secret satellites whose launches or orbits are not announced can be tracked by hobbyists and these present a classic set of challenges—to know the otherwise unknown. Many of these have been found by accident or by intent, using patterns that are recognized by those who study orbital characteristics, launch times, and previous observations.

Where might a rocket re-enter that boosted a satellite into orbit but was never intended to go into orbit itself? This is another hobbyist area to study since nations are required to announce notice to mariners (ocean navigation warnings) that allow specific water zones to become known and can therefore be outlined.

Finally, expected satellite behavior can be studied, which shows repeatedly what a particular type of satellite with certain orbit parameters, injected into orbit by a nation, will do. There are "rules" created by prior launches from known sites that can reveal anomalous events, such as delayed orbit injection, burn deviations, etc., that can provide clues to a new purpose, or a failure.

TIME

TIME AND TIME SCALES

BY ROY BISHOP

Time has been said to be nature's way of keeping everything from happening at once. In 1687, Sir Isaac Newton (1642–1727) perceived time as being separate from and more fundamental than the spinning of changeable planets or the oily mechanisms of clocks: "Absolute, true, and mathematical time, of itself, and from its own nature flows equably without regard to anything external." That is the common sense or intuitive view most people have of time.

Albert Einstein (1879–1955) was the first to understand that time is but an abstraction that does not exist independently of clocks. In his special theory of relativity (1905), Einstein predicted that clocks moving relative to an observer run slower, a phenomenon called time dilation or the second-order Doppler effect. For example, relative to a clock fixed beside a road, the wristwatch of a person driving past at a speed of 100 km/h loses 0.26 ps per minute (ps = picosecond = 10^{-12} s; see p. 32). A decade later, in his theory of gravitation, the general theory of relativity, Einstein predicted that clocks lower or higher than the observer in a gravitational field run slower or faster, respectively, than the observer's clock. In the case of a lower clock, it is called the gravitational redshift. For example, an alarm clock on the floor a metre below your bed loses 3.1 ps per 8-h night relative to a watch on your wrist. These counterintuitive effects are not only real, but in recent years they have found their way into the consumer marketplace in the form of GPS (Global Positioning System) receivers. These handheld units receive signals from orbiting atomic clocks and rely on programs that allow for time dilation and gravitational redshift (see *Physics Today*, May 2002, (p. 41). In astronomy, the general theory of relativity was mostly ignored until the last few decades of the 20th century, when increasing precision of clocks and advances in theoretical astrophysics and cosmology demanded its use.

As to understanding time, Lord Kelvin (1824–1907) said that you know a physical quantity if you can measure it. Time can indeed be measured, with mind-boggling precision. For those who feel compelled to state "We still don't know what time actually is," perhaps the mystery resides merely in the meaning of this statement.

The essence of time is that isolated material changes occur in invariant ratios one with respect to another. That is, as Sir Hermann Bondi (1919–2005) put it: "Time is that which is manufactured by clocks." Thus, to deal with time, clocks must be devised and units and time scales established. Readers who wish to pursue this topic beyond the brief overview presented here should consult *The Measurement of Time*, by C. Audoin and B. Guinot, Cambridge University Press, 2001, the *Explanatory Supplement to the Astronomical Almanac, 3rd ed.*, by S.E. Urban and P.K. Seidelmann (eds.), University Science Books, 2013, and *Time: From Earth Rotation to Atomic Physics, 2nd ed.*, by D.D. McCarthy and P.K. Seidelmann, Cambridge University Press, 2018.

Periodic Time Intervals and Clocks

There are three obvious, natural, periodic time intervals on Earth: the seasonal cycle (year), the cycle of lunar phases (month), and the day–night cycle (day). The cycle of the seasons is called the *tropical year* and contains 365.242 189 days. The cycle of lunar phases is known as the *synodic month* and equals 29.530 589 days. The average day–night (diurnal) cycle is the *mean solar day* and presently contains approximately

86 399.9999 s. Other types of year, month, and day have been defined and are listed along with brief definitions and durations on p. 29.

The problem of accurately subdividing these natural intervals to make time locally available at any moment (i.e. timekeeping) was satisfactorily solved in 1657 by Christiaan Huygens, who invented the first practical pendulum clock. Through successive refinements, the pendulum clock reigned supreme for nearly three centuries, until it was surpassed in precision by the quartz oscillator in the 1940s. Within another 20 years the quartz clock was, in turn, superseded by the cesium atomic clock, which by the year 2000 reached a precision of about 1 part in 10^{15}. Today, clocks based on single ions of other elements are approaching a short-term stability of one part in 10^{17} (one second in 3 billion years), and optical-lattice clocks are exceeding that figure (see *Physics Today*, March 2014, p. 12).

Earth's Rotation and Time Scales

Of the three obvious, natural, periodic time intervals on Earth (year, month, and day), the day dominates our lives and determines the various time scales we have created. The day is caused primarily by Earth's rotation on its axis. To count rotations, a reference or fiducial point is required. Four such points are of interest, and three of these are the basis of five time scales:

(1) Earth's rotation relative to the distant stars: Although the distant stars (or better, extragalactic sources) provide a reference frame to determine the "true" period of Earth's rotation (presently about 86 164.0988 s), because of Earth's orbital motion and its rotational precession, this true period is not that of either the solar day or the day relative to the RA/Dec coordinate grid used to specify astronomical positions. Hence no time scales are based on Earth's true rotational period.

(2) Earth's rotation relative to the equinox: The equator and poles of the RA/Dec celestial coordinate grid are aligned with Earth's mean equator and poles. ("Mean" denotes that small, periodic variations caused by the nutation of Earth's axis have been averaged out. Nutation involves the true pole moving relative to the mean pole with an amplitude of about 9″ and a variety of short periods up to 18.6 years.) Hence the RA/Dec grid slowly shifts relative to the distant stars as Earth's rotation axis and equator precess, a motion caused primarily by the torques exerted by the Moon and Sun on Earth's equatorial bulge (see p. 21). The other planets make a smaller contribution to this *precession of the equator* and also cause a *precession of the ecliptic*. The sum of these two precessions is called *general precession*. General precession causes the zero point of right ascension (the "Greenwich of the skies," the vernal equinox, or "first point of Aries") to drift westward (retrograde) along the ecliptic about 50″ per year. As a result, Earth's rotation period relative to the equinox (called the *mean sidereal day*, currently 86 164.0904 s) is 8.4 ms shorter than the time for one rotation (see p. 29). At any longitude on Earth, the RA of a star on the meridian (corrected for nutation) is the ***Local Mean Sidereal Time*** **(LMST)** at that instant. At the Greenwich meridian (0° longitude), this is called ***Greenwich Mean Sidereal Time*** **(GMST)**. LMST may be used to set a telescope on an object of known right ascension. The hour angle of the object equals the sidereal time less the RA. LMST may be available from a sidereal clock, or it can be calculated as explained in the middle of p. 47. Because Earth makes one more rotation with respect to the other stars than it does with respect to the Sun during a year, sidereal time gains relative to time scales linked to the Sun (see below) by about 3 min 56 s per day, or 2 h per month.

(3) Earth's rotation relative to the real Sun: A common misconception is that the Sun is highest in the sky and lies on the local north–south meridian at 12:00 noon. However, time based on the position of the Sun in the sky, known as local ***apparent solar***

time or *sundial time*, can differ by up to an hour or more from civil time (the time that we normally use). There are two reasons for this discrepancy. One reason is that the Sun's eastward annual apparent motion around the sky is far from uniform, both because of Earth's elliptical orbit and because of the inclination of the celestial equator to the ecliptic. Thus apparent solar time does not have a uniform rate (see the next paragraph). The second reason for the difference between sundial time and civil time is the use of standard time zones (see the penultimate paragraph of this article).

(4) Earth's rotation relative to the mean Sun: If the Sun is replaced by a fictitious mean sun moving uniformly along the celestial equator, Earth's rotation relative to this mean sun defines ***Local Mean (solar) Time*** **(LMT)**. Apparent solar time can differ by up to 16 min from LMT, depending upon the time of year (see the diagram on p. 185). Small, periodic shifts of Earth's crust relative to the axis of rotation *(polar motion)* affect astronomical time determinations through the resulting east–west shift in the meridian at latitudes away from the equator. LMT at the Greenwich meridian (0° longitude), when corrected for this polar motion, is called ***Universal Time*** **(UT1**, or often simply **UT**). UT1 is best determined using very-long-baseline interferometry measurements of distant point sources, such as quasars.

All the above mean time scales (LMST, GMST, LMT, and UT1), being based upon Earth's rotation, are only as uniform as that rotation. By the mid-19th century, discrepancies between theory and the observed motion of the Moon indicated that, over the long term, Earth's rotation is slowing down. However, not until clocks became better timekeepers than the spinning Earth (c. 1940, when crystal-controlled clocks exceeded precisions of 1 in 10^{10}) was it realized how complex is the variable rotation of our planet. There are (i) long-, (ii) medium-, and (iii) short-term accelerations:

(i) Over many centuries, there is a *secular* slowing caused by tidal friction of about 8 parts in 10^{13} per day (i.e. the day becomes one second longer about every 40 000 years).

(ii) Over a few decades, there are *random* accelerations (positive and negative), apparently caused by core–mantle interactions and possibly by changes in ocean currents. These are about 10 times larger than the tidal deceleration, and thus completely obscure the latter effect over time intervals of less than a century or so.

(iii) The largest accelerations in Earth's rotation rate are short-term ones: *periodic components* are associated mainly with lunar-induced tides (over two-week and monthly intervals) and seasonal meteorological factors (over semiannual and annual intervals); *nonperiodic* (chaotic) high-frequency variations are associated mainly with the global atmospheric wind and pressure distributions. These short-term accelerations are typically one or two orders of magnitude larger again than the random, decadal fluctuations on which they are superimposed (see the article by John Wahr in the June 1986 issue of *Sky & Telescope*, p. 545).

Uniform Time Scales

(1) Based on orbital motion: Although Earth's axial rotation is not sufficiently predictable to serve as a precise clock, the orbital motions of our Moon, Earth, and the other planets are predictable to high accuracy. Through the dynamical equations describing these motions plus extended astronomical observations, a uniform dynamical time scale can be derived. Such a scale, known as *Ephemeris Time* (ET), was for several years (1952–1984) the basis of astronomical ephemerides. The ephemeris second, defined in 1960 as a certain fraction of the tropical year 1900.0, was the fundamental unit of time. Early in the 20th century, the UT1 and ET scales coincided, but because Earth's rotation rate has been generally slower than the ET rate, by 1984 UT1 was 54 s behind ET and was losing about half a second per year.

Between 1984 and 2020, Earth's rotation rate has varied (part of the random decadal fluctuations), losing between 0.2 and 0.8 s per year relative to ET (actually TT, see below). Remarkably, since 2016 Earth's rotation has been accelerating such that, for the first time in several decades, by the second half of 2020 the mean solar day became less than the SI day (d) of exactly 86 400 s (by about 0.1 ms).

(2) Based on atomic transition frequency: The quantum nature of matter gives atoms a permanence and stability that macroscopic objects such as quartz crystals, planets, and pendulums do not possess. The idea of an atomic clock was proposed by the Austrian-American physicist Isidor Rabi in 1945. In 1967, the second was given an atomic definition: 9 192 631 770 periods of the radiation involved in the transition between the two hyperfine levels of the unperturbed ground state of the cesium 133 atom (the only stable isotope of cesium, an element that has a single valence electron). This is known as the SI (for Système International) second (abbreviation s, *not* sec). The number 9 192 631 770 was chosen so that on the rotating geoid (i.e. for clocks fixed on Earth at mean sea level), the SI second is identical to the older ET second to within the precision of measurement.

The previous sentence implies that clocks on the geoid run at the same rate. What about Earth's rotation? Clocks nearer the equator move faster, so does time dilation not make them run slower relative to clocks at higher latitudes? Ignoring the Moon and Sun, if Earth did not rotate and had an isotropic density distribution, its geoid (mean sea-level surface) would be spherical, and clocks fixed on this geoid would, by symmetry, all run at the same rate (they would all be at rest and have similar positions in Earth's gravitational field). For a rotating Earth, the equatorial bulge is such that clocks away from the poles are just enough higher in Earth's gravitational field that the resulting gravitational blueshift exactly cancels the time dilation associated with their rotational speed. This simple, elegant, and convenient result is a consequence of Einstein's principle of equivalence: A body at rest in a gravitational field is equivalent to a body being accelerated in a field-free space. As described by general relativity, gravitation is geometry, not a force, which is why no one has ever felt a force of gravity. The only force acting on Earth-based clocks, or on any stationary Earth-based objects, is the electromagnetic contact force supporting them. Any two nearby clocks located on the same surface perpendicular to the direction of this contact force (the plumb-bob direction) will have identical rates. Thus *all* clocks on the geoid run at the same rate. Whether or not the planet beneath is rotating is immaterial.

Five SI-second-based time scales are in use today. One of these (UTC) merely differs an integral number of seconds from one of the other four and is described in the last section. The fundamental time scale for unambiguously dating events within the Solar System and beyond (e.g. planet and interplanetary spacecraft motions, and pulsar signals) is **Barycentric Coordinate Time (TCB)**. TCB is the time base of a nonrotating coordinate system with its origin located at the center of mass of the Solar System, and it is not influenced by the gravitational fields of any bodies in the Solar System. It is as if the Solar System were not present.

The fundamental time scale for unambiguously dating events in the vicinity of Earth (e.g. motions of Earth-orbiting satellites) is **Geocentric Coordinate Time (TCG)**. TCG is the time base of a nonrotating coordinate system with its origin located at the center of mass of Earth, and it is not influenced by the gravitational field of Earth. It is as if all bodies of the Solar System except Earth were present.

TCG runs at a slower (and slightly variable) rate relative to TCB because of both time dilation associated with Earth's orbital motion and gravitational redshift associated with Earth's location within the Sun's gravitational well, and (to a much lesser extent) the gravitational wells of all the other bodies in the Solar System (except Earth). Relative to TCB, TCG loses about 467 ms per year.

One might expect that TCG would be the time scale of choice for Earth-based observers (e.g. for dealing with apparent geocentric ephemerides); however, cesium atomic clocks at Earth's surface are deep within Earth's gravitational well and lose about 22 ms per year relative to TCG. To avoid this inconvenience, a second geocentric coordinate time scale has been devised, **Terrestrial Time (TT)**. TT is defined as having a rate exactly $1 - 6.969290134 \times 10^{-10}$ as large as the TCG rate so that the unit of the TT scale is very close to the SI second on the rotating geoid, matching the rate of Earth-based atomic clocks. Thus TT is an idealized atomic time scale on the geoid, and is a derived scale, not fundamental. The TT rate definition is based upon TCG and not the geoid because of uncertainties surrounding the realization of the geoid (the geoid would coincide with Earth's sea surface *if* the waters of the oceans were homogeneous and at rest). TT loses about $22 + 467 = 489$ ms (nearly half a second) per year relative to TCB.

TCB, TCG, and TT are theoretical, ideal time scales. Real clocks are needed for measurements. To this end in 1972, ***International Atomic Time*** (**TAI** = Temps Atomique International) was introduced. TAI is based on a weighted average of more than 200 atomic clocks reduced to the geoid in more than 30 countries and presently is the most precise *achievable* time scale. Not even atomic clocks are perfect time keepers (they drift randomly one with respect to another), so TAI shifts unpredictably relative to the ideal TT rate by about 0.1 μs/year (a few parts in 10^{15}). The TAI scale was set to agree with UT1 on 1958 Jan. 1, which led to the definition that TT be exactly 32.184 s ahead of TAI on 1977 Jan. 1.0 (TAI) to ensure continuity of TT with ET, TT's predecessor for geocentric ephemerides.

TCB, TCG, and TT are defined to have had the same reading on 1977 Jan. 1.0 (TAI) at Earth's center of mass, all three being exactly 32.184 s ahead of TAI at that point in spacetime. At the beginning of 2022, TT is about 1.0 s behind TCG, and 22 seconds behind TCB. TCB, TCG, and TT are realized via TAI.

Three time scales no longer in use are associated with the SI second: ET, TDT, and TDB. ET and TDT have been abandoned, and TDB is deprecated. Unfortunately they still appear in some publications so they must be mentioned. *Ephemeris Time* (ET), introduced in section (1) above, was defined and adopted by the International Astronomical Union in 1952. The transition from ET to the modern TT took place in three steps: (i) Because of several difficulties surrounding both the original concept of ET and its determination (the most serious being that it ignored relativity), and because atomic clocks had become readily available, in 1984 ET was abandoned in favor of *Terrestrial Dynamical Time* (TDT). The unit of TDT was the SI second on the rotating geoid, and its scale was chosen to agree with the 1984 ET scale; (ii) In 1991, the general theory of relativity was explicitly adopted as the theoretical background for spacetime reference systems. To emphasize that TDT was no longer derived from observations of the dynamical aspects of Solar System bodies, TDT was renamed simply Terrestrial Time (TT); (iii) Because of uncertainties surrounding the realization of the geoid (mentioned above), TT was redefined in terms of TCG in 2000.

In 1976, *Barycentric Dynamical Time* (TDB) was introduced when it became necessary to acknowledge relativistic effects, but before the general theory of relativity was accepted by astronomers. It was similar to TCB, except its scale unit was adjusted to approximate ET (currently TT). TDB was needlessly complex and confusing; however, it was used extensively by the Jet Propulsion Laboratory for ephemerides in planetary exploration, so was not completely abandoned when TCB was introduced in 1991. This unsatisfactory situation was resolved in 2006 when TDB was redefined by a simple linear relation in terms of TCB. Although redundant and deprecated, TDB is now an alternative way to express TCB, with the minor convenience that it keeps nearly in step with TT at Earth's center.

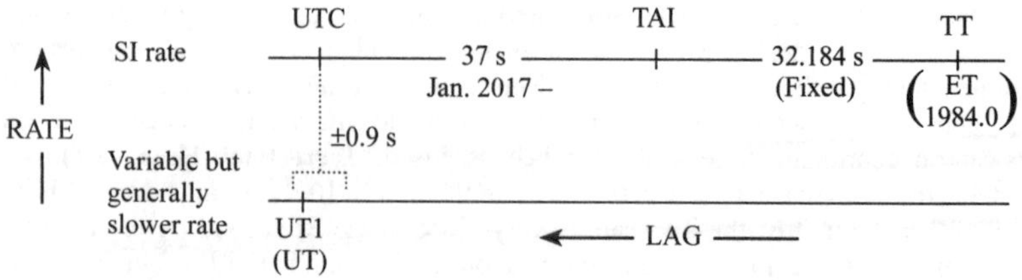

This diagram displays the rate and scale relations between Earth-based time scales that run at or near the SI rate at sea level and that are not longitude-dependent.

(3) Based on pulsars: Millisecond radio pulsars (old, rapidly spinning neutron stars) display extraordinary stability in their rotation. Their stability, after allowing for spin-down, is almost as good as the best atomic clocks. However, uncertainties in predicting the spin-down rate of a pulsar and in Earth's motion relative to a pulsar, the elaborate equipment needed to observe a pulsar, and the complex data analysis required all make it unlikely that a pulsar will ever replace cesium clocks as the basis for a uniform time scale. Like quartz crystals, planets, and pendulums, pulsars do not possess the permanence and stability of atoms.

Uniform Time Scales with Steps (to track the mean Sun)

Closely related to UT1 (which follows Earth's variable rotation relative to the mean Sun) is ***Coordinated Universal Time*** **(UTC)**, introduced in its present form in 1972. UTC, the basis of the world system of civil time, runs at the TAI rate and is offset an integral number of seconds from TAI so that it approximates UT1. When required (usually on Jun. 30 or Dec. 31), "leap seconds" are inserted into (or, if necessary, deleted from) UTC so that the difference UT1 – UTC = DUT1 does not exceed ±0.9 s. Current values of DUT1 are available in Bulletin A of the International Earth Rotation and Reference Systems Service (IERS): iers.org/IERS/EN/Organization/About/about.html. The present value of DUT1 is also coded in radio time signals (see p. 47).

The most recent insertion of a leap second occurred at the beginning of 2017, making the difference TAI – UTC = 37 s. Hence TT – UTC = 37 s + 32.184 s = 69.184 s exactly (see the diagram above). For announcements of leap seconds see ftp://hpiers.obspm.fr/iers/bul/bulc/bulletinc.dat. UTC is readily available via radio time signals and GPS receivers. (Note: The term *Greenwich Mean Time* (GMT) over the years has had three different meanings: the same as UT1, UTC, and mean solar time at the Greenwich meridian with 0 h corresponding to noon. To avoid confusion, the term *Greenwich Mean Time* should not be used.)

Local Mean (solar) Time (LMT) would suffice for the inhabitants of an isolated village, but with the advent in the 19th century of rapid travel and communication (railways, steamships, and the telegraph), it became essential that clocks over a range of longitudes indicate the same time. To keep these clocks reasonably in phase with the day–night cycle and yet avoid the inconvenience to travelers of a local time that varies continuously with longitude, in 1884, Earth was divided into 24 ***Standard Time*** zones, adjacent zones generally differing by one hour and each ideally 15° wide (see the time-zone map on p. 46). All clocks within the same zone read the same time. The Canadian railway surveyor and construction engineer Sir Sandford Fleming (1827–1915) was instrumental in establishing this system of standard time zones. The zero zone is centered on the Greenwich meridian (longitude 0°), and, since 1972, standard time in that zone is UTC. Thus the world system of civil time is based on UTC. Depending upon an observer's location within his or her standard time zone, standard time may differ by up to an hour or so from LMT (see the third paragraph on p. 205). That is the second reason why the Sun seldom, if ever, is on the observer's meridian at 12:00 noon, standard time.

Humans generally have an awake/asleep cycle that is delayed by a few hours relative to the day/night cycle. Consequently, in higher latitudes during the spring and summer, when the Sun rises before humans do, more energy is needed for lighting in the evening than would be the case if the two cycles coincided. To shift the lifestyles of their citizens to be more in phase with the day/night cycle, many countries adopt ***Daylight Saving Time***, advancing clocks by one hour during the spring and summer (a better term would be *Energy Saving Time* because it is energy that is being saved, not daylight). For most of Canada and the United States[1], clocks are advanced by one hour at 02:00 local time on the second Sunday in March, and return to standard time at 02:00 local time on the first Sunday in November: *spring ahead, fall back.*

[1] Some regions in northwestern Ontario, Saskatchewan, northeastern and southeastern British Columbia, Hawaii, and most of Arizona, do not observe Daylight Saving Time. For more information see webexhibits.org/daylightsaving.

STANDARD TIME ZONES

The map on the following page shows the world system of standard time zones. It was prepared and provided by Her Majesty's Nautical Almanac Office. Over the open oceans, the time zones are uniformly spaced and are bounded by lines of longitude 15° apart. In populated regions, political and other considerations have considerably modified the ideal geometry.

The standard time zones are generally designated by letters of the alphabet. The zero time zone, centered on the longitude 0° meridian passing through the Airy Transit Circle at the Old Royal Observatory in Greenwich, England, is denoted Z. Standard time within this zone is Coordinated Universal Time (UTC). Zones A, B, C,…, M (J excluded), increase eastward at one-hour intervals to the International Date Line (where, continuing eastward, the day of the week jumps discontinuously back by one day), while zones N, O, P,…, Y decrease westward at one-hour intervals to the same boundary (where, continuing westward, the day of the week jumps discontinuously ahead by one day). Zones M and Y are only one-half hour wide. Also, as indicated on the map, there are several partial zones that are one-half hour different from the adjacent main zones.

In Canada and the U.S., there is one partial zone and seven standard time zones. In terms of their name (and letter designation, hours behind the Greenwich zone, and the west longitude of the reference or standard meridian), these are:

(1)	Newfoundland	(P*,	3 h 30 min,	52.5°)
(2)	Atlantic	(Q,	4 h,	60°)
(3)	Eastern	(R,	5 h,	75°)
(4)	Central	(S,	6 h,	90°)
(5)	Mountain	(T,	7 h,	105°)
(6)	Pacific	(U,	8 h,	120°)
(7)	Alaska	(V,	9 h,	135°)
(8)	Hawaii	(W,	10 h,	150°)

Note: Caution is advised when relying on the time-zone information given in the map overleaf. The zones are drawn based on the best information available as of August 2022 (no change since 2020) and are subject to change. Also, local jurisdictions, especially those near depicted zone boundaries, often adopt a different time. For current official Canadian and U.S. time zones, visit nrc.canada.ca/en/node/1325 and time.gov, respectively.

WORLD MAP OF TIME ZONES

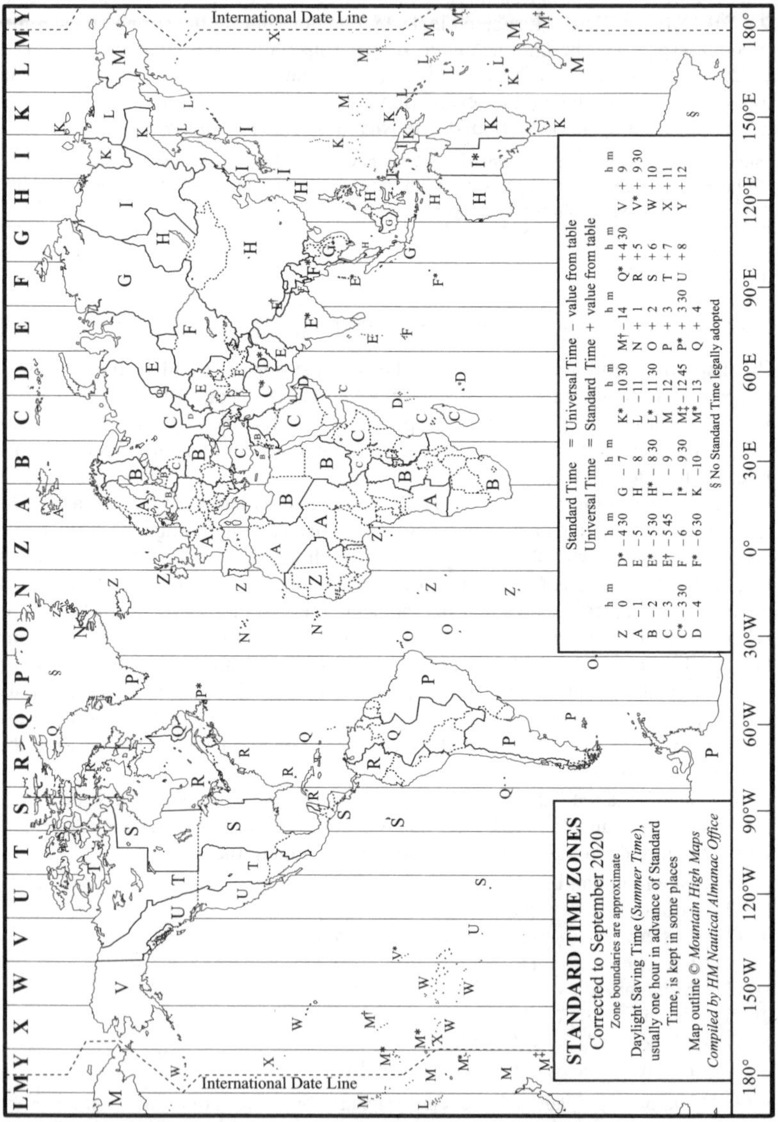

TIME SIGNALS

National time services distribute Coordinated Universal Time (UTC). UTC is coordinated through the Bureau International des Poids et Mesures (BIPM) in Sèvres, France, so that most time services are synchronized to a tenth of a millisecond. Radio time signals available in North America include:

CHU Ottawa, Ontario, Canada 3.330, 7.850, 14.670 MHz
WWV Fort Collins, Colorado, USA 2.5, 5, 10, 15, 20 MHz

For CHU, each minute starts at the *beginning* of the tone following the voice announcement, the tone for the 29th second is omitted, and the tones for seconds 31 through 39 have a different sound from the others.

The difference DUT1 = UT1 − UTC to the nearest tenth of a second is coded in the signals. If UT1 is ahead of UTC, second markers beginning at the 1-second mark of each minute are doubled, the number of doubled markers indicating the number of tenths of a second UT1 is ahead of UTC. If UT1 is behind UTC, the doubled markers begin at the 9-second point.

Time signals are also available by telephone from the National Research Council in Ottawa. Call 613-745-1576 for English, and 613-745-9426 for French; the call may be routed via one or two communications satellite hops, being delayed by 0.25 seconds per hop. See tinyurl.com/ybfjkjtz and time5.nrc.ca for internet time.

MEAN SIDEREAL TIME, 2022

The following is the Greenwich Mean Sidereal Time (GMST) in hours on day 0 at 0h UT of each month ("day 0" is the last day of the previous month):

Jan. 6.6430	Apr. 12.5568	Jul. 18.5364	Oct. 0.5817
Feb. 8.6800	May 14.5281	Aug. 20.5734	Nov. 2.6187
Mar. 10.5198	Jun. 16.5651	Sep. 22.6104	Dec. 4.5900

GMST (in hours) at hour t UT on day d of the month =
GMST at 0h UT on day 0 + $0.065710\,d + 1.002738\,t$
LMST (Local Mean Sidereal Time) = GMST − west longitude (or + east longitude)

LMST computed by this method is accurate to ±0.2 s provided t is stated to ±0.1 s or better and the observer's longitude is known to ±1″. Note that t must be expressed in decimal hours UT and longitude in hours, not degrees. Also, to achieve ±0.1 s accuracy in t, the correction DUT1 must be applied to UTC. See TIME SIGNALS above.

JULIAN DATE (JD), 2022

The Julian Date (JD) is commonly used by astronomers to refer to the time of astronomical events, because it avoids some of the annoying complexities of the civil calendar. Julian Date 0.0 was the instant of Greenwich mean noon on 4713 Jan. 1 BCE (see "The Origin of the Julian Day System" by G. Moyer, *Sky & Telescope*, April 1981, and en.wikipedia.org/wiki/Julian_day#Julian_Date).

The Julian day **commences at noon** (12h) UT. To find the JD at any time during 2022, determine the day of the month and time at the Greenwich meridian, convert this to a decimal day, and add it to one of the following numbers according to the month (these numbers are the JD for 0h UT on the 0th day of each month):

Jan. 245 9579.5	Apr. 245 9669.5	Jul. 245 9760.5	Oct. 245 9852.5
Feb. ... 245 9610.5	May 245 9699.5	Aug. ... 245 9791.5	Nov. ... 245 9883.5
Mar. ... 245 9638.5	Jun. 245 9730.5	Sep. 245 9822.5	Dec. 245 9913.5

For example, 21:36 EDT on May 18 = 1:36 UT on May 19 = May 19.07 UT = 245 9699.5 + 19.07 = JD 245 9718.57.

The JD for 0h UT Jan. 0 for the five proximate years are 245 0000.5 plus: 8483 (2019), and 8848 (2020), and 9214 (2021), and 9944 (2023), and 1 0309 (2024).

ASTRONOMICAL TWILIGHT AND SIDEREAL TIME

BY RANDALL BROOKS

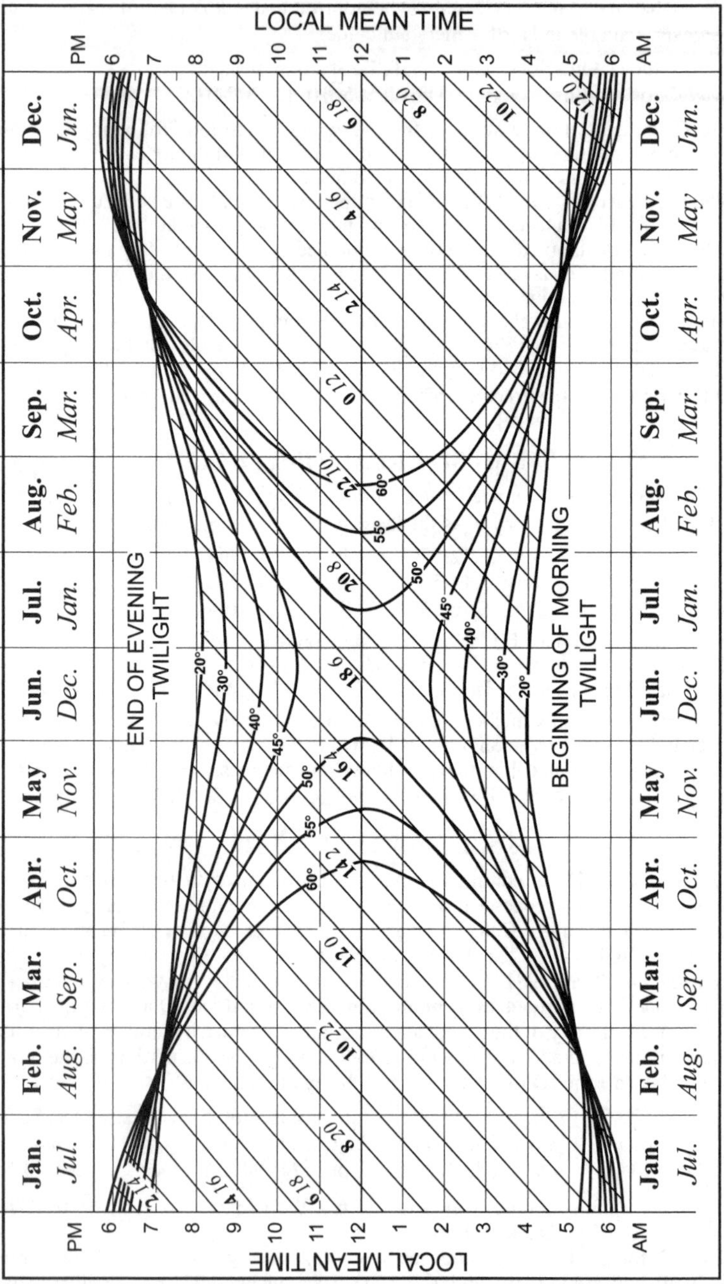

The diagram gives for any day of the year: **(1)** *the LMT of the end and beginning of astronomical twilight at seven specified latitudes (curved lines);* **(2)** *the (LMST = right ascension at the observer's meridian) as a function of LMT (diagonal lines). Months and right ascensions shown in* **boldface** *are for observers in the Northern Hemisphere, those in italics are for observers in the Southern Hemisphere.*

OPTICS AND OBSERVING

TELESCOPE PARAMETERS

BY ROY BISHOP

Equations

Objective: f_o = focal length; D = diameter; FR = focal ratio $\equiv f_o/D$

Eyepiece: f_e = focal length; d_f = diameter of field stop; θ_p = apparent angular field

Whole Instrument: M = angular magnification; d_p = diameter of exit pupil; θ_c = actual angular field

$$M \equiv \tan(\theta_p/2)/\tan(\theta_c/2) = f_o/f_e = D/d_p \approx \theta_p/\theta_c$$

$$d_f = 2f_o \tan(\theta_c/2) = 2f_e \tan(\theta_p/2)$$

Performance

D is assumed to be expressed in millimetres.

Light Grasp (LG) is the ratio of the light flux intercepted by a telescope's objective lens or mirror to that intercepted by a human eye having a 7-mm-diameter entrance pupil.

Limiting Visual Magnitude $m \approx 2.7 + 5 \log D$, assuming transparent, dark-sky conditions with good seeing and magnification $M \geq 1D$ (see *Sky & Telescope, 45*, 401, 1973; *77*, 332, 1989; *78*, 522, 1989).

Smallest Resolvable Angle $\alpha \approx \lambda/D \approx 555 \text{ nm}/D = 114/D$ seconds of arc. However, atmospheric conditions seldom permit values less than 0.5″.

Useful Magnification Range $\approx 0.2D$ to $2D$. The lower limit ($0.2D$) guarantees that, for most observers, all the light exiting a telescope can reach the retina. (The reciprocal of the coefficient to D is the diameter (in mm) of the telescope's exit pupil. Also, see the next section concerning exit pupils and magnification.) The upper limit ($2D$) is determined by the wave nature of light and the optical limitations of the eye, although atmospheric turbulence usually limits the maximum magnification to 400× or less. For examination of double stars, detection of faint stars, and studying structure in bright nebulae, magnifications of up to $3D$ are sometimes useful.

Chapman's Magnification Rule: For any telescope, an eyepiece of focal length FR mm provides $M = D$ and a 1-mm diameter exit pupil.

Values for some common apertures

D (mm):	**60**	**80**	**102**	**152**	**203**	**254**	**305**	**406**	**444**
LG:	73	130	210	470	840	1300	1900	3400	4000
m:	11.6	12.2	12.7	13.6	14.2	14.7	15.1	15.7	15.9
α:	1.9″	1.4″	1.1″	0.75″	0.56″	0.45″	0.37″	0.28″	0.26″
0.2*D*:	12×	16×	20×	30×	40×	50×	60×	80×	90×
2*D*:	120×	160×	200×	300×	400×	500×	600×	800×	900×

TELESCOPE EXIT PUPILS

BY ROY BISHOP

If a visual telescope (i.e. having an eyepiece, but no camera) is pointed toward the daytime sky, a small, bright, disk of light will be seen hovering immediately behind the eyepiece. That bright disk is the telescope's **exit pupil**. Insert a small piece of onion skin or paper in that vicinity to demonstrate that the exit pupil *really is located behind the eyepiece*. The exit pupil is the optical image of the telescope's objective lens or mirror formed by the eyepiece.

Another pupil is relevant: As seen by another person, the pupil of your eye, the black disk framed by the colored iris, is an image of your actual eye pupil magnified somewhat by the transparent, convex cornea immediately in front of it. That magnified pupil is the **entrance pupil** of your eye. (Incidentally, the reason your pupil appears black is because the other person's eye pupil *is in the way of the light* that would otherwise be illuminating the part of your retina that can reflect light to the other person's eye pupil.)

Maxwell's equations (see p. 33) describe how light travels, and those equations are symmetric in time. Thus, just as the eyepiece of a telescope forms an image of the telescope's objective, when the entrance pupil of your eye is placed at that image (the telescope's exit pupil), the eyepiece forms an image of the entrance pupil of your eye at the telescope's objective. Provided the entrance pupil of your eye is at least as large as the exit pupil, to incoming starlight that image fills the entire aperture of the telescope. In other words, optically an eyepiece gives you an eye entrance pupil as large as the objective lens or mirror of your telescope. You are transformed into a Cyclops!

The diagram on p. 52 may be used to display the relation between the diameter of the exit pupil (d_p) of a telescope and the focal lengths (f_e) of various eyepieces. Both d_p and f_e are expressed in millimetres. The numbered scale around the upper right-hand corner of the diagram indicates the focal ratio (FR) of the objective lens or mirror of the telescope. (The FR equals the focal length of the objective divided by its diameter; see p. 49.) To prepare the diagram for a particular telescope, locate the FR of the telescope's objective on the FR scale, and draw a straight diagonal line from there to the origin (the lower left-hand corner). The diagram provides a visual display of the standard relation $d_p = f_e/\text{FR}$. One can see at a glance what range of eyepiece focal lengths is suitable for a particular telescope. Concerning the "AGE" scale on the diagram, see the section Very Low (RFT) Magnifications below.

To determine, for example, the eyepiece focal length required to produce a 3-mm exit pupil on a certain telescope, locate $d_p = 3$ on the ordinate, run horizontally across to the diagonal line corresponding to the FR of that telescope, and from there drop vertically downward to the abscissa to find f_e. This procedure may, of course, be reversed: for a given f_e, find the corresponding d_p.

Magnification Ranges

The ranges H, M, L, and RFT blocked off along the ordinate of the diagram break the d_p scale into four sections, starting at 0.5 mm and increasing by factors of 2. Although this sectioning is somewhat arbitrary, it does correspond closely to what are usually considered to be the high (H), medium (M), low (L), and "richest-field telescope" (RFT) magnification ranges of any visual telescope—and the associated d_p ranges are easy to remember. Note that these magnification ranges are defined by d_p, not by the numerical value of the magnification; for example, a magnification of 100× is "high" for a telescope of aperture $D = 70$ mm, "medium" for $D = 150$ mm, "low" for $D = 300$ mm, "very low (RFT)" for $D = 600$ mm, and "ultra-low" for D larger than 0.8 m.

High Magnifications: In the case of the Moon, the planets, and all but the dimmest stars, the highest useful magnification is the point at which blurring due to diffraction (caused by the wave nature of light) becomes noticeable. That corresponds approximately to $d_p = 0.5$ mm, assuming good optics and negligible atmospheric turbulence (i.e. excellent "seeing"). Higher magnifications will not reveal any more detail in these images and will cause reductions in four desirable features: sharpness, brightness, field of view, and eye relief (the space between the eye and eyepiece). However, for double stars and for some objects requiring the use of averted vision (e.g. faint stars) very high magnifications ($d_p < 0.5$ mm) can sometimes be used to advantage.

Medium Magnifications: A problem with high magnifications is that exit-pupil diameters of about 1 mm and smaller cause "floaters" (mobile debris in the vitreous humor of the eye in front of the retina) to interfere with vision. That problem increases with the age of the observer and with decreasing d_p. To avoid the distraction of floaters, an observer might choose to keep exit-pupil diameters no smaller than 1.5 mm (i.e. in the "medium" magnification range). For this lower limit the diagram indicates a minimum eyepiece focal length of, for example, 7 mm for an FR = 4.5 telescope, 15 mm for an FR = 10 telescope, and 24 mm for an FR = 16 telescope. With this restriction, to achieve a magnification of 250× for observing planets, a telescope would need an aperture of at least $D = M \times d_p = 250 \times 1.5 = 375$ mm. Hence, in addition to providing more light and greater resolution, a large-aperture telescope makes floaters less noticeable and magnifications in the "high" range less necessary.

With magnifications greater than very low (RFT) magnifications and also possibly greater than low magnifications, structure in dim, extended objects, such as galaxies and bright and dark nebulae, will be more easily seen. To see such objects, observers use averted vision, which places the image on the peripheral retina, which is composed primarily of the very sensitive "rod" photoreceptor cells. However, the number of rod cells far exceeds the number of nerve axons available to carry the signals to the visual centers in the brain. To accommodate this limitation and to cope with spontaneous thermal noise in the rod cells, the cells are grouped into detector units of various sizes (analogous to binning of pixels in a CCD chip). Because of the thermal noise, only those signals triggered by almost simultaneous photon hits in several rod cells are allowed to produce a conscious sensation. Thus in very dim light only large retinal detector units receive enough photon hits to respond. As a consequence, our ability to see detail is greatly reduced in dim light. Hence extra magnification helps to reveal structure in galaxies and nebulae.

Low Magnifications: Low magnifications have several advantages over certain other magnification ranges:

(1) For most observers an exit-pupil diameter between 2 mm and 4 mm results in the sharpest optical image because the combined influence of optical aberrations in the eye of the observer (which increase with increasing d_p) and blurring due to diffraction (which decreases with increasing d_p) is at a minimum. Assuming, for example, that the optimum d_p for a "typical observer" is 2.5 mm, then to realize this and achieve a magnification of 250× for observing planets, a telescope needs an aperture of $D = M \times d_p = 250 \times 2.5 = 625$ mm. Once again, the superiority of a large telescope (by amateur standards) is apparent. Another example: the reason for the crisp images provided by Canon's image-stabilized binoculars is that their d_p is in the "low magnification" range, and their optical quality is up to the challenge.

(2) Low magnifications provide greater luminance than high or medium magnifications, enabling the eye to discern contrast variations over a wider range of spatial frequencies.

EXIT-PUPILS DIAGRAM

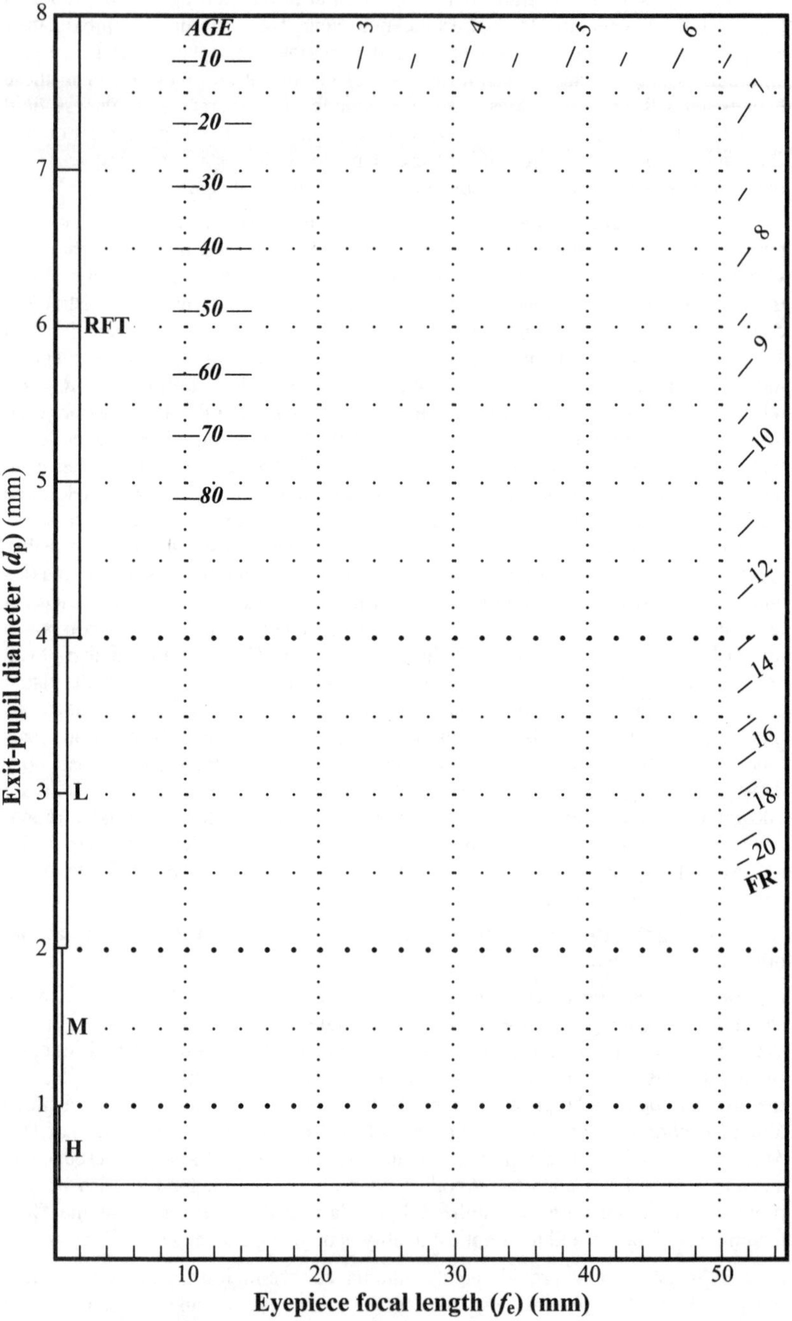

Diagram by Roy Bishop

(3) Viewing is more comfortable than with very low (RFT) magnifications, since the observer can move a bit (move the head and/or scan the field) without cutting into the light beam and dimming the image. As mentioned below, ultra-low magnifications have the same advantage, but light is wasted.

(4) Light entering near the edge of the pupil of the dark-adapted eye is not as effective in stimulating the rod cells in the retina—the "scotopic Stiles–Crawford effect" (see VanLoo and Enoch, *Vision Research, 15* (1975), p. 1005). Thus low magnifications make more effective use of the light than do very low (RFT) magnifications.

(5) Low magnifications provide a darker sky background than do very low (RFT) magnifications, producing views that some observers consider to be aesthetically more pleasing.

Very Low (RFT) Magnifications: Magnifications in the RFT range are useful because they yield wide fields of view, the brightest (greatest luminance) images of extended objects, and for common telescope apertures, the most stars visible in one view (hence the term *richest field*). The lowest magnification that still makes use of the full aperture of a telescope is determined by the point at which the diameter of the telescope's exit pupil matches the diameter of the entrance pupil of the observer's eye.

For the dark-adapted eye, the entrance-pupil diameter seldom equals the often-quoted figure of 7 mm, but depends, among other things, upon the age of the observer as indicated by the scale in the upper-left portion of the diagram (see Kadlecová et al., *Nature, 182* (1958), p. 1520; *Sky & Telescope*, May 1992, p. 502). Note that this scale indicates *average* values; the maximum diameter of the entrance pupil of the eye of any *one* individual may differ by up to a millimetre from these values. A horizontal line should be drawn across the diagram corresponding to the maximum diameter of one's own entrance pupil. This line will be an upper bound on d_p in the same sense that the line at $d_p = 0.5$ mm is a lower bound. Note that in daylight, the entrance pupil of the eye has a diameter in the range of 2 mm to 4 mm. Thus for daylight use of telescopes, the upper bound on d_p will be correspondingly reduced.

Ultra-Low Magnifications: If a d_p value larger than the entrance pupil of the eye is used, the iris of the observer's eye will cut off some of the light passing through the telescope to the retina; that is, the iris will have become the light-limiting aperture *(aperture stop)* of the system rather than the edge of the telescope's objective. In this case, the cornea of the eye together with the lenses of the telescope's eyepiece form an image of the observer's iris at the objective of the telescope; to the incoming starlight, a highly magnified image of the iris hovers as an annular skirt covering the outer region of the objective of the telescope! A telescope can be used at such "ultra-low" magnifications, but obviously a telescope of smaller aperture would perform as well. However, ultra-low magnifications have two advantages:

(1) A wider actual field of view, assuming the field stop of the eyepiece will permit this (an eyepiece having a 2-in. barrel diameter is usually necessary).

(2) Ease of alignment of the entrance pupil of the eye with the exit pupil of the telescope, an aspect of viewing that is usually troublesome when these two pupils are nearly the same size. An oversize exit pupil provides "slop," making alignment less critical. That is particularly helpful when using binoculars during activities involving motion, such as boating or bird watching, and is one advantage of using 7×50 ($= M \times D$) binoculars rather than 7×35 binoculars for daytime activities, although less than half of the light entering the larger binoculars can reach the observer's retinas.

MAGNIFICATION AND CONTRAST IN DEEP-SKY OBSERVING

BY LEE JOHNSON AND WILLIAM ROBERTS

For visual observation of point sources (stars), magnitude limits of common telescope apertures are given in TELESCOPE PARAMETERS (see p. 49). Additional challenges attend the observation of faint, extended, deep-sky objects. This article explores methods to determine the visibility of diffuse objects such as galaxies, dense star clusters, and gaseous nebulae. The main variables governing the visibility of such an object are its average luminance ("surface brightness" in older sources), its angular dimensions, the sky luminance, the telescope aperture, and the magnification used (or, equivalently, the exit pupil of the telescope). Additional factors include the effects of filters, atmospheric extinction, and the limitations of monocular vision. Addressing all these factors, this article builds on seminal research on visual contrast thresholds (Blackwell, 1946), and concludes by linking to an online **Magnification and Contrast Calculator** for estimating the visibility of deep-sky objects. (For an alternative treatment of the same research, especially in relation to the structure of the eye, see Clark, 1990.)

Luminance and Exit Pupils

Table 1 shows the magnitude, size, and luminance of two representative deep-sky objects, with luminance expressed in units of magnitude per square arcsecond (mag/arcsec^2). (For more details on these two objects, see the referenced pages in this Handbook.) When these luminance values are compared to those of skies corresponding to mountain-top observatories (22), dark country sites (21), sites with 5th-mag. stars visible (19.5), and a suburban setting with 4th-mag. stars visible (18.5), it is clear that an object can be dimmer than the sky background; that is, the contrast between the object and the sky is very low. A Sky Quality Meter (unihedron.com) provides a baseline luminance measurement for such a comparison.

TABLE 1—MAGNITUDE, SIZE, AND LUMINANCE

Object	Type	m_V	Size (arcmin)	Luminance (mag/arcsec^2)	OH Page Ref.
NGC 7317	galaxy	13.6	0.5×0.5	20.7	p. 323, 337
Jones 1	planetary nebula	12.1	5.5×5.5	24.4	p. 323

Size, magnitude, and luminance (surface brightness) of deep-sky objects can be found in *The Deep Sky Field Guide to Uranometria 2000.0* and (for a few objects) in A DEEP-SKY SELECTION (see p. 309). In addition, most tables in THE DEEP SKY (see p. 307) include magnitudes and sizes of objects. For any extended deep-sky object, the luminance, S, in mag/arcsec^2, can be estimated from size and magnitude by

$$S = m_V + 2.5\log(2827ab),$$

where a and b are, respectively, the object's major and minor diameters in arcminutes, assuming an elliptical shape. (Subtract 8.9 to convert units to mag/arcmin^2.)

The exit pupil of a telescope (objective diameter divided by magnification) determines the luminance of the image of both the object and the sky as viewed through the eyepiece (see TELESCOPE EXIT PUPILS, p. 50). When an extended object is magnified to the extent that the telescope exit pupil becomes smaller than the entrance pupil of the eye—nominally 7 mm—its luminance decreases relative to the naked-eye view. The decrease is the same for both the object and the sky; in other words, **magnification does not alter contrast**. Table 2 gives the reduction in luminance of both object and sky as the exit pupil decreases.

TABLE 2—DIMMING WITH RESPECT TO A 7-MM EXIT PUPIL

Exit Pupil (mm)	7	6	5	4	3	2	1	0.5
Dimming (mag)	0.0	0.3	0.7	1.2	1.8	2.7	4.2	5.7

Human binocular vision has a lower luminance limit of approximately 1 μcd/m^2, which, when adjusted for monocular vision, is about 27 mag/arcsec^2. When the dimming due to reduced exit pupils (from Table 2) is combined with the sky luminance, it is apparent that the luminance of a magnified dark sky may approach the detection limit of the eye; for example, a 1-mm exit pupil in a 22.0 mag/arcsec^2 sky reduces the apparent sky luminance to 26.2 mag/arcsec^2, which is near the limit of the eye.

The Relation Between Size and Threshold Luminance

Blackwell (1946), in a massive World War II study that is still the only one of its kind, analysed approximately 450 000 observations of threshold contrast over a wide range of background illumination. Table 3, derived from Blackwell's data, gives the minimum detectable luminance of an object for various combinations of object size and background luminance. The values are corrected for monocular vision and assume a 50% probability of detection; for 90% probability, subtract 0.5 from the entries in the table.

TABLE 3—THRESHOLD LUMINANCE OF EXTENDED OBJECTS

Object	**Background Luminance (mag/arcsec^2)**							
Size (′)	**26**	**25**	**24**	**23**	**22**	**21**	**20**	**19**
360	26.3	26.0	25.6	25.0	24.4	23.7	23.0	22.3
240	26.1	25.8	25.4	24.8	24.2	23.5	22.8	22.2
120	25.5	25.3	24.9	24.4	23.7	23.1	22.4	21.8
60	24.7	24.5	24.2	23.7	23.1	22.5	21.9	21.3
30	23.8	23.8	23.3	22.8	22.3	21.7	21.1	20.6
15	22.5	22.3	22.0	21.6	21.1	20.6	20.1	19.7

The table confirms that low-luminance objects of a given size are more easily seen against darker backgrounds. For a given background luminance, large objects are more easily detected than small ones of equal luminance. Applied to the case of an object viewed through a telescope, as magnification increases, one moves up in the table (larger apparent size) and also to the left (smaller exit pupil = darker sky). Hence, detectability benefits from higher magnifications, in agreement with observing experience. However, note that this benefit is smaller toward the upper-left corner of the table. As magnification increases, a point may be reached where the decreasing exit pupil reduces the object luminance faster than the increasing size raises the threshold luminance. Thus the object would become more difficult to detect, but the increased magnification might make it easier to identify bright detail within the object.

It is important to note that the table values are guidelines only. If Table 3 suggests that the detection of an object is marginal, do not be discouraged; try anyway. Other factors that affect object detection are: atmospheric extinction, light loss in the telescope optics, the difference between the nighttime and daytime response of the eye (see FILTERS, 64), and the observer's visual acuity. Typically, the cumulative effect of these factors is between −0.5 and +0.5 mag.; see Schaefer (1990) for further details.

An example using Table 3: Consider the galaxy NGC 7317 in a 21.0 mag/arcsec^2 sky. A magnification of 148× with a 445-mm telescope gives an apparent object size of 74′ with a telescope exit pupil of 3 mm. From Table 2, a 3-mm exit pupil dims both object and sky by 1.8 mag., resulting in luminance values of 22.5 (object) and 22.8 (sky). The entry in Table 3 for background luminance 23 and object size 60′ gives a threshold luminance of 23.7. That is more than one magnitude dimmer than the image of NGC 7317, which should therefore be clearly visible under the specified conditions. On the other hand, a smaller, 130-mm telescope with a magnification of 43× gives a reduced object size of 22′ with a 3-mm exit pupil, hence the values of object and sky luminance are the same as before. Again from the fourth column of Table 3, the interpolated threshold luminance of this smaller image is 22.2, so the object will likely not be visible in this smaller instrument at this magnification. Alternatively, finding the object luminance in that column, we see that the minimum apparent size is almost 30′, and since 22′ is less than this, the object is unlikely to be seen.

The Relation between Minimum Detectable Size and Contrast

Figure 1 shows another way of interpreting Blackwell's data, a graphical representation of Table 3, whose columns are now a set of curves (odd-valued sky luminance values are shown with dashed lines for clarity). The vertical axis represents the minimum detectable size of an object, and the horizontal axis is the object–sky magnitude contrast, that is, the magnitude difference between object luminance and sky luminance. Whereas Table 3 emphasizes detectability as a function of object luminance and size, Figure 1 emphasizes detectability as a function of the object–sky magnitude contrast and size.

FIGURE 1—MINIMUM DETECTABLE SIZE VS. CONTRAST

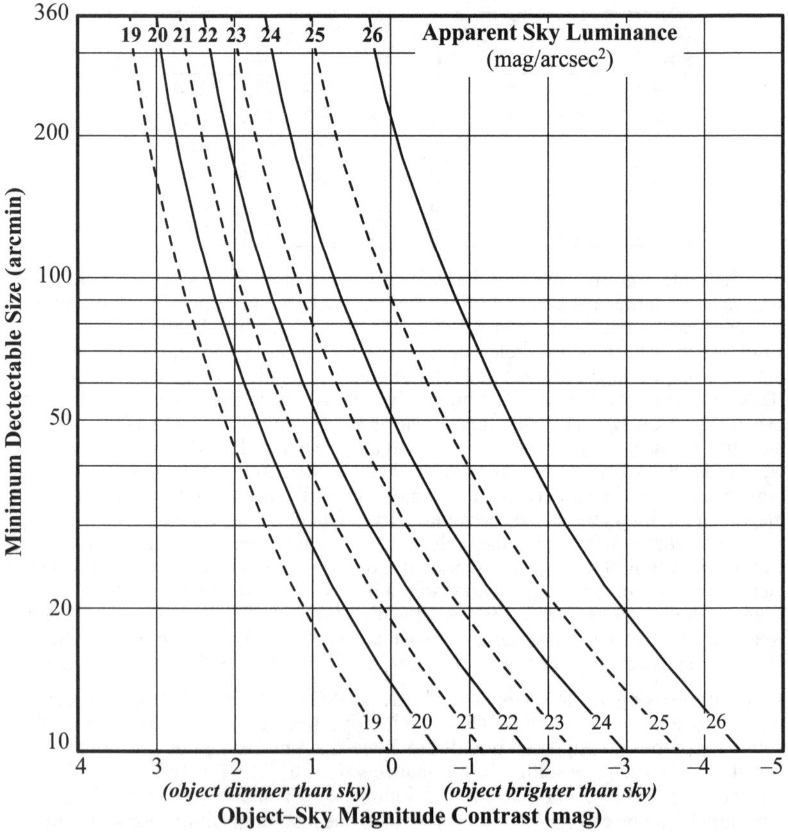

An example using Figure 1: Emission and planetary nebulae are special cases, as contrast can be improved using filters (see FILTERS, 64). Bandpass filters such as the UHC, OIII, and Hβ improve contrast by passing light near the emission wavelengths and rejecting broad-spectrum light from light pollution and natural skyglow at other wavelengths, effectively reducing the sky luminance by about 1.6 mag. through the UHC filter and about 2.6 mag. through the OIII and Hβ filters. The visible light from emission nebulae is mainly in the OIII and Hβ wavelengths, which lie close to the peak response of the dark-adapted eye. Filters such as the UHC pass all the light from these lines and do not significantly dim the nebulae. These filters therefore do not require an increase in exit pupil in order to maintain the object luminance. On the other hand, OIII filters—and especially Hβ filters—may pass only a portion of the light from an emission nebula, hence dimming the nebula. Here, restoring the object's luminance requires an increase in exit pupil and thus a decrease in magnification. The OIII filter passes most of the light from a typical planetary nebula and thus does not require an increase in exit pupil; it is therefore the filter of choice for these objects. The situation for other emission nebulae is not so clear.

Consider viewing Jones 1, a dim planetary nebula of luminance 24.4 mag/arcsec^2, in a sky of luminance 21.0, a magnitude contrast of +3.4. An exit pupil of 2 mm or smaller would reduce the object luminance below the eye's absolute threshold of 27. In a 250-mm aperture, a magnification of 50× gives an exit pupil of 5 mm, which results in a sky luminance of 21.7 and an object size of 275′. Figure 1 shows the minimum detectable size at a contrast of 3.4 to be greater than 360′, so Jones 1 would not be visible under these conditions. An OIII filter would reduce the sky luminance by 2.6 mag. without dimming Jones 1 appreciably and results in a sky luminance of 24.3. The magnitude contrast would be +0.8 mag., and the minimum apparent size is approximately 40′. The planetary nebula should be visible when viewed in that telescope with the filter.

Magnification and Contrast Calculator

Table 3 has been incorporated into a **Magnification and Contrast Calculator** spreadsheet, available online at rasc.ca/supplements. When data for an object, the sky, the telescope, and possible filters are entered, the spreadsheet calculates the observed image parameters and makes a detection prediction of YES, NO, or MAYBE.

Summary

Generally, experienced deep-sky observers select eyepieces that produce exit pupils in the range 2–3 mm when viewing a faint deep-sky object. This range of exit pupils corresponds to the middle of both Table 3 and Figure 1. Larger exit pupils correspond to the lower right of the table, where small, faint objects may fall below the threshold of visibility; and smaller exit pupils to the upper left, where excessive magnification may dim the object to invisibility. At any fixed apparent size, moving from right to left across the table results in a decrease in threshold brightness, which shows the benefit of observing in increasingly dark skies or with the aid of a filter.

References and Resources

- Blackwell, H.R., "Contrast thresholds of the human eye," *J. Opt. Soc. Am. 36*, 624–643 (1946).
- Clark, Roger N., *Visual Astronomy of the Deep Sky*, Sky Publishing Corp., Cambridge, Mass., 1990, p. 13 *ff.* Also see clarkvision.com/visastro
- Schaefer, Bradley "Telescopic Limiting Magnitudes," *Publ. Astron. Soc. Pac. 102*, 213–215 (February, 1990).
- Mel Bartels' internet page *Visual Astronomy*: bbastrodesigns.com/visual.html

NIGHT VISION, EYEGLASSES, AND OBSERVING

BY DAVID M.F. CHAPMAN

Visual observers take great care of their telescopes, eyepieces, and other gear to ensure a successful night under the stars, but the state of their personal vision is equally important. This article provides guidance on several aspects of vision that affect your observing experience.

Dark Adaptation, Glare, and "Red" Lights—The sensitivity of the eye is reduced by exposure to bright light, especially at the shorter (blue) wavelengths. Avoid bright sunlight during the day before observing, and especially avoid gazing into computer and mobile device screens. Allow at least 30 minutes in a dark place for the eye to biochemically adapt before attempting to observe dim objects (see LIGHT POLLUTION/Light and Vision, p.79). If you must use your device, make sure it is dimmed and/or reddened appropriately; many devices now have internal settings for that.

Any extraneous light that enters the eye while observing constitutes unwanted glare that interferes with your view. Reducing glare while observing is the responsibility of both you and your observing companions: such extraneous light needs to be shielded, dimmed, and reddened. Flashlights (including headlamps) must not trespass on the observing space of others, and should be as dim as possible, with even illumination (not concentrated at the center)—some observers add tissue paper to the unit to diffuse the glow. Many red flashlights and headlamps are simply too bright for visual observing at the telescope—inspect them thoroughly for improvement opportunities.

Floaters—day or night, if you are viewing through an optical instrument at high magnification, chances are you will notice out-of-focus "stuff" inside your eye, slowly drifting through your field of view, interfering with the observation. It's particularly noticeable with bright objects, such as the Sun, Moon, and planets. Floaters are still present while observing dim objects, although they may not be obvious, and may degrade the view. There's not much you can do about floaters, but they will limit the maximum usable magnification of your telescope. Getting a bigger telescope helps! (See TELESCOPE EXIT PUPILS/Medium Magnifications, p. 50.)

Eyeglasses at the Telescope—If you need glasses only to correct for simple far –or near-sightedness, you probably do not need to wear them at the eyepiece—the telescope focusing mechanism should provide all the adjustment you need. However, astigmatism is a condition in which the eye magnifies more in one lateral direction than the perpendicular direction: stars don't focus to small points, but to elliptical blobs, decreasing resolution and reducing the maximum useful magnification.

Rx	SPH	CYL	AXIS	ADD
OD	*–1.50*	*–0.25*	*020*	*+2.00*
OS	*–1.75*			*+2.00*

Sample optical prescription for weak myopia, with mild astigmatism in the right eye. OD = Oculus Dexter = right eye, OS = Oculus Sinister = left eye, SPH = spherical correction (overall focus) in diopters, CYL = cylindrical correction (astigmatism) in diopters AXIS = axis angle of cylindrical lens in degrees, ADD = additional correction for reading glasses.

If you have your eyeglass prescription handy, you have astigmatism if numbers occupy the boxes under the "CYL" column. The units are dioptres (D), a measure of lens power: $D = 1/FL$, in which FL is the lens focal length in metres. 0 is good, 0.25 not bad, anything larger needs to be addressed. Your two eyes will likely be different: The "OD" row denotes your right eye; the "OS" row denotes the left eye. If you have only mild astigmatism, you might get by without using your glasses. If you have strong astigmatism, you will need to wear your glasses—it's a personal choice, depending on your circumstances and observing goals.

If you need help with astigmatism, and must wear your glasses, consider using eyepieces known for "long eye relief" (Pentax XW/XL, Tele Vue Delos, Tele Vue DeLite, Noblex, and Vixen SLV are examples). Another solution is the Tele Vue DIOPTRX™ corrective lenses that attach to some of their eyepieces. The only good news is that you will probably save a lot of money NOT buying those fancy, ultra-wide panoramic eyepieces: if you can't place your eye at the required distance for optimal views, the outer reaches of the field of view will be wasted on you. The best advice is to "try before you buy" when it comes to any premium eyepiece.

Bifocal lenses create additional problems for the observer. The upper part of the lens is curved to provide correction for distant vision, like a typical eyeglass lens. The lower part is curved to provide corrections at mid –and reading distances; the problem is, almost all bifocals are "progressive" lenses that really only work looking directly ahead, and not to the side. In addition, the power of the lens varies along the vertical direction. Naturally, this creates havoc at the eyepiece, and you need to be careful how you position your eyes with bifocals. The simplest solution is to have a second pair of "single vision" eyeglasses for telescope use.

Laser Corrective Surgery—It is tempting to do away with eyeglasses completely, by having surgery on your corneas to alter their refraction; however, there are potential pitfalls. Typically, the treatment is applied only to the central area of the cornea, as the pupil of the eye only opens that far in daytime light levels. In the dark, when your pupil dilates to admit more light, any surgery-induced imperfections or ridges in the surface of the cornea will become evident, leading to unwelcome effects such as halos around bright sources and hazy vision from scattered light. Most patients are interested in improving their day-to-day vision, and often opt for convenience over visual acuity. As an observing amateur astronomer, you need to have a serious discussion with your eye health specialist or eye surgeon regarding your expectations before taking this irreversible course.

Cataracts and Lens Replacement—As you age, you might develop indistinct vision due to the formation of cataracts inside the internal lens of the eye. Eventually, your eye health specialist will refer you for intraocular lens replacement surgery. The improvement in vision is rapid and remarkable; however, as with laser correction, the amateur astronomer needs to balance day-to-day convenience and visual acuity, as there are many replacement lens options to consider, too many to recount here. Again, you need to have a heart-to-heart discussion with your eye surgeon to choose the right options for you. Most amateur astronomers who have undergone lens replacement surgery report that they experience a much-improved view of the sky. However, even after laser correction or lens replacement, you may still need eyeglasses!

Night Myopia—Most people become a little nearsighted in the dark, owing to the larger pupil aperture. You can compensate for this by adjusting your standard prescription and ordering special glasses only used for stargazing. Not only will your view of the sky be clearer, you could gain a half a star magnitude of sensitivity. To determine the best correction, you will need to obtain a set of optical "flippers" to try in front of your normal eyewear. It is possible that your eye health professional can assist you. For the new lenses, anti-reflection coatings are recommended, and polycarbonate material is to be avoided. See Joshua Roth's article "Spectacles for Spectacular Skies" on p. 30 of the September 2005 issue of *Sky&Telescope*, or online at skyandtelescope.org/astronomy-resources/spectacles-for-spectacular-skies.

[Author's note: thanks to Roy Bishop, Chris Beckett, Ralph Chou, and Rob Dick for their assistance.]

BINOCULARS

BY ROY BISHOP

For an experienced observer, binoculars are indispensable. For a beginning observer, binoculars are preferable to an astronomical telescope. For a beginner unfamiliar with the large-scale features of the sky, who cannot yet identify a dozen constellations on any clear night, a telescope's narrow field of view, confusing image orientations, and unfamiliar controls will quickly cause more frustration than fun. The beginner is at a double disadvantage because he or she also does not know enough about astronomical telescopes to distinguish those that are worthy of the name from the common camera/department-store "junk telescopes"—the $299 wonders with poor optics and wobbly mounts. How many such telescopes are gathering dust in closets, their young owners turned off astronomy and their parents a few hundred dollars poorer? Far better had the same investment been made in a good pair of binoculars. With their ease of use, wide field of view, and unreversed, upright images, binoculars are a great help in finding one's way around the sky, and provide many unique views of the heavens.

Binoculars magnifying 6 to 10 times are ideal for locating planets in the twilight, scanning the constellations, studying the larger dark nebulae and star fields of our galaxy, and viewing bright comets. Binoculars magnifying 10 to 20 times provide the best views of objects spanning a few degrees, such as the Hyades, the Pleiades, the North America Nebula, and the Andromeda Galaxy; they also give the finest view of the slender crescent Moon, or of the full Moon with broken clouds blowing by.

Binoculars permit us to view the Universe with both eyes, thereby providing more advantages: an improved sense of reality and depth (although parallax is negligible when viewing the heavens); more relaxed viewing; a complete view in the sense that the blind areas of one eye (associated with blood vessels and the region where the optic nerve attaches to the retina) are compensated by the field provided by the other eye; and dim objects appear brighter when viewed with two eyes.

Sizes: Binocular sizes are specified by numbers, for example, 7×50 and 8×30. The first number, including the "×," is the angular magnification or "power"; the second number is the diameter of the front (objective) lenses in millimetres. That is, in the notation on p. 49: $M \times D$. Thus the exit-pupil diameter is easily calculated from $D \div M$ (e.g. 7×35 binoculars have exit pupils of $35 \div 7 = 5$ mm). Another important parameter is field of view. Binoculars have apparent angular field diameters of about 50° when equipped with standard eyepieces, to near 70° with wide-angle eyepieces. The actual field of view on the sky (typically 3° to 10°) equals approximately the apparent field divided by the magnification. Thus the area of sky visible decreases rapidly with higher magnifications, making aiming binoculars at an object of interest more difficult.

What is the best binocular size for astronomical use? There is no simple answer. Almost *any* pair of binoculars will show far more than can be seen with the unaided eyes; however, for astronomical use the objective lenses should be at least 30 mm in diameter. Also, small binoculars of high quality are more enjoyable to use than a large pair of low quality.

Caveat emptor! Low-quality binoculars (and telescopes) are common. Images seen through low-quality binoculars are slightly fuzzy (usually not apparent to the inexperienced observer), one's eyes will be strained in trying to compensate for imperfectly aligned optics, and the focusing mechanism is usually flexible and crackling with an excess of grease used to mask poor workmanship. Avoid both zoom (variable magnification) binoculars and binoculars that do not have an adjustable focus—invariably these are of low quality.

Considering that binoculars contain at least 14 pieces of glass with 36 optical surfaces, antireflection coatings on (hopefully) all air-to-glass surfaces, plus two focusing mechanisms and an interpupillary adjustment, it is not surprising that top-quality instruments cost about $1000 or more. Such prices buy crisp, high-contrast images, accurately aligned optics, precise, rugged, dust –and moisture-proof construction, and pleasurable service for a lifetime. Nevertheless, there is a big market for $99 binoculars and $299 telescopes, and manufacturers are happy to satisfy the demand. When it comes to optical equipment, quality usually matches price.

Stability: One aspect of binocular use not often appreciated is how much more can be seen if the binoculars are mounted on a stable support, such as a camera tripod. That eliminates the constant jiggling associated with hand-holding and also supports the weight of the instrument. Adapters for attaching binoculars to a tripod are available, although usually it is not difficult to make your own. A recent major advance in binocular design is "image stabilization," an active optical system built into binoculars that compensates for the tremor associated with hand-holding. For example, the Canon company has introduced microprocessor-controlled binocular image stabilization that gives almost tripod-like stability with the convenience of hand-holding (see *SkyNews*, July/August 1998, p. 12; and *Sky & Telescope*, July 2000, p. 59). The Canon 10×42L model in particular, with its superb optics, convenient 6.5° diameter actual field, and close focusing ability, is the single best, hand-held set of binoculars ever created for both general daytime use and astronomy. It accepts 52-mm camera UV filters to protect the objective lenses.

Rating Binoculars

A frequently cited figure for binocular performance is "Relative Brightness," which equals the square of the diameter (in millimetres) of the instrument's exit pupils. For example, for 7×50 binoculars this figure is $(50 \div 7)^2 \approx 51$. Although this is a measure of the surface brightness *(luminance)* of an extended object seen through the binoculars under nighttime conditions, it is a totally inadequate measure of binocular performance on the night sky. For instance, using this figure of merit, large 14×100 binoculars have practically the same rating as the unaided eyes (which, when young and in dim light, are effectively 1×7 binoculars)!

Since seeing depends upon light, and the amount of light passing through a pair of binoculars depends primarily upon the *area* of the objective lenses (diameter D), a D^2 dependence appears reasonable. However, although the amount of light going into the point images of stars increases as D^2, assuming constant magnification the increase in the luminance of the background sky as D increases leads to a somewhat slower improvement in the visibility of these stars. A similar muted improvement occurs for dim extended images, resulting in an approximately D^1 dependence, rather than D^2.

Also, for constant D the detail that can be seen in the night sky increases with the magnification M. The resulting lower luminance of the background sky allows fainter stars to be seen, and the visibility of structure in extended images improves as M increases because the image is larger and of fixed contrast relative to the sky background.

The simplest figure of merit for the performance of binoculars in low-light conditions that combines both variables is the mathematical product $M \times D$ (which happens to look the same as the binocular size specification). In the case of two pairs of binoculars, one having twice the M and twice the D of the other, $M \times D$ indicates that "four times as much" should be visible in the larger instrument (e.g. 16×60 versus 8×30 binoculars). That is to be expected, since in the larger instrument stars will be four times brighter and extended images will have four times the area from which the eyes can glean information, with luminances being the same in both instruments.

For many decades the venerable Carl Zeiss optical company has cited $\sqrt{(M \times D)}$ as a "Twilight Performance Factor" for binoculars, its value said to be proportional to the distance at which various binoculars will show the same detail. That is equivalent to $M \times D$ being proportional to *the amount of detail that can be seen at the same distance.* The latter situation is relevant for astronomy since, unlike a bird or other object on Earth, a star or a galaxy is always at essentially the *same distance* from the observer. $M \times D$ could be called the *visibility factor.*

Binocular Performance Diagram

The diagram on the following page enables one to quickly compare binoculars in terms of their ability to reveal detail in the night sky. The vertical axis is magnification M; the horizontal axis is aperture D. The uniform grid of small dots is a guide to reading the diagram. The five straight lines indicate constant exit-pupil diameters of 3, 4, 5, 6, and 7 mm, as indicated both by numbers and by circles of these diameters near the top ends of the lines. The five curved arcs indicate constant values of $M \times D$ (the visibility factor), increasing by successive powers of 2 toward the upper right (100, 200, 400, 800, and 1600). Each large dot represents a common size of binoculars. The arrows in the lower-right corner indicate the directions on the diagram in which various quantities increase most rapidly.

Each straight line (constant exit-pupil diameter) also corresponds to constant luminance of extended areas, such as the Orion Nebula or the background sky glow, with the luminance being proportional to the square of the exit-pupil diameter (provided the entrance pupils of the observer's eyes are large enough to accommodate the exit pupils of the binoculars). However, exit pupils of 3 to 5 mm ensure that (i) all the light transmitted by the binoculars can enter the dark-adapted eyes no matter what the observer's age; (ii) alignment of exit pupils with dark-adapted eye pupils is relatively easy to achieve; (iii) the background sky glow will be subdued; and (iv) star images will be less distorted by aberrations in the observer's eyes (see TELESCOPE EXIT PUPILS, p. 50).

Examples (see the diagram): for viewing the night sky 10 × 50 binoculars will show about twice as much detail as 7 × 35s; 11 × 80 and 15 × 60 binoculars are equally capable, as are 8 × 30s and 6 × 42s (assuming one's eye pupils can accommodate the exit pupils of the instrument with the larger D); 10 × 50 binoculars are appreciably better than 7 × 50s for visibility (although, assuming equal apparent angular fields, 7 × 50s will show about twice as much sky area as will 10 × 50s). Canon's image-stabilized 15 × 45 binoculars are nearly equivalent to tripod-mounted 10 × 70s, with the *triple* advantage of smaller size, accommodating observers whose pupils will not open to 7 mm, and not requiring a tripod!

The visibility factor $(M \times D)$ is applicable to the usual range of binocular sizes (exit pupils between about 2 mm and 7 mm), but should not be extrapolated indefinitely. For instance, as the magnification is increased on a telescope and the exit pupil approaches 1 mm or less, a point will be reached (dependent upon the darkness of the sky) where the background sky glow is imperceptible. Also, stars will begin to show either seeing disks or diffraction disks. A further increase in M will not cause a noticeable improvement in the visibility of stars, and the perceived contrast between an extended object and the sky will decrease. In addition, the angular size of an extended object must be kept in mind. Once M is increased to the point at which the object fills the field of view of the instrument, the object may not be visible at all! For example, a large, dim comet coma may be visible in 15 × 60 binoculars $(M \times D = 900)$ but *invisible* in a 45 × 200 telescope $(M \times D = 9000)$.

BINOCULAR PERFORMANCE DIAGRAM

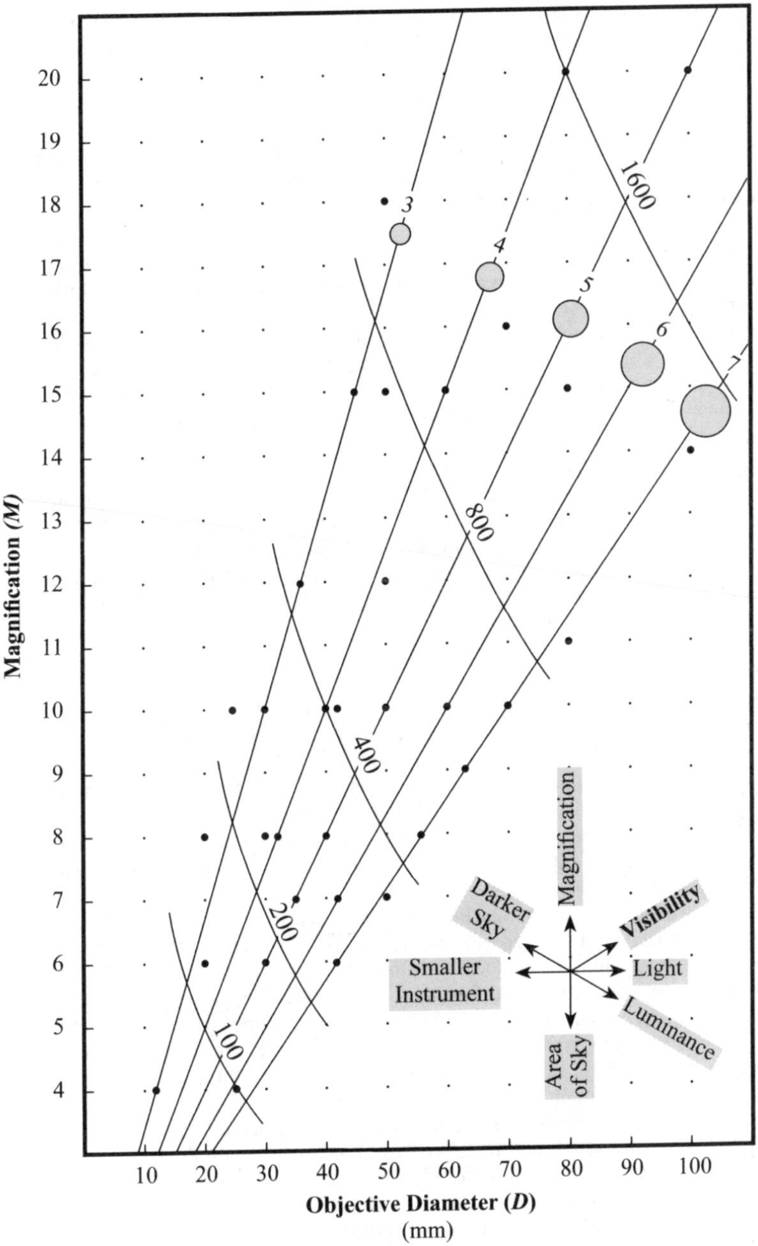

Diagram by Roy Bishop

FILTERS

BY ROY BISHOP

Optical filters reflect and absorb some portion of the incident light. *Neutral-density filters* reflect and absorb light more or less uniformly across the visible spectrum. *Colored (dye) filters* typically pass only one or two moderately broad portions of the spectrum. *Interference filters* are more selective and typically pass only one or two well-defined, narrow segments of the spectrum. All three types of filter are invaluable in astronomy.

In addition to categorization by physical type, filters may be categorized according to their intended use: lunar and planetary (neutral-density and dye filters), solar (neutral-density and interference filters), and nebular (interference filters).

Lunar and Planetary Filters

As viewed in a telescope, the Moon and the planets Venus, Mars, and Jupiter are often uncomfortably bright. A neutral-density filter, which passes only 13%–25% of the light, solves this problem while avoiding the loss in resolution that would accompany stopping down the aperture of the telescope to decrease the brightness to the same level. With a less-glaring image, light scattering in the observer's eye is reduced and fine details are easier to see. A neutral-density filter is typically about 26 mm in diameter and is attached to the forward-facing end of an eyepiece.

Dye filters can enhance the visibility of various planetary features. For instance, a red or yellow filter will absorb bluish light scattered by the Martian atmosphere and thereby improve the contrast of features on the surface of Mars. A green filter will increase the visibility of pale red and blue areas in the atmosphere of Jupiter (although the entire image will then appear green). Also, since they absorb an appreciable fraction of the light, dye filters or polarizing filters have the same advantage as a weak neutral-density filter when viewing bright objects.

Solar Filters

A filter is essential when observing the Sun. Solar filters must be designed not only to reduce the brightness of the solar surface to a comfortable level, but to block out the invisible but damaging infrared and ultraviolet radiation. Just because a filter makes the Sun dim enough to view comfortably is no guarantee that it is not transmitting damaging amounts of invisible radiation! This is no place to experiment with do-it-yourself filter designs—use only a proper solar filter from a reputable manufacturer. *Failure to use a proper filter when observing the Sun can cause immediate and irreversible damage to vision.*

A special warning: Heavy atmospheric haze near sunrise or sunset often dims the Sun so that it appears as a dull red disk, not uncomfortably bright to the eye. At such times resist the temptation to view the Sun with a telescope without using a solar filter. The atmosphere at such times is still relatively transparent in the invisible infrared portion of the spectrum, and the great light grasp of a telescope can result in thermal retinal damage! With the unaided eyes the retinal solar image, although just as bright, is much smaller and the eye can better dissipate the heat. Also, with unaided vision, one is less apt to fixate on the Sun for a prolonged period.

For white-light views of the Sun a dark, broad-spectrum, neutral-density solar filter is needed. Aluminized Mylar and metal-coated glass are common designs, although they usually do not attenuate light uniformly across the visible spectrum (i.e. they are not perfect neutral-density filters). Aluminized Mylar gives a bluish color to the solar image, while metal-coated glass filters usually give an orange color.

The filter should be 50 mm or more in diameter and must be positioned to cover the *front* of the telescope. Ensure that the filter is *securely attached* so that a gust of wind or a bump cannot dislodge it. (Some small telescopes are sold with a "Sun filter" designed to attach to the eyepiece, just before the observer's eye. Sunlight concentrated by the telescope can overheat and shatter a filter of this design. Such filters should be thrown in the garbage!)

For direct viewing of the Sun (not using binoculars or a telescope) shade #14 (no other shade) rectangular welder's glass may be used (available at welding supplies shops). These filters are not suitable for attaching to the front of binoculars or a telescope simply because their poor optical quality results in a fuzzy image.

Red, flame-like prominences at the Sun's limb and much structure in its chromosphere across the solar disk can be seen in hydrogen-alpha (Hα) light, a strong spectral line emitted by atomic hydrogen. This light is totally overwhelmed by the rest of the solar spectrum, so a neutral-density filter will not work. Advances in vacuum thin-film technology have made possible interference filters, filters that operate on the same principle as Fabry–Perot interferometers, involving the interference of multiply reflected beams of light. These filters can be constructed so they are transparent only to light having an extremely narrow range of wavelengths, typically 0.15 to 0.05 nm for solar viewing, although band-passes of up to 1 nm are used in solar-prominence viewers designed to occult the solar disk. If this band-pass is centered on the Hα wavelength (656.3 nm), nearly all the Sun's light will be blocked, leaving an image in Hα light.

Hα filters are expensive, particularly for band-passes near 0.05 nm that are needed for high-contrast images of the solar disk. These filters may be located either in front of the objective of a telescope or between the objective and the eyepiece. In the latter case, because the wavelength of the center of the narrow band-pass varies with the angle at which light rays enter the filter (a characteristic of interference filters), the focal ratio of the imaging telescope must be near *f*/20 for 0.15-nm band-pass filters and *f*/30 or higher for filters with narrower band-passes. Temperature control is usually required to keep the band-pass centered on the Hα wavelength, although some Hα filters are designed to be tilted in order to tune them to the Hα wavelength (the wavelength of peak transmittance is shifted toward shorter wavelengths when the filter is tilted away from 90° incidence).

Hα filters require a broadband "energy-rejection prefilter," located at the front of the telescope. The prefilter has a band-pass of about 100 nm in the red part of the spectrum and blocks essentially all the infrared, ultraviolet, and much of the visible part of the solar radiation from entering the telescope.

Nebular Filters

From the surface of Earth, the night sky is not completely dark. Even in the absence of light pollution (human-made and lunar), the air itself emits a feeble light called airglow. In higher latitudes, aurorae can also contribute to the glow of the atmosphere. Two other components of the light of the night sky are not associated with Earth's atmosphere, the zodiacal light and background starlight. The diffuse glow from all four sources reduces the contrast of celestial objects and, in the case of dim comets, galaxies, and nebulae, the object may be completely obscured by the brightness of the sky.

Filters transmit only a fraction of the incident light. Thus employing them to see faint objects may seem counterproductive. However, there are objects in the heavens that emit light only at certain wavelengths. This behavior is characteristic of plasmas—excited gases, matter composed of separate atoms energized either by ultraviolet radiation from nearby hot stars or by collisions such as occur in supernova explosion shock fronts. Such regions are called emission nebulae and include star-forming regions, planetary nebulae, and some supernova remnants. A filter that selectively blocks most of the background sky glow but is transparent to the wavelengths at which such objects emit most of their visible light will darken the sky background without appreciably dimming the object of interest. With narrow-band-pass interference-type filters the effect can be dramatic, improving contrast and revealing details that otherwise are completely invisible. It is the next best thing to observing these objects from above Earth's atmosphere!

Dark-adapted (scotopic) human vision responds to light having wavelengths from approximately 400 to 620 nm. In bright light (photopic vision) the spectral range extends to somewhat longer wavelengths, about 750 nm. For both types of vision the response curve (sensitivity vs. wavelength) is "bell-shaped," the wavelength of maximum sensitivity being in the middle of the visible range—near 507 nm for scotopic vision and 555 nm for photopic vision (see the figure "Nebular Filter Transmission" on the following page). The photopic sensation produced by 555-nm light is green; for scotopic vision color is not produced, but at photopic levels 507-nm light appears blue-green.

Hydrogen is the predominant element in the Universe. Atomic hydrogen, when excited by ultraviolet radiation from a nearby hot star, emits light in the visible spectrum at only four discrete wavelengths: 656, 486, 434, and 410 nm (designated as Hα, Hβ, Hγ, and Hδ, respectively, part of the *Balmer spectrum* of hydrogen). Scotopic vision is blind to 656-nm (Hα) light and relatively insensitive to the less intense 434 –and 410-nm light. However, 486 nm (Hβ) lies near the 507-nm peak sensitivity of scotopic vision, and an Hβ ("H-beta") filter having a narrow band-pass at this wavelength will greatly reduce the surrounding sky brightness and reveal Hβ-emitting nebulae.

The classic example is the Horsehead Nebula, a dark, silhouetted column of dust just southeast of the east end of Orion's belt. The surrounding hydrogen gas, excited by the nearby hot star σ Orionis, fluoresces dimly with Hβ light. If the obscuring airglow is blocked by an Hβ filter, the dark Horsehead can distinctly be seen in a telescope having an aperture of 400 mm or greater and an eyepiece giving an exit pupil near 5 mm (see pp. 50–53). However, the number of objects that can be viewed advantageously with an Hβ filter is very limited, apparently because few nebulae emit strongly in Hβ light.

Two other strong nebular emission lines lie at 496 and 501 nm, nearly at the peak sensitivity of scotopic vision. Originally detected in 1864 by the British astronomer William Huggins, the origin of these lines was unknown at that time, and they were attributed to a hypothetical new element, "nebulium." In 1927, the American astrophysicist Ira Bowen identified the lines as due to doubly ionized oxygen (O^{++} or OIII), which glows brightly when very low-density nebular gas is strongly excited (high temperature). A filter that has a narrow band-pass spanning these two wavelengths gives striking views of highly excited nebulae. A good example is the Veil Nebula, a supernova remnant in eastern Cygnus. Through an OIII filter on a dark, transparent night, the direct view of the Veil in a large amateur telescope is more spectacular than any photograph. Planetary nebulae (fluorescing, low-density shells of gas surrounding hot central stars) also show up well with an OIII filter; examples include the Helix Nebula (NGC 7293), the Owl Nebula (M97), the Dumbbell Nebula (M27), and the Ring Nebula (M57).

Because of their narrow band-passes, Hβ and OIII filters are sometimes called *line filters*, although their band-passes are much wider than that of an Hα filter. Filters encompassing both the Hβ and OIII lines are termed *narrowband filters*, for example the Lumicon Ultra High Contrast (UHC) filter. Although the background sky will be brighter than with a line filter, more and brighter stars will be visible, providing a more attractive setting for a view of a nebula, particularly in smaller telescopes. Stars emit light across the entire visible spectrum, thus line filters and narrowband filters impair views of single stars, reflection nebulae, star clusters, and galaxies.

Older types of streetlights (e.g. low –and high-pressure sodium, mercury vapor) are notorious for shining much of their light horizontally and upward, creating

NEBULAR FILTER TRANSMISSION

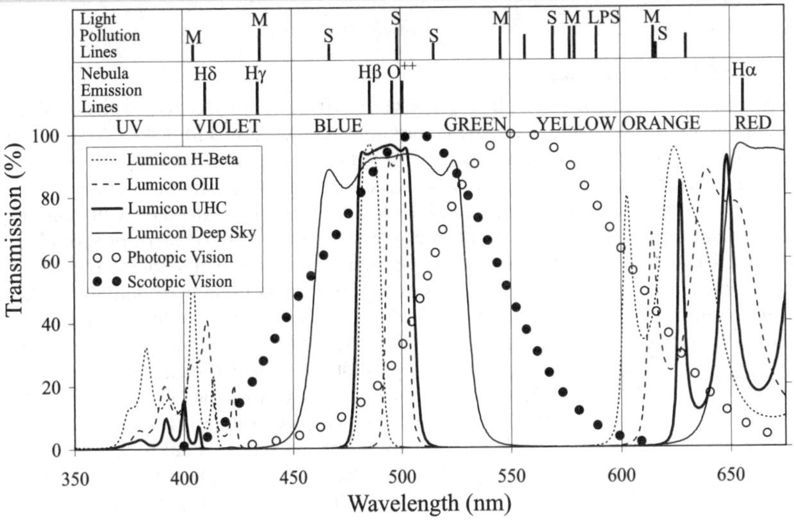

The dotted, dashed, and continuous curves show the transmission versus wavelength characteristic of four interference filters (in descending order in the legend): two line filters, a narrowband filter, and a broadband filter. The bell-shaped curves composed of small open and solid circles show the relative response of bright-adapted (photopic) vision and dark-adapted (scotopic) vision. In ascending sequence above the curves are spectral colors, nebula emission lines, and light-pollution lines (M = mercury, S = high-pressure sodium, and LPS = low-pressure sodium). High-pressure sodium light sources emit an additional broad continuum spectrum that is not shown. The two unlabeled light-pollution lines are strong airglow/auroral lines produced by atomic oxygen. (Dave Lane used a "Varian Model Cary 50 Conc UV-Visible Spectrophotometer" owned by the Chemistry Department at Saint Mary's University to obtain the filter curves; he also prepared the diagram.)*

*See p. 32 for basic information on optical wavelength and color.

glare, light trespass, and wasting energy, yet much of their light is emitted at only one or a few wavelengths such that filters with band-passes avoiding those wavelengths suppress much of the associated light pollution. LED streetlights are replacing those earlier types, and their usual full-cutoff designs direct their light downward where it is useful. Unfortunately, most of today's LED streetlights have two negative features: a continuous spectrum that is difficult to filter out, and more serious, their spectrum is particularly bright at short wavelengths (c. 450 nm). Those indigo wavelengths scatter much more readily in the air than do longer wavelengths (which is why scattered sunlight makes the clear sky blue), exacerbating the ever growing nighttime artificial sky glow that negatively impacts wildlife and human health, and prevents most people from ever experiencing the spectacle of a truly dark, star-filled sky.

Nowadays many astrophotographers impacted by light pollution resort to a set of line filters centered on the nebular wavelengths Hβ, OIII, Hα, and SII (singly ionized sulfur at 672 and 673 nm). Although Hα and SII filters are useless for viewing nebulae directly (scotopic vision being blind to those wavelengths), together with CCD cameras these line filters make possible impressive color composite images of nebulae taken from light-polluted sites, including when the bright Moon is in the sky.

LIMITING MAGNITUDES

BY DOUGLAS PITCAIRN

Limiting Visual Magnitude

One of the many difficulties with visual observing from the surface of our planet is the variability of the atmosphere. In any record of observations it is important to note the condition of the sky. Parameters such as brightness and contrast are greatly affected by the transparency of the sky and the presence of light pollution or aurorae.

One of the simplest ways to quantify local sky conditions is to note the magnitude of the faintest star visible with the unaided eye: the *limiting visual magnitude* (LVM). (See rasc.ca/lpa/sky-quality-measurement-project for an alternative method using an electronic *sky quality meter* that measures sky brightness in units of *magnitude per square arcsecond*.) Although individuals differ in their ability to detect faint stars, these differences are generally small, and for any one observer such observations provide a consistent measure of sky quality. The chart at the left shows a 9° field in the vicinity of Polaris (the brightest star on the chart) and is useful for observers at latitude 20°N or higher. For orientation, the solid lines mark the beginning of the handle of the Little Dipper (see MAPS OF THE NIGHT SKY, p. 339). Several stars have their visual magnitudes indicated (with decimal points omitted). Using this field to determine your LVM has several advantages: it is always above the horizon in mid-northern latitudes; its altitude does not change with the time of night or year, so the variation of atmospheric extinction with altitude is not a consideration; there are no bright stars or planets in the field to dazzle the eye; the faint stars are quite well spaced and therefore easy to identify; and being a simple field, it can be memorized. Especially note the dashed spiral of descending magnitudes labeled "A" through "F."

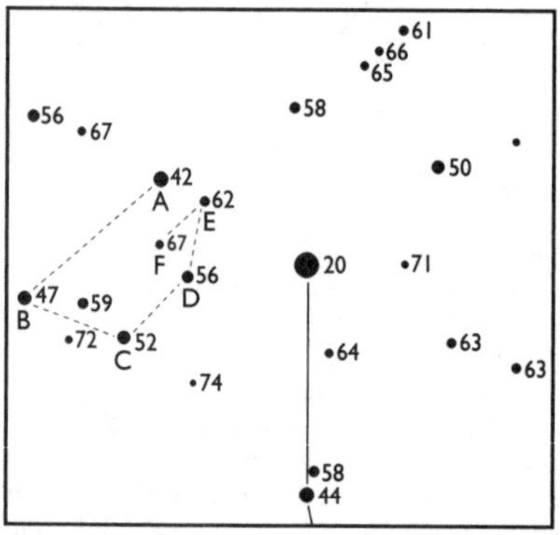

Limiting Telescopic Magnitude

Aperture, telescope design, eyepiece design, magnification, and the quality of optical surfaces are a few of the many variables that will determine the faintest stars visible through a given telescope and eyepiece. By determining an instrument's limiting magnitude—the *limiting telescopic magnitude* (LTM)—you can effectively assess the effect of these variables. The quality of the night sky will also affect the LTM. Therefore, changes in the LVM should be taken into account when determining the LTM. (The relationship between LTM and LVM is complex; readers may explore it using the excellent web-based calculator at bogan.ca/astro/optics/maglimit.html.) The LTM is a useful guide when attempting faint targets (Pluto in a 150-mm scope?), comparing the performance of different instruments, or determining whether a mirror or lens needs cleaning (many people clean their optics too often, assuming that dust degrades optical performance more than it actually does). For a study on sky brightness, telescope magnification, and contrast in deep-sky observing, see p. 54.

To help determine the LTM of your instrument, use the charts on the next page, which show an 8′-wide section of the northwest quadrant of M67 centered at RA 8 h 50.1 m and Dec +11° 53′. This old open cluster lies 8° south-southeast of M44, Cancer's famous Beehive Cluster. The accompanying table lists the visual magnitudes

STAR	VISUAL	B – V
A	10.60	1.10
B	11.19	0.43
C	11.59	0.42
D	12.01	0.57
E	12.26	0.68
F	12.57	0.59
G	13.04	0.85
H	13.35	0.59
I	13.61	0.59
J	13.96	0.62
K	14.34	0.56
L	14.66	0.67
M	14.96	0.69
N	15.30	0.79
O	15.58	0.84
P	16.06	0.74
Q	16.31	0.99
R	16.62	0.81
S	17.05	1.26
T	17.38	1.17
U	17.64	1.31
V	18.04	1.27
W	18.38	0.76
X	18.69	1.17
Y	19.07	1.56
Z	19.29	0.61
a	19.42	1.34
b	20.10	0.00
c	20.35	0.83
d	20.61	1.55
e	21.03	0.32

M67 Limiting Telescopic Magnitude Chart

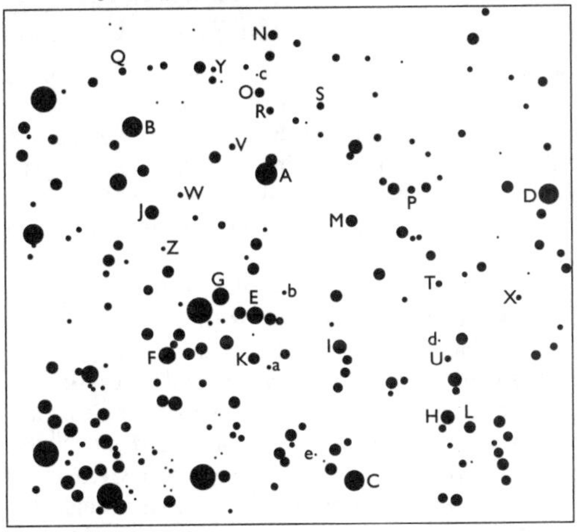

as above, mirror-reversed view

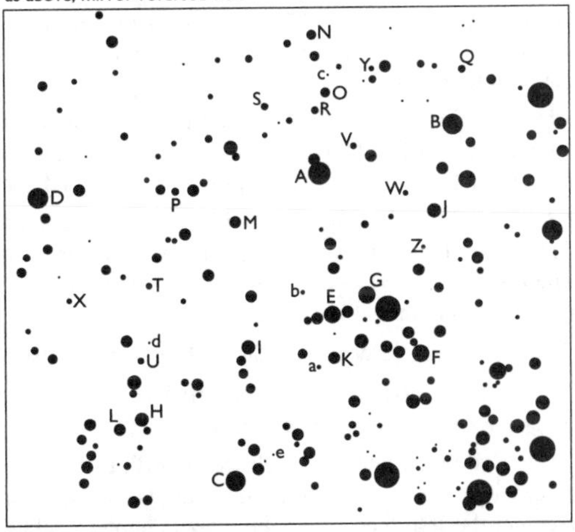

The upper chart is for telescopes with an even number of reflecting surfaces (e.g. Newtonian reflectors) and the "mirror-reversed" chart is for telescopes with an odd number of reflecting surfaces (e.g. a refractor with a diagonal). North is at top in both of these charts.

and the $B - V$ color indices of the labeled stars. The diagram was constructed from a photograph taken by René Racine of the Université de Montréal, who exposed a 103a-D plate at the *f*/3.67 focus of the Hale Reflector. The magnitudes are based on work by Racine and Ronald Gilliland of the Space Telescope Science Institute.

Correction for Atmospheric Extinction

Atmospheric extinction varies with altitude above the horizon. To normalize observations to the zenith (altitude 90°), the following values should be added to estimates of faintest visible magnitude obtained using the charts. The format is: (altitude range) **correction:**

(18°–20°) **0.5** (20°–24°) **0.4** (24°–29°) **0.3** (29°–36°) **0.2** (36°–52°) **0.1** (52°–90°) **0.0**

These corrections are for near sea level and would be reduced at higher elevations. Also, excellent sky conditions are assumed; under less-than-ideal conditions, the corrections are generally larger and can be quite uncertain, especially when the target area is closer to the horizon.

POLAR ALIGNMENT

BY BLAIR MACDONALD

Beginning observers are often confused by the concept of telescope mount alignment. With the advent of Go To mounts, this confusion is compounded by the fact that the *computer* of such a mount must also be oriented to the sky. Polar alignment applies only to equatorial mounts; it is an independent physical alignment of the polar axis of the mount with the north celestial pole (NCP) or the south celestial pole (SCP).

Ideally, the polar axis is parallel to Earth's rotational axis and therefore must point at a celestial pole. The required alignment accuracy depends on the observing goals. For casual visual observing, it is usually sufficient to align the polar axis of an equatorial mount with Polaris (in the Northern Hemisphere) or σ Octantis (in the Southern Hemisphere). The charts on the facing page show the location of the NCP and SCP in their surrounding star fields, and the caption describes the alignment procedure.

For long-exposure astrophotography or for an automated observing program, significantly more accurate polar alignment is necessary. A dedicated polar axis telescope with a Polaris-offset reticle on a German equatorial mount, makes it simple to achieve polar alignment. However, any equatorial mount can be polar aligned by the straightforward *drift alignment* method. As outlined below, the drift alignment method uses a reticle eyepiece and the viewing of two stars on the celestial equator, one near the meridian and the other near the eastern horizon. The method also works in the Southern Hemisphere: simply interchange north and south, clockwise and counterclockwise.

1. Roughly level the mount and point the polar axis at Polaris. A simple eyeball alignment is sufficient, but the closer you get now, the fewer drifting iterations you will have to make later. The rough alignment described above is usually good enough.

2. Install a reticle eyepiece with the lines aligned to the right ascension (RA) and declination (Dec) axes directions as follows: First, center a star on one of the lines. Then move the telescope slightly in RA and rotate the eyepiece until the star moves parallel to the line.

3. Point the telescope at a star on the celestial equator in the south near the meridian.

4. With the drive engaged, center the star on a reticle line aligned with the RA direction. Ignoring RA drift, note the Dec drift of the star over several minutes.

5. If you must move the telescope north to recenter the star, then adjust the mount clockwise in azimuth as seen from above. If you must move the telescope south to recenter the star, then adjust the mount counterclockwise in azimuth.

6. Repeat Steps 4 and 5 until there is no visible drift over several minutes.

7. Now point the telescope at a star near the eastern horizon on the celestial equator.

8. Center the star on a reticle line aligned with the RA axis as in Step 4. Ignoring RA drift, note the Dec drift of the star over several minutes.

9. If you must move the telescope north to recenter the star, then tilt the polar axis downward. If you must move the telescope south to recenter the star, then tilt the polar axis upward.

10. Repeat Steps 8 and 9 until there is no visible drift over several minutes.

Repeat Steps 3–10 for improved accuracy, because adjusting the elevation often requires further adjustment in azimuth and vice versa. The longer it takes to detect Dec drift, the more accurate the polar alignment. For a star near the equator, a Dec drift of d arcseconds over time t minutes indicates a polar axis misalignment of $p \approx 3.8\ d/t$

arcminutes. For example, a 10″ drift over 1 min indicates a polar axis misalignment of 38′, while a 5″ drift over 5 min indicates a polar axis misalignment of only 3.8′.

The drift method produces very accurate alignment even when the optical tube is not exactly aligned with the mount.

See backyardastronomy.com/Backyard_Astronomy/Downloads.html for a comprehensive treatment of polar alignment.

FINDER CHARTS FOR THE NORTH AND SOUTH CELESTIAL POLES

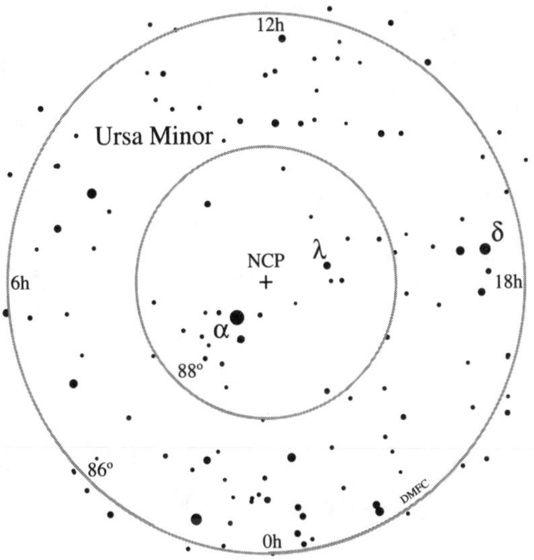

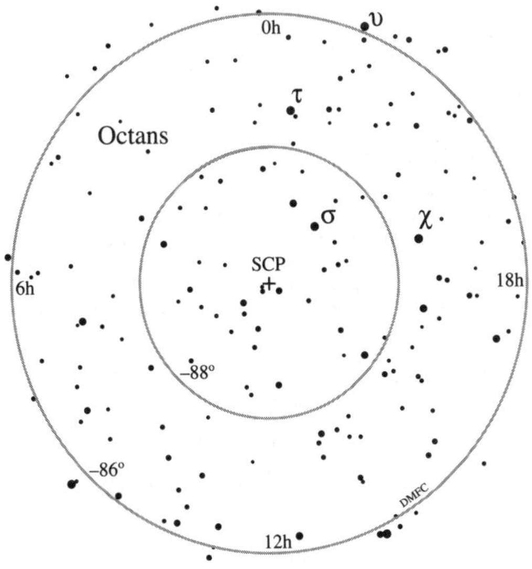

The finder charts depict mirror-correct fields of view with circles of diameter 4° and 8° centered on the celestial poles (Dec is indicated on the circles). Stars are shown to magnitude 9. δ UMi is the penultimate "handle" star in Ursa Minor.

For casual visual observing, it is sufficient to align the polar axis of an equatorial mount to Polaris (α UMi, magnitude 2.0), near the NCP, or to σ Oct (magnitude 5.5), near the SCP, as follows:

Roughly level the mount and orient the RA axis to true north (south) in azimuth. Set the RA axis elevation to the observing latitude. Lock the Dec axis to +90° (–90°). While viewing through the finder or telescope at low magnification, adjust the azimuth and elevation to center the pole star. For finer alignment, align to the estimated position of the NCP (SCP) relative to the star field.

For accurate polar alignment, the drift alignment method (described on the facing page) is recommended and works for all equatorial mounts.

(Finder charts were derived from sky charts generated with Voyager III, *a product of Carina Software.)*

Diagram by Dave Chapman

FREQUENCY OF NIGHTTIME CLOUD COVER

BY JAY ANDERSON

FEBRUARY–MAY MEAN NIGHTTIME CLOUD COVER IN PERCENT

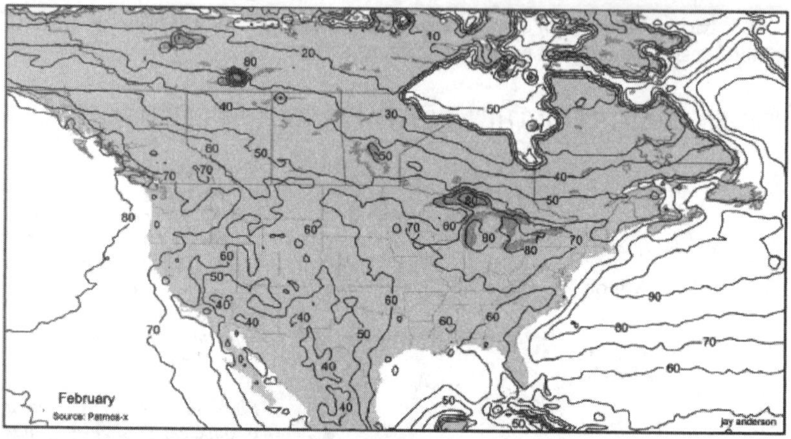

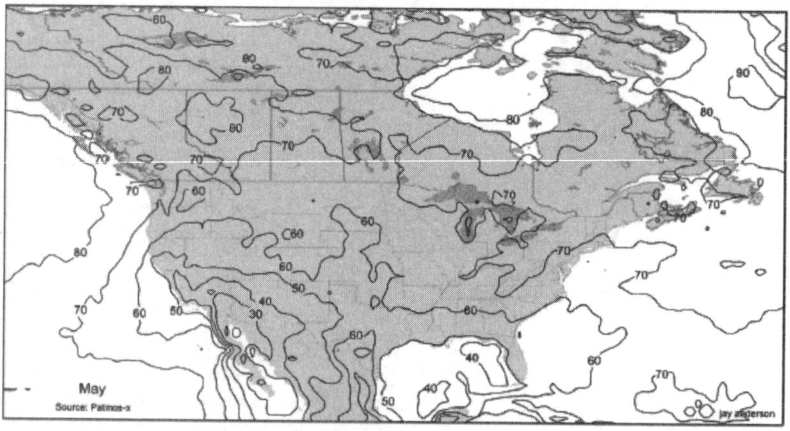

The maps on these pages are constructed from observations taken from 16 years of satellite observations ending in 2009. These sensors detect emitted and reflected radiation in several wavelengths and use a statistical, climatological, model-based algorithm to determine the amount of cloud in 1-degree longitude by 1-degree latitude bins. The Patmos-x dataset used in these maps is one of the best of several approaches to cloud measurement.

The months chosen give a good year-round depiction of annual cloud climatology, while avoiding June and July. Several notable trends are shown: the clearer skies over western Canada that come with frigid winter temperatures, the heavy winter cloudiness around the Great Lakes, the sunny Prairie summers, the higher cloud amounts in mountainous terrain, and the onset and decay of the mid-summer Southwest Monsoon of Arizona and New Mexico.

February cloud amounts follow a quasi-latitudinal pattern across Canada, interrupted by the very high cloudiness across the Great Lakes. The situation in the U.S. is more complex, with more cloud over the northern Rockies, Appalachians, and the northeast U.S, where the influence of the Great Lakes and east-coast storms dominates. The southwest states have the least cloudiness, mostly because their low latitude takes them out of the path of the major winter storms, along with the shelter provided by the mountain chains in the area. That protective topography has an influence farther north, creating a zone of low cloud that extends northward along the Front Range of the Rockies as far north as the Canadian border.

AUGUST–NOVEMBER MEAN NIGHTTIME CLOUD COVER IN PERCENT

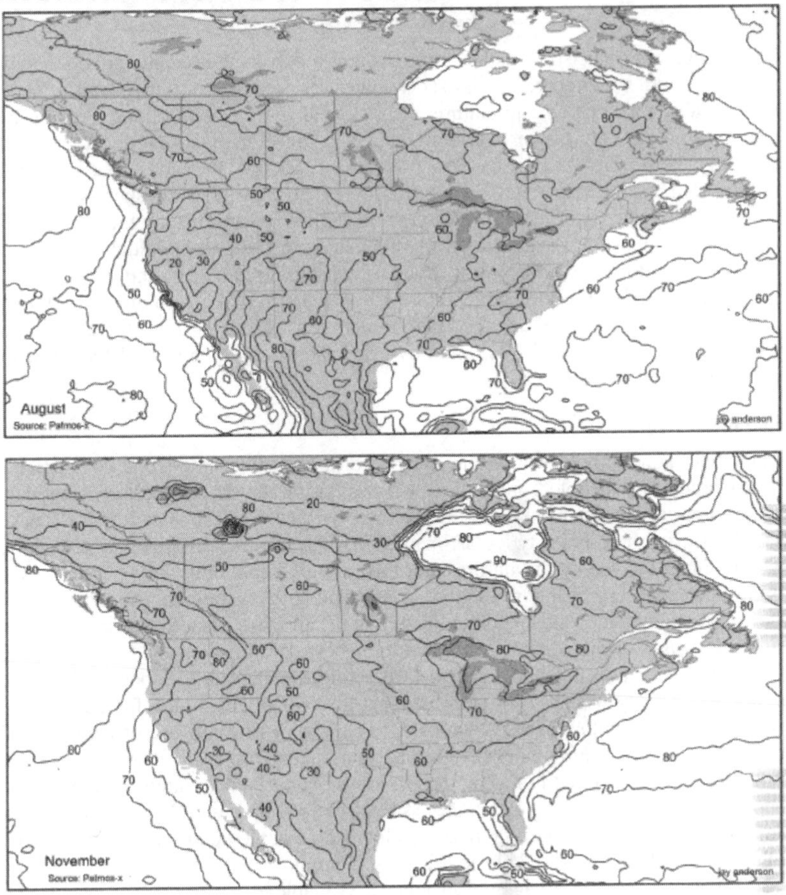

In May, the cold air retreats northward and much of Canada returns to a cloudier climatology. The protection provided by the Rockies fades away, leaving a broad band of moderate cloudiness across the Great Plains. The Appalachians north of Georgia retain their reputation for high cloudiness, but in the American Southwest May is the sunniest month, sandwiched between the winter months with their occasional low-latitude snows and the summer's onset of convective thunderstorms.

In August, the Southwest becomes one of the cloudiest regions, as Gulf of California moisture spreads north. Noteworthy is the very low cloud amount in central California. The plains retain a modest amount of cloud—it's still thunderstorm season, but the protection of the Rockies is still evident in the arc of below-50% contours from southern Saskatchewan and Alberta to Texas. The Appalachian states still hold onto high cloud frequencies, but eroded from earlier maximums.

November brings a hint of winter, though the low cloud amounts that come with freeze-up are still limited to the Northwest Territories. The monsoon season is long gone over the southwest, the Great Lakes have begun their role as winter cloud-makers, but winter has not reached the south; the Appalachians enjoy their sunniest season of the year. Rocky Mountain cloudiness has increased over British Columbia as the first of the fall storms arrive onshore, and the Prairies are gradually losing their sunny disposition.

Additional maps of global cloudiness may be found on the author's website at eclipsophile.com. Data source: Patmos-x/CIMMS/SSEC.

WEATHER RESOURCES ON THE INTERNET

BY ALLAN RAHILL

Despite public skepticism, weather forecasts are in fact quite accurate, provided they are from informed sources. Specialized weather services—usually involving a fee—are available for aviation, agriculture, forestry, and marine applications. Previously, there was no such service for astronomy, likely because there was no directly related economy. However, the Canada-France-Hawaii Telescope at Mauna Kea has been using a seeing and transparency forecast for more than eight years to "queue schedule" observing activities. Currently, professional observatories are making the best use of weather conditions and are able to effectively manage activities accordingly.

Similar information has been freely available to amateur and professional astronomers worldwide on the internet for many years. With light pollution becoming more and more pervasive, amateur astronomers must drive long distances to get to dark skies. They can avoid frustration by using the information and URLs below to plan their observing sessions.

Satellite Images

Many astronomers rely on satellite images to predict nighttime cloud cover. Real-time images are available from GOES satellites for the eastern and western Americas; other satellites such as Meteosat give the same service for Europe and Africa. These satellites give three main types of images: visible, infrared (IR), and water vapor. Visible images are easy to interpret, but they are available only during the day; for nighttime tracking of clouds, IR images are available. Water-vapor images do not track clouds; they indicate the total moisture in the air mass. Usually the darkest areas in those images have good correlation with the best sky transparency.

Particularly useful for short-term forecasting are IR satellite loops, which are available at many websites. IR images show the radiance emission from Earth and indicate the temperature of the ground and/or clouds. During cold seasons, the ground can be as cold as, if not colder than, the air mass, and single IR satellite images are not very helpful in identifying low-level clouds such as stratocumulus. One way to separate clouds from the ground in these situations is to use a time-lapse loop and look for motion: the ground doesn't move, but clouds do. People in northern latitudes from late fall to early spring should keep this trick in mind.

There are many IR image enhancements available at various websites, and you should be aware that many of them do not display *any* low clouds, even with the trick mentioned above. One way to familiarize yourself with low-cloud detection is to compare visible GOES images to IR enhancements in the early morning, when the ground is still cold. In some situations, you may be surprised by the amount of low cloud not displayed in the IR satellite images. By comparing IR and visible images, you can select a website that you feel gives accurate images and one that you are comfortable with. I recommend the following website for IR satellite images because it provides the ability to zoom into your region, to choose different satellite-image enhancements, and to do animation easily wunderground.com/maps/satellite/infrared.

To make the best use of weather-satellite images, you also should be aware of the behavior of certain types of cloud. Low-level clouds such as stratus usually develop locally and generally move much more slowly than high clouds. These clouds appear during the night and usually get burned off by the Sun during the day. Coastal regions will usually see the low clouds moving inland in the evening and out to sea in the morning.

In addition, cumulus, towering cumulus, and cumulonimbus clouds arise with daytime convective heating if the air mass is unstable. The depth or height of the cloud structure is related to the level of instability and can reach up to 20 000 m for severe thunderstorms. On satellite loops, these clouds appear as clear areas that are gradually filled with clouds during the day and that slowly vanish in the evening. In the summer, some of the most unstable cumulonimbus clouds will survive at night. Even though thunderstorms, associated with cumulonimbus clouds, can be far from your location, cirrus blowoff from these cells may reach you quite quickly, depending on the upper wind direction, and thus ruin your observing session. Satellite and radar loops are good ways to keep track of these thunderstorm lines.

Radar

Remote-controlled observatories, where the operator is not physically present, and star parties, where telescopes are often left set up and exposed, are becoming more popular. When the sky conditions are variable, there is one common worry: is there a fast-moving precipitation band approaching the observing site? The best way to track precipitation in the short term is with radar. The radar network is extensive across the United States; it also covers populated regions of Canada.

Radar images require careful interpretation. During the night, the air cools near the ground and creates a temperature inversion. On some nights with strong inversions, radar signals are refracted, or bent, toward the ground and scattered back to the radar, thus appearing as precipitation on the graphical displays. Similar situations occur in mountainous areas, where higher terrain interrupts the radar signal. A radar loop will help you distinguish these areas: sometimes they are nearly motionless; at other times they shift around in a chaotic jumble. Precipitation moves in a smoother fashion, at times linearly. The best websites for access to radar loops for Canada and the United States, respectively, are weather.gc.ca/radar and wunderground.com/radar.

Weather Forecasts for Astronomy

Cloud Forecasts: Local media and television "experts" cannot always be relied upon when conditions are uncertain. Usually their forecasts cover a large area, and the weather can be quite different within the region. Also, for most people, including many local weather forecasters, skies are considered clear despite thin, high cloudiness that may interfere with observing.

The best forecasts for clouds are from the direct output of numerical models. Weather models are not perfect, but they are surprisingly good at capturing local effects and predicting cloud formation and dissipation. The biggest problem with numerical forecasting is convection (thunderstorms): it is like trying to predict the next bubble in boiling water. Complex thunderstorm cells can be forecast much farther away than they actually appear, leading to poor cloud progression forecasts for regions hundreds of kilometres ahead.

Some weather channels and websites use animated forecasts to show cloud progression for the next day, but these animations generally have low resolution and are not very useful for astronomy. The only North American high-resolution cloud forecast I still know of is produced at the Canadian Meteorological Centre (CMC) and is at weather.gc.ca/astro/clds_vis_e.html.

Occasionally, especially in the fall when low clouds (stratocumulus) are omnipresent, a weather balloon can be launched into a cloud hole, and the resulting cloud forecast may be too optimistic for the surrounding regions. To avoid a bad forecast, always compare the cloud-cover forecast with the latest satellite picture. In these situations, an old forecast may be a better choice. This is why the most recent old forecast, in addition to the current forecast, is available at this website; hourly forecasts are now available.

Sky Transparency Forecasts: For deep-sky observing, sky transparency is critical because it largely determines how dark the sky will be. Aerosols—particles suspended in the atmosphere—and moisture reduce sky transparency and brighten the sky by diffusing the light in the sky. Aerosols include volcanic ash, pollen, sea salts, and smoke from forest fires. Spectacular examples of events that introduced aerosols into the atmosphere are the Mount St. Helens volcanic eruption, which spread roughly 540 million tonnes of ash into the atmosphere in 1980, and the more recent large forest fires: in summer 2003 over British Columbia, which spread smoke over large areas, and in 2002 in northern Québec, which spread smoke over all of northeastern North America. Specialized weather numerical models handle aerosol phenomena; websites that track aerosol envelopes with up to five-day forecasts across the world are ozoneaq.gsfc.nasa.gov and nrlmry.navy.mil/aerosol/#currentaerosolmodeling.

Moisture is the only weather element affecting sky transparency that can be forecast with confidence. For many northern-latitude residents, moisture is the most important contributor to reduced sky transparency; despite clear skies, very often, high-level ice crystals (extremely thin clouds) are present and can be seen only at sunset and sunrise. In addition, moisture from open waters, vegetation (evapotranspiration), or moist soil can keep the low-level atmosphere humid.

Over the years, I have compared water-vapor satellite images to various observers' estimates of background sky brightness. The resulting hourly sky transparency forecasts can be found at weather.gc.ca/astro/transparence_e.html.

There is a good correlation between the darkest areas in water-vapor images and the darkest observed sky conditions. There are some cases where the sky background is brighter than expected due to moisture trapped by a temperature inversion. Based on this observation and others, the forecasts in the above website emphasize humidity near the surface and also near the tropopause (cirrus heights).

Seeing Forecasts: Seeing conditions determine the steadiness of images through a telescope and are relevant for planetary as well as deep-sky observing. When highest resolution is necessary for planetary imaging or visual observing, seeing should be at its best.

Conditions are favorable when the atmosphere is turbulence-free all across the path of the light. The best weather pattern is weak wind circulation at all levels. These conditions occur more frequently over the southeastern United States than any other region of North America, with Atlantic Canada generally having the worst conditions among populated North American regions. Canadian and U.S. central prairies often experience blocking weather systems that give weak upper wind circulation and excellent seeing conditions.

Another pattern for excellent seeing takes place when moderate winds blow from the same direction at all levels, that is, when horizontal and vertical wind shear are weak at all levels. In other words, no jet stream (strong winds reaching 200 km/h–400 km/h at an altitude of 10 km–12 km) or sudden shifts or increase in wind speed with height are present.

At locations downwind from mountains when winds are moderate, it is best to be far away from the mountains, since "gravity waves"—vertical air-mass oscillations caused by the mountains—can downgrade seeing. In general, topography is quite important because rough terrain increases the wind shear in the low-level atmosphere, due to friction and gravity waves.

Temperature variation at the surface also plays a role in seeing conditions. Nights of excellent wind conditions as described above may nevertheless have marginal seeing. On such nights, temperatures quickly and steadily fall, and large telescopes have trouble cooling at the same rate as the surrounding air. This creates what is called "local seeing": thermal heat released from the optics (despite good ventilation) ruins the seeing despite the excellent weather pattern. The opposite is also true: the best planetary observations with a large telescope often take place just before thick clouds roll in or when looking through thin cirrostratus cloud. Under these conditions, the temperature usually rises a few degrees before the clouds appear. Thin cirrostratus clouds usually keep the temperature steady, eliminating any negative local seeing effects. Thin clouds also play the role of a neutral-density filter, increasing fine detail and contrast on bright planets. Ground fog can also be associated with excellent seeing conditions (until the fog thickens), if you can keep your optics dry.

Predicting favorable seeing conditions requires the ability to interpret weather charts, something that is difficult for most observers to do. The Canadian weather service has a seeing forecast, available at their astro-weather website, which attempts to simulate wind shears, topography, and temperature effects; it is at weather.gc.ca/astro/seeing_e.html.

Some Tips to Get the Most Out of Your Telescope: "Local seeing" is the term used to describe the effects of heat radiating from the components of a telescope (e.g. its optics) or from the immediate surroundings (e.g. observatory walls and floor, trees, flowing water, neighboring houses). If the local seeing is bad, the telescopic viewing will be significantly deteriorated. However, in contrast to atmospheric seeing, the effects of local seeing can be controlled.

Tube currents in particular will dramatically deteriorate telescopic images. Mirror-type instruments are more sensitive to such currents than refractors. Large mirrors can take hours to cool down during the night and in fact may never reach full thermal equilibrium. However, the amateur astronomer can accelerate the cooling of the primary mirror by installing one or more battery-type fans behind it. Their use will cool down the mirror to near the ambient temperature in one or two hours. Another approach is to use a high-quality but thin primary mirror. Many manufacturers offer mirror blanks of thickness 2.5 cm for mirror diameters up to 400 mm, in addition to the traditional mirrors of thickness 5–8 cm. The thinner mirrors will reach thermal equilibrium 2–3 times faster* than the thicker ones. Many amateurs also ventilate the front of their primary mirror with two fans placed on either side of the mirror, separated by 180°. One fan pulls air into the tube while the other pushes it out. Such ventilation has two benefits: it breaks up the thermal boundary layer near the mirror surface (and therefore reduces convective-type turbulence) and it cools the mirror up to 50% more quickly than without the fans*.

The popular Schmidt–Cassegrain telescopes do not come with cooling fans and they are known to suffer from internal turbulence, especially at large apertures. Only a few advanced amateur astronomers will have the courage to add fans to those telescopes. Any telescope, and particularly the Schmidt–Cassegrain type, should always be brought outside to cool it down at least two hours before the observing session. Better yet is to keep a telescope permanently outside in a backyard observatory.

To minimize the occurrence of poor local seeing, one must avoid all potential sources of heat in the surroundings. For example, concrete structures and buildings or houses have the capacity to retain daytime heat and then release it during the night. Even trees during the growing season can release heat at night, and so deteriorate the local seeing for astronomical objects found just above their canopy. Ideally, the amateur should choose an environment free from all these elements. If you are lucky enough to have an observatory, then remember that all the outside walls must be white, since even pale colors will allow the walls to heat up during the day and then create local seeing problems when they release the heat at night.

The local geography can also be used to one's advantage: observing can be better at the top of a hill than at its base. It appears that the local seeing is improved at the top of a hill, due to nighttime katabatic winds that drain air down the slope of the hill

***Sky & Telescope*, June 2004, p. 122 (Improving the Thermal Properties of Newtonian Reflectors—Part 2)

to its base. This means that air above the hill must also move downward to replace the air that moved away. This descent creates a dry subsidence inversion that, combined with the cool surface temperature at the top of the hill, stabilizes the air locally. This results in good seeing. Many of my best planetary observations took place on hill tops.

One final tip: near dusk and dawn, if you can spot planets, then there will often be a 20–60-min window during which the seeing will be one or two notches better than during the night. This seems to be related to large-scale tidal motions in the atmosphere that create more-stable conditions at those times, but the effect is not well understood. Give it a try in the early morning and the early evening.

The Clear Sky Chart

The Canadian Meteorological Centre's numerical weather forecasts, given in the URLs above, are unique because they are specifically designed for astronomers. They can be found on the "Weather forecast for astronomy" page of the Environment Canada website at weather.gc.ca/astro. There are several products for the astronomy community, including hourly forecast images of cloud cover, sky transparency, seeing, and near-ground weather. However, they include 842 forecast images per day, covering all of North America, so it can be a chore to find the precise one you need. All the above astronomical weather forecasts can be viewed at a glance for any particular observing site in North America using Attilla Danko's excellent Clear Sky Chart at cleardarksky.com/csk.

Editor's Note: Attilla Danko, a member of the Ottawa Centre of The Royal Astronomical Society of Canada, received the Ken Chilton Prize from the Society in 2005 for his creation of the Clear Sky Chart, which uses the Canadian Meteorological Centre's forecasts for astronomers created by Allan Rahill. Most popular observing locations in North America now have an associated chart, and many amateur astronomers rely on these forecasts to plan their observing sessions. Several websites give useful information similar to the Clear Sky Chart. The spatial resolution of these sites is quite low compared to the Canadian Meteorological Centre's products.

For the UK:	weatherweb.net/wxwebastronomy.php
For Australia:	philhart.com/content/cloud-forecasts-astronomers
For the U.S.:	accuweather.com (Click the + sign and choose "Astronomy")

The Milky Way in a clear, dark sky. (photo: James Edgar)

LIGHT POLLUTION

BY ROBERT DICK

Light becomes pollution only when its attributes exceed limits that compromise our ability to see and affects the abilities and biology of wildlife. Fortunately, what is good for astronomy is also good for wildlife, and vice versa.

Light and Vision

Vision is complicated. It involves everything from the light source to the mental algorithms used to construct images in the brain, whatever they may be. Most of these processes are beyond our conscious control. But with a limited amount of understanding and the development of conscious techniques, we can dramatically improve our ability to "see" and experience the night.

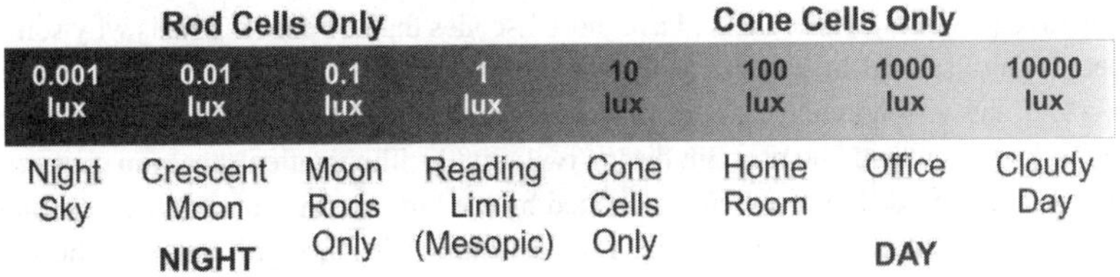

The range of illuminance that is accommodated by the rod and cone cells in the retina. Illuminance is the amount of light that shines upon an area.

Natural illumination has a range of about 10^8—remarkable! Full sunlight (about 120 000 lux) is at one limit. At the other end of the scale is the nighttime sky-lit countryside at only 0.001 lux. To accommodate this range requires some complicated photobiology and trade-offs. (You don't get something for nothing.)

The most critical visual cells for our daytime survival are the cone-shaped detectors that are concentrated in the center of our vision and give us our photopic vision. We have about 6 million of these. Three types of cone cells are sensitive to

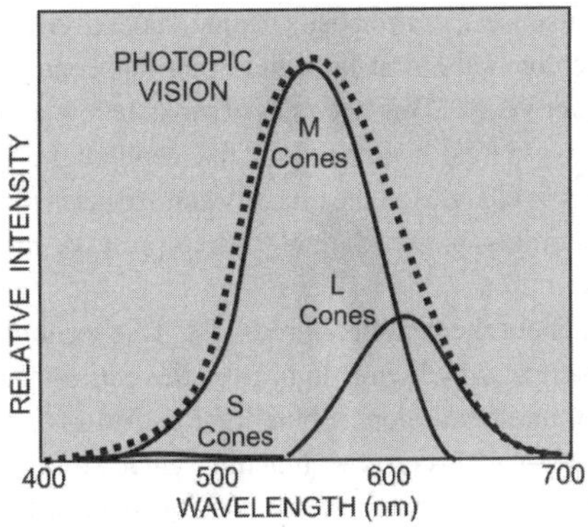

The relative sensitivity of our three sets of cone cells. Green to yellow = M-cones, orange to red = L-cones, and blue = S-cones. Our combined cone vision has a spectral sensitivity that peaks at 555 nm. Our reduced blue sensitivity results from the lack of physical threats in the environment that are colored blue.

different bands of wavelengths that give us the impressions of color from red to blue.

The natural environment has driven the evolution of our sensitivity to each of these spectral bands. Red and yellow are critical for identifying whether food is ripe or rotten. Surprisingly, for humans there is virtually nothing harmful in nature that is blue. The sky is blue, but humans have little to fear from predators in the sky, so only 6% of our cones are blue sensitive. Coupled with the poor optical quality to blue light of our lens and cornea, this cripples our "blue vision." Many of us have seen this with theatrical lighting when actors appear "fuzzy" under blue spotlights.

Our sensation of color depends on the combination of the three "colors" that, when combined, create "white." The limited blue image information is amplified and used by our brain to provide a "wash" of blue over the green-red image to help distinguish subtle hues of the scene.

However, not all people are the same. Some people have up to about 60% of their cones sensitive to green-yellow (M-cones), and the remaining cones are orange-red sensitive (L-cones), while others have more L-cones than M-cones. This is why some people can't see red-lit surfaces as well as others.

Our day vision evolved to be very good during the day, with the solar spectrum between 400 nm and 700 nm. But during twilight, the illumination spectrum changes. As the apparent disk of the Sun is occulted by the horizon, the countryside becomes illuminated primarily by the blue sky. You don't notice this change because the human brain subconsciously "white balances" the scene. Rather, the colors of the land slowly become desaturated as there is less color information.

There is a common error made by some people in the lighting industry who promote high color recognition at night. At illumination levels typical of street lighting, our cones do not work very well, so our color rendering is very poor. It remains poor until the illumination levels on streets are well in excess of industry best practice.

There are about 100 million rod cells crowded out of our cone-dominated fovea. Daylight "bleaches" these rods but they recover in step as evening twilight fades, halving in brightness every 5 minutes. However, this slow recovery is a problem in our modern society where artificial light is turned off at the flick of a switch, or by a single step outside into the night.

Below 5 lux (about 30 minutes after sunset), our rod cells begin to take over from our cone vision. The desaturation of color is the first indication that our cones are "failing" and the rods are dominating our vision. This becomes obvious below about 5 lux. Between 1 and 5 lux, even yellow-red light begins to look like candlelight.

The rods are sensitive to the shorter wavelengths of the blue sky and are insensitive to the other colors. This is why astronomers use red light—to help preserve night vision.

However, there is a misconception about the benefits of red light. This technique originated with filtered incandescent lamps, which emit light over the entire visual spectrum. Filtering out the somewhat limited emission of blue light helped save our rod vision and still allowed both our M –and L-cones to function. Under this "red light," we preserve the sensitivity of our rods and retain the help and visual acuity of our cones for reading fine detail.

This changed with modern red-light LED lamps that emit a narrow range (20 nm), which is only detected by the L-cone cells. This reduces our ability to see from 60% for L-cone sensitive people down to about 30% for M-cone sensitive people while also reducing our visual acuity, because there are fewer cones responding to the light. In this case, dim amber light (yellow+red) may be preferable (R.S. Dick, Seeing Red, *Sky & Telescope*, June 2016; Ken Wishaw, *Sky & Telescope, 34*, July 2019).

Does red LED light really save our night vision? Our rod vision is between 100 and 1000× more sensitive than our system of cone cells, depending on the degree of dark adaptation. At this sensitivity, our system of rod cells responds to red light as much as our cone cells. So, if you can "see" the red in the red illumination, you are already affecting your night vision. So, this red light must be well shielded. If the lamp is visible, then the luminance will be focused on your retina and will "bleach" the rod cells, even though our night vision is not particularly sensitive to the diffuse red luminance. Red LEDs on electronic equipment may have a luminance greater than Venus. To protect your night vision, use well-shielded lamps with the lowest practical luminance.

Dark-Sky Sites

Outdoor lighting is so ubiquitous in our society that most people give it little thought. The RASC, IDA, and other organizations want to change this by promoting Dark-Sky Sites that let visitors experience a dark sky and wildlife. What kind of lighting should you expect in a Dark-Sky Site? None! But, if deemed necessary by the manager, then there are practical limits.

The key is a lighting guideline that defines "Low-Impact Lighting." It sets limits on the spectrum, shielding, duration of outdoor lighting, and its brightness.

The spectrum, shielding, and the duration of the lighting must be controlled to the limits shown in the following figure. Since short wavelengths less than 500 nm are needed to make light look "white," white light is not permitted. Compliant light looks "amber," which is the combination of yellow and red light. The shielding prevents glare and light trespass beyond the targeted area, and the light source dims or turns off when most people have gone to bed.

In testing compliant luminaires, we can see quite well with compliant illumination.

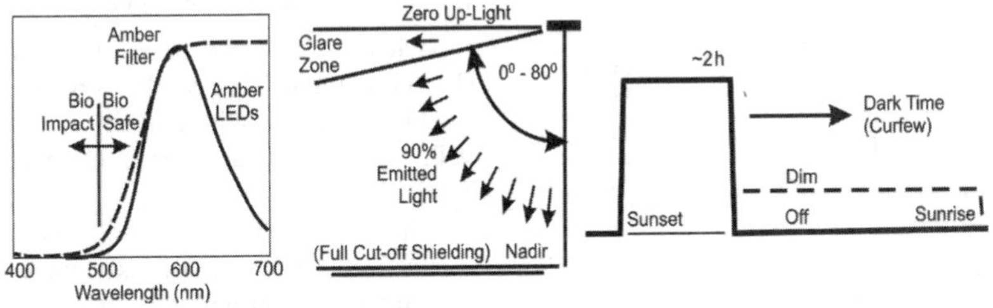

Main Attributes of Low-Impact Lighting. Requirements: 1) Spectral limits (amber filters may be used such as Roscolux #15 Deep Straw), 2) Shielding, and 3) Lighting Schedule. It also defines the brightness limit of <1 lux to 3 lux. For full details, see rasc.ca/dark-sky-site-guidelines*).*

ASTRONOMICAL LEAGUE OBSERVING PROGRAMS

BY AARON CLEVENSON, OBSERVING PROGRAM DIRECTOR

Observing is the keystone and core ingredient in Amateur Astronomy. Nothing can equal the joy and wonder of seeing new objects in the vastness of the universe. Today, with the availability of reasonably priced telescopes with very good optics, the gems of space are within reach of many people who might not have had the opportunity in the past.

On any clear night, when we decide that we are going to observe, amateur astronomers are faced with a difficult decision: "What shall I observe tonight?" The sky is literally the limit. There are thousands of objects available to even a modest telescope, with hundreds of objects available to a typical pair of binoculars. Many objects are worth repeat visits—the Orion Nebula, the Andromeda Galaxy, and the planets. But there are so many other things worth looking at, and many can be pleasant surprises.

Observing Programs from the Astronomical League

The Astronomical League has a broad selection of Observing Programs designed to help deal with this question. Each Observing Program has a list of objects to pursue. These are not single night endeavors. Some take months to complete and some take years. The lists of objects provide a clear direction for one's observing sessions. There is enough depth and breadth to provide observing challenges for a lifetime.

The goal of the Astronomical League's Observing Program Division is to provide Observing Programs that increase the observer's knowledge about celestial objects, and, at the same time, increase the observer's observing prowess. This is done through increasing levels of difficulty and by introducing the amateur astronomer to new techniques and equipment.

The Observing Programs are designed to provide something for everyone, and they include recognition for those who complete the requirements. There are programs for the novice as well as for very experienced observers. Some programs require no equipment, some use binoculars, some require only a modest telescope, and some necessitate large "light buckets" to catch faint and challenging objects. There are Observing Programs for almost every different type of celestial object: the Sun, the Moon, the solar system, stars, star clusters, nebulae, galaxies, and many more.

Master Observer Progression Awards

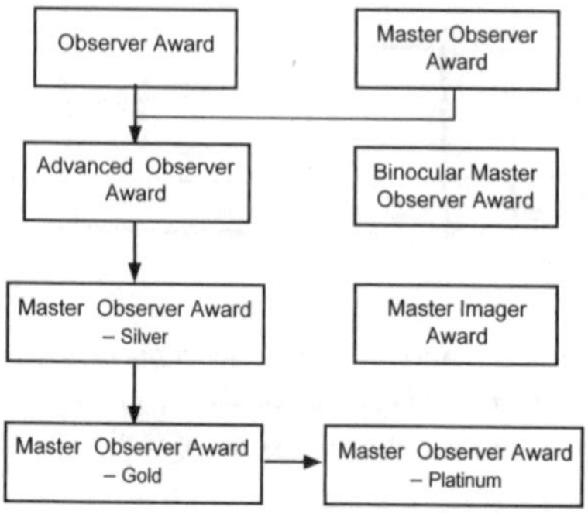

Master Observer Progression

So, where should the amateur begin? The Astronomical League has provided a roadmap to help with this question as well. It is called the Master Observer Progression.

The Master Observer Award, created in 2001, recognizes those astronomers who completed a group of ten Observing Programs. At that time, there were only 15 Observing Programs to choose from, but today, with 63 different Observing Programs and Observing Awards, the

Master Observer Award has been transformed into the Master Observer Progression.

The Progression has levels to recognize amateur astronomers as their knowledge and experience grow. The levels are Observer, Master Observer—Silver, Master Observer—Gold Master, and Master Observer—Platinum. Each level has requirements that encourage observers to broaden their knowledge and to hone observing skills. They challenge observers to branch out and to try new things and to see new objects.

In most cases, the awards require the completion of the top level of each of the Observing Programs. These levels go by different names, but they are typically achieved by completing all of the objects on the object lists (often 100 of them). The lists are designed to take you through the different seasons and to explore objects throughout the sky.

The Observer Award is designed for the novice observer. It is awarded to observers who complete five required Observing Programs: *Constellation Hunter*, *Messier*, *Binocular Messier*, *Lunar*, and *Solar System*. Additionally, the observer gets to pick one additional introductory level Program from this list: *Galileo*, *Sketching*, *Sky Puppy* (for youth ten years old and younger), *Youth Astronomer* (for youth 17 years old and younger), *Beyond Polaris* (introductory program for adults), *Two in the View*, *Universe Sampler*, or *Urban*.

The Master Observer Award is for observers who have mastered the basics of observing by completing ten Observing Programs. The required Observing Programs are: *Messier*, *Binocular Messier*, *Lunar*, *Double Star*, and the *Herschel 400*. The observer chooses the additional five Observing Programs.

The Advanced Observer Award is designed to introduce the Master Observer to five additional programs that are focused on various types of stellar objects (for a total of 15). Observing Programs that the observer may choose from are: *Asterisms*, *Asteroids*, *Bright Nebulae*, *Carbon Star*, *Comets*, *Dark Nebulae*, *Earth Orbiting Satellites*, *Globular Clusters*, *Meteors*, *Open Clusters*, one of the Solar Observing Programs, *Planetary Nebulae*, and one of the Galaxy-based Observing Programs.

The top three levels of the Master Observer Progression require the completion of additional Observing Programs. Silver requires an additional five (to give a total of 20), and must include: *Lunar II*, an Outreach Award, *Sketching*, and *Sunspotters*. Gold requires an additional ten (to give a total of 30), and must include: additional Outreach, the *Herschel II*, *Hydrogen Alpha—Solar*, *Stellar Evolution*, and a Variable Star Observing Program. Platinum requires an additional ten (to give a total of 40), and must include: the top-level Outreach Award, *Dark Sky Advocate*, *Target NEO*, *Radio Astronomy* (gold level), and *Asteroid* or *Comet*.

Pursuit of the higher levels of the Master Observer Progression is not for everyone. It requires decades of dedicated effort and a good deal of tenacity, but the feeling of accomplishment from seeing thousands of objects is profound.

Master Imager Award

Image:
- a Lunar Program
- a Solar Program
- a Solar System Program (main bodies)
- a Deep Space Program
- a Scientific Study Program

+ any 5 Observing Programs

Free Range Observing

We know that some observers enjoy freely roaming around the universe and seeing the wonders. They may not be interested in structured Observing Programs. For those amateur astronomers, the objects lists contain many jewels of the night sky, and are filled with potential targets. Other observers enjoy the structure and the challenge that the object lists provide.

Binocular Observing

Binocular Master Observer Award

Complete any 8 of these 9:
- Binocular Double Star
- Advanced Binocular Double Star
- Binocular Messier
- Binocular Variable Star
- Deep Sky Binocular
- Galileo Binocular
- Lunar Binocular Cerfticate
- Solar System Binocular Certificate
- Southern Skies Binocular

Recognizing that not all astronomers have telescopes, there is also a Binocular Master Observer Award. The observer must complete eight of the binocular-based Observing Programs. Currently, the list includes: *Binocular Double Star*, *Advanced Binocular Double Star*, *Binocular Messier*, *Binocular Variable Star*, *Deep Sky Binocular*, *Galileo*, the *Lunar Binocular Certificate*, the *Solar System Binocular Certificate*, and the *Southern Skies Binocular*.

Imaging

We also recognize that not all observers are visual observers. Many amateur astronomers prefer to image their targets. To recognize the accomplishments of these imagers, the Astronomical League has also added a Master Imager Award. To earn this award, the imager must complete ten Observing Programs through imaging. These must include: a Lunar Program, a Solar Program, and a Solar System (main bodies) Program, a Deep Space Program, and a Scientific Study Observing Program (Spectroscopy, Variable Stars, Novae, and more). The additional five can be any of the other Observing Programs that have been done through imaging.

Details on the requirements of each Observing Program and the process for receiving the certifications are on the Astronomical League's website. They differ from program to program. So, if you decide to pursue an Observing Program, it is important to be sure to understand what is required.

With the breadth of Observing Programs available, there is truly something for everyone. We hope you will expand your knowledge and skills by seeking out the objects in these programs. There is so much to see in our vast Universe, and so little time! The Universe awaits those who enter here.

For more information on the Astronomical League's Observing Programs, please access the Observe section of the League's website: www.astroleague.org, or contact an Observing Program Director through email at aaron@clevenson.org.

Aaron Clevenson teaches introductory astronomy at Lone Star College in Texas. He is also the Observatory Director at the Insperity Observatory in Humble ISD. He is one of five Observing Program Directors at the Astronomical League and has authored a number of the current Observing Programs.

DEEP-SKY OBSERVING HINTS

BY ALAN DYER

In the 1960s and 1970s, few observers owned telescopes larger than 200-mm aperture. Today, 250-mm to 600-mm Dobsonian-mounted reflectors are commonplace. Using computerized telescopes, observers can now find thousands of objects at the push of a button. As a result, deep-sky observing has soared in popularity.

However, owners of less-sophisticated, small-aperture instruments shouldn't think they are shut out of deep-sky viewing. In a dark sky, an 80-mm to 100-mm telescope will show all the Messier objects and reveal hundreds of brighter NGC (New General Catalogue) objects. In fact, many large objects are best seen in fast (*f*/4 to *f*/6), small-aperture telescopes or in giant 70-mm and 80-mm binoculars. Contrary to popular belief, even slow f-ratio instruments (*f*/11 to *f*/16) are useful; their only disadvantage is the difficulty of achieving a low-power wide field. No matter what telescope you use, follow these techniques to get the most out of a night's deep-sky viewing:

- Always plan each night's observing: Prepare a list of a dozen or so objects for the night. Hunt them down on star charts or with computer programs first during the day to become familiar with their location.
- Seek out dark skies; a black sky improves contrast and makes up for lack of aperture.
- To preserve night vision, always use a dim red flashlight for reading charts.
- Avoid prolonged exposure to bright sunlight earlier in the day (such as a day at the beach); it will reduce your ability to dark adapt and make for tired eyes at night.
- Use averted vision; looking to one side of an object places it on a more sensitive part of the retina.
- Another technique for picking out faint objects is to jiggle the telescope (and the image) slightly.
- Don't be afraid to use high power; it often brings out small, faint objects such as planetary nebulae and galaxies, and resolves detail in globulars, in small, rich open clusters, and in bright galaxies.
- Use a nebular filter on emission and planetary nebulae (see FILTERS on p. 64); even in a dark sky, filters can dramatically enhance the view of these kinds of objects, often making obvious an otherwise elusive nebula.
- Be comfortable; sit down while at the eyepiece and be sure to dress warmly.
- Collimate and clean your optics; a poorly maintained telescope will produce distorted star images, reduce image contrast, and make it more difficult to see faint stars and other threshold objects.
- Don't expect to use analog setting circles; in a portable telescope "dial-type" circles will rarely be accurate.
- Digital setting circles and Go To telescopes can find objects precisely. While they are wonderful observing aids, they can overwhelm observers with thousands of targets, often supplying scant information about each one. When making a list for a night's viewing, books such as the three-volume *Burnham's Celestial Handbook* and the two-volume *Night Sky Observer's Guide* by Kepple and Sanner are still the best guides.
- Don't be in a rush to check off targets; take time to examine each object, and take notes or make drawings. Both will help train your eye to see subtle detail; you'll learn to see the most through your telescope.
- Consider keeping a logbook or journal of your nightly tours of the sky; including eyepiece impressions and drawings provides a record of your improving observing skills that is fun to look back upon in future years. See the section THE OBSERVING LOGBOOK (immediately following) for suggestions on organizing a journal.

THE OBSERVING LOGBOOK

BY PAUL MARKOV

There are many good reasons for maintaining an observing logbook: A logbook is useful for recalling the details of previous observations and comparing past observations with current ones; maintaining one will make your observing organized and methodical; and having to describe an object forces you to *look* for more details, thus sharpening your observing skills. Finally, if you are planning to apply for one of the several RASC observing certificates (see note on p. 308), then a logbook with your observations may be required when submitting your application.

Logbooks can be chronological or sectional. In a chronological logbook, all observations are listed sequentially by date, regardless of object type. In a sectional logbook, observations are grouped by object type, such as open clusters and galaxies. With either format, you may want to keep a master index of objects for cross-referencing to the correct page in your logbook.

What about the book itself? Typical choices are the simple three-ring binder with standard lined paper, spiral-bound notebooks, and hardcover record/accounting books. In my opinion, the most practical is the three-ring binder because it allows you to insert auxiliary materials into your logbook with the help of a three-hole punch. With this choice, entering observations out of sequence is never an issue because you can easily rearrange the sheets. Also, should you wish to make a "soft" copy of your logbook using a scanner that generates Adobe Acrobat PDF files, it is much easier with loose sheets.

For recording observations, using a preprinted observing form offers these advantages: the fill-in-the-blank fields remind you to record the relevant data; many of these forms have a space for making a drawing of the observed object; and they give your book a neat and organized look. An example of an observing form can be found at rasc.ca/sites/default/files/obsform.pdf; you may prefer to design your own observing form by using the fields suggested below. However, I prefer to use plain, lined paper as there is less repetition when writing observing session details, and I do not have to worry about using different forms for different objects or running out of forms.

There are two choices for recording your observations: using full sentences and using acronyms and abbreviations. Using full sentences is the preferred method if you enjoy re-reading your observations from past years, or if you want others to be able to easily read your logbook. But if your intent is to keep a data book for reference purposes only, then acronyms and abbreviations are the recommended choices.

It is useful to record the following information for each observing session: date; time of arrival and departure (if you have traveled somewhere to observe); location; names of other people at the observing site; sky transparency (i.e. clarity of the atmosphere, which is generally noted by faintest visible stellar magnitude; see LIMITING MAGNITUDES, p. 68); seeing (i.e. the steadiness of the atmosphere: if stars and planets appear to shimmer, that indicates poor seeing; if they appear sharp and steady, that indicates good seeing), and environmental conditions (e.g. temperature, dew, wind, sources of light pollution, snow cover, and the presence of insects). You can also number each observing session sequentially for easy referencing within your logbook.

Be sure to standardize your time/date format. For recording time, choose either the 24-hour format or a.m./p.m. format. In addition, use alpha characters to specify the month rather than numbers. For example, use 2022 Aug. 5 instead of 8/5/22; this will avoid ambiguity in reading the date.

For each object observed, record the following information as a minimum: date and time of observation, object name or designation, type of object, constellation, telescope and magnification used, type of filter (if any), and visual description. Making drawings is highly recommended and adds substantially to the value of your logbook. It is also important to record failed observations because these entries will remind you to try again in your next observing session. Remember to update the observing notes if the sky conditions change, if you have equipment trouble, if you take extended "coffee breaks," or if you see something unusual like a fireball or aurora.

If you are able to write neatly while observing, it is best to enter observations directly into your logbook. However, if this proves too difficult given the environmental circumstances, you can record your observations in a temporary notebook and transcribe them into your logbook the next day. An audio recorder can also be used if you are careful to ensure its mechanical integrity while in the field and if you are diligent enough to transcribe the recorded observations into your observing logbook regularly. Below are some suggestions on what to look for when observing deep-sky objects.

All Object Types: What is the shape of the object? What is its size (based on the field of view of your eyepiece)? Is averted vision required to see the object? Does averted vision allow you to see more detail? (If yes, describe the extra detail.) Is the object near (or in the same field of view as) other deep-sky objects or bright stars? What magnification gives the best view of the object? Does a filter improve the view? (See FILTERS, p. 64.)

Open Cluster: Is there a greater concentration of stars in a specific part of the cluster? Is it fully resolved into its component stars, or are there any unresolved stars causing the cluster to appear nebulous? How many stars can you see (only if reasonable to count them)? Are there any bright stars within the cluster? Are there any colored stars? (If so, describe their tints and locations within the cluster.) Does the cluster stand out from the background star field?

Globular Cluster: What is the degree of star concentration (high, medium, low)? How much can be resolved to component stars (none, outer edges, middle, to the core)?

Galaxy: Is it uniform in brightness, or does it have a brighter nucleus? Is it diffuse or stellar? Can any detail or mottling be seen in the arms? Are any stars visible within the arms?

Emission or Reflection Nebula: Is the brightness even, or are there brighter/darker areas? Are the edges of the nebula well defined? Are there any stars within the nebula? Is there a hint of any color?

Planetary Nebula: Is it stellar in appearance, or can a disk be seen? Are the edges well defined or diffuse? Are there any brighter/darker areas? Can a central star be seen? Is there a hint of any color? Can it be "blinked" with a filter or averted vision?

Dark Nebula: Is it easy or difficult to discern the dark nebula from the background sky? Are there any stars within the nebula?

Logbooks and Databases

If you enjoy using computers, an electronic database can be a helpful complement to an observing logbook. You can obtain commercially available deep-sky databases that allow you to enter your own observations for any object. These databases are also useful for creating observing lists and planning observing sessions. A highly recommended database, which also happens to be freeware, is the Saguaro Astronomy Club (SAC) deep-sky database, available at **saguaroastro.org**. With minimal tweaking, the SAC database can be formatted to accept your own observations.

You can transcribe complete observations from your logbook into the database or simply enter four valuable pieces of information for each observed object: seen (Y/N), date, telescope used, and location. With these fields filled in, in a matter of seconds you can determine which and how many objects you have observed, and the date field for any object will direct you to the correct page in your observing logbook. You can also determine interesting facts such as from which observing location you observed the most objects or which telescope produced the most observations.

ASTROSKETCHING

BY KATHLEEN E. HOUSTON

Curiosity. Perseverance. Are these words familiar to you? Perhaps associated with the Mars rovers? And what about Ingenuity? These are also qualities in every sketcher of the mostly nocturnal variety. Sketching is about following your curiosity, or persevering through questions you have, and being ingenuous about ferreting out reluctant details. Perhaps you want to observe objects that you can actually see move, like a double transit on Jupiter, or a comet's motion against the backdrop stars. For me, during binocular viewing of Comet NEOWISE, 30 minutes showed noticeable motion.

Visual recording of celestial wonders is a deeply human activity. Here is a very compressed time line: Hall of Bulls, Lascaux Paleolithic image of Taurus and Pleiades (15 000–17 000 BCE), Chaco Culture petroglyphs in New Mexico (c. 1000 CE), Galileo's sketches of Jupiter's moons (1610), William Parsons' drawing of the Whirlpool Galaxy (1845), and David Levy's drawings of the impact sites of Comet Shoemaker–Levy 9 on Jupiter (1994). Going beyond the casual 10-second glance through a telescope, with binoculars or naked eye, is to take yourself on a unique, spell-bound adventure. Erika Rix wrote: "Every sketch rendered at the eyepiece is of value, meaning they don't need to be a work of art" (see reference below).

Drawing Toolkit: Make a grab-and-go sketching kit, and then you are always prepared! Keep it simple and let it evolve. Practicality sometimes means it's what you can fit in your hand or pocket. A selection of wooden pencils with a range of HB hardnesses offers drawing choices. An HB pencil makes a light grey color and is excellent for the mapping-out stage. For a darker black that stands out, try 2B, 4B, or 6B. Some sketchers include very light pencils in the 2H range for faint stars and edge-of-seeing details. Some swear by their Blackwing pencils. I prefer woodless graphite pencils, because I can use the side to create large areas of soft gray to deep black. Erika Rix likes to use sandpaper to sharpen and shape her pencil tip. A retractable eraser stick is perfect for defining fine detail. A good pencil sharpener keeps tips predictable. Include a blending stump (rolled paper) for smudging and blending and sculpting nebulosity.

Experiment with your toolkit: In daylight, take your toolkit for a spin on plain paper. Work from a photograph if you wish. Try pivoting your pencil to create stars in clusters. Hand pressure and pencil hardness help portray star magnitudes. You can modify a finger-smudged nebulosity with the blending stump, and an eraser to control and feather the shape. Learn about your toolkit's mark-making powers, and explore how the information from your eye to hand to paper actually works for you.

Red-light illumination: Dark-adapted eyes are least impacted by red filters, so try red cellophane or primary red theatre gel on your flashlight, headlamp, or book light. Some lights have an intensity adjustment; if yours does, set it to the lowest practical setting. Cover the light while viewing at the eyepiece to minimize impact at the telescope, and uncover the light to dive back into the details of the pencil work.

White paper (drawing in the negative): For typical projects, use medium-weight paper with medium-tooth finish. Consider using a template on a clipboard, with pre-drawn circles and text lines to write comments and notes. I usually prefer a blank sketchbook.

Gray or black paper (drawing in the positive): Gray paper allows for the exploration of a huge range of tones, from dark, deep dust lanes and up into tones lighter than the paper. Black paper allows you to draw the light you see, like you see it. I've used HB, 2B, 4B, and 6B pencils; white china marker for stars, and white smudgeable conté pencil work well.

Principal Drawing Steps

- Choose your object! New to sketching? Then choose something bright like the Moon or M42 in Orion. Page through some resources. Check out these Handbook sections: THE SKY MONTH BY MONTH; ECLIPSES; THE MOON; THE PLANETS IN 2022; METEORS, COMETS, AND DUST; and THE DEEP SKY. *SkyNews* publishes bi-monthly and showcases highlights for the year in the January/February edition. For lunar aficionados, the Isabel Williamson Lunar Observing Program is super. (See link in the resource list.)
- Decide what kind of drawing you are after: Landscape to show where you are with interesting local landmarks, wide field to draw meteors or map the star hopping involved, or deep-sky field with good seeing.

- Frame the subject in your binoculars or telescope optics. Pick out guide stars and unique details that catch your interest. Look at your subject for a while. Introduce yourself!
- Draw the brightest stars first. Use your natural spatial awareness to estimate apparent star distances. Imaginary horizontal and vertical lines help with understanding angles. Draw two stars, and build up from there to form triangles, polygons, or sprays of stars. Perhaps you notice shapes that suggest something to your mind's eye.
- Either work from object to periphery, or from the periphery in toward the object. One method may be more natural to you than the other. Experiment!
- Try different strategies for better seeing. Use pointers from Stephen James O'Meara; try averted vision; jiggle the scope to allow subtle seeing to emerge; breathe deeply. I use a cover over my head to block stray light. The best eye opener is to stay at the eyepiece to get dark adapted.
- Vary magnification. Use a variety of wide, medium, and narrow fields.
- Make a second sweep. Use an imaginary clock dial to divide the field into quadrants, go around the clock: 12, 3, 6, and 9 o'clock. O'Meara was fond of saying, "Exhaust all detail!" in each view.
- Mark west (the direction of drift) and north, especially if the view is mirror-reversed.
- Finish in the warm-up shelter or indoors. Adjust tones, make field notes, and tidy up.

Sharing sketches: Dear reader, what you have drawn is like gold to others, so it's really awesome to share. Scan or take a picture, invert or not, software process or not—my opinion is, please don't lose the character and uniqueness of the drawing itself! (See link to Astrosketchers in the resource list.)

OBSERVING SKILLS AND SKETCHING STRATEGIES

Subject	Observing Skills	Sketching Strategy
Stars and star clusters	Look for triangles and hockey sticks, stars that define a specific shape or pattern, curve, etc.	Pivot HB pencil point for small stars, 4B (softer) for larger stars.
Galaxies	Explore at high magnification to define edges and luminance details of galaxy structure.	Use the side of a 2B or 4B pencil to define the overall shape, then the fingertip to diffuse the edge and a blending stump to feather out shape and detail.
Nebulae and comets	Locate two or three field stars to orient and frame the general shape and size of the diffuse subject.	As for galaxies. Use a second sweep around the clock quadrants to detect edges and fainter stars.
Moon	Work at the terminator for high contrast. Observe the shape of a crater, like a shadow on an inverted apple, and how the shadow defines the cavity.	With craters, work from the rim, and draw the shapes of the shadow and subtle grays. Note details of surface texture. Dark adaptation of the eye is not important.

Drawing in color: Create a black-and-white drawing to write in color descriptors, for finishing later in the warm-up shelter, or at home. To record a lunar eclipse, create templates in advance, so you can concentrate on the shifting shadow and deepening orange color.

Guidelines to Facilitate Drawing

- Create a comfort zone with your binoculars or telescope. Stand or sit, as you wish, or use an adjustable chair to make yourself comfortable at the eyepiece during sustained drawing. On cool nights, take breaks to keep warm.
- Become dark adapted at the eyepiece. Take a really long, good look at your subject, and let your eyes open up. Minimize exposure to your drawing light. Sketch what you see in the finder scope to map how to get there.
- Sketching versus drawing. Sketching is generally a quick observation on one sheet of paper, taking 5–10 minutes. A drawing is a sustained effort with more attention to detail and contrast, taking 30–60 minutes, or perhaps multiple sessions.

The Seeing and Drawing Loop: Frederick Franck describes the experience of looking and drawing as mini-moments: The Three Nens (*The Awakened Eye*, Vintage, 1979). This natural process is interesting to play with.

The *1st Nen* is the simple act of seeing and sketching in short, quick glances. Draw what you see using speed as a friend, and use your natural spatial awareness.	The *2nd Nen* follows rapidly to build on 1st Nen ingenuity, expanding on the texture, fully mapping the field, and moving naturally from eye to hand to paper.	The *3rd Nen* engages the thinking mind to redraw or improve subject distances, refine contrast, define edges, name and judge what you are looking at.

Once you notice the freedom from the busy mind, of drawing in the 1st and 2nd Nen, it is a fluid, uninterrupted, and productive experience.

During the **First Sitting**, minimize eye travel between eyepiece and paper. Persevere with continuous 1st and 2nd Nen sketching. Draw everything you see, especially fleeting detail. Try a **Second Sitting**, because the inner eye accumulates the experience, and you observe and know more.

One to grow on: Set up future goals, or create something new for your equipment. I am curious about digital drawing and would like someone to invent a primary-red screen protector for tablet or iPad drawing, preferably paperlike.

Favorites, challenges: a night landscape; a meteor shower; use different filters on Mars and Jupiter; a binocular-field mosaic in Sagittarius; ashen light on Venus; extreme lunar libration objects; Jovian moon shadow transits; solar-filtered sunspots, prominences, filaments, light bridges, and transits; globular clusters (finding shapes in the complexity); the complete Veil Nebula; Barnard's Dark Nebulae (including B86, the Ink Spot Nebula).

Astrosketching Publications

- Franck, Frederick, The Awakened Eye theawakenedeye.com/pages/the-way-of-nen
- French, Sue, Celestial Sampler, *60 Small-Scope Tours for Starlit Nights* (*Sky & Telescope Stargazing Series*), Sky Publishing, 2005.
- O'Meara, Stephen James, *Deep-Sky Companions: The Messier Objects*, Cambridge University Press, 1998.
- O'Meara, Stephen James, *Observing the Night Sky with Binoculars: A Simple Guide to the Heavens.* Cambridge University Press, 2008.
- *The Patrick Moore's Practical Astronomy Series*, Springer–Verlag (in production order):
  –Handy, R., Moody, D.B., Perez, J., Rix, E., Robbins, S.,
  Astronomical Sketching, a Step-by-Step Introduction, 2007.
  –Grego, Peter,
  Astronomical Cybersketching: Observational Drawing with PDAs and Tablet PCs, 2009.
  (Very curious about tablet astrosketching!)
  –Handy, R., Kelleghan, D., McCague, T., Rix, E., Russell, S.,
  Sketching the Moon: An Astronomical Artist's Guide, 2012.
  –Rix, E., Hay, K., Russell, S., Handy, R.,
  Solar Sketching: A Comprehensive Guide to Drawing the Sun, 2015.

RASC Links

- www.rasc.ca/astrosketchers-group
- www.rasc.ca/carol-lakomiaks-astrosketching-tutorials-moon
- www.rasc.ca/carol-lakomiaks-astrosketching-tutorials-solar-and-dso-sketching
- www.rasc.ca/sketch-galleries
- www.rasc.ca/isabel-williamson-lunar-observing-program

Astrosketching Websites

- www.astroleague.org/content/sketching-resources Plethora of resources, includes video by Peter Vercauteren
- Bratton, Mark, skynews.ca/become-a-better-observer-sketch/
- www.perezmedia.net/beltofvenus/archives/000567.html Two tabs: "Drawn to the Universe"; "Astronomical Sketching Resources" (templates also)
- Rix, Erika, astronomy.com/magazine/erika-rix Impressive article list! For example: "Sandpaper Blocks"; "Get Stumped"; "Perseid Meteor Shower"; and "Tracking Asteroids," 2012–2017.

DIGITAL ASTROPHOTOGRAPHY: A PRIMER

BY TENHO TUOMI

In 1610, when Galileo turned his telescope to the heavens, he observed detail that he could not see with his eyes alone. The camera was the next step (c. 1850), capturing more detail than the eye and telescope together. Along with sketching, photography became an archiving tool for recording astronomical views and events. For many, the camera has become an artistic tool to produce beautiful pictures of astronomical objects. The recent digital camera revolution makes it possible for anyone to enjoy this endeavor. The second part of the revolution has been the rapid development of computer software for enhancing astronomical photographs. The following primer on astronomical photography is only the starting point: consult the books, websites, and user forums listed below for more information and guidance.

Field of view: The angular span of an astrophoto is determined by the focal length (f) of the image-forming optics and a linear dimension (d) of the sensor (width, height, or diagonal, accordingly). The field of view (FOV) is given by

$$\text{FOV} = 2\arctan(d/2f) \ (\approx 57.3\ d/f \text{ degrees when } f \text{ is much larger than } d).$$

For example, the 36×24-mm sensor of a professional "full-frame" camera on a telescope with $f = 1000$ mm has a FOV of $2.1° \times 1.4°$. The smaller 22.2×14.8-mm APS-C sensor (used in many prosumer cameras) gives a smaller $1.3° \times 0.9°$ FOV on the same telescope, a good size to frame the Orion Nebula. At the other extreme, a 50-mm lens on a camera with an APS-C sensor gives a FOV of $25° \times 17°$, large enough to capture most of the constellation Orion itself.

Camera-and-tripod astrophotography: Many good astrophotos can be taken with an ordinary camera using the supplied lens, mounted on a solid tripod. Typical subjects include: aurorae, conjunctions of planets (or of the planets with the Moon), solar eclipses, lunar eclipses, and wide-field views of constellations and the Milky Way. Exposures are typically longer than for daytime photography, requiring a tripod (or some other way of holding the camera steady). For best results, turn off image stabilization (if the lens has it) and use the self-timer or a remote shutter control to reduce camera shake. Some cameras have automatic settings for nighttime photos, but manual settings are recommended. Initially set the camera sensitivity (ISO number) as high as it will go and the f/stop one or two stops higher than wide open (for sharp stars). Set the focus to infinity (which may have to be verified visually with most modern lenses). Set the shutter speed long enough to register the background sky, up to about 30 s. (For cameras with exposure histograms, the peak levels would be in the 20–30% range.) Too long an exposure time will show elongated or streaked stars. To estimate the maximum exposure time t in seconds for a lens of focal length f mm, use the formula $t = 500/f$. If the camera does not have a "full-frame" sensor, use the "35-mm equivalent focal length" (check the camera manual). Experiment with different settings to find what works best for your camera, lens, and sky conditions.

Wide-field astrophotography with cameras on equatorial mounts: If your camera has a "bulb" setting, you can capture fainter objects without stars streaking by "piggy-backing" the camera on a telescope with an equatorial (EQ) mount, or by using a specialized commercial camera mount or homemade "barn-door" tracker aligned equatorially. The EQ mount can be driven manually, mechanically, or electrically to follow the motion of the heavens. For example, a tracked exposure of several minutes with a lens focal ratio (FR) of f/3.5 and sensor sensitivity of ISO 1600 will produce acceptable photos of the Milky Way or the zodiacal light. Any EQ mount that is used for long-exposure photography with standard camera lenses should be at least approximately polar-aligned (see POLAR ALIGNMENT, p. 70).

Afocal astrophotography of Solar System objects at the telescope eyepiece: It is possible to take an astrophoto simply by placing the camera and lens at the eyepiece of a telescope. For best results, use a mechanical adapter that aligns the lens to the eyepiece and clamps them together. This afocal technique works well with older cameras and lenses, but many modern cameras with zoom lenses suffer from bad vignetting with afocal photography, showing a black border around a small image in the middle. However, one can still take very pleasing astrophotos of bright subjects such as the filtered Sun, the Moon, Saturn, and Jupiter with its moons, using simple cameras (even cell phones!), just by using the viewscreen to align the picture.

Prime-focus astrophotography: High-quality deep-sky astrophotos usually require a Digital Single-Lens Reflex (DSLR) camera at prime focus with the camera lens replaced by the telescope objective lens or mirror, which—in effect—becomes a long telephoto lens. Adapters are available for attaching the camera to the telescope. In this case, the EQ mount must be carefully polar-aligned and the drive should be guided to follow the stars exactly. Most drives have irregularities that limit unguided exposure to times as short as 15 s. Good astrophotos may result from such short exposures if the telescope optics are "fast," i.e. *f*/6 or less. Longer exposures require guiding the photographic telescope on a star using the finder or another comounted telescope, either manually or with special automatic guiding electronics. Even better astrophotos can be obtained with a camera having a modified infrared filter over the sensor (such as the Canon 60Da), and from dedicated astronomical CCD cameras. With an acceptable image (or images) as a starting point, computer software can help tease out the interesting details in images and enhance the overall appearance of the composition.

The best deep-sky astrophotos result from taking multiple short exposures, often called "subframes," and combining them in software to create a master frame. The total exposure time may range from tens of minutes to hours. The following table suggests minimum *subframe* exposure times for various objects, using an *f*/5 telescope with a camera sensitivity of ISO 1600. For other configurations, multiply the suggested times by the factor $64\ \mathrm{FR}^2/\mathrm{ISO}$ (where FR denotes the focal ratio). For example, if the FR of the telescope is 10 instead of 5, multiply the time by 4; if the ISO is 800 instead of 1600, multiply the time by 2, and so on.

Deep-Sky Object	Exposure time for *f*/5 and ISO 1600
Star clusters, bright comets	30 s
Small planetary nebulae (M57, M76)	30 s
Larger planetary nebulae (M27, M97)	120 s (2 min)
Galaxies, faint comets	120 s (2 min)
Reflection and emission nebulae	120–300 s (2–5 min)
Dim nebulae (Veil Nebula)	300 s (5 min)

Some objects have large dynamic range, like M42 (the Orion Nebula), requiring different subframe exposure times for different parts. The nebula center and the Trapezium stars show best with a few seconds exposure. To show the entire nebula requires a several-minute exposure, but that overexposes the center. Computer software can be used to combine short and long exposures to show all parts of the nebula. M45 (the Pleiades) is another example where a short exposure shows the stars sharply, but a long exposure is required to show the nebulosity around the stars.

Long-focus and eyepiece projection astrophotography: The Sun, Moon, and planets are bright and can benefit from slower telescopes (larger FR) and lower ISO settings. To increase the apparent size of the planets or details of the Sun and Moon, use a Barlow lens or eyepiece (in a special adaptor) to project a magnified image to the sensor. This increases the effective telescope focal ratio (FR). The following suggested exposure times, using an *f*/10 telescope with a camera sensitivity of ISO 400, can be adjusted for other configurations by multiplying by the factor $4\,FR^2/ISO$.

Sun, Moon, and Planets	Exposure time for *f*/10 and ISO 400
Filtered Sun	1/2000 s
Moon	1/1000 s – 1/25 s
Planets	1/800 s – 1/50 s

Webcam astrophotography: Excellent astrophotos of the lunar detail and the brighter planets have been obtained with computer webcams, such as the *Logitech QuickCam Pro*, by removing the lens and making an adapter to attach to the telescope focuser. Capture a video of 100 to 1000 frames, and combine the best frames (those uncorrupted by atmospheric turbulence) with computer software, such as *RegiStax*. For planets, a Barlow lens can be used to increase the image size.

Postprocessing of astrophotos: Many methods can be used to reduce noise, graininess, and uneven illumination in astrophotos, most of which require specialized computer software. Steps relevant to the image data-collection stage include:

- Take multiple exposures and stack them using *RegiStax* or *DeepSkyStacker*.
- Expose "dark frames," stack them, and subtract them from the stacked "light frames." (With care, in-camera noise reduction may be used.)
- Use "flat frames" to adjust uneven exposure across the field.

Almost all astrophotos require some computer enhancement to obtain the best results. Usually the first aim is to stretch the image, that is, to darken the background and to brighten the faint detail of nebulae or galaxies without overbrightening the stars or galaxy cores. Another priority is to reduce the noise in the image without losing desirable low-level detail. No two astrophotographers enhance pictures the same way, for it is usually a matter of taste and compromise. Computer software supplied with cameras usually has some capabilities to enhance pictures. Good results can be obtained with freeware image-processing programs like *IrfanView* (irfanview.com) or *GIMP* (gimp.org), using the gamma and contrast adjustments in their menus. Best results usually require commercial image-processing software such as *Adobe Photoshop* (adobe.com) or astronomy-specific software like *MaxIm DL* (diffractionlimited.com/product/maxim-dl).

Suggested astrophotography resources

- Dickinson, T. and Dyer, A., "Digital Astrophotography," *The Backyard Astronomer's Guide*, Firefly Books, Ltd., 2010, Chapter 13.
- Dyer, A., *How to Photograph and Process Nightscapes and Timelapses* (interactive eBook, 2014) amazingsky.smugmug.com/NightscapesBook
- *Cloudy Nights* (several online imaging forums): cloudynights.com
- *RegiStax* (image-stacking and processing freeware): astronomie.be/registax
- *DeepSkyStacker* (image-stacking and registration freeware): deepskystacker.free.fr
- Lodriguss, Jerry, *Catching the Light*, astrophotography page: astropix.com
- *Tenho Tuomi Observatory*: lex.sk.ca/astro/index.htm

Editor's note: The author has completely photographed the Handbook lists THE MESSIER CATALOGUE, THE FINEST NGC OBJECTS, *and* DEEP-SKY GEMS.

THE SKY MONTH BY MONTH

BY BRUCE MCCURDY (TEXT), LARRY BOGAN (JUPITER'S SATELLITES), PATRICK KELLY (EVENTS), DAVE LANE (TABLES), AND ALISTER LING (LUNAR IMAGES)

INTRODUCTION

In the descriptions on the left-hand monthly pages (pp. 98–120), the right ascension (**RA**), declination (**Dec**) (both for equinox J2000.0), distance from Earth's center in astronomical units (**Dist**), visual magnitude (**Mag**), and equatorial angular diameter (**Size**) are tabulated for seven planets for 0h UT on the 1st, 11th, and 21st day of each month. The RA, Dec, distance, and diameter of the Sun are also given. **In the text below the tables, the meridian transit times at Greenwich (in UT) may be read as Standard Time at an observer's standard meridian (the error is no more than a minute or two). If the observer is west (east) of the standard meridian, the Standard Time of transit will be later (earlier) by 4 min per degree of longitude difference from the standard meridian. Remember to add one hour for Daylight Saving Time, if applicable.**

Sun

Data concerning the position, transit, orientation, rotation, and activity of the Sun plus times of sunrise and sunset appear on pp. 180–189, and 201–203. For detailed information on this year's solar eclipses, see ECLIPSES IN 2022 on p. 126.

Moon

Conjunctions of the Moon with the naked-eye planets and the bright Messier objects that lie near the ecliptic—the Beehive Cluster (M44), M35, and the Pleiades Cluster (M45)—are given in the right-hand monthly tables (pp. 99–121). Only events for which the elongation of the Moon is at least 14° are included, and only selected such events involving the Messier objects are listed. See p. 19 for the definition of conjunction and elongation.

The Moon's phases, perigees, and apogees (computed with *Multiyear Interactive Computer Almanac 1800–2050*, Willmann–Bell, 2005) are also given in the right-hand tables. The phases new Moon, first quarter, full Moon, and last quarter correspond, respectively, to the Moon having a longitude 0°, 90°, 180°, and 270° east of the Sun. The age of the Moon is the time since the new phase; first-quarter, full, and last-quarter phases correspond approximately to 7.4, 14.8, and 22.1 days, respectively. For times of moonrise and moonset, see pp. 150–157.

The Sun's selenographic colongitude (SSC), given on the left-hand monthly pages, indicates the position of the sunrise terminator as it moves across the face of the Moon and provides a method of ascertaining the angle of illumination of features on the Moon's surface. The SSC is the angle of the sunrise terminator measured toward the observer's east (i.e. westward on the Moon) starting from the lunar meridian that passes through the mean center of the apparent disk. Its value increases by nearly 12.2° per day, or about 0.5° per hour, and is approximately 0°, 90°, 180°, and 270° at the first-quarter, full, last-quarter, and new phases, respectively. Values of the SSC are given on pp. 98–120 for the 0th day of each month.

Selenographic longitude (λ) is measured toward the observer's west (i.e. eastward on the Moon) from the mean central lunar meridian. Thus sunrise will occur at a given point on the Moon when SSC = 360° – λ; values of 360° – λ for several lunar features are listed in the MAP OF THE MOON on p. 148. The longitude of the sunset terminator differs by 180° from that of the sunrise terminator.

Libration, also given on the left-hand pages, is the apparent rocking motion of the Moon as it orbits Earth. As a consequence, over time, about 59% of the lunar surface can be viewed from Earth (see *Sky & Telescope*, July 1987, p. 60). Libration in longitude (±8°) results from the nearly uniform axial rotation of the Moon combined with its varying orbital speed along its elliptical orbit, while libration in latitude (±7°) is caused by the tilt of the Moon's equator to its orbital plane. A smaller contribution (up to ±1°), called *diurnal libration*, is associated with the shifting of the observer due to Earth's rotation.

When the libration in longitude is positive, more of the Moon's east limb, the limb near Mare Crisium, is exposed to view (in reference to the lunar limbs, *east* and *west* are used in this lunar sense; see also the "E" and "W" labels on the MAP OF THE MOON, p. 148). When the libration in latitude is positive, more of the Moon's north limb is exposed to view. The monthly dates of the greatest positive and negative values of the libration in longitude and latitude and the dates of greatest northern and southern declination are given on the left-hand pages.

The lunar graphics on the right-hand pages give the geocentric appearance of the Moon at 0h UT on odd-numbered days of the month. They depict the Moon's phase, size, and libration. A small dot of size proportional to the amount of libration appears near the limb that is exposed. The graphics were prepared by Alister Ling with the aid of his *Lunar Calculator* software, jointly processed with the *JPL HORIZONS* ephemerides (ssd.jpl.nasa.gov/?horizons) to ensure accuracy.

The Moon's orbit is inclined 5° 09′ to the ecliptic. The gravitational influences of Earth and the Sun cause (i) the orbital plane to wobble, and (ii) the major axis of the orbit to precess: (i) The wobble shifts the line of nodes (see p. 122) westward (retrograde) along the ecliptic with a period of 18.60 years (18.61 years relative to the vernal equinox). During 2022, the ascending node regresses from longitude 59.5° to 40.2° from Taurus into Aries. The Moon's declination reaches a northern extreme of +27.5° on Nov. 12 and a southern extreme of –27.5° on Oct. 30. In 2015, around the September equinox, the Moon's declination range had minimum extremes of ±18.1° (a minor standstill); from then on, the extreme range of the Moon's declination continually increases, reaching a peak of ±29° in 2025; (ii) The precession shifts the perigee point eastward (prograde) with a period of 8.85 years, although the positions of successive perigees fluctuate considerably from the mean motion. The Moon's mean equatorial plane, its mean orbital plane, and the plane of the ecliptic intersect along a common line of nodes, the equator being inclined at 1°32′ to the ecliptic and at 1° 32′ + 5° 09′ = 6° 41′ to the orbit (i.e. the ascending node of the equator on the ecliptic coincides with the descending node of the orbit).

Jupiter's Satellites

The configurations of Jupiter's Galilean satellites, provided by Larry Bogan, are given on the right-hand monthly pages. In these diagrams, the vertical double line represents the equatorial diameter of the disk of Jupiter. Time is shown on the vertical scale, successive horizontal lines indicating 0h UT on the various days of the month with the last day in **bold**. The relative positions of the four satellites with respect to the disk of Jupiter are given by the four curves, each with the respective satellite's name. Note the "West–East" orientation given at the top of each diagram; these directions are those of the observer's sky, not Jupiter's limbs. Double-shadow transits of Jupiter's Galilean satellites that are not within 1.5 months of Jupiter's conjunction with the Sun are listed. Double-satellite transits that are not accompanied by a double-shadow event are generally also listed. For more information about the various transits, occultations, and eclipses of Jupiter's Galilean satellites, see PHENOMENA OF THE GALILEAN SATELLITES (p. 226).

Lunar Occultations of Bright Stars and Planetary Bodies

Occultations by the Moon of the bright stars that lie near the ecliptic (Aldebaran, Antares, Regulus, and Spica) are given in the right-hand tables along with those of the seven planets, the dwarf planet Ceres, and some bright minor planets (Pallas, Juno, and Vesta). If the elongation of the Moon is less than 14°, the event is not listed. Footnotes give areas of visibility; for more details on occultations visible in North America, including several involving members of the Pleiades (M45), see LUNAR OCCULTATIONS (p. 162) and PLANETARY OCCULTATIONS (p. 243).

Minima of Algol

Estimated predicted times of mid-eclipse are based on the formula heliocentric minimum = 2457675.717 + 2.86734E *(courtesy of AAVSO, 2021)* and are expressed as geocentric times for comparison with observations. The first number is the Julian Date for the minimum of 2016 Oct. 14.217, and the second is the period of Algol in days; E is an integer. The presence of a third stellar component introduces variations in these times, and careful timings by observers are encouraged (see VARIABLE STARS, p. 298).

Planets

Conjunctions of the planets with each other and the bright ecliptic stars and Messier objects are listed in the right-hand tables. Only events for which the elongation of the inner planet is greater than 11° are included, and not all events involving the Messier objects are listed. Also included are oppositions, conjunctions with the Sun, greatest elongations, and stationary times. See p. 19 for definitions of these terms, and TABLE OF CONTENTS or the INDEX for the location of more information on each of the planets. The following diagrams give an overview of the circumstances of the planets in 2022.

Miscellaneous Entries

The lunation number is the number of times the Moon has circled the Earth since January 1923, based on a series described by Ernest W. Brown in *Planetary Theory*, 1933. Peaks of major meteor showers (see also p. 254), equinoxes and solstices, heliocentric phenomena of the planets, phenomena of the bright dwarf planets and minor planets, and a few other events and occasional notes are given in the right-hand tables.

MAGNITUDES OF NAKED-EYE PLANETS IN 2022

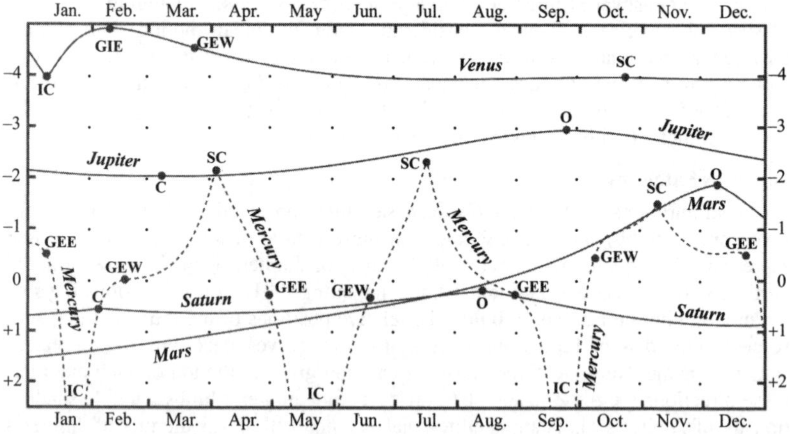

The visual magnitudes of the five classical (naked-eye) planets during 2022 are given. Oppositions (O), conjunctions (C), inferior and superior conjunctions (IC, SC), and greatest elongations east and west (GEE, GEW) are indicated. A diagram explaining these terms is on p. 20. Greatest illuminated extent, (GIE), if shown, occurs when the illuminated area of Venus, as viewed from Earth, covers the most square degrees. (Chart provided by Patrick Kelly.)

RIGHT ASCENSIONS OF THE SUN AND PLANETS IN 2022

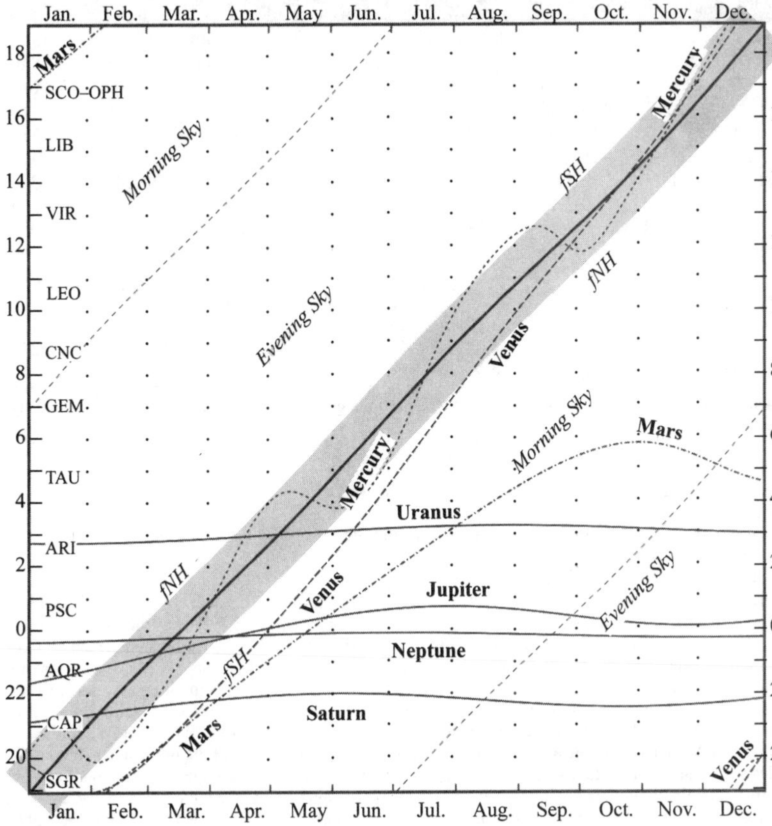

This diagram shows the variation during the year in the right ascension (vertical axis) of the Sun and planets. The slightly curved, heavy diagonal line represents the Sun; the shaded regions approximately indicate parts of the night sky affected by twilight. The two thin, dashed diagonal lines at the upper left and lower right represent the boundary between the evening sky and the morning sky.

The diagram may be used to determine in what part of the sky a planet may be found (including in which constellation—note the abbreviations along the vertical axis), when a superior planet is in conjunction with the Sun or at opposition (opposition is approximately where its curve intersects the dashed diagonal lines, and note that, due to retrograde motion, this point is also where the planet's curve has its maximum negative slope), when Mercury and Venus have their various greatest elongations and conjunctions, and when there are conjunctions of planets—that is, when the curves for planets intersect. For example, Mars and Venus are close before down from the start of Feb. to the end of Mar. At that time, Saturn passes Venus, and then Mars a week later. Jupiter meets Venus at the end of April; then Mars at the end of May. Nothing of note happens until the very end of the year when Venus and Mercury come together at sunset.

For observers in mid-latitudes, at certain times of the year the ecliptic stands steeply to the horizon in the western evening sky or the eastern morning sky, making apparitions of planets in these parts of the sky favorable from the Northern Hemisphere ("fNH" on the diagram) or favorable from the Southern Hemisphere ("fSH").

For more information on all these events, see the following 24 monthly pages and THE PLANETS IN 2022 *(p. 207). (Chart provided by Patrick Kelly; design by Roy Bishop.)*

THE SKY FOR JANUARY

		Mercury	Venus	Mars	Jupiter	Saturn	Uranus	Neptune	Sun
RA	1	20h 01m	19h 37m	16h 45m	22h 11m	20h 57m	2h 33m	23h 26m	18h 45m
	11	20h 46m	19h 12m	17h 16m	22h 18m	21h 02m	2h 33m	23h 27m	19h 28m
	21	20h 31m	18h 51m	17h 47m	22h 27m	21h 06m	2h 33m	23h 28m	20h 11m
Dec	1	−22° 22′	−18° 38′	−22° 28′	−12° 19′	−18° 06′	+14° 38′	−4° 52′	−23° 03′
	11	−18° 06′	−17° 07′	−23° 18′	−11° 35′	−17° 47′	+14° 36′	−4° 47′	−21° 53′
	21	−16° 01′	−16° 18′	−23° 46′	−10° 48′	−17° 28′	+14° 36′	−4° 41′	−20° 01′
Dist	1	1.14	0.27	2.34	5.57	10.75	19.21	30.24	0.983
	11	0.89	0.27	2.29	5.68	10.82	19.36	30.40	0.983
	21	0.68	0.29	2.23	5.78	10.87	19.53	30.54	0.984
Mag	1	−0.7	−4.3	1.5	−2.1	0.7	5.7	7.9	
	11	−0.3		1.5	−2.1	0.7	5.7	7.9	
	21	4.0	−4.5	1.5	−2.1	0.7	5.7	7.9	
Size	1	5.9″	60.9″	4.0″	35.4″	15.5″	3.6″	2.2″	32′ 32″
	11	7.5″	62.5″	4.1″	34.7″	15.4″	3.6″	2.2″	32′ 32″
	21	9.9″	57.8″	4.2″	34.1″	15.3″	3.6″	2.2″	32′ 30″

Moon: On January 0 at 0h UT, the Sun's selenographic colongitude is 234.49° and increases 12.2° each day thereafter.
Greatest N declination on the 16th (+26.2°)
Greatest S declination on the 3rd (−26.1°) and 30th (−26.4°)
Libration in longitude: E limb most exposed on the 8th (+7.6°)
W limb most exposed on the 23rd (−6.0°)
Libration in latitude: N limb most exposed on the 6th (+6.7°)
S limb most exposed on the 21st (−6.6°)
Large tides in the days following new Moon (Jan. 2)

Mercury: Begins the year in the early evening sky, trailing the Sun by 18° and shining brightly at mag. −0.7. Reaches maximum eastern elongation of 19.2° on the 7th, a week before the perihelion of its strongly elliptical orbit so brightly illuminated (mag. −0.5) in more intense sunlight but against a brighter background sky than is the case for an aphelic elongation. It is also moving relatively quickly, so this apparition is short-lived. Achieves a quasi-conjunction some 3.4° from Saturn on the 13th, but never quite overtakes the Ringed Planet. The two will share a wide binocular field each early evening from the 10th to 15th, during which time Mercury will fade an entire magnitude and become the fainter of the two planets. It quickly fades to obscurity thereafter as it falls back towards the Sun, reaching inferior conjunction on the 23rd.

Venus: Technically in the evening sky to open the year, though just 13° from the Sun and closing fast. Makes its (or any planet's) closest approach to Earth in a century on the 8th, when it is just 133 light-seconds (0.2658 AU) distant with an angular diameter of 62.8″. The razor-thin crescent passes 4°51′ north of the Sun at inferior conjunction on the 9th, and can be observed by an experienced telescopist taking thorough safety precautions. In retrograde motion until the 29th, Venus speeds into the morning sky and becomes visible to the unaided eye in the later stages of the month, reaching 31° elongation by the 31st.

Mars: The Red Planet begins its year-long approach toward a fine December opposition in understated fashion, shining meekly at mag. +1.5 in the dawn sky as it continues its emergence from behind the Sun. Crossing the border from Ophiuchus into Sagittarius in the second half of the month, it is joined by the waning crescent Moon 2° to its south on the 29th.

Jupiter: Readily visible in evening twilight as 2022 begins, low in the southwest sky. The waxing crescent Moon passes 4° to the south on the evening of the 5th as seen from the Americas. Its viewing window is closing, as its elongation from the Sun reduces from 50° to 25° during January.

Saturn: Located in central Capricornus, in which constellation it will be situated for the entirety of 2022. Saturn can be seen low in the southwest in the early evening at the beginning of the year, but is lost in the solar glare by mid-month. It has a quasi-conjunction with Mercury on the 13th (see Mercury entry above).

Uranus: Well placed for Northern Hemisphere observers in the evening sky nearly 15° north of the celestial equator in the constellation of Aries. At mag. +5.7 it is visible to the unaided eye from a dark location. As January begins it is 0.4° south of the mag. 6.0 star 29 Arietis and near its stationary point, which occurs on the 18th. Meridian transit times at Greenwich on the 1st, 11th, 21st–19:49, 19:09, 18:30 UT.

Neptune: Can be found with optical aid in early evening among the stars of extreme northeastern Aquarius.

Time (UT) d	h m	JANUARY EVENTS
Sat. 1	23	Moon at perigee (358 033 km) **Large tides**
Sun. 2	18 33	**new Moon (lunation 1225)**
Mon. 3	0 42	Algol at minimum
	21	**Quadrantid meteors peak**
Tue. 4	1	Mercury 3° N of Moon
	7	Earth at perihelion (147 105 052 km)
	17	Saturn 4° N of Moon
Wed. 5	21 31	Algol at minimum
Thu. 6	0	Jupiter 4° N of Moon
Fri. 7	11	**Mercury greatest elongation E (19°)**
Sat. 8	18 20	Algol at minimum
Sun. 9	1	Venus in inferior conjunction
	18 11	**first quarter**
Mon. 10		
Tue. 11		Mercury at ascending node
	11	Uranus 1.5° N of Moon
	15 09	Algol at minimum
	22	Juno in conjunction with the Sun
Wed. 12		
Thu. 13	0	**Ceres 1.2° S of Moon, occultation†**
	6 50	**Double shadow transit on Jupiter**
Fri. 14	1	Mercury stationary
	9	Moon at apogee (405 805 km)
	11 58	Algol at minimum
Sat. 15		Mercury at perihelion
	21	Moon 1.8° N of M35
Sun. 16	22	Ceres stationary
Mon. 17	8 47	Algol at minimum
	23 48	**full Moon (smallest in 2022)**
Tue. 18	20	Uranus stationary
Wed. 19		
Thu. 20	5 36	Algol at minimum
Fri. 21		
Sat. 22		
Sun. 23		Venus at perihelion
	2 24	Algol at minimum
	10	Mercury in inferior conjunction
Mon. 24		
Tue. 25	13 41	**last quarter**
	23 13	Algol at minimum
Wed. 26		Mercury at greatest heliocentric lat. N
Thu. 27		
Fri. 28	20 02	Algol at minimum
Sat. 29	8	Venus stationary
	15	**Mars 2° N of Moon**
Sun. 30	7	Moon at perigee (362 252 km)
Mon. 31	16 51	Algol at minimum

Jupiter's Satellites
West East

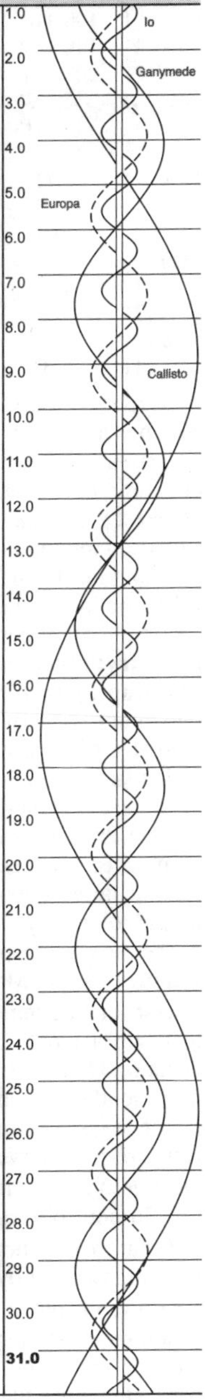

†Westernmost Canada, Alaska, NE edge of Russia

THE SKY FOR FEBRUARY

		Mercury	Venus	Mars	Jupiter	Saturn	Uranus	Neptune	Sun
RA	1	19h 44m	18h 45m	18h 22m	22h 36m	21h 12m	2h 33m	23h 29m	20h 57m
	11	19h 53m	18h 57m	18h 54m	22h 45m	21h 16m	2h 34m	23h 30m	21h 37m
	21	20h 34m	19h 21m	19h 26m	22h 54m	21h 21m	2h 35m	23h 32m	22h 16m
Dec	1	−18° 03′	−16° 16′	−23° 50′	−9° 53′	−17° 05′	+14° 38′	−4° 33′	−17° 15′
	11	−19° 31′	−16° 40′	−23° 28′	−9° 00′	−16° 45′	+14° 41′	−4° 25′	−14° 12′
	21	−19° 07′	−16° 59′	−22° 42′	−8° 06′	−16° 24′	+14° 46′	−4° 17′	−10° 45′
Dist	1	0.72	0.34	2.17	5.86	10.90	19.71	30.67	0.985
	11	0.88	0.40	2.11	5.92	10.89	19.88	30.77	0.987
	21	1.04	0.47	2.04	5.95	10.86	20.05	30.85	0.989
Mag	1	1.2	−4.8	1.4	−2.0	0.7	5.8	7.9	
	11	0.0	−4.9	1.4	−2.0	0.7	5.8	8.0	
	21	−0.1	−4.8	1.3	−2.0	0.7	5.8	8.0	
Size	1	9.4″	49.2″	4.3″	33.6″	15.3″	3.6″	2.2″	32′ 28″
	11	7.6″	41.7″	4.4″	33.3″	15.3″	3.5″	2.2″	32′ 25″
	21	6.5″	35.5″	4.6″	33.1″	15.3″	3.5″	2.2″	32′ 21″

Moon: On February 0 at 0h UT, the Sun's selenographic colongitude is 251.45° and increases 12.2° each day thereafter.
Greatest N declination on the 13th (+26.4°)
Greatest S declination on the 26th (−26.5°)
Libration in longitude: E limb most exposed on the 5th (+6.6°)
W limb most exposed on the 18th (−5.0°)
Libration in latitude: N limb most exposed on the 2nd (+6.5°)
S limb most exposed on the 17th (−6.5°)

Mercury: Emerging into the morning sky at the start of the month to begin the **best morning apparition of the year for Southern Hemisphere observers**. Reaches maximum western elongation of 26° on the 16th at mag. 0.0, when it forms an isosceles triangle with Venus and Mars to the west. It remains favorably elongated and at similar brightness for the rest of the month. The waning crescent Moon passes 4° to the south on the 28th.

Venus: Prominent in the dawn sky, Venus reaches greatest illuminated extent on the 12th, when it shines at mag. −4.9 at nearly 40° elongation from the Sun just five weeks after its inferior conjunction. It is technically in conjunction with Mars, 6 mag. fainter and 7° to the south, on the 13th. Earth's two neighbors remain in lockstep for the rest of the month, creeping eastward among the stars of Sagittarius, briefly joined by the waning crescent Moon on the 27th.

Mars: In Sagittarius throughout February, Mars overtakes Venus by mid-month to begin a month-long dalliance of Earth's nearest neighbors, albeit at a discreet distance. On the 13th, they have a wide conjunction nearly 7° apart, the Red Planet the more southerly. Venus is at its greatest brilliancy at this time and outshines Mars by a factor of ~300×, with atmospheric extinction increasing this differential for Northern Hemisphere observers. The waning crescent Moon passes still further south on the 27th.

Jupiter: Visible with increasing difficulty in early evening twilight early in the month. The 36-hour-old waxing crescent Moon passes 4° to the south on the 2nd.

Saturn: In conjunction with the Sun on the 4th, it is just beginning to emerge in bright morning twilight by month end.

Uranus: Visible in the early evening sky in south-central Aries. The waxing crescent Moon makes a close pass on the 7th, with an occultation taking place at the remote location shown on the bottom of the facing page. This is the first of a series of 15 consecutive occultations of Uranus extending into early 2023.

Neptune: Fading into bright evening twilight as it approaches its Mar. 13 solar conjunction.

Time (UT) d	h	m	FEBRUARY EVENTS
Tue. 1	5	46	**new Moon (lunation 1226)**
Wed. 2	21		Jupiter 4° N of Moon
Thu. 3	13	40	Algol at minimum
	22		Mercury stationary
Fri. 4	19		Saturn in conjunction with the Sun
Sat. 5			
Sun. 6	10	29	Algol at minimum
Mon. 7	20		**Uranus 1.2° N of Moon, occultation†**
Tue. 8	13	50	**first quarter**
Wed. 9	7	18	Algol at minimum
	11		**Ceres 0.03° S of Moon, occultation‡**
Thu. 10			
Fri. 11	3		Moon at apogee (404 897 km)
Sat. 12	4		Moon 1.9° N of M35
	4	07	Algol at minimum
	22		**Venus greatest illuminated extent**
Sun. 13			Venus at greatest heliocentric lat. N
	1		Venus 7° N of Mars
Mon. 14			
Tue. 15	0	56	Algol at minimum
Wed. 16	16	56	**full Moon**
	21		**Mercury greatest elongation W (26°)**
Thu. 17	21	45	Algol at minimum
Fri. 18			Mercury at descending node
			Zodiacal light vis. in N lat. in W after evening twilight for next two weeks
Sat. 19			
Sun. 20	18	34	Algol at minimum
Mon. 21			
Tue. 22			
Wed. 23	15	23	Algol at minimum
	22	32	**last quarter**
Thu. 24			
Fri. 25			
Sat. 26	12	12	Algol at minimum
	22		Moon at perigee (367 789 km)
Sun. 27	9		Mars 4° N of Moon
Mon. 28			Mercury at aphelion
	20		Mercury 4° N of Moon

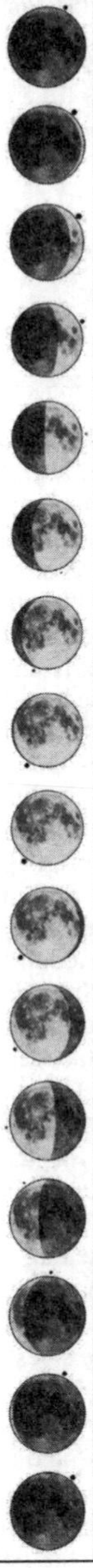

Jupiter's Satellites
West East

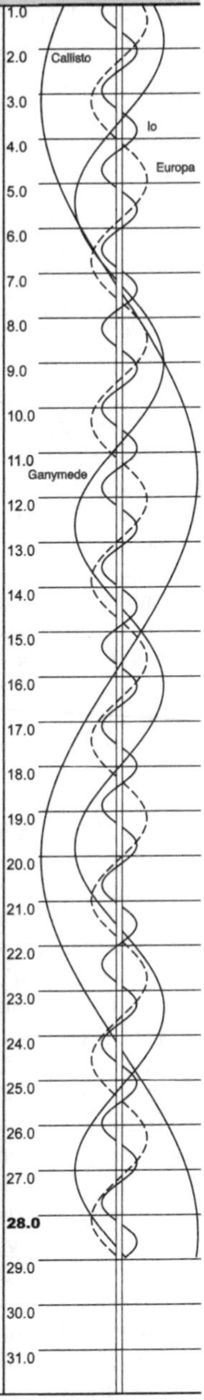

†Edge of Queen Maud Land, South Sandwich Islands
‡Seychelles, Maldives, S tip of India, Sri Lanka, most of SE Asia, SE China, Korean Peninsula, Japan, N Micronesia

THE SKY FOR MARCH

		Mercury	Venus	Mars	Jupiter	Saturn	Uranus	Neptune	Sun
RA	1	21h 17m	19h 46m	19h 52m	23h 01m	21h 25m	2h 36m	23h 33m	22h 46m
	11	22h 16m	20h 22m	20h 23m	23h 10m	21h 29m	2h 37m	23h 34m	23h 24m
	21	23h 19m	21h 01m	20h 54m	23h 19m	21h 33m	2h 39m	23h 36m	0h 00m
Dec	1	−17° 16′	−16° 56′	−21° 49′	−7° 22′	−16° 07′	+14° 50′	−4° 10′	−7° 48′
	11	−13° 03′	−16° 17′	−20° 22′	−6° 26′	−15° 47′	+14° 58′	−4° 01′	−3° 56′
	21	−6° 45′	−14° 53′	−18° 35′	−5° 30′	−15° 28′	+15° 06′	−3° 52′	+0° 01′
Dist	1	1.15	0.53	2.00	5.97	10.82	20.17	30.89	0.991
	11	1.26	0.60	1.93	5.97	10.75	20.32	30.91	0.993
	21	1.33	0.68	1.87	5.95	10.65	20.44	30.91	0.996
Mag	1	−0.1	−4.7	1.3	−2.0	0.8	5.8	8.0	
	11	−0.3	−4.6	1.2	−2.0	0.8	5.8	8.0	
	21	−0.7	−4.5	1.1	−2.0	0.8	5.8	8.0	
Size	1	5.9″	31.6″	4.7″	33.0″	15.4″	3.5″	2.2″	32′ 17″
	11	5.4″	27.6″	4.8″	33.0″	15.5″	3.4″	2.2″	32′ 12″
	21	5.1″	24.4″	5.0″	33.1″	15.6″	3.4″	2.2″	32′ 07″

Moon: On March 0 at 0h UT, the Sun's selenographic colongitude is 232.05° and increases 12.2° each day thereafter.
Greatest N declination on the 12th (+26.7°)
Greatest S declination on the 25th (–26.6°)
Libration in longitude: E limb most exposed on the 5th (+5.5°)
W limb most exposed on the 17th (–5.2°)
Libration in latitude: N limb most exposed on the 2nd (+6.5°) and 29th (+6.6°)
S limb most exposed on the 16th (–6.6°)

Mercury: The **best morning apparition of the year for Southern Hemisphere observers** continues. Mercury brightens through the first half of the month as its phase angle increases, but becomes increasingly lost in bright morning twilight, falling within 15° elongation of the Sun at mid-month. Passes 1.3° from Jupiter on the 20th, when the two bright planets, rising just ahead of the Sun, may be glimpsed with difficulty by Southern Hemisphere observers.

Venus: Shines brilliantly in the dawn sky, still accompanied by Mars with which it is again in conjunction (4° separation) on the 12th. Achieves maximum western elongation on the 20th when it is 47° from the Sun. Achieves conjunction 2° north of Saturn on the 29th, with all three of Venus, Mars, and Saturn visible in a single 7° binocular field for the last week of March. The waning crescent Moon passes well to the south of the trio on the 28th, although the angle of the morning ecliptic is unfavorable for Northern Hemisphere observers.

Mars: Passes from Sagittarius into Capricornus on the 6th. Remains to the south of much brighter Venus during the first half of the month, the duo achieving another conjunction separated by some 4° on the 12th. The waning crescent Moon passes to the south of the widening pair on 28th, with Saturn also in the frame.

Jupiter: In conjunction with the Sun on the 5th. Just beginning to emerge in morning twilight at the end of March when it achieves 20° elongation, with Southern Hemisphere observers best placed to see it.

Saturn: Emerging in the morning sky, it separates significantly from the Sun in March, its elongation stretching from 22° on the 1st to 49° on the 31st. Late in the month it joins Venus and Mars in a single binocular field, with the Moon passing to the south of the group on the 28th. Venus closes to 2° to Saturn's north on the 29th.

Uranus: Its evening viewing window is closing rapidly as its elongation from the Sun narrows from 60° on the 1st to 32° on the 31st. Occulted by the waxing crescent Moon on the 7th; see facing page for details.

Neptune: Too close to the Sun to be seen. In solar conjunction on the 13th.

Time (UT)	d	h	m	MARCH EVENTS
Tue.	1	0		Saturn 4° N of Moon
		9	01	Algol at minimum
Wed.	2	13		Mercury 0.7° S of Saturn
		17	35	**new Moon (lunation 1227)**
Thu.	3			
Fri.	4	5	50	Algol at minimum
Sat.	5	14		Jupiter in conjunction with the Sun
Sun.	6			
Mon.	7	2	39	Algol at minimum
		6		**Uranus 0.8° N of Moon, occultation†**
Tue.	8			
Wed.	9	7		**Ceres 0.3° N of Moon, occultation‡**
		23	28	Algol at minimum
Thu.	10	10	45	**first quarter**
		23		Moon at apogee (404 268 km)
Fri.	11			
Sat.	12	14		Venus 4° N of Mars
		20	17	Algol at minimum
Sun.	13			**Daylight Saving Time Begins**
		12		Neptune in conjunction with the Sun
Mon.	14			
Tue.	15	17	06	Algol at minimum
Wed.	16			
Thu.	17			
Fri.	18	7	18	**full Moon**
		13	55	Algol at minimum
Sat.	19			
Sun.	20			**Zodiacal light vis. in N lat. in W after evening twilight for next two weeks**
		9		**Venus greatest elongation W (47°)**
		15	33	**Equinox**
		22		**Mercury 1.3° S of Jupiter**
Mon.	21			Mercury at greatest heliocentric lat. S
		10	44	Algol at minimum
Tue.	22			
Wed.	23			
Thu.	24	0		Moon at perigee (369 760 km)
		7	33	Algol at minimum
Fri.	25	5	37	**last quarter**
Sat.	26			
Sun.	27	4	22	Algol at minimum
Mon.	28	3		Mars 4° N of Moon
		10		Venus 7° N of Moon
		12		Saturn 4° N of Moon
Tue.	29	13		**Venus 2° N of Saturn**
Wed.	30	1	11	Algol at minimum
		15		Jupiter 4° N of Moon
Thu.	31			

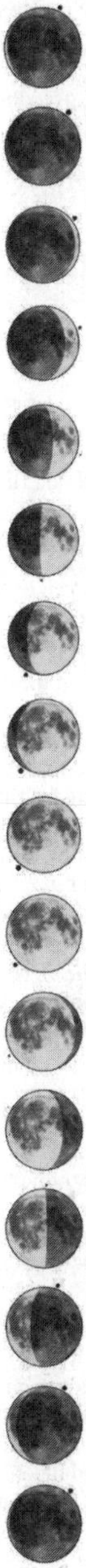

Jupiter's Satellites
West East

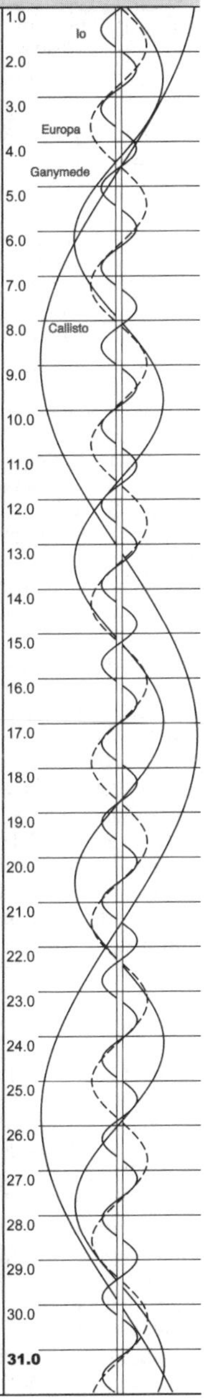

†Parts of E Antarctica, SE Australia, SE Melanesia, SW Polynesia
‡W and N Australia, E Indonesia, Papua New Guinea, N Melanesia, Micronesia, N Polynesia (except Hawaii)

THE SKY FOR APRIL

		Mercury	Venus	Mars	Jupiter	Saturn	Uranus	Neptune	Sun
RA	1	0h 35m	21h 47m	21h 27m	23h 29m	21h 38m	2h 41m	23h 37m	0h 40m
	11	1h 49m	22h 29m	21h 57m	23h 37m	21h 41m	2h 43m	23h 38m	1h 17m
	21	3h 01m	23h 12m	22h 26m	23h 45m	21h 44m	2h 45m	23h 40m	1h 54m
Dec	1	+2° 20′	−12° 27′	−16° 16′	−4° 30′	−15° 09′	+15° 16′	−3° 42′	+4° 20′
	11	+11° 36′	−9° 30′	−13° 54′	−3° 36′	−14° 54′	+15° 26′	−3° 34′	+8° 07′
	21	+19° 14′	−6° 00′	−11° 20′	−2° 44′	−14° 40′	+15° 36′	−3° 26′	+11° 40′
Dist	1	1.35	0.77	1.81	5.90	10.52	20.55	30.87	0.999
	11	1.26	0.85	1.75	5.84	10.39	20.63	30.81	1.002
	21	1.05	0.92	1.69	5.76	10.24	20.68	30.72	1.005
Mag	1	−1.9	−4.4	1.1	−2.0	0.8	5.9	8.0	
	11	−1.5	−4.3	1.0	−2.1	0.9	5.9	8.0	
	21	−0.8	−4.2	0.9	−2.1	0.9	5.9	7.9	
Size	1	5.0″	21.7″	5.2″	33.4″	15.8″	3.4″	2.2″	32′ 01″
	11	5.3″	19.7″	5.4″	33.7″	16.0″	3.4″	2.2″	31′ 56″
	21	6.4″	18.1″	5.5″	34.2″	16.2″	3.4″	2.2″	31′ 50″

Moon: On April 0 at 0h UT, the Sun's selenographic colongitude is 249.66° and increases 12.2° each day thereafter.
Greatest N declination on the 8th (+26.8°)
Greatest S declination on the 22nd (−26.9°)
Libration in longitude: E limb most exposed on the 1st (+4.9°) and 28th (+5.5°)
W limb most exposed on the 14th (−6.0°)
Libration in latitude: N limb most exposed on the 25th (+6.8°)
S limb most exposed on the 12th (−6.8°)

Partial solar eclipse on Apr. 30, visible from extreme northern Antarctica, southern South America, the south Pacific Ocean, and the south Atlantic Ocean.

Mercury: In superior conjunction on the 2nd. At mid-month Mercury emerges into an evening sky otherwise bereft of bright planets to begin its **best evening apparition of the year for Northern Hemisphere observers**. Achieves maximum eastern elongation of 21° on the 29th, by which time it has faded to mag. +0.2. In conjunction 1.4° south of the Pleiades on the same date, making for a rich binocular field in deepening twilight.

Venus: Gradually pulling away from Mars and Saturn throughout April, Venus overtakes two more outer planets late in the month. First comes an exceptionally close approach just 0.01° south of Neptune on the 27th, although the extreme brightness difference of 12 mag. will be a challenging observation for even the experienced telescopist. Venus passes just 0.2° south of Jupiter on the 30th, 43° ahead of the Sun in the dawn sky.

Mars: Achieves a close conjunction 0.3° south of Saturn on the 4th, when the two are also separated by just 0.2 mag. (+0.9 and +1.1 respectively). Their similar brightness will allow for a fine comparison of their contrasting colors against the deep blue of morning twilight. Mars crosses from Capricornus into Aquarius on the 11th, just as it achieves mag. +1.0. The waning crescent Moon passes 4° to the south on the 25th.

Jupiter: Achieves a very close conjunction just 0.1° from Neptune on the 12th, though the 10-mag. difference will make for an exceedingly challenging telescopic observation in morning twilight. Crosses the border from Aquarius to Pisces at mid-month, around which time it is situated at the eastern end of a regularly spaced line of planets including Venus, Mars, and Saturn. Achieves a close conjunction with Venus on the 30th, when the two brightest planets are separated by just 0.2° at a favourable elongation of 42–43°.

Saturn: Begins the month in between Venus and Mars in the morning sky, achieving a fine conjunction with the latter on the 4–5. Around this time it passes north of −15° declination for the first time since 2014. By the third week of the month, Saturn forms the westernmost of a line of four regularly spaced naked-eye planets at intervals of about 10°. The waning crescent Moon makes a wide pass 5° to its south on the 24–25th.

Uranus: Quickly fading into evening twilight. Occulted by the waxing crescent Moon on the 3rd; see facing page for details.

Neptune: Gradually emerging in morning twilight among the stars of northeastern Aquarius for telescopic observers. It has extremely close conjunctions with bright Jupiter on the 12th and brighter Venus on the 27th; see the entries under those planets for further details.

Time (UT)	d	h m	APRIL EVENTS
Fri.	1	6 24	**new Moon (lunation 1228)**
		22 00	Algol at minimum
Sat.	2	23	Mercury in superior conjunction
Sun.	3	17	**Uranus 0.6° N of Moon, occultation**†
Mon.	4	18 49	Algol at minimum
		22	**Mars 0.3° S of Saturn**
Tue.	5		
Wed.	6	9	**Ceres 0.2° N of Moon, occultation**‡
Thu.	7	15 38	Algol at minimum
		19	Moon at apogee (404 438 km)
Fri.	8		
Sat.	9		Mercury at ascending node
		6 48	**first quarter**
Sun.	10		Venus at descending node
		12 27	Algol at minimum
Mon.	11		
Tue.	12	3	Pallas in conjunction with the Sun
		20	**Jupiter 0.1° N of Neptune**
Wed.	13		Mercury at perihelion
		9 16	Algol at minimum
Thu.	14		
Fri.	15		
Sat.	16	6 05	Algol at minimum
		18 55	**full Moon**
Sun.	17		
Mon.	18	13	Mercury 2° N of Uranus
Tue.	19	2 54	Algol at minimum
		15	Moon at perigee (365 143 km)
Wed.	20		
Thu.	21	23 43	Algol at minimum
Fri.	22	18	Lyrid meteors peak
Sat.	23	11 56	**last quarter**
Sun.	24		Mercury at greatest heliocentric lat. N
		20 31	Algol at minimum
		21	Saturn 5° N of Moon
Mon.	25	22	Mars 4° N of Moon
Tue.	26		
Wed.	27	2	Venus 4° N of Moon
		8	Jupiter 4° N of Moon
		17 20	Algol at minimum
		19	**Venus 0.01° S of Neptune**
Thu.	28		
Fri.	29	8	**Mercury greatest elongation E (21°)**
		19	**Mercury 1.4° S of Pleiades (M45)**
Sat.	30	14 09	Algol at minimum
		19	**Venus 0.2° S of Jupiter**
		20 28	**new Moon (lunation 1229)**
			Partial Solar Eclipse (p. 126)

Jupiter's Satellites
West East

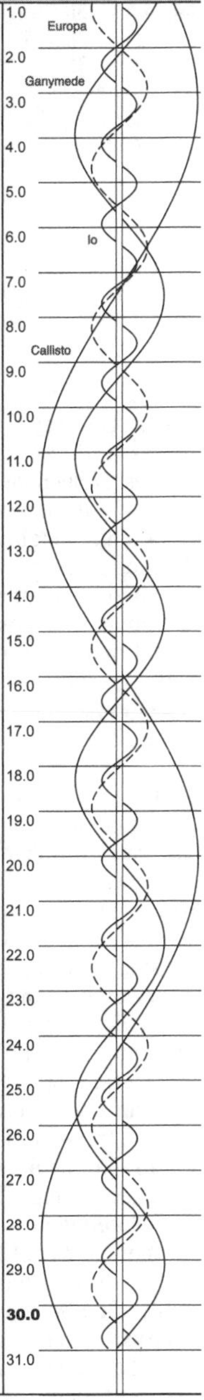

†S and E S. America, Ascension Island, St. Helena, edge of W Central Africa
‡Madagascar, parts of E Africa, S and E India, most of SE Asia, SE China, Papua New Guinea, most of Micronesia

THE SKY FOR MAY

		Mercury	Venus	Mars	Jupiter	Saturn	Uranus	Neptune	Sun
RA	1	3h 51m	23h 54m	22h 55m	23h 53m	21h 47m	2h 48m	23h 41m	2h 32m
	11	4h 09m	0h 37m	23h 23m	0h 01m	21h 48m	2h 50m	23h 42m	3h 10m
	21	3h 56m	1h 20m	23h 51m	0h 08m	21h 50m	2h 52m	23h 43m	3h 50m
Dec	1	+22° 56′	−2° 05′	−8° 36′	−1° 54′	−14° 30′	+15° 46′	−3° 20′	+14° 55′
	11	+22° 39′	+2° 06′	−5° 45′	−1° 08′	−14° 22′	+15° 56′	−3° 14′	+17° 44′
	21	+19° 21′	+6° 20′	−2° 51′	−0° 25′	−14° 17′	+16° 06′	−3° 09′	+20° 04′
Dist	1	0.82	1.00	1.63	5.67	10.08	20.71	30.61	1.007
	11	0.63	1.07	1.57	5.55	9.92	20.71	30.48	1.010
	21	0.55	1.14	1.52	5.43	9.75	20.68	30.33	1.012
Mag	1	0.4	−4.1	0.9	−2.1	0.8	5.9	7.9	
	11	2.6	−4.1	0.8	−2.2	0.8	5.9	7.9	
	21		−4.0	0.7	−2.2	0.8	5.9	7.9	
Size	1	8.2″	16.7″	5.7″	34.8″	16.5″	3.4″	2.2″	31′ 45″
	11	10.6″	15.6″	6.0″	35.5″	16.8″	3.4″	2.2″	31′ 41″
	21	12.2″	14.6″	6.2″	36.3″	17.1″	3.4″	2.2″	31′ 37″

Moon: On May 0 at 0h UT, the Sun's selenographic colongitude is 255.58° and increases 12.2° each day thereafter.
Greatest N declination on the 6th (+26.9°)
Greatest S declination on the 19th (-27.0°)
Libration in longitude: E limb most exposed on the 24th (+6.7°)
W limb most exposed on the 12th (-7.0°)
Libration in latitude: N limb most exposed on the 22nd (+6.8°)
S limb most exposed on the 9th (-6.8°)

Total lunar eclipse on May 16, visible from western Europe, the Middle East, Africa, North America, South America, Antarctica, the Atlantic Ocean, and the Pacific Ocean.

Mercury: Fading into evening twilight early in the month. The waxing crescent Moon passes nearby on the 1st and 2nd of the month. Not easily visible from either hemisphere for the rest of the month, achieving inferior conjunction on the 21st.

Venus: Begins the month near Jupiter in the morning sky, but soon pulls away. Has a close conjunction with the waning crescent Moon on the 28th, best seen from the Eastern Hemisphere, with an occultation visible from those locales designated at the bottom of the facing page.

Mars: Becoming more prominent in the morning sky as its elongation from the Sun extends to 60° and beyond, Mars passes 0.6° south of Neptune on the 17th before crossing from Aquarius into Pisces on the 19th. The waning crescent Moon passes 3° to the south on the 24th. Steadily overtakes Jupiter as the month progresses, and the two achieve a close conjunction just 0.6° apart on May 28–29.

Jupiter: Still near Venus as the month begins in the aftermath of their fine Apr. 30 conjunction. Spends most of May seemingly bridging the gap from Venus to Mars, with the waning crescent Moon joining the frame on the 24–25. At their closest on the 28–29, Jupiter is just 0.6° north of Mars and shines three full magnitudes brighter; in a low-to-medium-power telescopic view, Jupiter appears roughly 6× the diameter of its rocky neighbor and actually has a lower surface brightness than the tinier but shinier Red Planet.

Saturn: Shines at mag. +0.8 among the stars of eastern Capricornus, its prograde motion slowing throughout the month. The last-quarter Moon passes 4° to its south on the 22nd.

Uranus: In conjunction with the Sun on the 5th. Not easily observed throughout the month, but emerges to 20° elongation by the 28th when it is occulted by the waning crescent Moon; see facing page for details.

Neptune: In the morning sky, it creeps across the border from Aquarius into Pisces early in the month. Achieves conjunction 0.6° north of Mars on the 17–18.

Time (UT) d	h	m	MAY EVENTS
Sun. 1			
Mon. 2	14		**Mercury 1.8° N of Moon**
Tue. 3	10	58	Algol at minimum
Wed. 4	14		**Ceres 0.01° N of Moon, occultation**†
Thu. 5	7		Uranus in conjunction with the Sun
	13		Moon at apogee (405 285 km)
Fri. 6	7	47	Algol at minimum
	8		η-Aquariid meteors peak
Sat. 7			
Sun. 8			
Mon. 9	0	21	**first quarter**
	4	36	Algol at minimum
Tue. 10	23		Mercury stationary
Wed. 11			
Thu. 12	1	25	Algol at minimum
Fri. 13			
Sat. 14	22	14	Algol at minimum
Sun. 15			Venus at aphelion
Mon. 16	4	14	**full Moon**
			Total Lunar Eclipse (p. 127)
Tue. 17			Mercury at descending node
	15		Moon at perigee (360 298 km)
	19	03	Algol at minimum
	23		**Mars 0.6° S of Neptune**
Wed. 18			
Thu. 19			
Fri. 20	15	52	Algol at minimum
Sat. 21	19		Mercury in inferior conjunction
Sun. 22	5		Saturn 4° N of Moon
	18	43	**last quarter**
Mon. 23	12	41	Algol at minimum
Tue. 24	19		Mars 3° N of Moon
Wed. 25	0		Jupiter 3° N of Moon
Thu. 26			Mars at greatest heliocentric lat. S
	9	30	Algol at minimum
Fri. 27			Mercury at aphelion
	3		**Venus 0.2° N of Moon, occultation**‡
Sat. 28	14		**Uranus 0.3° N of Moon, occultation**††
Sun. 29	0		**Mars 0.6° S of Jupiter**
	6	19	Algol at minimum
Mon. 30	11	30	**new Moon (lunation 1230)**
Tue. 31			

Jupiter's Satellites
West East

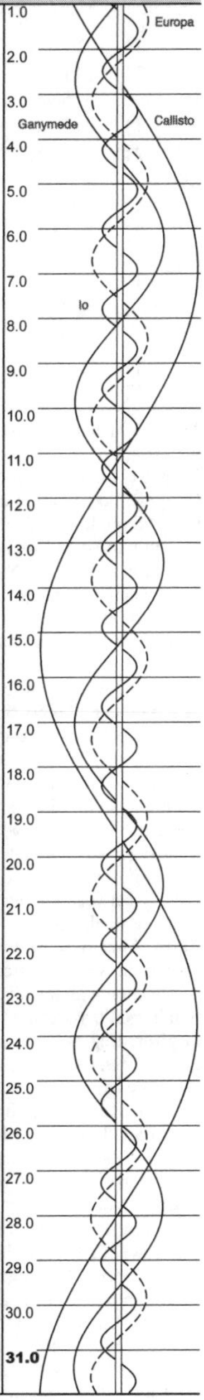

†NE S. America, Cape Verde Islands, Madeira, N Africa, southernmost Europe, parts of Middle East, W and S India
‡S Madagascar, most of SE Asia, SE China, most of Micronesia
††Easter Island, most of S. America, Cape Verde Islands, most of W Africa

THE SKY FOR JUNE

		Mercury	Venus	Mars	Jupiter	Saturn	Uranus	Neptune	Sun
RA	1	3h 38m	2h 08m	0h 21m	0h 14m	21h 50m	2h 55m	23h 43m	4h 34m
	11	3h 47m	2h 54m	0h 48m	0h 20m	21h 50m	2h 57m	23h 44m	5h 16m
	21	4h 22m	3h 42m	1h 15m	0h 25m	21h 50m	2h 59m	23h 44m	5h 57m
Dec	1	+15° 48′	+10° 51′	+0° 21′	+0° 18′	−14° 16′	+16° 17′	−3° 05′	+21° 59′
	11	+15° 50′	+14° 38′	+3° 12′	+0° 51′	−14° 18′	+16° 26′	−3° 02′	+23° 03′
	21	+18° 35′	+17° 54′	+5° 58′	+1° 18′	−14° 23′	+16° 34′	−3° 01′	+23° 26′
Dist	1	0.59	1.22	1.46	5.28	9.57	20.62	30.16	1.014
	11	0.72	1.28	1.40	5.13	9.41	20.54	29.99	1.015
	21	0.91	1.35	1.35	4.98	9.27	20.44	29.82	1.016
Mag	1	2.9	−3.9	0.7	−2.3	0.7	5.9	7.9	
	11	1.0	−3.9	0.6	−2.3	0.7	5.8	7.9	
	21	0.0	−3.9	0.5	−2.4	0.6	5.8	7.9	
Size	1	11.3″	13.7″	6.4″	37.3″	17.4″	3.4″	2.2″	31′ 33″
	11	9.3″	13.0″	6.7″	38.4″	17.7″	3.4″	2.2″	31′ 30″
	21	7.4″	12.4″	6.9″	39.6″	17.9″	3.4″	2.2″	31′ 29″

Moon: On June 0 at 0h UT, the Sun's selenographic colongitude is 274.19° and increases 12.2° each day thereafter.
Greatest N declination on the 2nd (+27.0°) and 29th (+26.9°)
Greatest S declination on the 15th (–26.7°)
Libration in longitude: E limb most exposed on the 21st (+7.7°)
W limb most exposed on the 9th (–7.5°)
Libration in latitude: N limb most exposed on the 18th (+6.7°)
S limb most exposed on the 6th (–6.8°)
Large tides in the days following full Moon (Jun. 14)

Mercury: Emerging into the morning sky as June begins though too faint to be easily seen until around the 10th. Achieves greatest elongation west (23°) on the 16th when it shines relatively weakly at mag. +0.5. Continues to brighten for the rest of the month. As it comes to visibility, it defines the eastern end of a **line of naked-eye planets that are distributed along the morning ecliptic in order: Mercury, Venus, Mars, Jupiter, Saturn**. The waning crescent Moon bridges the gap between Mars and Venus on the 23–25, assuming its "rightful place" in the line of planets as best observed on the 24th. In fact, all seven planets including Uranus and Neptune will be loosely clustered in the morning sky, all to the west of the rising Sun but east of the meridian in a 110° swath. This unusual collection is best seen from the Southern Hemisphere due to the northerly declination of the Sun at this time.

Venus: Remains prominent in the dawn sky even as it is gradually being reined in by the Sun, its elongation reducing from 37° to 30° during the month. The waning crescent Moon passes 3° to its north on the 26th, directly between the famous open clusters Pleiades and Hyades, with Mercury rising late to the party some 9° to the southeast.

Mars: Already separating from Jupiter as the month begins, Mars continues to speed eastward, primarily among the stars of Pisces with a brief pass through northwestern Cetus early in the month. Has a close conjunction with the thick crescent Moon on the 22nd, with an occultation visible from certain islands in the South Pacific as detailed at the bottom of the facing page.

Jupiter: Begins the month near Mars but is soon left behind by the Red Planet as the bright planets string out in order. (See Mercury entry above.) The last-quarter Moon passes 3° to the south on the 21st. Still in prograde (eastward) motion, Jupiter crosses the border from Pisces into Cetus late in the month.

Saturn: Reaches its first stationary point on the 5th, marking the beginning of a leisurely 20-week retrograde loop that will see it reverse its tracks in western Capricornus by some 6°. This period, which brackets its Aug. 14 opposition, roughly defines its best telescopic observing window of 2022. The waning gibbous moon passes 4° to the south on the 18th. By the second half of June, Saturn rises around midnight local daylight time, the westernmost among the seven planets adorning the morning sky. With all five outer planets in the same sector of the sky and all achieving opposition within a four-month span in the second half of the year, 2022 offers an outstanding opportunity for the careful observer to track their rrespective retrograde loops, as detailed in this section at the first stationary point for each.
Meridian transit times at Greenwich on the 1st, 11th, 21st–05:13, 04:34, 03:54 UT.

Uranus: Emerging in the morning sky, its elongation from the Sun doubling from 25° to 50° during the month. Venus, fully 10 magnitudes brighter, passes 1.6° to its south on the 11th. Occulted by the waning crescent Moon on the 24th; see facing page for details.

Neptune: In the morning sky in Pisces. Reaches its first stationary point on the 28th, after which its tiny retrograde motion will slowly begin. The second stationary point won't happen until early December, just 2.5° to the west. As befitting the most distant planet, its retrograde motion takes the longest, yet covers the least amount of sky.

Time (UT)	d	h	m	JUNE EVENTS
Wed.	1	3	08	Algol at minimum
		21		**Ceres 0.1° S of Moon, occultation†**
Thu.	2	1		Moon at apogee (406 192 km)
Fri.	3	0		Mercury stationary
		23	57	Algol at minimum
Sat.	4			
Sun.	5	14		Saturn stationary
Mon.	6			Venus at greatest heliocentric lat. S
		20	46	Algol at minimum
Tue.	7	14	48	**first quarter**
Wed.	8			
Thu.	9	17	35	Algol at minimum
Fri.	10			
Sat.	11	13		Venus 1.6° S of Uranus
Sun.	12	14	24	Algol at minimum
Mon.	13			
Tue.	14	11	52	**full Moon**
		23		Moon at perigee (357 432 km) **Large tides**
Wed.	15	11	13	Algol at minimum
Thu.	16	15		**Mercury greatest elongation W (23°)**
Fri.	17			Mercury at greatest heliocentric lat. S
Sat.	18	8	02	Algol at minimum
		12		Saturn 4° N of Moon
Sun.	19	8		**Vesta 0.7° N of Moon, occultation‡**
Mon.	20			
Tue.	21			Mars at perihelion
		3	11	**last quarter**
		4	51	Algol at minimum
		9	14	**Solstice**
		14		Jupiter 3° N of Moon
Wed.	22	18		**Mars 0.9° N of Moon, occultation††**
Thu.	23			
Fri.	24	1	40	Algol at minimum
		22		**Uranus 0.05° N of Moon, occultation‡‡**
Sat.	25			
Sun.	26	8		**Venus 3° S of Moon**
		22	29	Algol at minimum
Mon.	27	8		Mercury 4° S of Moon
Tue.	28	23		Neptune stationary
Wed.	29	2	52	**new Moon (lunation 1231)**
		6		Moon at apogee (406 580 km)
		19	18	Algol at minimum
Thu.	30			

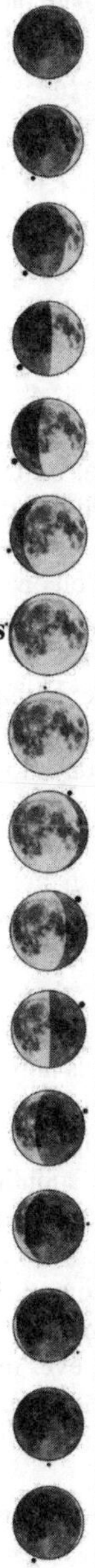

Jupiter's Satellites
West East

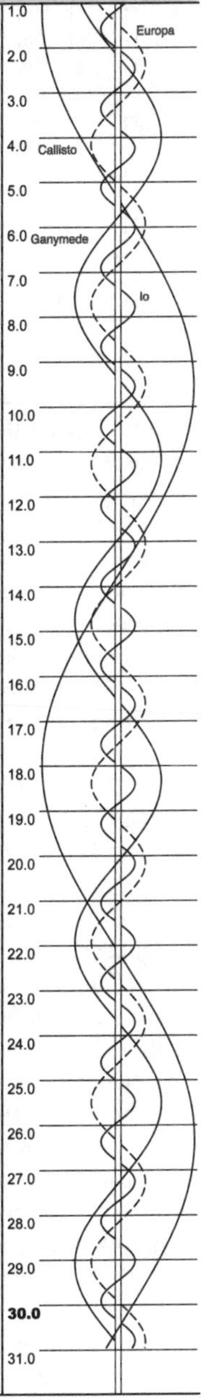

†N Polynesia, Hawaii, cont. USA, most of Mexico, S edge of Canada, Caribbean, NE edge of S. America
‡Most of Antarctica, tip of S. America, Falkland Islands, SW Africa
††George V Land, Oates Land, Marie Byrd Land, SE Polynesia
‡‡W and N Australia, E Indonesia, NW Melanesia, Micronesia, Hawaii

THE SKY FOR JULY

		Mercury	Venus	Mars	Jupiter	Saturn	Uranus	Neptune	Sun
RA	1	5h 24m	4h 31m	1h 42m	0h 28m	21h 48m	3h 00m	23h 44m	6h 39m
	11	6h 50m	5h 22m	2h 08m	0h 31m	21h 47m	3h 02m	23h 44m	7h 20m
	21	8h 22m	6h 14m	2h 35m	0h 33m	21h 44m	3h 03m	23h 44m	8h 00m
Dec	1	+22° 08′	+20° 28′	+8° 36′	+1° 39′	−14° 31′	+16° 41′	−3° 01′	+23° 08′
	11	+23° 46′	+22° 10′	+11° 03′	+1° 54′	−14° 42′	+16° 48′	−3° 03′	+22° 10′
	21	+21° 15′	+22° 51′	+13° 18′	+2° 01′	−14° 55′	+16° 53′	−3° 05′	+20° 34′
Dist	1	1.12	1.40	1.30	4.83	9.14	20.31	29.66	1.017
	11	1.29	1.46	1.24	4.67	9.03	20.17	29.50	1.017
	21	1.34	1.51	1.19	4.53	8.95	20.02	29.35	1.016
Mag	1	−0.8	−3.9	0.5	−2.4	0.6	5.8	7.9	
	11	−1.7	−3.8	0.4	−2.5	0.5	5.8	7.9	
	21	−1.7	−3.8	0.3	−2.6	0.4	5.8	7.8	
Size	1	6.0″	11.9″	7.2″	40.8″	18.2″	3.4″	2.3″	31′ 28″
	11	5.2″	11.4″	7.5″	42.2″	18.4″	3.5″	2.3″	31′ 28″
	21	5.0″	11.1″	7.9″	43.5″	18.6″	3.5″	2.3″	31′ 29″

Moon: On July 0 at 0h UT, the Sun's selenographic colongitude is 280.82° and increases 12.2° each day thereafter.
Greatest N declination on the 26th (+26.9°)
Greatest S declination on the 13th (–26.9°)
Libration in longitude: E limb most exposed on the 19th (+7.9°)
W limb most exposed on the 7th (–7.4°)
Libration in latitude: N limb most exposed on the 16th (+6.6°)
S limb most exposed on the 3rd (–6.7°) and 30th (–6.6°)
Large tides in the days following full Moon (Jul. 13)
Mercury: Visible with difficulty very early in the month in bright morning twilight, and again very late in the month in bright evening twilight. Otherwise is within 15° of the Sun, achieving superior conjunction on the 16th.
Venus: Gradually becoming less conspicuous in the dawn sky, its elongation from the Sun closing from 30° to 22° during July. The waning crescent Moon passes 4° to its north on the 26th.
Mars: Continues its rise to prominence, brightening from mag. +0.5 to +0.2 during the month as it crawls northward up the ecliptic from Pisces into Aries. Has another close conjunction with the thick crescent Moon on the 21st, with an occultation visible from northern-latitude locales as detailed at the bottom of the facing page.
Jupiter: Spends the month in extreme northwestern Cetus, rising around midnight local (daylight) time by mid-month. The waning gibbous Moon passes 2° to the south on the 18–19. Slows to its first stationary point on the 29th, setting the stage for its 4-month retrograde loop tracking some 9° in right ascension westward. Meridian transit times at Greenwich on the 1st, 11th, 21st–05:53, 05:16, 04:38 UT.
Saturn: Becoming ever more prominent in the late evening sky as it approaches its mid-August opposition. The waning gibbous Moon passes 4° to its south on the 15th. Meridian transit times at Greenwich on the 1st, 11th, 21st–03:13, 02:32, 01:50 UT.
Uranus: Occulted by the waning crescent Moon on the 22nd, a near-central event that can be widely seen across much of Eurasia; see facing page for details.
Neptune: Visible in the overnight and morning hours among the stars of Pisces. Meridian transit times at Greenwich on the 1st, 11th, 21st–05:08, 04:29, 03:49 UT.

Time (UT) d		h	m	JULY EVENTS
Fri.	1			
Sat.	2	16	07	Algol at minimum
Sun.	3			
Mon.	4	7		Earth at aphelion (152 098 455 km)
Tue.	5	12	56	Algol at minimum
Wed.	6			Mercury at ascending node
Thu.	7	2	14	**first quarter**
Fri.	8	9	45	Algol at minimum
Sat.	9			
Sun.	10			Mercury at perihelion
Mon.	11	6	34	Algol at minimum
Tue.	12	6		Vesta stationary
Wed.	13	9		Moon at perigee (357 264 km) **Large tides**
		18	38	**full Moon (largest in 2022)**
Thu.	14	3	23	Algol at minimum
Fri.	15	20		Saturn 4° N of Moon
Sat.	16	20		Mercury in superior conjunction
Sun.	17	0	12	Algol at minimum
Mon.	18	1		Neptune 3° N of Moon
Tue.	19	1		**Jupiter 2° N of Moon**
		21	01	Algol at minimum
Wed.	20	0		Venus 1.5° S of M35
		2		Pluto at opposition
		14	19	**last quarter**
Thu.	21			Mercury at greatest heliocentric lat. N
		17		**Mars 1.1° S of Moon, occultation†**
Fri.	22	1		Ceres in conjunction with the Sun
		6		**Uranus 0.2° S of Moon, occultation‡**
		17	50	Algol at minimum
Sat.	23			
Sun.	24			
Mon.	25	14	39	Algol at minimum
Tue.	26	10		Moon at apogee (406 274 km)
		14		**Venus 4° S of Moon**
Wed.	27			
Thu.	28	10		Juno stationary
		11	27	Algol at minimum
		17	55	**new Moon (lunation 1232)**
Fri.	29	10		S. δ-Aquariid meteors peak
		12		Jupiter stationary
Sat.	30			
Sun.	31	8	16	Algol at minimum

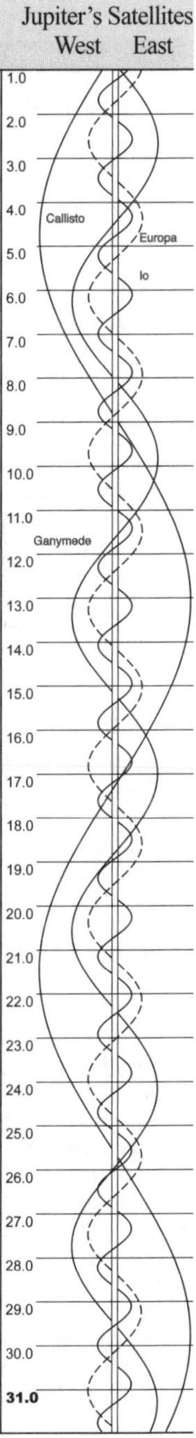

†Japan, NE Russia, NW Alaska, Svalbard, N Greenland
‡NE S. America, Cape Verde Islands, Madeira, NW Africa, Europe (except British Isles and Scandinavia), SW Russia, most of Middle East, W China, N India

THE SKY FOR AUGUST

		Mercury	Venus	Mars	Jupiter	Saturn	Uranus	Neptune	Sun
RA	1	9h 47m	7h 12m	3h 03m	0h 33m	21h 42m	3h 04m	23h 43m	8h 43m
	11	10h 48m	8h 04m	3h 28m	0h 32m	21h 39m	3h 05m	23h 42m	9h 22m
	21	11h 36m	8h 55m	3h 53m	0h 30m	21h 36m	3h 05m	23h 41m	9h 59m
Dec	1	+14° 53′	+22° 22′	+15° 30′	+2° 00′	−15° 12′	+16° 57′	−3° 10′	+18° 09′
	11	+8° 00′	+20° 47′	+17° 15′	+1° 51′	−15° 27′	+16° 59′	−3° 14′	+15° 26′
	21	+1° 19′	+18° 12′	+18° 44′	+1° 35′	−15° 42′	+17° 00′	−3° 20′	+12° 18′
Dist	1	1.27	1.56	1.13	4.37	8.89	19.84	29.21	1.015
	11	1.16	1.59	1.08	4.25	8.86	19.67	29.10	1.014
	21	1.02	1.63	1.02	4.14	8.86	19.51	29.01	1.012
Mag	1	−0.6	−3.8	0.2	−2.7	0.4	5.8	7.8	
	11	−0.2	−3.8	0.1	−2.7	0.3	5.8	7.8	
	21	0.1	−3.9	0.0	−2.8	0.3	5.7	7.8	
Size	1	5.3″	10.7″	8.3″	45.1″	18.7″	3.5″	2.3″	31′ 31″
	11	5.8″	10.5″	8.7″	46.4″	18.8″	3.6″	2.3″	31′ 34″
	21	6.6″	10.3″	9.2″	47.6″	18.8″	3.6″	2.3″	31′ 37″

Moon: On August 0 at 0h UT, the Sun's selenographic colongitude is 299.73° and increases 12.2° each day thereafter.
Greatest N declination on the 23rd (+27.0°)
Greatest S declination on the 9th (−27.0°)
Libration in longitude: E limb most exposed on the 16th (+7.3°)
W limb most exposed on the 4th (−6.6°)
Libration in latitude: N limb most exposed on the 12th (+6.5°)
S limb most exposed on the 26th (−6.6°)

Mercury: The **best evening apparition of the year for Southern Hemisphere observers** gets underway as the calendar turns, though the geometry is poor for those situated at mid-northern latitudes. Passes just 0.7° from Regulus on the 4th (evening of the 3rd in the Americas) when both objects are 18° from the Sun. Achieves greatest elongation east of the year at 27° on the 27th when it shines at mag. +0.2.

Venus: Rising with the Gemini twins Castor and Pollux early in the month, Venus draws ever closer to the Sun throughout September. By month-end its elongation is just 14°, though it can be observed in bright morning twilight. The waning crescent Moon passes 4° to its north on the 25th.

Mars: In conjunction with Uranus on the 1st, red Mars shining ~150× brighter than greenish-blue Uranus 1.4° to its north. On the 9th it crosses the border from Aries into Taurus, where it will remain for the rest of the year. The last-quarter Moon passes 3° to its north on the 19th. Mars reaches mag. 0.00 on the 21st, and 90° elongation from the Sun on the 27th.

Jupiter: In extreme northwestern Cetus all month long, as its retrograde loop oh so gradually picks up the pace. The waning gibbous Moon passes 2° to the south on the 15th. Meridian transit times at Greenwich on the 1st, 11th, 21st–03:55, 03:15, 02:34 UT.

Saturn: Achieves opposition on the 14th, when it is 74 light-minutes (8.857 AU) from Earth, mag. +0.3, the northern side of the ring plane exposed at a 13° tilt. The rings span 43.7″, the disk of the planet nearly 18.8″, and 15.5° south of the celestial equator. Saturn will be visible throughout the night in retrograde motion against the background stars of eastern Capricornus. The full Moon passes 4° to the south on the 11–12.
Meridian transit times at Greenwich on the 1st, 11th, 21st–01:04, 00:22, 23:36 UT.

Uranus: In conjunction with Mars on the 1st, which passes 1.4° to its south. Occulted by the waning gibbous Moon on the 18th, technically visible in Canada though in the daylight hours; see facing page for details. Now rising close to local midnight local daylight time, Uranus reaches its first stationary point on the 24th. Its subtle retrograde loop will take 22 weeks and cover 5° of sky. Meridian transit times at Greenwich on the 1st, 11th, 21st–06:26, 05:47, 05:08 UT.

Neptune: Rises in mid-evening as it approaches its Sep. 16 opposition. Its minuscule retrograde motion sees it reverse back over the Pisces-Aquarius border at mid-month. Meridian transit times at Greenwich on the 1st, 11th, 21st–03:05, 02:25, 01:45 UT.

Time (UT) d	h	m	AUGUST EVENTS
Mon. 1	9		**Mars 1.4° S of Uranus**
Tue. 2			Venus at ascending node
Wed. 3	5	05	Algol at minimum
Thu. 4	5		**Mercury 0.7° N of Regulus**
Fri. 5	11	07	**first quarter**
Sat. 6	1	54	Algol at minimum
Sun. 7			
Mon. 8	22	43	Algol at minimum
Tue. 9	1	30	**Double shadow transit on Jupiter**
Wed. 10	17		Moon at perigee (359 828 km)
Thu. 11	19	32	Algol at minimum
Fri. 12	1	36	**full Moon**
	4		Saturn 4° N of Moon
Sat. 13			Mercury at descending node
	1		**Perseid meteors peak**
Sun. 14	10		Neptune 3° N of Moon
	16	21	Algol at minimum
	17		**Saturn at opposition**
Mon. 15	10		**Jupiter 1.9° N of Moon**
Tue. 16	3	59	**Double shadow transit on Jupiter**
Wed. 17	13	10	Algol at minimum
Thu. 18	15		**Uranus 0.6° S of Moon, occultation**†
Fri. 19	4	36	**last quarter**
	12		Mars 3° S of Moon
Sat. 20	9	59	Algol at minimum
Sun. 21			
Mon. 22	19		Vesta at opposition
	22		Moon at apogee (405 418 km)
Tue. 23			Mercury at aphelion
	6	48	Algol at minimum
Wed. 24	15		Uranus stationary
Thu. 25	19		**Ceres 0.7° N of Moon, occultation**‡
	21		**Venus 4° S of Moon**
Fri. 26	3	37	Algol at minimum
Sat. 27	8	17	**new Moon (lunation 1233)**
	16		**Mercury greatest elongation E (27°)**
Sun. 28			
Mon. 29	0	26	Algol at minimum
Tue. 30			
Wed. 31	21	15	Algol at minimum

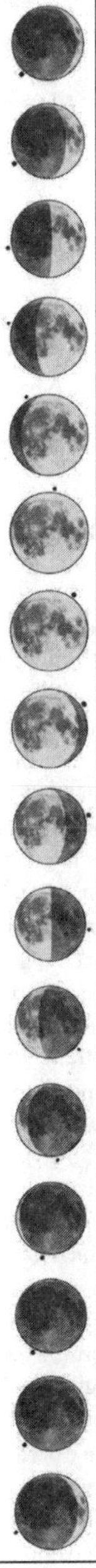

Jupiter's Satellites
West East

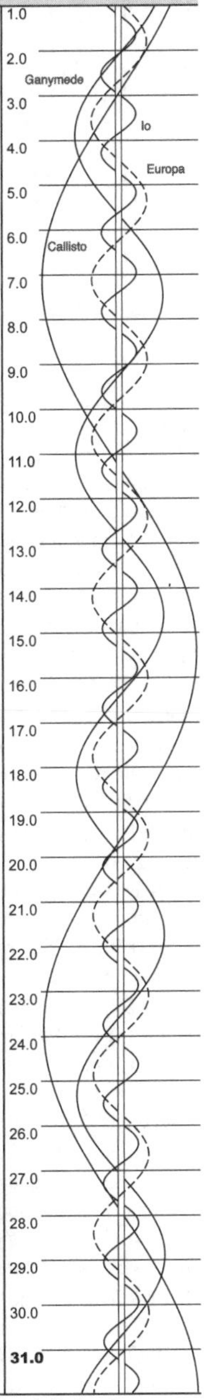

†Micronesia, most of Hawaii, Alaska, northernmost USA, Canada, Greenland, Iceland
‡Most of S and E Polynesia, S tip of S. America

THE SKY FOR SEPTEMBER

		Mercury	Venus	Mars	Jupiter	Saturn	Uranus	Neptune	Sun
RA	1	12h 14m	9h 49m	4h 18m	0h 27m	21h 33m	3h 05m	23h 40m	10h 40m
	11	12h 25m	10h 37m	4h 40m	0h 22m	21h 30m	3h 05m	23h 39m	11h 16m
	21	12h 03m	11h 23m	4h 59m	0h 18m	21h 28m	3h 04m	23h 38m	11h 52m
Dec	1	−4° 39′	+14° 23′	+20° 04′	+1° 09′	−15° 58′	+17° 00′	−3° 27′	+8° 29′
	11	−7° 08′	+10° 12′	+21° 02′	+0° 41′	−16° 10′	+16° 58′	−3° 33′	+4° 46′
	21	−4° 05′	+5° 32′	+21° 47′	+0° 10′	−16° 21′	+16° 55′	−3° 40′	+0° 55′
Dist	1	0.86	1.66	0.96	4.05	8.90	19.33	28.94	1.009
	11	0.72	1.68	0.90	3.99	8.97	19.17	28.91	1.007
	21	0.64	1.70	0.84	3.96	9.06	19.03	28.91	1.004
Mag	1	0.3	−3.9	−0.1	−2.9	0.3	5.7	7.8	
	11	1.1	−3.9	−0.3	−2.9	0.4	5.7	7.8	
	21	4.6	−3.9	−0.4	−2.9	0.4	5.7	7.8	
Size	1	7.8″	10.1″	9.8″	48.7″	18.7″	3.6″	2.3″	31′ 41″
	11	9.3″	9.9″	10.4″	49.4″	18.5″	3.7″	2.3″	31′ 46″
	21	10.4″	9.8″	11.1″	49.8″	18.4″	3.7″	2.3″	31′ 51″

Moon: On September 0 at 0h UT, the Sun's selenographic colongitude is 318.42° and increases 12.2° each day thereafter.
Greatest N declination on the 19th (+27.3°)
Greatest S declination on the 6th (−27.1°)
Libration in longitude: E limb most exposed on the 13th (+6.4°)
W limb most exposed on the 1st (−5.3°) and 27th (−4.5°)
Libration in latitude: N limb most exposed on the 8th (+6.6°)
S limb most exposed on the 22nd (−6.7°)

Mercury: Still well placed in the evening sky for Southern Hemisphere observers as September begins, though fading ever more rapidly from night to night and into obscurity by mid-month. Reaches inferior conjunction on the 23rd.

Venus: Can be seen in bright morning twilight early in the month, especially in the Northern Hemisphere where the angle of the morning ecliptic is favorable. Now a full but tiny disk just 10″ in diameter, it drops to 10° elongation by the 15th and just 6° by month-end.

Mars: Rising before midnight local (daylight) time in most locales as September begins, shining at mag −0.1 and brightening near mag −0.6 by month end. In Taurus throughout the month, it passes some 4° to the north of Aldebaran on the 9th. During this meeting, Mars is a full magnitude brighter than the similarly ruddy star. The last-quarter Moon passes 3° to the north on the 19th. Meridian transit times at Greenwich on the 1st, 11th, 21st–05:39, 05:21, 05:01 UT.

Jupiter: Achieves opposition on the 26th when it is 33 light-minutes (3.953 au) from Earth, mag. −2.9 with a 49.9″ disk and within 1′ of the celestial equator. At this time its four largest (Galilean) satellites are also at their brightest and with their widest apparent separation. Jupiter's retrograde motion is also at its maximum at this time, having crossed the border from Cetus back into Pisces on the 1st. Visible throughout the night all month, with the full Moon passing 2° to its south on the 11th. Meridian transit times at Greenwich on the 1st, 11th, 21st–01:47, 01:03, 00:20 UT.

Saturn: Now rising well before sunset and well-placed for observation throughout the evening hours. The assiduous binocular observer can track its leisurely retrograde motion against 4th-mag. Iota Capricorni, as Saturn pulls from 2.5° east of the star on the 1st to within 1° on the 30th. The waxing gibbous Moon slips by 4° to its south on the 8-9. Meridian transit times at Greenwich on the 1st, 11th, 21st–22:49, 22:07, 21:26 UT.

Uranus: Rising in the late evening hours, its retrograde motion gradually gathers steam in southeastern Aries. Occulted again by the waning gibbous Moon on the 14th; see facing page for details. Meridian transit times at Greenwich on the 1st, 11th, 21st–04:25, 03:45, 03:05 UT.

Neptune: Achieves opposition on the 16th, 4.0 light-hours (28.9 au) from Earth, mag. +7.8 with a 2.3″ disk. Neptune will be in the sky all night long throughout the month, in extreme northeastern Aquarius. Meridian transit times at Greenwich on the 1st, 11th, 21st–01:01, 00:21, 23:36 UT.

Time (UT) d	h m	SEPTEMBER EVENTS
Thu. 1		
Fri. 2		
Sat. 3	18 04	Algol at minimum
	18 08	**first quarter**
Sun. 4		Venus at perihelion
Mon. 5	1	Venus 0.8° N of Regulus
Tue. 6	14 53	Algol at minimum
Wed. 7	17	Juno at opposition
	18	Moon at perigee (364 492 km)
Thu. 8	11	Saturn 4° N of Moon
Fri. 9	11 42	Algol at minimum
	20	Mercury stationary
Sat. 10	9 59	**full Moon**
	19	Neptune 3° N of Moon
Sun. 11	15	**Jupiter 1.8° N of Moon**
Mon. 12	8 31	Algol at minimum
Tue. 13		Mercury at greatest heliocentric lat. S
Wed. 14	23	**Uranus 0.8° S of Moon, occultation**†
Thu. 15	5 20	Algol at minimum
Fri. 16	23	**Neptune at opposition**
Sat. 17	2	Mars 4° S of Moon
	21 52	**last quarter**
Sun. 18	2 09	Algol at minimum
Mon. 19	15	Moon at apogee (404 555 km)
Tue. 20	8	Pollux 1.9° N of Moon
	22 58	Algol at minimum
Wed. 21		
Thu. 22		
Fri. 23		**Zodiacal light vis. in N lat. in E before morning twilight for next two weeks**
	1 04	**Equinox**
	7	Mercury in inferior conjunction
	19 47	Algol at minimum
Sat. 24		
Sun. 25	21 54	**new Moon (lunation 1234)**
Mon. 26		Venus at greatest heliocentric lat. N
	16 36	Algol at minimum
	20	**Jupiter at opposition**
Tue. 27		
Wed. 28		
Thu. 29	13 25	Algol at minimum
Fri. 30		

Jupiter's Satellites
West East

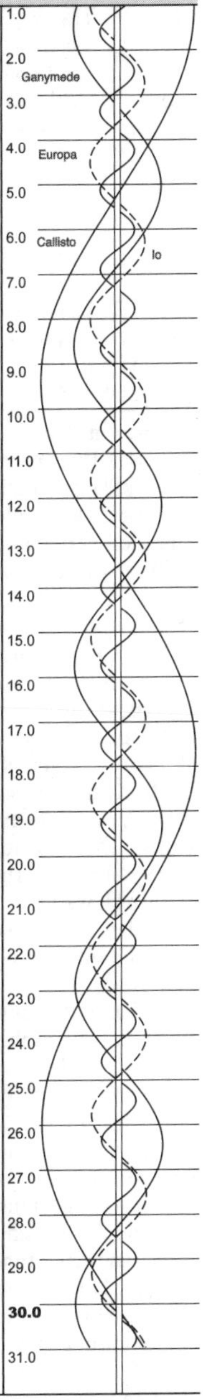

†Most of N Africa, Europe, parts of Middle East, most of Russia, Greenland, northernmost Canada, NW Alaska

THE SKY FOR OCTOBER

		Mercury	Venus	Mars	Jupiter	Saturn	Uranus	Neptune	Sun
RA	1	11h 38m	12h 09m	5h 16m	0h 13m	21h 26m	3h 03m	23h 37m	12h 28m
	11	12h 02m	12h 55m	5h 28m	0h 08m	21h 25m	3h 02m	23h 36m	13h 04m
	21	12h 58m	13h 41m	5h 37m	0h 04m	21h 25m	3h 00m	23h 36m	13h 41m
Dec	1	+2° 01′	+0° 36′	+22° 24′	−0° 22′	−16° 29′	+16° 51′	−3° 46′	−2° 58′
	11	+1° 44′	−4° 25′	+22° 54′	−0° 52′	−16° 34′	+16° 45′	−3° 53′	−6° 49′
	21	−4° 07′	−9° 18′	+23° 22′	−1° 19′	−16° 35′	+16° 39′	−3° 58′	−10° 30′
Dist	1	0.76	1.71	0.78	3.96	9.17	18.91	28.94	1.001
	11	1.02	1.72	0.73	3.99	9.30	18.81	29.00	0.998
	21	1.26	1.72	0.67	4.05	9.45	18.74	29.09	0.996
Mag	1	1.4	−3.9	−0.6	−2.9	0.5	5.7	7.8	
	11	−0.8	−4.0	−0.8	−2.9	0.5	5.7	7.8	
	21	−1.0		−1.0	−2.9	0.6	5.6	7.8	
Size	1	8.9″	9.8″	11.9″	49.8″	18.1″	3.7″	2.3″	31′ 57″
	11	6.6″	9.7″	12.9″	49.4″	17.9″	3.7″	2.3″	32′ 02″
	21	5.3″	9.7″	13.9″	48.7″	17.6″	3.7″	2.3″	32′ 08″

Moon: On October 0 at 0h UT, the Sun's selenographic colongitude is 324.49° and increases 12.2° each day thereafter.
Greatest N declination on the 16th (+27.4°)
Greatest S declination on the 3rd (−27.4°) and 30th (−27.5°)
Libration in longitude: E limb most exposed on the 11th (+5.5°)
W limb most exposed on the 24th (−5.0°)
Libration in latitude: N limb most exposed on the 5th (+6.7°)
S limb most exposed on the 19th (−6.8°)

Partial solar eclipse on Oct. 25, visible from Europe, the Middle East, northern Africa, western Asia, the north Atlantic Ocean, and the north Indian Ocean.

Mercury: Just beginning the **best morning apparition of the year for Northern Hemisphere observers** as the month begins, though a brief one. Reaches the perihelion of its orbit on the 6th and its greatest western elongation just 2 days later when it is just 18° from the Sun, shining at mag −0.5. Continues to brighten in the mornings that follow, but dropping into ever brighter twilight and seen only with difficulty after mid-month.

Venus: Too close to the Sun to be seen. Reaches superior conjunction on the 22nd.

Mars: Steadily brightening from mag. −0.6 to −1.2 during October, Mars's eastward motion slows in eastern Taurus and its elongation from the Sun increases dramatically. It reaches its first stationary point between the horns of The Bull on the 30th, setting the stage for a retrograde loop that will extend until 2023 Jan. 12 and cover 19° in right ascension.
Meridian transit times at Greenwich on the 1st, 11th, 21st–04:38, 04:11, 03:40 UT.

Jupiter: Now in the evening sky as October begins and becoming ever more prominent in early evening twilight on each subsequent day. Still in retrograde motion, it creeps westward closer toward the Circlet of Pisces throughout the month. The nearing-full Moon cruises by 2° to the south on the 8th.
Meridian transit times at Greenwich on the 1st, 11th, 21st–23:31, 22:47, 22:03 UT.

Saturn: Its retrograde motion slows to a standstill just 0.5° east of 4th-mag. Iota Capricorni, reaching its second stationary point on the 24th. The Moon passes 4° to its south on the evening of Oct. 4–5.
Meridian transit times at Greenwich on the 1st, 11th, 21st–20:45, 20:05, 19:25 UT.

Uranus: Up most of the night as it approaches its Nov. 9 opposition. Occulted by the waning gibbous Moon, an event visible in most of North America in the overnight hours of the 11–12. See facing page as well as LUNAR OCCULTATIONS p. 162. The disappearance against the Moon's bright limb will be challenging, the reappearance on the dark limb more accessible.
Meridian transit times at Greenwich on the 1st, 11th, 21st –02:25, 01:44, 01:03 UT.

Neptune: Visible most of the night, just past opposition, in extreme northeastern Aquarius. Meridian transit times at Greenwich on the 1st, 11th, 21st–22:56, 22:16, 21:35 UT.

Time (UT) d	h	m	OCTOBER EVENTS
Sat. 1	15		Mercury stationary
Sun. 2			Mercury at ascending node
	10	14	Algol at minimum
Mon. 3	0	14	**first quarter**
Tue. 4	17		Moon at perigee (369 325 km)
Wed. 5	7	03	Algol at minimum
	16		Saturn 4° N of Moon
Thu. 6			Mercury at perihelion
Fri. 7	6		Vesta stationary
Sat. 8	3		Neptune 3° N of Moon
	3	52	Algol at minimum
	18		**Jupiter 2° N of Moon**
	21		**Mercury greatest elongation W (18°)**
Sun. 9	20	55	**full Moon**
Mon. 10			
Tue. 11	0	41	Algol at minimum
Wed. 12	7		**Uranus 0.8° S of Moon, occultation†**
	14	43	**Double shadow transit on Jupiter**
Thu. 13	21	30	Algol at minimum
Fri. 14			
Sat. 15	5		Mars 4° S of Moon
Sun. 16	18	19	Algol at minimum
Mon. 17			Mercury at greatest heliocentric lat. N
	10		Moon at apogee (404 328 km)
	16		**Pollux 1.8° N of Moon**
	17	15	**last quarter**
Tue. 18			
Wed. 19	0		Juno stationary
	15	08	Algol at minimum
	17	19	**Double shadow transit on Jupiter**
Thu. 20			Mars at ascending node
Fri. 21	18		Orionid meteors peak
Sat. 22	11	57	Algol at minimum
	21		Venus in superior conjunction
Sun. 23			**Zodiacal light vis. in N lat. in E before morning twilight for next two weeks**
	9		Saturn stationary
Mon. 24			
Tue. 25	8	46	Algol at minimum
	10	49	**new Moon (lunation 1235)**
			Partial Solar Eclipse (p. 131)
Wed. 26	20	20	**Double shadow transit on Jupiter**
Thu. 27			
Fri. 28	5	35	Algol at minimum
Sat. 29	15		Moon at perigee (368 290 km)
Sun. 30	11		Mars stationary
Mon. 31	2	23	Algol at minimum

Jupiter's Satellites
West East

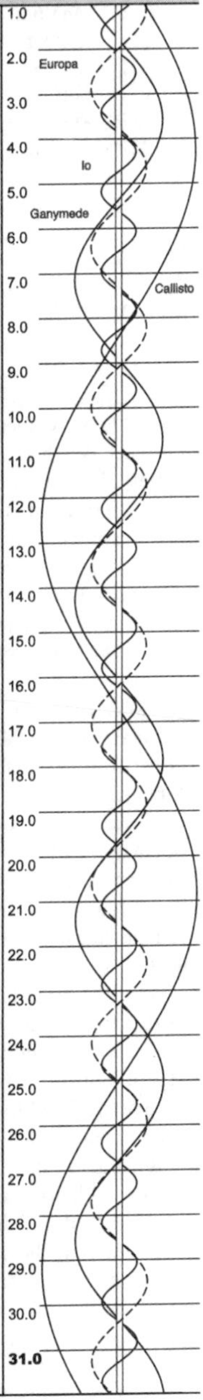

†NW Mexico, W USA including Alaska, most of Canada, N edge of Russia, Greenland, Iceland, Scandinavia

THE SKY FOR NOVEMBER

		Mercury	Venus	Mars	Jupiter	Saturn	Uranus	Neptune	Sun
RA	1	14h 06m	14h 34m	5h 39m	0h 00m	21h 25m	2h 58m	23h 35m	14h 23m
	11	15h 09m	15h 23m	5h 35m	23h 58m	21h 26m	2h 57m	23h 34m	15h 03m
	21	16h 13m	16h 15m	5h 25m	23h 57m	21h 27m	2h 55m	23h 34m	15h 44m
Dec	1	−11° 45′	−14° 15′	+23° 52′	−1° 41′	−16° 33′	+16° 32′	−4° 03′	−14° 15′
	11	−17° 48′	−18° 08′	+24° 19′	−1° 53′	−16° 28′	+16° 25′	−4° 06′	−17° 16′
	21	−22° 24′	−21° 13′	+24° 42′	−1° 57′	−16° 20′	+16° 18′	−4° 08′	−19° 47′
Dist	1	1.40	1.71	0.62	4.14	9.63	18.70	29.21	0.993
	11	1.45	1.71	0.58	4.25	9.79	18.69	29.35	0.990
	21	1.43	1.70	0.55	4.38	9.96	18.71	29.50	0.988
Mag	1	−1.2	−4.0	−1.2	−2.8	0.6	5.6	7.8	
	11	−1.4	−3.9	−1.5	−2.7	0.7	5.6	7.8	
	21	−0.8	−3.9	−1.7	−2.7	0.7	5.6	7.9	
Size	1	4.8″	9.7″	15.1″	47.6″	17.3″	3.7″	2.3″	32′ 13″
	11	4.7″	9.8″	16.1″	46.4″	17.0″	3.7″	2.3″	32′ 18″
	21	4.7″	9.8″	16.9″	45.0″	16.7″	3.7″	2.3″	32′ 22″

Moon: On November 0 at 0h UT, the Sun's selenographic colongitude is 342.26° and increases 12.2° each day thereafter.
Greatest N declination on the 13th (+27.4°)
Greatest S declination on the 26th (–27.3°)
Libration in longitude: E limb most exposed on the 7th (+5.3°)
W limb most exposed on the 20th (–6.1°)
Libration in latitude: N limb most exposed on the 2nd (+6.8°) and 29th (+6.7°)
S limb most exposed on the 16th (–6.8°)

Total lunar eclipse on Nov. 8, visible from South America, North America, Australia, Asia, the north Atlantic Ocean, and the Pacific Ocean.

Mercury: Too close to the Sun to be seen throughout the month, formally reaching superior conjunction on the 8th.

Venus: Too close to the Sun to be seen as it oh so slowly pulls out of superior conjunction.

Mars: As the month begins, Mars is slowly commencing its retrograde loop that will see it sweep nearly 20° westward across Taurus over the next 2.5 months. It brightens significantly from mag. –1.2 to –1.8 during November, as its disk swells from 15″ to 17″. The waning gibbous Moon passes 2° to its north on the 11th. In the Americas, it technically reaches its closest approach to Earth during the evening hours of the 30th (see next month's entry for details.) Meridian transit times at Greenwich on the 1st, 11th, 21st–02:59, 02:16, 01:26 UT.

Jupiter: Dominates the evening sky throughout the month, far outshining the stars of its temporary home in Pisces and surrounding constellations. The waxing gibbous Moon slides by 2° to the south on the 4th. Reaches its second stationary point on the 24th. Meridian transit times at Greenwich on the 1st, 11th, 21st–21:17, 20:35, 19:55 UT.

Saturn: Slowly resuming prograde motion against the now-familiar backdrop of western Capricornus. The Moon makes two more passes 4° to its south in November, the first in waxing gibbous phase on the 1st, the second as a waxing crescent on Nov. 28–29.
Meridian transit times at Greenwich on the 1st, 11th, 21st–18:42, 18:04, 17:26 UT.

Uranus: Achieves opposition on the 9th, 2.6 light-hours (18.7 au) from Earth, mag. +5.6 with a 3.7″ disk. Uranus will be occulted by the full Moon just coming out of eclipse in the morning hours of the 8th, less than a day before opposition. This unusual event is theoretically visible in northwestern North America, but the extreme brightness difference will render it impossible. By the 20th, with the glare of the Moon now long gone, mag. 5.6 Uranus forms a near-equilateral triangle, 1.8° to a side, with 5.3-mag. Pi Arietis and 5.6-mag. Rho Arietis, the latter a binocular double of similarly bright stars. Meridian transit times at Greenwich on the 1st, 11th, 21st–00:18, 23:33, 22:52 UT.

Neptune: Well placed in the evening sky among the stars of extreme northeastern Aquarius. Meridian transit times at Greenwich on the 1st, 11th, 21st–20:51, 20:12, 19:32 UT.

Time (UT) d	h m	NOVEMBER EVENTS
Tue. 1	6 37	**first quarter**
	21	Saturn 4° N of Moon
Wed. 2	23 12	Algol at minimum
Thu. 3	0 22	**Double shadow transit on Jupiter**
	8	**Juno 1.0° N of Moon, occultation†**
Fri. 4	8	Neptune 3° N of Moon
	20	**Jupiter 2° N of Moon**
Sat. 5	18	S. Taurid meteors peak
	20 01	Algol at minimum
Sun. 6		**DAYLIGHT SAVING TIME ENDS**
Mon. 7		
Tue. 8	11 02	**full Moon**
		Total Lunar Eclipse (p. 132)
	13	**Uranus 0.8° S of Moon, occultation‡**
	16 50	Algol at minimum
	17	Mercury in superior conjunction
Wed. 9		Mercury at descending node
	8	**Uranus at opposition**
Thu. 10		
Fri. 11	13 39	Algol at minimum
	14	**Mars 2° S of Moon**
Sat. 12	18	N. Taurid meteors peak
Sun. 13		
Mon. 14	0	**Pollux 1.7° N of Moon**
	7	Moon at apogee (404 921 km)
	10 28	Algol at minimum
Tue. 15		
Wed. 16	13 27	**last quarter**
Thu. 17	7 17	Algol at minimum
Fri. 18	0	Leonid meteors peak
Sat. 19		Mercury at aphelion
Sun. 20	4 06	Algol at minimum
Mon. 21		Venus at descending node
Tue. 22		
Wed. 23	0 55	Algol at minimum
	22 57	**new Moon (lunation 1236)**
Thu. 24	13	Jupiter stationary
	13	Pallas stationary
Fri. 25	21 44	Algol at minimum
Sat. 26	2	Moon at perigee (362 826 km)
Sun. 27		
Mon. 28	18 33	Algol at minimum
Tue. 29	5	Saturn 4° N of Moon
Wed. 30	14 36	**first quarter**

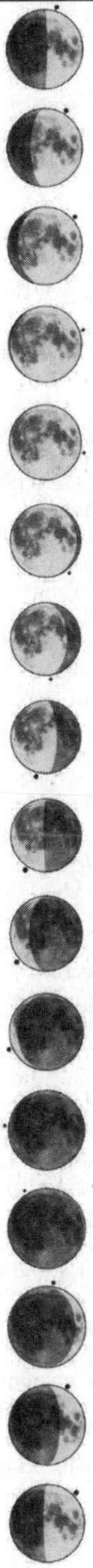

Jupiter's Satellites
West East

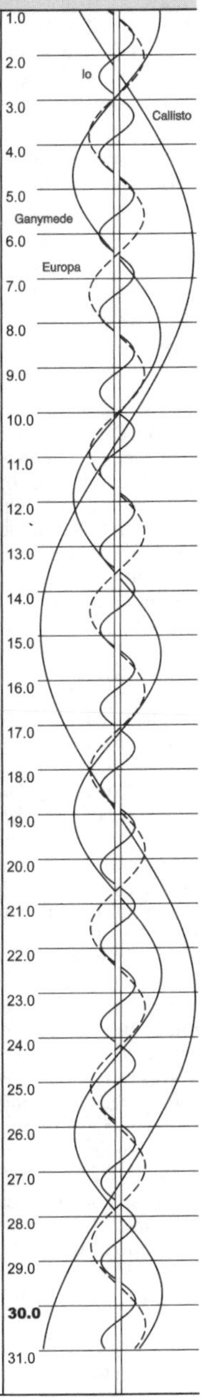

†Most of Antarctica, southeasternmost Polynesia
‡Asia (except W and S India), most of Russia, Alaska, Svalbard, N half of Greenland, most of N and W Canada

THE SKY FOR DECEMBER

		Mercury	Venus	Mars	Jupiter	Saturn	Uranus	Neptune	Sun
RA	1	17h 19m	17h 09m	5h 09m	23h 57m	21h 29m	2h 53m	23h 34m	16h 27m
	11	18h 25m	18h 03m	4h 52m	23h 58m	21h 32m	2h 52m	23h 34m	17h 10m
	21	19h 23m	18h 58m	4h 37m	0h 01m	21h 35m	2h 51m	23h 34m	17h 55m
Dec	1	−25° 07′	−23° 17′	+24° 56′	−1° 53′	−16° 09′	+16° 12′	−4° 09′	−21° 43′
	11	−25° 38′	−24° 12′	+24° 56′	−1° 40′	−15° 56′	+16° 06′	−4° 08′	−22° 57′
	21	−23° 48′	−23° 52′	+24° 46′	−1° 20′	−15° 39′	+16° 01′	−4° 06′	−23° 26′
Dist	1	1.36	1.68	0.54	4.53	10.12	18.76	29.66	0.986
	11	1.22	1.66	0.55	4.68	10.27	18.84	29.83	0.985
	21	1.02	1.64	0.58	4.84	10.41	18.95	30.01	0.984
Mag	1	−0.6	−3.9	−1.8	−2.6	0.8	5.6	7.9	
	11	−0.6	−3.9	−1.8	−2.5	0.8	5.7	7.9	
	21	−0.6	−3.9	−1.6	−2.4	0.8	5.7	7.9	
Size	1	4.9″	9.9″	17.2″	43.6″	16.4″	3.7″	2.3″	32′ 26″
	11	5.5″	10.0″	16.9″	42.1″	16.2″	3.7″	2.2″	32′ 29″
	21	6.6″	10.2″	16.0″	40.8″	16.0″	3.7″	2.2″	32′ 31″

Moon: On December 0 at 0h UT, the Sun's selenographic colongitude is 347.38° and increases 12.2° each day thereafter.
Greatest N declination on the 10th (+27.4°)
Greatest S declination on the 24th (−27.4°)
Libration in longitude: E limb most exposed on the 3rd (+6.3°) and 31st (+7.4°)
W limb most exposed on the 19th (−7.3°)
Libration in latitude: N limb most exposed on the 26th (+6.6°)
S limb most exposed on the 13th (−6.7°)

Mercury: Emerges into the evening sky in the second week of the month. Reaches maximum eastern elongation (its fourth of 2022) on the 21st, when it shines at mag. −0.6 some 20° east of the Sun, and some 5° east of brilliant Venus. The two inner planets achieve conjunction 1.4° apart on the 28–29, by which time Mercury will have faded nearly a full magnitude. Binoculars will be a must to enjoy this pairing.

Venus: Slowly emerging into early evening twilight, low in the southwest after sunset. Joins fading Mercury late in the month, with the one-day-old waxing crescent Moon entering the frame on the 24th. The two inner planets achieve conjunction 1.4° apart on the 29th (see above).

Mars: Above the horizon throughout the hours of darkness all month long, its declination of 25° N among the stars of Taurus makes it extremely accessible to Northern Hemisphere observers. Begins December at its closest point to Earth of the current apparition, gleaming at mag. −1.8 with a 17.2″ disk, just 4.5 light-minutes (0.544 AU) away. Opposition doesn't occur until a full week later on the 8th, the lag time due to the asymmetric nature of the Red Planet's orbit. Extraordinarily, **Mars is occulted by the full Moon** when both objects are exactly opposite the Sun (although far enough north of the ecliptic that no lunar eclipse occurs) and 100% illuminated. This event favors observers in the Northern Hemisphere including most of North America (evening hours of the 7th for most of the continent) and much of Europe (morning hours of the 8th). (See: LUNAR OCCULTATIONS p. 162.) Meridian transit times at Greenwich on the 1st, 11th, 21st, 31st–00:31, 23:30, 22:36, 21:46 UT.

Jupiter: Gradually resuming its prograde motion in southern Pisces, where it is prominent throughout the evening hours. The Moon passes to its south twice in December, in waxing gibbous phase on the 1st and as a thick, waxing crescent on the 29th. By month-end, Jupiter is setting around midnight local standard time. Meridian transit times at Greenwich on the 1st, 11th, 21st, 31st–19:16, 18:38, 18:01, 17:26 UT.

Saturn: Ends the year some 10° east of where it began, still among the stars of Capricornus. Now exclusively in the evening sky, its viewing window is closing rapidly; the Ringed Planet's elongation from the Sun is reduced from 70° to 42° during December. The waxing crescent Moon passes 4° to the south on the 25–26th.

Uranus: Now well past opposition, Uranus is well placed in the evening sky at the onset of darkness. It will have yet another close encounter with the now-waxing gibbous Moon on the 5th, with an occultation visible from those parts of the world detailed on the facing page.

Meridian transit times at Greenwich on the 1st, 11th, 21st, 31st–22:12, 21:31, 20:50, 20:10 UT.

Neptune: In the SW evening sky in extreme northeastern Aquarius, setting before midnight local standard time. Reaches its second stationary point on the 4th, and gradually resumes prograde motion thereafter. Meridian transit times at Greenwich on the 1st, 11th, 21st 31st–18:52, 18:13, 17:34, 16:55 UT.

Time (UT) d	h	m	DECEMBER EVENTS
Thu. 1	0		**Juno 1.2° S of Moon, occultation†**
	2		**Mars at closest approach**
	13		Neptune 3° N of Moon
	15	22	Algol at minimum
Fri. 2	1		Jupiter 3° N of Moon
Sat. 3			
Sun. 4	10		Neptune stationary
	12	11	Algol at minimum
Mon. 5	18		**Uranus 0.7° S of Moon, occultation‡**
Tue. 6			
Wed. 7	9	00	Algol at minimum
Thu. 8	4		***Mars 0.5° S of Moon, occultation††***
	4	08	**full Moon**
	6		**Mars at opposition**
Fri. 9			
Sat. 10			Mercury at greatest heliocentric lat. S
	5	49	Algol at minimum
Sun. 11	8		**Pollux 1.8° N of Moon**
Mon. 12			Jupiter at greatest heliocentric lat. S
	0		Moon at apogee (405 888 km)
Tue. 13	2	38	Algol at minimum
Wed. 14	13		Geminid meteors peak
Thu. 15	23	27	Algol at minimum
Fri. 16	8	56	**last quarter**
Sat. 17			
Sun. 18	20	16	Algol at minimum
Mon. 19			
Tue. 20			
Wed. 21	15		**Mercury greatest elongation E (20°)**
	17	05	Algol at minimum
	21	48	**Solstice**
Thu. 22	22		Ursid meteors peak
Fri. 23	10	17	**new Moon (lunation 1237)**
Sat. 24	8		Moon at perigee (358270 km) **Large tides**
	11		**Venus 3° N of Moon**
	13	54	Algol at minimum
	18		Mercury 4° N of Moon
Sun. 25			
Mon. 26			Venus at aphelion
	16		Saturn 4° N of Moon
Tue. 27	10	43	Algol at minimum
Wed. 28	20		Neptune 3° N of Moon
Thu. 29			Mercury at ascending node
	3		Mercury stationary
	9		**Mercury 1.4° N of Venus**
	11		**Jupiter 2° N of Moon**
Fri. 30	1	20	**first quarter**
	7	32	Algol at minimum
	10	27	**Double shadow transit on Jupiter**
Sat. 31			

Jupiter's Satellites
West East

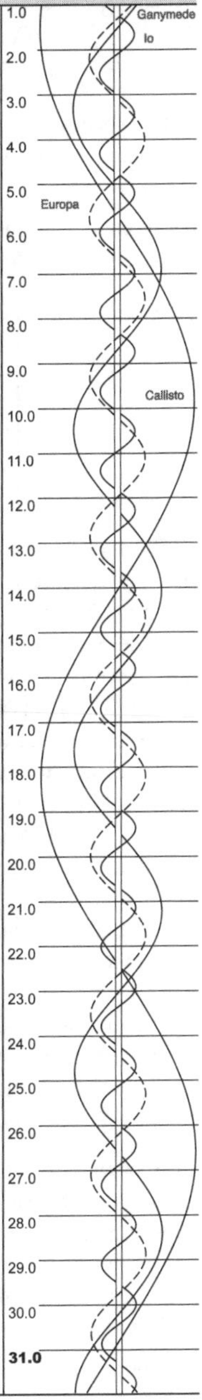

†W. USA (including E Alaska), most of Canada
‡Most of N Africa, Azores, Europe (except Iceland), parts of Middle East, Russia, N Japan
††NW Mexico, most of USA (except Alaska), Canada, Greenland, Svalbard, Europe, W Russia, parts of N Africa

ECLIPSES

ECLIPSE PATTERNS

BY ROY BISHOP

Eclipse Seasons

The plane of the Moon's orbit is tilted about 5° to the plane of Earth's orbit, the ecliptic. Since 5° is considerably larger than both the north–south range of lunar parallax for various localities on Earth (≈1.9°) and the angular radii of the Sun and Moon (each ≈0.25°), solar eclipses can occur only when the Sun is near (within about

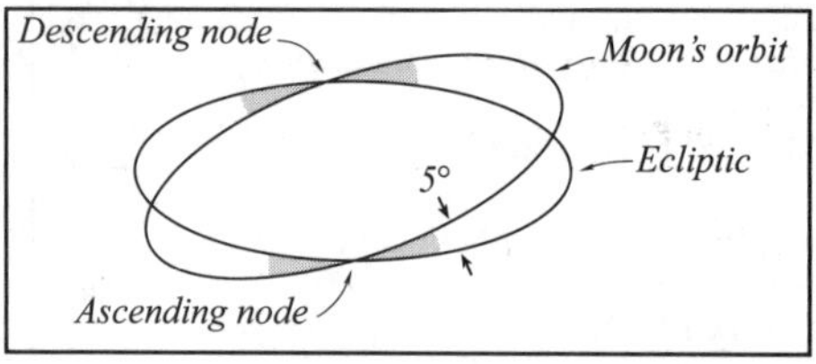

±15° to ±18°) one of the two points at which the Moon's orbit crosses the ecliptic (nodes). Lunar eclipses have a comparable restriction. The *ascending* node is the one at which the Moon crosses to the *north* side of the ecliptic.

The Sun moves eastward along the ecliptic about 1° per day; thus the interval during which an eclipse can occur is at most about $(2 \times 18°) \div 1°/\text{d} = 36$ d, an *eclipse season*. The interval between new moons (29.5 days) is somewhat less, thus one or two solar eclipses will occur in each eclipse season. Six months later, when the Sun is near the other node, another eclipse season occurs. However, the plane of the Moon's orbit wobbles, making the nodes regress slowly westward along the ecliptic with a period of 18.60 years (see p. 95); thus the two eclipse seasons drift backward through the year, occurring about 19 days earlier each year. *The eclipse seasons of 2022 occur in April/May, and October/November.*

In a calendar year,

- there can be as many as seven eclipses (solar and lunar combined, as last occurred in 1982) and as few as four (the usual number);
- there can be as many as five solar or lunar eclipses and as few as two;
- the number of total or annular solar eclipses can range from zero to two, the number of total lunar eclipses from zero to three.

In 2022, there are four eclipses: two solar (both partial) and two lunar (both total).

The Saros

Eclipses of the Sun and Moon recur with various periodicities that are more or less approximate. These periodicities are interesting both as numerical curiosities and because they may be used to predict eclipses. The most famous periodicity, the *Saros*, has been known since ancient times. It is a consequence of a remarkable commensurability between three lunar average periods:

Synodic month *(S)* (new to new)	= 29.530 589 d,	$223S$	= 6585.3213 d
Draconic month *(N)* (node to node)	= 27.212 221 d,	$242N$	= 6585.3575 d
Anomalistic month *(P)* (perigee to perigee)	= 27.554 550 d,	$239P$	= 6585.5375 d

Several aspects of this arithmetic are relevant to the pattern of eclipses (for brevity, the following comments are restricted primarily to the case of solar eclipses):

(1) An integer number of Ss (223) ensures a new Moon and hence the possibility of a second solar eclipse.

(2) $242N \approx 223S$ means that the new Moon will be at almost the same position relative to a node, ensuring that an eclipse *will* occur again and that it will occur on Earth's globe about the same distance north or south of the ecliptic plane as did the first eclipse.

(3) The Saros ($223S$) = 6585.3213 d = 18 years + *only* 10.3213 d or 11.3213 d (depending on the number of intervening leap years). Thus one Saros later Earth will be at almost the same point in its elliptical orbit and hence at nearly the same distance

(text continues on next page)

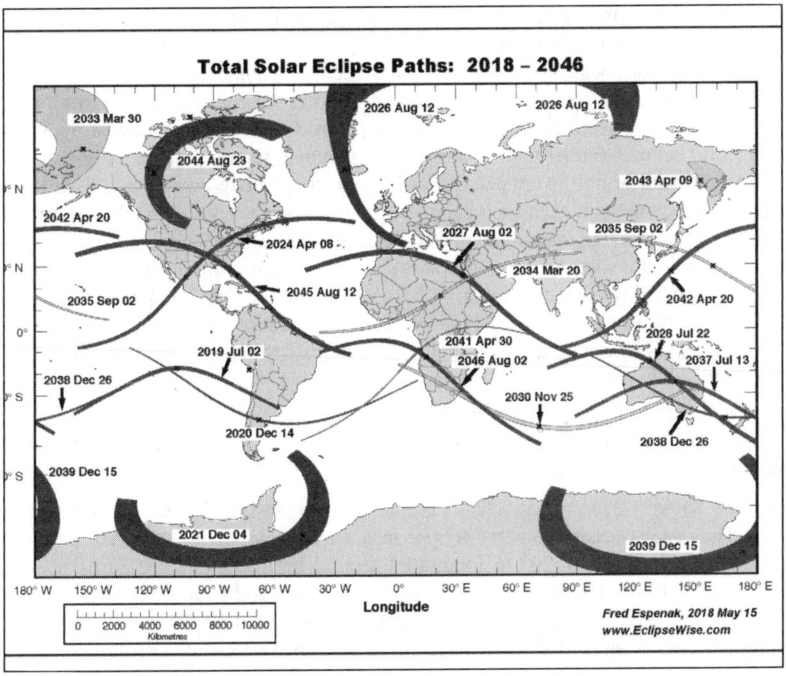

The figure shows the paths of all total solar eclipses, excluding hybrid annular/total eclipses, occurring during the years 2018–2046. There are 20 eclipses, one in each of the years 2019, 2020, 2021, 2024, 2026, 2027, 2028, 2030, 2033, 2034, 2035, 2037, 2038, 2039, 2041, 2042, 2043, 2044, 2045, and 2046. Because the 29-year period covered by the figure is somewhat longer than the 18-year Saros interval, the first seven and seven of the last nine eclipses drawn with heavy shading, make up seven Saros pairs, with Saros numbers 127, 142, 152, 139, 126, 136, and 146, respectively. Note that the members of each pair are both total eclipses, are separated in time by one Saros, have similar path shapes, and occur at similar latitudes; note also that the later member is shifted 120° westward in longitude (see items (2) through (6) of the text explaining these features). The figure was kindly produced by Fred Espenak for the Observer's Handbook. *For figures showing total solar eclipses, annular eclipses, and hybrid annular/total eclipses for the period –1999 to +3000 (2000 BCE to 3000 CE), see* eclipsewise.com/solar/solar.html.

from the Sun. Moreover, the inclination of Earth toward the Sun (season) will be nearly the same; thus the same latitude region of Earth will be exposed to the eclipse.
(4) $239P \approx 223S$ means that one Saros later the new Moon will be at almost the same point in its elliptical orbit and thus at the same distance from Earth. With the same lunar and solar distances, the type of eclipse (total or annular) will be the same. Since the eclipse will occur near the same geographic latitude (see **(2)** and **(3)**), the duration of totality or annularity, or the magnitude of partial eclipse if the eclipse is not central, will be almost the same as it was one Saros earlier.
(5) $242N - 223S = 0.0361$ d $= 0.87$ h. This, together with the 0.55°/h eastward speed of the Moon in its orbit, means that after one Saros the Moon will be about 0.5° west of its former position relative to its node. Thus a Saros series does not last forever; there will be about $36°/0.5° \approx 72$ eclipses in a Saros series (the number ranges from 69 to 87). Furthermore, any one Saros series will last for about $72 \times 18 \approx 1300$ years (the range is 1226 to 1551 years).

A Saros series begins with about 10 partial eclipses of increasing magnitude in the north or south polar region, depending upon whether the eclipses are occurring near the ascending or descending lunar node, respectively. These are followed by about 50 central eclipses (either total or annular), which over many centuries progressively shift southward or northward across Earth (on average an approximate 300-km shift in latitude occurs with each successive eclipse). The series ends with 10 or so partial eclipses of decreasing magnitude in the opposite polar region.

Currently, for solar eclipses, 40 Saros series are running simultaneously, numbers 117 through 156 (for lunar eclipses, 41 Saros series are running, numbers 110 through 150). That is, in any 18-year 11-day interval, one eclipse from each of these 40 (and 41) series takes place, after which the whole pattern repeats. Those series occurring at the lunar ascending node are given odd numbers; those at the descending node, even numbers (vice versa for lunar eclipses).

The four eclipses of 2022 belong to the same four Saros series as the four eclipses of 2004.

(6) The Saros $= 223S = 6585.3213$ d, and the fractional 0.3213 d $\approx$ one-third of a day. Thus each successive solar eclipse in a Saros series will be shifted one-third of the way westward (120° in longitude) around Earth. After three Saros periods (3×6585.3213 d $\approx 19\,756$ d, or approximately 54 years and 1 month), a cycle known as the *Exeligmos*, the eclipse will be back at approximately the same geographic longitude, although shifted about 1000 km in latitude. Two examples follow:

(a) One of the most historically significant total solar eclipses was that of 1919 May 29. Its path of totality crossed Africa. Data from that eclipse confirmed a prediction of Einstein's general theory of relativity, making him world famous. The first Exeligmos of that eclipse occurred on 1973 Jun. 30, again across Africa, and its second Exeligmos will occur 5 years from now, on 2027 Aug. 2, six Saroses or twice "54 years + 1 month" after the 1919 eclipse, again across Africa.

(b) The total solar eclipse of 2024 Apr. 8 (no. 30 of Saros 139), which sweeps northeastward across eastern North America, will be geographically similar to that of 1970 Mar. 7 (no. 27 of Saros 139), which followed the eastern seaboard of North America one Exeligmos earlier. Also, one Saros earlier we had the similar total solar eclipse of 2006 Mar. 29 (no. 29 of Saros 139), which occurred about 120° to the east, across Africa and the Mediterranean.

The Metonic Cycle

The sequence of lunar phases and the year repeat their relative pattern at 19-year intervals, a cycle known to astronomers in ancient Babylon and that was discovered independently around 430 BCE by Meton, a Greek astronomer. We have $235S = 235 \times 29.530\,589 = 6939.6884$ d;

$$19 \text{ years} = 6939 \text{ d or } 6940 \text{ d (depending on leap years).}$$

Moreover, $255N$ is also very close to 19 years,

$$255N = 255 \times 27.212\,221 = 6939.1164 \text{ d.}$$

Thus solar and lunar eclipses also repeat on a 19-year "Metonic" cycle. Since $255N$ is less than $235S$, the Moon does not reach the same phase (new or full for an eclipse) until it has moved eastward relative to the node by

$$(235S - 255N) \times 24 \text{ h} \times 0.55°/\text{h} = 7.5°.$$

Thus a Metonic eclipse series will have only

$$\text{eclipse season width on the ecliptic } (36°) \div 7.5° \approx 4 \text{ or } 5 \text{ eclipses;}$$

and the geographic latitude of successive solar eclipses in a series will change substantially (north or south, depending upon whether the Moon is at its ascending node or descending node, respectively).

What about the Moon's position in its orbit relative to its perigee? Using the anomalistic month P (the Moon returns to perigee on average every 27.554 550 d),

$$235S \div P = 251.85, \text{ which is } \textit{not} \text{ near an integer.}$$

Thus in a Metonic series the Moon's distance is not the same from one eclipse to another. Hence the type of solar eclipse (total or annular) will vary within the series.

With only about four eclipses in a series, a mix of eclipse types, and scattered geographic occurrence, a Metonic eclipse series is not as elegant or useful as a Saros series. The main feature of a Metonic eclipse series is that, like lunar phases, the successive eclipses occur on (almost) the *same day* of the year.

Examples of the Metonic cycle for a lunar phase, lunar eclipses, and the 2024 Western Hemisphere total solar eclipse are given below. The numbers in parentheses are Saros numbers.

Full Moon	Lunar Eclipses	Solar Eclipses
1965 May 15	1965 May 15 (no eclipse)	1967 Apr. 9 (no eclipse)
1984 May 15	1984 May 15 Penumbral (111)	1986 Apr. 9 Partial (119)
2003 May 16	2003 May 16 Total (121)	2005 Apr. 8 Ann/Tot (129)
2022 May 16	**2022** May 16 Total (131)	**2024** Apr. 8 Total (139)
2041 May 16	2041 May 16 Partial (141)	2043 Apr. 9 Total (149)
2060 May 15	2060 May 15 (no eclipse)	2062 Apr. 9 (no eclipse)
2079 May 15	2079 May 15 (no eclipse)	2081 Apr. 9 (no eclipse)

Canons of Eclipses

Detailed information, including maps showing the areas on Earth from which each eclipse is visible, is available in two books by Fred Espenak: *Thousand Year Canon of Solar Eclipses 1501 to 2500*, and *Thousand Year Canon of Lunar Eclipses 1501 to 2500*. In those ten centuries there are 2389 solar eclipses, and 2424 lunar eclipses. See: eclipsewise.com/pubs/TYCSE.html and eclipsewise.com/pubs/TYCLE.html. For several more publications about eclipses by Espenak see: www.astropixels.com/pubs/index.html.

ECLIPSES IN 2022

BY FRED ESPENAK

In 2022, there are two solar eclipses and two lunar eclipses:

2022 Apr. 30:	Partial Solar Eclipse
2022 May 16:	Total Lunar Eclipse
2022 Oct. 25:	Partial Solar Eclipse
2022 Nov. 08:	Total Lunar Eclipse

Predictions for the eclipses are summarized in Tables 1 through 4. World maps show the regions of visibility for each eclipse. The lunar eclipse diagrams also include the path of the Moon through Earth's shadow. Contact times for each principal phase are tabulated along with the magnitudes and geocentric coordinates of the Sun and the Moon at greatest eclipse. All times are given in terms of UT1[1].

Partial Solar Eclipse of April 30

The first solar eclipse of 2022 is a Southern Hemisphere event visible from South America and the South Pacific (Figure 1, p. 128). Greatest eclipse[2] takes place at 20:41:26 UT1 when the eclipse magnitude reaches 0.6396. The contact times of the Moon's penumbral shadow with Earth are as follows:

Partial eclipse begins: 18:45:19 UT1
Partial eclipse ends: 22:38:01 UT1

Local circumstances for a number of cities are given in Table 1 (below). All times are provided in Local Time. The Sun's altitude and azimuth, the eclipse magnitude, and obscuration are all listed for the instant of maximum eclipse.

This is the 66th eclipse of Saros[3] series 119, an old series, which produced its last central eclipse (annular) on 1950 Mar. 18. The entire series is composed of 71 solar eclipses in the following sequence: 8 partial, 2 total, 1 hybrid, 51 annular, and 9 partial eclipses (Espenak and Meeus, 2021a). Saros series 119 runs from the years 850 to 2112.

Complete details for Saros 119 may be found at
www.EclipseWise.com/solar/SEsaros/SEsaros119.html

For additional information about this eclipse, see
www.EclipseWise.com/solar/SEprime/2001-2100/SE2022Apr30Pprime.html

All times below are Local Time.

TABLE 1—LOCAL CIRCUMSTANCES FOR THE PARTIAL SOLAR ECLIPSE OF 2022 APRIL 30

Country/City	Eclipse Begins	Maximum Eclipse	Eclipse Ends	Sun Altitude	Sun Azimuth	Eclipse Magnitude	Eclipse Obscuration
Argentina							
Buenos Aires	17:43	—	—	0	288	0.268	0.158
Cordoba	17:46	—	—	0	287	0.340	0.222
Bolivia							
La Paz	17:39	18:02	18:24	2	286	0.053	0.014
Chile							
Santiago	16:33	17:37	—	5	291	0.404	0.285
Paraguay							
Asuncion	18:12	—	—	0	286	0.089	0.031
Uruguay							
Montevideo	17:44	—	—	0	288	0.184	0.091

[1] *Universal Time* (UT1) is within 0.9 second of Coordinated Universal Time (UTC) See p. 44.

[2] *The instant of greatest eclipse* for solar eclipses occurs when the distance between the Moon's shadow axis and Earth's geocenter reaches a minimum.

[3] *The Saros* is a period of 6,585.3 days (18 years 11 days 8 hours) in which eclipses (both solar and lunar) repeat. The alignment does not repeat exactly but close enough for a Saros series to last 12 or more centuries.

Total Lunar Eclipse of May 16

The second eclipse of the year is a total lunar eclipse occurring at the lunar orbit's descending node in Libra. It occurs 1.5 days before perigee (May 17 19:23 UT1). Consequently, the apparent diameter of the Moon (33.0″) is much larger than its mean diameter (31.1″). This perigean full Moon will likely be hyped by the general media as a so-called Blood Supermoon.

The Moon's orbital trajectory takes it through the southern part of Earth's dark umbral shadow. The times of the major eclipse phases are as follows:

Penumbral Eclipse Begins:	01:31:44 UT1
Partial Eclipse Begins:	02:27:31 UT1
Total Eclipse Begins:	03:28:40 UT1
Greatest Eclipse:	04:11:31 UT1
Total Eclipse Ends:	04:54:11 UT1
Partial Eclipse Ends:	05:55:27 UT1
Penumbral Eclipse Ends:	06:51:11 UT1

The beginning and end of a penumbral eclipse are not visible to the eye. In fact, no shading can be detected until about 2/3 of the Moon's disk is immersed in the penumbra. This would correspond to about 02:10 UT1 when the penumbral eclipse is first detectable. Keep in mind that this is only an estimate. Atmospheric conditions and the observer's visual acuity are important factors to consider. An interesting exercise is to note when penumbral shading is first and last detected with the naked eye or binoculars.

At the instant of greatest eclipse[4] (04:11:31 UT1), the Moon lies at the zenith for a point near the border between Bolivia and Paraguay. The umbral eclipse magnitude[5] peaks at 1.4154. At this time, the Moon's northern limb passes 1.2″ south of the shadow's axis. In contrast, the Moon's southern limb will lie 31.8″ from the shadow center and 13.9″ from the southern edge of the umbra. Consequently, the southern half of the Moon will appear considerably brighter than the northern half, which will lie deeper in the shadow.

Since the Moon samples a large range of umbral depths during totality, its appearance will likely change dramatically with time. The exact brightness distribution in the umbra is difficult to predict, so observers are encouraged to estimate the Danjon value at mid-totality (see Danjon Scale of Lunar Eclipse Brightness). It may also be necessary to assign different Danjon values to different portions of the Moon (e.g. north vs. south).

Nearly 40 years ago (1982 Jul. 6), the author watched another total lunar eclipse with the Moon in nearly the same part of the sky. I was amazed at how brilliantly the summer Milky Way glowed since it was all but invisible during the partial phases. Observers will have a similar opportunity during May's eclipse. In this case, the totally eclipsed Moon will lie in eastern Libra 30° west of the brightest Sagittarian star clouds. The summer constellations are well placed for viewing, so a number of bright stars can be used for magnitude comparisons with the totally eclipsed Moon.

Antares (mag. +0.92) is 15° to the southeast, Shaula (mag. +1.63) is 31° southeast, Epsilon Sgr (mag. +1.85) is 40° southeast, Arcturus (mag. –0.05) stands 43° to the northwest, and Spica (mag. +0.97) is 32° northwest of the Moon

The Moon's brightness during totality can be easily estimated using a pair of binoculars (see *Moon's Apparent Magnitude During Total Lunar Eclipses*).

The entire event is visible from the Western Hemisphere (eastern Pacific Ocean, most of North and South America). Europe will miss the later stages of the eclipse because they

---

[4] *The instant of greatest eclipse* for *lunar* eclipses occurs when the distance between the Moon's midpoint and Earth's shadow axis reaches a minimum.

[5] Umbral *eclipse magnitude* is defined as the fraction of the Moon's diameter occulted by Earth's umbral shadow.

FIGURE 1—PARTIAL SOLAR ECLIPSE OF 2022 APRIL 30

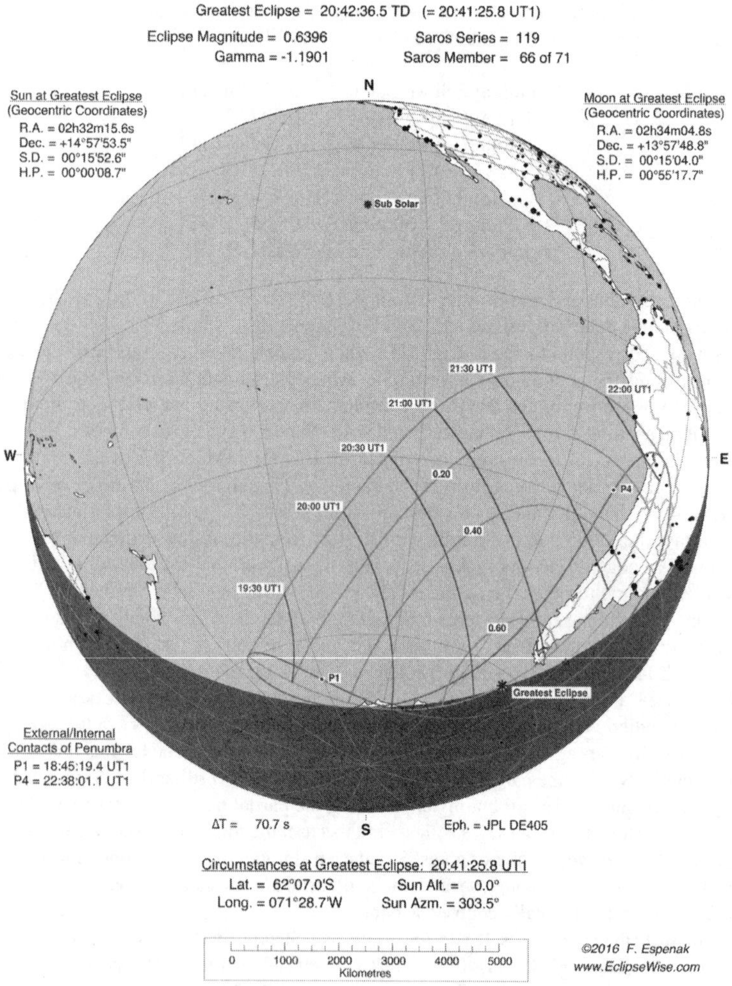

Courtesy of ***21st Century Canon of Solar Eclipses***, Fred Espenak, Astropixels Publishing, 2016.

See p. 134 for an explanation of this figure.

FIGURE 2—TOTAL LUNAR ECLIPSE OF 2022 MAY 16

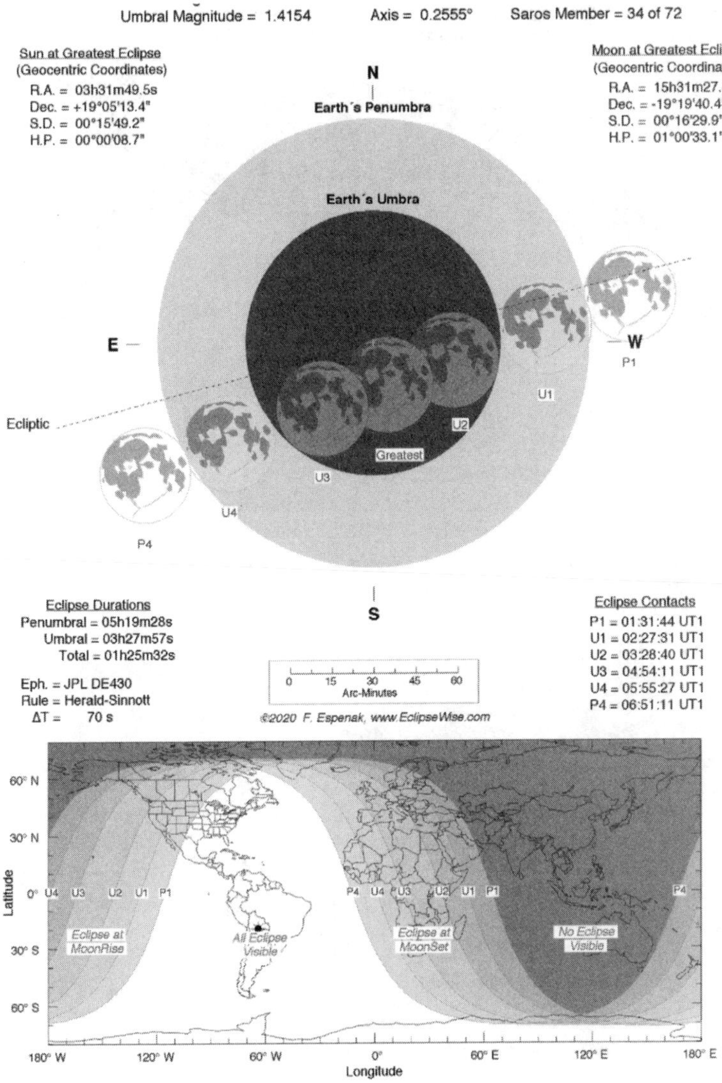

Courtesy of ***21st Century Canon of Lunar Eclipses***, Fred Espenak, Astropixels Publishing, 2020.

See p. 136 for an explanation of this figure.

FIGURE 3—PARTIAL SOLAR ECLIPSE OF 2022 OCTOBER 25

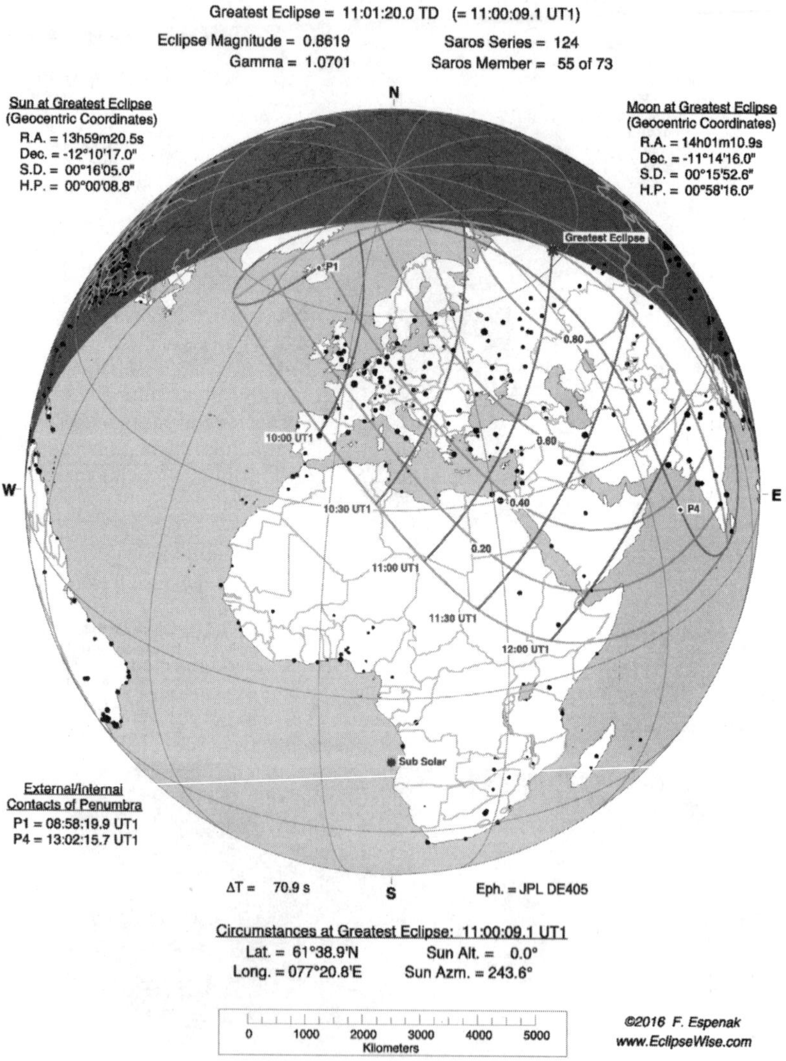

Courtesy of ***21st Century Canon of Solar Eclipses***, Fred Espenak, Astropixels Publishing, 2016.

See p. 134 for an explanation of this figure.

TABLE 2—TOTAL LUNAR ECLIPSE OF 2022 MAY 16
CRATER IMMERSION AND EMERSION TIMES

UT1 of Immersion	Crater Name	UT1 of Emersion	Crater Name
02:30	Riccioli	05:00	Riccioli
02:31	Grimaldi	05:01	Grimaldi
02:37	Aristarchus	05:04	Billy
02:38	Billy	05:09	Campanus
02:40	Kepler	05:11	Tycho
02:48	Pytheas	05:13	Kepler
02:48	Copernicus	05:14	Aristarchus
02:50	Campanus	05:21	Copernicus
02:51	Timocharis	05:23	Pytheas
02:54	Plato	05:27	Timocharis
02:57	Autolycus	05:32	Plato
03:02	Tycho	05:34	Autolycus
03:02	Manilius	05:35	Manilius
03:02	Aristoteles	05:37	Dionysius
03:03	Eudoxus	05:39	Menelaus
03:05	Menelaus	05:40	Eudoxus
03:07	Dionysius	05:40	Aristoteles
03:09	Plinius	05:42	Plinius
03:11	Endymion	05:42	Censorinus
03:15	Censorinus	05:43	Goclenius
03:18	Proclus	05:47	Messier
03:19	Taruntius	05:48	Langrenus
03:21	Messier	05:48	Taruntius
03:21	Goclenius	05:48	Endymion
03:25	Langrenus	05:50	Proclus

Predictions include the enlargement of the umbral shadow due to Earth's atmosphere.
Courtesy of Fred Espenak, *Eclipses During 2022*,
2022 *Observer's Handbook*, The Royal Astronomical Society Of Canada.

occur after moonset. None of the eclipse is visible from Asia or Australia (see visibility map in Figure 2, p. 129).

Table 2 (above) lists predicted umbral immersion and emersion times for 25 well-defined lunar craters. The timing of craters is useful in determining the atmospheric enlargement of Earth's shadow (see *Crater Timings During Lunar Eclipses*).

The May 16 eclipse is the 34th eclipse of Saros series 131. The series is composed of 72 lunar eclipses in the following sequence: 7 penumbral, 22 partial, 15 total, 20 partial, and 8 penumbral eclipses (Espenak and Meeus, 2021b). Saros 131 spans 1280.1 years and runs from the years 1427 to 2707.

Complete details for Saros 131 (including all eclipses in the series) can be found at:
www.EclipseWise.com/lunar/LEsaros/LEsaros131.html

Additional information about the May 16 total lunar eclipse can be found at:
www.EclipseWise.com/lunar/LEprime/2001-2100/LE2022May16Tprime.html

Partial Solar Eclipse of October 25

The second solar eclipse of 2022 is visible from the Northern Hemisphere. Most of Europe, the Middle East, Central Asia and northeastern Africa will be in the path of the Moon's penumbral shadow (Figure 3, opposite). Greatest eclipse takes place at 11:00:09 UT1 when the eclipse magnitude will reach 0.8619. The contact times of the Moon's penumbral shadow with Earth are as follows:

(text continues on next page)

Partial eclipse begins: 08:58:20 UT1
Partial eclipse ends: 13:02:16 UT1

Local circumstances for a number of cities are given in Table 3 (opposite). All times are provided in Local Time. The Sun's altitude and azimuth, the eclipse magnitude, and obscuration are all listed for the instant of maximum eclipse.

The **2022 October 25 Solar Eclipse Calculator** is an interactive webpage that can quickly calculate the local circumstances for the eclipse from any geographic location not included in the table. The URL for the calculator is

www.EclipseWise.com/solar/SEcirc/2001-2100/SE2022Oct25Pcirc.html

This is the 55th eclipse of Saros series 124, another old series that produced its last central eclipse on 1986 Oct. 3. That event was an unusual beaded annular eclipse with a very short path just off the west coast of Iceland. The entire series is composed of 73 solar eclipses in the following sequence: 9 partial, 43 total, 1 annular, and 20 partial eclipses (Espenak and Meeus, 2021a). Saros 124 lasts 1298 years running from 1049 to 2347.

Complete details for Saros 124 may be found at
www.EclipseWise.com/solar/SEsaros/SEsaros124.html
For additional information about this eclipse, see
www.EclipseWise.com/solar/SEprime/2001-2100/SE2022Oct25Pprime.html

Total Lunar Eclipse of November 08

The last eclipse of the year is another total lunar eclipse. Once again, the event will be well placed for North Americans. The eclipse occurs at the ascending node of Luna's orbit in southern Aries. Since the Moon is 5.8 days shy of apogee (Nov. 14 10:41 UT1), it will appear 7% smaller (30.6″) than it was during May's eclipse. The Moon's trajectory takes it deep into the northern umbral shadow, resulting in a total eclipse that lasts ~86 minutes, and with an umbral eclipse magnitude of 1.3607.

The Moon's path through Earth's shadow and a map illustrating worldwide visibility of the event are shown in Figure 4 (p. 135). The times of the major eclipse phases are listed as follows.

Penumbral Eclipse Begins: 08:01:52 UT1
Partial Eclipse Begins: 09:08:49 UT1
Total Eclipse Begins: 10:16:12 UT1
Greatest Eclipse: 10:59:11 UT1
Total Eclipse Ends: 11:41:52 UT1
Partial Eclipse Ends: 12:49:24 UT1
Penumbral Eclipse Ends: 13:56:32 UT1

At mid-eclipse the Moon's southern limb is just 0.9″ from the umbra's center. In contrast, the northern limb is 11.0″ from the umbra's edge and 29.7″ from its center. Since different parts of the Moon will probe radically different portions of Earth's umbral shadow, a large variation in shadow brightness can be expected. The northern half of the totally eclipsed Moon will appear noticeably brighter than its southern half. Observers are encouraged to estimate the Danjon value at mid-totality (see *Danjon Scale of Lunar Eclipse Brightness* below).

The instant of greatest eclipse (10:59:11 UT1) occurs with the Moon in the zenith for a point in the Pacific Ocean west of the Hawaiian Islands. Most of North America will be treated to the entire eclipse. However, the partial phases will still be in progress at moonset for observers in the eastern United States and Canada. Most of Australia will see the beginning of totality just after moonrise, but observers in the western quarter of the country will see the Moon already in total eclipse when it rises.

TABLE 3—LOCAL CIRCUMSTANCES FOR THE PARTIAL SOLAR ECLIPSE OF 2022 OCTOBER 05

COUNTRY,CITY	Eclipse Begins	Maximum Eclipse	Eclipse Ends	Sun Altitude	Sun Azimuth	Eclipse Magnitude	Eclipse Obscuration
EUROPE							
Austria, Vienna	11:16	12:21	13:27	30	175	0.415	0.300
Belarus, Minsk	12:17	13:29	14:41	24	190	0.607	0.512
Belgium, Brussels	11:10	12:04	13:01	25	158	0.301	0.189
Bulgaria, Sofia	12:27	13:37	14:46	35	188	0.436	0.322
Czech Rep, Prague	11:13	12:17	13:22	27	172	0.416	0.301
Denmark, Copenhagen	11:07	12:11	13:17	22	169	0.469	0.356
Finland, Helsinki	12:12	13:22	14:31	18	184	0.631	0.540
France, Paris	11:13	12:03	12:55	26	155	0.241	0.137
Germany, Berlin	11:10	12:14	13:19	25	170	0.436	0.322
Germany, Munchen	11:14	12:15	13:17	29	168	0.351	0.236
Greece, Athens	12:36	13:44	14:51	39	191	0.377	0.262
Hungary, Budapest	11:18	12:25	13:33	30	179	0.441	0.327
Ireland, Dublin	10:07	10:53	11:40	18	145	0.224	0.123
Italy, Rome	11:26	12:22	13:19	35	170	0.265	0.157
Netherlands, Amsterdam	11:08	12:04	13:03	23	159	0.334	0.219
Poland, Warsaw	11:14	12:23	13:33	26	181	0.521	0.414
Romania, Bucharest	12:26	13:38	14:50	33	191	0.494	0.384
Russia, Moscow	12:25	13:39	14:51	20	202	0.709	0.633
Spain, Barcelona	11:33	12:08	12:43	33	154	0.096	0.035
Sweden, Stockholm	11:08	12:15	13:23	18	176	0.564	0.461
Switzerland, Zurich	11:15	12:11	13:09	29	164	0.298	0.186
Ukraine, Kiev	13:23	14:37	15:50	26	195	0.607	0.512
UK, London	10:09	10:59	11:51	22	152	0.259	0.151
AFRICA							
Algeria, Algiers	10:58	11:13	11:29	38	156	0.017	0.003
Egypt, Cairo	12:00	13:09	14:16	43	211	0.373	0.257
Ethiopia, Addis Abeba	11:27	11:59	12:29	43	244	0.069	0.022
Sudan, Khartoum	12:53	13:39	14:22	49	230	0.139	0.061
Tunisia, Tunis	10:41	11:24	12:09	40	168	0.140	0.061
ASIA							
Armenia, Jerevan	13:53	15:11	16:25	28	221	0.647	0.559
Azerbaijan, Baku	14:00	15:18	16:30	24	227	0.686	0.606
Iran, Tehran	14:41	15:58	17:09	24	232	0.643	0.554
Iraq, Baghdad	13:06	14:23	15:35	31	226	0.565	0.463
Israel, Tel Aviv	12:58	14:11	15:22	39	214	0.448	0.335
Saudi Arabia, Riyadh	13:31	14:43	15:48	32	236	0.449	0.335
Turkey, Istanbul	12:34	13:47	14:59	35	198	0.491	0.380
Uzbekistan, Taskent	15:23	16:35	-	9	245	0.750	0.683
India, Delhi	16:29	17:30	-	2	255	0.546	0.440
Pakistan, Karachi	15:58	17:02	-	11	251	0.500	0.390

All times are Universal Time (UT1).
Courtesy of Fred Espenak, *Eclipses During 2022*,
2022 *Observer's Handbook*, The Royal Astronomical Society Of Canada.

During totality, the winter constellations are well placed for viewing so a number of bright stars can be used for magnitude comparisons. Aldebaran (mag. +0.75 > +0.95) is 25° east of the eclipsed Moon, Hamal (mag. +2.00) is 12° to the northwest, Capella (mag. +0.08) is 42° to the northeast, while Betelgeuse (mag. ~ +0.60) and Rigel (mag. +0.13) are 46° and 43°, respectively, to the east-southeast.

The Moon's brightness during totality can be easily estimated using these stars and a pair of binoculars (see Moon's Apparent Magnitude During Total Lunar Eclipses).

Table 4 (p. 134) lists predicted umbral immersion and emersion times for 25 well-defined lunar craters. The timing of craters is useful in determining the atmospheric enlargement of Earth's shadow (see *Crater Timings During Lunar Eclipses*).

TABLE 4—TOTAL LUNAR ECLIPSE OF 2022 NOVEMBER 8
CRATER IMMERSION AND EMERSION TIMES

UT1 of Immersion	Crater Name	UT1 of Emersion	Crater Name
09:10	Riccioli	11:49	Aristarchus
09:11	Grimaldi	11:50	Riccioli
09:15	Billy	11:51	Grimaldi
09:21	Kepler	11:56	Kepler
09:22	Aristarchus	11:56	Plato
09:25	Campanus	11:57	Billy
09:29	Copernicus	12:00	Pytheas
09:32	Pytheas	12:01	Timocharis
09:33	Tycho	12:03	Copernicus
09:37	Timocharis	12:05	Aristoteles
09:46	Autolycus	12:06	Autolycus
09:46	Manilius	12:07	Eudoxus
09:47	Plato	12:09	Campanus
09:49	Dionysius	12:12	Endymion
09:50	Menelaus	12:15	Manilius
09:54	Plinius	12:18	Menelaus
09:56	Eudoxus	12:19	Tycho
09:57	Censorinus	12:22	Plinius
09:57	Aristoteles	12:23	Dionysius
10:01	Goclenius	12:31	Proclus
10:03	Messier	12:32	Censorinus
10:04	Taruntius	12:35	Taruntius
10:05	Proclus	12:38	Messier
10:07	Langrenus	12:39	Goclenius
10:09	Endymion	12:44	Langrenus

Courtesy of Fred Espenak, *Eclipses During 2022*,
2022 *Observer's Handbook*, The Royal Astronomical Society Of Canada.

The Nov 08 eclipse is the 20th eclipse of Saros 136. This series is composed of 72 lunar eclipses in the following sequence: 8 penumbral, 7 partial, 27 total, 8 partial, and 22 penumbral eclipses (Espenak and Meeus, 2021b). Saros 136 spans 1280.1 years and runs from 1680 Apr 13 to 2960 Jun 01.

Complete details for Saros 136 (including all eclipses in the series) can be found at:
www.EclipseWise.com/lunar/LEsaros/LEsaros136.html

For more information about the eclipse, visit
www.EclipseWise.com/lunar/LEprime/2001-2100/LE2022Nov08Tprime.html

Solar Eclipse Figures

For each solar eclipse, an orthographic projection map of Earth shows the path of penumbral (partial) eclipse. North is to the top in all cases and the daylight terminator is plotted for the instant of greatest eclipse. An asterisk (*) indicates the sub-solar point[6] on Earth.

Current political borders are plotted for easy reference. The black dots represent major cities, where the size of the dot is an indication of the population size.

The limits of the Moon's penumbral shadow delineate the region of visibility of the partial solar eclipse. This irregular or saddle shaped region often covers more than half of the daylight hemisphere of Earth and consists of several distinct zones or limits. At the northern and/or southern boundaries lie the limits of the penumbra's path. Partial eclipses have only one of these limits.

Great loops at the western and eastern extremes of the penumbra's path identify

[6] The sub-solar point is the geographic location where the Sun appears directly overhead (zenith).

FIGURE 4—TOTAL LUNAR ECLIPSE OF 2022 NOVEMBER 8

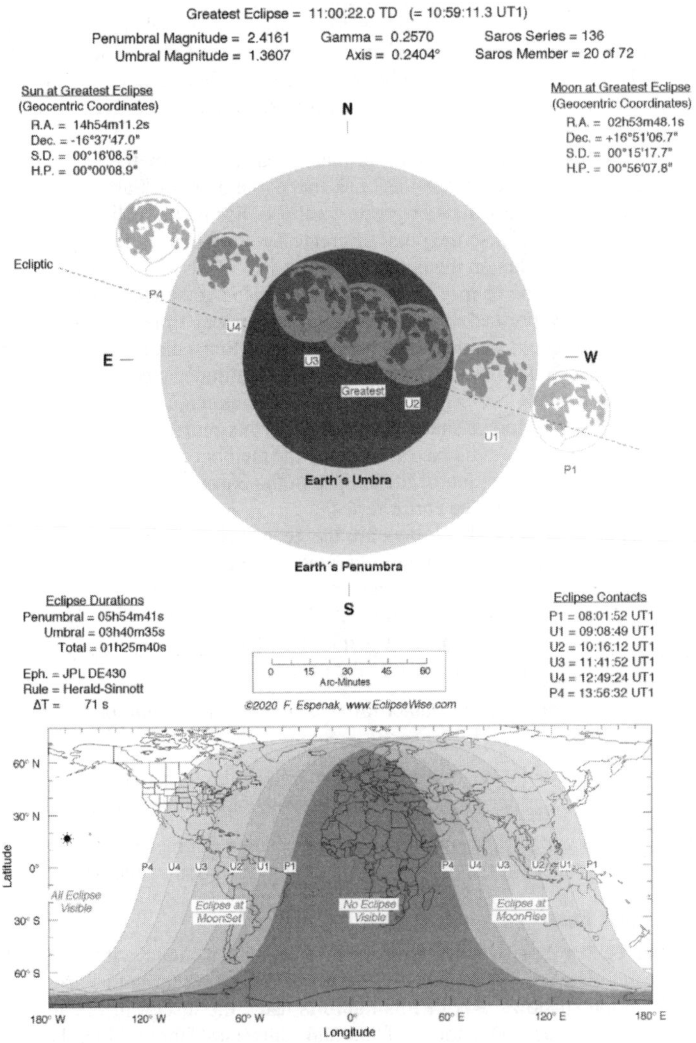

Courtesy of ***21st Century Canon of Lunar Eclipses***, Fred Espenak, Astropixels Publishing, 2020.

See p. 136 for an explanation of this figure

the areas where the eclipse begins/ends at sunrise and sunset, respectively. The curves are connected in a distorted figure eight. Bisecting the "eclipse begins/ends at sunrise and sunset" loops is the curve of maximum eclipse at sunrise (western loop) and sunset (eastern loop). The points P1 and P4 mark the coordinates where the penumbral shadow first contacts (partial eclipse begins) and last contacts (partial eclipse ends) Earth's surface. These correspond to the coordinates where the penumbral shadow cone is internally tangent to Earth's disk.

A curve of maximum eclipse is the locus of all points where the eclipse is at maximum at a given time. Curves of maximum eclipse are plotted at each half-hour Universal Time. They generally run between the penumbral limits in the north/south direction, or from the maximum eclipse at sunrise and sunset curves to one of the limits.

Greatest eclipse is defined as the instant when the axis of the Moon's shadow passes closest to Earth's center. An asterisk marks the point on Earth's surface intersected by the lunar shadow axis at greatest eclipse. For partial eclipses, the shadow axis misses Earth entirely, so the point of greatest eclipse lies on the day/night terminator and the Sun appears on the horizon.

Data pertinent to the eclipse appear with each map. At the top is listed the instant of greatest eclipse, expressed in both Terrestrial Dynamical Time and Universal Time. The eclipse magnitude is defined as the fraction of the Sun's diameter obscured by the Moon at greatest eclipse. For central eclipses, the magnitude listed is actually the geocentric ratio of diameters of the Moon and the Sun. Gamma is the minimum distance (in Earth radii) of the Moon's shadow axis from Earth's center at greatest eclipse. The Saros series of the eclipse is listed, followed by the member position. The first number identifies the sequence position of the eclipse in the Saros, while the second number is the number of eclipses in the entire series.

In the upper left and right corners are the geocentric coordinates of the Sun and the Moon, respectively, at the instant of greatest eclipse. They are:

R.A.– Right Ascension
Dec.– Declination
S.D.– Apparent Semi-Diameter
H.P.– Horizontal Parallax

To the lower left are exterior contact times of the Moon's penumbral shadow with Earth, which are defined:

P1—Instant of first exterior tangency of Penumbra with Earth's limb. (Partial Eclipse Begins)
P4—Instant of last exterior tangency of Penumbra with Earth's limb. (Partial Eclipse Ends)

At bottom are the geographic coordinates of the position of greatest eclipse along with the local circumstances at that location (i.e. Sun altitude, Sun azimuth).

Lunar Eclipse Figures

Each lunar eclipse has two diagrams associated with it along with data pertinent to the eclipse. The top figure shows the path of the Moon through Earth's penumbral and umbral shadows. Above this figure is listed the instant of greatest eclipse, expressed in Terrestrial Dynamical Time and Universal Time (UT1). The penumbral and umbral magnitudes are defined as the fraction of the Moon's diameter immersed in the two shadows at greatest eclipse. The radii of the penumbral and umbral shadows, P. Radius and U. Radius, are also listed. Gamma is the minimum distance in Earth radii of the Moon's center from Earth's shadow axis at greatest eclipse, and Axis is the same parameter expressed in degrees. The Saros series of the eclipse is listed, followed by a pair of numbers. The first number identifies the sequence position of the eclipse in the Saros; the second is the total number of eclipses in the series.

In the upper left and right corners are the geocentric coordinates of the Sun and the Moon, respectively, at the instant of greatest eclipse. They are:

R.A.– Right Ascension
Dec.– Declination

S.D.– Apparent Semi-Diameter
H.P.– Horizontal Parallax

To the lower left are the semi-durations (half-durations) of the penumbral, umbral (partial), and total eclipses. Below them are the extrapolated value of ΔT (the difference between Terrestrial Dynamical Time and Universal Time) and the Sun/Moon ephemerides used in the predictions. To the lower right are the contact times of the Moon with Earth's penumbral and umbral shadows, defined as follows:

P1–	Instant of first exterior tangency of Moon with Penumbra. (Penumbral Eclipse Begins)
U1–	Instant of first exterior tangency of Moon with Umbra. (Partial Umbral Eclipse Begins)
U2–	Instant of first interior tangency of Moon with Umbra. (Total Umbral Eclipse Begins)
U3–	Instant of last interior tangency of Moon with Umbra. (Total Umbral Eclipse Ends)
U4–	Instant of last exterior tangency of Moon with Umbra (Partial Umbral Eclipse Ends)
P4–	Instant of last exterior tangency of Moon with Penumbra. (Penumbral Eclipse Ends)

The bottom figure is a cylindrical equidistant projection map of Earth that shows the regions of visibility for each stage of the eclipse. In particular, the moonrise/moonset terminator is plotted for each contact and is labeled accordingly. An asterisk indicates the point where the Moon is at the zenith at greatest eclipse. The region that is unshaded will observe the entire eclipse, while the darkly shaded area will witness no eclipse. The remaining lightly shaded areas will experience moonrise or moonset while the eclipse is in progress. The lightly shaded zones east of the asterisk (*) will witness moonset before the eclipse ends, and the lightly shaded zones west will witness moonrise after the eclipse has begun.

Danjon Scale of Lunar Eclipse Brightness

The Moon's appearance during a total lunar eclipse can vary enormously from one eclipse to the next. Obviously, the geometry of the Moon's path through the umbra plays an important role. Not as apparent is the effect that Earth's atmosphere has on total eclipses. Although the physical mass of Earth blocks all direct sunlight from the umbra, the planet's atmosphere refracts some of the Sun's rays into the shadow. Earth's atmosphere contains varying amounts of water (clouds, mist, precipitation) and solid particles (meteoric dust, organic debris, volcanic ash). This material significantly filters and attenuates the sunlight before it is refracted into the umbra. For instance, very dark, red eclipses often follow large or frequent volcanic eruptions, which dump huge quantities of ash into the atmosphere for several years. Extensive cloud cover along Earth's limb also tends to darken the eclipse by blocking sunlight.

The French astronomer André-Louis Danjon proposed a useful five-point scale for evaluating the visual appearance and brightness of the Moon during total lunar eclipses. L values for various luminosities are defined as follows:

- L=0 Very dark eclipse.
  (Moon almost invisible, especially at mid-totality)
- L=1 Dark eclipse, grey or brownish in coloration.
  (details distinguishable only with difficulty)
- L=2 Deep red or rust-colored eclipse.
  (very dark central shadow, while outer umbra is relatively bright)
- L=3 Brick-red eclipse.
  (umbral shadow usually has a bright or yellow rim)
- L=4 Very bright copper-red or orange eclipse.
  (umbral shadow has a bluish, very bright rim)

The assignment of an L value to lunar eclipses is best done with the naked eye, binoculars, or a small telescope near the time of mid-totality. It is also useful to examine the Moon's appearance just after the beginning and just before the end of totality. The Moon is then near the edge of the shadow, providing an opportunity to assign an L value to the outer umbra. In making any evaluations, the instrumentation used and the time should both be recorded. Also note any variations in color and brightness in different parts of the umbra, as well as the apparent sharpness of the shadow's edge. Pay attention to the visibility of lunar features within the umbra. Notes and sketches made during the eclipse are often invaluable in recalling important details, events, and impressions.

Moon's Apparent Magnitude During Total Lunar Eclipses

The Moon's apparent magnitude during the total phase of a lunar eclipse can be estimated with a pair of binoculars. The idea here is to use the binoculars "backwards"—look at the Moon through the objective end of the binoculars with the eyepiece end pointed toward the Moon. This method will reduce size of the Moon's image so that it appears star-like. The brightness of the Moon through the inverted binoculars can then be compared to the brightness of nearby stars that are viewed without binoculars.

This measurement should be done at mid-totality when the Moon is deepest in Earth's umbral shadow. Use a star atlas to identify nearby stars and record which star the Moon appears closest to in brightness. Taking the star's apparent magnitude as a starting point, the Moon's apparent magnitude must be corrected for a factor introduced by the binoculars. The corrections for 8×, 7×, and 6× binoculars are 4.5, 4.2, and 3.9 magnitudes, respectively. The correction factor should be subtracted from the comparison star's magnitude to get the Moon's estimated magnitude during totality.

For example, if the totally eclipsed Moon through a pair of inverted 7×35 binoculars appears as bright as Altair (mag. +0.77), the Moon's estimated apparent magnitude is −3.43 (= 0.77 − 4.2).

Dr. Richard A. Keen (University of Colorado) has been using these measurements to estimate the amount of volcanically produced stratospheric aerosols in Earth's atmosphere (Keen, 1983). He welcomes measurements of the Moon's brightness during both of the total lunar eclipses in 2022. He can be reached at
richard.keen@colorado.edu.

Crater Timings During Lunar Eclipses

In 1702, Pierre de La Hire made a curious observation about Earth's umbra. In order to accurately predict the duration of a lunar eclipse, he found it necessary to increase the radius of the shadow about 1% more than is warranted by geometric considerations. Although the effect is clearly related to Earth's atmosphere, it is not completely understood, since the shadow enlargement seems to vary from one eclipse to the next. The enlargement can be measured through careful timings of lunar craters as they enter and exit the umbra.

Such observations are best made using a low-power telescope and a clock or watch synchronized with radio time signals. Timings should be made to a precision of about 5 seconds. Record the instant when the most abrupt gradient at the umbra's edge crosses the apparent center of the crater. In the case of large craters like Tycho and Copernicus, record the times when the shadow touches the two opposite edges of the crater. The average of these times is equal to the instant of crater bisection.

As a planning guide, Tables 2 and 4 list a number of well-defined craters with predicted umbral immersion and emersion times during the two lunar eclipses of 2022. You should be thoroughly familiar with these features before viewing an eclipse in order to prevent confusion and misidentification. The four umbral contacts with the Moon's limb can also be used in determining the shadow's enlargement. However, these events are less distinct and therefore difficult to time accurately. Observers are encouraged to make crater timings and to send their results to *Sky & Telescope* (*Sky & Telescope*, 90 Sherman Street, Cambridge MA 02140-3264, USA) for analysis.

Enlargement of Earth's Shadows and Lunar Eclipses

In 1707, Philippe de La Hire made a curious observation about Earth's umbra. The predicted radius of the shadow needed to be enlarged by about 1/41 in order to fit timings made during a lunar eclipse. The enlargement is attributed to Earth's atmosphere, which becomes increasingly less transparent at lower levels. Additional observations over the next two centuries revealed that the shadow enlargement was somewhat variable from one eclipse to the next.

William Chauvenet (1891) formulated one method to account for the shadow enlargement while André-Louis Danjon (1951) devised another. Both methods assumed a circular cross section for the umbral shadow. However, Earth is flattened at the poles and bulges at the Equator, so an oblate spheroid more closely represents its shape. The projection of each of the planet's shadows is an ellipse rather than a circle. Furthermore, Earth's axial tilt towards or away from the Sun throughout the year means the elliptical shape of the penumbral and umbral shadows varies as well.

In an analysis of 22 539 observations made at 94 lunar eclipses from 1842 to 2011, Herald and Sinnott (2014) found that the size and shape of the umbra are consistent with an oblate spheroid at the time of each eclipse, enlarged by the empirically determined occulting layer that uniformly surrounds Earth. The effective height of this layer was found to be 87 kilometres. Based on this work, the authors developed a new method to calculate the shadow enlargement including their elliptical shape.

In *Eclipses During 2022*, the Herald and Sinnott method is used in calculating lunar eclipse circumstances and magnitudes.

Eclipse Altitudes and Azimuths

The altitude a and azimuth A of the Sun or Moon during an eclipse depends on the time and the observer's geographic coordinates. They are calculated as follows:

h = 15 (GST + UT – α) + λ,
a = arcsin [sin δ sin φ + cos δ cos h cos φ], and
A = arctan [– (cos δ sin h) / (sin δ cos φ – cos δ cos h sin φ)],

in which:

h = Hour Angle of Sun or Moon,
a = Altitude,
A = Azimuth,
GST = Greenwich Sidereal Time at 0:00 UT,
UT = Universal Time,
α = RA of Sun or Moon,
δ = Dec of Sun or Moon,
λ = Observer's Longitude (East +, West –), and
φ = Observer's Latitude (North +, South –).

During the eclipses of 2022, the values for GST and the geocentric RA and Dec of the Sun or the Moon (at greatest eclipse) are as follows:

Eclipse	**Date**	**GST**	**α**	**δ**
Partial Solar	Apr. 30	14.585	2.538	14.965
Total Lunar	May 16	15.591	15.524	–19.328
Partial Solar	Oct. 25	2.255	13.989	–12.171
Total Lunar	Nov. 08	3.174	2.897	16.852

Two web-based tools can also be used to calculate the local circumstances for all solar and lunar eclipses visible from any location. They are the *Javascript Solar Eclipse Explorer* and the *Javascript Lunar Eclipse Explorer*. The URLs for these two tools are

www.EclipseWise.com/solar/JSEX/JSEX-index.html
www.EclipseWise.com/lunar/JLEX/JLEX-index.html

Eclipses During 2023

In 2023, there are two solar eclipses and two lunar eclipses:

Apr. 20: Hybrid Solar Eclipse
May 5: Penumbral Lunar Eclipse
Oct. 14: Annular Solar Eclipse
Oct. 28: Partial Lunar Eclipse

A full report on these eclipses will be published in *Observer's Handbook 2023*. Additional information may be found at www.eclipsewise.com/oh/ec2023.html

Eclipse Websites

EclipseWise.com is a website dedicated to predictions and information on eclipses of the Sun and the Moon. It offers a graphically intuitive interface and contains maps, diagrams, tables, and information about every solar and lunar eclipse from 2000 BCE to 3000 CE. This period includes 11 898 solar eclipses and 12 064 lunar eclipses.

Much of EclipseWise is based on the *Thousand Year Canon of Solar Eclipses: 1501 to 2500* (Espenak 2014a) and the *Thousand Year Canon of Lunar Eclipses: 1501 to 2500* (Espenak 2014b). These eclipse predictions use the Jet Propulsion Laboratory's DE405—a computer ephemeris used for calculating high-precision coordinates of the Sun and the Moon for thousands of years into the past and future.

Detailed information on solar and lunar eclipse photography, and tips on eclipse observing and eye safety may be found at www.MrEclipse.com/MrEclipse.html

Acknowledgments

All eclipse predictions were generated on a Macintosh G4 PowerPC using algorithms developed from the *Explanatory Supplement* [1974] with additional algorithms from Meeus [1989]. The solar and lunar coordinates used in the eclipse predictions are based on the JPL DE405. For lunar eclipses, the elliptical shape of the umbral and penumbral shadows were calculated using Herald and Sinnott (2014) method of enlarging Earth's radius to compensate for the opacity of the terrestrial atmosphere (including corrections for the oblateness of Earth).

All calculations, diagrams, tables, and opinions presented in this paper are those of the author, and he assumes full responsibility for their accuracy.

References and Bibliography

Chauvenet, W., *Manual of Spherical and Practical Astronomy, Vol.1*, 1891 (Dover edition 1961).

Danjon, A., "Les éclipses de Lune par la pénombre en 1951," *L'Astronomie, 65,* 51–53 (Feb. 1951).

Espenak, F., and Meeus, J., *Five Millennium Canon of Solar Eclipses: 1 to 3000 (2nd Edition)*, Astropixels Publishing, Portal, AZ (2021a).

Espenak, F., and Meeus, J., *Five Millennium Canon of Lunar Eclipses: 1 to 3000 (2nd Edition)*, Astropixels Publishing, Portal, AZ (2021b).

Espenak, F., *Thousand Year Canon of Solar Eclipses: 1501 to 2500*, Astropixels Publishing, Portal, AZ (2014a).

Espenak, F., *Thousand Year Canon of Lunar Eclipses: 1501 to 2500*, Astropixels Publishing, Portal, AZ (2014b).

Espenak, F., *21st Century Canon of Solar Eclipses*, Astropixels Publishing, Portal, AZ (2016).

Espenak, F., *21st Century Canon of Lunar Eclipses*, Astropixels Publishing, Portal, AZ (2020).

Explanatory Supplement to the Astronomical Ephemeris and the *American Ephemeris and Nautical Almanac*, Her Majesty's Nautical Almanac Office, London, 1974.

Herald, D., and Sinnott, R.W., "Analysis of Lunar Crater Timings, 1842–2011," *J. Br. Astron. Assoc., 124,* 5 (2014)

Keen, R.A., "Volcanic Aerosols and Lunar Eclipses", *Science, vol. 222,* p. 1011–1013, Dec. 2, 1983.

Meeus, J., *Elements of Solar Eclipses 1951–2200*, Willmann-Bell, Richmond, VA (1989).

HOW TO WATCH A SOLAR ECLIPSE

BY JAY ANDERSON

There are no central solar eclipses in 2022, and so the pause afforded by the mis-aligned orbits of the Earth and Moon provides us with an opportunity to reflect on the phenomena in advance of the coming eclipses of 2023 and 2024 over North America. A solar eclipse, especially a total eclipse, is more than a view of the corona and chromosphere. It is a chance to investigate solar and atmospheric physics in a setting of unparalleled cosmic beauty—a chance to add "science" to our appreciation of a Sun-Moon-Earth alignment.

For most eclipse watchers, totality is a time to revel in the corona and the chromosphere and take note of any prominences that might be visible. There are also supplementary events that go along with the eclipse: shadow bands, meteorological changes, crescent-shaped pin-hole images, the sight of an onrushing shadow, changes in animal (including human) behavior, the daytime appearance of planets, and so on. These are visually exciting and sought-after events, but with some simple instrumentation, there are a few other intriguing elements to be revealed.

First among these is the flash spectrum, visible for a few seconds at second and third contact during a total eclipse. These are the moments just before and after totality when the solar photosphere (the visible surface) is covered but the chromosphere, the solar atmosphere's innermost layer, either still lingers above, or emerges from behind, the lunar limb. Visually, the chromosphere is a brilliant red crescent that subtends a large part of the solar limb (and which may appear as a complete circle in very short eclipses). That color signals the presence of hydrogen, which glows at a deep red wavelength of 656.3 nm. The chromosphere is readily visible in H-alpha telescopes—it is the surface of the Sun in such instruments. However, there is much more to the chromosphere than hydrogen.

To view the chemical composition of the Sun, it is usually necessary to build a spectroscope, which consists of a narrow slit through which the Sun is viewed, a prism or diffraction grating to disperse the light from the Sun, and a set of lenses to configure the light passing through the slit as it passes through the grating and comes to focus. It's not a difficult instrument to make, though the light coming through the slit must be first made parallel to pass through the grating or prism and then focused to be viewed on a screen or viewed by eye (where the eye itself acts as the focusing lens). You can buy direct-vision spectroscopes online for $100 or so.

However, during an eclipse, the encroaching limb of the Moon turns the solar disk into a very narrow crescent, mimicking the function of the slit in a direct-vision spectroscope. Because the solar "slit" is at infinity (for all intents and purposes), no collimating lens is needed ahead of the dispersion mechanism, and the eye can be used to bring the image to focus. All that is needed, then, is a dispersion mechanism—a prism or a diffraction grating. Diffraction gratings are $4 each. Prisms are more complicated to use, cost more, and are best avoided.

In the moments before the start of totality, the solar photosphere shrinks into a very thin crescent that then breaks up into a series of photospheric beads (Baily's beads) embedded in a red arc of chromosphere. As the last of the beads evaporate behind the encroaching lunar limb, the eclipse watcher is left with a narrow crescent of chromosphere that in turn disappears behind the lunar edge a few seconds later. Within the last half-minute or so before totality begins, the grating will display this sequence of events in a continuously evolving display of colors. At first, a continuous rainbow band of colors marks where the photosphere is showing, but as the solar crescent shrinks, the rainbow will be joined by a half-dozen or so narrow, curved horns of intense color at its top and bottom. As more and more of the photosphere is covered, the continuous spectrum narrows and then disappears, while at the same time, the colored horns on each side of the spectrum grow toward their middle, eventually joining to form a crescent. The first few colored arcs with be joined by many others as the instant of second contact approaches, some extending for a considerable distance along the limb of the Moon, others for a short arc and visible only as the last of the beads are dissipating and the total eclipse is imminent.

The rainbow of colors visible in the grating is the light from the photosphere, blended into a band of continuous color from indigo to red. The distinct colored horns emerging from above and below the continuous spectrum comes from the chromosphere and each one is associated with a particular element in the solar atmosphere. A deep red line will mark the position where H-alpha wavelengths appear, while another fainter line in the blue-green may mark the location of H-beta wavelengths and yet another in the deep blue for H-gamma (see p. 32). Sodium wavelengths may appear in the yellow section of the spectrum and emissions from iron in the orange. There will be many lines—tens at least—some long and some short, gradually appearing as the photospheric spectrum fades and then disappearing as the chromosphere is covered by the Sun. Short lines come from low in the chromosphere; longer from gases dispersed more widely.

The whole transition, from photosphere to chromosphere to eclipse, lasts for perhaps 10 seconds and so it is tagged with the name "flash spectrum." There is far too much detail for the mind to capture in the brief duration of the flash spectrum, but fortunately, a second flash spectrum is waiting for third contact, when the chromosphere is uncovered again. This time, the arcing lines will emerge from the centre and grow outward (though this depends on the limb profile to some extent) until overwhelmed by the growing photosphere. This evolution of the flash spectrum is a visual and scientific treat, but too quick to register in the instants available, leaving the mind wondering what the eye actually saw.

The diffraction grating has its uses during totality as well. Prominences will be visible as beads, showing only the emission in alpha, beta and gamma—an interesting departure from the many more lines of the chromosphere and telling you something distinctive about the makeup of prominences. The coronal spectrum is also visible, but it's typically a continuous spectrum with few details, since it's largely made up of reflected (photospheric) sunlight. If coronal emission is visible, it will show as a ring of emission (as opposed to the arcs from the chromosphere), likely in the green and perhaps in the red, both of which are due to highly ionized iron.

If the flash spectrum piques your interest, how about examining the polarization of the corona as well?

Light from the corona comes from five sources of which three, labelled K, E, and F, are important for eclipse observations: The E-corona is found relatively close to the Sun and is formed where the million-degree coronal plasma emits light at discrete wavelengths, primarily from highly ionized iron. The F-corona is a reflection of photospheric light from interplanetary dust grains; it is bright close to the Sun and can be traced out to 10 or more solar radii, perhaps merging into the Zodiacal light. The K-corona is formed from sunlight scattering off free electrons and is the only polarized component of the outer solar atmosphere.

If you were able to look directly at a beam of light, it would appear as linked electric and magnetic waves, which could be oscillating at any angle: up and down, side to side, or any direction in between. If all or a part of the light is oscillating in one direction (say up and down), then it is said to be polarized or partly polarized; unpolarized light has beams oscillating randomly in all orientations. Light becomes polarized in many ways, but most particularly, for astronomical purposes, when it is reflects off of particles, particularly if those particles are organized in some fashion, perhaps by a magnetic field. In the corona, the electrons in the K-corona can provide just this capability and so the K-corona light is partly polarized.

Polarization is a subtle feature and is best detected by comparing light that is polarized in two different directions or by comparing polarized light with unpolarized light, typically by use of a polarizing filter. Depending on their design, these filters pass light in only one plane (called linear polarization) and that plane can be changed by simply rotating the filter. If you have polarizing sunglasses, you can detect the atmosphere's polarization by looking at the clear sky in a direction away from the Sun and rotating your glasses. Expect some questioning looks if you are caught wearing sunglasses at a solar eclipse, however!

Because polarization of the corona may be a subtle effect, with polarization amounts from 20 to 50%, a quick change from one orientation to another is probably necessary to see changes in the corona. Two orthogonally oriented polarization filters, side-by-side, will allow "blinking" from one view to the other and help make changes in the corona structure visible. Large sheets of polarizing film is readily available online, as are sheets of diffraction film.

In the three minutes or so of a typical solar eclipse, you may find that fiddling with viewing equipment during an eclipse takes too much time away from the event, so try constructing an eclipse "viewer" such as that shown in the diagram. With this instrument, you can watch the filtered partial phases, the naked-eye eclipse, the flash spectrum, and evaluate polarization in very short order. If you restrict yourself to just the flash spectrum, you can still watch the eclipse evolve naked eye. Diffraction gratings create a color spectrum on each side of the Sun and so you will always have the Sun in view while the flash spectrum is making its display off to the side.

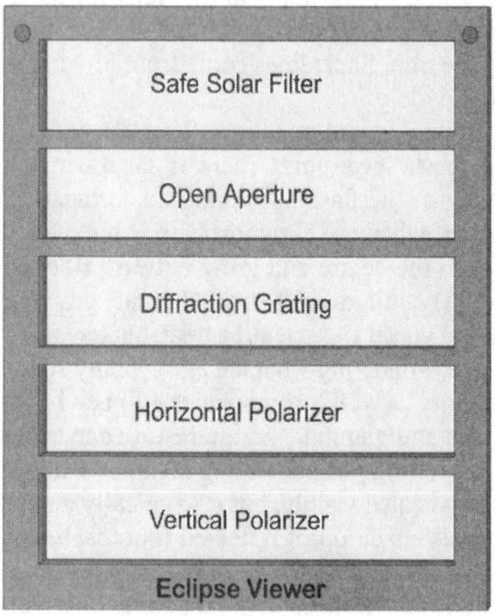

Temperatures fall during a solar eclipse—a feature that is well known to any eclipse chaser, but did you know that it falls at different rates in the atmosphere? Set out two thermometers, one at the ground and one at chest height, and you will find that the ground temperature drops much more than the chest-height thermometer and that the individual minimums will occur at a different time. Better yet, put out three thermometers, each at a different height, and see how the atmosphere responds through a greater depth. Some eclipse experimenters have even buried a thermometer a few centimetres into the ground, but you'll have to wait for some time after central eclipse for the wave of cooler temperatures to penetrate below the surface.

Measuring temperature changes may require some stand-alone thermometers but simple digital thermometers with an inside/outside display may be enough. If they don't record values, someone will have to read them through the eclipse, though you could point a small camera at them are take a photo every minute or so. Take readings every few minutes on the approach to totality and then more frequently for the few minutes before and after eclipse. Expect temperatures to reach a minimum about 5 to 10 minutes after central eclipse.

One of the more intriguing events during an eclipse is the change in the tone and color of the sky. It's a phenomenon that's hard to define, but the air seems to become "oppressive" or "ominous" from about half way between first and second contact until totality begins. There are often comments made about changes in the color of the sky—it seems more metallic in the closing moments before the main event. One way to investigate any color changes would be to set up a camera to photograph a plain white target from first to last contact and then use graphics software to separate the red, green, and blue color components in the series of images.

If this is your first eclipse, perhaps you should just watch. Pull out the camera after eclipse number two or three, and then go into more in-depth analysis later in your eclipse career. If you are the experimental type, carry a diffraction grating and steal a look as the Moon begins to cover or uncover the Sun.

ECLIPSE HISTORY
BY JAMES EDGAR

Eclipses have been recorded in history for as long as there have been records. Ancient Greeks used the term ekleipsis, meaning "the abandonment" or "the darkening of a heavenly body," from which we derive the current term. Experiencing a total solar eclipse is unforgettable, and such events created great fear in early observers.

Even though early astrologers (for it was they who kept track of heavenly events) generally understood the movements in the Solar System, their calculations weren't precise enough to establish that the Sun is at the center of the Solar System. Nor did they know at first what caused the Sun to suddenly darken for part of a day.

A standing-stone monument inscribed with petroglyphs at the Loughcrew Cairn L in Ireland is believed to record the solar eclipse of 3340 Nov. 30 BCE. Another record from China likely marks the day when "the Sun and Moon did not meet harmoniously" on 2134 Oct. 22 BCE. Such events struck fear into the inhabitants—fear that the Sun may not come back was quite real at that time. According to Chinese tradition, loud noises, banging drums and pots, and even shouting scared away the "dragon" that was eating the Sun.

Later scribes in Babylon kept careful records of celestial events on clay tablets, some of which exist to this day. We know from one of these records that on 1063 Jul. 31 BCE, a total solar eclipse "turned day into night." Assyrian observers in Nineveh wrote of the eclipse of 763 Jun. 15 BCE. These careful records led to the predictions and series we know today as the Saros cycle (see p. 122). By about 610 BCE, Thales of Greece was able to predict a solar eclipse, but his method does not survive. Ptolemy's writings in the Almagest around CE 150 show that he had a method for predicting both lunar and solar eclipses. The findings of Meton were widely known around the Mediterranean by then, as well (see p. 125).

For many, an eclipse was no longer something to be feared, but an interesting orbital regularity—something to anticipate with joy and excitement—much like today.

Science enters the picture

Many discoveries have occurred in the years since Ptolemy: solar prominences were first reported in CE 334; a comet was observed during an eclipse in 418; Johannes Kepler wrote an accurate description of a total solar eclipse in 1605; Edmund Halley made an extremely accurate prediction of the solar eclipse of 1715 May 3, only missing the mark by 4 min and 30 km. The substance of the solar corona puzzled many observers, but by 1724, the proposal that it was part of the Sun met with acceptance. Francis Baily, in 1836, noted the "beads" of light that now bear his name—rays of light streaming through the mountain passes on the lunar landscape as totality approaches and then recedes. Helium was discovered as an element from a spectral line during a total solar eclipse in 1868, and a new element, "coronium," caused a brief flurry of excitement in 1869, until it was finally confirmed in 1941 to be ionized iron.

Sir Arthur Eddington is famously known for confirming Albert Einstein's prediction in his GTR that a massive object's gravity "warps" spacetime, such that light traveling from a distant star moves along the shortest path, appearing to "bend" around the edge of the massive object. The first proposal to measure the amount of bend came in the middle of WW I, but was postponed until after the war's end. Eddington chose the island of Principe off Africa's western coast to observe and photograph the eclipse of 1919 May 29, where the Moon's shadow, having crossed South America and the southern Atlantic Ocean, would pass right over his vantage point as it continued over central Africa.

The stars Eddington chose for his experiment were the bright ones in the Hyades Cluster (including κTauri), which, of course, would be obscured by the Sun's glare except during an eclipse. Even though the images recorded were of poor quality, the measurements derived from them showed that the prediction is correct—light does indeed bend around the edge of a massive object. This effect has been measured to exquisite accuracy, even with stars occulted by Jupiter. Gravitational lensing is a similar effect, and observations of such events are now commonly used to study the nature of very distant stars and galaxies.

Lunar Eclipses

Although not as spectacular as solar eclipses, lunar eclipses have been equally studied since ancient times, contributing to myths in many cultures. Was it a sow eating the Moon, as the Egyptians thought? Did a jaguar eat the Mayan Moon? Did a three-legged toad in China swallow the Moon whole? Many cultures—many myths. Careful study, though, especially by the ancient Greeks, led to the discovery of cycles such as the Saros and the Metonic series. The early Greeks even declared that Earth is round like a globe, because the umbral shadow cast on the Moon during an eclipse is always round.

Columbus is remembered for his "discovery" of the Americas, but he also famously predicted a lunar eclipse, stating that he could make the Moon disappear and then reappear to frighten the natives in Jamaica who were rebelling against the Spaniards eating all their food. He had the calculations correct and pulled off the stunt. The next day the natives gave over their food.

Superstition has generally given way to scientific study and accurate measurement of events. As explained by Fred Espenak in the preceding pages, measuring crater timings—the moment when Earth's shadow encroaches on a crater's central point—gives valuable information about the size of the shadow. A better way to measure is to accurately note the time when the shadow touches the crater rims, then divide the difference by 2 to get the average central time. It's known that Earth's shadow will be slightly larger than geometry requires, but what is still not well understood is why the enlargement varies from one eclipse to another, or what it is about Earth's atmosphere that causes such variation.

Eclipsophiles

When Eddington travelled to Principe to observe and measure during the 1919 eclipse, it was a big deal. Travel wasn't easy, and he travelled with a lot of baggage. These days, with easy travel arrangements, eclipsophiles can go anywhere in the world to bask in the glory of the Moon's shadow. And they do. There are at least two solar eclipses per year, and often one of them proves to be spectacular. Many are the photos from people who travel to wherever the eclipse track takes them—the Australian Outback, Africa, onboard a ship, and even flying in a specially chartered aircraft to chase the shadow!

People continue to talk about the Great Eclipse of 2009, during which totality lasted over 6 min. This included travel to East Asia to see it. How about the one over northern Australia in 2013? Or Svalbard in 2015? Many were the astronomers who visited those countries to see the Sun blotted out by the Moon. The hobby is more than a passion to some, who will continue to calculate, plan, and seek out places to get a fleeting glimpse of nature's amazing wonder—a total solar eclipse.

VIEWING A SOLAR ECLIPSE—A WARNING
BY ROY BISHOP

When viewing the Sun, the safety rule is simple: **Never look at the Sun without a suitable filter, either directly with the unaided eyes or through binoculars or a telescope.** To do so one risks permanent partial blindness, and this can occur almost instantly in the case of telescopic viewing. Viewing our Sun is just as dangerous on any clear day, but at the time of an eclipse people have a reason to want to look at it—and often resort to dangerous methods.

A direct view of the Sun is safe only if a suitable filter is used in a proper manner. In the case of binoculars or a telescope, the filter must be one that attaches *securely* to the *front* end of the instrument, never one that attaches to the eyepiece end (the heat developed near the eyepiece can shatter such a filter). Specially designed so-called "solar viewing glasses" are suitable for an unmagnified look at the Sun.

Filters specifically designed for solar viewing include aluminized Mylar and glass filters plated with a slightly transparent, metallic film. Such filters may be purchased online from telescope dealers. Shade #14 (no other shade) rectangular welder's glass may be used; however, as these filters are of low optical quality, they are useful only for views not involving binoculars or a telescope. All of these are commercial items and cannot be replaced with ordinary household items. For example, layers of photographic color film, colored glass, stacked sunglasses, crossed polarizers, smoked glass, or photographic neutral-density filters must never be used. Although one may devise a combination that dims the *visible* sunlight to a comfortable level, the makeshift filter may be quite transparent in the infrared part of the solar spectrum, and this invisible radiation will damage the observer's eye. For the same reason, one must never rely on clouds or heavy atmospheric haze to dim the solar image when using a telescope.

A simple-to-arrange, safe, versatile, yet almost unknown method to observe the partial phases of a solar eclipse is *mirror projection*. Take an ordinary, small, flat mirror and cover its surface with masking tape or duct tape, leaving a small area open near its center. For projecting an image of the Sun across a room, a square opening about 6 mm (a quarter inch) on a side works well. Prop the mirror up on a sunny windowsill and aim the reflected sunlight onto a convenient viewing screen within the room—but not directly into anyone's eyes! Even the ceiling or a wall can be used as the viewing screen. The spot of light on the viewing screen is a surprisingly good image of the solar disk. Mirror projection has a great advantage over the usual "pinhole" technique: the image can be aimed across a substantial distance to a convenient viewing screen. The greater the distance, the larger the image of the Sun. Furthermore, it is easy to adjust the size of the opening on the mirror for the best compromise between image brightness and image sharpness. With this elegantly simple device the progress of a partial solar eclipse can be viewed safely by a group of children in a darkened room. Furthermore, on any sunny day the children can watch the rotation of their classroom as the room's viewing screen moves slowly and silently past the Sun's image.

A sharper and brighter image of the solar disk may be projected onto a white viewing screen placed 30 or 40 cm behind the eyepiece of binoculars or a small telescope (the telescope aperture should be stopped down to about 50 mm in order to limit the intensity of sunlight passing through the instrument, and the viewing screen should be shielded from direct sunlight). However, one must ***never*** look through the instrument when aiming it at the Sun, and, especially if children are present, a physical barrier must be used to prevent anyone from attempting to look into the eyepiece. If the telescope has a finderscope, it must be either covered or removed.

THE MOON

MAP OF THE MOON

BY ROY BISHOP

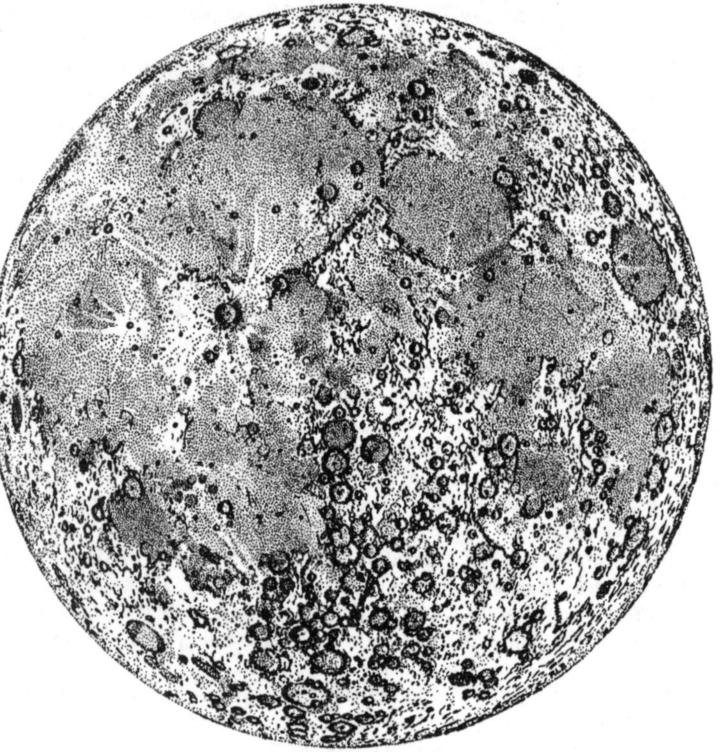

Maria	
LS	Lacus Somniorum (Lake of Dreams) (330°)
MC	Mare Crisium (Sea of Crises) (300°)
MFe	Mare Fecunditatis (Sea of Fertility) (310°)
MFr	Mare Frigoris (Sea of Cold) (0°)
MH	Mare Humorum (Sea of Moisture) (40°)
MI	Mare Imbrium (Sea of Rains) (20°)
MNe	Mare Nectaris (Sea of Nectar) (325°)
MNu	Mare Nubium (Sea of Clouds) (15°)
MS	Mare Serenitatis (Sea of Serenity) (340°)
MT	Mare Tranquillitatis (Sea of Tranquillity) (330°)
MV	Mare Vaporum (Sea of Vapors) (355°)
OP	Oceanus Procellarum (Ocean of Storms) (50°)
SA	Sinus Aestuum (Seething Bay) (8°)
SI	Sinus Iridum (Bay of Rainbows) (32°)
SM	Sinus Medii (Central Bay) (0°)
SR	Sinus Roris (Bay of Dew) (60°)

Lunar Probes	
2	*Luna 2,* First to reach Moon (1959-9-13) (0°)
7	*Ranger 7,* First close pictures (1964-7-31) (21°)
9	*Luna 9,* First soft landing (1966-2-3) (64°)
11	*Apollo 11,* First men on Moon (1969-7-20) (337°)
12	*Apollo 12* (1969-11-19) (23°)
14	*Apollo 14* (1971-2-5) (17°)
15	*Apollo 15* (1971-7-30) (356°)
16	*Apollo 16* (1972-4-21) (344°)
17	*Apollo 17* (1972-12-11) (329°)

Angles in parentheses equal 360°– λ, where λ is the selenographic longitude of the center of the feature. 0° marks the mean center of the lunar disk and the angles increase toward the observer's east (i.e. westward on the Moon). These angles facilitate locating the feature on the accompanying map, and may be correlated with the Sun's selenographic colongitude (see *THE SKY MONTH BY MONTH (p. 98)* *to determine the optimum times for viewing the feature.*

Mountains

A Alpine Valley (356°)
B Alps Mountains (359°)
E Altai Scarp (336°)
F Apennine Mountains (2°)
G Carpathian Mountains (24°)
H Caucasus Mountains (352°)
K Haemus Mountains (349°)
M Jura Mountains (34°)
N Pyrenees Mountains (319°)
R Rheita Valley (312°)
S Riphaeus Mountains (27°)
V Spitzbergen (5°)
W Straight Range (20°)
X Straight Wall (8°)
Y Taurus Mountains (319°)
Z Teneriffe Mountains (13°)

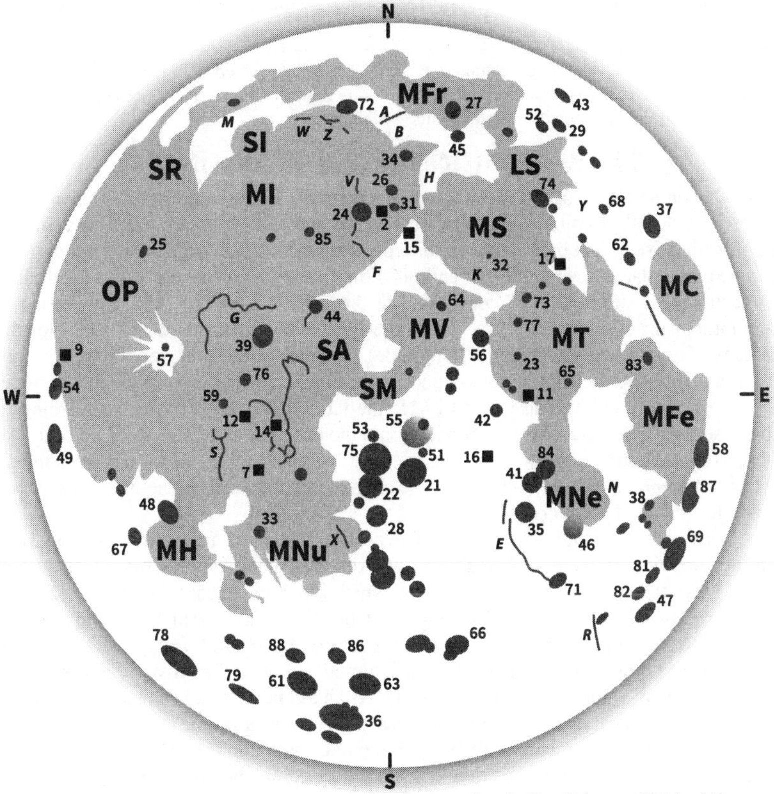

chart by Roy Bishop and Michael Gatto

Craters

21 Albategnius (356°)
22 Alphonsus (3°)
23 Arago (338°)
24 Archimedes (4°)
25 Aristarchus (47°)
26 Aristillus (358°)
27 Aristoteles (342°)
28 Arzachel (2°)
29 Atlas (315°)
31 Autolycus (358°)
32 Bessel (342°)
33 Bullialdus (22°)
34 Cassini (355°)
35 Catharina (336°)
36 Clavius (15°)
37 Cleomedes (304°)
38 Cook (311°)
39 Copernicus (20°)
41 Cyrillus (336°)
42 Delambre (342°)
43 Endymion (305°)
44 Eratosthenes (11°)
45 Eudoxus (343°)
46 Fracastorius (326°)
47 Furnerius (299°)
48 Gassendi (40°)
49 Grimaldi (68°)
51 Halley (354°)
52 Hercules (321°)
53 Herschel (2°)
54 Hevelius (66°)
55 Hipparchus (354°)
56 Julius Caesar (345°)
57 Kepler (38°)
58 Langrenus (299°)
59 Lansberg (27°)
61 Longomontanus (21°)
62 Macrobius (314°)
63 Maginus (6°)
64 Manilius (351°)
65 Maskelyne (330°)
66 Maurolycus (345°)
67 Mersenius (49°)
68 Newcomb (316°)
69 Petavius (298°)
71 Piccolomini (327°)
72 Plato (10°)
73 Plinius (336°)
74 Posidonius (330°)
75 Ptolemaeus (2°)
76 Reinhold (23°)
77 Ross (338°)
78 Schickard (55°)
79 Schiller (40°)
81 Snellius (304°)
82 Stevinus (305°)
83 Taruntius (313°)
84 Theophilus (333°)
85 Timocharis (13°)
86 Tycho (11°)
87 Vendelinus (298°)
88 Wilhelm (20°)

For expanded photographic views of the lunar surface see wms.LROC.asu.edu/LROC (a *Lunar Reconnaissance Orbiter* Camera mosaic).

UNIVERSAL TIME OF NEW-MOON DATES

2022			2023		
Jan. 2.8	May 30.5	Sep. 25.9	Jan. 21.9	May 19.7	Sep. 15.1
Feb. 1.2	Jun. 29.1	Oct. 25.5	Feb. 20.3	Jun. 18.2	Oct. 14.7
Mar. 2.7	Jul. 28.7	Nov. 24.0	Mar. 21.7	Jul. 17.8	Nov. 13.4
Apr. 1.3	Aug. 27.3	Dec. 23.4	Apr. 20.2	Aug. 16.4	Dec. 13.0
Apr. 30.9					

These dates will be useful for planning observing sessions, determining favorable dates for observing very thin lunar crescents, and setting Moon dials on clocks. The dates are indicated to lower precision in the calendars on the inside back cover.

TIMES OF MOONRISE AND MOONSET

The table on pp. 152–157 gives the times of moonrise and moonset for locations ranging from 20°N to 60°N latitude. Dates of new Moon and full Moon are given in **bold** and *italic* respectively. The table may be interpolated linearly for nontabular latitudes and can be extrapolated beyond the 20° and 60° limits a few degrees without significant loss of accuracy. "Rise" and "Set" correspond to the upper limb of the Moon appearing at the horizon for an observer at sea level. The times are local mean time (LMT) for the Greenwich meridian (i.e. UT at 0° longitude). Because of the relatively rapid eastward motion of the Moon, unlike the sunrise and sunset table, for observers not near 0° longitude, the times cannot be read directly as LMT; the table must be interpolated according to the observer's longitude. Also, to convert from the observer's LMT to standard time, the observer's longitude correction relative to his or her standard meridian must be applied. After it is prepared for a given location, the chart at the right enables the sum of these two corrections to be determined in one step.

To prepare the **Moonrise/Moonset Correction Diagram**, first mark your longitude on the *West or East Longitude* scale. Draw a diagonal line from this mark to the (0,0) point. Next, the *Correction in minutes* axis (which is subdivided at two-minute intervals) must be labeled. As a guide, the first three divisions have been tentatively labeled 0, ±2, ±4 *(use + if you are west of the prime meridian in Greenwich, England, − if east)*; but, to these numbers must be added your longitude correction relative to your standard meridian (see the third paragraph on p. 201). As an aid both for labeling and for reading the chart, the vertical lines at 10-min intervals are wider. **Examples:** For Omaha, which is 6° W of its standard meridian of 90°W, the longitude correction is +24 min, so an observer in Omaha would label the Correction axis 24, 26, 28,…; an observer in Boston (longitude correction −16) would label the axis −16, −14, −12,…; an observer in Hong Kong (east longitude, longitude correction +24) would label the axis 24, 22, 20,…; an observer in Vienna (longitude correction −6) would label the axis −6, −8, −10,….

The chart is now ready for use on any day from your position. Interpolating for nontabular latitudes, from the table obtain today's time for the event (moonrise, or moonset) and tomorrow's time if you are west of Greenwich, yesterday's time if east, enter the difference on the *Tabular Delay* axis, and run horizontally across to meet the diagonal line. The correction, to the nearest minute, can then be read directly below off the Correction axis. This correction is applied to the tabular "today's time" and results in the standard time of the event for your position. **Example:** The longitude of Chicago, Illinois, is 88°W, and latitude is 42°N. Interpolating the 40°N and 45°N entries, the table gives for 42°N a moonrise time of 21:21 on May 17. The Correction corresponding to a 73-min Tabular Delay, when the chart is prepared for Chicago as described above, is –3 min; hence the time of moonrise is 21:33 – 3 min = 21:30 CST May 17, or, adding one hour for Daylight Saving Time, 22:30 CDT.

A blank PDF chart for download and personal use is available on the site www.rasc.ca/supplements.

MOONRISE/MOONSET CORRECTION DIAGRAM

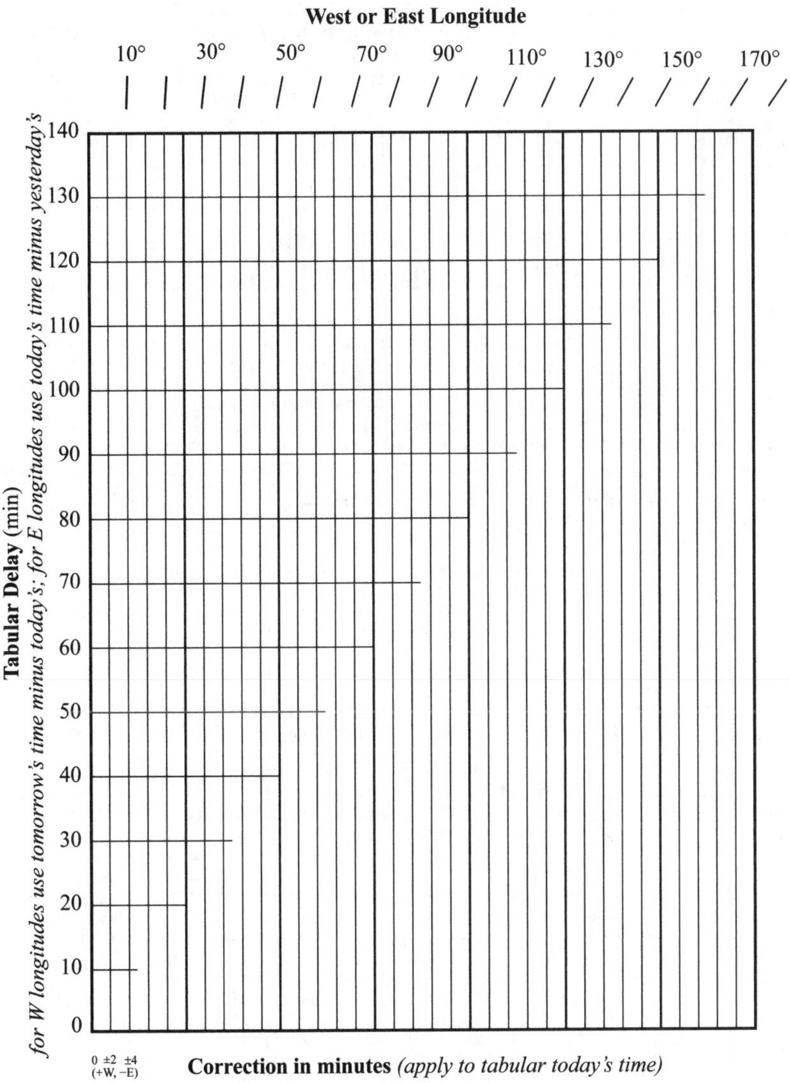

Note: Due to a difference in elevation between the observer and the actual horizon, the observed time may differ by several minutes from the predicted time.

The correction in minutes can also be calculated from the formula:

$$(L/360) \times (\text{Tabular Delay}) + 4(L - Ls)$$

in which L = longitude of the observer from Greenwich, and Ls = longitude of the observer's time-zone standard meridian (L and Ls are in degrees, and are negative if east of Greenwich). The term 4(L – Ls) is tabulated for American capital or major cities on p. 205.

Alternatively, see p. 10 for computer-based planetarium programs or applications for mobile devices.

MOONRISE AND MOONSET, JANUARY AND FEBRUARY 2022
UNIVERSAL TIME AT GREENWICH MERIDIAN

Latitude:	+20°		+30°		+35°		+40°		+45°		+50°		+55°		+60°	
Event:	RISE	SET	RISE	SET	RISE	SET	RISE	SET	RISE	SET	RISE	SET	RISE	SET	RISE	SET
Jan. 1	05:06	16:15	05:30	15:50	05:44	15:35	06:01	15:18	06:20	14:58	06:45	14:32	06:45	14:32	08:10	13:05
2	**06:15**	**17:20**	**06:41**	**16:54**	**06:56**	**16:39**	**07:14**	**16:21**		**15:59**	**00:00**	**15:32**	**08:03**	**15:32**	**09:40**	**13:55**
3	07:20	18:28	07:46	18:04	08:01	17:49	08:18	17:32	08:39	17:12	09:05	16:47	09:05	16:47	10:34	15:19
4	08:19	19:36	08:42	19:15	08:55	19:03	09:10	18:49	09:28	18:32	09:50	18:11	09:50	18:11	11:00	17:03
5	09:11	20:40	09:29	20:24	09:39	20:14	09:51	20:04	10:05	19:51	10:22	19:36	10:22	19:36	11:12	18:49
6	09:55	21:39	10:08	21:29	10:16	21:23	10:24	21:16	10:34	21:07	10:46	20:57	10:46	20:57	11:19	20:28
7	10:35	22:35	10:43	22:30	10:47	22:27	10:52	22:23	10:58	22:19	11:04	22:14	11:04	22:14	11:24	22:01
8	11:11	23:28	11:13	23:28	11:15	23:28	11:16	23:28	11:18	23:28	11:20	23:28	11:20	23:28	11:26	23:28
9	11:45		11:43		11:41		11:39		11:37		11:35		11:35		11:29	
10	12:19	00:18	12:11	00:24	12:07	00:27	12:02	00:30	11:57	00:34	11:50	00:39	11:50	00:39	11:32	00:52
11	12:53	01:09	12:41	01:19	12:34	01:25	12:26	01:31	12:17	01:39	12:06	01:48	12:06	01:48	11:35	02:16
12	13:30	01:59	13:13	02:14	13:04	02:22	12:53	02:32	12:40	02:44	12:25	02:58	12:25	02:58	11:40	03:39
13	14:09	02:51	13:48	03:09	13:37	03:20	13:23	03:33	13:07	03:48	12:48	04:06	12:48	04:06	11:48	05:04
14	14:51	03:43	14:28	04:05	14:15	04:18	13:59	04:33	13:40	04:51	13:17	05:14	13:17	05:14	12:02	06:27
15	15:38	04:36	15:13	05:00	14:58	05:15	14:41	05:32	14:20	05:52	13:55	06:17	13:55	06:17	12:26	07:45
16	16:29	05:28	16:03	05:54	15:48	06:09	15:30	06:26	15:09	06:47	14:42	07:14	14:42	07:14	13:09	08:48
17	*17:22*	*06:18*	*16:57*	*06:43*	*16:43*	*06:58*	*16:26*	*07:15*	*16:06*	*07:36*	*15:40*	*08:02*	*15:40*	*08:02*	*14:13*	*09:29*
18	18:16	07:06	17:54	07:29	17:41	07:43	17:26	07:58	17:09	08:16	16:47	08:39	16:47	08:39	15:34	09:53
19	19:11	07:50	18:53	08:10	18:42	08:21	18:30	08:35	18:15	08:50	17:58	09:09	17:58	09:09	17:02	10:07
20	20:05	08:31	19:52	08:47	19:44	08:56	19:35	09:06	19:24	09:18	19:11	09:33	19:11	09:33	18:32	10:15
21	20:59	09:09	20:50	09:20	20:45	09:27	20:39	09:34	20:33	09:42	20:24	09:52	20:24	09:52	20:01	10:20
22	21:52	09:46	21:49	09:52	21:47	09:55	21:44	09:59	21:42	10:03	21:38	10:09	21:38	10:09	21:29	10:23
23	22:46	10:21	22:48	10:22	22:49	10:22	22:50	10:23	22:52	10:24	22:54	10:24	22:54	10:24	22:59	10:26
24	23:42	10:57	23:49	10:53	23:53	10:50	23:58	10:47		10:44		10:40		10:40		10:29
25		11:36		11:26		11:20		11:14	00:04	11:06	00:11	10:58	00:11	10:58	00:31	10:33
26	00:40	12:17	00:53	12:02	01:00	11:54	01:09	11:44	01:19	11:32	01:31	11:18	01:31	11:18	02:07	10:38
27	01:42	13:04	02:00	12:44	02:10	12:33	02:22	12:20	02:37	12:04	02:55	11:45	02:55	11:45	03:50	10:46
28	02:47	13:58	03:09	13:34	03:22	13:20	03:38	13:04	03:56	12:45	04:19	12:21	04:19	12:21	05:35	11:02
29	03:53	14:58	04:19	14:32	04:34	14:17	04:51	13:59	05:12	13:38	05:39	13:11	05:39	13:11	07:13	11:36
30	04:59	16:04	05:25	15:38	05:41	15:23	05:59	15:06	06:20	14:44	06:47	14:17	06:47	14:17	08:23	12:42
31	06:01	17:12	06:25	16:49	06:39	16:35	06:56	16:20	07:15	16:01	07:39	15:37	07:39	15:37	09:00	14:19
Feb. 1	**06:56**	**18:18**	**07:16**	**17:59**	**07:28**	**17:49**	**07:42**	**17:36**	**07:58**	**17:21**	**08:17**	**17:03**	**08:17**	**17:03**	**09:18**	**16:06**
2	07:44	19:21	08:00	19:08	08:09	19:00	08:19	18:51	08:31	18:41	08:45	18:28	08:45	18:28	09:27	17:51
3	08:27	20:20	08:37	20:12	08:43	20:08	08:49	20:03	08:57	19:57	09:06	19:50	09:06	19:50	09:32	19:29
4	09:05	21:15	09:10	21:13	09:13	21:12	09:16	21:10	09:19	21:09	09:24	21:07	09:24	21:07	09:36	21:01
5	09:41	22:08	09:41	22:12	09:40	22:13	09:40	22:16	09:40	22:18	09:39	22:21	09:39	22:21	09:38	22:29
6	10:16	23:00	10:10	23:09	10:07	23:13	10:04	23:19	09:59	23:25	09:54	23:33	09:54	23:33	09:41	23:55
7	10:51	23:52	10:40		10:34		10:28		10:20		10:10		10:10		09:44	
8	11:27		11:12	00:05	11:03	00:12	10:53	00:21	10:42	00:31	10:28	00:44	10:28	00:44	09:48	01:20
9	12:05	00:43	11:46	01:01	11:35	01:11	11:22	01:23	11:07	01:37	10:49	01:54	10:49	01:54	09:54	02:46
10	12:47	01:36	12:24	01:57	12:11	02:09	11:56	02:24	11:38	02:41	11:16	03:02	11:16	03:02	10:05	04:11
11	13:32	02:28	13:07	02:53	12:53	03:07	12:36	03:23	12:16	03:43	11:50	04:08	11:50	04:08	10:25	05:32
12	14:21	03:21	13:55	03:47	13:40	04:02	13:22	04:19	13:01	04:40	12:34	05:07	12:34	05:07	11:00	06:41
13	15:14	04:12	14:48	04:38	14:33	04:53	14:16	05:10	13:55	05:31	13:29	05:58	13:29	05:58	11:57	07:30
14	16:08	05:01	15:45	05:25	15:31	05:39	15:15	05:55	14:57	06:15	14:33	06:39	14:33	06:39	13:14	07:59
15	17:03	05:47	16:44	06:08	16:32	06:20	16:19	06:34	16:03	06:51	15:44	07:11	15:44	07:11	14:42	08:15
16	*17:59*	*06:29*	*17:43*	*06:46*	*17:34*	*06:56*	*17:24*	*07:07*	*17:12*	*07:21*	*16:57*	*07:37*	*16:57*	*07:37*	*16:13*	*08:24*
17	18:53	07:08	18:43	07:21	18:37	07:28	18:30	07:36	18:22	07:46	18:12	07:57	18:12	07:57	17:44	08:30
18	19:48	07:46	19:43	07:53	19:40	07:58	19:36	08:03	19:32	08:08	19:28	08:15	19:28	08:15	19:14	08:34
19	20:42	08:22	20:43	08:24	20:43	08:26	20:43	08:27	20:43	08:29	20:44	08:31	20:44	08:31	20:45	08:37
20	21:38	08:58	21:43	08:55	21:47	08:53	21:51	08:52	21:55	08:49	22:01	08:47	22:01	08:47	22:17	08:39
21	22:35	09:36	22:46	09:27	22:53	09:23	23:01	09:17	23:09	09:11	23:20	09:03	23:20	09:03	23:52	08:42
22	23:35	10:16	23:52	10:02		09:54		09:45		09:35		09:22		09:22		08:46
23		11:01		10:42	00:01	10:31	00:13	10:19	00:26	10:04	00:42	09:46	00:42	09:46	01:32	08:53
24	00:37	11:51	00:59	11:28	01:12	11:14	01:26	10:59	01:44	10:41	02:05	10:18	02:05	10:18	03:16	09:05
25	01:42	12:47	02:07	12:21	02:22	12:06	02:39	11:49	02:59	11:28	03:25	11:01	03:25	11:01	04:56	09:30
26	02:46	13:49	03:13	13:23	03:28	13:07	03:46	12:49	04:08	12:27	04:36	12:00	04:36	12:00	06:15	10:20
27	03:48	14:54	04:13	14:29	04:28	14:15	04:45	13:58	05:06	13:38	05:32	13:12	05:32	13:12	07:02	11:45
28	04:44	15:59	05:06	15:39	05:19	15:26	05:34	15:12	05:52	14:55	06:14	14:35	06:14	14:35	07:24	13:27

Bold = new Moon, *italic* = full Moon. A gap in a column indicates the event will take place early the next day.

MOONRISE AND MOONSET, MARCH AND APRIL 2022
UNIVERSAL TIME AT GREENWICH MERIDIAN

Latitude:	+20°		+30°		+35°		+40°		+45°		+50°		+55°		+60°	
Event:	RISE	SET	RISE	SET	RISE	SET	RISE	SET	RISE	SET	RISE	SET	RISE	SET	RISE	SET
Mar. 1	05:34	17:03	05:52	16:47	06:02	16:38	06:14	16:27	06:28	16:14	06:45	15:59	06:45	15:59	07:35	15:13
2	**06:18**	**18:03**	**06:31**	**17:53**	**06:38**	**17:47**	**06:47**	**17:40**	**06:56**	**17:32**	**07:08**	**17:22**	**07:08**	**17:22**	**07:41**	**16:53**
3	06:58	19:00	07:06	18:56	07:10	18:53	07:15	18:50	07:20	18:46	07:27	18:42	07:27	18:42	07:45	18:29
4	07:36	19:55	07:37	19:56	07:38	19:56	07:40	19:57	07:41	19:57	07:43	19:58	07:43	19:58	07:48	20:00
5	08:11	20:48	08:08	20:54	08:06	20:58	08:04	21:02	08:01	21:07	07:58	21:12	07:58	21:12	07:50	21:29
6	08:46	21:41	08:38	21:52	08:33	21:59	08:27	22:06	08:21	22:15	08:14	22:25	08:14	22:25	07:52	22:56
7	09:22	22:33	09:09	22:49	09:01	22:59	08:53	23:09	08:43	23:22	08:30	23:37	08:30	23:37	07:56	
8	10:00	23:26	09:42	23:46	09:32	23:58	09:21		09:07		08:50		08:50		08:01	00:24
9	10:41		10:19		10:07		09:52	00:12	09:35	00:28	09:15	00:48	09:15	00:48	08:09	01:51
10	11:25	00:19	11:01	00:43	10:46	00:57	10:30	01:13	10:10	01:32	09:46	01:56	09:46	01:56	08:24	03:16
11	12:13	01:12	11:47	01:38	11:31	01:53	11:14	02:10	10:52	02:31	10:26	02:58	10:26	02:58	08:51	04:32
12	13:04	02:04	12:38	02:30	12:22	02:46	12:05	03:04	11:43	03:25	11:16	03:52	11:16	03:52	09:39	05:29
13	13:57	02:54	13:33	03:19	13:18	03:34	13:02	03:51	12:42	04:11	12:16	04:37	12:16	04:37	10:50	06:05
14	14:52	03:40	14:31	04:03	14:18	04:16	14:04	04:32	13:46	04:50	13:25	05:12	13:25	05:12	12:15	06:24
15	15:48	04:24	15:30	04:43	15:20	04:54	15:08	05:07	14:55	05:22	14:38	05:40	14:38	05:40	13:46	06:35
16	16:43	05:05	16:30	05:19	16:23	05:28	16:15	05:37	16:05	05:48	15:53	06:02	15:53	06:02	15:18	06:41
17	17:38	05:43	17:31	05:53	17:27	05:58	17:22	06:04	17:16	06:12	17:10	06:20	17:10	06:20	16:50	06:45
18	*18:33*	*06:20*	*18:32*	*06:24*	*18:31*	*06:27*	*18:30*	*06:30*	*18:28*	*06:33*	*18:27*	*06:37*	*18:27*	*06:37*	*18:22*	*06:47*
19	19:30	06:57	19:34	06:56	19:36	06:55	19:39	06:54	19:42	06:53	19:46	06:52	19:46	06:52	19:56	06:50
20	20:28	07:34	20:38	07:28	20:43	07:24	20:50	07:20	20:57	07:15	21:06	07:09	21:06	07:09	21:33	06:52
21	21:28	08:14	21:44	08:02	21:52	07:55	22:03	07:47	22:15	07:38	22:30	07:27	22:30	07:27	23:15	06:55
22	22:31	08:58	22:52	08:41	23:03	08:31	23:17	08:19	23:34	08:06	23:54	07:49	23:54	07:49		07:01
23	23:36	09:47		09:25		09:12		08:58		08:40		08:18		08:18	01:00	07:10
24		10:42	00:01	10:16	00:14	10:02	00:31	09:44	00:51	09:24	01:16	08:58	01:16	08:58	02:43	07:29
25	00:40	11:42	01:07	11:15	01:22	10:59	01:40	10:41	02:02	10:19	02:30	09:51	02:30	09:51	04:11	08:10
26	01:42	12:45	02:08	12:19	02:23	12:04	02:41	11:47	03:03	11:25	03:30	10:59	03:30	10:59	05:06	09:24
27	02:38	13:49	03:02	13:26	03:16	13:13	03:32	12:58	03:51	12:40	04:15	12:17	04:15	12:17	05:33	11:01
28	03:29	14:51	03:49	14:34	04:00	14:23	04:13	14:11	04:29	13:57	04:48	13:39	04:48	13:39	05:46	12:45
29	04:14	15:51	04:29	15:39	04:38	15:31	04:47	15:23	04:59	15:13	05:12	15:01	05:12	15:01	05:52	14:25
30	04:55	16:49	05:04	16:41	05:10	16:37	05:16	16:33	05:23	16:27	05:32	16:20	05:32	16:20	05:56	16:01
31	05:32	17:43	05:36	17:42	05:38	17:41	05:41	17:40	05:44	17:39	05:48	17:37	05:48	17:37	05:59	17:33
Apr. 1	**06:07**	**18:37**	**06:06**	**18:41**	**06:06**	**18:43**	**06:05**	**18:46**	**06:04**	**18:48**	**06:03**	**18:52**	**06:03**	**18:52**	**06:01**	**19:02**
2	06:42	19:30	06:36	19:39	06:32	19:44	06:28	19:50	06:24	19:57	06:18	20:06	06:18	20:06	06:02	20:30
3	07:18	20:23	07:07	20:37	07:00	20:45	06:53	20:54	06:44	21:05	06:34	21:19	06:34	21:19	06:05	21:59
4	07:18	20:23	07:39	21:35	07:30	21:45	07:19	21:58	07:07	22:13	06:52	22:31	06:52	22:31	06:09	23:28
5	07:55	21:16	08:15	22:32	08:03	22:45	07:50	23:00	07:34	23:18	07:14	23:41	07:14	23:41	06:15	
6	08:35	22:10	08:54	23:28	08:41	23:43	08:25	00:01	08:06		07:42		07:42		06:26	00:56
7	09:18	23:03	09:39		09:23		09:06		08:45	00:21	08:18	00:47	08:18	00:47	06:47	02:18
8	10:04	23:56	10:28	00:22	10:12	00:37	09:54	00:56	09:32	01:17	09:04	01:45	09:04	01:45	07:25	03:24
9	10:54		11:21	01:12	11:06	01:27	10:48	01:45	10:27	02:06	10:01	02:33	10:01	02:33	08:27	04:08
10	11:46	00:46	12:17	01:58	12:04	02:12	11:48	02:28	11:29	02:48	11:06	03:12	11:06	03:12	09:47	04:32
11	12:40	01:34	13:16	02:39	13:04	02:51	12:51	03:05	12:36	03:21	12:16	03:42	12:16	03:42	11:16	04:45
12	13:35	02:18	14:15	03:16	14:06	03:26	13:56	03:37	13:45	03:50	13:30	04:05	13:30	04:05	12:47	04:52
13	14:30	02:59	15:15	03:50	15:09	03:57	15:03	04:05	14:55	04:14	14:46	04:25	14:46	04:25	14:19	04:56
14	15:25	03:38	16:15	04:22	16:13	04:26	16:10	04:30	16:07	04:35	16:03	04:42	16:03	04:42	15:51	04:59
15	16:20	04:15	17:17	04:53	17:18	04:54	17:19	04:55	17:20	04:56	17:21	04:57	17:21	04:57	17:25	05:01
16	*17:16*	*04:52*	*18:21*	*05:25*	*18:26*	*05:23*	*18:30*	*05:20*	*18:36*	*05:17*	*18:43*	*05:13*	*18:43*	*05:13*	*19:03*	*05:03*
17	18:14	05:29	19:28	05:59	19:36	05:53	19:45	05:47	19:55	05:39	20:07	05:31	20:07	05:31	20:45	05:05
18	19:15	06:09	20:38	06:37	20:49	06:28	21:01	06:17	21:16	06:06	21:35	05:51	21:35	05:51	22:33	05:09
19	20:19	06:52	21:49	07:20	22:02	07:08	22:18	06:54	22:37	06:38	23:01	06:18	23:01	06:18		05:17
20	21:25	07:40	22:58	08:10	23:14	07:56	23:32	07:39	23:54	07:19		06:54		06:54	00:22	05:31
21	22:32	08:35		09:08		08:52		08:34		08:12	00:21	07:44	00:21	07:44	02:01	06:03
22	23:36	09:34	00:03	10:12	00:19	09:56	00:37	09:38	00:59	09:16	01:27	08:48	01:27	08:48	03:09	07:08
23		10:38	01:00	11:19	01:15	11:05	01:32	10:49	01:52	10:29	02:17	10:05	02:17	10:05	03:42	08:42
24	00:35	11:42	01:49	12:26	02:01	12:14	02:15	12:01	02:32	11:46	02:53	11:26	02:53	11:26	03:57	10:25
25	01:28	12:45	02:30	13:31	02:40	13:23	02:51	13:13	03:03	13:02	03:19	12:48	03:19	12:48	04:05	12:06
26	02:14	13:45	03:06	14:33	03:13	14:28	03:20	14:22	03:29	14:15	03:39	14:07	03:39	14:07	04:09	13:42
27	02:55	14:42	03:38	15:33	03:42	15:31	03:46	15:29	03:50	15:26	03:56	15:23	03:56	15:23	04:11	15:13
28	03:32	15:37	04:08	16:32	04:09	16:33	04:09	16:34	04:10	16:35	04:10	16:37	04:10	16:37	04:13	16:42
29	04:07	16:30	04:37	17:29	04:35	17:33	04:32	17:38	04:29	17:43	04:25	17:50	04:25	17:50	04:14	18:09
30	**04:42**	**17:22**	**05:07**	**18:26**	**05:01**	**18:33**	**04:55**	**18:42**	**04:48**	**18:51**	**04:40**	**19:03**	**04:40**	**19:03**	**04:16**	**19:36**

MOONRISE AND MOONSET, MAY AND JUNE 2022
UNIVERSAL TIME AT GREENWICH MERIDIAN

Latitude:	+20°		+30°		+35°		+40°		+45°		+50°		+55°		+60°	
Event:	**RISE**	**SET**	**RISE**	**SET**	**RISE**	**SET**	**RISE**	**SET**	**RISE**	**SET**	**RISE**	**SET**	**RISE**	**SET**	**RISE**	**SET**
May 1	05:16	18:14	05:38	19:24	05:30	19:34	05:21	19:45	05:10	19:59	04:57	20:15	04:57	20:15	04:19	21:05
2	05:52	19:07	06:12	20:22	06:02	20:34	05:49	20:48	05:35	21:05	05:17	21:26	05:17	21:26	04:24	22:34
3	06:31	20:01	06:50	21:19	06:37	21:33	06:22	21:50	06:04	22:10	05:42	22:35	05:42	22:35	04:32	00:01
4	07:13	20:55	07:33	22:14	07:18	22:29	07:01	22:47	06:41	23:09	06:15	23:36	06:15	23:36	04:48	
5	07:58	21:48	08:20	23:06	08:04	23:21	07:46	23:39	07:25		06:57		06:57		05:18	01:15
6	08:46	22:39	09:12	23:53	08:56		08:38		08:17	00:01	07:49	00:29	07:49	00:29	06:11	02:08
7	09:38	23:28	10:06		09:52	00:07	09:36	00:25	09:16	00:45	08:51	01:11	08:51	01:11	07:25	02:38
8	10:31		11:03	00:35	10:51	00:48	10:37	01:03	10:20	01:21	09:58	01:43	09:58	01:43	08:50	02:54
9	11:24	00:13	12:01	01:13	11:51	01:24	11:40	01:36	11:26	01:51	11:10	02:09	11:10	02:09	10:19	03:02
10	12:18	00:54	13:00	01:48	12:52	01:56	12:44	02:05	12:35	02:16	12:23	02:29	12:23	02:29	11:49	03:07
11	13:12	01:33	13:59	02:20	13:55	02:25	13:50	02:31	13:45	02:38	13:38	02:46	13:38	02:46	13:19	03:10
12	14:06	02:10	14:59	02:50	14:58	02:53	14:57	02:55	14:56	02:58	14:54	03:02	14:54	03:02	14:51	03:12
13	15:00	02:46	16:01	03:21	16:04	03:20	16:06	03:19	16:10	03:18	16:14	03:17	16:14	03:17	16:25	03:14
14	15:57	03:22	17:06	03:54	17:12	03:50	17:19	03:45	17:27	03:40	17:37	03:34	17:37	03:34	18:05	03:16
15	16:56	04:01	18:15	04:29	18:25	04:22	18:36	04:14	18:48	04:04	19:04	03:52	19:04	03:52	19:52	03:19
16	*17:59*	*04:42*	*19:28*	*05:10*	*19:40*	*05:00*	*19:55*	*04:48*	*20:12*	*04:33*	*20:34*	*04:16*	*20:34*	*04:16*	*21:44*	*03:24*
17	19:06	05:28	20:41	05:58	20:56	05:45	21:13	05:29	21:34	05:11	22:00	04:48	22:00	04:48	23:34	03:35
18	20:15	06:21	21:50	06:55	22:06	06:39	22:25	06:21	22:47	06:00	23:15	05:33	23:15	05:33		03:58
19	21:23	07:21	22:53	07:58	23:08	07:43	23:26	07:24	23:47	07:02		06:33		06:33	01:00	04:49
20	22:27	08:25	23:46	09:07	23:59	08:52		08:35		08:15	00:13	07:49	00:13	07:49	01:46	06:18
21	23:23	09:32		10:17		10:04	00:14	09:50	00:32	09:33	00:55	09:12	00:55	09:12	02:06	08:03
22		10:38	00:31	11:24	00:41	11:14	00:53	11:04	01:07	10:51	01:24	10:35	01:24	10:35	02:16	09:48
23	00:12	11:40	01:08	12:28	01:16	12:21	01:24	12:14	01:34	12:06	01:46	11:56	01:46	11:56	02:20	11:26
24	00:55	12:38	01:42	13:28	01:46	13:25	01:51	13:22	01:57	13:18	02:04	13:13	02:04	13:13	02:23	12:59
25	01:34	13:33	02:12	14:26	02:13	14:26	02:15	14:26	02:17	14:27	02:19	14:27	02:19	14:27	02:25	14:27
26	02:09	14:26	02:41	15:23	02:39	15:26	02:37	15:30	02:35	15:34	02:33	15:39	02:33	15:39	02:26	15:53
27	02:43	15:18	03:10	16:20	03:05	16:26	03:00	16:33	02:54	16:41	02:47	16:51	02:47	16:51	02:28	17:20
28	03:17	16:09	03:40	17:17	03:33	17:26	03:24	17:36	03:15	17:48	03:03	18:03	03:03	18:03	02:30	18:47
29	03:53	17:01	04:13	18:14	04:03	18:26	03:51	18:39	03:38	18:55	03:22	19:14	03:22	19:14	02:34	20:16
30	**04:30**	**17:54**	**04:49**	**19:11**	**04:37**	**19:25**	**04:22**	**19:41**	**04:06**	**20:00**	**03:45**	**20:23**	**03:45**	**20:23**	**02:41**	**21:43**
31	05:10	18:48	05:30	20:07	05:15	20:22	04:59	20:40	04:39	21:01	04:15	21:28	04:15	21:28	02:54	23:02
Jun. 1	05:54	19:41	06:15	21:00	06:00	21:16	05:42	21:34	05:21	21:56	04:53	22:23	04:53	22:23	03:18	
2	06:41	20:34	07:05	21:49	06:50	22:04	06:32	22:21	06:10	22:43	05:42	23:09	05:42	23:09	04:02	00:04
3	07:32	21:23	07:59	22:33	07:44	22:47	07:27	23:02	07:06	23:21	06:40	23:45	06:40	23:45	05:09	00:41
4	08:24	22:09	08:55	23:12	08:42	23:24	08:27	23:37	08:09	23:53	07:46		07:46		06:31	01:01
5	09:17	22:52	09:52	23:47	09:41	23:56	09:29		09:14		08:56	00:12	08:56	00:12	07:59	01:12
6	10:11	23:31	10:49		10:41		10:32	00:07	10:20	00:19	10:07	00:34	10:07	00:34	09:27	01:17
7	11:03		11:46	00:19	11:41	00:26	11:35	00:33	11:28	00:42	11:19	00:52	11:19	00:52	10:55	01:21
8	11:56	00:08	12:44	00:49	12:42	00:53	12:39	00:57	12:36	01:02	12:33	01:07	12:33	01:07	12:23	01:23
9	12:48	00:43	13:44	01:19	13:45	01:20	13:46	01:20	13:47	01:21	13:48	01:22	13:48	01:22	13:53	01:25
10	13:42	01:18	14:46	01:50	14:50	01:47	14:55	01:44	15:01	01:41	15:07	01:37	15:07	01:37	15:27	01:27
11	14:38	01:54	15:52	02:23	15:59	02:17	16:08	02:10	16:18	02:03	16:31	01:54	16:31	01:54	17:08	01:29
12	15:38	02:33	17:02	03:00	17:13	02:51	17:25	02:41	17:40	02:29	17:59	02:15	17:59	02:15	18:57	01:33
13	16:43	03:16	18:15	03:44	18:29	03:32	18:45	03:18	19:04	03:02	19:28	02:42	19:28	02:42	20:50	01:40
14	*17:51*	*04:05*	*19:28*	*04:36*	*19:43*	*04:22*	*20:02*	*04:05*	*20:23*	*03:45*	*20:51*	*03:20*	*20:51*	*03:20*	*22:33*	*01:56*
15	19:01	05:01	20:36	05:38	20:52	05:22	21:10	05:04	21:32	04:42	22:00	04:13	22:00	04:13	23:40	02:31
16	20:09	06:05	21:35	06:47	21:50	06:32	22:06	06:14	22:26	05:52	22:50	05:24	22:50	05:24		03:45
17	21:11	07:13	22:25	07:59	22:37	07:46	22:50	07:30	23:06	07:11	23:25	06:48	23:25	06:48	00:11	05:30
18	22:05	08:22	23:07	09:10	23:16	08:59	23:25	08:47	23:37	08:33	23:51	08:15	23:51	08:15	00:24	07:20
19	22:52	09:28	23:43	10:17	23:48	10:10	23:54	10:02		09:52		09:40		09:40	00:31	09:04
20	23:33	10:30		11:21		11:17		11:12	00:01	11:07	00:10	11:00	00:10	11:00	00:34	10:41
21		11:28	00:14	12:21	00:17	12:20	00:19	12:19	00:22	12:18	00:26	12:16	00:26	12:16	00:36	12:12
22	00:10	12:22	00:44	13:18	00:43	13:21	00:43	13:23	00:42	13:26	00:41	13:30	00:41	13:30	00:38	13:40
23	00:45	13:14	01:13	14:15	01:09	14:20	01:05	14:26	01:01	14:33	00:55	14:42	00:55	14:42	00:39	15:06
24	01:19	14:06	01:43	15:12	01:36	15:20	01:29	15:29	01:20	15:40	01:10	15:53	01:10	15:53	00:42	16:33
25	01:54	14:58	02:14	16:09	02:05	16:19	01:55	16:32	01:43	16:46	01:28	17:04	01:28	17:04	00:45	18:00
26	02:30	15:50	02:49	17:05	02:38	17:19	02:24	17:34	02:09	17:52	01:50	18:14	01:50	18:14	00:51	19:28
27	03:09	16:43	03:28	18:02	03:15	18:16	02:59	18:33	02:40	18:54	02:17	19:20	02:17	19:20	01:01	20:50
28	03:52	17:37	04:12	18:56	03:57	19:11	03:40	19:29	03:19	19:51	02:52	20:18	02:52	20:18	01:21	21:58
29	**04:38**	**18:29**	**05:01**	**19:46**	**04:46**	**20:01**	**04:27**	**20:19**	**04:06**	**20:40**	**03:38**	**21:07**	**03:38**	**21:07**	**01:58**	**22:43**
30	05:28	19:20	05:54	20:31	05:39	20:45	05:21	21:02	05:00	21:21	04:33	21:46	04:33	21:46	02:59	23:07

Bold = new Moon, *italic* = full Moon. A gap in a column indicates the event will take place early the next day.

MOONRISE AND MOONSET, JULY AND AUGUST 2022

UNIVERSAL TIME AT GREENWICH MERIDIAN

Latitude:	**+20°**		**+30°**		**+35°**		**+40°**		**+45°**		**+50°**		**+55°**		**+60°**	
Event:	**RISE**	**SET**	**RISE**	**SET**	**RISE**	**SET**	**RISE**	**SET**	**RISE**	**SET**	**RISE**	**SET**	**RISE**	**SET**	**RISE**	**SET**
Jul. 1	06:20	20:07	06:49	21:12	06:36	21:24	06:20	21:38	06:01	21:55	05:37	22:16	05:37	22:16	04:17	23:20
2	07:13	20:51	07:46	21:48	07:35	21:58	07:21	22:09	07:05	22:23	06:46	22:39	06:46	22:39	05:44	23:27
3	08:06	21:31	08:43	22:21	08:34	22:28	08:24	22:36	08:11	22:46	07:56	22:58	07:56	22:58	07:12	23:31
4	08:58	22:08	09:39	22:51	09:33	22:55	09:26	23:00	09:18	23:06	09:08	23:14	09:08	23:14	08:38	23:34
5	09:50	22:43	10:36	23:20	10:33	23:21	10:29	23:23	10:25	23:26	10:19	23:28	10:19	23:28	10:04	23:35
6	10:42	23:17	11:33	23:49	11:33	23:48	11:33	23:46	11:32	23:45	11:32	23:42	11:32	23:42	11:31	23:37
7	11:34	23:51	12:32		12:35		12:38		12:42		12:47	23:58	12:47	23:58	13:01	23:39
8	12:27		13:34	00:20	13:40	00:15	13:47	00:10	13:56	00:05	14:06		14:06		14:35	23:42
9	13:23	00:27	14:40	00:54	14:50	00:46	15:00	00:38	15:13	00:28	15:29	00:16	15:29	00:16	16:17	23:47
10	14:24	01:07	15:50	01:33	16:02	01:23	16:17	01:10	16:34	00:56	16:56	00:39	16:56	00:39	18:06	23:57
11	15:29	01:52	17:02	02:20	17:17	02:07	17:34	01:51	17:55	01:33	18:22	01:10	18:22	01:10	19:55	
12	16:37	02:43	18:13	03:16	18:29	03:01	18:47	02:43	19:09	02:22	19:38	01:55	19:38	01:55	21:22	00:20
13	*17:46*	*03:43*	*19:17*	*04:22*	*19:32*	*04:06*	*19:50*	*03:48*	*20:11*	*03:25*	*20:38*	*02:57*	*20:38*	*02:57*	*22:09*	*01:13*
14	18:51	04:49	20:13	05:34	20:26	05:19	20:41	05:02	20:58	04:42	21:20	04:16	21:20	04:16	22:29	02:47
15	19:51	05:59	20:59	06:48	21:09	06:36	21:21	06:22	21:34	06:05	21:51	05:45	21:51	05:45	22:39	04:39
16	20:42	07:08	21:39	07:59	21:46	07:50	21:53	07:40	22:02	07:28	22:13	07:14	22:13	07:14	22:43	06:30
17	21:27	08:14	22:13	09:06	22:17	09:01	22:21	08:55	22:25	08:48	22:31	08:39	22:31	08:39	22:46	08:13
18	22:07	09:15	22:44	10:10	22:45	10:08	22:45	10:05	22:46	10:03	22:46	09:59	22:46	09:59	22:48	09:50
19	22:44	10:13	23:14	11:10	23:12	11:11	23:09	11:12	23:05	11:14	23:01	11:16	23:01	11:16	22:50	11:21
20	23:19	11:08	23:44	12:08	23:39	12:12	23:32	12:17	23:25	12:23	23:16	12:30	23:16	12:30	22:52	12:50
21	23:54	12:01		13:06		13:13	23:58	13:21	23:47	13:31	23:33	13:43	23:33	13:43	22:54	14:18
22		12:53	00:16	14:03	00:07	14:13		14:24		14:38	23:54	14:55	23:54	14:55	22:59	15:46
23	00:30	13:46	00:50	15:00	00:39	15:12	00:26	15:27	00:11	15:44		16:05		16:05	23:08	17:14
24	01:09	14:39	01:27	15:56	01:14	16:11	00:59	16:27	00:41	16:47	00:19	17:13	00:19	17:13	23:24	18:39
25	01:50	15:32	02:10	16:51	01:55	17:07	01:38	17:24	01:17	17:46	00:52	18:14	00:52	18:14	23:55	19:52
26	02:35	16:25	02:57	17:43	02:42	17:58	02:23	18:16	02:02	18:38	01:34	19:05	01:34	19:05		20:44
27	03:24	17:16	03:49	18:30	03:34	18:44	03:16	19:01	02:54	19:21	02:27	19:47	02:27	19:47	00:49	21:13
28	**04:15**	**18:05**	**04:44**	**19:12**	**04:30**	**19:25**	**04:13**	**19:40**	**03:53**	**19:57**	**03:29**	**20:19**	**03:29**	**20:19**	**02:04**	**21:29**
29	05:08	18:49	05:41	19:49	05:28	20:00	05:14	20:12	04:57	20:27	04:37	20:44	04:37	20:44	03:29	21:37
30	06:02	19:31	06:38	20:23	06:28	20:31	06:17	20:40	06:04	20:51	05:47	21:04	05:47	21:04	04:58	21:41
31	06:55	20:09	07:35	20:54	07:28	20:59	07:20	21:05	07:10	21:12	06:59	21:20	06:59	21:20	06:25	21:44
Aug. 1	07:47	20:44	08:31	21:23	08:27	21:25	08:22	21:28	08:17	21:31	08:10	21:35	08:10	21:35	07:52	21:46
2	08:38	21:18	09:28	21:51	09:27	21:51	09:25	21:50	09:24	21:50	09:22	21:49	09:22	21:49	09:18	21:47
3	09:30	21:52	10:25	22:21	10:27	22:17	10:30	22:13	10:32	22:09	10:36	22:04	10:36	22:04	10:45	21:49
4	10:22	22:27	11:25	22:53	11:30	22:46	11:36	22:39	11:43	22:30	11:51	22:20	11:51	22:20	12:16	21:51
5	11:16	23:04	12:27	23:29	12:36	23:19	12:45	23:08	12:57	22:55	13:11	22:40	13:11	22:40	13:52	21:55
6	12:13	23:45	13:34		13:45	23:58	13:58	23:44	14:14	23:27	14:34	23:06	14:34	23:06	15:35	22:02
7	13:14		14:43	00:11	14:57		15:13		15:33		15:58	23:43	15:58	23:43	17:22	22:17
8	14:19	00:32	15:52	01:01	16:08	00:46	16:26	00:29	16:48	00:09	17:16		17:16		18:59	22:52
9	15:26	01:26	16:58	02:01	17:14	01:45	17:32	01:26	17:54	01:04	18:22	00:36	18:22	00:36	20:03	
10	16:31	02:28	17:57	03:09	18:12	02:53	18:28	02:35	18:48	02:14	19:12	01:46	19:12	01:46	20:33	00:06
11	17:33	03:35	18:48	04:21	19:00	04:08	19:13	03:52	19:28	03:34	19:48	03:10	19:48	03:10	20:46	01:52
12	*18:28*	*04:44*	*19:31*	*05:34*	*19:39*	*05:24*	*19:49*	*05:12*	*20:00*	*04:58*	*20:13*	*04:40*	*20:13*	*04:40*	*20:52*	*03:46*
13	19:16	05:52	20:08	06:45	20:13	06:38	20:19	06:30	20:25	06:20	20:33	06:09	20:33	06:09	20:56	05:35
14	19:59	06:57	20:41	07:52	20:43	07:48	20:45	07:44	20:47	07:39	20:50	07:34	20:50	07:34	20:58	07:17
15	20:38	07:58	21:13	08:55	21:11	08:55	21:09	08:55	21:08	08:54	21:05	08:54	21:05	08:54	20:59	08:53
16	21:15	08:55	21:43	09:56	21:39	09:59	21:33	10:02	21:28	10:07	21:21	10:12	21:21	10:12	21:01	10:26
17	21:51	09:50	22:15	10:55	22:07	11:01	21:59	11:09	21:49	11:17	21:37	11:27	21:37	11:27	21:03	11:57
18	22:28	10:44	22:48	11:54	22:38	12:03	22:26	12:14	22:13	12:26	21:56	12:41	21:56	12:41	21:07	13:27
19	23:06	11:38	23:25	12:52	23:12	13:04	22:58	13:18	22:41	13:34	22:20	13:54	22:20	13:54	21:14	14:57
20	23:47	12:32		13:50	23:52	14:04	23:35	14:20	23:15	14:39	22:50	15:03	22:50	15:03	21:26	16:25
21		13:26	00:06	14:45		15:01		15:18	23:57	15:40	23:29	16:07	23:29	16:07	21:51	17:44
22	00:31	14:19	00:52	15:38	00:36	15:54	00:18	16:12		16:34		17:02		17:02	22:37	18:44
23	01:18	15:11	01:43	16:27	01:27	16:42	01:09	16:59	00:47	17:20	00:19	17:47	00:19	17:47	23:47	19:19
24	02:09	16:01	02:37	17:10	02:22	17:24	02:05	17:40	01:44	17:59	01:18	18:22	01:18	18:22		19:38
25	03:02	16:47	03:33	17:49	03:20	18:01	03:05	18:14	02:47	18:30	02:25	18:49	02:25	18:49	01:11	19:47
26	03:56	17:29	04:31	18:24	04:20	18:33	04:08	18:44	03:53	18:56	03:36	19:10	03:36	19:10	02:40	19:52
27	**04:49**	**18:09**	**05:29**	**18:56**	**05:21**	**19:02**	**05:11**	**19:09**	**05:01**	**19:18**	**04:48**	**19:27**	**04:48**	**19:27**	**04:09**	**19:55**
28	05:42	18:45	06:26	19:26	06:21	19:29	06:15	19:33	06:08	19:37	06:00	19:42	06:00	19:42	05:37	19:57
29	06:34	19:20	07:23	19:55	07:21	19:55	07:19	19:55	07:16	19:56	07:13	19:56	07:13	19:56	07:04	19:58
30	07:26	19:54	08:21	20:24	08:22	20:21	08:23	20:18	08:25	20:15	08:26	20:11	08:26	20:11	08:32	19:59
31	08:19	20:28	09:20	20:55	09:24	20:49	09:29	20:42	09:35	20:35	09:42	20:26	09:42	20:26	10:02	20:01

MOONRISE AND MOONSET, SEPTEMBER AND OCTOBER 2022
UNIVERSAL TIME AT GREENWICH MERIDIAN

Latitude:	+20°		+30°		+35°		+40°		+45°		+50°		+55°		+60°	
Event:	RISE	SET	RISE	SET	RISE	SET	RISE	SET	RISE	SET	RISE	SET	RISE	SET	RISE	SET
Sep. 1	09:12	21:04	10:21	21:29	10:29	21:20	10:37	21:10	10:47	20:58	11:00	20:44	11:00	20:44	11:36	20:03
2	10:08	21:44	11:25	22:08	11:36	21:56	11:48	21:43	12:03	21:27	12:21	21:08	12:21	21:08	13:17	20:09
3	11:07	22:28	12:32	22:54	12:46	22:40	13:01	22:24	13:20	22:04	13:43	21:40	13:43	21:40	15:01	20:19
4	12:09	23:18	13:40	23:49	13:55	23:33	14:13	23:15	14:35	22:53	15:02	22:25	15:02	22:25	16:42	20:44
5	13:14		14:45		15:01		15:20		15:43	23:55	16:12	23:26	16:12	23:26	17:58	21:40
6	14:18	00:16	15:45	00:52	16:01	00:36	16:18	00:17	16:39		17:06		17:06		18:37	23:13
7	15:20	01:19	16:38	02:01	16:51	01:46	17:06	01:29	17:24	01:09	17:45	00:43	17:45	00:43	18:54	
8	16:16	02:25	17:23	03:12	17:33	03:00	17:45	02:46	17:58	02:30	18:14	02:09	18:14	02:09	19:02	01:03
9	17:06	03:33	18:02	04:23	18:09	04:14	18:16	04:04	18:25	03:52	18:36	03:38	18:36	03:38	19:06	02:54
10	*17:51*	*04:38*	*18:37*	*05:31*	*18:40*	*05:25*	*18:44*	*05:19*	*18:48*	*05:12*	*18:53*	*05:04*	*18:53*	*05:04*	*19:08*	*04:39*
11	18:31	05:40	19:09	06:36	19:09	06:34	19:09	06:32	19:09	06:30	19:09	06:27	19:09	06:27	19:09	06:19
12	19:09	06:39	19:40	07:39	19:37	07:40	19:33	07:42	19:29	07:44	19:24	07:47	19:24	07:47	19:11	07:54
13	19:45	07:36	20:11	08:40	20:05	08:45	19:58	08:50	19:50	08:57	19:40	09:05	19:40	09:05	19:12	09:28
14	20:22	08:31	20:45	09:40	20:35	09:48	20:25	09:58	20:13	10:08	19:58	10:22	19:58	10:22	19:15	11:01
15	21:00	09:26	21:21	10:40	21:09	10:51	20:55	11:04	20:39	11:18	20:20	11:37	20:20	11:37	19:20	12:34
16	21:41	10:21	22:01	11:39	21:47	11:53	21:31	12:08	21:11	12:26	20:48	12:49	20:48	12:49	19:29	14:05
17	22:24	11:17	22:45	12:37	22:30	12:52	22:12	13:09	21:50	13:30	21:23	13:57	21:23	13:57	19:48	15:31
18	23:11	12:11	23:34	13:31	23:18	13:47	23:00	14:05	22:37	14:28	22:09	14:56	22:09	14:56	20:25	16:40
19		13:04		14:22		14:37	23:54	14:55	23:33	15:17	23:05	15:45	23:05	15:45	21:27	17:24
20	00:01	13:55	00:27	15:07	00:12	15:22		15:38		15:58		16:23		16:23	22:48	17:47
21	00:53	14:42	01:23	15:48	01:09	16:00	00:53	16:15	00:34	16:32	00:10	16:53	00:10	16:53		17:58
22	01:47	15:26	02:21	16:24	02:09	16:34	01:55	16:45	01:39	16:59	01:19	17:15	01:19	17:15	00:16	18:04
23	02:41	16:06	03:19	16:57	03:09	17:04	02:59	17:12	02:47	17:22	02:32	17:34	02:32	17:34	01:47	18:07
24	03:34	16:44	04:16	17:27	04:10	17:32	04:03	17:37	03:55	17:42	03:45	17:49	03:45	17:49	03:16	18:09
25	**04:27**	**17:19**	**05:14**	**17:56**	**05:11**	**17:58**	**05:07**	**17:59**	**05:03**	**18:01**	**04:58**	**18:04**	**04:58**	**18:04**	**04:44**	**18:10**
26	05:19	17:54	06:12	18:26	06:12	18:24	06:12	18:22	06:13	18:20	06:13	18:18	06:13	18:18	06:13	18:11
27	06:12	18:28	07:12	18:56	07:15	18:51	07:19	18:46	07:23	18:40	07:29	18:32	07:29	18:32	07:44	18:12
28	07:06	19:04	08:14	19:30	08:20	19:22	08:28	19:13	08:37	19:02	08:48	18:50	08:48	18:50	09:19	18:14
29	08:02	19:43	09:18	20:07	09:28	19:57	09:39	19:44	09:53	19:29	10:09	19:11	10:09	19:11	10:59	18:17
30	09:01	20:26	10:25	20:52	10:38	20:38	10:53	20:22	11:10	20:04	11:32	19:40	11:32	19:40	12:45	18:25
Oct. 1	10:03	21:15	11:33	21:43	11:48	21:28	12:05	21:10	12:27	20:48	12:53	20:21	12:53	20:21	14:29	18:43
2	11:07	22:10	12:39	22:43	12:55	22:27	13:14	22:08	13:37	21:45	14:06	21:16	14:06	21:16	15:55	19:26
3	12:11	23:10	13:40	23:49	13:55	23:34	14:14	23:16	14:36	22:54	15:04	22:27	15:04	22:27	16:43	20:48
4	13:13		14:33		14:47		15:03		15:22		15:46	23:49	15:46	23:49	17:04	22:33
5	14:09	00:15	15:19	00:58	15:31	00:45	15:43	00:30	15:59	00:11	16:17		16:17		17:13	
6	15:00	01:20	15:59	02:07	16:07	01:57	16:16	01:45	16:27	01:31	16:40	01:14	16:40	01:14	17:17	00:22
7	15:45	02:24	16:34	03:14	16:39	03:07	16:45	03:00	16:51	02:51	16:58	02:40	16:58	02:40	17:20	02:07
8	16:26	03:26	17:06	04:19	17:08	04:16	17:10	04:12	17:12	04:07	17:14	04:02	17:14	04:02	17:21	03:47
9	*17:04*	*04:25*	*17:37*	*05:22*	*17:36*	*05:22*	*17:34*	*05:22*	*17:32*	*05:22*	*17:29*	*05:22*	*17:29*	*05:22*	*17:22*	*05:23*
10	17:40	05:22	18:08	06:23	18:03	06:27	17:58	06:31	17:52	06:35	17:44	06:41	17:44	06:41	17:23	06:57
11	18:17	06:17	18:41	07:24	18:33	07:31	18:24	07:39	18:13	07:48	18:01	07:58	18:01	07:58	17:25	08:30
12	18:54	07:13	19:16	08:25	19:05	08:35	18:53	08:46	18:38	08:59	18:21	09:15	18:21	09:15	17:28	10:04
13	19:34	08:09	19:54	09:26	19:41	09:38	19:26	09:52	19:08	10:09	18:46	10:31	18:46	10:31	17:35	11:39
14	20:17	09:04	20:37	10:25	20:22	10:39	20:05	10:56	19:44	11:16	19:18	11:42	19:18	11:42	17:48	13:10
15	21:03	10:00	21:25	11:21	21:09	11:37	20:51	11:56	20:28	12:18	20:00	12:46	20:00	12:46	18:16	14:30
16	21:52	10:55	22:17	12:14	22:01	12:30	21:43	12:49	21:20	13:11	20:52	13:40	20:52	13:40	19:07	15:25
17	22:44	11:47	23:12	13:02	22:57	13:17	22:40	13:35	22:20	13:56	21:54	14:22	21:54	14:22	20:23	15:54
18	23:37	12:36		13:44	23:56	13:58	23:41	14:13	23:23	14:32	23:01	14:55	23:01	14:55	21:50	16:08
19		13:21	00:09	14:22		14:33		14:46		15:01		15:19		15:19	23:19	16:15
20	00:30	14:02	01:06	14:55	00:56	15:04	00:44	15:14	00:30	15:25	00:12	15:39	00:12	15:39		16:19
21	01:24	14:40	02:03	15:26	01:56	15:32	01:47	15:39	01:37	15:46	01:25	15:55	01:25	15:55	00:49	16:21
22	02:16	15:16	03:01	15:56	02:56	15:59	02:51	16:02	02:45	16:05	02:38	16:10	02:38	16:10	02:17	16:22
23	03:09	15:51	03:59	16:25	03:58	16:25	03:56	16:24	03:54	16:24	03:52	16:24	03:52	16:24	03:46	16:22
24	04:01	16:25	04:58	16:55	05:00	16:52	05:03	16:48	05:05	16:43	05:08	16:38	05:08	16:38	05:17	16:23
25	**04:55**	**17:01**	**06:00**	**17:28**	**06:06**	**17:21**	**06:12**	**17:14**	**06:19**	**17:05**	**06:27**	**16:54**	**06:27**	**16:54**	**06:52**	**16:25**
26	05:51	17:39	07:05	18:05	07:14	17:55	07:24	17:44	07:35	17:30	07:50	17:15	07:50	17:15	08:33	16:27
27	06:50	18:22	08:13	18:47	08:25	18:35	08:39	18:20	08:55	18:02	09:15	17:41	09:15	17:41	10:20	16:33
28	07:53	19:09	09:23	19:38	09:37	19:23	09:54	19:05	10:14	18:44	10:40	18:18	10:40	18:18	12:09	16:47
29	08:58	20:03	10:31	20:36	10:47	20:20	11:06	20:01	11:29	19:38	11:58	19:09	11:58	19:09	13:46	17:20
30	10:04	21:04	11:35	21:41	11:51	21:25	12:10	21:07	12:32	20:45	13:01	20:16	13:01	20:16	14:47	18:31
31	11:08	22:08	12:31	22:50	12:46	22:36	13:03	22:19	13:23	22:00	13:48	21:36	13:48	21:36	15:14	20:12

Bold = new Moon, *italic* = full Moon. A gap in a column indicates the event will take place early the next day.

MOONRISE AND MOONSET, NOVEMBER AND DECEMBER 2022

UNIVERSAL TIME AT GREENWICH MERIDIAN

Latitude:	+20°		+30°		+35°		+40°		+45°		+50°		+55°		+60°	
Event:	RISE	SET	RISE	SET	RISE	SET	RISE	SET	RISE	SET	RISE	SET	RISE	SET	RISE	SET
Nov. 1	12:06	23:13	13:19	23:58	13:31	23:47	13:45	23:34	14:02	23:19	14:22	23:00	14:22	23:00	15:25	22:01
2	12:58		14:00		14:09		14:19		14:32		14:46		14:46		15:30	23:45
3	13:44	00:17	14:35	01:05	14:41	00:57	14:48	00:48	14:56	00:37	15:05	00:24	15:05	00:24	15:32	
4	14:25	01:18	15:07	02:09	15:10	02:04	15:13	01:59	15:17	01:53	15:21	01:46	15:21	01:46	15:33	01:24
5	15:03	02:17	15:38	03:11	15:37	03:09	15:37	03:08	15:36	03:07	15:36	03:05	15:36	03:05	15:34	02:59
6	15:39	03:13	16:08	04:11	16:04	04:13	16:00	04:16	15:56	04:18	15:50	04:22	15:50	04:22	15:35	04:31
7	16:14	04:08	16:39	05:11	16:32	05:17	16:25	05:23	16:16	05:30	16:06	05:38	16:06	05:38	15:36	06:03
8	*16:51*	*05:02*	*17:12*	*06:11*	*17:03*	*06:20*	*16:52*	*06:30*	*16:39*	*06:41*	*16:24*	*06:55*	*16:24*	*06:55*	*15:39*	*07:36*
9	17:29	05:57	17:49	07:12	17:37	07:23	17:23	07:36	17:07	07:52	16:46	08:11	16:46	08:11	15:43	09:11
10	18:10	06:53	18:31	08:12	18:16	08:26	18:00	08:42	17:40	09:01	17:15	09:25	17:15	09:25	15:53	10:45
11	18:55	07:49	19:17	09:10	19:01	09:26	18:43	09:44	18:21	10:05	17:53	10:33	17:53	10:33	16:13	12:11
12	19:43	08:44	20:07	10:05	19:51	10:21	19:33	10:40	19:10	11:03	18:41	11:31	18:41	11:31	16:54	13:18
13	20:34	09:38	21:01	10:55	20:46	11:11	20:28	11:29	20:07	11:51	19:40	12:18	19:40	12:18	18:02	13:57
14	21:27	10:29	21:57	11:40	21:44	11:54	21:28	12:10	21:09	12:30	20:45	12:55	20:45	12:55	19:25	14:16
15	22:21	11:15	22:54	12:19	22:43	12:31	22:29	12:45	22:14	13:02	21:55	13:22	21:55	13:22	20:54	14:26
16	23:14	11:58	23:51	12:54	23:42	13:03	23:32	13:15	23:20	13:28	23:06	13:43	23:06	13:43	22:22	14:30
17		12:37		13:25		13:32		13:40		13:49		14:01		14:01	23:50	14:32
18	00:06	13:13	00:47	13:55	00:41	13:59	00:34	14:03	00:27	14:09	00:17	14:15	00:17	14:15		14:34
19	00:57	13:47	01:44	14:23	01:41	14:24	01:38	14:26	01:34	14:27	01:29	14:29	01:29	14:29	01:16	14:34
20	01:49	14:21	02:41	14:52	02:42	14:50	02:42	14:48	02:43	14:46	02:43	14:43	02:43	14:43	02:45	14:35
21	02:41	14:55	03:42	15:23	03:45	15:18	03:49	15:13	03:54	15:06	04:00	14:58	04:00	14:58	04:17	14:36
22	03:35	15:32	04:45	15:58	04:52	15:50	05:00	15:40	05:09	15:29	05:21	15:16	05:21	15:16	05:55	14:38
23	**04:33**	**16:13**	**05:52**	**16:39**	**06:03**	**16:27**	**06:15**	**16:14**	**06:29**	**15:58**	**06:46**	**15:40**	**06:46**	**15:40**	**07:40**	**14:42**
24	05:35	16:58	07:03	17:27	07:17	17:12	07:32	16:56	07:51	16:36	08:14	16:12	08:14	16:12	09:32	14:52
25	06:40	17:51	08:15	18:24	08:30	18:08	08:49	17:49	09:10	17:27	09:38	16:58	09:38	16:58	11:20	15:15
26	07:48	18:51	09:23	19:29	09:39	19:12	09:58	18:53	10:21	18:31	10:51	18:01	10:51	18:01	12:41	16:12
27	08:56	19:56	10:24	20:38	10:40	20:24	10:57	20:07	11:19	19:46	11:46	19:20	11:46	19:20	13:19	17:48
28	09:58	21:03	11:17	21:49	11:30	21:37	11:45	21:23	12:02	21:06	12:24	20:46	12:24	20:46	13:34	19:39
29	10:54	22:10	12:00	22:58	12:10	22:49	12:22	22:38	12:35	22:26	12:52	22:12	12:52	22:12	13:41	21:27
30	11:43	23:13	12:38		12:45	23:57	12:52	23:51	13:01	23:43	13:12	23:34	13:12	23:34	13:44	23:08
Dec. 1	12:26		13:10	00:03	13:14		13:18		13:23		13:29		13:29		13:45	
2	13:04	00:12	13:41	01:05	13:41	01:03	13:42	01:00	13:43	00:57	13:44	00:54	13:44	00:54	13:46	00:43
3	13:40	01:09	14:10	02:05	14:08	02:06	14:05	02:07	14:02	02:08	13:58	02:10	13:58	02:10	13:47	02:15
4	14:15	02:03	14:40	03:04	14:35	03:08	14:28	03:13	14:21	03:19	14:12	03:25	14:12	03:25	13:48	03:45
5	14:50	02:56	15:12	04:03	15:04	04:10	14:54	04:19	14:43	04:28	14:29	04:41	14:29	04:41	13:50	05:16
6	15:27	03:50	15:47	05:02	15:36	05:12	15:23	05:24	15:08	05:38	14:50	05:56	14:50	05:56	13:54	06:49
7	16:07	04:45	16:27	06:02	16:13	06:15	15:57	06:30	15:39	06:47	15:16	07:09	15:16	07:09	14:01	08:22
8	*16:50*	*05:40*	*17:11*	*07:01*	*16:56*	*07:15*	*16:38*	*07:33*	*16:17*	*07:53*	*15:50*	*08:20*	*15:50*	*08:20*	*14:17*	*09:51*
9	17:37	06:35	18:00	07:57	17:44	08:13	17:25	08:31	17:03	08:53	16:34	09:22	16:34	09:22	14:49	11:07
10	18:27	07:30	18:53	08:49	18:37	09:05	18:19	09:23	17:57	09:45	17:29	10:14	17:29	10:14	15:47	11:56
11	19:19	08:22	19:48	09:35	19:34	09:50	19:17	10:07	18:57	10:28	18:32	10:54	18:32	10:54	17:06	12:22
12	20:13	09:10	20:45	10:16	20:32	10:29	20:18	10:44	20:01	11:02	19:41	11:24	19:41	11:24	18:33	12:34
13	21:06	09:54	21:41	10:53	21:31	11:03	21:20	11:15	21:07	11:30	20:51	11:47	20:51	11:47	20:01	12:40
14	21:58	10:34	22:36	11:25	22:29	11:33	22:21	11:42	22:12	11:53	22:01	12:06	22:01	12:06	21:28	12:43
15	22:49	11:11	23:32	11:54	23:28	12:00	23:23	12:06	23:18	12:13	23:11	12:21	23:11	12:21	22:52	12:44
16	23:39	11:45		12:22		12:25		12:28		12:31		12:35		12:35		12:45
17		12:18	00:27	12:50	00:26	12:50	00:25	12:49	00:24	12:49	00:22	12:48	00:22	12:48	00:17	12:46
18	00:29	12:51	01:25	13:19	01:27	13:16	01:29	13:12	01:32	13:07	01:35	13:02	01:35	13:02	01:45	12:46
19	01:21	13:26	02:25	13:51	02:30	13:45	02:36	13:37	02:43	13:28	02:52	13:18	02:52	13:18	03:17	12:48
20	02:15	14:03	03:29	14:28	03:37	14:18	03:47	14:07	03:59	13:54	04:13	13:38	04:13	13:38	04:56	12:50
21	03:14	14:45	04:37	15:12	04:49	14:59	05:03	14:44	05:19	14:26	05:39	14:05	05:39	14:05	06:44	12:57
22	04:17	15:34	05:49	16:04	06:03	15:49	06:20	15:31	06:41	15:10	07:07	14:44	07:07	14:44	08:37	13:12
23	**05:24**	**16:30**	**07:00**	**17:07**	**07:17**	**16:51**	**07:35**	**16:32**	**07:58**	**16:09**	**08:27**	**15:39**	**08:27**	**15:39**	**10:16**	**13:50**
24	06:33	17:34	08:07	18:17	08:23	18:02	08:42	17:43	09:04	17:21	09:33	16:54	09:33	16:54	11:15	15:12
25	07:40	18:43	09:06	19:31	09:20	19:17	09:36	19:02	09:56	18:44	10:20	18:20	10:20	18:20	11:40	17:04
26	08:42	19:53	09:55	20:43	10:06	20:33	10:19	20:21	10:34	20:08	10:53	19:51	10:53	19:51	11:49	18:58
27	09:35	21:01	10:36	21:52	10:44	21:45	10:53	21:38	11:04	21:29	11:17	21:18	11:17	21:18	11:54	20:46
28	10:22	22:04	11:11	22:57	11:16	22:54	11:21	22:50	11:28	22:46	11:35	22:41	11:35	22:41	11:56	22:26
29	11:03	23:03	11:43	23:59	11:45	23:59	11:46	23:59	11:48	23:59	11:51	23:59	11:51	23:59	11:57	00:01
30	11:41	23:59	12:13		12:12		12:10		12:07		12:05		12:05		11:58	
31	12:16		12:43	00:59	12:38	01:02	12:33	01:06	12:27	01:10	12:19	01:16	12:19	01:16	11:59	01:31

LUNAR OBSERVING

BY BRUCE MCCURDY

I feel quite sure that I first viewed the moon in my small scope with just as much incredible delight as Galileo did in his. It is true that I had seen photographs of the moon and therefore had some vague idea of what its appearance would be like, but I was still wholly unprepared for all the wonders which I found on that first night as I explored the lunar surface. No photograph has yet been made which is not cold and flat and dead when compared with the scenes that meet one's eyes when the moon is viewed through even a small telescope.

Leslie Peltier, *Starlight Nights*

The Moon is the first astronomical object to grab anyone's eye in the night sky, and has provided "first light" for countless telescopes in the four centuries from Galileo's time to the present. Galileo himself was beaten to the punch by the underappreciated Englishman, Thomas Harriot, who was likely the first telescopic visual observer of Earth's satellite, and certainly the first to sketch an eyepiece view, on 1609 Jul. 26. This was some four months before Galileo did the same.

While the invention of the telescope may be considered the birth of modern astronomy, the Moon has been an object of fascination and mystique since the earliest annals of history, and presumably long before that. Early scientists in ancient observatories carefully tracked lunar cycles and recorded the extremes of its rising and setting points along the horizon. Some 23 centuries ago, the enterprising Aristarchus of Samos carefully observed a total lunar eclipse and derived impressively accurate measurements of the Moon's diameter ($^1/_3$ that of Earth; the actual percentage is 27.2) and distance (30 Earth diameters, similar to the modern accepted mean value).

One hardly needs a telescope to enjoy the Moon. If observed even briefly on a regular basis, Earth's only natural satellite has much to offer the modern-day naked-eye observer. Noteworthy phenomena include its wandering path through the constellations of the zodiac, the inexorable progression of phases, frequent conjunctions with planets and bright stars, occasional eclipses, libration, earthshine, and atmospheric effects.

Many of the cycles that fascinated the ancients can be observed directly. Understanding these cycles is interesting in its own right. It is also of value to telescopic lunar observers who can benefit when the Moon is favorably placed in the sky, as well as to dark-sky enthusiasts who may be more interested in knowing when it is below the horizon.

Every child learns that the Moon, like the Sun, rises in the east and sets in the west. Relative to a terrestrial landmark (or when viewed through an unpowered telescope!) the Moon appears to move its own diameter (~0.5°) westward in about 2 min. When measured against the background stars, however, it moves about its own diameter *eastward* in an hour, the same direction that Earth rotates. The 30:1 ratio between these rates nicely squares with the time periods involved: one day for Earth to rotate, one sidereal month (about 27.3 d) for the Moon to complete an orbit.

If one observes the Moon at about the same time from night to night, its eastward motion against the background stars becomes apparent. The Moon transits the meridian about 50 min later from one day to the next, a period that rules the tides (see TIDES AND THE EARTH–MOON SYSTEM, p. 175). However, rise and set times vary much more as the Moon's eastward motion also contains a significant northward or southward component, causing moonrise times to bunch together for part of each month, and moonset times to similarly cluster two weeks later. This is famously manifest in the Harvest Moon, an observation of interest to almost everyone. Every two weeks, a rise or set event occurs just after midnight, explaining why one day has no moonrise and another no moonset; over the course of a synodic month (new Moon to new Moon), Luna transits the meridian one fewer time than does the Sun (see TIMES OF MOONRISE AND MOONSET, p. 150).

Note the Moon's phase during a conjunction with a bright star, and again the following month when it returns: the phase is 2 d less (see the table). The extra couple of days it needs to get back to the same phase means traveling almost an additional 30°. This is due to the Sun's own apparent motion across the sky, also about 30° per month. If one tracks its position among the stars from, for example, one full Moon to the next, it is easy to see that the full Moon appears to be shifted eastward by about one zodiacal constellation each lunar month.

2022 passages of the Moon through 6 h RA (highest declination, in northeastern Taurus)

Date	Age (d)	Phase
Jan. 15	13	high-phase waxing gibbous
Feb. 12	11	moderate waxing gibbous
Mar. 11	9	just past first quarter
Apr. 07	6	just before first quarter
May 04	4	waxing crescent
Jun. 01	2	thin waxing crescent
Jun. 28	29	new Moon
Jul. 25	27	thin waning crescent
Aug. 21	24	waning crescent
Sep. 18	22	last quarter
Oct. 15	20	low-phase waning gibbous
Nov. 12	18	moderate waning gibbous
Dec. 08	15	full moon

No two months are the same: the lunar orbit is significantly out of round (e = 0.0549) and its path ever-changing. While mean distances and periods are known to high accuracy, the Moon's distance from Earth is not constant, rather it is constrained between 356 000 and 407 000 km. Each month, the Moon's perigee (closest approach to Earth) ranges from 35 000 to 50 000 km closer than its apogee, depending on the orientation of these orbital positions relative to the Sun. Thus the Moon varies in size from about 30′ to 34′. Nor is its speed constant; the Moon near perigee and apogee can be traveling as much as 5% faster and slower, respectively, than its mean orbital speed of 1.023 km/s. Our perception of the Moon's ever-changing path is further enhanced through the effects of parallax.

Among the major satellites of the Solar System, only the Moon and Neptune's Triton do not orbit in the plane of the equator of its planet. The Moon roughly orbits in the plane of the ecliptic, causing it to ride high or low at different points in the month, and at different phases throughout the calendar year. For example, a first-quarter Moon always cruises high in the sky around the time of the spring equinox but low around the autumn equinox; a full Moon is high around the time of the winter solstice but low around the summer solstice. The same statements apply to both Northern and Southern Hemispheres; however, the seasons themselves are six months out of phase.

Moreover, the Moon's orbit is tilted some 5° 09′ to the ecliptic, with the nodes (crossing points) of its orbit regressing rapidly, completing a full cycle (the regression of the nodes) in just 18.61 years. The combination of these two tilts can be constructive or destructive, exaggerating or muting the seasonal effects noted above. The extremes of azimuth for rise and set points, and of altitude for meridian transits, are likewise modulated. In 2022, this effect is additive, with the Moon having a declination range from + to –24.8° in January, increasing to a range of – to +27.5° in October–November (see THE SKY MONTH BY MONTH, p. 95 and pp. 98 to 120). Occultation series for stars near the ecliptic, the brightest of which are listed in the Zodiacal Catalog, also follow the 18.61-year cycle (see LUNAR OCCULTATIONS p. 162).

A period quite similar to the 18.61 year period of "lunar nodes regression" is the 6585 $^1/_3$ day (or 18.03 year) period of the Saros. Used for many centuries to explain and predict solar and lunar eclipses, the Saros also explains near-repetitions of the lunar librations and such phenomena as extreme perigees and apogees. Remarkably, the major lunar and solar cycles (draconic, sidereal, anomalistic, and synodic month, eclipse year, and calendar year) all have near-integer values during this important cycle, with the result that all three bodies return to very nearly their starting positions (see ECLIPSE PATTERNS, p. 122 and SOME ASTRONOMICAL AND PHYSICAL DATA, p. 29).

At the eyepiece, the closest astronomical target offers the greatest wealth of detail available to any given telescope, binocular, or camera, regardless of its size or quality. Of the countless recognizable features on the lunar nearside, over 1000—virtually all of them within reach of a moderate amateur telescope—have been formally named by the International Astronomical Union. Many of the greatest names in astronomy, exploration, and discovery are so commemorated. Observation of the Moon can be a lesson in the history of science. Six Canadians have been immortalized by having observable lunar craters named after them: Ostwald Avery (1877–1955), Frederick Banting (1891–1941), Carlyle Beals (1899–1979), Reginald Daly (1871–1957), Simon Newcomb (1835–1909), and John S. Plaskett (1865–1941). Remarkably, three of the six—Avery, Beals, and Newcomb—were born in Nova Scotia. Both Newcomb and Plaskett have been commemorated with RASC awards.

The face of the Moon is itself a history lesson of the early bombardment period of the inner Solar System. On a world devoid of erosion processes like wind, water, weather, glaciation, volcanism, plate tectonics, sedimentation, and life itself that have modified Earth, most of the Moon's features were sculpted billions of years ago. The largest of the ancient impact basins were subsequently filled with lava flows from its then-molten interior that hardened into basaltic rock and formed the distinctively dark, primarily circular regions wrongly but permanently identified as lunar maria, or seas. The brighter white areas, highlands that surround the maria and dominate the southern portion of the Earth-facing hemisphere, feature innumerable smaller but similarly ancient impact craters. With bombardment slowed to a relative trickle and the Moon remaining geologically inert since those ancient lava flows, Luna's appearance has changed but little over the past three billion years. Today, only the cosmic sandblasting of micrometeorites serves to gradually soften her features.

Observation of the Moon is nonetheless a very dynamic activity, due to the ever-changing angles of illumination. The terminator (the sunrise/sunset line) shifts westward across lunar features at ~0.5° per hour, a consequence of its 360° rotation in one month, about 12° per 24 hours. (Note that lunar east and west are reversed to celestial east and west, having been changed to the terrestrial standard during the early days of lunar exploration so as not to confuse the astronauts.) This slow but inexorable progression is particularly dramatic near the lunar terminator, where oblique sunlight reveals "in-depth" details of lunar features.

During the Moon's waxing phases (from new Moon to full), the sunrise terminator advances across new ground, exposing the most elevated features first. It can be a fascinating experience to look a little beyond the terminator for little points of light that might be mountain peaks or raised crater rims, and over the course of a single observing session, watch these features gradually expand under the oblique illumination of the rising Sun. It may take a few hours or even days before all the features on the crater floors are completely lighted. It is well worth revisiting an area of interest night after night to observe its changing appearance, even as the advancing Sun is revealing new wonders by the hour. Or, as the eloquent Peltier put it, "the geography of a whole new world…turning page by nightly page."

Under magnification, the darker areas, including the maria and the floors of large craters called "walled plains," are primarily flat and smooth. Occasional shift features such as scarps, wrinkle ridges, rilles, and rounded domes catch the eye, especially under low angles of illumination. Relatively few craters dot the landscape, proof positive of the greatly reduced rate of bombardment since those lava plains were formed. Frequently, they are surrounded by circular mountain ranges that represent the vestiges of the outer rings of the ancient impact structures. At low Sun angles, these cast long and impressive shadows whose jagged forms give a false impression of the rounded mountain tops. Long shadows yield interesting information about the topography under careful measurement, yet they often obscure features of interest in the lower terrain beyond. Hadley Rille of *Apollo 15* fame is theoretically well placed near the terminator at first quarter, but is lost in the shadows of towering Mount Hadley and the Apennine Mountains, which take days to recede. A return to this area just before last quarter will reveal the same scene lit from the opposite direction, the western faces of the mountains bathed in sunlight and the rille nicely illuminated.

At times of high angles of illumination around full Moon, a different aspect of the Moon is revealed. The three-dimensional context created in the brain from the pattern of light and dark is lost when the shadows are cast directly behind the features. Depth perception is problematic except right along the terminator, which now effectively encircles the Moon. Although the surface looks flat, a huge range of tonality is gained. Relatively young craters and their splash effects, such as ray systems and ejecta blankets, appear especially bright. Many small and otherwise unremarkable features stand out as brilliant points of light.

Full Moon is also the best time to observe the lunar libration zones. For line-of-sight reasons, explained on p. 95, the Moon displays a gentle rocking motion, revealing, over time, about 59% of its total surface area to the Earth-bound observer. Librations of longitude are zero when the Moon is at perigee or apogee; librations of latitude are zero when the Moon crosses the ecliptic at its ascending or descending node. Therefore, these librations follow the anomalistic month and draconic month, respectively, and thus gradually change with respect to each other, to bring different quadrants into favorable position. Libration has a more general effect on every lunar observing session, as even accessible nearside features can become more or less favorably situated to the line of sight, offering a more vertical or horizontal aspect from one viewing to the next. Details on current librations can be found in THE SKY MONTH BY MONTH, p. 98 and following.

The RASC's Isabel Williamson Lunar Observing Program is a detailed guide containing key information about the lunar surface and how to observe it. The program booklet lists 135 specific observing objectives (with sub-objectives) and optional activities such as Libration Challenge Features, lunar surface drawings, imaging, Observable Craters with Canadian Connections, and more. It also provides a detailed overview of the history of the Moon and the various geological eras that have shaped its surface, explaining each type of lunar feature and providing tips for observing each of them. See rasc.ca/isabel-williamson-lunar-observing-program (open to all to download, but RASC membership is required to earn the pin and certificate). See also the new Explore the Moon program for beginners, based on the Moon map in this Handbook, rasc.ca/observing/explore-the-moon-observing-certificate.

From Aristarchus to Galileo, from Peltier to the 21st-century amateur astronomer, the Moon has remained among the most reliable and rewarding celestial targets for observers of all experience levels.

Recommended Reading:

- Brunier, S. and Legault, T., *New Atlas of the Moon*, Firefly Books Ltd., 2006.
- Peltier, L., *Starlight Nights: The Adventures of a Sky-Gazer*, Sky Publishing, 2007.
- Rükl, A., *Atlas of the Moon*, Sky Publishing, 2004.
- Sheehan, W. and Dobbins, T., *Epic Moon: A History of Lunar Exploration in the Age of the Telescope*, Willmann–Bell Inc., 2001.
- Westfall, J., *Atlas of the Lunar Terminator*, Cambridge University Press, 2000.
- Wood, C., *The Modern Moon: A Personal View*, Sky Publishing, 2003.

[Ed. See rasc.ca/supplements for a listing by John Read and a near-side map of craters named for women.]

LUNAR OCCULTATIONS

BY DAVID W. DUNHAM

The Moon often passes between Earth and a star, an event called an occultation. During an occultation, a star suddenly disappears as the east limb of the Moon crosses the line between the star and the observer. The star reappears from behind the west limb some time later. Because the Moon moves through an angle about equal to its own diameter every hour, the longest time for an occultation is about an hour. The time is shorter if the occultation is not central. Solar eclipses are actually occultations: the star being occulted by the Moon is the Sun.

Since observing occultations is rather easy, amateur astronomers should try this activity. The slow, majestic drift of the Moon in its orbit is interesting, with the disappearance or reappearance of a star at the Moon's limb a remarkable sight, particularly when it occurs as a graze near the Moon's northern or southern limb. During a graze, a star may disappear and reappear several times in succession as mountains and valleys in the Moon's polar regions drift by it. On rarer occasions the Moon occults a planet. There will be four, one a difficult daytime event on Oct. 24, when a 1%-waning Moon will occult Mercury near noon for much of North America, and a better one of Mars by the full Moon on Dec. 8. There will be two occultations of Uranus, by a 94%-sunlit Moon on Oct. 12 and an impossible one on Nov. 8 in northwesternmost North America an hour after the last umbral contact of a total lunar eclipse. That event will be very interesting in western Asia, during the total lunar eclipse, with a southern-limit partial occultation over northern Luzon Island. There will be no occultations of 1st-magnitude stars in 2022, and the only 2nd-magnitude star will be 2.3-mag. δ Scorpii (Dschubba) that will be occulted in parts of North America on Apr. 19, Jun. 13, Aug. 6, Sep. 3, and Oct. 27. There will be two bright occultations during the May 16 total lunar eclipse, with one of 5.5-mag. ZC 2217 visible from Mexico and the southwestern USA, and the other, of 6.3-mag. ZC 2214 visible from the rest of North America. For lucky observers in a 100-km-wide strip extending from northern California to southern Texas, both occultations can be seen; see the graze lines on the map on page 173.

Lunar occultation and graze observations refine our knowledge of the shape of the lunar profile and fundamental stellar data. These observations complement those made by other techniques, such as *Kaguya* and *Lunar Reconnaissance Orbiter* laser ranging. Especially grazing occultation observations have revealed small errors whose source is still being investigated. Occultation observations are also useful for detecting double stars and measuring their separations. Binaries with separations as small as 0.02″ have been discovered visually during grazes. Doubles with separations in this range are useful for filling the gap between doubles that can be directly resolved and those whose duplicity has been discovered spectroscopically.

Observations

The International Occultation Timing Association (IOTA) analyzes lunar occultation observations and is now the world clearinghouse for such observations. Anyone interested in pursuing a systematic program of lunar occultation observations should consult the lunar and grazing occultation sections of Chasing the Shadow: The IOTA Occultation Observer's Manual that is available as a free downloaded Acrobat (.pdf) file at poyntsource.com/IOTAmanual/Preview.htm. If you don't have your own web access, obtain the file online at any public library or write to IOTA's North American coordinator of lunar occultation observations, Derek Breit, 17370 B Hawkins Lane, Morgan Hill, CA 95037, email breit_ideas@poyntsource.com. For general information, write to IOTA, see their Web site at occultations.org, or contact IOTA at PO Box 423, Greenbelt, MD 20768, USA; email: business@occultations.org. IOTA provides predictions and coordination services for occultation observers, but now, most observers can calculate their own predictions using IOTA's free Windows program *Occult4*; see lunar-occultations.com/iota/iotapredictions.pdf. If you have difficulty generating your own predictions, we can put you in touch with one of our members in your region who can help. Most IOTA services are free, including access to their prediction software and quarterly publication *Journal for Occultation Astronomy*, available through IOTA's main website at www.occultations.org. Annual IOTA membership costs $15; see occultations.org/about-us/iota-membership. Worldwide lunar occultation predictions of the brighter objects and other technical information is at www.lunar-occultations.com/iota. IOTA primarily serves North America, but there are sections providing similar services in Europe, Australia, New Zealand, Japan, India, the Middle East, and South America; links to their websites are at occultations.org/community/international-iota-sections.

The main information required in a lunar occultation observation is the time of the event and the observer's location. Supplementary data include the seeing conditions, telescope size, timing method, estimate of the observer's reaction time (if visual) and the accuracy of the timing, and whether or not the reaction time correction has been applied. A shortwave-radio time signal and audio recorder provide a simple, permanent time record, but a video record gives higher accuracy. The observer's longitude, latitude, and altitude should be reported to the nearest tenth of an arcsecond and 10 m, respectively, and should be accurate to at least 0.5″ or 16 m. These can be determined from either GPS measurements (5 min of position averaging and an unobstructed view of the sky above about 15° altitude are needed) or a suitable topographical map. For Canada, the maps are available from Regional Distributors, who are listed at maps.nrcan.gc.ca/distrib_centres_e.php. Email topo.maps@NRCan.gc.ca or call 800-465-6277 for more information. For the United States (except Alaska), write to US Geological Survey, Map Sales, PO Box 25286, Denver CO 80225, asking for an index to topographical maps in the desired state, or call 800-USA-MAPS. For Alaska, write to US Geological Survey, Map Sales, 4230 University Dr, Room 101, Anchorage AK 99508-4664, or phone 907-786-7011. Parts of USGS maps can be viewed and printed at certain websites such as nationalmap.gov/ustopo—enter a location or click on the USA map to zoom in and click on the Topo map tab. Detailed imagery is also available at some other websites, and with Google Earth. IOTA is using these resources for predictions; they are usually, but not always, accurate enough for reporting lunar occultation observations.

Observers are encouraged to learn how to videotape occultations in order to obtain reliable and accurate timings. Inexpensive yet sensitive video cameras are now available. Visual timings must be accurate to ±0.2 s to be good enough for further improvement of the lunar profile and other parameters, except for grazes, where ±0.5 s is adequate. Information about video recording occultations is in the Observing section of IOTA's main website and in its manual given above. Forms and reporting procedures are at occultations.org/observing/reporting-observations. If you have questions, correspond with the North American coordinator specified on the previous page.

Pages 165–170 give tables of occultation predictions and a table and a map of northern or southern limits for grazing occultations is on pp. 173–174.

1. TOTAL LUNAR-OCCULTATION PREDICTIONS

BY DAVID HERALD AND DAVID W. DUNHAM

The total lunar-occultation predictions listed in the tables on pp. 165–170 are for the 18 standard stations identified on the map on p. 164; the longitudes and latitudes of these stations are given in the table headings. The predictions were computed for IOTA by David Herald in Murrumbateman, Australia.

The predictions are limited to stars of magnitude 7 at the best phases and brighter otherwise. The first five columns give for each occultation the **Date**, the Zodiacal Catalog (**ZC**) number of the star, its magnitude (**mag.**), the phenomenon (**PH**), and the sunlit % of the Moon (**%sl**), with "+" for waxing and "–" for waning phases. if the occultation occurs during a lunar eclipse, "E" is used and the value is the percent of the Moon's disk not in the umbral shadow. Under each station are given the event time (**UT**), factors **A** and **B** (see below), and the cusp angle **CA** (measured around the Moon's limb from the north or south cusp, positive on the dark side, negative on the sunlit side, to the point of occurrence of the phenomenon);

during a lunar eclipse, the fractional distance of the star from the center of the Moon's umbra (0) to its edge (100) is given with "U" instead of "N" or "S". If no data are given for an occultation for a given station, it is due to no occultation, below the horizon, or sunlight there. If A or B have values larger than 5 min/degree, as can happen in the case of near grazes, they will not give a reliable prediction for other places.

The terms A and B are for determining corrections to the times of the events for stations within 300 km of the standard stations. If Lo* and La* represent the longitude and latitude of the standard station, and Lo and La those of the observer, then for the observer,

$$\text{UT of event} = \text{UT of event at the standard station} + A(\text{Lo} - \text{Lo}^*) + B(\text{La} - \text{La}^*),$$

where Lo, etc. are expressed in degrees, and A and B are in minutes of time per degree. Longitude measured west of Greenwich is assumed to be *negative* (which is now the IAU convention and that used by IOTA's *Occult* software). Due regard must be paid to the algebraic signs of the terms. To convert UT to the standard time of the observer, see the section STANDARD TIME ZONES on p. 45.

As an example, consider the occultation of 6.1-mag. ZC 3413 on 2022 Jan. 7 as seen from Seattle, Washington. For Seattle, Lo = –122.3° and La = 47.6°. The nearest standard station is Vancouver, for which Lo* = –123.1° and La* = 49.2°. Therefore, the UT of the disappearance at the dark limb (DD) is 4:35.5 + 0.3 × (–122.3° +123.1°) min –0.2 × (47.6°–49.2°) min = 4:36.1. The % illumination of the Moon is 24+, showing the Moon is crescent, about five days old. The cusp angle of disappearance is approximately 68° from the northern cusp on the Moon's dark limb. At Seattle, mainly south of Vancouver, the cusp angle should be a little more; accurate data from *Occult* shows it will be 73°. The local time is 8:36.1 p.m. PST, since that is 8h behind UT (that is, PST = UT –8 hours) on the night before, on Jan. 6 PST. With the thin crescent Moon, the event should be readily observable with any small telescope, if the sky is clear.

The number of events observable from any location increases *rapidly* as predictions are extended to fainter stars. Observers who wish to pursue such work can obtain software or more extensive lists from Walter Robinson, 515 W Kump, Bonner Springs KS 66012–1439, USA, by providing accurate geographical coordinates, your largest telescope aperture, and a long, self-addressed envelope (with postage); or, better, email webmaster@lunar-occultations.com.

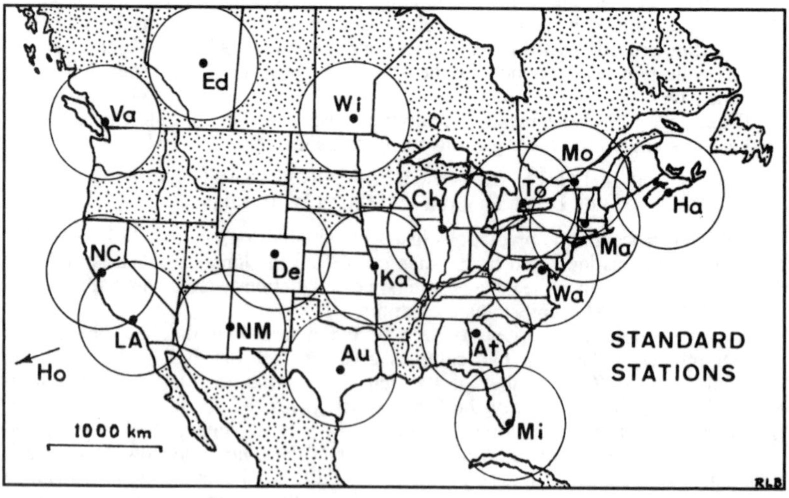

TOTAL LUNAR OCCULTATIONS FOR 2022

Date	ZC	mag.	PH	%sl	HALIFAX 44.6°N, 63.6°W				MONTRÉAL 45.5°N , 73.6°W				TORONTO 43.7°N, 79.4°W			
					UT	A m/deg	B m/deg	CA °	UT	A m/deg	B m/deg	CA °	UT	A m/deg	B m/deg	CA °
Jan. 14	709	4.3	DD	87+	05:15.6	+1.0	–1.2	90N	05:03.2	+1.3	–1.1	88S	04:57.1	+1.6	–1.3	80S
15	822	5.8	DD	93+	02:39.6	+1.8	+3.5	30N	02:28.9	+1.0	+5.5	16N	02:14.4	+0.8	+4.9	19N
28	2442	5.9	RD	19–					11:03.0	+1.3	+0.9	90N	10:53.5	+1.3	+1.3	78S
28	2443	5.7	RD	19–					11:05.0	+1.0	+0.4	66N	10:58.3	+1.0	+0.7	78N
Feb. 5	49	6.1	DD	17+					01:10.4	+0.5	–1.5	71S	01:09.8	+0.7	–1.7	67
6	283	6.6	DD	34+	23:27.0	+1.5	–0.5	86S	23:11.7	+1.5	+0.4	81N				
10	634	5.3	DD	64+	01:19.2	+1.8	–3.5	45S	00:55.6	+2.3	–2.2	55S	00:45.0	+2.7	–2.3	52S
10	656	4.2	DD	65+	04:43.2	+0.5	–0.5	68N	04:36.1	+0.8	–0.7	74N	04:32.7	+0.9	–0.9	84N
10	657	5.3	DD	64+	04:40.3	+0.3	–1.2	90S	04:34.4	+0.6	–1.4	84S	04:33.4	+0.7	–1.7	74S
10	767	5.5	DD	72+	23:27.8	+2.3	–0.4	72S	23:07.2	+1.8	+0.8	86S	22:55.3	+1.7	+1.1	89S
11	900	4.8	DD	80+	22:09.2	+0.1	+4.5	19N								
Mar. 10	742	5.8	DD	47+					04:10.6	–0.1	–2.2	57S	04:15.8	–0.2	–2.8	44S
10	852	5.2	DD	55+	22:29.8	+1.4	+4.5	26N								
16	1484	3.5	DD	94+	00:08.3	+1.5	+1.3	58N	23:57.0	+1.1	+1.6	56N	23:48.8	+0.8	+1.3	62N
19	1821	2.8	RD	99–	06:05.4	+1.6	–1.1	77N	05:47.1	+1.9	–0.2	88S	05:34.0	+2.5	+0.8	71S
Apr. 5	531	5.7	DD	13+	00:25.8	+0.2	–1.8	68S	00:20.8	+0.5	–2.0	64S	00:21.7	+0.6	–2.6	53S
5	533	6.1	DD	13+	01:16.7	–0.5	–2.9	37S	01:18.8	–0.6	–4.3	27S				
6	693	6.0	DD	21+	02:28.9	+0.2	–0.4	60N	02:25.7	+0.3	–0.6	70N	02:25.0	+0.4	–0.9	81N
7	822	5.8	DD	30+	03:08.0	–1.0	–3.1	28S								
18	2118	2.8	RD	98–	01:05.7	+0.1	–0.2	55N								
19	2290	2.3	DB	92–	06:22.9	+1.2	–0.9	–50S	06:12.8	+0.7	–0.9	–37S	06:12.9	+0.0	–1.7	–21S
19	2290	2.3	RD	91–	07:27.9	+1.9	–0.3	67S	07:07.8	+2.1	+0.4	58S	06:52.4	+2.8	+1.4	44S
May 6	1061	6.2	DD	23+	03:11.3	–0.6	–1.7	57S	03:15.6	–0.6	–2.1	47S	03: 23.7	–0.8	–2.6	34S
10	1514	6.2	DD	61+	03:05.6	+0.5	–2.1	73S	02:58.3	+0.5	–2.3	61S	02:59.8	+0.4	–2.6	48S
12	1733	5.4	DD	80+	04:31.1	+0.6	–2.0	68S	04:23.2	+0.6	–2.1	58S	04:24.0	+0.5	–2.3	47S
13	1821	2.8	DD	87+	00:06.2	–0.9	–4.3	13S								
13	1821	2.8	RB	87+	00:36.7	+3.6	+2.8	–36S								
13	1825	5.9	DD	87+	00:50.3	+1.2	–1.0	70S								
20	2910	4.7	RD	77–	06:23.1	+1.0	–1.3	19N								
20	2914	4.8	RD	77–	08:07.6	+2.5	–1.6	28N	07:44.0	+1.7	–1.9	17N	07:37.8	+1.3	–0.9	24N
Jun. 13	2290	2.3	DD	97+	02:24.8	+1.1	–0.7	45S	02:15.4	+0.6	–0.7	32S	02:15.2	+0.0	–1.5	16S
13	2290	2.3	RB	97+	03:30.7	+1.9	–0.2	–80S	03:11.3	+2.1	+0.5	–69S	02:56.5	+2.6	+1.4	–55S
Jul. 20	219	4.8	RD	53–	05:52.8	+0.7	+1.8	89N	05:48.8	+0.4	+1.7	80N	05:43.8	+0.3	+1.6	78N
24	716	6.3	RD	16–	07:23.3	–0.1	+1.8	70S	07:26.0	–0.2	+1.6	81S	07:24.6	–0.3	+1.4	84S
25	852	5.2	RD	10–	08:23.4	+0.9	+0.4	55N								
Aug. 8	2479	5.1	DD	78+					02:43.1	+1.5	–0.6	83N	02:34.5	+1.7	–0.4	84N
8	2480	5.2	DD	78+					02:43.2	+1.5	–0.6	83N	02:34.6	+1.7	–0.4	84N
20	660	4.3	RD	40–	05:02.6	–0.1	+1.7	74S	05:05.9	–0.2	+1.5	84S	05:05.0	–0.3	+1.4	87S
20	664	5.5	RD	40–	05:34.5	+0.2	+1.5	86N	05:34.0	+0.1	+1.3	73N	05:31.5	+0.0	+1.1	70N
23	1089	6.7	RD	14–					08:37.6	+0.6	+0.6	71N	08:33.3	+0.5	+0.5	68N
Sep. 6	2784	3.3	DD	76+	03:56.2	+0.7	–0.9	83N	03:48.2	+0.8	–0.5	69N	03:43.9	+0.9	–0.3	65N
13	257	4.3	RD	90–	09:47.1	+1.3	–1.9	62N	09:27.8	+2.3	–3.2	46N	09:18.9	+2.8	–3.2	45N
16	621	6.1	RD	65–	07:19.8	+0.6	+3.2	35S	07:15.1	+0.8	+2.4	53S	07:06.5	+0.7	+2.3	58S
20	1169	5.3	RD	28–	06:55.3	+0.6	+0.9	84N	06:51.1	+0.4	+0.5	69N	06:48.0	+0.3	+0.4	66N
23	1514	6.2	RD	6–									10:49.5	+0.5	+2.6	38S
Oct. 19	1373	6.5	RD	34–	09:59.5	+1.8	–0.1	88N	09:43.2	+1.5	+0.3	88N	09:34.0	+1.4	+0.7	86S
20	1484	3.5	DB	24–									11:34.0	+1.8	+0.7	–73N
21	1569	6.9	RD	17–	07:42.3	+0.4	–0.1	69N								
24	Mercury	–1.1	RD	1–					15:12.1	–1.7	–4.7	12N	15:20.4	+0.2	–2.4	36N
29	2660	6.2	DD	24+	22:16.0	+1.5	–1.0	83S								
Nov. 13	1088	5.8	RD	78–	10:02.6	+1.4	–1.6	79N	09:44.9	+1.8	–0.9	86N	09:34.7	+2.1	–0.2	84S
14	1206	5.9	RD	70–	07:43.1	+2.0	+0.5	80S	07:25.1	+1.7	+0.8	83S	07:13.7	+1.5	+1.2	79S
17	1544	5.4	RD	41–	10:26.0	+1.6	–1.2	76N	10:09.3	+1.6	–0.4	85N	09:59.7	+1.7	+0.3	84
19	1733	5.4	RD	23–	07:42.0	+0.5	+1.1	75S	07:39.2	+0.2	+1.1	77S	07:36.1	+0.1	+1.2	70S
Dec. 7	599	4.4	DD	99+					04:04.1	+3.9	–5.8	38S	03:50.2	+4.2	–4.7	41S
8	Mars	–1.9	DD	100+	04:19.6	+9.9	+9.9	75N	03:41.8	+2.6	–1.8	45N	03:29.4	+2.6	–1.3	43N
8	Mars	–1.9	RD	100+	04:29.9	+9.9	+9.9	88N	04:29.7	+1.0	+4.1	69S	04:17.3	+0.7	+4.2	70S
11	1169	5.3	RD	91–	08:10.0	+2.2	+0.0	69S	07:47.4	+2.4	+1.2	61S	07:29.4	+2.6	+3.0	47S
12	1274	5.7	RD	85–	04:41.8	+1.8	–2.5	35N	04:19.7	+2.3	–5.6	18N	04:15.0	+2.1	–4.0	23N
14	1484	3.5	RD	70–	03:58.6	+0.9	–1.4	42N	03:48.1	+1.0	–2.8	26N	03:47.3	+0.8	–2.3	30N
26	3202	6.2	DD	17+	22:53.1	–0.3	+1.5	23N								

DB/DD = Disappearance at Bright/Dark limb; RB/RD = Reappearance at Bright/Dark limb

See p. 163 for additional explanation of these tables.

TOTAL LUNAR OCCULTATIONS FOR 2022 (continued)

					WINNIPEG 49.9°N , 97.2°W				EDMONTON 53.6°N , 113.4°W				VANCOUVER 49.2°N , 123.1°W			
Date	ZC	mag.	PH	%sl	UT	A m/deg	B m/deg	CA °	UT	A m/deg	B m/deg	CA °	UT	A m/deg	B m/deg	CA °
Jan. 7	3413	6.1	DD	24+									04:35.5	+0.3	−0.2	68N
8	3529	6.6	DD	33+									01:57.7	+2.3	−1.1	56S
14	709	4.3	DD	87+	04:23.6	+1.7	+0.4	77N	04:04.6	+1.2	+2.0	54N	03:44.5	+1.1	+2.2	56N
Feb. 5	49	6.1	DD	17+	00:49.8	+0.8	−0.2	76N								
8	422	5.5	DD	46+					06:07.2	+1.5	+9.2	7N	05:47.0	+0.9	+1.2	42N
10	634	5.3	DD	63+	00:06.8	+1.5	+1.3	85N								
10	656	4.2	DD	65+	04:07.9	+1.4	−0.1	71N	03:47.0	+1.4	+1.2	56N	03:27.3	+1.6	+1.4	65N
10	657	5.3	DD	65+	04:05.2	+1.4	−1.0	87S	03:39.9	+1.5	+0.3	78N	03:22.4	+1.8	+0.5	86N
22	2117	5.2	RD	66−					11:44.8	+0.3	−1.2	26N	11:43.3	+0.8	−0.6	51N
22	2118	2.8	DB	66−	11:41.4	+3.6	+1.7	−30N	11:05.4	+1.8	+1.1	−58N	10:46.4	+1.3	+0.8	−83N
22	2118	2.8	RD	66−	12:04.2	−0.7	−3.0	6N	11:55.5	+0.4	−1.1	31N	11:52.6	+0.9	−0.6	54N
Mar. 10	742	5.8	DD	47+	03:54.1	+0.6	−3.1	48S	03:28.5	+1.2	−2.5	55S	03:30.0	+1.8	−5.7	30S
11	900	4.8	DD	58+	08:07.8	+1.9	+2.4	15N	07:53.4	+0.8	−0.2	38N	07:48.8	+0.7	−0.9	64N
19	1821	2.8	RD	99−	05:03.3	+2.1	+2.8	57S	04:48.2	+1.3	+3.9	49S				
20	1962	5.0	RD	94−									10:31.0	+0.7	−1.6	37N
Apr. 6	693	6.0	DD	21+	02:07.7	+0.9	−0.8	78N								
6	716	6.3	DD	23+					06:30.4	−0.1	−0.9	70N	06:36.0	−0.1	−1.2	89N
20	2479	5.1	RD	82−									12:19.1	+1.6	−0.1	62S
20	2480	5.2	RD	82−									12:19.1	+1.6	−0.1	61S
May 3	656	4.2	DD	5+					04:43.2	−1.0	−2.8	27S				
3	660	4.3	DD	5+									05:20.0	+0.3	+0.2	41N
6	1061	6.2	DD	23+	03:19.0	−1.0	−4.2	18S								
10	1514	6.2	DD	61+	02:36.3	+0.2	−3.2	30S								
10	1544	5.4	DD	63+									08:20.8	+1.4	−0.6	27N
12	1733	5.4	DD	80+	04:03.4	−0.1	−2.8	25S								
14	1962	5.0	DD	95+	04:39.1	+2.3	+0.6	50N	04:12.5	+1.4	+0.8	69N	03:58.9	+0.9	+0.3	87S
Jun. 5	1393	6.5	DD	27+					06:06.5	−0.2	−1.8	78S	06:16.4	−0.2	−1.9	66S
6	1484	3.5	DD	35+									02:29.7	+2.7	+0.7	46N
11	2053	4.5	DD	86+									09:01.0	+0.8	−1.5	75N
Jul. 13	2784	3.3	DD	100+									08:53.3	+1.4	−0.4	49S
Aug. 2	1821	2.8	DD	25+									22:31.5	+3.3	+3.9	37N
7	2347	4.6	DD	69+									05:41.7	+1.3	−1.1	81S
19	531	5.7	RD	48−	07:52.2	−0.5	+2.8	24S	08:05.7	−0.2	+2.1	50S				
20	693	6.0	RD	38−	09:57.0	−0.2	+3.3	26S	10:05.6	+0.2	+2.2	56S	09:55.6	+0.0	+2.0	61S
Sep. 6	2784	3.3	DD	76+	03:28.5	+0.9	+0.6	34N					02:52.1	+2.0	+2.2	29N
16	621	6.1	RD	65−	07:05.6	+0.7	+1.6	86N								
23	1514	6.2	RD	6−	10:55.8	+0.1	+1.3	70S	10:59.1	−0.1	+0.8	89N				
Oct. 2	2554	4.5	DD	40+									03:37.9	+1.1	−0.8	69N
7	3349	4.1	DD	91+	03:56.2	+1.9	+0.1	54S	03:33.9	+1.2	+1.1	76S	03:16.9	+1.1	+1.4	80S
12	Uranus	5.7	RD	94−	06:23.0	+0.3	+2.8	33S	06:23.8	+0.5	+2.0	63S	06:10.1	+0.4	+2.0	69S
13	599	4.4	RD	86−					13:51.7	+1.0	+0.3	53S	13:33.5	+1.4	+3.2	28S
14	743	5.8	RD	78−									14:09.1	+1.5	+0.8	53S
18	1270	6.1	RD	42−					12:13.9	+1.4	−1.2	54N	12:03.2	+1.4	−0.2	69N
18	1274	5.7	RD	42−									13:41.9	+1.5	−2.5	45N
19	1373	6.5	RD	34−	09:17.9	+0.8	+0.0	65N								
20	1484	3.5	DB	24−	11:16.6	+1.0	+2.0	−57N	11:14.2	+0.4	+3.1	−39N				
20	1484	3.5	RD	24−	12:20.3	+1.1	−1.3	56N	12:00.1	+0.8	−1.4	44N	11:55.7	+0.8	−0.3	61N
Nov. 8	423	6.3	DD	39E	12:09.2	+0.3	−0.3	77S	12:01.3	+0.6	−0.1	77S	11:56.1	+0.8	−0.5	74S
13	1088	5.8	RD	78−	08:59.5	+1.7	−0.1	78N	08:33.9	+1.4	−0.2	57N	08:20.2	+1.3	+0.3	63N
14	1206	5.9	RD	70−	06:56.9	+1.0	+0.5	69N								
17	1544	5.4	RD	41−	09:39.7	+0.9	+0.4	84N	09:30.0	+0.5	+0.3	70N	09:23.9	+0.3	+0.6	81N
20	1849	6.1	RD	14−	11:33.9	+1.2	+3.1	42S	11:31.4	+0.5	+2.7	46S				
29	3141	5.8	DD	33+									04:20.0	+0.8	−0.9	89N
Dec. 1	3428	5.0	DD	57+									06:49.1	+0.5	−0.5	83N
4	257	4.3	DD	86+	09:08.2	+0.2	+0.2	59N	09:03.9	+0.4	+0.7	46N	08:56.2	+0.7	+0.4	62N
7	599	4.4	DD	99+	03:10.8	+1.2	+1.4	85N	03:05.0	+0.4	+2.1	59N	02:53.1	+0.1	+2.1	54N
8	Mars	−1.9	DB	100+	03:05.4	+0.8	+1.5	−1N	03:04.6	+0.2	+2.1	−27N	02:55.5	−0.1	+2.0	−32N
8	Mars	−1.9	RB	100−	04:15.7	+1.0	+1.8	29N	04:06.2	+0.9	+1.4	3N	03:52.5	+0.7	+1.4	0N
11	1169	5.3	RD	91−	07:08.0	+1.5	+1.6	71S	06:53.2	+1.0	+1.3	90S	06:38.2	+0.7	+1.6	84S
14	1514	6.2	RD	67−					13:13.7	+0.8	−2.1	50N	13:10.9	+1.4	−1.3	74N
27	3227	6.3	DD	19+									02:51.0	+0.6	−0.4	72N

DB/DD = Disappearance at Bright/Dark limb; RB/RD = Reappearance at Bright/Dark limb

See p. 163 for additional explanation of these tables.

Editor's Note:
A great synchronized video of observations of a spectacular grazing occultation of Aldebaran in 2017, produced by Andreas Gada, is very instructive; view it when you can at vimeo.com/209854850

TOTAL LUNAR OCCULTATIONS FOR 2022 (continued)

					MASSACHUSETTS 42.5°N, 72.5°W				WASHINGTON, D.C. 38.9°N, 77.0°W				CHICAGO 41.9°N, 87.7°W			
Date	ZC	mag.	PH	%sl	UT	A m/deg	B m/deg	CA °	UT	A m/deg	B m/deg	CA °	UT	A m/deg	B m/deg	CA °
Jan. 14	709	4.3	DD	87+	05:08.6	+1.3	−1.5	78S	05:09.1	+1.4	−2.2	62S	04:45.1	+2.0	−1.4	72S
15	822	5.8	DD	93+	02:17.9	+1.5	+3.3	34N	02:00.1	+1.6	+2.8	44N				
28	2442	5.9	RD	19−	11:01.8	+1.5	+0.9	86S	10:50.5	+1.7	+1.5	69S	10:38.8	+1.5	+2.3	57S
28	2443	5.7	RD	19−	11:04.9	+1.1	+0.4	71N	10:57.5	+1.3	+0.7	85N	10:48.5	+1.0	+1.2	86S
Feb. 5	49	6.1	DD	17+	01:16.3	+0.5	−2.1	57S	01:23.2	+0.9	−3.7	40S	01:05.5	+1.1	−1.6	67S
6	283	6.6	DD	34+	23:12.9	+1.8	+0.0	89S								
9	631	5.6	DD	63+									23:46.0	+9.9	+9.9	24S
10	631	5.6	RD	63+									00:00.3	+9.9	+9.9	6S
10	634	5.3	DD	64+	01:08.3	+2.7	−4.9	37S					00:24.5	+3.0	−1.4	56S
10	656	4.2	DD	64+	04:39.3	+0.7	−0.9	83N	04:40.0	+0.7	−1.3	82S	04:25.9	+1.2	−1.2	85S
10	657	5.3	DD	65+	04:39.6	+0.5	−1.6	75S	04:44.3	+0.5	−2.2	59S	04:29.8	+1.0	−2.2	62S
10	767	5.5	DD	72+	23:07.7	+2.2	+0.3	76S	22:56.7	+2.3	+0.2	70S				
22	2118	2.8	DB	66−									12:03.8	+3.6	+1.6	−29N
22	2118	2.8	RD	66−									12:28.1	−0.1	−4.0	7N
24	2398	6.1	RD	44−					10:55.2	+1.9	−0.1	81N				
Mar. 10	742	5.8	DD	47+	04:17.2	−0.3	−2.4	49S	04:30.1	−0.9	−3.8	27S	04:25.7	−0.9	−5.4	20S
15	1484	3.5	DD	94+	23:54.2	+1.1	+1.0	67N	23:46.6	+1.0	+0.5	80N				
19	1821	2.8	RD	99−	05:50.0	+2.2	−0.1	83S	05:35.5	+3.7	+1.8	60S				
Apr. 5	531	5.7	DD	13+	00:27.8	+0.3	−2.4	53S	00:38.3	+0.0	−4.3	30S				
6	693	6.0	DD	21+	02:28.2	+0.2	−0.8	77N	02:30.5	+0.2	−1.1	88S	02:23.2	+0.5	−1.3	85S
19	2290	2.3	DB	92−	06:16.6	+0.6	−1.2	−33S	06:22.8	−0.8	−3.2	−10S				
19	2290	2.3	RD	91−	07:09.1	+2.4	+0.5	54S	06:51.6	+3.9	+2.5	34S				
May 6	1061	6.2	DD	23+	03:21.3	−0.7	−2.2	41S								
10	1514	6.2	DD	61+	03:05.8	+0.5	−2.4	57S	03:13.5	+0.2	−2.8	43S	03:03.7	−0.2	−3.5	27S
12	1733	5.4	DD	80+	04:30.4	+0.6	−2.2	56S	04:36.8	+0.4	−2.6	43S	04:26.1	+0.0	−3.0	28S
13	1825	5.9	DD	87+	00:44.3	+0.7	−1.5	50S								
14	1962	5.0	DD	95+					05:33.6	+4.1	+1.9	25N	05:00.4	+2.8	+0.2	48N
20	2910	4.7	RD	77−	06:16.2	+0.8	−0.2	33N	06:12.4	+0.9	+0.2	46N				
20	2914	4.8	RD	77−	07:50.3	+1.9	−1.2	27N	07:45.1	+1.8	−0.6	36N	07:29.3	+1.0	−0.2	35N
Jun. 13	2290	2.3	DD	97+	02:18.6	+0.6	−1.1	27S	02:24.2	−0.7	−2.7	5S				
13	2290	2.3	RB	97+	03:12.2	+2.3	+0.6	−66S	02:55.4	+3.6	+2.3	−45S				
Jul. 7	1866	5.8	DD	50+									03:30.3	+2.1	+0.3	27N
20	219	4.8	RD	53−	05:44.2	+0.4	+1.7	84N	05:36.7	+0.3	+1.6	86N				
24	716	6.3	RD	16−	07:21.1	−0.2	+1.6	76S	07:17.0	−0.4	+1.4	75S				
25	852	5.2	RD	10−	08:14.9	+1.0	−0.2	42N	08:12.0	+0.7	−0.2	45N				
Aug. 2	1728	6.7	DD	17+	01:30.6	+0.2	−1.7	90N	01:35.8	+0.3	−1.8	84S				
8	2479	5.1	DD	78+	02:46.8	+1.6	−0.7	86N	02:41.4	+1.9	−0.6	89S	02:19.7	+1.9	−0.1	89N
8	2480	5.2	DD	78+	02:47.0	+1.6	−0.7	87N	02:41.5	+1.9	−0.6	89S	02:19.8	+1.9	−0.2	89N
20	660	4.3	RD	40−	05:01.1	−0.3	+1.5	79S	04:57.5	−0.4	+1.4	78S				
20	664	5.5	RD	40−	05:30.1	+0.1	+1.3	79N	05:25.8	−0.1	+1.2	80N				
23	1089	6.7	RD	14−	08:36.0	+0.5	+0.8	81N	08:31.1	+0.3	+0.8	84N	08:29.0	+0.4	+0.2	60N
Sep. 6	2784	3.3	DD	76+	03:50.7	+0.9	−0.6	76N	03:48.0	+1.1	−0.4	77N	03:35.4	+1.2	+0.1	58N
13	257	4.3	DD	90−									08:43.9	+9.9	+9.9	12N
13	257	4.3	RD	90−	09:37.0	+1.8	−1.7	62N	09:33.2	+2.0	−1.0	72N	08:51.6	+9.9	+9.9	24N
16	621	6.1	RD	65−	07:08.1	+0.6	+2.8	44S	06:55.9	+0.4	+2.8	43S	06:57.2	+0.6	+2.1	67S
20	1169	5.3	RD	28−	06:49.6	+0.4	+0.7	78N	06:45.8	+0.2	+0.7	82N	06:45.2	+0.2	+0.1	58N
23	1514	6.2	RD	6−					10:30.1	−0.3	+9.6	3S	10:42.5	+0.1	+2.6	35S
Oct 19	1373	6.5	RD	34−	09:43.6	+1.6	+0.6	82S	09:32.9	+1.5	+1.3	68S	09:22.6	+1.1	+0.9	82S
20	1484	3.5	DB	24−									11:19.3	+1.5	+0.4	−85N
20	1484	3.5	RD	24−									12:41.9	+1.7	−1.0	77N
24	Mercury	−1.1	RD	1−	15:22.9	−0.7	−3.6	21N	15:32.6	+0.6	−2.3	44N	15:19.1	+0.9	−1.4	59N
Nov 8	423	6.3	DD	49E									12:14.0	−0.1	−0.6	75S
13	1088	5.8	RD	78−	09:49.5	+2.0	−0.6	85S	09:39.5	+2.5	+0.6	68S	09:15.7	+2.3	+0.8	74S
14	1206	5.9	RD	70−	07:23.8	+1.8	+1.3	72S	07:09.7	+1.6	+2.1	60S	07:00.0	+1.2	+1.4	78S
17	1544	5.4	RD	41−	10:11.9	+1.9	−0.2	87S	10:01.7	+2.2	+0.9	69S	09:45.1	+1.5	+1.1	71S
19	1733	5.4	RD	23−	07:35.7	+0.3	+1.4	65S	07:28.7	+0.1	+2.0	50S				
Dec 7	599	4.4	DD	99+									03:24.5	+3.1	−1.2	55S
8	Mars	−1.9	DD	100+									03:10.8	+2.1	−0.1	33N
8	Mars	−1.9	RD	100+									04:04.9	+0.6	+3.5	64S
11	1169	5.3	RD	91−	07:45.0	+2.9	+2.6	48S					07:01.6	+2.1	+5.9	31S
12	1274	5.7	RD	85−	04:30.7	+1.7	−1.7	40N	04:27.7	+1.5	−0.8	53N				
14	1484	3.5	RD	70−	03:54.2	+0.7	−1.1	45N	03:54.3	+0.5	−0.5	56N				
21	2290	2.3	RD	5−					10:39.4	−1.5	−3.4	3N				
26	3202	6.2	DD	17+	22:54.1	−1.1	+3.0	8N	22:48.2	−0.8	+2.8	11N				

DB/DD = Disappearance at Bright/Dark limb; RB/RD = Reappearance at Bright/Dark limb

See p. 163 for additional explanation of these tables.

TOTAL LUNAR OCCULTATIONS FOR 2022 (continued)

					MIAMI 25.8°N, 80.3°W				ATLANTA 33.8°N, 84.3°W				AUSTIN 30.2°N, 97.8°W			
Date	ZC	mag.	PH	%sl	UT	A m/deg	B m/deg	CA °	UT	A m/deg	B m/deg	CA °	UT	A m/deg	B m/deg	CA °
Jan. 10	219	4.8	DD	53+	02:51.3	+1.2	+1.1	67N	03:02.5	+0.5	+3.1	29N	02:43.5	+0.3	+4.0	23N
14	709	4.3	DD	87+					05:15.2	+1.6	−5.6	33S				
15	822	5.8	DD	92+	01:29.8	+2.4	+1.0	82N	01:36.1	+1.4	+2.4	51N	01:14.0	+0.5	+2.8	39N
27	2282	5.8	RD	29−	09:56.0	+0.5	−1.0	48N	09:45.9	−0.2	−1.4	29N	09:46.6	+0.3	−0.1	66N
28	2443	5.7	RD	19−	10:31.9	+3.3	+3.8	43S	10:41.8	+1.6	+1.6	68S				
Feb. 10	656	4.2	DD	65+	05:10.5	−0.7	−5.3	22S	04:43.2	+0.8	−2.3	58S	04:44.0	+0.9	−6.8	25S
10	657	5.3	DD	65+					04:58.5	−0.2	−5.4	25S				
22	2117	5.2	RD	66−									12:38.0	+1.5	−2.1	47N
22	2118	2.8	DB	66−					12:08.3	+2.7	+0.2	−48N	11:31.8	+2.6	−0.4	−81N
22	2118	2.8	RD	66−	13:25.3	+1.4	−2.5	48N	12:57.7	+1.1	−3.0	28N	12:48.9	+1.6	−2.1	51N
24	2398	6.1	RD	44−	10:42.9	+3.1	+1.1	65S	10:39.2	+2.2	+0.7	79S				
26	2721	3.2	RD	23−	09:06.7	+0.3	+0.2	59N								
27	2910	4.7	DD	13−					11:17.1	−4.0	−9.0	8S				
27	2910	4.7	RD	13−					11:26.7	+9.9	+9.9	23S				
Mar. 15	1484	3.5	DD	94+	23:54.2	+1.4	−3.3	46S	23:38.9	+0.9	−0.2	84S				
20	1962	5.0	RD	94−									11:32.6	+0.8	−2.8	35N
23	2359	5.0	RD	70−									09:13.3	+0.3	−1.9	27N
Apr. 4	434	6.9	DD	8+									02:45.6	+0.4	+0.7	57N
6	693	6.0	DD	21+	02:51.6	−0.6	−2.4	40S	02:36.3	+0.1	−1.7	64S	02:45.0	−0.2	−4.1	29S
May 5	912	7.0	DD	16+					02:28.4	+1.0	+0.4	49N	02:17.8	+0.9	−0.8	84N
12	1733	5.4	DD	80+					04:53.4	−1.1	−4.4	13S				
14	1962	5.0	DD	95+	05:25.3	+2.4	−0.8	71N	05:10.5	+2.6	−0.4	60N	04:41.6	+1.9	−1.0	84S
20	2910	4.7	RD	77−	06:03.1	+1.3	+0.7	79N	06:04.0	+0.9	+0.6	65N				
20	2914	4.8	RD	76−	07:42.1	+2.1	+0.1	68N	07:34.7	+1.6	−0.1	51N0	07:15.7	+1.1	+0.6	70N
23	3349	4.1	RD	44−	06:45.5	+0.2	+0.6	55N								
Jun. 6	1484	3.5	DD	35+									03:35.0	+2.5	+0.5	40N
6	1484	3.5	RB	35+									04:05.4	−1.2	−4.0	−14N
16	2848	5.6	RD	95−	06:37.3	+2.5	−0.6	68N								
20	3458	6.2	RD	58−	08:49.5	+1.2	+2.5	50S	09:00.9	+1.4	+1.8	71S				
Jul. 7	1866	5.8	DD	50+	03:48.6	+0.9	−0.9	64N	03:38.1	+1.3	−0.6	47N	03:19.4	+1.9	−1.2	72N
8	1973	6.2	DD	61+									02:29.5	+2.0	−1.4	83S
10	2228	5.8	DD	82+									04:16.5	+1.8	−1.6	58S
20	219	4.8	RD	53−					05:27.7	+0.0	+1.5	90N				
25	852	5.2	RD	10−					08:09.6	+0.3	−0.3	48N				
Aug. 2	1728	6.7	DD	17+	01:59.7	+0.1	−2.0	59S	01:43.1	+0.3	−1.9	72S				
2	1821	2.8	DD	25+									23:37.1	+9.9	+9.9	28N
2	1821	2.8	RD	25+									23:48.6	+9.9	+9.9	12N
5	2053	4.5	DD	45+	01:10.1	+4.5	+3.9	27N								
8	2479	5.1	DD	78+	02:45.0	+2.4	−1.2	66S	02:29.3	+2.2	−0.5	81S	02:02.0	+2.0	−0.5	64S
8	2480	5.2	DD	78+	02:45.2	+2.4	−1.2	65S	02:29.5	+2.2	−0.5	80S	02:02.2	+2.0	−0.5	64S
10	2848	5.6	DD	94+	02:50.6	+2.4	+1.5	69N0	02:56.5	+2.1	+2.3	47N				
23	1089	6.7	RD	14−	08:18.2	−0.2	+1.1	66S	08:25.8	+0.1	+0.7	87N				
Sep 5	2583	5.8	DD	65+					01:21.7	+2.3	−2.3	30S	01:07.4	+0.6	−5.6	6S
6	2784	3.3	DD	76+	03:49.7	+1.9	−0.7	79S	03:39.8	+1.5	−0.1	78N	03:14.9	+2.1	+0.6	71N
13	257	4.3	RD	90−	09:24.5	+1.8	+1.3	68S	09:20.6	+2.3	−0.2	79N	08:42.4	+3.8	−0.8	59N
16	621	6.1	RD	65−					06:40.0	+0.2	+2.6	44S				
20	1169	5.3	RD	28−	06:34.8	−0.4	+1.0	67S	06:42.2	−0.1	+0.6	86N				
Oct. 4	2910	4.7	DD	63+									04:44.9	+0.7	+0.2	67N
19	1373	6.5	RD	34−					09:14.1	+1.0	+2.3	50S				
20	1484	3.5	DB	24−					11:28.1	+1.7	−1.3	−68S	11:14.0	+1.4	−2.5	−47S
20	1484	3.5	RD	24−									12:16.4	+2.4	+2.2	49S
24	Mercury	−1.1	RD	1−	15:52.6	+2.2	−1.5	83N	15:33.9	+1.5	−1.4	73N	15:09.9	+2.2	+0.6	67S
Nov. 4	3428	5.0	DD	79+	00:14.0	−1.7	+5.9	8N								
8	423	6.3	DD	76E									12:28.9	−0.4	−2.0	74S
13	1088	5.8	RD	78−					09:08.5	+3.0	+4.1	39S	08:18.0	+0.9	+7.6	18S
14	1206	5.9	RD	70−					06:47.1	+1.0	+3.0	45S	06:29.6	+0.3	+2.4	48S
17	1544	5.4	RD	41−					09:33.3	+2.4	+4.5	34S				
26	2784	3.3	DD	12+	22:35.4	+0.7	+1.1	37N								
26	2784	3.3	RB	12+	23:31.8	+1.8	−1.6	−67N								
29	3130	5.4	DD	33+									03:51.1	−0.3	+1.2	41N
Dec. 8	Mars	−1.9	DD	100+									02:56.9	+5.8	−5.7	60N
8	Mars	−1.9	RD	100+									03:12.4	−4.1	+9.3	83N
12	1274	5.7	RD	85−	04:21.4	+1.1	+0.9	83S	04:19.9	+1.2	−0.1	65N				
14	1484	3.5	RD	70−	03:52.0	+0.0	+0.6	80S	03:53.4	+0.2	−0.2	69N				
21	2290	2.3	RD	5−	10:53.1	+0.2	−0.2	63N	10:50.4	−0.2	−0.5	43N				
27	3214	6.8	DD	18+	01:14.5	+0.2	+0.5	62N								
28	3358	6.9	DD	28+									01:51.5	+1.2	+0.1	85N

DB/DD = Disappearance at Bright/Dark limb; RB/RD = Reappearance at Bright/Dark limb

See p. 163 for additional explanation of these tables.

TOTAL LUNAR OCCULTATIONS FOR 2022 (continued)

					KANSAS CITY 39.0°N, 94.5°W				DENVER 39.8°N, 105.0°W				NEW MEX., ARIZ. 34.0°N, 109.0°W			
Date	ZC	mag.	PH	%sl	UT	A m/deg	B m/deg	CA °	UT	A m/deg	B m/deg	CA °	UT	A m/deg	B m/deg	CA °
Jan. 14	709	4.3	DD	87+	04:34.8	+2.5	−1.9	63S	04:06.9	+2.6	−0.5	75S	04:01.0	+3.5	−1.9	56S
20	1484	3.5	RD	94−									11:20.4	+0.0	−3.6	21N
Feb. 5	49	6.1	DD	17+	01:01.6	+1.5	−1.7	63S								
8	422	5.5	DD	46+					05:57.1	+0.5	−0.2	73N	05:57.9	+0.5	−0.8	85S
10	634	5.3	DD	64+	00:07.0	+3.1	−0.9	57S								
10	656	4.2	DD	65+	04:21.1	+1.5	−1.7	71S	04:01.4	+2.0	−1.3	73S	04:04.6	+2.5	−3.3	48S
10	657	5.3	DD	65+	04:30.4	+1.2	−3.4	45S	04:11.1	+2.0	−3.4	46S				
22	2117	5.2	RD	66−	12:20.7	+0.6	−2.7	22N	12:10.2	+1.0	−1.8	39N	12:14.3	+1.5	−1.4	57N
22	2118	2.8	DB	66−	11:40.4	+2.9	+0.3	−54N	11:13.4	+2.3	+0.2	−73N	11:05.0	+1.9	−0.3	−86S
22	2118	2.8	RD	66−	12:33.1	+0.9	−2.5	28N	12:20.9	+1.1	−1.7	43N	12:24.6	+1.6	−1.4	60N
25	2558	6.3	RD	32−					12:22.1	+1.9	+1.2	74S				
Mar. 11	900	4.8	DD	58+					08:04.1	+0.2	−0.6	65N	08:08.3	+0.0	−0.9	85N
20	1962	5.0	RD	94−					11:01.2	+0.5	−2.7	23N	11:12.8	+1.0	−2.3	41N
23	2359	5.0	RD	70−					08:54.4	−1.1	−2.9	9N	09:03.7	+0.4	−0.9	41N
Apr. 4	434	6.9	DD	8+									02:42.2	+0.7	+0.9	51N
06	693	6.0	DD	21+	02:23.7	+0.6	−1.7	70S	02:13.8	+1.0	−2.0	64S	02:26.8	+0.7	−4.3	34S
May 5	912	7.0	DD	16+0	02:18.4	+1.3	+0.3	49N								
14	1962	5.0	DD	95+	04:43.3	+2.3	−0.2	70N	04:22.1	+1.7	−0.3	88N	04:19.7	+1.3	−1.0	71S
16	2217	5.5	DD	0E									03:38.9	+2.7	+4.0	22U
16	2217	5.5	RD	0E									04:03.2	−1.5	−3.8	18U
20	2914	4.8	RD	77−	07:22.8	+0.9	+0.2	47N								
Jun. 6	1484	3.5	DD	35+									03:08.0	+2.3	−0.6	60N
6	1484	3.5	RB	35+									04:00.2	−0.3	−3.1	−31N
Jul. 7	1866	5.8	DD	50+	03:17.6	+2.0	−0.7	48N	02:54.8	+2.2	−0.9	65N	02:52.3	+2.1	−1.2	83N
10	2228	5.8	DD	82+0					03:52.3	+1.6	−0.9	66S	03:51.9	+1.5	−1.3	51S
Aug. 2	1821	2.8	DD	25+									22:48.6	+3.2	+0.5	63N
7	2347	4.6	DD	69+									06:25.2	+1.5	−2.2	52S
8	2479	5.1	DD	78+	02:06.6	+2.0	+0.0	83S								
8	2480	5.2	DD	78+	02:06.8	+2.0	+0.0	83S								
19	531	5.7	RD	48−					07:28.5	−1.0	+3.2	15S				
20	693	6.0	RD	38−					09:25.0	−1.3	+4.2	10S				
Sep. 6	2784	3.3	DD	76+	03:25.5	+1.5	+0.5	56N	03:09.4	+1.7	+1.2	47N	02:54.4	+2.2	+1.3	58N
23	1514	6.2	RD	6−	10:35.2	−0.3	+3.0	26S	10:40.8	−0.4	+1.9	41S				
Oct. 2	2554	4.5	DD	40+									04:11.3	+1.3	−1.6	70
4	2910	4.7	DD	63+	04:48.4	+0.2	+0.4	49N0	04:50.0	−0.6	+1.9	22N	04:41.6	+0.2	+1.4	34N
4	2914	4.8	DD	63+									05:59.4	+0.6	−0.2	72N
7	3349	4.1	DD	91+					03:37.0	+2.5	+0.3	49S	03:25.3	+2.7	+0.1	44S
12	Uranus	5.7	RD	94−					05:52.1	−0.3	+3.3	23S				
18	1270	6.1	RD	42−					12:33.6	+2.3	+0.5	77S	12:16.7	+2.4	+2.2	53S
19	1373	6.5	RD	34−	09:13.4	+0.8	+1.1	76S								
20	1484	3.5	DB	24−	11:09.3	+1.3	+0.0	−83S	10:57.8	+0.9	+0.3	−87S	10:55.0	+1.0	−0.7	−67S
20	1484	3.5	RD	24−	12:31.1	+1.9	−0.1	87S	12:13.7	+1.5	+0.4	84S	12:02.5	+1.4	+1.5	61S
24	Mercury	−1.1	RD	1−	15:14.7	+1.2	−0.6	79N								
Nov. 8	423	6.3	DD	53E	12:16.4	+0.0	−0.9	74S	12:14.5	+0.2	−1.2	74S	12:22.8	+0.1	−2.1	74S
13	1088	5.8	RD	78−	08:56.7	+2.2	+1.8	63S	08:37.7	+1.7	+1.6	71S	08:19.4	+1.3	+2.6	53S
14	1206	5.9	RD	70−	06:48.6	+0.9	+1.5	74S	06:41.8	+0.6	+1.1	88S				
17	1544	5.4	RD	41−	09:30.8	+1.3	+2.0	56S	09:21.8	+0.7	+1.8	59S	09:04.9	+0.3	+3.6	32S
Dec. 4	257	4.3	DD	86+					09:09.3	+0.4	−0.8	83S	09:14.3	+0.4	−1.6	60S
7	599	4.4	DD	99+	03:06.6	+2.7	−0.3	61S	02:47.3	+1.3	+1.2	85S	02:35.5	+1.3	+1.0	79S
8	Mars	−1.9	DD	100+	02:57.1	+1.8	+0.3	29N	02:44.7	+0.8	+1.2	9N	02:35.2	+0.8	+0.9	16N
8	Mars	−1.9	RD	100+	03:51.6	+0.4	+3.3	63S	03:48.2	+0.6	+2.3	44N	03:32.7	+0.2	+2.5	52N
11	1169	5.3	RD	91−					06:28.0	+0.6	+5.0	30S				
21	2305	5.9	RD	5−					13:32.2	+2.1	+2.9	51S				

DB/DD = Disappearance at Bright/Dark limb; RB/RD = Reappearance at Bright/Dark limb

See p. 163 for additional explanation of these tables.

Author's note:
The occultation of Mars on Dec. 8 will occur within an hour of full Moon for most locations. In this case, the usual distinction between the sunlit and dark limb is irrelevant; the whole lunar disk will be brightly sunlit. Also, the cusp angle, which we use to specify where on the Moon's limb an event will occur, is too poorly defined. The program used to compute the predictions generates values, but they are meaningless for this event. Sometime before the occultation, we'll post at occultations.org/publications/rasc/2022/nam22grz.htm a diagram of the Moon for the occultation showing where the D and R events will occur for the standard stations used for the predictions given here.

TOTAL LUNAR OCCULTATIONS FOR 2022 (continued)

					LOS ANGELES 34.1°N, 118.3°W				N. CALIFORNIA 38.0°N, 122.0°W				HONOLULU 21.3°N, 157.9°W			
Date		ZC	mag.	PH %sl	UT	A m/deg	B m/deg	CA °	UT	A m/deg	B m/deg	CA °	UT	A m/deg	B m/deg	CA °
Jan.	7	3428	5.0	DD 25+									07:22.2	+0.0	+1.6	45N
	14	709	4.3	DD 87+	03:31.9	+2.7	+0.2	74S	03:26.5	+1.9	+1.2	88N				
	20	1484	3.5	RD 94–	11:15.1	+1.0	–2.7	42N	11:00.7	+1.0	–2.8	38N				
	22	1702	4.0	RD 80–									11:02.4	+1.6	–0.1	87S
Feb.	8	422	5.5	DD 46+	05:01.1	+0.9	–0.9	81S	05:44.9	+1.1	–0.4	85N	04:34.4	+4.0	–0.8	65S
	9	531	5.7	DD 56+									07:09.3	+2.6	–0.6	77S
	10	656	4.2	DD 65+	03:37.3	+3.2	–2.1	57S	03:22.3	+2.6	–0.3	77S				
	10	657	5.3	DD 65+					03:31.4	+3.3	–2.6	50S				
	22	2117	5.2	RD 66–	11:59.2	+1.7	–0.7	73N	11:50.8	+1.5	–0.5	71N				
	22	2118	2.8	DB 66–	10:50.2	+1.3	–0.5	–69S	10:44.4	+1.1	–0.2	–72S				
	22	2118	2.8	RD 66–	12:08.7	+1.8	–0.7	75N	12:00.0	+1.6	–0.5	74N				
Mar.	11	900	4.8	DD 58+	08:07.7	+0.1	–1.3	83S	08:01.7	+0.3	–1.3	88S				
	13	1169	5.3	DD 75+									06:14.4	+3.1	–0.3	86N
	20	1962	5.0	RD 94–	11:01.7	+1.3	–1.8	56N	10:50.1	+1.3	–1.7	55N				
	22	2217	5.5	RD 79–									11:15.2	+1.3	–0.2	82N
	23	2359	5.0	RD 70–	08:59.2	+0.5	–0.2	58N	08:56.9	+0.3	–0.2	53N				
Apr.	7	852	5.2	DD 31+									08:09.2	–0.2	–2.2	47S
	12	1484	3.5	DD 79+									11:39.2	+1.5	+0.0	46N
	17	2053	4.5	RD 99–									13:25.3	+3.0	+0.7	51S
	20	2479	5.1	RD 82–	12:24.1	+2.2	+1.2	36S	12:19.3	+2.2	+0.6	45S				
	20	2480	5.2	RD 82–	12:24.0	+2.2	+1.2	36S	12:19.4	+2.2	+0.7	45S				
	22	2848	5.6	RD 60–									13:31.1	+1.9	+0.4	76N
May	3	664	5.5	DD 5+									06:12.7	–0.4	–1.8	48S
	10	1544	5.4	DD 63+	08:36.9	+0.4	–0.9	54N	08:31.1	+0.7	–1.0	51N	08:37.2	+0.0	–3.2	35S
	14	1962	5.0	DD 95+	04:10.0	+0.7	–1.3	53S	04:02.9	+0.7	–1.0	58S				
	16	2217	5.5	DD 3E	03:24.4	+0.9	+1.7	33U	03:28.5	+1.1	+2.4	30U				
	16	2217	5.5	RD 0E	04:08.5	–0.2	–1.3	26U	04:04.1	–0.5	–1.7	27U				
	19	2784	3.3	RD 84–									12:32.2	+2.7	+1.6	59S
Jun.	3	1169	5.3	DD 12+									07:05.8	+1.6	+1.6	40N
	6	1484	3.5	DD 35+	02:47.5	+2.1	–1.2	81N	02:35.3	+2.2	–1.0	78N				
	6	1484	3.5	RB 35+	03:59.3	+0.4	–2.6	–49N	03:47.2	+0.5	–2.7	–48N				
	9	1821	2.8	DD 68+									11:05.9	+0.4	–1.5	87S
	11	2053	4.5	DD 86+	09:28.0	+0.7	–1.6	85S	09:18.9	+0.8	–1.6	88N	09:05.3	+0.9	–3.2	30S
	19	3343	5.7	RD 67–									12:49.9	+1.0	+3.8	26S
	19	3349	4.1	RD 66–									14:43.2	+1.8	+1.9	61S
	26	660	4.3	RD 5–									15:54.9	+0.4	+1.2	81S
Jul.	13	2784	3.3	DD 100+					09:00.6	+2.0	–0.7	34S				
Aug.	2	1821	2.8	DD 25+	22:24.3	+2.1	–0.1	85N	22:17.2	+1.9	+0.3	81N				
	7	2347	4.6	DD 69+	06:10.6	+1.7	–1.9	59S	05:58.1	+1.6	–1.5	67S				
	18	Uranus	5.7	RD 56–									13:34.2	–1.2	+4.9	10S
Sep.	3	2290	2.3	DD 43+									02:31.3	+2.8	+0.4	77N
	3	2290	2.3	RB 43+									03:47.5	+1.7	–2.1	–43N
	6	2784	3.3	DD 76+	02:33.6	+2.3	+1.6	60N	02:31.9	+2.2	+1.8	54N				
	8	3130	5.4	DD 94+	08:54.1	–1.6	+3.8	21N								
Oct.	2	2554	4.5	DD 40+	03:58.0	+1.5	–1.2	82S	03:48.5	+1.5	–0.9	86N				
	4	2914	4.8	DD 63+	05:54.1	+0.6	+0.4	55N	05:55.3	+0.1	+1.0	36N	04:51.1	+1.7	+5.7	21N
	7	3349	4.1	DD 91+	03:04.6	+1.8	+0.9	57S	03:02.8	+1.5	+1.2	67S				
	12	Uranus	5.7	RD 94–	05:37.5	–0.1	+2.6	37S	05:46.7	+0.1	+2.3	51S				
	18	1274	5.7	RD 42–					13:59.0	+2.3	–0.5	87N	12:38.5	+0.3	+2.1	45S
	20	1484	3.5	RD 24–	11:51.8	+0.9	+1.4	62S	11:53.2	+0.8	+0.9	78S				
	28	2371	4.8	DD 9+									04:49.6	+1.9	–3.0	45S
Nov.	14	1233	5.7	RD 69–									10:35.2	+2.6	–3.7	35N
	15	1363	5.2	RD 58–									16:44.9	+1.1	–3.6	39N
	17	1544	5.4	RD 41–	09:04.4	–0.1	+2.6	40S	09:12.2	+0.1	+1.6	60S				
	29	3158	5.7	DD 35+									08:10.9	+0.6	–0.5	81S
Dec.	1	3425	4.4	DD 57+	07:14.5	–0.8	+4.1	15N								
	1	3428	5.0	DD 57+					07:01.3	+1.0	–1.8	56S	06:05.6	+2.9	+0.1	74S
	4	257	4.3	DD 86+	09:08.1	+0.9	–1.6	61S	08:59.9	+1.0	–0.9	78S	07:52.8	+3.6	–0.2	66S
	7	599	4.4	DD 99+	02:27.1	+0.6	+1.4	85N	02:31.7	+0.3	+1.7	72N				
	8	Mars	–1.9	DB 100+	02:30.6	+0.2	+1.2	1N	02:35.5	+0.0	+1.5	–11N				
	8	Mars	–1.9	RD 100–	03:30.5	+0.3	+1.9	37N	03:36.2	+0.4	+1.7	24N				
	11	1169	5.3	RD 91–	05:59.6	–0.9	+5.7	20S	06:15.1	+0.2	+2.9	47S				
	17	1821	2.8	DB 37–									13:39.0	+1.0	–0.2	–90S
	17	1821	2.8	RD 37–									14:52.4	+1.1	–1.5	62N
	19	2053	4.5	RD 18–									15:16.0	+0.4	–1.1	56N
	25	2910	4.7	DD 4+	02:08.4	+0.5	–0.8	81N	02:04.2	+0.4	–0.5	64N				

DB/DD = Disappearance at Bright/Dark limb; RB/RD = Reappearance at Bright/Dark limb

See p. 163 for additional explanation of these tables.

NAMES OF STARS OCCULTED IN 2022

ZC	Name	ZC	Name	ZC	Name
215	96 Psc	1062	40 Gem	2105	5 Lib
238	CY Psc	1088	47 Gem	2118	α^2 Lib (Zubenelgenubi)
257	ο Psc (Torcular)	1149	υ Gem	2172	ι Lib
422	σ Ari	1169	76 Gem	2290	δ Sco (Dschubba)
531	13 Tau	1211	4 Cnc	2305	V929 Sco
533	14 Tau	1251	λ Cnc	2347	19 Sco
582	32 Tau	1263	24 Cnc	2443	26 Oph
599	37 Tau	1270	28 Cnc	2452	28 Oph
601	39 Tau	1274	υ^1 Cnc	2455	31 Oph
621	V1137 Tau	1279	υ^2 Cnc	2479	36 Oph N
631	51 Tau	1363	ξ Cnc	2480	26 Oph S
634	56 Tau	1365	79 Cnc	2554	X Sgr
656	κ Tau	1484	η Leo	2558	V3894 Sgr
657	67 Tau	1544	46 Leo	2601	7 Sgr
660	υ Tau	1733	7 Vir	2784	τ Sgr
664	72 Tau	1749	10 Vir	2910	ω Sgr (Terebellum)
693	V1116 Tau	1821	γ Vir (Porrima)	2914	60 Sgr
709	τ Tau	1849	38 Vir	3130	33 Cap
742	99 Tau	1866	44 Vir	3141	35 Cap
852	125 Tau	1869	46 Vir	3349	τ Aqr
867	V1165 Tau	1962	82 Vir	3358	75 Aqr
900	139 Tau	2034	EV Vir	3428	ψ^3 Aqr
1061	39 Gem	2053	λ Vir		

Names of occulted stars

The stars that are occulted by the Moon are stars that lie along the zodiac; hence they are known by their number in the Zodiacal Catalogue (ZC) compiled by James Robertson and published in the *Astronomical Papers Prepared for the Use of the American Ephemeris and Nautical Almanac, Vol. 10*, Part 2 (U.S. Government Printing Office, Washington, 1940). Robertson's ZC has been out of print for several years. In 1986, Isao Sato, a member of the Lunar Occultation Observers Group in Japan, republished the ZC. This new edition is based on the epoch J2000 and includes much new data, particularly on double stars. Since stars are not usually recognized by their ZC numbers, the equivalent Bayer designations or Flamsteed numbers of the stars occulted during the year are given in the table above. The ZC and XZ (now version XZ80Q) catalogs, updated in 2018 by D. Herald using *Gaia* data, are available through IOTA's website.

2. GRAZING OCCULTATIONS: PREDICTIONS AND STAR DATA

BY EBERHARD RIEDEL AND DAVID W. DUNHAM

Grazing occultation predictions

The table on pp. 174 lists lunar grazing occultation predictions for the 22 brighter stars and planets visible from much of North America in 2022. The events are limited to stars of magnitude 5.5 or brighter that will graze the limb of the Moon when it is at a favorable elongation from the Sun and at least as high above the horizon in degrees as the star's magnitude (e.g. a third-magnitude star is included only if its altitude is at least 3°). Some stars fainter than mag. 5.5 are included, to provide a good geographical distribution of paths. The map on pp. 173 shows the predicted graze tracks; the map is a "false" projection, since the latitude and longitude scales are both linear. This makes it much easier for measuring coordinates or plotting locations with known coordinates than is possible with any other type of projection. The longitude scale is compressed by a factor of cos 50°. The maps are not detailed enough for locating oneself in the 2- or 3-km-wide zone where multiple disappearances of the star may occur. To obtain detailed predictions of any graze for plotting on larger-scale maps of your region, write to (or email) IOTA (see p. 162). For some grazes, IOTA overlays the predicted limit line on the very detailed maps and imagery of maps.google.com, but further corrections are needed based on the predicted lunar profile and the observer's height above sea level. A Web .htm file to do this is generated by the free *Occult4* program (see above).

The 2022 month and day of month, and the star or planet's name or number are given along each track on the map. Conditions are represented by three different types of lines:

solid line = dark limb, night
dashed line = bright limb, night
dotted line = dark or bright limb, day

Thicker lines are drawn for first-magnitude stars and planets. Many tracks begin and/or end with the letter A, B, or S: A denotes that the Moon is at a low altitude, B that the bright limb interferes, and S that sunlight or twilight interferes. The tick marks along the tracks indicate multiples of 10 min of every hour. For example, if the time for the west end of the track is 3:16.2, the tick marks proceeding eastward correspond to 3:20, 3:30, etc. Time always increases from west to east along the path. The time ticks are on the side of the limit with an occultation, that is north of southern limits and south of northern limits. The locations for the North American standard stations for lunar total occultation predictions are indicated by asterisks on the graze map (see the map on p. 164). 248 grazes are shown on six maps and tables, similar to what we published in the Handbook for previous years, at occultations.org/publications/rasc/2022/nam22grz.htm. We are using the pages saved in this way, to add some maps of the more valuable asteroidal occultations in the Planetary Occultations section on pages 243 to 251.

Occulted stars known to be double

In the table at right are data on double stars for which graze predictions are given. This information is from DSFILE, a comprehensive file of zodiacal double-star data compiled by Don Stockbauer, Henk Bulder, Mitsuru Sôma, David Herald, and David Dunham; most of the data for the ZC stars are in the Sato ZC catalog. The successive columns give the ZC number of the star, the 2022 date, the double star code (d), the magnitudes of the brighter (A) and fainter (B) components, the separation in arcseconds, and the position angle (PA) of B from A measured eastward from north. If the star is triple, the third component's magnitude is given under C, and its separation and PA from A are given in the last columns.

The parameters are given for the epoch of the occultation, computed from orbital elements when available or from extrapolations from a long series of observations. If there is little change in the available observations, the last-observed separation and PA are used. Most components fainter than magnitude 12.0 are not listed, and some very close doubles whose parameters are not known, generally with separations less than 0.2□, are also not listed. The latter include spectroscopic binaries (code U, or sometimes V) and visual occultation doubles (most codes K and X, and many Vs).

The codes have the following meanings:

A	Double listed by Aitken and/or Burnham (ADS, BDS)
C	Double listed by Innes, Couteau, or other visual observers
D	primary of wide pair; secondary has separate catalog entry
K	U or V, but duplicity doubtful, only reported "gradual" from a past visual occultation observation
L	close triple star (only two stars often listed because inner pair is often spectroscopic; J or U, & V; all V; or all J)
O	orbital elements available and used to calculate the separation and PA
U	Double, separation 0.05″ or less, usually a 2-line spectroscopic binary
V	Close double discovered by occultation or by interferometry
W	Triple, J or U, and A or C
Y	triple, K or X (visual A component) and A or C (C component)

Some close pairs have rapid orbital motion such that the current PA is unknown.

STARS OCCULTED IN 2022 AND KNOWN TO BE DOUBLE

ZC#	Date	d	A	B	Sep. ″	PA °	C	Sep. ″	PA °
852	Jul. 25	L	5.2	7.2	0.0003		8.5	0.3	313
1484	Dec. 14	C	4.1	4.6	0.1	93			
1821	Mar. 19	O	3.5	3.5	3.0	357			
2214	May 16	Y	7.0	7.0	0.03	60	8.5	11.1	281
2290*	Apr. 19	O	2.5	4.5	0.006	350			
2617	Nov. 26	K	5.1	5.9	0.3	12			
3428	Dec. 1	A	5.2	11.2	1.8	131			

*ZC 2290 = δ Scorpii (Dschubba) will be near periastron of its 10.8-year period. During the last two periastrons, the star brightened to magnitude 1.6; this is likely to be the case for the April occultation. We have not found good information about the magnitude of the B-component; maybe it can be measured with a high-speed recording of the occultation. During the April 19th graze, the cusp angle will be 12S with a 92% sunlit waning Moon; at central graze, the star will be 8″ from the terminator, but with high mountains catching sunlight, the star might pass within 2″ of sunlit mountains. The total occultation reappearance visible 20 km or more north of the southern limit should not have any close terminator sunlit feature interference.

> *"Because the Moon moves through an angle about equal to its own diameter every hour, the longest time for an occultation is about an hour. The time is shorter if the occultation is not central. Solar eclipses are actually occultations: the star being occulted by the Moon is the Sun."*

GRAZING LUNAR OCCULTATIONS FOR 2022

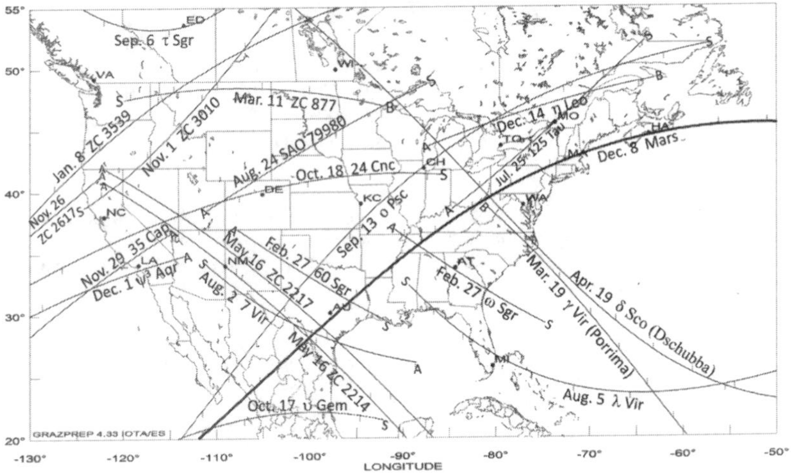

GRAZING LUNAR OCCULTATIONS FOR 2022

This table lists lunar grazing occultations for the brighter stars grazes under favorable conditions for much of North America. Their graze tracks are shown on the map on p. 173. For each graze, the table provides:

Date..............The 2022 date
Object name....Planet name, or star's proper name, Bayer Greek letter or Flamsteed number designation
ZC/SAO.........The star's ZC or Smithsonian Astrophysical Observatory (SAO) catalog number
d.................. double star code (if the star is double or triple) – see p. 172
m.................. its visual magnitude
%sl...............the percent of the Moon sunlit (+ for waxing, – for waning, E for lunar eclipse)
L..................whether the track is a northern (N) or southern (S) limit
W.U.T........... the Universal Time at the west end of the track
Lo., La........... the longitude and latitude of the west end of the track

Date	Object Name	ZC/SAO	d	*m*	%sl	L	W.U.T.	Lo.	La.
Jan. 8		ZC 3529	K	6.5	33+	S	02:03.8	−130	38
Feb. 27	ω Sgr	ZC 2910	K	4.7	14–	S	11:19.8	−90	37
Feb. 27	60 Sgr	ZC 2914	V	4.8	14–	S	12:31.0	−107	37
Mar. 11		ZC 877		6.5	55+	S	02:08.7	−120	48
Mar. 19	Porrima	ZC 1821	O	2.8	99–	S	05:10.8	−80	39
Apr. 19	Dschubba	ZC 2290	L	2.3	92–	S	06:13.2	−101	55
May 16		ZC 2217		5.5	0E	N	03:48.0	−122	42
May 16		ZC 2214	Y	6.3	0E	S	03:52.4	−122	41
Jul. 25	125 Tauri	ZC 852	L	5.2	10–	N	08:01.0	−84	39
Aug. 2	7 Vir	ZC 1733		5.4	17+	N	02:33.5	−111	34
Aug. 5	λ Vir	ZC 2053	U	4.5	45+	N	00:51.6	−89	32
Aug. 24		SAO 79980		7.3	8–	N	10:34.2	−111	39
Sep. 6	t Sgr	ZC 2784	V	3.3	76+	N	03:07.5	−124	55
Sep. 13	o Psc	ZC 257		4.3	90–	N	07 32.8	−114	20
Oct. 17	n Gem	ZC 1149	W	4.1	53–	N	10:54.5	−114	20
Oct. 18	24 Cancri	ZC 1263	D	6.9	44–	N	09:51.6	−130	33
Nov. 1		ZC 3010		6.4	47+	S	01:26.3	−124	39
Nov. 26		ZC 2617	K	4.5	6+	S	01:39.0	−130	37
Nov. 29	35 Cap	ZC 3141		5.8	34+	S	04:51.0	−130	28
Dec. 1	ψ^3 Aqr	ZC 3428	A	5.0	57+	S	07:19.0	−130	30
Dec. 8	Mars			−1.9	100+	S	02:41.2	−112	20
Dec. 14	ν Leonis	ZC 1484	C	3.5	71–	N	03:34.6	−87	44

"The Moon often passes between Earth and a star, an event called an occultation. During an occultation, a star suddenly disappears as the east limb of the Moon crosses the line between the star and the observer. The star reappears from behind the west limb some time later."

Lunar-occultation and graze observations refine our knowledge of the shape of the lunar profile and the fundamental star-coordinate system. These observations complement those made by other techniques, such as Kaguya *and* Lunar Reconnaissance Orbiter *laser ranging and photographs.*

TIDES AND THE EARTH–MOON SYSTEM

BY ROY BISHOP

The tidal aspect of gravitation produces some of the most interesting phenomena in the Universe, from the structure of interacting galaxies, such as M51, to the volcanoes of Io, the fragmentation of Comet Shoemaker–Levy 9 by Jupiter in 1992, the synchronous rotation of our Moon, and the pulse of the seas on our planet. Because they occur at our feet, the tides of the oceans are often overlooked when considering the heavens; yet the pulse of the tides is the heartbeat of a greater Universe beyond Earth.

Newtonian Tides

Tides have been known for millennia, but an understanding of their origin came just over three centuries ago with the publication of Newton's *Principia* (1687). In the Newtonian context, the decrease of the force of gravity with distance causes the tides. The Moon exerts a force on Earth, and Earth responds by accelerating toward the Moon; however, the waters on the hemisphere facing the Moon, being closer to the Moon, accelerate more and fall ahead of Earth. Similarly, Earth itself accelerates more than the waters on the other hemisphere and falls ahead of those waters; the Moon is yanking Earth out from under the waters on the more distant hemisphere, leaving those waters behind. Thus two tidal bulges are produced, one on the side of Earth facing the Moon and one on the side facing away from the Moon. Because the Moon is quite far from Earth (about 60 Earth radii), the two tidal bulges are essentially equal in size.

Note that the waters directly under the Moon and the waters farthest from the Moon do not rise up because of the slightly larger and smaller, respectively, lunar gravity at these two locations; all that results from the Moon's action on the waters at these two points is a slight decrease in the pressure on the floor of the sea. The two tidal bulges form because the variation in the Moon's gravity causes the *surrounding* waters on each hemisphere to flow horizontally across Earth's surface into these regions:

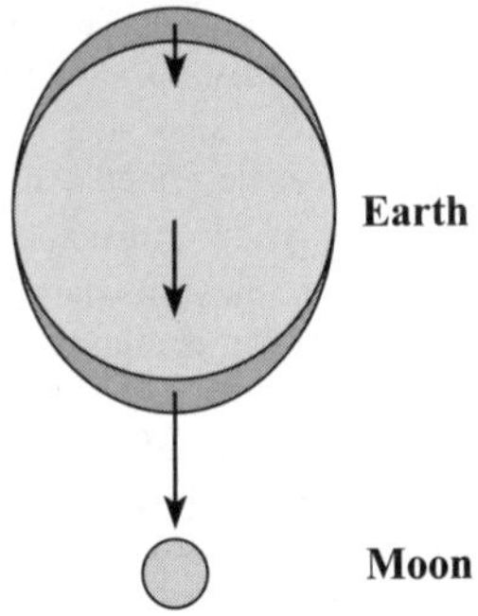

In order of decreasing length, the arrows indicate the force per unit mass (acceleration) produced by the Moon's gravity on the near side, center, and far side of Earth. It is the resulting horizontal flow of the water across Earth's surface toward the two points nearest and farthest from the Moon that produces the two tidal bulges (indicated by heavy shading).

As Earth rotates on its axis, the orientation of the two bulges relative to the Moon remains fixed; hence the rise and fall of the oceans on Earth. The solid Earth is not perfectly rigid. It too responds to the tidal influences of Moon and Sun, resulting in an elastic *body tide* (vertical range ~0.4 m). Lesser, more-localized deformations of the solid Earth are caused indirectly by *ocean tide loading*.

Because of the Moon's orbital motion, it transits on average 50.47 min later each day. Thus on successive days, high tides recur about 50 min later; or for the many regions experiencing two high tides daily, these tides recur at intervals of 12 h 25 min.

The Sun exerts a gravitational force 180 times stronger than that exerted by the Moon on Earth; however, because the Moon is so much closer, the *variation* in the Moon's force across Earth's diameter is about 2.2 times larger than the variation in the Sun's force. As described above, it is this variation that produces tides; thus the pair of bulges raised by the Moon is considerably larger than the pair raised by the Sun. As the Moon goes through its monthly cycle of phases, the two pairs of tidal bulges get in and out of step, combining in step to produce *spring tides* (no connection with the season) when the Moon is new or full (syzygy) and out of step to produce *neap tides* when the Moon is near first or last quarter (quadrature).

Another factor having a substantial influence on tidal ranges is the elliptical shape of the Moon's orbit. The Moon is only 8% to 12% closer at perigee than at apogee; however, because the *variation* in its gravitational force varies inversely as the cube of its distance (the force itself varies inversely as the square of the distance), the Moon's tidal influence is 30% to 49% greater at perigee than at apogee. Because the Sun tidally influences the shape of the Moon's orbit, exceptionally close perigees coincide with full or new Moon, and the resulting extreme tides are known as *perigean spring tides* (colloquially known along some coasts as *king tides*). If the lunar orbit were fixed in orientation, such tides would recur at half-year intervals, alternately with new and full Moon; however, the major axis of the lunar orbit rotates prograde with a period of 8.85 years, making the average interval between perigean spring tides about 23 days longer than half a year (205.9 days).

The day to day variation in the vertical range of the tides at a given locality is determined both by the energy being put into the tides and by the energy being lost through friction with the seabed. As long as the input is greater than the loss, the tide range will increase even though the input may have peaked and already be decreasing. Hence the tide range is greatest not when the astronomical influences peak, but a day or two later when the decreasing input equals the increasing loss. At that point the energy in the tides is at a maximum.

Influences on the Tides

Five, basic, astronomical periods significantly impact the tides. In increasing length these are: Earth's mean rotation day, the draconic, sidereal, and anomalistic months, and the sidereal year (see p. 29). The resulting periods that show up in the tides include (in ascending order):

(1) semidiurnal, 12 h 00 min (two solar-induced tidal bulges, as described above);

(2) semidiurnal, 12 h 25 min (two lunar-induced tidal bulges, as described above);

(3) diurnal, 24 h 00 min (the usual nonzero declination of the Sun shifts the pair of solar tidal bulges out of Earth's equatorial plane, resulting in a tidal component with a one-day period);

(4) diurnal, 24 h 50 min (the usual nonzero declination of the Moon shifts the pair of lunar tidal bulges out of Earth's equatorial plane, resulting in a tidal component with a one-day period; that is the dominant tide in some areas, such as parts of the southern coast of Canada's Gulf of St. Lawrence);

(5) semimonthly, 13.66 days (variation in the Moon's declination);

(6) semimonthly, 14.77 days (spring–neap cycle, described above);

(7) monthly, 27.55 days (perigee–apogee cycle, described above);

(8) semiannual, 182.63 days (variation in the Sun's declination);

(9) semiannual, 205.9 days (perigean spring cycle, described above);

(10) annual, 365.26 days (perihelion–aphelion cycle);

(11) 4.43 years (perigean-spring tides near an equinox recur at half the prograde precession period of the major axis of the lunar orbit); and

(12) 18.61 years (retrograde precession of the nodes of the lunar orbit).

In addition to astronomical factors, the tides on Earth are strongly influenced by the sizes, boundaries, and depths of ocean basins and inlets and by Earth's rotation, winds, and barometric pressure fluctuations. Using Newton's gravitation and laws of motion, the French physicist Pierre-Simon Laplace (1749–1827) developed the dynamical theory of the tides on the rotating Earth (*Mécanique Céleste*, 1799), but because of the complexity of the tides the full application of his theory was not possible until the advent of the digital computer in the last third of the 20th century.

Tides typically have ranges (vertical high to low) of a metre or two, but there are regions in the oceans where the various influences conspire to produce virtually no tides at all (called amphidromic points) and others where the tides are greatly amplified. Among the latter regions are the Sea of Okhotsk, the Gulf of Alaska, the northwest coast of Australia, the English Channel, and in Canada, Ungava Bay in northern Québec, and the Bay of Fundy between New Brunswick and Nova Scotia. The tidal ranges in these regions are of the order of 10 m.

Fundy Tides

Only two localities on Earth sometimes have a vertical tide range exceeding 16 m (52 ft.), and both are in Canada: Minas Basin, the eastern extremity of the Bay of Fundy in Nova Scotia, and Leaf Basin, a remote inlet on the southwestern side of Ungava Bay in northern Québec. The current best data give Minas Basin a slight edge; however, several years of tide gauge data continuing through a peak in the 18.61-year tide cycle are needed to determine which site, if either (to the precision that measurements can be made), has the greater tide range.

The primary cause of the immense tides of Fundy is a resonance of the Bay of Fundy/Gulf of Maine system. The system is effectively bounded at its outer end by the edge of the continental shelf with its approximately 40:1 increase in depth. The system has a natural period of approximately 13 hours, a *Q*-value* of about 5, and is driven near resonance, not directly by the Moon, but by the dominant semidiurnal tides of the Atlantic Ocean. Like a father pushing his daughter on a swing, the gentle Atlantic tidal pulse pushes the waters of the Bay of Fundy/Gulf of Maine basin at nearly the optimum frequency to cause a large oscillation. The seventh Astronomer Royal, Sir G.B. Airy (1801–1892), first developed the theory of the behavior of tides in restricted arms of the ocean such as the Fundy system.

Fundy tides are unique in that they respond more to the perigee–apogee influence than they do to the spring–neap influence. That is because the lunar tidal period (12.42 hours) is closer to the system's resonant period than is the solar tidal period (12.00 hours). Although the variation in the Moon's distance is not obvious when viewing the Moon directly, near the head of the Bay of Fundy the 3-m to 6-m *increase* in the vertical tidal range makes it obvious when the Moon is near perigee, clear skies or cloudy!

The most dramatic view of the vertical range of Fundy tides is at the Minas Basin Pulp & Power Company wharf in the town of Hantsport, Nova Scotia. That site is practically unknown and, unfortunately, it is not open to the public.

Perhaps the most awesome display of the tides on our planet occurs at Cape Split, Nova Scotia, on the southern side of the entrance to Minas Basin. (Cape Split may be reached by a pleasant two-hour walk along a popular hiking trail from the village of Scots Bay.) Here, at the time of the midpoint of an incoming tide, for a considerable distance the forest on the towering cliffs is filled with a hollow roar produced by

* The *Q*-value, or quality-value, of an oscillator indicates its efficiency. A large *Q* means low energy loss per cycle and a well-defined resonant frequency. A *Q* of 5 is relatively small, indicative of considerable damping in the Fundy system, yet it is large enough to make these tides among the highest on Earth.

the turbulence of the waters surging over the submarine ridges below. The currents exceed 8 knots (4 m/s), and the flow in the deep, 5-km-wide channel on the north side of Cape Split equals the combined flow of all the streams and rivers of Earth (approximately 1 million tonnes per second, or 4 cubic kilometres per hour). Three hours later the spectacle pauses and then begins flowing in the opposite direction.

The highest of the high tides in the Bay of Fundy occur when a perigean spring high tide coincides with a low-barometric-pressure storm system sweeping northward across New Brunswick, accompanied by hurricane-force southerly winds over the Gulf of Maine and the Bay of Fundy. The close Moon, the in-phase solar tide, the reduced air pressure above the water, and the wind drag pushing more water into the Bay of Fundy (the last two effects are called a storm surge) all contribute to an especially high tide. An additional favorable influence is if all this occurs near an equinox, for then the axis of the tidal bulges of the spring tide is at a right angle to Earth's rotation axis, optimizing the semidiurnal tidal range at all latitudes (see item (11), above). This right-angle-axes enhancement of the tides is strengthened in those years when the declination range of the Moon (±18° to ±29°) is near a minimum, a situation that recurs with the 18.61-year period of the retrograde motion of the nodes of its orbit relative to the equinoxes. (The declination range was at its ±18° minimum in 1959, 1978, 1997, and 2015, and will be again in 2034 and 2052. See p. 95 for the shift in the longitude of the ascending node of the Moon's orbit during 2022.) Furthermore, since perihelion occurs in January, the highest tides of all tend to occur just prior to the March equinox or after the September equinox. The infamous Bay of Fundy "Saxby gale" of 1869 Oct. 5 was a time when all seven of these factors approximately coincided (perigee, spring tide, low pressure, south wind, equinox, minimum declination range, and perihelion enhancement). Weather is unpredictable. Thus, so too is the next major tidal flood in the Bay of Fundy.

Paradoxically, the large tides of Fundy protect its shores from flooding associated with most storm surges, since the normal variation in its high tide levels is already several metres. Only those rare storm surges that happen to coincide with a perigean spring high tide will be a problem. In contrast, shorelines with small tides are much more susceptible to storm surges.

Sea level is slowly increasing in the Bay of Fundy/Gulf of Maine region. That is bringing the resonant period of the system closer to the lunar tidal period which, in turn, is causing Fundy tides to gradually become even larger (by a few centimetres per decade).

Tidal Friction

Tidal friction, which occurs primarily in shallow seas around the margins of the oceans, transforms Earth's rotational kinetic energy into heat at a rate of about 3.7 TW, comparable to humankind's total rate of energy use. Approximately 1% of this energy transformation occurs in the Bay of Fundy, and, since 1984, a tiny portion of this (20 MW peak) is being turned into commercial electric power at the Annapolis Basin tidal power plant in Nova Scotia. Two larger tidal power plants exist: the Rance in France (240 MW) and the Sihwa Lake in South Korea (254 MW peak).

The aforementioned tidal power plants use turbines located in dams (also called barrages). At a few sites, including the Bay of Fundy, studies presently are underway for using isolated turbines located in tidal currents—effectively underwater windmills. The problem with this approach is that the power available in currents of 8 knots or less is dilute. To generate significant electrical power (100 MW or more), large turbine cross-sections are required, with attendant high capital and maintenance costs.

Tidal friction also transfers angular momentum from Earth to the Moon, lengthening the day and increasing the size of the orbit of the Moon. The day is lengthening by about 1 s every 40 000 years—imperceptible on a human time scale but of profound significance to Earth's rotation over a few billion years. (For example, 900 million years ago, when Earth was already 80% of its present age, there were about 480 18-hour days in a year.) The Moon is receding about 3.8 cm per year, with the result that about one billion years from now total solar eclipses will cease. Presently we are well into the transitional phase: Annular eclipses already outnumber total solar eclipses.

General Relativity and Tides

Einstein's theory of gravitation, general relativity, superseded Newton's theory more than a century ago, yet descriptions of the tides almost invariably ignore Einstein (as has this article to this point). There are three reasons for using the older, wrong theory: (1) Newton's theory describes the gentle tides on Earth to high accuracy; (2) the mathematics involved is much simpler than that of general relativity; (3) the Newtonian description of the tides is compatible with cultivated common sense. Because of (3), Newton's concepts regarding motion and gravitation form the essential foundation for anyone attempting to understand the tides. One must climb up on Newton's towering shoulders before it is possible to focus clearly on Einstein.

As mentioned in the section ORBITAL MOTION (see p. 27), Newton's Euclidean universe with its force of gravity never did exist. Although Newton's ideas are more than adequate for describing the tides on Earth, for some purposes, such as the Global Positioning System (GPS), Newton's concepts of space, time, and gravitation are inadequate. We inhabit an Einsteinian universe, a universe in which gravitation is a manifestation of the structure of spacetime, the four-dimensional stage of our existence in which space and time are interwoven. The geometry of spacetime is curved by the mass–energy of matter, and the curvature instructs matter how to move. That instruction has an astounding grip. If spacetime were not curved, a mind-boggling 300-km diameter steel cable, stressed to its breaking point, would be required to connect Earth and Moon in order to maintain their mutual orbit.

The Moon's mass alters the structure of spacetime at its location, and this distortion propagates outward, becoming more dilute with the volume encompassed according to the inverse cube of the distance. At Earth, the distortion results in the waters of the oceans following slightly different paths through spacetime than does the rigid planet beneath, producing the characteristic egglike shape of the tidal effect. The tidal heartbeat is that of the very fabric of spacetime. The tides at our feet carry a profound message, a message that Albert Einstein was the first to fully grasp.

References

For more information, see the superb introduction *The Tides* by E.P. Clancy, Anchor Books, Doubleday and Co., 1969 (now, unfortunately, out of print). For a detailed account of the evolution of our understanding of the tides see *Tides, A Scientific History*, by D.E. Cartwright, Cambridge University Press, 1999. An excellent book covering tides, storm surges, tsunamis, and sea level in general is *Sea-Level Science* by D. Pugh and P. Woodworth, Cambridge University Press, 2014. (Note, however, that none of these four authors mentions general relativity.) For a popular account of general relativity, see *A Journey into Gravity and Spacetime*, by J.A. Wheeler, Scientific American Library, 1990. The major astronomical factors influencing the tides (the phases, perigees, and apogees of the Moon) are tabulated in THE SKY MONTH BY MONTH section (see p. 94) of this Handbook. For tide predictions at many sites world-wide, see tbone.biol.sc.edu/tide/index.html.

THE SUN

EPHEMERIS FOR THE SUN

BY PATRICK KELLY

Sundial Correction

The **Greenwich Transit** time in the table opposite may be used to calculate the sundial correction at the observer's position. For example, to find the correction at New York on 2022 Jul. 18, determine the following: At Greenwich, the Sun transits at 12:06:03 on Jul. 16 and at 12:06:22 on Jul. 20. Thus, to the nearest min, on Jul. 18 at both Greenwich and New York, the Sun will transit at 12:06 local mean solar time (LMT), or 12:02 Eastern Standard Time (EST) since New York has a longitude correction of –4 min (see the 3rd paragraph on p. 201). Thus a 6-min correction must be added to the reading of a simple sundial to obtain LMT (compare with the horizontal position of the light dot marking Jul. 9 on the analemma, on the bottom right of the facing page). An additional 4 min must be subtracted to obtain EST, and 1 hour must be added for Eastern Daylight Time (EDT). Thus solar noon will occur at 1:02 p.m. EDT

Even with these corrections, a sundial may still read incorrectly. For the horizontal sundial, the *gnomon* (vertical part) must be aligned to true north with the *dial* (horizontal part) level. The angle of the gnomon and the hour angles on the dial must be appropriate for the latitude. Beware of "consumer" sundials with poorly marked hour angles and crooked styles. (The *style* is the edge of the gnomon that casts the shadow.) Thick gnomons should taper to an edge, otherwise they have two styles, neither casting a shadow in the right place. The 6 a.m. and 6 p.m. hour angles should form a straight line perpendicular to the gnomon, meeting where the style meets the dial.

Orientation of the Sun

The table on the next page gives three angles that specify the orientation of the Sun.

P is the position angle of the axis of rotation, measured eastward in the observer's sky from the north point on the disk (i.e. counterclockwise). Note that *P* varies between +26° (solar north pole tilted eastward) and –26° (tilted westward) during the year. This tilt is associated mainly with the inclination of the ecliptic in the observer's sky, with a smaller contribution from the Sun's 7.2° inclination to the ecliptic (the longitude of the ascending node of the solar equator on the ecliptic is 76°).

B_0 is the heliographic latitude of the center of the disk, and is the result of the Sun's 7.2° inclination to the ecliptic. Note that positive values of B_0 correspond to the solar equator passing south of the center of the disk, with the solar north pole being tipped toward the observer.

L_0 is the heliographic longitude of the center of the disk measured from Carrington's solar prime meridian in the direction of rotation. L_0 decreases about 13° per day. The dates during the year when L_0 = 0° are given in the table below. The rotation period of the Sun depends upon heliographic latitude. The synodic and sidereal periods of rotation at the solar equator are 27.2753 days and 25.38 days, respectively.

Commencement (UT) of Numbered Synodic Solar Rotations

No.*	Commences	No.	Commences	No.	Commences	No.	Commences
2252 '21	Dec. 15.49	2256	Apr. 3.81	2260	Jul. 21.69	2264	Nov. 7.74
2253 '22	Jan. 11.82	2257	May 1.07	2261	Aug. 17.91	2265 '22	Dec. 5.05
2254	Feb. 8.17	2258	May 28.29	2262	Sep. 14.17	2266 '23	Jan. 1.38
2255	Mar. 7.50	2259	Jun. 24.49	2263	Oct. 11.44	2267	Jan. 28.72

*Based on R.C. Carrington's Greenwich photoheliocentric series, in which rotation No. 1 commenced 1853 Nov. 9.

EPHEMERIS FOR THE SUN, 2022

Date 0h UT	Apparent RA (2022) h m	Apparent Dec ° ′	Greenwich Transit UT	Orientation P	Orientation B_0	Orientation L_0
Jan 1	18 45.8	−23 01	12:03:17	2.1	−3.0	142.5
5	19 03.4	−22 38	12:05:08	0.1	−3.5	89.9
9	19 20.9	−22 08	12:06:53	−1.8	−3.9	37.2
13	19 38.3	−21 31	12:08:28	−3.7	−4.3	344.5
17	19 55.5	−20 47	12:09:53	−5.6	−4.7	291.8
21	20 12.5	−19 57	12:11:07	−7.4	−5.1	239.2
25	20 29.3	−19 01	12:12:09	−9.2	−5.5	186.5
29	20 45.9	−18 00	12:12:59	−10.9	−5.8	133.8
Feb 2	21 02.3	−16 53	12:13:36	−12.6	−6.1	81.2
6	21 18.4	−15 41	12:13:59	−14.1	−6.4	28.5
10	21 34.4	−14 26	12:14:10	−15.6	−6.6	335.8
14	21 50.1	−13 06	12:14:08	−17.0	−6.8	283.2
18	22 05.7	−11 43	12:13:54	−18.4	−6.9	230.5
22	22 21.0	−10 17	12:13:30	−19.6	−7.1	177.8
26	22 36.2	−8 49	12:12:55	−20.7	−7.2	125.1
Mar 2	22 51.3	−7 18	12:12:12	−21.7	−7.2	72.5
6	23 06.2	−5 46	12:11:21	−22.7	−7.3	19.8
10	23 21.0	−4 12	12:10:23	−23.5	−7.2	327.1
14	23 35.7	−2 38	12:09:19	−24.2	−7.2	274.3
18	23 50.3	−1 03	12:08:11	−24.9	−7.1	221.6
22	0 04.9	+0 32	12:07:00	−25.4	−7.0	168.9
26	0 19.5	+2 07	12:05:48	−25.8	−6.8	116.1
30	0 34.1	+3 40	12:04:36	−26.0	−6.7	63.4
Apr 3	0 48.7	+5 13	12:03:25	−26.2	−6.5	10.6
7	1 03.3	+6 44	12:02:16	−26.3	−6.2	317.8
11	1 18.0	+8 14	12:01:10	−26.2	−5.9	265.0
15	1 32.7	+9 41	12:00:09	−26.0	−5.6	212.2
19	1 47.5	+11 06	11:59:13	−25.7	−5.3	159.4
23	2 02.5	+12 27	11:58:24	−25.3	−5.0	106.6
27	2 17.6	+13 46	11:57:43	−24.8	−4.6	53.7
May 1	2 32.8	+15 00	11:57:10	−24.1	−4.2	0.9
5	2 48.1	+16 11	11:56:45	−23.4	−3.8	308.0
9	3 03.6	+17 18	11:56:29	−22.5	−3.4	255.1
13	3 19.3	+18 20	11:56:21	−21.5	−2.9	202.2
17	3 35.1	+19 17	11:56:23	−20.4	−2.5	149.3
21	3 51.0	+20 08	11:56:34	−19.2	−2.0	96.4
25	4 07.1	+20 54	11:56:53	−17.9	−1.5	43.5
29	4 23.4	+21 35	11:57:21	−16.5	−1.1	350.6
Jun 2	4 39.7	+22 09	11:57:56	−15.1	−0.6	297.7
6	4 56.2	+22 38	11:58:37	−13.5	−0.1	244.7
10	5 12.7	+23 00	11:59:23	−11.9	0.4	191.8
14	5 29.3	+23 15	12:00:12	−10.2	0.9	138.8
18	5 45.9	+23 24	12:01:03	−8.5	1.4	85.9
22	6 02.6	+23 26	12:01:55	−6.8	1.8	32.9
26	6 19.2	+23 22	12:02:47	−5.0	2.3	340.0
30	6 35.8	+23 11	12:03:36	−3.2	2.7	287.0
Jul 4	6 52.3	+22 54	12:04:22	−1.4	3.2	234.1
8	7 08.8	+22 30	12:05:03	0.5	3.6	181.2
12	7 25.1	+22 00	12:05:37	2.3	4.0	128.2
16	7 41.3	+21 24	12:06:03	4.0	4.4	75.3
20	7 57.4	+20 42	12:06:22	5.8	4.8	22.4
24	8 13.3	+19 55	12:06:32	7.5	5.1	329.4
28	8 29.1	+19 02	12:06:33	9.2	5.5	276.5
Aug 1	8 44.7	+18 04	12:06:24	10.8	5.8	223.6
5	9 00.2	+17 02	12:06:05	12.3	6.1	170.7
9	9 15.5	+15 55	12:05:36	13.8	6.3	117.8
13	9 30.6	+14 44	12:04:58	15.3	6.5	64.9
17	9 45.6	+13 29	12:04:11	16.6	6.7	12.1
21	10 00.5	+12 11	12:03:16	17.9	6.9	319.2
25	10 15.2	+10 50	12:02:14	19.1	7.0	266.3
29	10 29.8	+9 26	12:01:06	20.2	7.1	213.5
Sep 2	10 44.4	+8 00	11:59:51	21.3	7.2	160.7
6	10 58.8	+6 31	11:58:32	22.2	7.2	107.8
10	11 13.2	+5 01	11:57:10	23.1	7.3	55.0
14	11 27.6	+3 30	11:55:44	23.8	7.2	2.2
18	11 41.9	+1 58	11:54:19	24.5	7.2	309.4
22	11 56.3	+0 24	11:52:53	25.1	7.1	256.6
26	12 10.6	−1 09	11:51:30	25.5	6.9	203.8
30	12 25.1	−2 42	11:50:09	25.9	6.8	151.0
Oct 4	12 39.5	−4 15	11:48:52	26.1	6.6	98.2
8	12 54.1	−5 48	11:47:41	26.2	6.4	45.4
12	13 08.8	−7 18	11:46:36	26.3	6.1	352.7
16	13 23.6	−8 48	11:45:39	26.2	5.8	299.9
20	13 38.6	−10 15	11:44:52	25.9	5.5	247.1
24	13 53.8	−11 40	11:44:15	25.6	5.2	194.4
28	14 09.1	−13 02	11:43:49	25.1	4.8	141.6
Nov 1	14 24.7	−14 21	11:43:35	24.5	4.4	88.9
5	14 40.4	−15 36	11:43:34	23.8	4.0	36.1
9	14 56.4	−16 47	11:43:45	22.9	3.6	343.4
13	15 12.6	−17 54	11:44:11	21.9	3.1	290.7
17	15 29.0	−18 55	11:44:50	20.9	2.7	237.9
21	15 45.6	−19 51	11:45:42	19.6	2.2	185.2
25	16 02.5	−20 42	11:46:48	18.3	1.7	132.5
29	16 19.5	−21 26	11:48:05	16.9	1.2	79.8
Dec 3	16 36.7	−22 04	11:49:34	15.3	0.7	27.0
7	16 54.2	−22 35	11:51:12	13.7	0.2	334.3
11	17 11.7	−22 58	11:52:58	12.0	−0.4	281.6
15	17 29.4	−23 15	11:54:50	10.2	−0.9	228.9
19	17 47.1	−23 24	11:56:47	8.4	−1.4	176.2
23	18 04.8	−23 26	11:58:46	6.5	−1.9	123.5
27	18 22.6	−23 20	12:00:45	4.6	−2.4	70.8
31	18 40.3	−23 07	12:02:42	2.7	−2.9	18.1

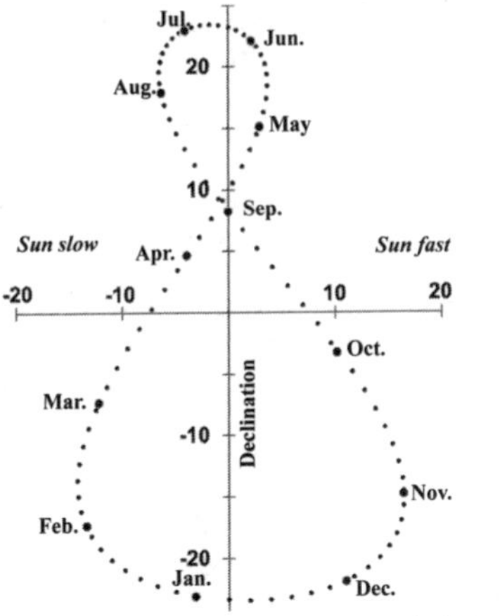

The bowling-pin-shaped ***analemma*** *depicts the drift of apparent solar time or sundial time relative to LMT (horizontal axis) and the changing declination of the Sun (vertical axis) during 2022. For points to the left of the vertical axis ("Sun slow"), the Sun transits after 12:00 LMT. To the right ("Sun fast"), the Sun transits before 12:00 LMT. For each month, a heavy dot marks day 1 with small dots for days 5, 9, 13, 17, 21, 25, and 29.* *See p. 40 for further details.*

SOLAR OBSERVING

BY KIM HAY

The Sun, our closest star, is a wonderful Solar System object to observe with any type of telescope, if used **SAFELY**. Never look directly at the Sun, and always use a **full-aperture solar filter**. The solar filters that screw into the base of an eyepiece should be **thrown out** and **never used**. The telescope objective concentrates sunlight on such an eyepiece filter, making it very hot, leading to possible breakage, with a high risk of vision loss. The only safe filter is the kind that covers the full aperture of the telescope, at the front, allowing only 1/100 000th of the sunlight through the telescope, thus lowering the heating effect and allowing you to view the Sun safely. Ensure that the filter material is specifically certified as suitable for solar observing.

The preferred solar filters come from Thousand Oaks Optical (Solarlite) or Baader film. The Thousand Oaks glass gives the Sun a golden-orange color. The Baader film gives the Sun a natural, white look, which can provide good contrast if there are any plages on the Sun (see below). Other options include lightweight Mylar film (which gives a blue-white tint) and eyepiece projection. Projecting the image from the eyepiece onto white card-stock paper or a wall produces an image that can be safely shared with others.

For safety, the finder must be kept covered. Since your telescope and finder are aligned, look at the shadow of the telescope on the ground and move the telescope until you have the smallest shadow on the ground. The Sun should be in the eyepiece, or close to it. Alternatively, make a small filter for your finder, if you want to use it.

For the amateur, there are alternatives for observing the Sun in various wavelength bands—the simplest method involves a wide spectrum of sunlight, using the solar filters described above. For the enthusiast, narrowband filters, such as the hydrogen-alpha (Hα) red filter (656.3 nm) or the calcium K-line (CaK) violet filter (393.4 nm), can be fitted to existing telescopes (but they also need a broadband pre-filter). Recently, dedicated solar telescopes with built-in narrowband filters have become affordable. An Hα filter shows solar prominences at the solar limb and possibly granulation on the disk. The CaK filter (especially in photographs) enhances granularity and flares.

A Herschel wedge (a type of prism used for white-light observing and photography) can be used, but **with caution**. Only 5% of the light is reflected to the eyepiece. The remaining 95% that is directed out the end of the diagonal is very intense and can burn. Herschel wedges should only be used with refractors or a telescope with an aperture stop to avoid the buildup of heat, which could damage internal components. The cover should only be taken off after the telescope has been set up. You will also need a neutral-density filter (optical density 3.0–4.0, 0.01%–0.001% transmittance). For enhanced viewing comfort, a filter (either green or polarizing) may help, depending on the sky conditions. **A Herschel wedge should only be used by an experienced observer.**

The Sun is best observed at high angular altitude, minimizing the optical effects of the unstable lower 100 m of atmosphere. Try to observe when the Sun is at least 25° above the horizon. Keep in mind that daytime atmospheric seeing conditions are usually very poor, so even a small telescope can be used without loss of detail. Another observing tip is to use a dark hood to cover your head and the eyepiece to block stray light, improving views of fine details.

Observing the morphology of prominences, filaments, flares, sunspots, and other solar phenomena is a great way to witness the dynamics of the Sun. These phenomena result from the strong magnetism within the Sun, which erupts to the surface. An active area can start with plages (white areas) and faculae, turn into a pore, and then blossom into a small dark spot. As a pore grows into a sunspot (umbra), a grey area (penumbra) surrounds the sunspot. The umbra is cooler than the surrounding penumbra. Prominences are solar plasma ejections, some of which fall back to the Sun in the form of teardrops or loops; against the Sun's disk, prominences appear as dark filaments. In a turbulence-free atmosphere, look for white-light flares, which are flash-points produced from

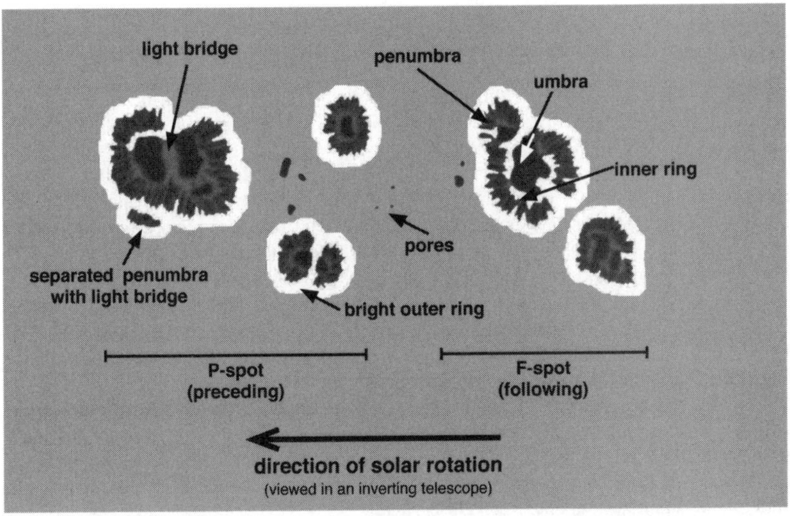

Nomenclature of phenomena related to sunspots. As the morphology of a sunspot changes, growing into a larger group, it eventually starts to dissipate and show trailing sunspots. Light bridges are formed early and stay with a sunspot over its lifetime. The formation of a light bridge is a slow process taking several days. The light-bridge material generally appears first on the outside of the umbra-penumbra boundary then extends across the umbra. When the light bridge is seen, it can signify the division or final dissolution of the spot. Light bridges have three general features: classic light bridges, islands, and streamers. (Image used with permission from the Solar Astronomy Handbook *and adapted for publication.)*

sudden discharges of energy. Flares can last from a few moments to several hours, but they are generally measured in minutes. There are also limb flares, flare kernels/hot cores, two-ribbon/two-strand flares, Hyder/impact flares, homologous flares, and Moreton waves, which are shock waves emanating from a white-light flare. An intense solar flare can eject charged particles, which may reach Earth, possibly exciting the upper atmosphere to create aurorae.

Counting sunspots and groups is another interesting activity. For consistency, observing should be done at the same time each day. Start at the limb of the Sun, because this is where you will notice plages and faculae. Then sweep across the disk in a grid pattern to look for disturbances or sunspots. These can be in either hemisphere and at any latitude, depending on the progression of the sunspot cycle. The relative sunspot number (also Wolf number or Zurich number) is $R = 10g + s$, where g is the number of groups (including groups of one) and s is the number of individual spots (including those in groups). Individuals may submit their observations to the Solar Section of the American Association of Variable Star Observers (AAVSO, see below), which compiles monthly averages from all observers. To help locate the latitude and longitude of a sunspot, and to find instructions and a template (called the Stonyhurst disk) to place over your sketch or image, see the weblinks below. See also the EPHEMERIS FOR THE SUN on p. 180, which lists the orientation of the Sun (P, B_0, and L_0) in four-day increments. Solar activity can be mapped as an exercise, using disk templates (Stonyhurst, Porter, or grid) and solar orientation elements (see BAA Solar Section and Atmospheric Optics websites, below).

The Sun takes 25 to 29 days to make a full rotation, with an average of 27 days. The Carrington rotation number, invented by Richard Carrington, counts the number of rotations of the Sun since 1895 Nov. 3. The Solar Section of the Association of Lunar & Planetary Observers (ALPO) uses Carrington rotation numbers for the study and archiving of solar morphology and prominence activity. For an updated Carrington list, visit alpo-astronomy.org/solarblog. ALPO accepts sketches and photographs (at all wavelengths) on the Sun Forms that are available on the solar blog webpage. All submissions are stored on the online Solar Gallery. (For instruction on astronomical sketching see ASTRONOMICAL SKETCHING, p. 88; for a primer on astrophotography, see DIGITAL ASTROPHOTOGRAPHY, p. 91.)

A wide range of digital cameras and webcams, combined with various filters, can produce phenomenal images of the Sun. Numerous computer programs allow the combination of multiple images to create an enhanced image or video. Libraries, online chat rooms, and email lists provide a wealth of information on solar photography. The best way to learn is to read and ask questions of experienced solar imagers.

A solar cycle takes 10–13 years (11 years on average) to complete, and we have started Solar Cycle 25. This was stated back in December 2020 that we were starting Solar Cycle 25, but in January and in March 2021 more spots in the Northern Hemisphere were showing up. The Solar Flux was also increasing and staying at a higher level.

NOAA stated in April 2021 that we were in Solar Cycle 25 but there was some debate with two models on how active the cycle would be. The SIDC modelling has one showing a weak cycle like Cycle 24 (based on 100 years of data) and another to be a strong cycle (based on 60 years of data). It goes to show that each Solar Cycle can be different, and this will certainly be an interesting one. Keep Observing!

Also, keep watching the adventure of the *Parker Solar Probe*. It's now into its 8th perihelion orbit, studying the Sun's chromosphere (see website below).

If you do not have the proper equipment to observe the Sun, you can always visit the *Solar and Heliospheric Observatory* (SOHO) and the *Solar Dynamics Observatory* (SDO) websites to see the daily activity of the Sun.

The following Handbook sections contain related information: FILTERS (p. 64), SOLAR ACTIVITY (opposite) and VIEWING A SOLAR ECLIPSE—A WARNING (p. 147).

[1]en.wikipedia.org/wiki/Solar_cycle_25

References

ALPO Solar Astronomy Handbook, ALPO Solar Section
Bray, R.J. and Loughhead, R.E., *Sunspots*, Dover Publications, 1964.
Broxton, T., *Solar Observer's Handbook*, Authorhouse, 2009.
Jenkins, J.L., *The Sun and How to Observe It*, Springer, 2009.
Rix E., Hay, K., Russell, S., and Handy, R., *Solar Sketching: A Comprehensive Guide to Drawing the Sun*, Springer, 2015.

Websites for Solar Observing and Astrophysics

aavso.org/solar (AAVSO)
almanac.com/content/solar-cycle-updates-and-predictions
alpineastro.com/collections/solar-observation (Alpine Astronomical)
alpo-astronomy.org/solar (ALPO)
atoptics.co.uk/tiltsun.htm (Atmospheric Optics Tilting Sun)
britastro.org/section_front/21 (BAA: Stonyhurst, Porter, and Grid disks)
halpha.nso.edu (H Alpha Network Monitor)
nasa.gov/content/goddard/parker-solar-probe (*Parker Solar Probe*)
oneminuteastronomer.com/999/choose-solar-filter (choosing solar filters)
petermeadows.com/html/stonyhurst.html (Stonyhurst disks and instructions)
radiojove.gsfc.nasa.gov (NASA Solar and Planetary Radio Astronomy for Schools)
sdo.gsfc.nasa.gov (*Solar Dynamics Observatory*)
sohowww.nascom.nasa.gov (*Solar and Heliospheric Observatory*)
solarham.net (solar page by amateur radio station VE3EN)
spaceweatherwoman.com (Dr. Tamitha Skov—Heliosphere Physicist)
stce.be (Solar-Terrestrial Centre of Excellence—Belgium)
swpc.noaa.gov (NOAA Space Weather Prediction Center)

SOLAR ACTIVITY
BY KEN TAPPING

After a relatively long activity minimum, Cycle 25 is at last under way.* Predictions for this cycle range from another small cycle, maybe even smaller than Cycle 24, to a somewhat larger one. The complex processes underlying the rhythm of solar activity probably make it beyond accurate prediction. In Cycles 23 and 24 a decline in photospheric activity (sunspot numbers), compared with the level of activity in the corona (10.7 cm solar flux), hinted that solar behavior is trending toward either another Maunder or Dalton Minimum event. However, at this point, there are only hints. What the Sun does during Cycle 25 should hopefully tell us more.

Solar activity is fundamentally a magnetic phenomenon. Deep below the photosphere, differential rotation and convection cause the solar material to move in a complex manner. The density of this material is high enough for its movement to drag the magnetic fields along with it. This generates electric currents, which in turn produce magnetic fields. The result is a complex system of subphotospheric "magnetic flux ropes." The penetration of sections of these flux ropes through the photosphere and into the chromosphere and corona gives rise to the many observed forms of solar activity. Above the photosphere the situation is strikingly different: the density is much lower, and the magnetic fields trap and confine the ionized gas of the solar atmosphere, supporting loops and filaments, and forming the diverse menagerie of photospheric, chromospheric, and coronal structures with which we are familiar, such as sunspots, active regions, complexes of activity, and systems of loops. Changing emissions in the X-ray and ultraviolet wavelengths, and at radio wavelengths, are due to the changing amount of trapped plasma and the strengths of the magnetic fields containing them. The Sun's total energy output is also affected by magnetic activity, fortunately only slightly.

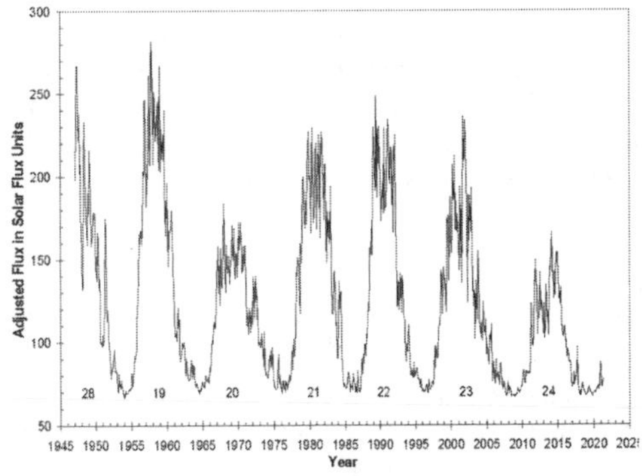

The 10.7-cm solar radio flux, averaged monthly (see p. 193). This index, which originates in the low solar corona overlying active regions, is a more global index of magnetic activity than sunspot number. The 10–13-year solar activity cycle is clearly visible. The shorter-term spikes are shorter episodes of activity as active regions and clusters of regions form, evolve, and decay. There is some level of activity even during solar minima. The Activity Cycle numbers are shown.

The organization of the subphotospheric magnetic fields gives rise to a consistent pattern in the magnetic configuration of active regions. Each region is magnetically bipolar, with the bipoles arranged east–west on the disk. All bipoles lying in the same hemisphere are arranged with the same magnetic polarity leading (facing in the direction in which the region appears to move as it is carried across the disk by solar rotation—westward in the observer's sky). In the other hemisphere, the leading and following magnetic polarities are reversed.

*The numbering system for solar activity cycles was started by Rudolph Wolf, who arbitrarily designated the activity maximum of 1750 as that of Cycle 1.

Exceptions do occur. Regions are sometimes formed that have a magnetic orientation perpendicular to or even the reverse of the norm for that hemisphere. Such regions usually try to move into the conventional orientation but are impeded by the magnetic linkages formed with their surroundings. These regions tend to produce flares as potential energy builds up in their magnetic structures and is subsequently released catastrophically.

The "conventional" magnetic configurations for active regions reverse on alternate activity cycles. For example, during Cycle 22, active regions in the northern solar hemisphere were oriented with their "negative" (i.e. south-seeking) magnetic polarity ends leading and "positive" (north-seeking) ends following, with the reverse situation in the southern hemisphere. In Cycle 23, this arrangement was reversed. Cycle 24 re-establishes the pattern of Cycle 22. A *magnetic* activity cycle, which is probably a more realistic description of the rhythms of solar activity, is equal to two of Wolf's activity cycles and takes about 22 years to complete.

Active regions are not isolated phenomena; they occur in complexes, comprising several active regions at various stages of development, together with the network of elements remaining from decayed regions. This localization of activity gives rise to a rotational modulation of the 10.7-cm flux as active-region clusters are carried across the disk and disappear around the east limb. To smooth out this modulation in long-term studies of solar activity, the data are averaged over solar rotations rather than by month. Active regions can persist for one or more solar rotations and the complexes for a dozen or so.

The large-scale organization of solar magnetic activity is also apparent in the spatial distribution of active regions during the solar cycle. The first activity of the new cycle is marked by the formation of active regions at high latitudes. As activity builds toward the maximum of the cycle, the number of active regions increases, and they tend to form at lower latitudes. As the activity wanes toward the next minimum, the number of regions decreases, but the average latitude continues to decrease until the last activity of the cycle is located near the equator. Then, as the new cycle starts, new active regions form at high latitudes.

The formation of a new active region begins with the emergence of magnetic loops through the photosphere and into the overlying chromosphere and corona. This is heralded by the appearance of small pores, about 1000 km across, which coalesce and spread into a patch of magnetic flux that may exceed 50 000 km in length. The average magnetic-field strength in such patches is of the order of 0.01 T (100 gauss). The emergence of these magnetic fields modifies the spatial and density structure of the chromosphere, giving rise to enhanced emission in the calcium and magnesium II K spectral lines. These bright patches (called plages), which stand out prominently in filtergrams, are the most conspicuous aspect of active regions. In some areas of the new active region, magnetic field strengths reach or exceed 0.1 T. These magnetic fields are strong enough to impede the transfer of energy from within the Sun, leading to these patches being cooler (3000 K) compared with the surrounding photosphere, which has a temperature of about 6000 K. Although actually quite hot and shining quite brightly, in contrast with their hotter surroundings, these flux concentrations appear as dark spots: sunspots. As a region grows, one or more large spots form at the leading end, and a scattering of smaller ones form at the trailing end. Sunspots are a prominent feature of active regions and are the aspect of solar activity that has been longest known.

The growth of the new active region continues through repeated episodes of magnetic flux emergence. In general, the size is directly proportional to the total magnetic flux in the region. Growth stops when the emergence of new magnetic flux ceases. Soon after, the region starts to decay. This proceeds partly by the resubmergence of magnetic flux and partly by fragmentation. The spots disappear, and eventually, all that remains is a large area of magnetic flux arranged in a network pattern, blending in slowly with the remains of other decayed active regions.

Repeated episodes of magnetic-flux emergence, together with motions of the footpoints, which are the photospheric anchors of magnetic loops, lead to the magnetic field overactive regions becoming complex and tangled and storing enormous amounts of energy. The relaxation of these fields is an important aspect of the evolution and dissipation of active regions. In some cases, this can occur noncatastrophically; otherwise, stresses increase until various plasma instabilities allow rapid relaxation and reconnection of the magnetic fields and a rapid release of the stored energy. These energy releases are known as flares.

The Solar Wind and Aurorae

The solar atmosphere is not stable. It is constantly flowing outward as a stream of particles and magnetic fields—the *solar wind.* The flow is strongest where the magnetic loops are very large and impose the least drag on the outwardly flowing particles. Because of their lower coronal densities, these regions produce a lower flux of X-rays and appear in X-ray images as dark patches, known as "coronal holes." The solar wind is not homogeneous or steady; its speed, density, and direction can change according to the positions of coronal holes and the nature of current solar activity.

The solar wind profoundly changes Earth's magnetic field. The wind pressure pushes the field out of its dipole shape into a long teardrop. The magnetic geometry in the tail of the drop makes it the site of many plasma instabilities. The flow of the solar wind over the boundary of Earth's magnetic field (the magnetopause) excites many types of waves, which move along Earth's magnetic field lines and which can be detected on the ground at high magnetic latitudes. Increases in the density or velocity of the solar wind change the pressure equilibrium between the solar wind and the magnetosphere, producing fluctuations in the strength and direction of the magnetic field lines at ground level. If the fluctuations are strong enough, the events are referred to as magnetic storms and substorms. These can disrupt any human activity that involves connected metal networks covering large geographical areas, especially at high magnetic latitudes.

Complex interactions between the solar wind and Earth's magnetic field lead to an accumulation of trapped particles in the magnetosphere. During magnetic storms, instabilities and waves excited in the magnetosphere by the solar wind accelerate some of the trapped particles downward along Earth's magnetic field into increasingly dense atmosphere, where they collide with the atmospheric constituents, exciting them with sufficient energy to produce light. These displays are called aurorae, or the northern and southern lights: *aurora borealis* and *aurora australis*, respectively. Views from space show that aurorae fall in a rough circle (the auroral oval), centered around the magnetic pole, that is, in a definite band of magnetic latitudes. As activity increases, the auroral oval expands, covering lower and lower magnetic latitudes. It also becomes increasingly distorted. During the period of very high activity in March 1989, auroral displays were seen as far south as the Caribbean.

Aurorae occur in many forms and can be steady, moving, or rapidly pulsating, depending upon the nature of the particle streams causing them. Aurorae can appear green or red, although if they are faint, the eye cannot respond in color and they appear grey. The greenish color is due to spectral lines from oxygen (558 nm) and a range of lines from nitrogen covering the band 391 nm to 470 nm. Under highly disturbed conditions, red spectral-line emissions at 630 nm and 636 nm and in a series of bands between 650 nm and 680 nm can also be seen. The green emissions are

AURORAL FORMS

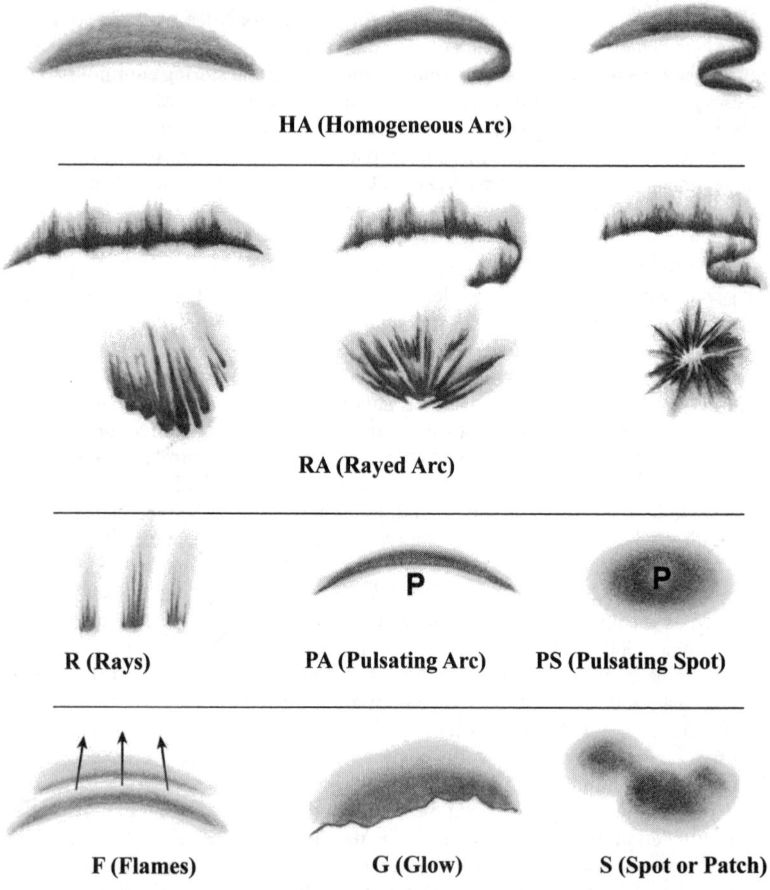

The above sketches illustrate standard auroral forms. This simplified classification was devised for visual observers during the International Geophysical Year six decades ago (1957–58). Although there is great variety in auroral patterns, the sketches emphasize fundamental features and minimize variations that depend on the location of the observer. The light of the aurora is emitted by the upper fringes of Earth's atmosphere (heights of 100 to 400 km) as it is bombarded by electrons of the solar wind (solar-wind protons contribute a smaller amount of energy). The modification of the trajectories of these particles by Earth's magnetic field restricts activity to high latitudes, producing the "aurora borealis" in the Northern Hemisphere and the "aurora australis" in the Southern Hemisphere. The wavelengths of four atmospheric molecular and atomic emission lines that can contribute strongly to auroral light are included in the list on p. 32. Whether aurorae appear colored depends on their luminance—light that is too faint will not activate color vision and appears grey. When the luminance is sufficiently great, the relative contributions of blue, green, and red emission lines can result in a variety of auroral hues.

produced at a height of about 110 km; the red, 630-nm and 636-nm emissions, due to atomic oxygen, originate at heights between 200 km and 400 km; the 650-nm to 680-nm emissions are produced at about 90 km.

The Impact and Measurement of Solar Activity

We find evidence of the profound effects of solar activity upon Earth extending as far back in time as we have been able to look. The rhythm of the solar activity cycle is reflected in cores from ocean beds, ice cores, and sediments from lakes that dry up in summer. It is also apparent in the growth rates of trees (determined from the study of tree rings) in recently living timber, wood from medieval buildings, and fossilized trees.

Solar activity can dramatically affect our lives. Magnetic storms due to solar activity induce currents in communications and power-transmission systems having long-distance wires, disrupting their operation for hours. The power blackouts in Québec and Scandinavia produced by a large flare on 1989 Mar. 10 are a particularly outstanding example. Railway signaling systems might also be affected. Increased X-ray emissions from flares cause enhanced ionization of Earth's atmosphere at D-region heights (about 90 km), producing blackouts of shortwave communications.

Solar activity heats the upper atmosphere, causing it to expand further into space, increasing the drag experienced by artificial satellites in low orbits. It is ironic that the lifetime of the *Solar Max* satellite was dramatically shortened in this way. Above the atmosphere, satellites have no protection from high-energy particle fluxes produced by the Sun. Their electronic systems can be damaged, leading to catastrophic failures in some cases, as occurred with two *Anik* communications satellites in January 1994.

The oldest index of solar activity is the sunspot number. A number of techniques, many empirical, have been developed to combine observations from various observatories and observers to form the International Sunspot Number. This is a rather poor index; however, it has given us a database extending back to at least the 17th century.

Probably the best available index of solar activity, at least covering the last six decades or so, is the *10.7-cm flux*, or $F_{10.7}$. This index is an objective measurement of the integrated emission at the 10.7-cm wavelength (a frequency of 2.8 GHz) from all sources present on the solar disk. It has been measured daily by the National Research Council of Canada for over 65 years and is now used worldwide as a primary index of solar activity. In 2003, the program became a joint one with the Canadian Space Agency. $F_{10.7}$ is expressed in solar-flux units (1 sfu = 10^{-22} W·m^{-2}·Hz^{-1}). The 10.7-cm flux has the great advantage that it can be measured in all weather conditions and requires no human involvement or "interpretation." When quiet, the Sun produces a $F_{10.7}$ value of 64 sfu, due to free-free thermal emission from the quiet solar corona. Also, $F_{10.7}$ can be used as an objective proxy for other activity-related quantities. The strength of the radio emission constituting $F_{10.7}$ is modulated by the annual variation in the distance between Earth and Sun. When considering solar-driven phenomena at the Earth and in near-Earth space, this is not important, so the "Observed" value of the flux may be applicable. On the other hand, when considering solar activity, this modulation has to be removed from the data. In such instances, the "Adjusted" flux, which is scaled to an Earth–Sun distance of 1 au, should be used.

We are a long way from understanding the nature and the extent of the effects solar activity has upon Earth. Some correlations, like that between the length of miniskirts and solar activity, are probably spurious; others might not be. As we exploit our environment more fully, we become increasingly sensitive to things that might affect it, even slightly.

(See pp. 64, 147, and 182 for safe methods of observing the Sun.)

RAINBOWS AND SOME OTHER SKY PHENOMENA

BY ROY BISHOP

Sunlight, and more rarely moonlight, interacting with water drops or ice crystals in the sky can result in aerial patterns displaying striking symmetry. This brief account is restricted to the more common sky phenomena. For more extensive treatments, including a dozen relatively rare patterns involving ice crystals, see the book by Greenler in the references and the websites listed there. For comprehensive accounts of the history and physics of the rainbow, see the books by Boyer, and Lee and Fraser.

In order of increasing angular distance from the Sun, ice crystals produce coronae, pillars, halos, sundogs, and circumhorizontal (or circumzenithal) arcs. (Other small particles, including water drops, also produce coronae.) In the half of the sky opposite the Sun, water drops produce rainbows and, surrounding the antisolar point, glories. The heiligenschein is not an atmospheric phenomenon, but like the glory is a bright area in the vicinity of the antisolar point.

Because the rainbow is the most famous, most beautiful, and most complex of these apparitions, I begin with rainbows and devote the greater part of this article to them. Also, if you understand the rainbow, it is easy to understand halos, sundogs, circumhorizontal arcs, circumzenithal arcs, and pillars.

Rainbows

The rainbow has challenged natural philosophers over the centuries, including Aristotle, Roger Bacon, Theodoric of Freiberg, René Descartes, Sir Isaac Newton, Edmund Halley, Thomas Young, Sir George Airy, and Gustav Mie. It was Descartes (1596–1650) who first understood the basic geometry of the rainbow, and it was Newton (1642–1727) who first understood the origin of the colors of the rainbow. In 1803, 1838, and 1908, Young, Airy, and Mie, respectively, gave successively more accurate treatments of the influence of the wave nature of light on the structure of the rainbow. Recently, Alistair Fraser and Raymond Lee, using the power of the computer, provided additional insights concerning the physics of the rainbow. A few poets, including Keats and Goethe, have derided science for analyzing the rainbow, but understanding only deepens one's admiration for the beauty and subtle nature of this phantom.

The Shape of a Raindrop: The shape of a raindrop is relevant for rainbows. Surface tension arising from molecular attraction shrinks raindrops into the shape with the least surface area per unit volume—a sphere. (Raindrops resemble teardrops only after they have crashed against a surface such as a windowpane.) Aerodynamic forces deform large raindrops into a hamburger-bun shape with the short axis vertical, but an average raindrop is essentially spherical.

The Origin of the Rainbow: Sunlight is refracted and reflected by a raindrop (see Figure 1). The *primary* rainbow involves two refractions (where the light ray enters and leaves the drop) and *one* internal reflection. A portion of a ray that enters a drop head-on is deviated through 180° by the internal reflection, but when the ray is shifted off-center, the reflection produces a smaller deviation. When the ray is shifted 86% of the way toward grazing the drop (as in Figure 1), because of the increasing refraction, a *minimum angle of deviation* of approximately 138° is reached. This *stationary* angle concentrates some of the light leaving a raindrop after one reflection near this direction. Dispersion associated with the two refractions makes the minimum angle vary with wavelength, resulting in a spectrum. This interplay of sunlight with single raindrops

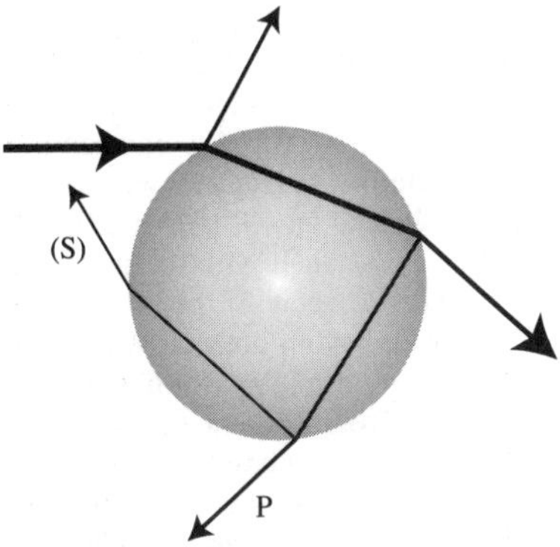

Figure 1 *The path of a ray of sunlight interacting with a spherical raindrop is displayed. The ray is shown entering the drop at 86% of the drop radius from head-on entry, causing ray P, exiting after one internal reflection, to be at a minimum angle of deviation of 138° and contributing to the primary rainbow. Ray (S) exiting after two internal reflections is close to but not at the minimum deviation for the secondary rainbow (231°); the ray entering the drop must be shifted closer to grazing incidence (to 95% of the drop radius) before a minimum deviation of 231° is attained. Rays undergoing three or more reflections within the drop are not shown, and neither is chromatic dispersion in the three rays exiting the drop. The widths of the various rays give an approximate indication of their relative intensities.*

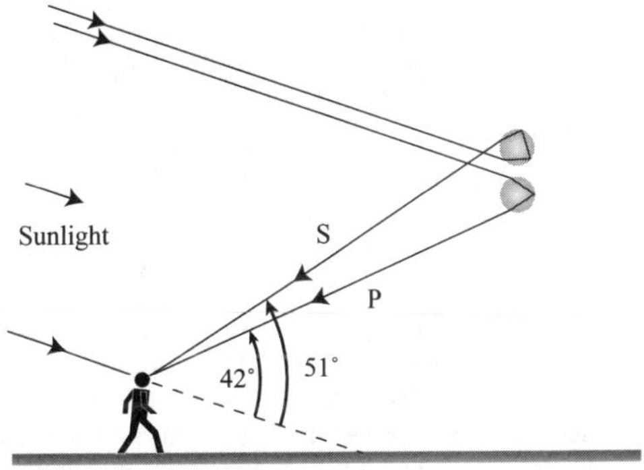

Figure 2 *Two raindrops are shown, greatly magnified, each with a ray of sunlight striking it such that the exiting ray is at the minimum angle of deviation and heading toward the observer. The drop with one internal reflection is contributing light to the observer's primary rainbow, and the drop with two internal reflections is contributing to the observer's secondary rainbow. Other drops (not shown) located along the rays P and S contribute in the same fashion to the two rainbows, and the whole array has rotational symmetry about the dashed line, the extended shadow of the observer's head. The observer, looking from the apices of these conical shells, sees two, circular, colored bands of light.*

in the sky is symmetric about an axis extending from the Sun through the eye of the observer; thus the circular arc of a rainbow is centered on that axis. To look at the primary rainbow, the observer's eyes must be turned toward 138° + 180° = 318° or 42° from the antisolar point, the shadow of the observer's head (see Figure 2).

To Predict Where a Rainbow Might Appear: If the Sun is shining where you are, with the Sun at your back extend your arms together straight out in front of you, splay your fingers and thumbs horizontally, and touch the tips of your thumbs together. Close one eye and align the tip of one little finger with the shadow of your head. As you tilt your hands, the tip of the other little finger will trace out the location of the primary rainbow in the sky. (A double hand-span at arm's length subtends approximately 40°, about the same as the 42° angular radius of the primary rainbow.)

Rainbows: None, Semicircular, and Circular: Don't expect to see a rainbow in the sky at midday in tropical latitudes, or at midday in spring or summer at higher latitudes. The Sun has to be less than 42° above the horizon for the top of the primary rainbow to be above the horizon (see Figure 2). At sunrise or sunset, the antisolar center of a rainbow is at the horizon, resulting in a semicircular rainbow that meets the horizon at 90°. From an airplane, or by spraying a garden hose, it is possible to see a complete circular rainbow at any time of day, provided there are many water drops and sunlight in the entire region 42° from the antisolar point.

A Rainbow Is Not a Bow: Angle, not distance, determines which raindrops send rainbow light to an observer's eye. Hence, the raindrops contributing to a rainbow lie in a conical shell with its tip at the observer's eye, and its axis coinciding with the extended shadow of the observer's head (see Figure 2). Only those parts of the conical shell having both raindrops and sunlight contribute to the rainbow. Thus, in spatial extent, a rainbow is like an immense, mouse-nibbled, ice-cream cone (sans ice cream). From the perspective of the observer located at the tip of this fragmented conical shell, a rainbow *looks* like a section of a flat circular arc or bow, but the only place a flat bow exists is on the observer's retina. Despite how rainbows are sometimes depicted in art and advertising, a rainbow cannot be viewed obliquely (it always appears circular), and it always has the same immense angular size. (Its 84° diameter spans almost one-quarter of the entire horizon.)

A Filled Cone of Light: Sunlight strikes an entire hemisphere of a raindrop, so in the case of the emerging rays that have undergone one internal reflection, sunlight is deviated over the entire range of possible angles, from 180° to the stationary, minimum, frequency-dependent angle of approximately 138°. Hence the conical shell of enhanced brightness that constitutes the primary rainbow is the outer surface of a filled cone of light (the portion thereof that lies above the observer's horizon) that brightens the disk of sky lying within the primary rainbow. Refractive dispersion occurs at all deviation angles less than 180° down to the approximate 138° minimum, but because of overlap, colors are perceived only near 138° where the overlap is not complete and the frequency-dependent stationary angle enhances the luminance, thereby creating the primary rainbow.

Your Rainbow: A rainbow is located at a particular angle relative to the Sun–observer axis (see Figure 2). When the observer moves, the axis moves, and the rainbow moves. The observer's shadow moves too, but a rainbow is subtler than a shadow; you can see someone else's shadow, but you cannot see their rainbow. Each observer has his or her own private rainbow. Although an observer's eyes image different rainbows, the two rainbows are in the same parallel direction, so when the images fuse, the observer sees one rainbow at infinity. Obviously a rainbow is not an object in the normal sense of the word; it is a pattern of light specific to the observer. Unlike the case of a normal object like a tree, there are as many rainbows as there are observers. If there is no observer, there is no rainbow; only raindrops in the sky, each raindrop independently scattering sunlight symmetrically about its own Sun-raindrop axis.

The Secondary Rainbow: If conditions are favorable (lots of rain and sunlight, and a dark sky background), a secondary rainbow will be visible. The *secondary* rainbow involves *two* internal reflections in each raindrop (see Figure 1). A light ray that enters a drop head-on is deviated through 360° by the two internal reflections, but when the ray is shifted off-center the reflections produce a smaller deviation. When the ray is shifted 95% of the way toward grazing the drop, because of the increasing refraction, a minimum angle of deviation of approximately 231° is reached. This stationary angle concentrates some of the light leaving a raindrop after two reflections near this direction. Dispersion associated with the two refractions makes the minimum angle vary with wavelength, resulting in a spectrum. To look at the secondary rainbow, the observer's eyes must be turned toward 231° + 180° = 411° or 51° from the antisolar point (see Figure 2). Thus the secondary rainbow lies (51° – 42°) = 9° outside of the primary rainbow (9° is about one fist-width at arm's length).

Width of the Secondary Rainbow: A light ray contributing to the secondary rainbow enters a raindrop closer to the edge of the raindrop than does a light ray contributing to the primary rainbow. Consequently, the amount of refraction and associated spectral dispersion are greater. The additional reflection from the curved inner surface of the raindrop further increases the dispersion, making the spectrum of the secondary bow about 60% wider than that of the primary bow (after taking the 0.5° diameter of the Sun into account).

Reversed Spectra: A light ray contributing to the primary rainbow enters the side of a raindrop nearest the convex side of the rainbow, is deviated through 138°, and exits near the opposite side of the drop heading toward the observer (see Figure 2). Long wavelengths are refracted least, emerging at a steeper angle to the rainbow axis, so the convex side of the primary rainbow appears red. A light ray contributing to the secondary rainbow is deviated through 231°. To reach the observer, the ray must rotate through the raindrop in the *opposite* sense to the path followed by the primary rainbow ray. Long wavelengths are refracted least, emerging at a shallower angle to the rainbow axis, so the concave side of the secondary rainbow appears red. Thus the spectral sequences are reversed, with the red of both bows bordering upon the space that is between the bows.

Alexander's Dark Band: The two rays, P and S, shown in Figure 2 undergo minimum deviations of 138° and 231°, the first approaching its minimum counter-clockwise, the other clockwise. Therefore there is a 138° + 231° – 360° = 9° gap into which such rays cannot enter. Thus the sky between the bows is darker than elsewhere, a feature called *Alexander's Dark Band* after Alexander of Aphrodisias, a Greek philosopher who drew attention to it c. 200 CE. The "dark" band is only moderately darker than the region beneath the primary rainbow because of three sources of light between the bows: skylight, external reflections off raindrops (see Figure 1), and diffraction of light waves by the raindrops.

The Tertiary Rainbow: Edmund Halley (1656–1742) first calculated that light rays exiting a raindrop after *three* reflections have a minimum angle of deviation of 318°, placing the *tertiary* rainbow only 42° from the Sun. For at least 2000 years, people had been looking for a tertiary rainbow in the vicinity of the primary and secondary rainbows. They had been looking in the wrong part of the sky! The luminance (surface brightness) of the secondary rainbow is less than that of the primary, and the luminance of the tertiary rainbow is less than that of the secondary because of three effects: (1) Light rays contributing to successively higher-order rainbows strike raindrops closer to grazing incidence, causing a greater fraction of the light to reflect without entering the drops; (2) Some light exits the drops at each internal reflection leaving less for higher-order rainbows; (3) Rainbow width increases as the order increases, spreading the light over a greater area. There is little hope of seeing the faint tertiary rainbow because it is almost invariably overwhelmed by two sources of white light in that region of the sky (see Figure 1): (a) *Most* of the sunlight entering raindrops passes through without being internally reflected and illuminates the sunward half of the sky. (The lack of a stationary angle in the deviation of these bright, unreflected rays is why there is no "zero-order" rainbow.); (b) Sunlight externally reflected from raindrops. The quaternary rainbow, fainter again than the tertiary, also occurs in the bright sunward half of the sky, about 44° from the Sun. Higher-order rainbows also occur, but usually only the primary and secondary bows are visible in the sky (see atoptics.co.uk/rainbows/ord34.htm).

Banding Beneath: The concave side of a primary rainbow may display two or three narrow bands, called *supernumerary bows* or *supernumerary arcs*. They are caused by the interference of two emerging parallel light rays that have entered a raindrop slightly nearer to and farther from grazing incidence than a ray that undergoes minimum deviation. The two paths have different lengths causing interference. Similar pairs of rays emerging at various angles produce the supernumerary bow pattern. British physicist Thomas Young (1773–1829) was the first to present this explanation, although more accurate descriptions involving diffraction were later provided by British Astronomer Royal, Sir George Airy (1801–1892); German physicist Gustav Mie (1868–1957); and Canadian meteorologist Alistair Fraser (in 1983).

Hamburger Buns and a Pot of Gold: The hamburger-bun distortion of raindrops with increasing drop size has the greatest effect on the top part of a rainbow because light rays in that region traverse a vertical cross section of a raindrop. The distortion has two consequences for the rainbow:

First, the distortion substantially increases the minimum deviation angle such that light from large raindrops of various diameters is spread into a white haze beneath the primary rainbow. Only spherical drops (diameters of about 0.5 mm and smaller) contribute to the upper part of a rainbow, often causing it to be less bright and its colors less vivid than in the lower part of the bow (assuming the Sun is low in the sky so the lower part of the rainbow is at a steep angle to the horizon). In the lower part, drops of all sizes present circular cross sections to light rays that are redirected toward the observer. Thus *all* drops contribute to the lower part of the rainbow, making it the brightest part when there is a heavy rainfall with a wide range of drop sizes. As Lee and Fraser surmise in their book *The Rainbow Bridge*, the bright glow of vivid colors near the end of the rainbow may be the origin of the pot-of-gold myth.

Second, the distortion-induced modification in the shift of the position of supernumerary bows with drop size causes distinct supernumerary bows to occur only for raindrops having diameters in the range of about 0.4 to 0.8 mm, and only in the upper part of a rainbow. The contributions of larger and smaller drops are blurred due to overlap. A bright rainbow *without* supernumerary bows typically involves a heavy rain shower during which there is a wide range of drop diameters. Drops in the 0.4 to 0.8 mm range are present, but the bright area beneath the primary rainbow caused by larger raindrops obscures their otherwise distinct supernumerary bows.

Beware of Sunglasses: The reflection that rainbow light undergoes inside a raindrop occurs very near *Brewster's angle* at which light reflected from a nonmetallic surface becomes 100% polarized (named in honor of Scottish physicist Sir David Brewster (1781–1868), who discovered this phenomenon). Thus the light of a rainbow is almost 100% polarized. The direction of polarization (the direction of the electric field) is tangent to the bow, which for the upper part of a rainbow has the same orientation as that of partially polarized light reflecting from the dash of a car, a highway, or a body of water. Polarizing sunglasses are designed to block polarized light from the latter three sources and will obliterate a rainbow!

Rainbows at Night: Observations of lunar rainbows are rare. The Moon is bright enough to produce a noticeable rainbow only when it is near its full phase. Also, people are usually indoors at night, and when they do step outside it is often into a light-polluted environment, which rules out any chance of seeing a lunar rainbow. Even when conditions are favorable, few people would notice a lunar rainbow because it is usually too dim to activate color vision and therefore appears white.

Not a Good Spectrum: The rainbow is often cited as the paragon of a white-light spectrum. However, five factors make the rainbow spectrum inferior to that produced by a laboratory spectroscope: (1) The minimum property of the stationary angle that produces a rainbow means that light of each wavelength is spread over larger angles, resulting in some overlap of the spectral colors; (2) The Sun is not a point source of light. The 0.5° spread of its rays smears the rainbow spectrum (see Bishop and Dyer in the references, p. 200); (3) Sunlight reflected from the front of the raindrops and skylight from behind dilutes the colors making them less saturated;

(4) The increase in the minimum angle of deviation associated with aerodynamic drop distortion (significant for drop diameters of 0.5 mm and larger) causes additional spectral smearing in the upper part of a rainbow; (5) Diffraction broadening results in further overlap of the spectral colors, particularly for small raindrops. In the case of fog or cloud (drop diameters in the range 0.01 to 0.1 mm), diffraction broadening causes the various colors to overlap sufficiently to produce a white rainbow, called a *fogbow*. Also known as a *cloudbow*, it may sometimes be seen from an airplane, a large white arc moving along on a cloud layer below the airplane.

Fog and Flashlight: A dark, foggy night provides an opportunity to see the stationary angle that is the key to a primary rainbow. Place a bright, well-collimated flashlight on the ground with its beam directed vertically upward into the fog. Step back a short distance and examine the vertical shaft of light. Look for a bright patch about 40° from the zenith. Fog droplets at that position preferentially redirect the light downward toward your eyes. Diffraction causes the stationary angle to deviate somewhat from the nominal 42° produced by larger drops. Diffraction broadening may make the faint patch of light from the secondary bow undetectable. It will be located about 54° from the zenith, below the fragment of the primary bow.

Rainbow Light on the Moon: The greater part of Earth's albedo is due to clouds. An observer on the Moon would see Earth brighten noticeably for several hours when the Sun–Earth–Moon angle is near 40° and the cloud droplets provide a 2°-diameter fragment of a cloudbow. At this point, the Moon is in its crescent phase, about three days from new, and earthshine will be enhanced. At Sinus Iridum, the Bay of Rainbows, twice each lunar night the plains and surrounding mountains are bathed in the light of a tattered fragment of a white primary rainbow enveloping Earth. Unfortunately, as viewed from Earth at such times, the substantial glare from the fat, sunlit, lunar crescent, plus scattering of moonlight in Earth's atmosphere and in the observer's eyes or camera tends to obscure the enhanced earthshine.

We Are Part of the Rainbow: Although rain and sunlight have been part of Earth's environment for four billion years, colored rainbows occurred quite recently with the appearance of animals possessing color vision. Our visual world with its brightness and colors occurs within our skull. Nevertheless, by some feat of mental projection we think that our visual world coincides spatially with the external world. Thus we confuse the neural rainbow with the external rainbow, and naively attribute the indescribable colors of the former to the latter. Three centuries ago, Sir Isaac Newton, aware of this overpowering illusion, wrote: "The rays to speak properly are not colored. In them there is nothing else than a certain power and disposition to stir up a sensation of this or that color." Yet, even today, most people regard the cone cells of the retina as "color receptors," as if colors existed in the external world. They speak of "the true colors of moonbows and nebulae revealed by time-exposure photographs," unaware that they are attributing a unique property of the neural photograph in their brain to the external photograph in their hands, and subsequently to moonbows and nebulae in the sky. The eye does not detect the colors of the rainbow; the brain creates them. *We* are part of the rainbow, its most beautiful part.

Halos

Under normal conditions of temperature and pressure, the wave and statistical properties of electrons impose hexagonal crystalline structure on water ice. When sunlight interacts with ice crystals in the frosty sky, it translates the atomic architecture into macroscopic aerial patterns of striking symmetry.

Small ice crystals suspended in the air can have a variety of shapes, including multi-crystalline fragments in which the sixfold symmetry is not obvious, rods that resemble pieces of a hexagonal pencil, flat six-sided plates, and snowflakes with their

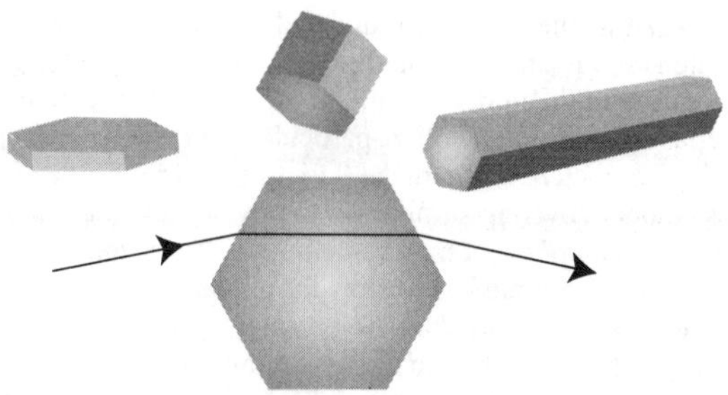

Figure 3 *The bottom diagram shows a light ray undergoing a net minimum deviation of 22° when it refracts symmetrically through alternate sides of a hexagonal ice crystal (in effect, a 60° ice prism). The top three diagrams show hexagonal ice crystals having, from left-to-right, increasing length-to-width ratios: a plate, a block, and a pencil. When falling, aerodynamic forces cause the plate and the pencil to orient horizontally, as shown. The block and clusters of crystals can have any orientation. Plates produce sundogs (refraction)* ***and*** *pillars (reflection). Randomly oriented crystals produce halos (refraction).* ***Pencils produce*** *pillars (reflection) and tangent arcs (refraction).*

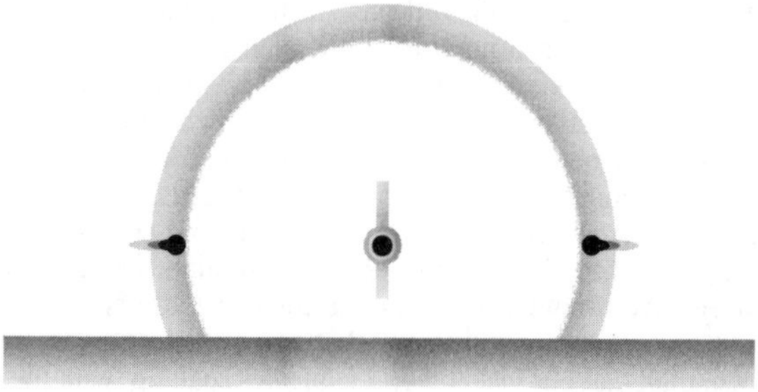

Figure 4 *A schematic diagram of a 22° halo with sundogs, and a corona and pillar adjacent to the Sun low near the horizon in the center. Hexagonal ice crystals are in the sky: plates (refraction/sundogs, reflection/pillar); blocks (refraction/halo); and both types of crystal (diffraction/corona). The absense of an upward-curving tangent arc at the top of the halo indicates that pencil crystals are not present.*

elegant symmetry.

Alternate sides of a hexagonal ice crystal form a 60° prism (see Figure 3). Light passing through this prism is deviated by the two refractions, the angle of deviation being a minimum (about 22°) when the passage is symmetric, with equal refractions at the two surfaces. As in the case of minimum deviation in a water drop, a significant fraction of the light passing through randomly oriented 60° ice prisms is deviated by approximately 22°, enhancing the brightness at that angle.

Adjacent sides of a hexagonal crystal form a 120° prism, but light cannot pass through such a prism; the light undergoes total internal reflection at the second surface. Opposite sides of a hexagonal crystal are parallel and, like a windowpane, provide no net deviation. End faces of the crystal form 90° prisms with the sides; light passing through a 90° ice prism undergoes a minimum deviation of about 46° when the passage is symmetric.

Crystals having lengths about equal to their widths (called “blocks”; see Figure 3) or clusters of two or more single crystals assume random orientations as they fall. Consequently, the refraction of light rays toward an observer by such crystals has symmetry about the Sun–observer axis, and the observer sees a *halo* of light in the sky, centered on the Sun and having an angular radius of 22° (about one hand-span from the Sun at arm’s length; see Figure 4). More rarely, refraction in 90° randomly oriented prisms results in an immense but fainter 46° halo, concentric with the 22° halo. Like the rainbow, a halo is not a circular hoop but a fragmented conical structure seen from its apex. Moonlight can also produce halos, particularly if the Moon is bright, near its full phase.

Because the 22° stationary angle of deviation is a minimum, the halo has a relatively sharp inner edge and a diffuse outer edge, the sky being brighter on the convex side of the halo. Because the deviation is least at the red end of the spectrum, the inner edge of a halo may appear reddish; however, ice crystals are not as optically perfect as raindrops, so the spectral colors of halos are not as pronounced as in rainbows.

The first person to understand the geometry of the 22° halo (i.e. minimum deviation in 60° ice prisms) was the French scientist Edme Mariotte (1620–1684). Sir Isaac Newton, apparently independently, arrived at the same explanation when writing his book *Opticks* (1704), but abandoned it in the published editions in favor of an erroneous explanation by the Dutch physicist Christiaan Huygens (1629–1695). Mariotte’s theory was largely ignored for more than a century until revived by Thomas Young in 1807.

The ice crystals that produce halos are often in the leading edge of a low-pressure system, so a halo is a fairly reliable sign that within 24 hours the weather will be overcast and possibly stormy.

Sundogs

Like a small twig or leaf falling from a tree, pencil crystals and flat crystals such as snowflakes and plates are dynamically stable when oriented horizontally as they fall, maximizing air resistance (see Figure 3). If ice crystals in the air are predominately plates, only those crystals at the same altitude as the Sun can refract light to the observer (provided the Sun is low in the sky), resulting in two bright spots 22° on either side of the Sun (see Figure 4). Called *sundogs* or *parhelia*, under favorable conditions these spots can be almost too bright to look at. Although sundogs appear as spots in the sky, the contributing 60° ice prisms lie along the arms of a 44° “V” with the observer’s eye at its vertex.

Rays passing nonsymmetrically through 60° plate prisms are deviated more than 22°, resulting in tails or smearing of the sundogs away from the Sun (see Figure 4). Also, like the 22° halo, sundogs often display a hazy spectrum with red on their sunward side.

Sundogs (or *moondogs*, if the Moon is the light source) may appear singly or in pairs (plate crystals) and may be accompanied by a 22° halo (randomly oriented crystals in addition to plates). Or only a 22° halo may be present (only randomly oriented crystals, or if plates are also present the Sun is too high in the sky for its rays to access the 60° prisms of these horizontally oriented crystals). If the Sun is moderately high in the sky (altitude ~30°), thick plates can still result in sundogs, but the skew rays involved displace the sundogs somewhat farther than 22° from the Sun.

Circumhorizontal and Circumzenithal Arcs

Closely related to the rare 46° halo, produced by refraction through the 90° faces of randomly oriented crystals, are two uncommon arcs, produced by refraction through the 90° faces of horizontally oriented plates. The 46° minimum deviation corresponds to the incident and exiting light rays making an almost grazing angle of 22° with the crystal faces.

If the incident ray enters a vertical face, the Sun must be at an altitude near 68° and the arc so formed will be only 22° above the horizon—a circumhorizontal arc —bright and rainbow-hued, with its red edge uppermost. Skew rays account for the extent of the arc perpendicular to the vertical plane containing the Sun and observer. Unlike a rainbow, it is not concentric with the observer's shadow, and it is in the same half of the sky as the Sun. If the Sun is much higher or lower, the arc is diffuse and dim, and cannot exist at all if the altitude of the Sun is much less than 60°. Thus the circumhorizontal arc cannot be seen at latitudes more than about 50° from the equator, and at that latitude only at solar noon near the summer solstice.

If the incident ray enters a horizontal face, the Sun must be relatively low in the sky at an altitude near 22°, and the arc so formed will be high in the sky, 68° above the horizon—a circumzenithal arc—bright and rainbow-hued, with its red edge lowermost, resembling an upside-down rainbow. Unlike the circumhorizontal arc, there are no geographical restrictions on a circumzenithal arc; a 22°-altitude Sun can occur anywhere.

Pillars

In cold weather when the Sun or Moon is near or just below the horizon, a vertical column or *pillar* of light sometimes is seen, extending upward from the Sun or Moon (see Figure 4). On winter nights, tall narrow pillars sometimes extend into the sky, the light sources being unshielded streetlights, often not in direct line of sight. Pillars (also known as *snow pillars*) are caused by plate crystals and/or snowflakes with their mirror-like faces oriented horizontally in the air. Reflections from pencil crystals can also produce pillars. *All* these miniature mirrors throughout the sky reflect light, but only those lying near the vertical plane passing through the light source and an observer reflect light toward the observer; hence the observer sees a vertical pillar. The crystals producing the pillar are located between the light source and the observer.

When sundogs accompany a Sun pillar, plate crystals provide at least some of the mirrors causing the pillar. When a short, upward-curving arc tangent to the top of a 22° halo accompanies a Sun pillar, reflections off the sides of pencil crystals contribute to the pillar, the *tangent arc* being due to refraction in the 60° prisms of the horizontally oriented pencils.

Coronae

In the presence of thin high cloud, hazy bright rings may closely surround the Sun or Moon, a pattern called a *corona* (not to be confused with the solar corona, the hot outer atmosphere of the Sun itself). Lying within several diameters of the Sun or Moon (see Figure 4), a corona often displays pale colors, including a reddish outer border—the reverse of the refraction-based reddish *inner* border of halos and sundogs. The red-reversal indicates that the corona is caused not by refraction but by diffraction scattering of light waves.

The scattering bodies are usually cloud droplets, but can be small ice crystals or even pollen grains. The smaller the scattering bodies, the larger the corona; the more uniform their size, the more obvious the ring structure. Thin clouds passing near the Sun or Moon may display a colorful iridescence associated with evaporation-induced variations in drop size, although in the case of the Sun the display may be too bright to view. Very small particles, such as are injected high into the atmosphere by volcanic eruptions, result in a large corona called a *Bishop's Ring*.

When cloud droplets are involved, a corona is caused by light rays that graze the sides of the water drops without entering the drops, and by rays that pass directly through the drops. The theory describing diffraction scattering is complex, and it is not possible to give a simple explanation of the structure and size of the corona. Note that the corona involves scattering of each light ray by only one drop; scattering by multiple drops eliminates the iridescence and structure of the corona.

Glories

The *glory* resembles the corona and is also caused by diffraction scattering of light waves by fog or cloud droplets; however, the glory occurs on the opposite side of the sky, surrounding the antisolar point. Like the corona, the angular size of the glory (seldom more than a few degrees) varies inversely with the size of the scattering drops. Despite the similarity of the corona and the glory, it is easy to remember which is which: the corona is in the same part of the sky as the solar corona (assuming the Sun, not the Moon, to be the light source of the corona).

Usually seen from an airplane on a cloud layer below, the glory appears as a ring-like pattern of hazy colors centered on the observer's position in the shadow of the airplane. If the cloud layer is sufficiently far from the plane, the plane's shadow (then penumbral only) will not be visible. Mountain climbers sometimes see a glory in a cloud (fog) layer below them. If the fog is close, the climber's shadow, distorted by perspective, will appear to the climber as a dark cavity in the fog with its head centered in the glory, a strange apparition called *the spectre of the Brocken* after a mountain in Germany where the phenomenon has often been observed.

In religious art, the rings or disks of light surrounding the heads of saintly figures were likely inspired by observations of the glory, and possibly the heiligenschein (see below). Certainly it flatters an observer to see an aureole surrounding the shadow of one's own head and not those of others!

The glory involves scattering of a light ray by one drop, whereas a white cloud involves scattering of a light ray by more than one drop—which is why clouds are otherwise white. As in the case of the corona, the theory describing the glory is complex, and it is not possible to give a simple explanation of the structure and size of the glory. Light waves moving along the surface of small water drops and reflections within the drops are both involved.

Heiligenschein

Heiligenschein (German for "holy light") refers to a diffuse colorless glow surrounding the shadow of the observer's head when that shadow is projected on a rough surface or on vegetation covered in dewdrops. Unlike the patterns described above, the heiligenschein is not an atmospheric phenomenon; however, like the glory, it surrounds the antisolar point, so it should be mentioned.

A rough surface appears brightest when viewed in the antisolar direction because the shadows associated with the roughness are hidden behind the objects casting the shadows. For example, on a sunny day, a person walking past shrubbery or a field of grass will see a glowing aura surrounding the shadow of his or her head. A forest viewed from an airplane displays a bright patch surrounding the shadow of the airplane. In the case of vegetation covered in dewdrops, the spherical drops redirect the incident light whence it came, enhancing the brightness associated with hidden shadows. Tiny glass spheres imbedded in highway-marker paint or on automobile license plates do the same. If the Moon had a perfectly diffuse matte surface, at full phase it would provide π times more light than at quarter phase when it is half illuminated; however, because of heiligenschein, at full phase the Moon provides more than ten times as much light—the multitude of shadows on the lunar surface are hidden, and impact-produced glass beads littering the lunar surface redirect sunlight toward Earth. When Saturn is near opposition, heiligenschein enhances the brightness of its rings.

Some people call the hidden shadow phenomenon *the Seeliger Effect* or *the Opposition Effect*, and restrict the term *heiligenschein* to the glow caused by dewdrops, glass spheres, or similar optics. However, etymologically, heiligenschein fits both contributions. Also, in the case of dewdrops, hidden shadows usually contribute too.

Concluding Thoughts

None of these apparitions—rainbows, halos, sundogs, circumhorizontal arcs, circumzenithal arcs, pillars, coronae, glories, and heiligenschein—are objects in the normal sense of the word. They are patterns of light specific to the individual observer. Anyone who understands them will find the world to be a more interesting place.

References

Benn, C.R., "Rainbows, Haloes, and Earthshine," *The Observatory 114*, No. 1120 (1994), p. 115.

Berry, M.V., "Nature's optics and our understanding of light," *Contemporary Physics 56*, No. 1 (2015), p. 2–16.

Bishop, R.L. and Dyer, A., "Rainbow Modification by a Partial Solar Eclipse," *JRASC, 108*, (2014), p. 21–23

Bishop, R.L. and Newton, I., "Rainbow over Woolsthorpe Manor," *Notes Rec. R. Soc. Lond., 36*, No. 1, (1981), p. 1–11

Boyer, C.B., *The Rainbow: From Myth to Mathematics*, Princeton University Press, 1987.

Fraser, A.B., "Why Can the Supernumerary Bows Be Seen in a Rain Shower?" *J. Opt. Soc. Am. 73* (1983), p. 1626.

Greenler, R., *Rainbows, Halos, and Glories*, Cambridge University Press, 1980.

Haussmann, A., "Rainbows in nature: recent advances in observation and theory," *Eur. J. Phys. 37*, No. 6 (2016), p. 1–30.

Lee, R.L., Jr., "Mie Theory, Airy Theory, and the natural rainbow," *Appl. Opt. 37* (1998), p. 1506.

Lee, R.L., Jr. and Fraser, A.B., *The Rainbow Bridge*, Pennsylvania State University Press, 2001.

Minnaert, M., *Light and Colour in the open air*, Bell and Sons, 1940.

Newton, I., *Opticks* (4th ed. 1730), Dover Publications, 1952.

Nussenzveig, H.M., "The Theory of the Rainbow," *Sci. Am. 236* (4) (1977), p. 116.

Shapiro, A.E., "Newton and Huygens' Explanation of the 22° Halo," *Centaurus 24* (1980), p. 273.

Walker, J., "Rainbows in a Water Drop," *Sci. Am.*, July 1977, p. 138.

Walker, J., "Mysteries of Rainbows," *Sci. Am.*, June 1980, p. 174.

Wright, W.D., *The Rays are not Coloured*, Adam Hilger Ltd., London, 1967.

Websites:

atoptics.co.uk
old.meteoros.de/haloe.htm
philiplaven.com/index1.html

Editor's Note:

For three additional sky phenomena, see the notes at the bottom of pages 202 and 203.

TIMES OF SUNRISE AND SUNSET

The table on the following two pages gives the times of sunrise and sunset at 4-day intervals for locations ranging from 20° to 60° north latitude. "RISE" and "SET" correspond to the upper limb of the Sun appearing at the horizon for an observer at sea level. The times are local mean time (LMT) for the Greenwich meridian (i.e. UT at 0° longitude), although for North American observers the stated values may be read directly as LMT at the observer's position with an error less than 1 min. The table may be interpolated linearly for both nontabular latitudes and dates, and can be extrapolated beyond the 20° and 60° latitude limits a few degrees without significant loss of accuracy.

It is a common misconception that extreme values for sunrise and sunset times occur on the shortest and the longest days of the year. That is not the case and is due to the tilt of Earth's spin axis to the axis of its orbit, and to Earth's varying speed along its elliptical orbit (as Kepler described in his second law). At mid-northern latitudes, the earliest sunset occurs early in December and the latest sunrise in early January whereas the shortest day (in the sense of hours of daylight) is Dec. 21 or 22. For more information see *Sky & Telescope*, December 1988, p. 674 and July 1972, p. 20, and an article by Terence Hicks in *JRASC, 88*, p. 86, February 1994.

The standard time of an event at a particular location must take account of the observer's longitude relative to his or her standard meridian (see STANDARD TIME ZONES on p. 45). The table below lists the latitude and the longitude correction (in minutes of time) for a number of cities in the United States. For example, to find the time of sunset in Atlanta on 2022 Aug. 5: the latitude is 34°, and from the table the time of sunset at 0° longitude is 18:57 UT (after interpolating for date and latitude). At Atlanta the time of sunset will be approximately 18:57 LMT. Atlanta is in the Eastern time zone (E) and is 37 min west of the standard meridian for this zone (75° W); thus, sunset in Atlanta will occur at 19:34 EST (Eastern Standard Time). Adding one hour to account for Daylight Saving Time makes it 20:34 EDT.

The longitude correction for any location may be found by converting the difference between the longitude of the place and that of its standard meridian to time (1° = 4 min of time), the correction being + if the place is west of its standard meridian, − if east. **Note**: Due to a difference in elevation between the observer and the actual horizon, the observed time may differ by several minutes from the predicted time.

American Cities

Albuquerque NM	35°	+7M	Hartford CT	42°	−9E	New Orleans LA	30°	0C
Atlanta GA	34°	+37E	Honolulu HI	21°	+31H	New York NY	41°	−4E
Austin TX	30°	+31C	Huntington WV	38°	+30E	Omaha NE	41°	+24C
Baltimore MD	39°	+6E	Indianapolis IN	40°	+45E	Pittsburgh PA	40°	+20E
Bangor ME	45°	−25E	Jackson MS	32°	+1C	Providence RI	42°	−14E
Billings MT	46°	+14M	Jefferson City MO	39°	+9C	Raleigh NC	36°	+15E
Birmingham AL	34°	+47E	Lansing MI	43°	+38E	Richmond VA	38°	+10E
Bismarck ND	47°	+43C	Laramie WY	41°	+2M	Salem OR	45°	+12P
Boise ID	44°	+45M	Las Vegas NV	36°	−19P	Salt Lake City UT	41°	+28M
Boston MA	42°	−16E	Lexington KY	38°	+38E	San Francisco CA	38°	+10P
Chicago IL	42°	−9C	Little Rock AR	35°	+9C	Seattle WA	48°	+9P
Columbia SC	34°	+24E	Los Angeles CA	34°	−7P	Sioux Falls SD	44°	+27C
Columbus OH	40°	+32E	Madison WI	43°	−2C	Trenton NJ	40°	−1E
Concord NH	43°	−14E	Miami FL	26°	+21E	Tucson AZ	32°	+24M
Denver CO	40°	0M	Minneapolis MN	45°	+13C	Tulsa OK	36°	+24C
Des Moines IA	42°	+14C	Montpelier VT	44°	−10E	Wichita KS	38°	+29C
Fairbanks AK	65°	+51A	Nashville TN	36°	+47E	Wilmington DE	40°	+2E

SUNRISE AND SUNSET, 2022 JANUARY–JUNE
UNIVERSAL TIME AT GREENWICH MERIDIAN

Latitude:	+20°		+30°		+35°		+40°		+45°		+50°		+55°		+60°	
Event:	RISE	SET	RISE	SET	RISE	SET	RISE	SET	RISE	SET	RISE	SET	RISE	SET	RISE	SET
Jan. –2	6:34	17:30	6:55	17:09	7:07	16:57	7:21	16:43	7:38	16:26	7:58	16:06	8:25	15:39	9:03	15:01
2	6:35	17:33	6:56	17:12	7:08	17:00	7:22	16:46	7:38	16:30	7:58	16:10	8:25	15:44	9:02	15:07
6	6:37	17:35	6:57	17:15	7:09	17:03	7:22	16:50	7:38	16:34	7:58	16:14	8:23	15:49	8:59	15:13
10	6:37	17:38	6:57	17:18	7:08	17:07	7:22	16:54	7:37	16:38	7:56	16:19	8:20	15:55	8:55	15:21
14	6:38	17:41	6:57	17:22	7:08	17:11	7:20	16:58	7:35	16:43	7:53	16:25	8:17	16:02	8:49	15:29
18	6:38	17:43	6:56	17:25	7:07	17:14	7:19	17:02	7:33	16:48	7:50	16:31	8:12	16:09	8:43	15:39
22	6:38	17:46	6:55	17:28	7:05	17:18	7:16	17:07	7:30	16:54	7:46	16:37	8:07	16:17	8:35	15:48
26	6:37	17:48	6:53	17:32	7:03	17:22	7:14	17:12	7:26	16:59	7:42	16:44	8:01	16:25	8:27	15:58
30	6:36	17:51	6:51	17:35	7:00	17:27	7:10	17:17	7:22	17:05	7:36	16:51	7:54	16:33	8:19	16:09
Feb. 3	6:35	17:53	6:49	17:39	6:57	17:31	7:07	17:21	7:18	17:11	7:31	16:58	7:47	16:41	8:09	16:19
7	6:33	17:55	6:46	17:42	6:54	17:35	7:03	17:26	7:12	17:16	7:24	17:04	7:40	16:50	7:59	16:30
11	6:31	17:57	6:43	17:45	6:50	17:39	6:58	17:31	7:07	17:22	7:18	17:11	7:31	16:58	7:49	16:40
15	6:29	17:59	6:40	17:49	6:46	17:43	6:53	17:36	7:01	17:28	7:11	17:18	7:23	17:06	7:38	16:51
19	6:27	18:01	6:36	17:52	6:42	17:46	6:48	17:40	6:55	17:33	7:03	17:25	7:14	17:15	7:27	17:01
23	6:24	18:03	6:32	17:55	6:37	17:50	6:42	17:45	6:48	17:39	6:56	17:32	7:05	17:23	7:16	17:12
27	6:21	18:04	6:28	17:58	6:32	17:54	6:37	17:49	6:42	17:44	6:48	17:39	6:55	17:31	7:05	17:22
Mar. 3	6:18	18:06	6:24	18:00	6:27	17:57	6:31	17:54	6:35	17:50	6:39	17:45	6:45	17:40	6:53	17:32
7	6:15	18:07	6:19	18:03	6:22	18:01	6:24	17:58	6:28	17:55	6:31	17:52	6:36	17:48	6:41	17:42
11	6:12	18:08	6:15	18:06	6:16	18:04	6:18	18:02	6:20	18:01	6:23	17:58	6:26	17:56	6:29	17:52
15	6:09	18:10	6:10	18:08	6:11	18:07	6:12	18:07	6:13	18:06	6:14	18:05	6:15	18:04	6:17	18:02
19	6:05	18:11	6:05	18:11	6:05	18:11	6:05	18:11	6:05	18:11	6:05	18:11	6:05	18:11	6:05	18:12
23	6:02	18:12	6:00	18:13	6:00	18:14	5:59	18:15	5:58	18:16	5:57	18:17	5:55	18:19	5:53	18:22
27	5:58	18:13	5:56	18:16	5:54	18:17	5:52	18:19	5:50	18:21	5:48	18:24	5:45	18:27	5:41	18:31
31	5:55	18:14	5:51	18:18	5:49	18:20	5:46	18:23	5:43	18:26	5:39	18:30	5:35	18:35	5:29	18:41
Apr. 4	5:51	18:15	5:46	18:20	5:43	18:24	5:40	18:27	5:36	18:31	5:31	18:36	5:25	18:43	5:17	18:51
8	5:48	18:16	5:41	18:23	5:38	18:27	5:33	18:31	5:28	18:36	5:22	18:43	5:14	18:50	5:05	19:01
12	5:45	18:17	5:37	18:25	5:32	18:30	5:27	18:35	5:21	18:41	5:14	18:49	5:05	18:58	4:53	19:10
16	5:41	18:19	5:32	18:28	5:27	18:33	5:21	18:39	5:14	18:47	5:05	18:55	4:55	19:06	4:41	19:20
20	5:38	18:20	5:28	18:30	5:22	18:36	5:15	18:43	5:07	18:52	4:57	19:01	4:45	19:14	4:29	19:30
24	5:36	18:21	5:24	18:33	5:17	18:40	5:10	18:47	5:01	18:57	4:50	19:08	4:36	19:22	4:18	19:40
28	5:33	18:22	5:20	18:35	5:13	18:43	5:04	18:51	4:54	19:02	4:42	19:14	4:27	19:29	4:07	19:50
May 2	5:30	18:24	5:16	18:38	5:08	18:46	4:59	18:56	4:48	19:07	4:35	19:20	4:18	19:37	3:56	20:00
6	5:28	18:25	5:13	18:41	5:04	18:49	4:54	19:00	4:43	19:11	4:28	19:26	4:10	19:45	3:45	20:10
10	5:26	18:27	5:10	18:43	5:01	18:53	4:50	19:03	4:37	19:16	4:22	19:32	4:02	19:52	3:35	20:20
14	5:24	18:28	5:07	18:46	4:57	18:56	4:46	19:07	4:32	19:21	4:16	19:38	3:54	19:59	3:25	20:29
18	5:23	18:30	5:05	18:48	4:54	18:59	4:42	19:11	4:28	19:26	4:10	19:43	3:48	20:06	3:16	20:39
22	5:22	18:32	5:03	18:51	4:52	19:02	4:39	19:15	4:24	19:30	4:05	19:49	3:41	20:13	3:07	20:48
26	5:21	18:33	5:01	18:53	4:50	19:05	4:37	19:18	4:21	19:34	4:01	19:54	3:36	20:19	3:00	20:56
30	5:20	18:35	5:00	18:55	4:48	19:07	4:34	19:21	4:18	19:38	3:58	19:58	3:31	20:25	2:53	21:04
Jun. 3	5:20	18:37	4:59	18:57	4:47	19:10	4:33	19:24	4:16	19:41	3:55	20:02	3:27	20:30	2:47	21:11
7	5:20	18:38	4:59	18:59	4:46	19:12	4:31	19:27	4:14	19:44	3:52	20:06	3:24	20:34	2:42	21:17
11	5:20	18:39	4:58	19:01	4:46	19:14	4:31	19:29	4:13	19:46	3:51	20:09	3:22	20:38	2:38	21:21
15	5:20	18:41	4:59	19:03	4:46	19:15	4:31	19:30	4:13	19:48	3:50	20:11	3:21	20:41	2:36	21:25
19	5:21	18:42	4:59	19:04	4:46	19:17	4:31	19:32	4:13	19:50	3:50	20:12	3:20	20:42	2:36	21:27
23	5:22	18:42	5:00	19:05	4:47	19:18	4:32	19:33	4:14	19:51	3:51	20:13	3:21	20:43	2:36	21:28
27	5:23	18:43	5:01	19:05	4:48	19:18	4:33	19:33	4:15	19:51	3:53	20:13	3:23	20:43	2:39	21:27

Noctilucent clouds: *During summer twilight, particularly in the latitude range 53°–60° (in either hemisphere) look for silver-blue, cirrus-like clouds low in the polar sky. These are ice clouds about 80 km high, catching the Sun's light long after it sets (see the newly revised* rasc.ca/handbook/supplements*).*
From notes by Mark Zalcik and Mike Boschat.

SUNRISE AND SUNSET, 2022 JULY–DECEMBER
UNIVERSAL TIME AT GREENWICH MERIDIAN

Latitude:	+20°		+30°		+35°		+40°		+45°		+50°		+55°		+60°	
Event:	RISE	SET	RISE	SET	RISE	SET	RISE	SET	RISE	SET	RISE	SET	RISE	SET	RISE	SET
Jul. 1	5:24	18:43	5:02	19:05	4:50	19:18	4:35	19:33	4:17	19:50	3:55	20:12	3:26	20:42	2:42	21:25
5	5:26	18:44	5:04	19:05	4:52	19:17	4:37	19:32	4:20	19:49	3:58	20:11	3:29	20:39	2:47	21:21
9	5:27	18:43	5:06	19:04	4:54	19:17	4:39	19:31	4:22	19:48	4:01	20:09	3:33	20:36	2:53	21:16
13	5:28	18:43	5:08	19:03	4:56	19:15	4:42	19:29	4:26	19:45	4:05	20:06	3:38	20:32	3:00	21:10
17	5:30	18:42	5:10	19:02	4:59	19:13	4:45	19:27	4:29	19:42	4:10	20:02	3:44	20:27	3:07	21:04
21	5:31	18:41	5:12	19:00	5:01	19:11	4:49	19:24	4:33	19:39	4:14	19:58	3:50	20:22	3:16	20:56
25	5:33	18:40	5:15	18:58	5:04	19:08	4:52	19:21	4:37	19:35	4:20	19:53	3:57	20:15	3:24	20:47
29	5:34	18:38	5:17	18:55	5:07	19:05	4:56	19:17	4:42	19:30	4:25	19:47	4:03	20:08	3:33	20:38
Aug. 2	5:36	18:37	5:20	18:53	5:10	19:02	4:59	19:13	4:46	19:25	4:31	19:41	4:10	20:01	3:43	20:28
6	5:37	18:34	5:22	18:49	5:13	18:58	5:03	19:08	4:51	19:20	4:36	19:35	4:18	19:53	3:52	20:18
10	5:38	18:32	5:24	18:46	5:16	18:54	5:07	19:03	4:56	19:14	4:42	19:28	4:25	19:45	4:02	20:07
14	5:40	18:29	5:27	18:42	5:19	18:50	5:10	18:58	5:00	19:08	4:48	19:20	4:32	19:36	4:12	19:56
18	5:41	18:27	5:29	18:38	5:22	18:45	5:14	18:53	5:05	19:02	4:54	19:13	4:40	19:27	4:21	19:45
22	5:42	18:24	5:31	18:34	5:25	18:40	5:18	18:47	5:10	18:55	5:00	19:05	4:47	19:17	4:31	19:33
26	5:43	18:20	5:34	18:30	5:28	18:35	5:22	18:41	5:15	18:48	5:06	18:57	4:55	19:08	4:40	19:22
30	5:44	18:17	5:36	18:25	5:31	18:30	5:26	18:35	5:19	18:41	5:12	18:48	5:02	18:58	4:50	19:10
Sep. 3	5:45	18:14	5:38	18:20	5:34	18:24	5:29	18:29	5:24	18:34	5:18	18:40	5:10	18:48	4:59	18:58
7	5:46	18:10	5:40	18:15	5:37	18:19	5:33	18:22	5:29	18:26	5:24	18:31	5:17	18:38	5:09	18:46
11	5:47	18:06	5:42	18:11	5:40	18:13	5:37	18:16	5:34	18:19	5:30	18:23	5:25	18:27	5:18	18:34
15	5:47	18:03	5:44	18:06	5:43	18:07	5:41	18:09	5:38	18:11	5:36	18:14	5:32	18:17	5:28	18:21
19	5:48	17:59	5:47	18:01	5:46	18:01	5:45	18:02	5:43	18:04	5:42	18:05	5:40	18:07	5:37	18:09
23	5:49	17:55	5:49	17:56	5:49	17:56	5:48	17:56	5:48	17:56	5:48	17:56	5:47	17:57	5:46	17:57
27	5:50	17:52	5:51	17:51	5:52	17:50	5:52	17:49	5:53	17:48	5:54	17:47	5:55	17:46	5:56	17:45
Oct. 1	5:51	17:48	5:53	17:46	5:55	17:44	5:56	17:43	5:58	17:41	6:00	17:39	6:02	17:36	6:05	17:33
5	5:52	17:45	5:56	17:41	5:58	17:39	6:00	17:36	6:03	17:33	6:06	17:30	6:10	17:26	6:15	17:21
9	5:53	17:41	5:58	17:36	6:01	17:33	6:04	17:30	6:08	17:26	6:12	17:22	6:17	17:16	6:24	17:09
13	5:54	17:38	6:00	17:32	6:04	17:28	6:08	17:24	6:13	17:19	6:18	17:13	6:25	17:06	6:34	16:57
17	5:55	17:35	6:03	17:27	6:07	17:23	6:12	17:18	6:18	17:12	6:25	17:05	6:33	16:57	6:44	16:46
21	5:57	17:32	6:06	17:23	6:11	17:18	6:17	17:12	6:23	17:05	6:31	16:57	6:41	16:47	6:54	16:34
25	5:58	17:30	6:09	17:19	6:14	17:13	6:21	17:07	6:29	16:59	6:38	16:50	6:49	16:38	7:04	16:23
29	6:00	17:27	6:11	17:16	6:18	17:09	6:25	17:01	6:34	16:53	6:44	16:42	6:57	16:29	7:14	16:12
Nov. 2	6:02	17:25	6:14	17:12	6:22	17:05	6:30	16:57	6:40	16:47	6:51	16:35	7:05	16:21	7:24	16:02
6	6:04	17:23	6:18	17:09	6:26	17:01	6:35	16:52	6:45	16:42	6:58	16:29	7:14	16:13	7:35	15:51
10	6:06	17:22	6:21	17:07	6:29	16:58	6:39	16:48	6:51	16:37	7:04	16:23	7:22	16:05	7:45	15:42
14	6:08	17:21	6:24	17:04	6:33	16:55	6:44	16:45	6:56	16:32	7:11	16:17	7:30	15:58	7:55	15:32
18	6:10	17:20	6:27	17:03	6:37	16:53	6:48	16:42	7:01	16:28	7:17	16:12	7:38	15:52	8:05	15:25
22	6:13	17:19	6:31	17:01	6:41	16:51	6:53	16:39	7:07	16:25	7:24	16:08	7:45	15:47	8:15	15:17
26	6:15	17:19	6:34	17:00	6:45	16:49	6:57	16:37	7:12	16:22	7:30	16:05	7:52	15:42	8:24	15:10
30	6:18	17:19	6:37	17:00	6:49	16:49	7:01	16:36	7:17	16:20	7:35	16:02	7:59	15:38	8:33	15:04
Dec. 4	6:20	17:20	6:40	17:00	6:52	16:48	7:05	16:35	7:21	16:19	7:40	16:00	8:05	15:35	8:41	14:59
8	6:23	17:21	6:43	17:00	6:55	16:48	7:09	16:35	7:25	16:18	7:45	15:58	8:11	15:33	8:48	14:56
12	6:25	17:22	6:46	17:01	6:58	16:49	7:12	16:35	7:29	16:18	7:49	15:58	8:16	15:32	8:53	14:54
16	6:28	17:23	6:49	17:02	7:01	16:50	7:15	16:36	7:32	16:19	7:53	15:59	8:20	15:32	8:58	14:53
20	6:30	17:25	6:51	17:04	7:03	16:52	7:18	16:37	7:35	16:21	7:55	16:00	8:22	15:33	9:01	14:54
24	6:32	17:27	6:53	17:06	7:05	16:54	7:20	16:40	7:36	16:23	7:57	16:02	8:24	15:35	9:03	14:56
28	6:34	17:30	6:55	17:08	7:07	16:56	7:21	16:42	7:38	16:25	7:58	16:05	8:25	15:38	9:03	15:00
32	6:35	17:32	6:56	17:11	7:08	16:59	7:22	16:45	7:38	16:29	7:59	16:09	8:25	15:42	9:02	15:05

***Earth's shadow** is visible during a lunar eclipse, but if the sky is clear and transparent, from locations with a low horizon the shadow may be seen twice on any day, projected as a dark band hugging the western or eastern horizon during the half hour before sunrise or after sunset, respectively. Before sunrise, the band lowers in the west, becoming more contrasty until it vanishes at sunrise. After sunset, the band rises in the east, becoming more diffuse as the sky darkens. Immediately above the dark shadow, the sky is illuminated directly by sunlight, pink in color because blue light has been scattered out during the long, grazing path those rays have traversed through the atmosphere. That pink band is called the **Belt of Venus**, after the Roman goddess, not after the planet Venus that can never occupy that part of the sky. However, when full, the Moon always occupies that part of the sky, contributing to the beauty of the scene.*

TWILIGHT

Twilight is the interval of time in the morning or evening when the Sun is below the horizon yet perceptibly contributes to sky glow. There are three geometrical definitions for the end of evening twilight or the start of morning twilight: (1) *Civil twilight*—center of the Sun 6° below the horizon, brightest stars and planets visible, marks start and end of night for the purposes of aviation and artificial lighting of ordinary outdoor activities; (2) *Nautical twilight*—center of the Sun 12° below the horizon, horizon indistinct; (3) *Astronomical twilight*—center of the Sun 18° below the horizon, negligible solar component of sky glow. The following table gives the start of morning and the end of evening astronomical twilight in UT at 0° longitude. For observers in North America the times may be handled in the same way as those of sunrise and sunset (see p. 201).

Latitude:	+20°		+30°		+35°		+40°		+45°		+50°		+55°		+60°	
	Morn.	Eve.	Morn.	Eve.	Morn.	Eve.	Morn.	Eve.	Morn.	Eve.	Morn.	Eve.	Morn.	Eve.	Morn.	Eve.
Jan. 0	5:16	18:50	5:30	18:36	5:37	18:29	5:44	18:22	5:52	18:15	6:00	18:07	6:08	17:58	6:18	17:48
10	5:19	18:56	5:32	18:43	5:39	18:36	5:45	18:30	5:52	18:24	5:59	18:17	6:06	18:09	6:15	18:01
20	5:21	19:01	5:32	18:50	5:38	18:45	5:43	18:40	5:48	18:34	5:54	18:29	5:59	18:23	6:06	18:17
30	5:20	19:07	5:29	18:58	5:33	18:54	5:37	18:50	5:41	18:46	5:45	18:43	5:48	18:40	5:51	18:37
Feb. 9	5:18	19:11	5:24	19:05	5:27	19:02	5:29	19:00	5:30	18:59	5:32	18:58	5:32	18:57	5:32	18:58
19	5:13	19:15	5:16	19:12	5:17	19:11	5:17	19:11	5:17	19:12	5:15	19:13	5:13	19:16	5:08	19:21
Mar. 1	5:07	19:18	5:07	19:19	5:06	19:20	5:04	19:22	5:01	19:25	4:56	19:29	4:50	19:36	4:40	19:46
11	4:59	19:21	4:55	19:25	4:52	19:28	4:48	19:33	4:43	19:38	4:35	19:46	4:24	19:58	4:09	20:13
21	4:50	19:25	4:43	19:32	4:38	19:37	4:31	19:44	4:23	19:53	4:11	20:05	3:56	20:21	3:33	20:44
31	4:41	19:28	4:30	19:39	4:23	19:46	4:13	19:56	4:02	20:08	3:46	20:24	3:24	20:46	2:52	21:19
Apr. 10	4:31	19:32	4:17	19:46	4:07	19:56	3:55	20:09	3:40	20:24	3:19	20:45	2:50	21:15	2:03	22:05
20	4:22	19:36	4:04	19:55	3:52	20:07	3:37	20:22	3:17	20:42	2:51	21:09	2:11	21:50	0:44	23:30
30	4:14	19:41	3:52	20:03	3:37	20:18	3:19	20:37	2:55	21:01	2:21	21:36	1:22	22:37	—	—
May 10	4:07	19:46	3:41	20:13	3:24	20:30	3:02	20:52	2:33	21:21	1:49	22:06	—	—	—	—
20	4:01	19:52	3:32	20:22	3:13	20:41	2:48	21:06	2:13	21:42	1:14	22:43	—	—	—	—
30	3:58	19:58	3:26	20:30	3:04	20:51	2:36	21:19	1:56	22:00	0:26	23:38	—	—	—	—
Jun. 9	3:56	20:02	3:23	20:36	3:00	20:59	2:29	21:30	1:44	22:15	—	—	—	—	—	—
19	3:57	20:06	3:22	20:40	2:59	21:04	2:28	21:35	1:40	22:23	—	—	—	—	—	—
29	4:00	20:07	3:25	20:41	3:02	21:05	2:31	21:35	1:44	22:22	—	—	—	—	—	—
Jul. 9	4:04	20:06	3:31	20:39	3:09	21:01	2:40	21:30	1:57	22:13	—	—	—	—	—	—
19	4:09	20:04	3:38	20:34	3:18	20:54	2:51	21:20	2:14	21:57	1:03	23:05	—	—	—	—
29	4:14	19:58	3:47	20:26	3:28	20:44	3:05	21:07	2:33	21:38	1:43	22:27	—	—	—	—
Aug. 8	4:19	19:52	3:55	20:15	3:39	20:31	3:19	20:51	2:53	21:17	2:14	21:54	0:56	23:08	—	—
18	4:24	19:43	4:04	20:03	3:50	20:17	3:34	20:33	3:12	20:54	2:42	21:24	1:54	22:10	—	—
28	4:28	19:34	4:11	19:50	4:01	20:01	3:47	20:14	3:29	20:32	3:06	20:55	2:32	21:28	1:30	22:26
Sep. 7	4:31	19:24	4:19	19:37	4:10	19:45	3:59	19:56	3:46	20:09	3:27	20:27	3:02	20:52	2:23	21:30
17	4:34	19:14	4:25	19:23	4:19	19:29	4:11	19:37	4:01	19:47	3:47	20:01	3:28	20:19	3:01	20:46
27	4:37	19:05	4:31	19:10	4:27	19:14	4:22	19:19	4:14	19:26	4:05	19:36	3:51	19:49	3:32	20:08
Oct. 7	4:39	18:56	4:37	18:58	4:35	19:00	4:32	19:03	4:28	19:07	4:21	19:13	4:12	19:22	4:00	19:34
17	4:42	18:49	4:43	18:47	4:43	18:47	4:42	18:48	4:40	18:50	4:37	18:53	4:32	18:57	4:25	19:04
27	4:45	18:43	4:50	18:38	4:51	18:36	4:52	18:35	4:53	18:34	4:52	18:35	4:51	18:36	4:48	18:38
Nov. 6	4:49	18:39	4:56	18:31	4:59	18:28	5:02	18:24	5:05	18:22	5:07	18:20	5:09	18:18	5:10	18:16
16	4:53	18:36	5:03	18:26	5:08	18:22	5:12	18:17	5:17	18:12	5:21	18:08	5:25	18:04	5:30	17:59
26	4:58	18:36	5:10	18:24	5:16	18:18	5:22	18:13	5:28	18:07	5:34	18:00	5:40	17:54	5:47	17:47
Dec. 6	5:04	18:38	5:17	18:25	5:24	18:18	5:30	18:11	5:37	18:04	5:45	17:57	5:53	17:49	6:02	17:40
16	5:09	18:42	5:23	18:28	5:30	18:21	5:38	18:13	5:45	18:06	5:53	17:58	6:02	17:49	6:12	17:39
26	5:14	18:47	5:28	18:33	5:36	18:26	5:43	18:18	5:50	18:11	5:58	18:03	6:07	17:54	6:18	17:44
Jan. 5	5:18	18:53	5:32	18:39	5:38	18:32	5:45	18:26	5:52	18:19	6:00	18:11	6:08	18:03	6:17	17:54

SKY BRIGHTNESS AT MIDNIGHT
BY ROY BISHOP

Astronomers generally desire dark skies, free of moonlight and light pollution by *Homo sapiens*. As mentioned on the previous page, the beginning or end of *astronomical twilight* corresponds to the center of the Sun being 18° below the horizon. At that point the amount of sunlight scattered by the upper layers of Earth's atmosphere is negligible; that is, it is less than the combined illuminance (about 2×10^{-3} lux) from starlight, airglow, and zodiacal light, the three main contributors to the light of the "dark" night sky.

For observers in countries at high latitudes (e.g. the United Kingdom, Norway, southern Argentina and Chile, and most of Canada), around the time of the summer solstice the Sun always lies less than 18° below the horizon, and the sky does not get dark at night. This "midnight twilight" phenomenon can be displayed in a graph as a function of latitude and time of year.

The following diagram indicates the brightness of the sky at local midnight at any time of the year for any latitude north of 45°N or south of 45°S. Below the lower curve the natural sky is dark. Between the two curves twilight prevails. Above the upper curve the Sun is in the sky. Place names in roman type (left-hand side) are in the Northern Hemisphere; place names in *italic* type (right-hand side) are in the *Southern Hemisphere*. On the horizontal axis use the roman-type months for the former, *italic*-type months for the latter. The diagram is simplified slightly in that the months are assumed to be of equal duration, and the seasonal pattern of months and summer solstices for Earth's two hemispheres are assumed to be identical except for a 6-month phase shift.

The latitude of the Arctic and Antarctic Circles (90° subtract the obliquity of the ecliptic = 66°34′) is indicated by the dashed line. This line is *not* tangent to the Midnight Sun curve because at midnight on the summer solstice at either the Arctic or the Antarctic Circle the Sun is above the horizon. Atmospheric refraction raises the apparent Sun about 34′ above the true Sun. Also, rise/set is defined as the top limb of the Sun at a sea-level horizon; thus the 16′ semidiameter of the Sun must also be taken into account. To see the top limb of the Sun on the horizon at local midnight on the summer solstice, an observer must be 34′ + 16′ = 50′ south of the Arctic Circle (or north of the Antarctic Circle), at latitude 65°44′.

By running a horizontal line across the chart at a selected latitude, the reader can determine the approximate dates when midnight twilight and, possibly, midnight Sun begin and end for any locality at north or south latitudes above 48.6°, the lower limit for midnight twilight on the summer solstice. (Remarkably, when rounded to the nearest degree, the latter figure is the latitude of the longest east–west international border: the 2000-km-long 49th parallel between the United States and western Canada.)

Some examples: The diagram shows that Earth's poles are astronomically dark for less than three months of the year. At Grise Fiord, a village on Ellesmere Island and Canada's northern-most community, the sky is never dark from about Mar. 10 until early October, and the midnight Sun lasts from late April until mid-August. Cape Horn at midnight is bathed in dim Antarctic twilight from early November until early February. Even at the latitude of Vancouver there is a period of almost a month each year when the sky never gets astronomically dark. Although the midnight sky should be dark at all latitudes below the lower curve, that is no longer the case in or near populated areas where the natural night sky is immersed in a perpetual twilight: the baleful pall of light pollution (see p. 79). For such areas the TWILIGHT table on the previous page is irrelevant.

SKY BRIGHTNESS AT MIDNIGHT

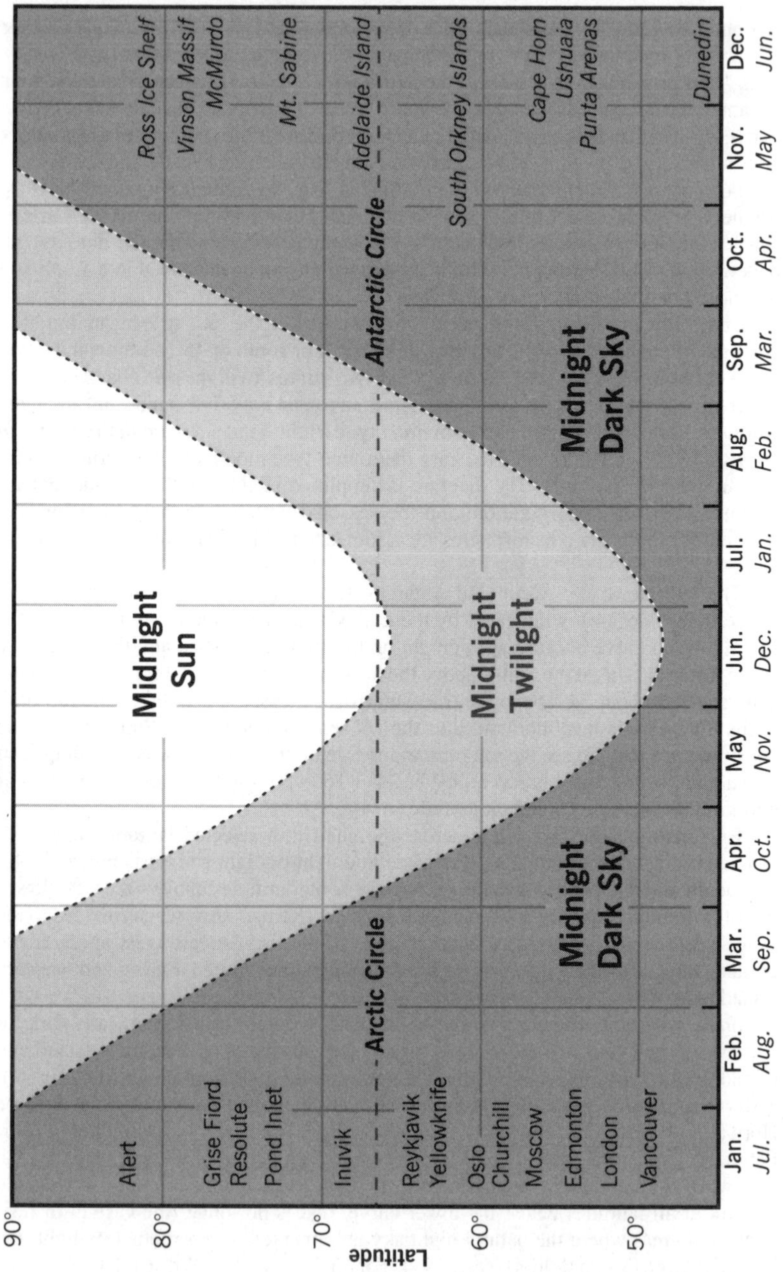

Diagram by Roy Bishop, drawn by Michael Gatto

PLANETS AND SATELLITES

THE PLANETS IN 2022
BY MURRAY PAULSON

INTRODUCTION

You would think that with the internet and today's technology, you would never need a telescope. But nothing replaces that "being there" moment at the eyepiece when, with persistent effort, you see those subtle details obscured by distance and atmosphere revealed for fleeting moments. Seeing the changing face of the planets in real time is something that many of us find alluring. We get to be explorers in that last frontier, and we get to see the beauty of our neighboring planets firsthand. Sometimes we even discover something new and point it out to the rest of the world, like the famous impacts in Jupiter's atmosphere. There is still a role for amateurs to play in discovery.

Optics: When observing the planets, it is important to minimize optical aberrations. To get the most out of your observing sessions, use high magnification with high-quality optics. If you are unable to change the optics, make sure they are clean and well-collimated. If you are considering a change, the best telescopes for the planets are high-quality refractors. The cost of these telescopes may be prohibitive, and "large" refractor apertures are only around 200 mm. The aperture is limited, but quality optics provide for astounding views. There are other high-end optical systems to choose from: Maksutovs, Dall–Kirkhams, and optimized Newtonians work very well.

Also important is resolution. One of the axioms of optics is: The larger the diameter of the telescope, the higher the resolution (see TELESCOPE PARAMETERS, p. 49 and TELESCOPE EXIT PUPILS, p. 50). In the world of amateur planetary imaging, some of the best work is being done with the larger, commercial, Schmidt–Cassegrain telescopes (SCTs) of aperture 300–400 mm. There are some excellent quality, larger SCTs that, when coupled with image-processing software, can do amazing things. Software can produce excellent images by stretching the contrast that central obstructions tend to reduce. There are also good-quality Newtonian telescopes and other

The apparent minimum and maximum observable size of seven planets.

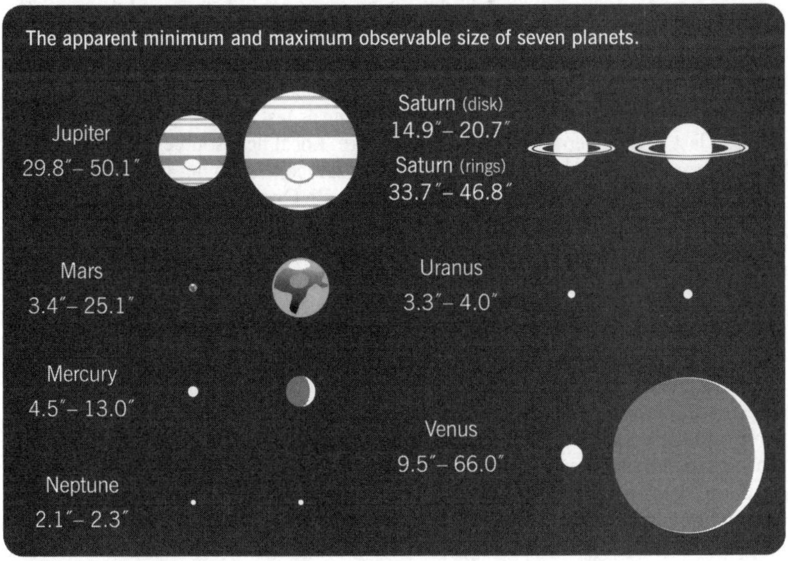

Illustration by Michael Gatto

Cassegrain designs. To evaluate telescope quality for planetary work, H.R. Suiter's book *Star Testing Astronomical Telescopes: A Manual for Optical Evaluation and Adjustment* (Willmann–Bell, Inc., Richmond, 2nd Ed., 2009) provides the appropriate tools.

With a high-quality telescope, you need good eyepieces. The general rule is: The higher the quality and the fewer optical elements, the better. Every surface scatters light, and the features on the planets are subtle. Orthoscopic eyepieces are the benchmark for planetary eyepieces, with Zeiss "orthos" at the top of the scale. These eyepieces produce very clean, high-contrast images. There are other manufacturers that produce Abbe Orthos, notably Takahashi and University Optics, but a few others make a variation on the orthoscopic design that have observers praising them. Try a variety of eyepieces when you can (e.g. at star parties) to see how they work for you. Be critical of what you see, and note the contrast and the color each eyepiece lends to its subject. Then check your wallet! If you are using a nondriven telescope, a wide, flat-field eyepiece like the Tele Vue Nagler or Ethos is indispensable, because the large fields of view of these eyepieces give you ample time to observe at high power before having to reposition the telescope. An alternative is the Nikon NAV SW series, with oculars exhibiting very little distortion or false color. The view in these eyepieces is sharp to the edge of the field. My best view of Mars was with a binoviewer. The use of both eyes gives your brain the chance to combine the image and ignore "floaters" and other visual defects. It is more expensive to purchase the viewer and the extra eyepieces, but it is effective.

Cleanliness of eyepieces and diagonals is also important. These surfaces are close to the observer, and will contribute the most degradation to image contrast if they are not clean. Do your homework before you clean your eyepieces, and make sure you do not damage them in the cleaning process (skyandtelescope.org/astronomy-resources/caring-for-your-optics, for example).

The next step is to get a drive for the telescope, which gives the observer uninterrupted time to concentrate on the planetary image and to discern the details.

Now consider the optical tube. If the telescope is warmer than the surrounding air, the warm air rising from the optical surfaces in the tube assembly will mix with the cold ambient air, causing localized turbulence, which degrades the image. Adequate thermal equalization of the telescope is critical for good images. The general rule is: The smaller the thermal mass, the shorter the cool-down period. To avoid long cool-down periods, some amateurs use a cooling fan to flush the heat out of the telescope or to blow cool air onto the mirror. Closed-tube assemblies will limit the mixing of the warm and cool air, and they do not cool quite as fast as an open-tube assembly.

The last of the aberrations is the atmosphere. Local heat sources, such as furnace flues, warm cars, paved parking lots, and even someone standing near the telescope, will cause heat plumes that could degrade the seeing. One way of ascertaining whether there are thermal sources affecting the seeing is to defocus your telescope while observing a bright star, and examine the image for any slow-moving anomalous structure. This movement is evidence of a heat plume aberrating the star's image. You may have to move the telescope. Sometimes the atmosphere is just not cooperative, and the jet stream or some other phenomenon will bloat the planet's image to resemble a fuzzy tennis ball. The defocused image will show a river of structure moving in one direction across it. There is not much you can do but try again on another night.

Daytime observing: The inner planets are often very close to the horizon after sunset, and this puts the observer at a disadvantage. Down that low, the shimmering of the atmosphere obscures the fine details on the inner planets. Just finding Mercury is a challenge in the twilight. Daytime observing of the inner planets is possible, but it does take some equipment and planning. The easiest way is to use a Go To telescope. Failing that, use a polar-aligned equatorial mount with setting circles. Both options will get the telescope aimed in the right area of the sky. Note: If the sky is hazy, the task of finding the planet in the daytime becomes significantly more difficult, or next to impossible.

Mars, Jupiter, and Saturn are observable in the daytime hours, so you are not limited to just the inner planets: The outer planets are more challenging, but fun to find. It is especially fun to observe a planetary conjunction in the daytime. My favorites have been Venus and Jupiter, and Mercury and Venus.

It is difficult to locate and acquire focus on planets in the daytime sky, so the recommended procedure is to first set up the telescope with a solar filter and a low-power eyepiece, then focus on the Sun. Once you have a good focus on the Sun, lock the focuser, if possible. You can also use calibrated or marked focusers, or simply use the same eyepiece/focuser combination from the previous night's observing session.

Do not remove the solar filter yet. **Do not hunt for planets within 5° of the Sun because of the hazard that accidental unfiltered exposure to the Sun poses.** Remember that blindness is not a desirable observing attribute! (See VIEWING A SOLAR ECLIPSE—A WARNING, p. 147.) If you are not using a Go To scope, set the coordinates on the mount to the Sun's position, and then move off to the location of the planet you are hunting. With the Go To, just enter the command to go to the planet. **Now it is safe to remove the solar filter.** To make absolutely sure that the Sun is not in the field of view, pass your hand over the eyepiece to see if it is safe, then look.

The resolution of the eye is acute only near the center of vision, so if you are not looking directly at the planet, you probably will not see it, and you will have to scan the field of view to find it. With Venus, this is not a problem, but it is with Mercury and the outer planets. Once the planet is in the field of view, center it and try higher-power eyepieces. Parfocal eyepieces provide easy eyepiece exchange with minimal refocusing. A light-orange filter like the Wratten #21 darkens the light-blue sky and improves the contrast.

If the planet is not in the field, either there is an error in your mount alignment or the planet is very low in contrast. You can scan for the planet, being very careful about sweeping toward the Sun. **Do not sweep too far!** The second choice is to try to improve the mount alignment. Try the drift alignment method (see p. 70) on the Sun or obtain a better north–south reference. The atmosphere heats up throughout the day, so it is most stable in the morning. Objects in the foreground, such as asphalt parking lots, may affect the seeing. If possible, for best stability, observe over grass or water.

Drawing the planets is encouraged (see ASTRONOMICAL SKETCHING, p. 88). I now mostly image the planets, but I am glad for the time I put in to drawing them. Drawing compels the observer to critically observe the planet. This is a worthwhile activity because it gives you multiple opportunities to observe the details that appear in the fleeting moments of good seeing, and this effort teaches your eye and brain how to see the subtle features. You become a much better observer. As a bonus, drawing also provides a record of what you saw during that session, for future reference.

For drawing, use a pair of soft and hard pencils (e.g. an HB and an H), a logbook, and a template (wikihow.com/Observe-Mars). Mars is typically drawn with a 42-mm circular template, corresponding to the ~4200-mile (6792-km) diameter of Mars. The templates for other planets can be of a convenient size, but do not make them too small. Jupiter and Saturn need an oblate template to make them easier to draw. Draw major features first, then fill in the little details as you see them. It is very important that you record the time and date on the drawing, as well as the aperture and eyepiece you are using, filters (if any), the general observing conditions, and your name and location. For example, Jupiter rotates very rapidly, and the features will visibly shift over a 20-min interval. The Association of Lunar and Planetary Observers is interested in amateur contributions and is happy to receive amateur drawings.

Editor's Note: All dates are UT and some events, as viewed from North America, may occur on the evening of the previous date. Check THE SKY MONTH BY MONTH (p. 98) for exact times, especially for phenomena involving the Moon.

MERCURY

Mercury is a planet of extremes: It is the smallest of the eight planets, it is closest to the Sun and therefore the fastest moving, and it is nearly the hottest planet. Mercury also has the longest solar day, lasting two of its orbital periods, or 176 days. In the peak of its "noonday" heat, Mercury's surface warms to 427 °C, and on the far side the temperature goes down to –163 °C. The coldest place is deep in the shadows of craters near the poles, –183 °C. These extremes give the planet a temperature range of 610 C°.

Mercury has an orbital period of 87.96 days, and it rotates on its axis every 58.65 days, locked in a 3:2 resonance with its orbital period around the Sun. This is due to the high eccentricity of its orbit, in which perihelic tidal forces dominate the spin period. Accordingly, every elongation is different, ranging from 18° to 28°. Mercury's orbit has a high inclination of 7.0°, which can place it well above or below the ecliptic during a given apparition. Since Mercury never strays more than 28° from the Sun, it is only visible near the horizon at dusk or dawn.

Most people have never seen Mercury, because the window of opportunity is so narrow near dusk and dawn. (They may have seen it and not realized it!) That fact, coupled with the general poor quality of the atmosphere close to the horizon, makes daytime observation of Mercury the better option, when the planet is higher in the sky and you are looking through less atmosphere. If you can observe early in the day, thermal effects are reduced. (Try observing over a body of water during the daytime, when the air and water temperatures are not too different, leading to improved seeing.) One difficulty of observing Mercury in twilight is that the high luminance of the planet makes the subtle markings difficult to see. By observing in the daytime, when Mercury is higher than the Sun, the luminance contrast is less, which makes the markings easier to see.

Any telescope equipped with Go To or setting circles can be used to find Mercury (see the daytime observing tips on p. 212). Details on Mercury can be seen in a 130-mm telescope using high magnifications of 1.5× to 3.0× per millimetre of diameter. A red or an orange filter (Wratten #21) can be used to boost the contrast with the blue of the sky. Anecdotally, the best phases to see the subtle details on the planet are between mid-gibbous and a wide crescent, near the greatest elongations. Views of Mercury with 250-mm Maksutovs show surprising detail.

MERCURY—ELONGATION AND APPARENT SIZE DURING 2022

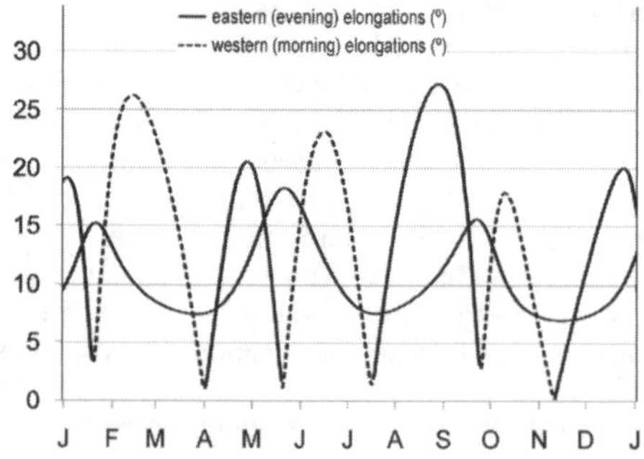

Elongation is plotted in degrees and angular diameter in arcseconds. The first day of each month is marked on the horizontal axis. Visibility depends not only on the elongation but also on the angle between the ecliptic and the horizon.

Mercury's mean synodic period (time between successive inferior conjunctions) is 115.88 days, so there are generally three opportunities to see it both after sunset and in the dawn sky every year. The angle of the ecliptic makes fall-evening and spring-morning apparitions at higher latitudes very poor—in both Northern and Southern Hemispheres—because the ecliptic is almost parallel to the horizon, and Mercury sets shortly after the Sun, or rises shortly before the Sun, in bright twilight. One disparity is that the Southern Hemisphere gets the better of the fall-morning and spring-evening elongations, because the inclination of Mercury's orbit to the ecliptic provides a more favorable geometry for Southern Hemisphere observers.

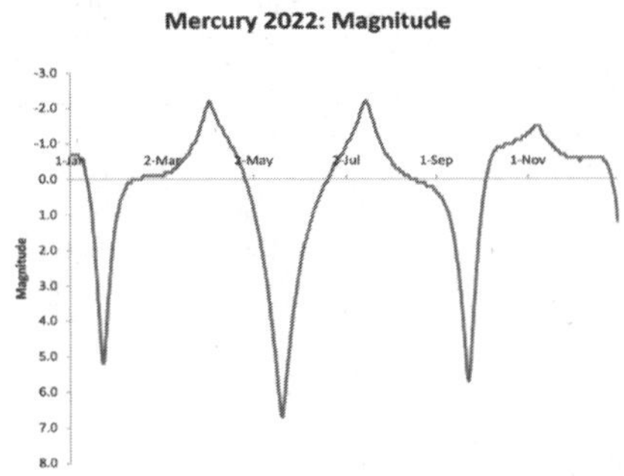

The year 2022 starts off with Mercury rising to its GEE on Jan. 7. It will move out to a 19° elongation and shine at mag. –0.6. In the eyepiece it will show a 7″ 56%-illuminated phase. Mercury sets about 1.5 h after the Sun and should be visible in the southwest for a week around the time of the GEE. On Jan. 12–13, Mercury will sit 3.4° west of Saturn. Mercury shines at mag. 0.0 and Saturn at 0.7. Mercury then plunges to its Jan. 23 inferior conjunction. Then it moves into the morning sky and reaches its GEW on Feb. 16. It will sit 26° from the Sun, shining at mag. 0.0, and it will show a 6.9″ 60%-illuminated disk. Mercury encounters Saturn again on its way back to the Sun on Mar. 2 when it passes quite close at 40′ south of Saturn. This is a Southern Hemisphere treat, since it will be out of view for the Northern Hemisphere.

The next event is Mercury's superior conjunction on Apr. 2 when it will pass 45′ below the Sun. It will shine at mag. –2.0, but this is not a challenge observation—far too close to the Sun! Mercury then moves on to its Apr. 29 GEE, where it will shine at mag. 0.3 and show an 8″ 36%-illuminated fat crescent at 20.6° elongation from the Sun. A few days later, on May 2, a crescent Moon passes 2.5° below Mercury, which will be visible near the longitude of 100° east. North American observers will see the Moon about 5° north and east of Mercury, while the Pleiades will be just to the southwest. On May 21, Mercury arrives at its inferior conjunction, where it passes 1° below the Sun. Jun. 16 marks the next GEW, where Mercury will sit at an elongation of 23° from the Sun in the morning sky. It shines at mag. 0.6 and shows a 6.9″ 36%-illuminated disk. In the northern latitudes, Mercury is just not visible in the twilight glare, so it is best hunted for in the daytime with a telescope that has GoTo capability or setting circles. A month later, on Jul. 16, Mercury is at superior conjunction and passes 1.25° above the Sun.

We move on to the Aug. 27 GEE, which is the greatest elongation of 2022. Mercury swings out to 27.3° from the Sun, shining at mag. 0.2 with a 50%-illuminated disk. Mercury will sit more than 20° from the Sun for over 36 days—plenty of opportunity to observe that disk evolve over the apparition. The interval is Aug. 7 to Sep. 11. It's a great show but mostly in the daytime Northern Hemisphere; if you are in the Southern Hemisphere, it sets 2.5 h after the Sun. Mercury falls to its next inferior conjunction on Sep. 23. It will pass 2.9° below the Sun but shine at a diminutive mag. 5.6. Three days later, Mercury passes 3.2° below Venus, but its 3.8 magnitude makes this an exceedingly difficult observation, 6.5° from the Sun. Venus would be fine at mag. –3.9, but the 8-magnitude difference makes sighting Mercury impossible. Only 15 days later, on Oct. 8, Mercury rises to its GEW. It will shine at mag. –0.6 and will stay in the negative magnitudes above –0.5 until Dec. 24, fading to 0.0 on Dec. 27.

The next big event is the occultation of Mercury by the Moon on the morning of Oct. 24. Check the LUNAR OCCULTATIONS section for details (p. 162). Next comes the superior conjunction on Nov. 8. Mercury spends 13.5 h behind the Sun and then pops out into the last evening apparition of the year. Mercury catches up with Venus and passes only 1.3° below it on Nov. 21. They sit 8° from the Sun, offering a good daytime challenge to see both of them. Venus shines at mag. –3.9 and Mercury at –0.7. Both are small disks, Venus 10.5″ and Mercury 5.6″; they will slowly separate, so you have a week to see them drift apart. Mercury's final GEE is on Dec. 21, where it will shine at mag. –0.6 and show a 60%-illuminated, slightly gibbous disk of 6.8″ diameter. Venus trails behind it. The pair will make for a delightful view in the hour after sunset. Venus sets 1 h after sunset with Mercury following 20 min later. On Dec. 24, a 37-h-old Moon joins the group for a nice photo opportunity.

VENUS

Known as both the morning star and the evening star, Venus has impressed us throughout the ages with the brilliance and purity of its light. Ranging inmagnitude from –4.9 to –3.8, Venus is bright enough to cast a visible shadow. If you know when and where to look, it is visible to the naked eye in full daylight.

In the pre-spacecraft era, people thought that our sister planet might bear habitable zones somewhat like Earth. Nothing could be further from the truth. The surface temperature on Venus is a fairly constant 460 °C, under a runaway greenhouse effect. The dense carbon dioxide atmosphere has a pressure of over 9300 kPa (92 atm) at the surface and a density of 65 kg/m^3, 6.5% the density of water and about 60 times that of Earth's atmosphere. Wind friction would be serious on Venus.

Thick sulphur-dioxide clouds with sulphuric-acid droplets veil the surface of Venus; little light reaches the surface. Occasional detail is seen in the cloud structure in amateur telescopes, but for the most part it appears as a featureless white disk. The subtle structure in the cloud tops is difficult to observe, but too few observers even give it a try. The best times to look are from just between thick crescent and mid-gibbous phases. A violet filter can enhance the visibility of atmospheric structure, and imaging through a UV filter will show cloud details. The Association of Lunar and Planetary Observers (ALPO on p. 221) is interested in your images of Venus seen this way.

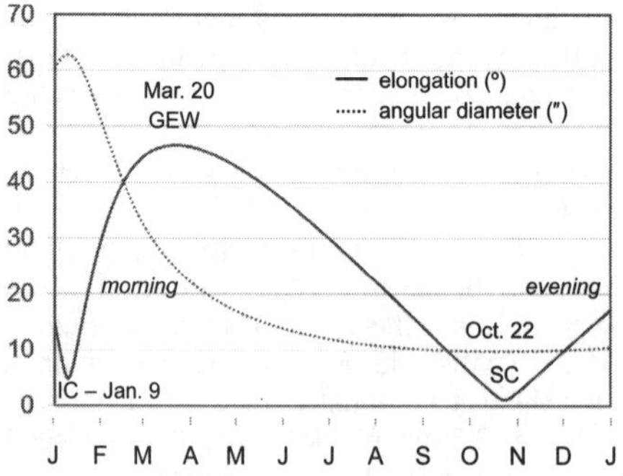

Elongation is plotted in degrees and apparent angular diameter in arcseconds. The first day of each month is marked on the horizontal axis.

Never far from the Sun, Venus may be found in a telescope during the daytime, when high in the sky, far from the deleterious effects of our thick near-horizon atmosphere. The daytime sky is favorable for viewing the bright disk of Venus, because of the lower luminance contrast. This is a popular daytime activity at star parties (see the discussion on daytime planet viewing in the INTRODUCTION of this section, p. 218).

The year 2022 starts off with Venus headed to a Jan. 9 inferior conjunction. These conjunctions with the Sun are an opportunity to see Venus as a large, razor-thin crescent. This year, the crescent will span an incredible 65″ due to Earth being near perihelion. Venus will shine at mag. –4.4, with the Sun only 5° south. Due to the proximity of the Sun, do take extreme caution if trying this observation. (I recommend using a refractor with clean optics for it. Review the section in the introduction on daytime viewing of the planets, and see VIEWING A SOLAR ECLIPSE—A WARNING, p. 147.) Venus moves out to its GEW on Mar. 20, where it shines at mag. –4.4 and shows a 24.5″ 50%-illuminated disk. Due to the Northern Hemisphere spring ecliptic hugging the morning horizon, Venus will be difficult to glimpse. On Mar. 28, Venus moves into a nice grouping with Saturn, Mars, and the Moon, where Saturn will sit 2.1° south of Venus; Mars will be 5.3° to the southwest with the Moon passing 7° south. Conversely, the Southern Hemisphere will get a great show.

The next set of conjunctions is even more spectacular. The first event is a tight conjunction with Neptune, with the pair passing only 14″ apart on the morning of Apr. 27 at 19:09 UT. Closest approach can be seen in the longitude of Sydney, Australia. Observers in the Americas see the pair around 24′ apart just after Venus rises in the morning sky. A thin crescent Moon may be visible 5° below the pair. On Apr. 30, Venus passes 14′ below Jupiter, with the closest approach visible in Australia and East Asia. North American viewers will see the pair 28′ apart.

May 27 sees a close encounter with a thin crescent Moon, where it passes 52′ below Venus. This is visible around the Greenwich meridian, but in North America it will expand out to 3° on the east coast and to 4.3° on the west coast. Our next stop is the Venus–Uranus conjunction on Jun. 11, where they pass 1.5° apart. This is near summer solstice, so Uranus will be difficult to see in the morning twilight, even if using a telescope. On Jun. 26, a crescent Moon joins Venus in the morning sky. It will be 3° north of Venus in North America with its closest approach visible on Newfoundland's meridian (60° W). About a lunar month later, Venus and Mercury join in a favorable conjunction on the morning of Jul. 26. The Moon will be well placed 3.5° above Venus.

On Oct. 22, Venus comes to its superior conjunction and will pass 0.75° above the Sun. When Venus is on the far side of its orbit, it moves very slowly with respect to the Sun, only 0.233° per day, so it won't be visible for a while in the twilight glare. Mercury is in hot pursuit and catches up with Venus on Nov. 20, with Venus a 10.3″ disk shining at mag. –3.9, and 1.3° south is Mercury with a 5.6″ disk shining at mag. –0.8. The problem is they are now only 7° east of the Sun, but with great care they can be observed in a daytime telescope. The pair will be close for two weeks following Nov. 20 and will shine together in the evening sky as they get higher in December. On Dec. 29, Mercury will have slowed its upward pace as it turns back to the Sun, and Venus will once again be up close. By then, Venus will be 16° elongation from the Sun and more prominent in the evening sky.

MARS

Mars is a planet that inspires us, a place we could envision walking on and exploring, a destination where our grandchildren may go. A web of imagined canals has ensnared us, and generations of observers and scientists have devoted their lives to the study of the Red Planet. Despite the unveiling of the mysteries of Mars, with neither Martians nor canals to be found, many of us are still infatuated with the planet.

About every 2 years and 50 days, on average, we renew our acquaintance with

Mars, as Earth—on the inside track—overtakes the fourth planet. Over the roughly 15-year cycle between extreme close approaches near perihelion, there are seven oppositions with diverse separations (see OPPOSITIONS OF MARS on p. 216). The Martian day is about 3% longer than our day; this results in us observing the same central meridian of Mars about 38 min later on successive nights. Equivalently, the longitude of the center of the Martian disk reduces by 9.5° per Earth day. Accordingly, near opposition, the same surface features will be visible at the same time of night 41 days later. When the view is near its best, you can expect to enjoy two full rotations of Mars in stroboscopic form.

Mars is accompanied by two small moons, Deimos and Phobos, discovered by Asaph Hall in 1877 with the 66-cm (26-in.) refractor at the U.S. Naval Observatory. These two moons undoubtedly are captured minor planets, given their angular shape and proximity to the asteroid belt. Deimos is the smaller, at 16 × 12 km, and completes one orbit in 30.3 h. Phobos, at 26 × 22 km, orbits Mars in a speedy 7.7 h. Viewed from the Martian surface, Phobos would rise in the west and set in the east. Detecting this pair is a real challenge, because Mars outshines them by 13 to 14 magnitudes, and they never venture very far from the planet. Observe near opposition with an occulting-bar eyepiece to block out the brilliance of the Martian disk (see p. 25), using lots of magnification and a finder chart, so you know where to look.

This year, we get to watch Mars grow from 4″ as it moves toward its December opposition to where it will culminate in a 17.2″ disk. But first check it out in January and compare it to Uranus, which is less than 10% smaller at 3.67″. The ambitious observer can get up early to see Mars rising 2 h before the Sun. We have a nice conjunction of Mars and the Moon on the morning of Jan. 29, with the thin, crescent Moon rising 3.3° south of Mars. A month later, on Feb. 24, Mars arrives at its autumnal equinox. On Apr. 4, Mars and Saturn will pass only 18′ apart. The closest approach will be visible in the longitudes around Australia, but North American viewers will see the pair at 24′ apart. Use binoculars to find the color-contrasting pair. Red Mars will shine at mag. 1.0 and cream-yellow Saturn will be mag. 0.9. While out viewing, you can see Venus 7° north in azimuth in the Northern Hemisphere and 7° south in the Southern Hemisphere.

On the morning of May 18, Mars will pass 31′ below Neptune. This will be a challenge with a 7.8-mag. planet lurking in the twilight and a mag. 0.8 Red Planet as your guide. But it does get better with Jupiter rising 6° down the ecliptic. Once again, this conjunction will be best viewed in the Southern Hemisphere. On May 29, Mars is in conjunction with Jupiter, and it will pass 35′ below the gas giant. Jupiter will shine at mag. –2.2 and is 37″ in diameter, whereas Mars is 6.4″, shining at mag. 0.7. Mars arrives at its winter solstice with the northern polar cap turned at its maximum to Earth. Mars shines at mag. 0.3 and has expanded to 7.9″. A close conjunction with the Moon occurs with the close approach visible in the western Pacific-Australian region where the Moon passes 35′ north of Mars. North America will see it on its lead-in about 4° west of Mars. The last planetary encounter of the year is with Uranus on Aug. 1. Mars has now expanded to 8.2″ in diameter, shining at mag. 0.1, while 1.3° above it sits mag. 5.1 Uranus at 3.6″ diameter. The pair rise just around 1:00 a.m. local time, so you will be up late or early for this observation.

As we roll into September, Mars breaks above 10″ diameter, and it will brighten into the negative magnitudes. For the next four months, Mars will be in Taurus and high in our sky above +20° declination. At three months away from its December opposition, Mars rises at near midnight, local time. On Oct. 29, Mars begins its retrograde motion, becoming the brightest object in the night sky with the exception of the Moon and Jupiter. Mars culminates around the time of opposition on Dec. 7 at mag. –1.9. The disk appears to swell to a maximum size of 17.20″ a week before opposition and is 17.01″ at opposition. This incongruity is due to the fact that Mars's orbit is carrying it farther away from Earth as we catch up and overtake it. We are actually closer on Dec. 1 than on the 8th, but Mars is not (yet) opposite the Sun as seen from Earth on the 1st. On the evening of the opposition (Dec. 7 in North America), Mars is occulted by the full Moon over most of North America except the eastern seaboard of the United States, through east Texas, and Mexico. See the section on LUNAR OCCULTATIONS, p. 162 for details on this event. It will be worth seeing and imaging. Mars will sit high in our skies and will be prominent over the month of December. Dec. 26 marks Mars's spring equinox. The Red Planet will dim slightly to mag. –1.2, and the disk will shrink slightly to 14.7″ by the end of the month.

TABLE 1–PROMINENT FEATURES ON MARS BY DATE

Date	Feature on disk at 5 UT	Size (″)	
Sep. 22	Mare Cimmerium with Syrtis Major rotating on	11.26	
Sep. 29	Tharsis / M Sirenum–Solus Lacus	11.84	
Oct. 6	Mare Erythaeum & Aurorae Sinus	12.47	
Oct. 13	Mare Erythraeum Sinus Meridiani	13.16	
Oct. 20	Syrtis major, Hellas Sinus Meridiani rotating on	13.89	
Oct. 27	Syrtis major–Mare Cimmerium	14.65	L
Nov. 3	Mare Cimmerium–Mare Sirenum	15.41	A
Nov. 10	Tharsis / M Sirenum–Solus Lacus	16.11	R
Nov. 17	Mare Erythaeum & Aurorae Sinus Solus Lacus	16.69	G
Nov. 24	Meridiani Sinus Mare Erythaeum	17.08	E
Dec. 1	Syrtis major, Hellas Sinus Meridiani rotating on	17.20	R
Dec. 8	Syrtis major–Mare Cimmerium	17.01	
Dec. 15	Mare Cimmerium–Mare Sirenum	16.54	than
Dec. 22	Tharsis / M Sirenum–Solus Lacus	15.83	
Dec. 29	Mare Erythaeum & Aurorae Sinus	14.96	13″
Jan. 5	Meridiani Sinus and Mare Sirenum	14.02	
Jan. 12	Syrtis major, Hellas	13.07	
Jan. 19	Mare Cimmerium–Mare Sirenum	12.11	
Jan. 26	Tharsis / M Sirenum–Solus Lacus	11.26	

What's up on Mars?

Table 1, above, lists the prominent features visible on Mars at 7-day intervals around the time of 5 UT, Sep. 2022 to Jan. 2023. This places it at 11 p.m. in a central North American time zone; you can refer to the MAP OF MARS on p. 217. Mars's winter solstice occurred on Jun. 21, so the table above begins a little after halfway to Mars's spring equinox on Dec. 26. Around the time of opposition, Dec. 8, Mars's north pole will be tipped to the west and about half of the north polar cap will be visible; refer to the diagram overleaf.

JUPITER

Other than Venus when near inferior conjunction, Jupiter is the largest planet to view in a telescope, with an angular diameter ranging from 44″ to 50″ at opposition. Jupiter moves just over 30° per year in its orbit around the Sun, visiting a new constellation of the zodiac about every year. It is the king of planets with an array of 79 attendant moons, of which 4 are readily visible and a 5th is a tough hunt.

Jupiter does not have a solid surface; however, unlike Venus, it has high-contrast, semi-stationary cloud features that have been observed for many centuries. Jupiter rotates on its axis in 9 h 51 m, slightly slower toward the poles, easily

continued on p. 218

OPPOSITIONS OF MARS, 2018–2033

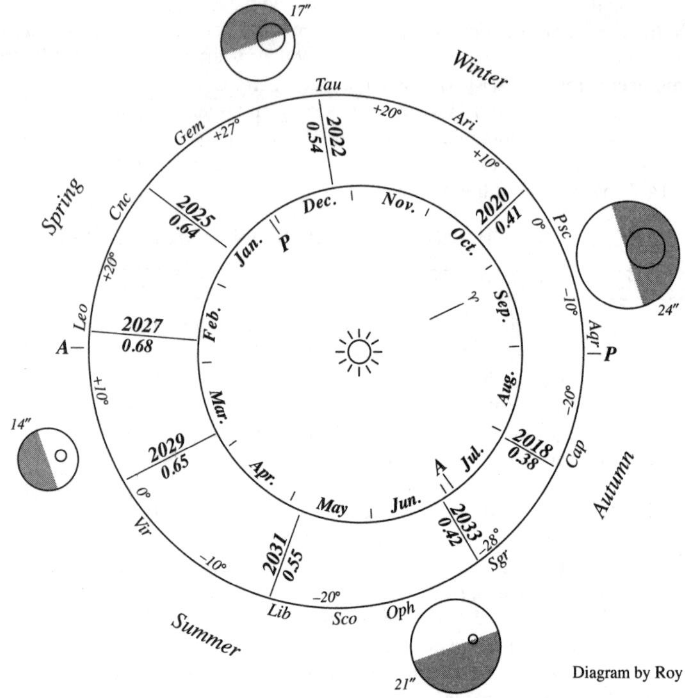

Diagram by Roy Bishop

The above diagram represents the orbits of Earth and Mars as viewed from the north ecliptic pole. Straight lines link simultaneous positions of the two planets for eight successive oppositions of Mars, beginning with that of the year 2018. The separation of the two planets (in astronomical units) at the various oppositions is indicated beside each of the connecting lines. The months inside of Earth's orbit indicate the position of Earth during the year (both planets orbit counterclockwise). For each orbit, two tick marks labeled A and P indicate the aphelion point and the perihelion point, respectively. The direction of the vernal equinox is shown (toward the late-September position of Earth). Around the orbit of Mars is indicated its declination (ranges between +27° and −28°) and the constellation in which Mars resides when at opposition.

Four views of Mars are shown: at its two equinoxes and two solstices. These views show the portion of Mars illuminated by the Sun, the location and approximate size of its north polar cap, and the apparent size of Mars (labeled in arcseconds) for oppositions occurring at these points in its orbit. The seasons of the Martian northern hemisphere are indicated around the outer margin of the diagram, and are very nearly one season ahead of those on Earth at the same orbital position. (For the southern hemisphere of Mars, the season and the configuration of the south polar cap are the same as those of the diametrically opposite view.) Note that the maximum angular diameter Mars can attain (25") occurs near its perihelion, at a late-August opposition.

As an example of the information that can be read from this diagram: The 2022 opposition of Mars occurs in early December with Mars located near declination +25° in the constellation Taurus, 0.54 au from Earth, and about 17" in diameter. It will be almost spring in the Martian northern hemisphere, and the north polar cap will be prominent. For observers residing in mid-northern latitudes, none of the succeeding five Martian oppositions will be as favorable as that of 2022.

MAP OF MARS

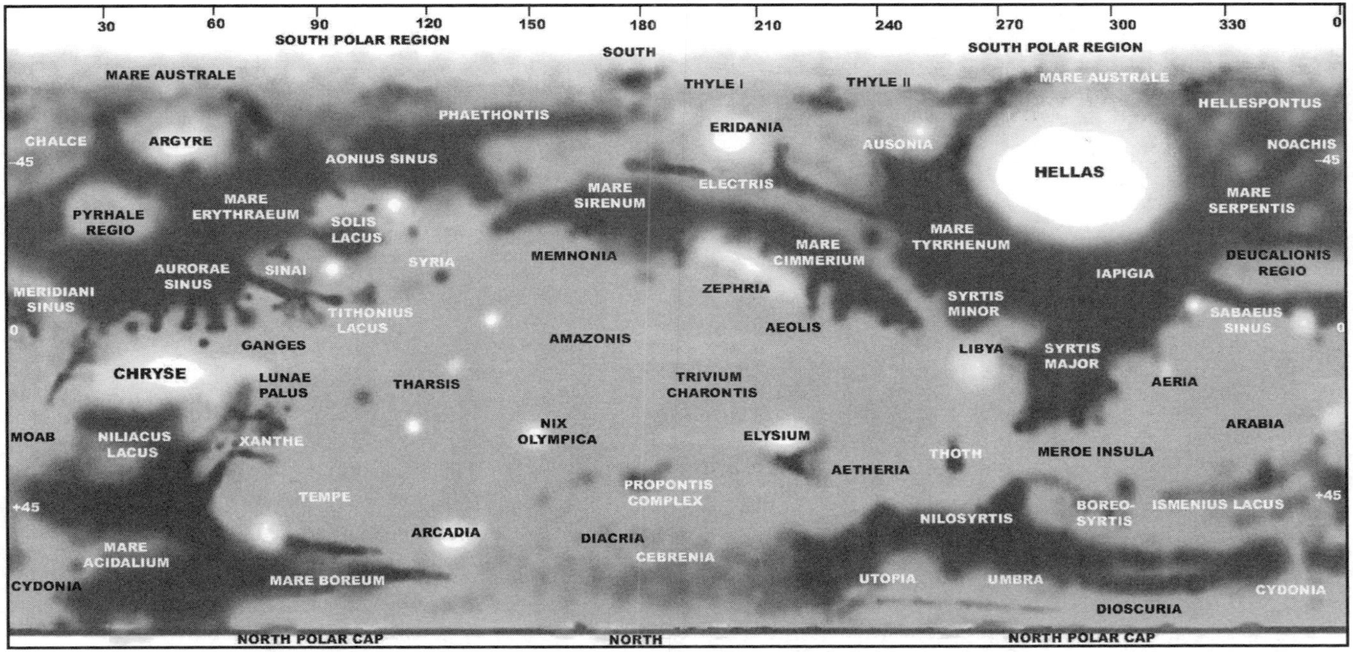

This map has south at top and north at bottom, and represents the view through a telescope having an even number (0, 2, 4) of reflections. It was computer-generated by Daniel Troiani, using all the data (CCD images, drawings, and photographs) from the Mars section of the Association of Lunar and Planetary Observers (ALPO) during the 2001 apparition. The map is intended to represent the appearance of Mars, as viewed from Earth through moderate-sized telescopes, during favorable apparitions, or electronic images that have been digitally processed. For recent observations of Mars, visit the Mars section of the ALPO website, alpo-astronomy.org.

noticeable over a period of half an hour. In fact, when drawing Jupiter, sketch the major features in the first 10 min, because their locations will noticeably change if you dwell on it. Then fill in the details relative to the major features. A 50-mm telescope will show the equatorial belts, the polar hoods, and the four Galilean moons. A 75-mm-aperture telescope will easily show the shadows of the moons and some structure in the various cloud belts. Fifty years ago, my old 50-mm refractor showed a brick-red Great Red Spot (GRS), but now the spot has faded and then reddened lately; you need a 90-mm refractor just to see it, under good conditions. In recent years, it has been determined that the GRS has been shrinking for quite some time. In the 1800s, the spot was estimated to have been 41 000 km in its long axis, whereas present-day measurements by the *Hubble Space Telescope* show it to be only 16 500 km in length. It is notable that recent amateur observations have determined that the spot has experienced an acceleration in its rate of shrinkage. We may bear witness to the disappearance of the Great Red Spot in our lifetime. Jupiter's belts are dynamic and occasionally disappear only to reappear again a few years later. If the GRS disappears, it may be a long time before a similar long-lived major feature emerges. Stay tuned.

The views of Jupiter in 125-mm to 175-mm apochromatic refractors or high-quality 200-mm to 320-mm obstructed apertures are spectacular. Wait for those rare moments of excellent seeing, and you will be rewarded. These apertures (with high-quality optics, properly collimated) will reveal the ovals, festoons, and many structures recorded in the best images of Jupiter. With a 130-mm refractor at magnifications above 200×, the contrast on Jupiter starts to get soft. Larger apertures have a higher magni-

Observable features on Jupiter

The following diagram illustrates the names of the major observable and photographic features of Jupiter.

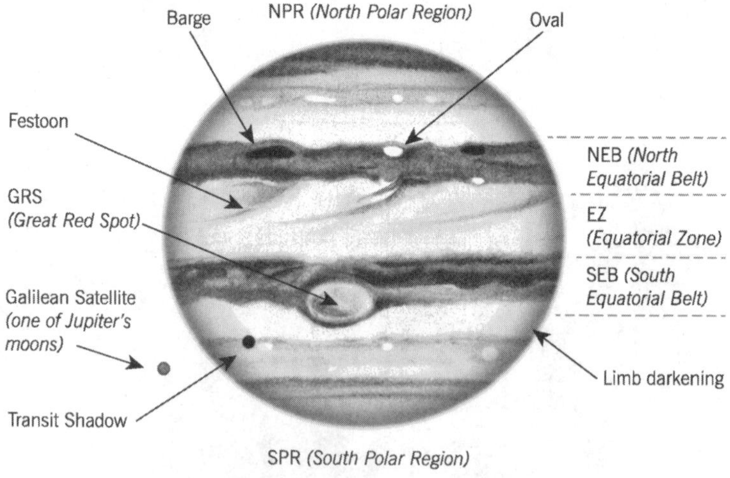

This composite drawing by Michael Gatto illustrates and names the principal observable features of Jupiter, including one of the Galilean satellites and its shadow.

fication limit and will improve the contrast, color, and amount of fine detail visible on Jupiter. In the last few years, several long-lived white ovals and additional red spots have been observed in Jupiter's southern regions, while the north equatorial belt has shown more dark markings along its margins. Because some of Jupiter's cloud features are colored, you can improve contrast and visibility by observing with color filters. The contrast of red spots and the belt features improves with a green filter, and the bluish festoons will darken with an orange or a red filter.

Jupiter is one of the better planets for imaging. The most recent generation of video imagers have improved the quality of amateur planet images. It is now easy to get images that push the limits of the optical system, and the dynamic range of the image can be stretched to reveal low-contrast details. Amateurs are producing images nearly as good as those from Hubble, and they are making discoveries such as "Red Spot, Jr." and impacts in Jupiter's atmosphere. As deep-sky observers search for locations with the darkest skies, leading imagers seek observing locations with stable atmospheres.

The year 2022 is a good one for observing Jupiter—we will see it at its closest approach in 70 years. The year starts off with Jupiter in the western evening sky. There are a couple of conjunctions with the Moon that will be favorable to North American viewers. The first is on the evening of Jan. 6, where a thin crescent Moon sits 4.6° below Jupiter. We get a repeat of this on Feb. 3, but with a more slender crescent. On Mar. 5, Jupiter is in conjunction with the Sun and will move into the morning sky. Jupiter will be in conjunction with Mercury on Mar. 21, but the pair will sit 12° west of the Sun, so hunt for them in a daytime sky. Mag. –0.8 Mercury will sit 1.2° below Jupiter shining at mag. –2.0. This will be a tough hunt unless the sky is pristine. On Apr. 30, Jupiter and Venus pass only 14′ apart. The closest approach is visible in the Australia–Eastern Asia region. In North America, we will see the pair 28′ apart. On the morning of May 29, Jupiter is in close conjunction with Mars, and they pass 35′ apart. Mars shines at mag. 0.7 with Jupiter at –2.2, and they rise just over 2 h before the Sun.

Jul. 27 marks the start of Jupiter's entry into retrograde motion. On the evening of Aug. 15, a nearly full Moon passes under Jupiter, and a lunar month later, on Sep. 11, it repeats this for observers in North America (passing over, as viewed from the Southern Hemisphere). Then on Sep. 26, Jupiter comes to opposition where it will shine at mag. –2.9 with its disk at 49.88″. It sits on the celestial equator, 0°, well positioned for observers in both hemispheres. We are seeing Jupiter near its perihelion and closest approach to Earth. We have a few nice conjunctions with the Moon over the next few months. On Oct. 8, a nearly full Moon rises just after Jupiter. Closest approach is visible in the Eastern Hemisphere at 2.6°, but North American viewers will see the pair close to 4° apart. On Nov. 4, a similar pairing occurs at 2.8° as seen in Europe's time zone, and 3° separation in North America. Nov. 23 marks the end of Jupiter's retrograde and it resumes a proper eastward motion. Dec. 2 (1 UT) marks another nice conjunction, with the waxing gibbous Moon well placed for Western Hemisphere observers.

TABLE 2: JOVIAN MOONS AT OPPOSITION

Moon	Diameter (″)	Magnitude
Io	1.25	4.9
Europa	1.07	5.1
Ganymede	1.81	4.4
Callisto	1.66	5.5

JUPITER—TABLE OF DAILY CENTRAL MERIDIANS, 2022

Date 0h UT	System I	System II	Date 0h UT	System I	System II	Date 0h UT	System I	System II	Date 0h UT	System I	System II	Date 0h UT	System I	System II
MARCH			**MAY**			**JULY**			**SEPTEMBER**			**NOVEMBER**		
1	353.8	129.3	1	253.2	283.1	1	159.8	84.3	1	234.2	45.6	1	152.8	218.8
2	151.5	279.3	2	50.9	73.3	2	317.7	234.6	2	32.3	196.0	2	310.7	9.1
3	309.1	69.3	3	208.7	223.4	3	115.6	24.9	3	190.3	346.5	3	108.7	159.4
4	106.8	219.3	4	6.4	13.5	4	273.5	175.1	4	348.3	136.9	4	266.6	309.7
5	264.5	9.4	5	164.2	163.6	5	71.4	325.4	5	146.4	287.3	5	64.5	100.0
6	62.1	159.4	6	321.9	313.7	6	229.3	115.7	6	304.4	77.7	6	222.4	250.2
7	219.8	309.4	7	119.7	103.9	7	27.2	266.0	7	102.5	228.1	7	20.3	40.5
8	17.4	99.4	8	277.4	254.0	8	185.1	56.2	8	260.5	18.5	8	178.2	190.8
9	175.1	249.5	9	75.2	44.1	9	343.1	206.5	9	58.6	168.9	9	336.1	341.0
10	332.8	39.5	10	233.0	194.3	10	141.0	356.8	10	216.6	319.3	10	134.0	131.3
11	130.4	189.5	11	30.7	344.4	11	298.9	147.1	11	14.6	109.8	11	291.9	281.6
12	288.1	339.6	12	188.5	134.5	12	96.8	297.4	12	172.7	260.2	12	89.7	71.8
13	85.7	129.6	13	346.3	284.7	13	254.7	87.7	13	330.7	50.6	13	247.6	222.1
14	243.4	279.6	14	144.0	74.8	14	52.7	238.0	14	128.8	201.0	14	45.5	12.3
15	41.1	69.7	15	301.8	224.9	15	210.6	28.3	15	286.8	351.4	15	203.4	162.5
16	198.8	219.7	16	99.6	15.1	16	8.5	178.6	16	84.9	141.8	16	1.2	312.8
17	356.4	9.8	17	257.3	165.2	17	166.5	328.9	17	242.9	292.2	17	159.1	103.0
18	154.1	159.8	18	55.1	315.4	18	324.4	119.2	18	40.9	82.7	18	316.9	253.2
19	311.8	309.8	19	212.9	105.5	19	122.3	269.5	19	199.0	233.1	19	114.8	43.4
20	109.4	99.9	20	10.7	255.7	20	280.3	59.8	20	357.0	23.5	20	272.6	193.7
21	267.1	249.9	21	168.5	45.8	21	78.2	210.1	21	155.1	173.9	21	70.5	343.9
22	64.8	40.0	22	326.3	196.0	22	236.2	0.4	22	313.1	324.3	22	228.3	134.1
23	222.5	190.0	23	124.1	346.2	23	34.1	150.8	23	111.2	114.7	23	26.1	284.3
24	20.2	340.1	24	281.9	136.3	24	192.1	301.1	24	269.2	265.1	24	184.0	74.5
25	177.8	130.1	25	79.6	286.5	25	350.0	91.4	25	67.2	55.5	25	341.8	224.7
26	335.5	280.2	26	237.4	76.7	26	148.0	241.7	26	225.3	205.9	26	139.6	14.9
27	133.2	70.2	27	35.2	226.8	27	306.0	32.1	27	23.3	356.3	27	297.4	165.1
28	290.9	220.3	28	193.0	17.0	28	103.9	182.4	28	181.3	146.7	28	95.3	315.3
29	88.6	10.4	29	350.9	167.2	29	261.9	332.8	29	339.4	297.1	29	253.1	105.4
30	246.3	160.4	30	148.7	317.4	30	59.9	123.1	30	137.4	87.5	30	50.9	255.6
31	43.9	310.5	31	306.5	107.5	31	217.8	273.4						

Date 0h UT	System I	System II	Date 0h UT	System I	System II	Date 0h UT	System I	System II	Date 0h UT	System I	System II	Date 0h UT	System I	System II
APRIL			**JUNE**			**AUGUST**			**OCTOBER**			**DECEMBER**		
1	201.6	100.5	1	104.3	257.7	1	15.8	63.8	1	295.4	237.9	1	208.7	45.8
2	359.3	250.6	2	262.1	47.9	2	173.8	214.1	2	93.4	28.3	2	6.5	195.9
3	157.0	40.7	3	59.9	198.1	3	331.8	4.5	3	251.5	178.7	3	164.3	346.1
4	314.7	190.7	4	217.7	348.3	4	129.8	154.8	4	49.5	329.1	4	322.1	136.3
5	112.4	340.8	5	15.6	138.5	5	287.8	305.2	5	207.5	119.5	5	119.8	286.4
6	270.1	130.9	6	173.4	288.7	6	85.7	95.6	6	5.5	269.9	6	277.6	76.6
7	67.8	280.9	7	331.2	78.9	7	243.7	245.9	7	163.5	60.3	7	75.4	226.7
8	225.5	71.0	8	129.0	229.1	8	41.7	36.3	8	321.5	210.6	8	233.2	16.9
9	23.2	221.1	9	286.9	19.3	9	199.7	186.6	9	119.5	1.0	9	31.0	167.0
10	180.9	11.2	10	84.7	169.5	10	357.7	337.0	10	277.5	151.4	10	188.7	317.2
11	338.6	161.2	11	242.5	319.7	11	155.7	127.4	11	75.6	301.8	11	346.5	107.3
12	136.4	311.3	12	40.4	109.9	12	313.7	277.8	12	233.6	92.1	12	144.2	257.4
13	294.1	101.4	13	198.2	260.1	13	111.7	68.1	13	31.5	242.5	13	302.0	47.6
14	91.8	251.5	14	356.1	50.3	14	269.7	218.5	14	189.5	32.9	14	99.8	197.7
15	249.5	41.6	15	153.9	200.5	15	67.8	8.9	15	347.5	183.2	15	257.5	347.8
16	47.2	191.6	16	311.8	350.7	16	225.8	159.3	16	145.5	333.6	16	55.3	137.9
17	204.9	341.7	17	109.6	141.0	17	23.8	309.7	17	303.5	123.9	17	213.0	288.0
18	2.6	131.8	18	267.5	291.2	18	181.8	100.0	18	101.5	274.3	18	10.7	78.1
19	160.4	281.9	19	65.3	81.4	19	339.8	250.4	19	259.5	64.6	19	168.5	228.3
20	318.1	72.0	20	223.2	231.6	20	137.8	40.8	20	57.4	215.0	20	326.2	18.4
21	115.8	222.1	21	21.1	21.9	21	295.9	191.2	21	215.4	5.3	21	123.9	168.5
22	273.5	12.2	22	178.9	172.1	22	93.9	341.6	22	13.4	155.7	22	281.7	318.6
23	71.3	162.3	23	336.8	322.3	23	251.9	132.0	23	171.3	306.0	23	79.4	108.7
24	229.0	312.4	24	134.7	112.6	24	49.9	282.4	24	329.3	96.3	24	237.1	258.8
25	26.7	102.5	25	292.5	262.8	25	208.0	72.8	25	127.2	246.6	25	34.8	48.8
26	184.5	252.6	26	90.4	53.1	26	6.0	223.2	26	285.2	37.0	26	192.6	198.9
27	342.2	42.7	27	248.3	203.3	27	164.0	13.6	27	83.1	187.3	27	350.3	349.0
28	139.9	192.8	28	46.2	353.6	28	322.1	164.0	28	241.1	337.6	28	148.0	139.1
29	297.7	342.9	29	204.1	143.8	29	120.1	314.4	29	39.0	127.9	29	305.7	289.2
30	95.4	133.0	30	1.9	294.1	30	278.1	104.8	30	197.0	278.2	30	103.4	79.3
						31	76.2	255.2	31	354.9	68.5	31	261.1	229.3

JUPITER—DAILY CENTRAL MERIDIANS AND TIME OF TRANSIT OF GREAT RED SPOT

The table on the facing page can be used to calculate the longitude of the central meridian of the observed disk of Jupiter throughout 2022, except for the interval Jan. 1 to Feb. 28, when Jupiter is too close to the Sun to observe. System I is the most rapidly rotating region, between the middle of the North Equatorial Belt and the middle of the South Equatorial Belt. System II applies to the rest of the planet, from the equatorial belts to the poles. The rotation rate of System I is +36.577 ± 0.008 °/h and that of System II is +36.259 ± 0.008 °/h. These figures, together with the closest tabular value, can be used to determine the longitude of a system's central meridian for any given date and time (UT) of observation. **Example:** At 9:00 p.m. CDT Jul. 17 = 2:00 UT Jul. 18, the longitude of the central meridian of System I is

$$324.4 + (36.577 \times 2) = 397.6°;$$

putting this angle in the range 0°–360° by subtracting 360° leaves a longitude of 37.6°.

The table may also be used to estimate when the Great Red Spot (GRS) will cross the central meridian of Jupiter's disk. Based on drift measurements, the GRS is predicted to be near longitude 7° in System II on 2022 Jan. 0, drifting by about +14° per year. See jupos.privat.t-online.de for an up-to-date value.

Example: Suppose an observer in Toronto is viewing Jupiter on the evening of Apr. 3 (time zone: EDT, –4 h). At 0 h UT Apr. 4 (20 h EDT Apr. 3), the table gives 190.7° for the longitude of the central meridian in System II. Ignoring GRS drift, a further rotation of 7°–190.7° = –183.7° (+176.3°) will bring the GRS to the central meridian, which takes place 176° ÷ 36.259°/h = 4.85 h = 4 h 51 min later. Thus the GRS will transit at 4:51 UT Apr. 4 = 0:51 EDT Apr. 4. (Correcting for the annual drift in GRS longitude would add 14° × 3/12 ÷ 36.259°/h = 0.10 h, or 6 min to the transit time.) By timing a transit of the GRS and using the table, you can update its longitude for yourself. Alternatively, you can use a specialized GRS transit calculator, such as skyandtelescope.com/observing/objects/planets/3304091.html.

SATURN

Saturn is the second-largest planet in the Solar System, with a maximum equatorial angular diameter of 21″ (excluding the rings). The ringed planet takes 29.4 y to orbit the Sun, and moves only 12.2° per year in its eastward journey along the ecliptic. Saturn is the most oblate of the planets, with a polar/equatorial diameter ratio of 0.90.

With its incredible system of rings, Saturn is possibly the most spectacular planet in the Solar System. The rings subtend 40″–47″ near opposition, and are visible even in steadied (or image-stabilized) high-power binoculars and small spotting scopes. Saturn's rings are composed mostly of ice particles of sizes ranging from dust to boulders, in complex subsystems of rings within rings. The more you zoom in on the rings, the more structure there is to see. The *Cassini* probe has found fine structure right down to the limits of its image resolution.

Visually, in earthbound telescopes, the rings divide into three distinct sectors

JUPITER AND SATURN IN 2022

	JUPITER		SATURN		
Date UT	Mag.	Equatorial Diameter ″	Mag.	Equatorial Diameter ″	Ring Inclination °
Jan. 1.0	–2.1	35	+0.7	15	17.6
Feb. 1.0	–2.0	33	+0.7	15	16.1
Mar. 1.0	–2.0	33	+0.8	15	14.8
Apr. 1.0	–2.0	33	+0.9	16	13.5
May 1.0	–2.1	35	+0.9	16	12.6
Jun. 1.0	–2.2	38	+0.8	18	12.3
Jul. 1.0	–2.4	42	+0.6	18	12.6
Aug. 1.0	–2.6	46	+0.4	19	13.4
Sep. 1.0	–2.8	49	+0.3	18	14.5
Oct. 1.0	–2.9	49	+0.5	18	15.2
Nov. 1.0	–2.8	48	+0.6	17	15.3
Dec. 1.0	–2.6	43	+0.7	16	14.7
Jan. 1.0	–2.4	39	+0.8	15	13.7

(see opposite). The outer (A) ring is separated from the first inner (B) ring by the Cassini Division, which J.D. Cassini discovered in 1675. The Cassini Division is visible in a 50-mm telescope, yet it is only 0.8″ wide at opposition. The A ring itself is divided by the Encke Gap, a very fine division about one-fifth of the way between the outer edge of the ring and the Cassini Division. The Encke Gap is extremely difficult to observe and requires a large aperture (250 mm or greater), high-quality optics, and high magnification (~500×), which in turn demands excellent atmospheric seeing. There is also a minimum in luminance called the Encke minimum, about halfway between the outer edge of the A ring and the Cassini Division. This is easier to see and is often confused with the Encke Gap.

The next ring inward is the B ring, which is the broadest and brightest of the rings. The inner edge of this ring fades a bit in brightness and often appears to have a stranded nature, like grooves in a vinyl record. The inner edge sometimes exhibits spokes in the ansae (the part of the rings seen on either side of the planet). You need high magnification and a very clean optical system to see these subtle features. They may only be visible on one side of the planet.

The innermost ring is the Crepe Ring (also called the C ring). It goes largely unnoticed because it is so dim in comparison to the outer two rings and the glare from Saturn. It is a ghostly ring about the same width as the A ring, and it appears dark where it passes in front of the planet. It looks like a shadow cast on the planet, but it is actually blocking the planet's reflected light from our view. A very clean optical system is essential to get a good view of the Crepe Ring. Contrast-robbing dust and debris on eyepiece and diagonal surfaces have a pronounced effect, because they are close to the eye. You know you have seen the Crepe Ring when you notice that the black space within the ansae next to the ball of the planet is only slightly darker than the Crepe Ring.

At a distance of 9.5 au from the Sun, Saturn does not receive enough solar energy to sustain as lively an atmosphere as that of Jupiter. There are a few belts, and the occasional storm or outbreak of activity. The average observer will see an equatorial-region belt and the dark polar hood, but not much else. The experienced observer may see much more, but the details are subtle. White spots have been seen in the south tropical zone, and a south equatorial disturbance was recorded in 2009. In late 2010, a dramatic storm appeared in the north temperate zone, and the white spot spread and was followed for many months in 2011. These subtle phenomena are more readily captured with a camera.

Saturn begins the year with a brief meeting with Mercury on Jan. 13. Mag. 0.7 Saturn sits 3.4° above mag. 0.3 Mercury, and they set 1.5 h after the Sun. Saturn is quite low in the sky. Its next stop is a conjunction with the Sun on Feb. 4. A month later, on Mar. 2, we get a repeat of the Saturn–Mercury conjunction in the morning sky. Mercury, at mag. –0.1, passes 40′ below mag. 0.8 Saturn. This spectacle is best viewed in the Southern Hemisphere due to the shallow morning ecliptic in the Northern Hemisphere, where the two rise only 40 min before the Sun. But do give it a try if the skies are co-operative. On Mar. 29, Venus joins Saturn in the morning twilight. Venus will be a mag. –4.4 beacon, and Saturn will sit 2.1° below, shining at mag. 0.9.

Jun. 4 marks the beginning of Saturn's retrograde motion and the planet's minimum ring tilt of the year at 12.3°. Saturn moves on to its Aug. 14 opposition just above γ Cap. The rings will be tilted up at 13.9°, and Saturn's 18.8″ disk shines at mag 0.3. Saturn has been climbing the ecliptic from its southerly location, and it now sits at a –15° declination. This is certainly an improvement for northern observers, but it will be a

SATURN—MAIN RING FEATURES VISIBLE FROM EARTH

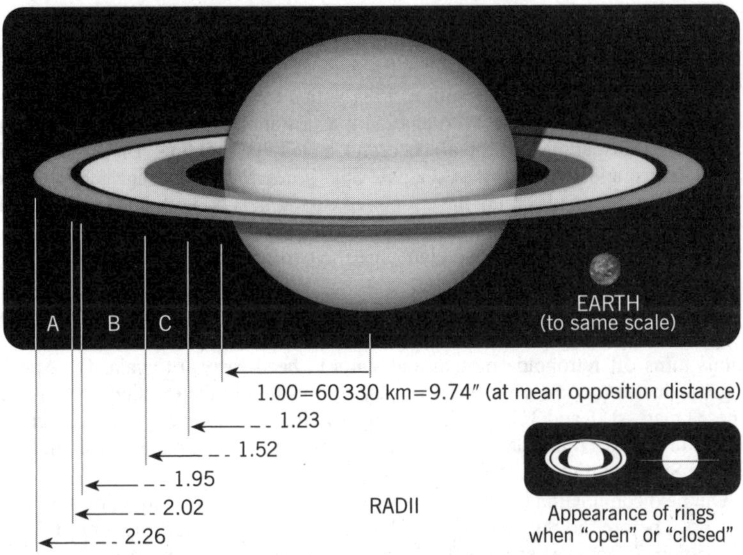

SATURN'S RING SYSTEM—MAIN STRUCTURAL REGIONS

Ring	Radius**	Discoverer
D	1.11 – 1.23	*Voyager 1* (1980)
C*	1.23 – 1.52	W.C. & G.P. Bond, W.R. Dawes (1850)
B*	1.52 – 1.95	Galileo (1610), C. Huygens (1659),
A*	2.02 – 2.26	J.D. Cassini (1675)
F	2.33	*Pioneer 11* (1979)
G	2.8	*Voyager 1* (1980)
E	3. – 8.	W.A. Feibelman (1966)

* *Visible from Earth; also, the tenuous E ring can be detected when Saturn's ring system appears edge-on.*

** *In units of Saturn's equatorial radius (60 330 km)*

Diagram by Roy Bishop/Michael Gatto

few more years before we return to positive declination numbers. From opposition, Saturn moves southward down the ecliptic until Oct. 22, when it finishes retrograding and returns to eastward motion. At this point, it will exhibit a maximum ring tilt of 15.3°. Over the remainder of the year, Saturn moves back north to where we saw it at opposition just above γ Cap, where it ends the year.

Saturn has 82 natural satellites, of which 8 are visible in amateur telescopes (see p. 26). Of those, only Titan shows a disk in large telescopes. At opposition this year, Titan presents a 0.8″ disk; the others, less than 0.25″.

The satellite Iapetus (mag. 10.5–12.8) is tidally locked to Saturn, with its leading hemisphere as dark as coal and the other side quite white. (The actual albedos are 0.05 and 0.5, respectively.) Because of this, when Iapetus is near elongation on the west side of Saturn, it is about two magnitudes brighter than it is on the east side. The 79.3-day orbit of Iapetus takes it as far as 9.1′ from Saturn. It is directly north of Saturn on Jul. 24 and Oct. 10, and directly south on Aug. 31 and Nov. 18. Since it is displaying both faces at these times, it will shine at an intermediate magnitude of 11.1.

URANUS

Uranus is the faintest of the planets visible to the naked eye and the third-largest overall, yet its tremendous distance means that its maximum angular diameter is only 4.0″. Uranus's orbital period is 84.4 y, and it moves along the ecliptic only about 4.3°/y. William Herschel discovered Uranus in 1781 with a 160-mm reflector, but it had been recorded by earlier observers, who charted it as a star. At mag. 5.7, it would require a clear and transparent sky for a successful naked-eye sighting. Binoculars easily reveal Uranus, and it blossoms into a pale blue-green disk under high magnification in a telescope. Some observers have reported seeing details on the planet, even with amateur-sized instruments. Fred Price, in *The Planet Observer's Handbook*, states that the only features seen on the planet are the two faint belts, and that you need at least a 250-mm telescope to see these.

Uranus starts off the year well placed for evening viewing. At +14° declination you can use some high power to examine the 3.7″ pale blue disk. Jan. 18 marks when Uranus turns off retrograde motion and starts to head eastward again. On Apr. 18, we get a chance to view a Uranus–Mercury conjunction in the evening sky. Mercury shines at mag. –1.0, and 2° below it sits mag. 5.7 Uranus. This event is in twilight, so it will require at least binoculars to tease out Uranus. On May 5, Uranus is in conjunction with the Sun, and it moves into the morning sky.

Our next conjunction is with the planet Venus on Jun. 11 in the morning sky. Venus rises 1.5 h before the Sun and sits 1.7° below Uranus. Binoculars are a must for this observation. It gets easier with the Mars–Uranus conjunction on Aug. 2, which is visible in a dark sky. Mars passes 1.3° below Uranus and shines at mag. 0.2 versus Uranus's mag. 5.6. Mars shows an 8.4″ disk compared to Uranus's 3.7″ disk. This would be a good opportunity to see if you can catch a sixth planet naked eye. It will make for a nice color comparison in a low-power field: red Mars and blue Uranus. Aug. 24 marks Uranus's switch to retrograde; it now moves westward across the sky. On Nov. 9, Uranus comes to its opposition. It shines at mag. 5.6 and will display a 3.77″ disk. The late fall will give plenty of opportunities to try to find Uranus's four "easy" moons.

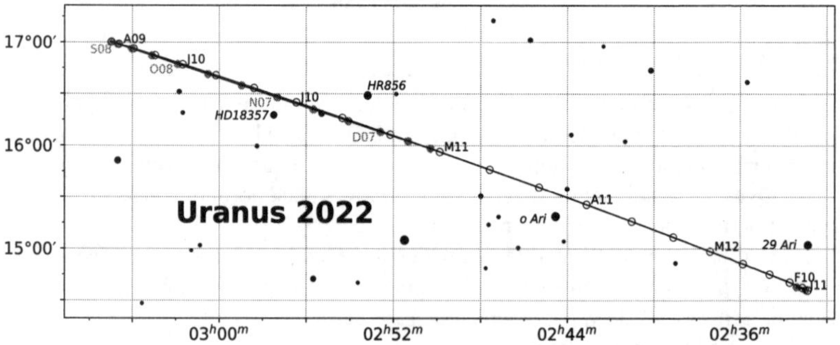

Uranus is shown as a mag.-6 object among stars ranging from mag. 6 to mag. 9 (chart limit). (See 134340 Pluto's finder chart for full attribution of all chart generation, p. 243.)

NEPTUNE

Neptune is the outermost planet in the Solar System, with a maximum angular diameter of only 2.4″. It was found at Berlin Observatory by Johann Galle on 1846 Sep. 23, near a position calculated from irregularities in the motion of Uranus; credit for this prediction has historically been shared by Urbain le Verrier of France and John Couch Adams of England, but le Verrier is the real champion here (see tinyurl.com/j23quw3). Neptune was at aphelion in 1959, at mag. 7.9. Its next perihelion, at mag. 7.7, is in 2041, in Aries.

The year starts off with Neptune low in the southwestern sky after dark. It is 6° below κ Cap, shining at mag. 7.9 and showing a 2.3″ disk. It is still well placed for evening viewing. Neptune goes into conjunction with the Sun on Mar. 13. The next event is a spectacular conjunction with Venus. The pair will pass 14″ apart on the morning of Apr. 27 at 19:09 UT. Closest approach can be seen in the longitudes of Sydney, Australia. In North America, we see the pair around 24′ apart just after Venus rises in the morning sky. A thin crescent Moon may be visible 5° below the pair.

On Jun. 27, Neptune moves into retrograde motion and will move to the west. On Sep. 16, Neptune comes to opposition and will brighten slightly to mag. 7.8. Its diameter will now be 2.34″, and it will be well placed for viewing. On Dec. 3, Neptune resumes prograde motion and its easterly course across the sky.

Neptune's one large moon, Triton, is within easy reach of medium-sized amateur telescopes (250+ mm). Triton is easier to find than any of the satellites of Uranus, primarily because Neptune is two magnitudes fainter than Uranus, so its glare is much reduced. At opposition, Triton is mag. 13.4, and from our perspective, its orbit describes a fat ellipse with a 10″ minor axis pointed along the polar axis and a major axis of 17″. Triton (when viewed from the north side) moves in a clockwise, retrograde direction around its primary, the only major satellite in the Solar System to do so.

Editor's note: To see the planet's disk requires more magnification than binoculars provide, so a telescope is a must.

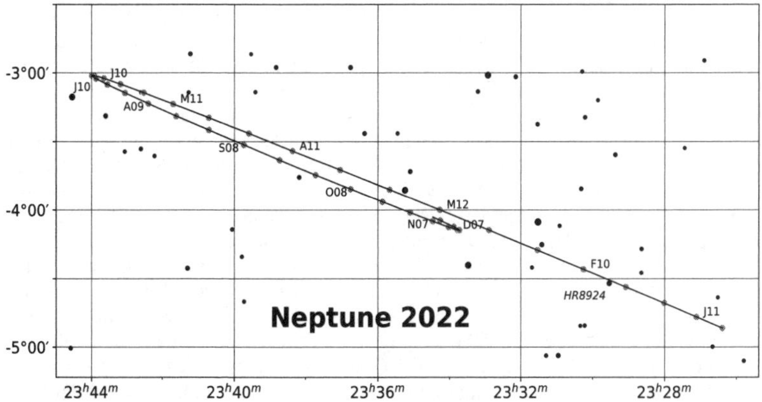

Neptune is shown as a mag. 8 object among stars ranging from mag. 6 to mag. 11 (chart limit). The star HR8924 is a mag. 6 red-giant variable star in Aquarius.

(See 134340 Pluto's finder chart for full attribution of all chart generation, p. 243.)

PHENOMENA OF THE GALILEAN SATELLITES
BY PATRICK KELLY

The table on the following six pages gives the various transits, occultations, and eclipses of the four great satellites of Jupiter up to mid-January and from mid-April to the end of the year. Jupiter is not well-placed for observing between mid-January and mid-April as it is in conjunction with the Sun on 2022 Mar. 5. Double-shadow transits are indicated in **bold**. Double-satellite transits are indicated in *italics*. When a bold and italic event are close that often indicates that two moons and two shadows can simultaneously be seen on Jupiter. Since the satellite phenomena are not instantaneous but take up to several minutes, the predicted times are for the middle of each event. The predictions were generated by the Institut de Mécanique Céleste et de Calcul des Ephémérides in Paris.

Satellites designations are: I = Io II = Europa III = Ganymede IV = Callisto
Events abbreviations are:
Ec = eclipse Oc = occultation Tr = satellite transit Sh = shadow transit
I = ingress E = egress D = disappearance R = reappearance

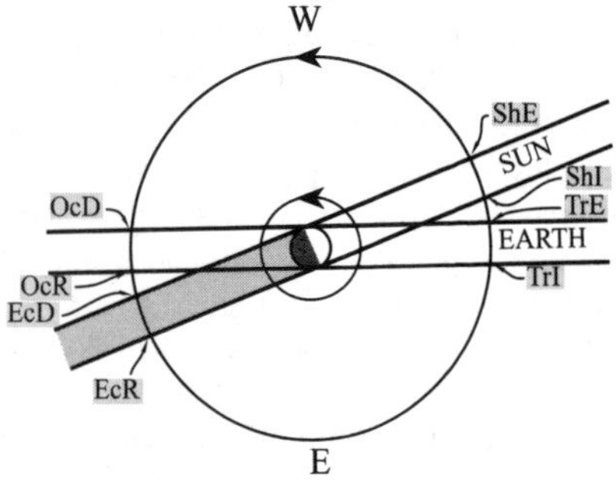

The general motion of the satellites and the successive phenomena are shown in the diagram at right, which is a view of Jupiter and the orbit of one of its satellites, looking down from the north side. Satellites move from east to west across the face of the planet and from west to east behind it (here "east" and "west" are used in the sense of the observer's sky, not in the Jovian sense). Before opposition, shadows fall to the west, and after opposition, to the east (as in the diagram).

The sequence of phenomena for the outer satellite shown in the diagram, counterclockwise beginning at the lower right, is transit ingress (TrI), transit egress (TrE), shadow ingress (ShI), shadow egress (ShE), occultation disappearance (OcD), occultation reappearance (OcR), eclipse disappearance (EcD), and eclipse reappearance (EcR). The actual sequence will depend on the actual Sun–Jupiter–Earth angle and the size of the satellite's orbit.

Over 3/4 of the phenomena listed will **not** be visible from any one location because they occur when Jupiter is near or below the horizon or when daylight interferes. In practice, an observer usually knows when Jupiter will be conveniently placed in the night sky; if not, consult THE SKY MONTH BY MONTH section (p. 99). The table can then be scanned to see if there are any events during the intended observing period. For example, an observer in San Francisco would know that Jupiter is well placed near midnight from July to September as Jupiter is at opposition on Sep. 26. If planning to observe from 22:00 on Aug. 15 to 4:00 PDT on Aug. 16 (7 h behind UT), scanning the table for events in the interval Aug. 16 from 5:00 to 11:00 UT would show five events. When they start observing, they will note that there are two shadows on Jupiter, those of Io and Ganymede. At 22:38 PDT on Aug. 15, Io's shadow leaves Jupiter followed 57 minutes later by Io itself. At 23:58 PDT Ganymede's shadow leaves Jupiter's disk, and a little over an hour later, Ganymede begins a transit of Jupiter, which will end two and a half hours later at 3:40 PDT. The configuration of the four Galilean satellites during that night is given in the diagram on the right-hand side of p. 113 in the THE SKY MONTH BY MONTH section.

A total of 1786 events (342 eclipse, 328 occultation, 562 shadow, and 554 transit) appear in the table, an average of one event every 3 h 42 min.

SATELLITES OF JUPITER, UT OF 2022 GEOCENTRIC PHENOMENA

JANUARY

Day	UT	Sat.	Event
1	4:01	II	TrI
	6:06	II	ShI
	6:52	II	TrE
	8:53	II	ShE
	13:26	I	TrI
	14:26	I	ShI
	15:43	I	TrE
	16:42	I	ShE
2	5:07	III	OcD
	8:44	III	OcR
	9:14	III	EcD
	10:34	I	OcD
	12:44	III	EcR
	13:52	I	EcR
	23:13	II	OcD
3	4:01	II	EcR
	7:56	I	TrI
	8:55	I	ShI
	10:13	I	TrE
	11:11	I	ShE
4	5:04	I	OcD
	8:21	I	EcR
	13:08	IV	OcD
	17:26	II	TrI
	17:38	IV	OcR
	19:25	II	ShI
	20:16	II	TrE
	22:12	II	ShE
	22:33	IV	EcD
5	2:26	I	TrI
	2:29	IV	EcR
	3:24	I	ShI
	4:43	I	TrE
	5:40	I	ShE
	19:25	III	TrI
	23:00	III	TrE
	23:22	III	ShI
	23:34	I	OcD
6	2:50	I	EcR
	2:50	III	ShE
	12:37	II	OcD
	17:19	II	EcR
	20:57	I	TrI
	21:53	I	ShI
	23:13	I	TrE
7	0:09	I	ShE
	18:05	I	OcD
	21:19	I	EcR
8	6:50	II	TrI
	8:44	II	ShI
	9:41	II	TrE
	11:31	II	ShE
	15:27	I	TrI
	16:22	I	ShI
	17:44	I	TrE
	18:38	I	ShE
9	9:32	III	OcD
	12:35	I	OcD
	13:08	III	OcR
	13:16	III	EcD
	15:47	I	EcR
	16:45	III	EcR
10	2:01	II	OcD
	6:37	II	EcR
	9:57	I	TrI
	10:51	I	ShI
	12:14	I	TrE
	13:07	I	ShE
11	7:05	I	OcD
	10:16	I	EcR
	20:15	II	TrI
	22:03	II	ShI
	23:06	II	TrE
12	0:50	II	ShE
	4:27	I	TrI
	5:19	I	ShI
	6:44	I	TrE
	7:35	I	ShE
	22:18	IV	TrI
	23:50	*III*	*TrI*
13	1:36	I	OcD
	2:45	IV	TrE
	3:23	III	ShI
	3:26	III	TrE
	4:45	I	EcR
	6:50	**IV**	**ShI**
	6:51	III	ShE
	10:42	IV	ShE
	15:25	II	OcD
	19:55	II	EcR
	22:58	I	TrI
	23:48	I	ShI
14	1:14	I	TrE
	2:04	I	ShE
	20:06	I	OcD
	23:14	I	EcR
15	9:40	II	TrI
	11:22	II	ShI
	12:31	II	TrE
	14:09	II	ShE
	17:28	I	TrI
	18:17	I	ShI
	19:45	I	TrE
	20:33	I	ShE

APRIL

Day	UT	Sat.	Event
16	0:38	I	ShI
	1:20	I	TrI
	2:50	II	EcD
	2:53	I	ShE
	3:35	I	TrE
	6:55	II	OcR
	7:43	III	ShI
	10:37	III	TrI
	11:00	III	ShE
	13:54	III	TrE
	21:54	I	EcD
17	0:54	I	OcR
	19:06	I	ShI
	19:50	I	TrI
	21:21	I	ShE
	21:39	II	ShI
	22:05	I	TrE
	23:10	II	TrI
18	0:22	II	ShE
	1:52	II	TrE
	16:22	I	EcD
	19:24	I	OcR
19	13:35	I	ShI
	14:20	I	TrI
	15:50	I	ShE
	16:07	II	EcD
	16:35	I	TrE
	20:19	II	OcR
	21:40	III	EcD
20	4:04	III	OcR
	10:51	I	EcD
	13:54	I	OcR
21	8:04	I	ShI
	8:50	I	TrI
	10:18	I	ShE
	10:59	II	ShI
	11:05	I	TrE
	12:36	II	TrI
	13:41	II	ShE
	15:18	II	TrE
22	5:20	I	EcD
	8:25	I	OcR
23	2:32	I	ShI
	3:20	I	TrI
	4:47	I	ShE
	5:25	II	EcD
	5:35	I	TrE
	9:43	II	OcR
	11:43	III	ShI
	15:00	III	ShE
	15:05	III	TrI
	18:19	III	TrE
	20:50	IV	ShI
	23:42	IV	ShE
	23:48	I	EcD
24	2:55	I	OcR
	4:57	IV	TrI
	7:36	IV	TrE
	21:01	I	ShI
	21:50	I	TrI
	23:15	I	ShE
25	0:05	I	TrE
	0:17	II	ShI
	2:01	II	TrI
	3:00	II	ShE
	4:42	II	TrE
	18:17	I	EcD
	21:25	I	OcR
26	15:29	I	ShI
	16:20	I	TrI
	17:44	I	ShE
	18:35	I	TrE
	18:42	II	EcD
	23:06	II	OcR
27	1:42	III	EcD
	4:59	III	EcR
	5:17	III	OcD
	8:30	III	OcR
	12:46	I	EcD
	15:55	I	OcR
28	9:58	I	ShI
	10:51	I	TrI
	12:12	I	ShE
	13:05	I	TrE
	13:36	II	ShI
	15:27	II	TrI
	16:19	II	ShE
	18:07	II	TrE
29	7:14	I	EcD
	10:25	I	OcR
30	4:26	I	ShI
	5:20	I	TrI
	6:41	I	ShE
	7:35	I	TrE
	8:00	II	EcD
	12:29	II	OcR
	15:44	III	ShI
	18:59	III	ShE
	19:32	III	TrI
	22:42	III	TrE

MAY

Day	UT	Sat.	Event
1	1:43	I	EcD
	4:55	I	OcR
	22:55	I	ShI
	23:50	I	TrI
2	1:09	I	ShE
	2:05	I	TrE
	2:55	II	ShI
	4:51	II	TrI
	5:37	II	ShE
	6:31	IV	EcD
	7:31	II	TrE
	9:22	IV	EcR
	15:38	IV	OcD
	18:04	IV	OcR
	20:12	I	EcD
	23:25	I	OcR
3	17:23	I	ShI
	18:20	I	TrI
	19:38	I	ShE
	20:34	I	TrE
	21:17	II	EcD
4	1:52	II	OcR
	5:43	III	EcD
	8:59	III	EcR
	9:42	III	OcD
	12:53	III	OcR
	14:40	I	EcD
	17:55	I	OcR
5	11:52	I	ShI
	12:50	I	TrI
	14:06	I	ShE
	15:04	I	TrE
	16:14	II	ShI
	18:16	II	TrI
	18:56	II	ShE
	20:55	II	TrE
6	9:09	I	EcD
	12:25	I	OcR
7	6:20	I	ShI
	7:20	I	TrI
	8:35	I	ShE
	9:34	I	TrE
	10:35	II	EcD
	15:15	II	OcR
	19:45	III	ShI
	23:00	III	ShE
	23:57	III	TrI
8	3:05	III	TrE
	3:37	I	EcD
	6:55	I	OcR
9	0:49	I	ShI
	1:50	I	TrI
	3:03	I	ShE
	4:04	I	TrE
	5:33	II	ShI
	7:40	II	TrI
	8:14	II	ShE
	10:19	II	TrE
	22:06	I	EcD
10	1:25	I	OcR
	15:10	IV	ShI
	17:49	IV	ShE
	19:17	I	ShI
	20:20	I	TrI
	21:31	I	ShE
	22:34	I	TrE
	23:52	II	EcD
11	1:44	IV	TrI
	3:39	IV	TrE
	4:38	II	OcR
	9:44	III	EcD
	12:59	III	EcR
	14:06	III	OcD
	16:35	I	EcD
	17:14	III	OcR
	19:55	I	OcR
12	13:46	I	ShI
	14:50	I	TrI
	16:00	I	ShE
	17:03	I	TrE
	18:52	II	ShI
	21:05	II	TrI
	21:33	II	ShE
	23:42	II	TrE
13	11:03	I	EcD
	14:25	I	OcR
14	8:14	I	ShI
	9:19	I	TrI
	10:28	I	ShE
	11:33	I	TrE
	13:10	II	EcD
	18:00	II	OcR
	23:46	III	ShI
15	2:59	III	ShE
	4:20	III	TrI
	5:32	I	EcD
	7:25	III	TrE
	8:54	I	OcR

I = Io; II = Europa; III = Ganymede; IV = Callisto

SATELLITES OF JUPITER, UT OF 2022 GEOCENTRIC PHENOMENA (cont.)

MAY (continued)			
16	2:43	I	ShI
	3:49	I	TrI
	4:57	I	ShE
	6:03	I	TrE
	8:10	II	ShI
	10:28	II	TrI
	10:51	II	ShE
	13:05	II	TrE
17	0:00	I	EcD
	3:24	I	OcR
	21:11	I	ShI
	22:19	I	TrI
	23:25	I	ShE
18	0:32	I	TrE
	2:27	II	EcD
	7:22	II	OcR
	13:44	III	EcD
	16:58	III	EcR
	18:28	III	OcD
	18:29	I	EcD
	21:32	III	OcR
	21:54	I	OcR
19	0:48	IV	EcD
	3:27	IV	EcR
	12:07	IV	OcD
	13:47	IV	OcR
	15:40	I	ShI
	16:48	I	TrI
	17:54	I	ShE
	19:02	I	TrE
	21:29	II	ShI
	23:52	II	TrI
20	0:09	II	ShE
	2:28	II	TrE
	12:58	I	EcD
	16:24	I	OcR
21	10:08	I	ShI
	11:18	I	TrI
	12:22	I	ShE
	13:31	I	TrE
	15:45	II	EcD
	20:44	II	OcR
22	3:48	III	ShI
	7:00	III	ShE
	7:26	I	EcD
	8:42	III	TrI
	10:53	I	OcR
	11:43	III	TrE
23	4:37	I	ShI
	5:47	I	TrI
	6:51	I	ShE
	8:01	I	TrE
	10:48	II	ShI
	13:15	II	TrI
	13:27	II	ShE
	15:50	II	TrE
24	1:55	I	EcD
	5:23	I	OcR
	23:05	I	ShI
25	0:17	I	TrI
	1:19	I	ShE
	2:30	I	TrE
25	5:02	II	EcD
	10:05	II	OcR
	17:45	III	EcD
	20:23	I	EcD
	20:58	III	EcR
	22:47	III	OcD
	23:52	I	OcR
26	1:49	III	OcR
	17:34	I	ShI
	18:46	I	TrI
	19:47	I	ShE
	21:00	I	TrE
27	0:07	II	ShI
	2:37	II	TrI
	2:46	II	ShE
	5:13	II	TrE
	9:32	IV	ShI
	11:56	IV	ShE
	14:52	I	EcD
	18:22	I	OcR
	22:23	IV	TrI
	22:54	IV	TrE
28	12:02	I	ShI
	13:16	I	TrI
	14:16	I	ShE
	15:29	I	TrE
	18:20	II	EcD
	23:27	II	OcR
29	7:49	III	ShI
	9:20	I	EcD
	11:00	III	ShE
	12:51	I	OcR
	13:00	III	TrI
	15:58	III	TrE
30	6:31	I	ShI
	7:45	I	TrI
	8:44	I	ShE
	9:58	I	TrE
	13:25	II	ShI
	15:59	II	TrI
	16:04	II	ShE
	18:34	II	TrE
31	3:49	I	EcD
	7:21	I	OcR
JUNE			
1	0:59	I	ShI
	2:15	I	TrI
	3:13	I	ShE
	4:27	I	TrE
	7:37	II	EcD
	12:48	II	OcR
	21:46	III	EcD
	22:18	I	EcD
2	0:58	III	EcR
	1:50	I	OcR
	3:04	III	OcD
	6:03	III	OcR
	19:28	I	ShI
	20:44	I	TrI
	21:41	I	ShE
	22:57	I	TrE
3	2:44	II	ShI
3	5:22	II	ShE
	5:22	II	TrI
	7:56	II	TrE
	16:46	I	EcD
	20:19	I	OcR
4	13:56	I	ShI
	15:13	I	TrI
	16:10	I	ShE
	17:26	I	TrE
	19:06	IV	EcD
	20:55	II	EcD
	21:31	IV	EcR
5	2:08	II	OcR
	11:15	I	EcD
	11:50	III	ShI
	14:48	I	OcR
	14:59	III	ShE
	17:15	III	TrI
	20:10	III	TrE
6	8:24	I	ShI
	9:42	I	TrI
	10:38	I	ShE
	11:55	I	TrE
	16:02	II	ShI
	18:40	II	ShE
	18:43	II	TrI
	21:16	II	TrE
7	5:43	I	EcD
	9:18	I	OcR
8	2:53	I	ShI
	4:12	I	TrI
	5:07	I	ShE
	6:24	I	TrE
	10:13	II	EcD
	12:52	II	EcR
	12:54	II	OcD
	15:28	II	OcR
9	0:12	I	EcD
	1:47	III	EcD
	3:47	I	OcR
	4:58	III	EcR
	7:17	III	OcD
	10:13	III	OcR
	21:21	I	ShI
	22:41	I	TrI
	23:35	I	ShE
10	0:53	I	TrE
	5:20	II	ShI
	7:59	II	ShE
	8:04	II	TrI
	10:37	II	TrE
	18:40	I	EcD
	22:16	I	OcR
11	15:50	I	ShI
	17:10	I	TrI
	18:03	I	ShE
	19:22	I	TrE
	23:30	II	EcD
12	2:09	II	EcR
	2:14	II	OcD
	4:48	II	OcR
	13:09	I	EcD
12	15:50	III	ShI
	16:45	I	OcR
	18:59	III	ShE
	21:26	III	TrI
13	0:18	III	TrE
	3:54	IV	ShI
	6:01	IV	ShE
	10:18	I	ShI
	11:39	I	TrI
	12:32	I	ShE
	13:51	I	TrE
	18:39	II	ShI
	21:16	II	ShE
	21:24	II	TrI
	23:56	II	TrE
14	7:37	I	EcD
	11:14	I	OcR
15	4:47	I	ShI
	6:08	I	TrI
	7:00	I	ShE
	8:20	I	TrE
	12:48	II	EcD
	15:27	II	EcR
	15:35	II	OcD
	18:08	II	OcR
16	2:06	I	EcD
	5:43	I	OcR
	5:48	III	EcD
	8:58	III	EcR
	11:28	III	OcD
	14:21	III	OcR
	23:15	I	ShI
17	0:37	I	TrI
	1:29	I	ShE
	2:49	I	TrE
	7:57	II	ShI
	10:35	II	ShE
	10:45	II	TrI
	13:16	II	TrE
	20:34	I	EcD
18	0:11	I	OcR
	17:44	I	ShI
	19:05	I	TrI
	19:57	I	ShE
	21:18	I	TrE
19	2:06	II	EcD
	4:44	II	EcR
	4:54	II	OcD
	7:27	II	OcR
	15:03	I	EcD
	18:40	I	OcR
	19:51	III	ShI
	22:58	III	ShE
20	1:35	III	TrI
	4:24	III	TrE
	12:12	I	ShI
	13:34	I	TrI
	14:26	I	ShE
	15:46	I	TrE
	21:15	II	ShI
	23:52	II	ShE
21	0:04	II	TrI
	2:35	II	TrE
	9:31	I	EcD
21	13:09	I	OcR
	13:24	IV	EcD
	15:33	IV	EcR
22	6:41	I	ShI
	8:03	I	TrI
	8:54	I	ShE
	10:15	I	TrE
	15:23	II	EcD
	18:02	II	EcR
	18:13	II	OcD
	20:46	II	OcR
23	4:00	I	EcD
	7:38	I	OcR
	9:49	III	EcD
	12:58	III	EcR
	15:35	III	OcD
	18:25	III	OcR
24	1:09	I	ShI
	2:32	I	TrI
	3:23	I	ShE
	4:44	I	TrE
	10:34	II	ShI
	13:11	II	ShE
	13:23	II	TrI
	15:54	II	TrE
	22:28	I	EcD
25	2:06	I	OcR
	19:38	I	ShI
	21:00	I	TrI
	21:51	I	ShE
	23:12	I	TrE
26	4:41	II	EcD
	7:20	II	EcR
	7:32	II	OcD
	10:04	II	OcR
	16:57	I	EcD
	20:35	I	OcR
	23:52	III	ShI
27	2:58	III	ShE
	5:40	III	TrI
	8:26	III	TrE
	14:06	I	ShI
	15:29	I	TrI
	16:20	I	ShE
	17:41	I	TrE
	23:51	II	ShI
28	2:28	II	ShE
	2:41	II	TrI
	5:11	II	TrE
	11:25	I	EcD
	15:03	I	OcR
29	8:35	I	ShI
	9:57	I	TrI
	10:48	I	ShE
	12:09	I	TrE
	17:59	II	EcD
	20:38	II	EcR
	20:50	II	OcD
	22:17	IV	ShI
	23:22	II	OcR
30	0:05	IV	ShE
	5:54	I	EcD

I = Io; II = Europa; III = Ganymede; IV = Callisto

SATELLITES OF JUPITER, UT OF 2022 GEOCENTRIC PHENOMENA (cont.)

JUNE (continued)			
30	9:32	I	OcR
	13:50	III	EcD
	16:57	III	EcR
	19:38	III	OcD
	22:24	III	OcR
JULY			
1	3:03	I	ShI
	4:26	I	TrI
	5:16	I	ShE
	6:38	I	TrE
	13:10	II	ShI
	15:46	II	ShE
	16:00	II	TrI
	18:29	II	TrE
2	0:22	I	EcD
	4:00	I	OcR
	21:32	I	ShI
	22:54	I	TrI
	23:45	I	ShE
3	1:06	I	TrE
	7:17	II	EcD
	9:55	II	EcR
	10:08	II	OcD
	12:39	II	OcR
	18:51	I	EcD
	22:28	I	OcR
4	3:53	III	ShI
	6:58	III	ShE
	9:41	III	TrI
	12:24	III	TrE
	16:00	I	ShI
	17:23	I	TrI
	18:13	I	ShE
	19:35	I	TrE
5	2:28	II	ShI
	5:04	II	ShE
	5:17	II	TrI
	7:46	II	TrE
	13:19	I	EcD
	16:57	I	OcR
6	10:28	I	ShI
	11:51	I	TrI
	12:42	I	ShE
	14:03	I	TrE
	20:35	II	EcD
	23:13	II	EcR
	23:26	II	OcD
7	1:56	II	OcR
	7:48	I	EcD
	11:25	I	OcR
	17:50	III	EcD
	20:57	III	EcR
	23:36	III	OcD
8	2:19	III	OcR
	4:57	I	ShI
	6:19	I	TrI
	7:10	I	ShE
	7:44	IV	EcD
	8:31	I	TrE
	9:35	IV	EcR
8	15:46	II	ShI
	18:22	II	ShE
	18:34	II	TrI
	21:02	II	TrE
9	2:16	I	EcD
	5:53	I	OcR
	23:25	I	ShI
10	0:47	I	TrI
	1:39	I	ShE
	2:59	I	TrE
	9:53	II	EcD
	12:31	II	EcR
	12:42	II	OcD
	15:13	II	OcR
	20:45	I	EcD
11	0:21	I	OcR
	7:55	III	ShI
	10:59	III	ShE
	13:38	III	TrI
	16:18	III	TrE
	17:54	I	ShI
	19:15	I	TrI
	20:07	I	ShE
	21:27	I	TrE
12	5:04	II	ShI
	7:39	II	ShE
	7:50	II	TrI
	10:18	II	TrE
	15:13	I	EcD
	18:49	I	OcR
13	12:22	I	ShI
	13:43	I	TrI
	14:36	I	ShE
	15:55	I	TrE
	23:11	II	EcD
14	1:49	II	EcR
	1:59	II	OcD
	4:29	II	OcR
	9:42	I	EcD
	13:17	I	OcR
	21:50	III	EcD
15	0:56	III	EcR
	3:30	III	OcD
	6:10	III	OcR
	6:51	I	ShI
	8:11	I	TrI
	9:04	I	ShE
	10:23	I	TrE
	18:22	II	ShI
	20:57	II	ShE
	21:06	II	TrI
	23:33	II	TrE
16	4:10	I	EcD
	7:45	I	OcR
	16:42	IV	ShI
	18:06	IV	ShE
17	1:19	I	ShI
	2:39	I	TrI
	3:33	I	ShE
	4:51	I	TrE
	12:29	II	EcD
	15:07	II	EcR
17	15:14	II	OcD
	17:44	II	OcR
	22:39	I	EcD
18	2:12	I	OcR
	11:56	III	ShI
	14:58	III	ShE
	17:30	III	TrI
	19:48	I	ShI
	20:08	III	TrE
	21:07	I	TrI
	22:01	I	ShE
	23:19	I	TrE
19	7:39	II	ShI
	10:15	II	ShE
	10:21	II	TrI
	12:48	II	TrE
	17:07	I	EcD
	20:40	I	OcR
20	14:16	I	ShI
	15:35	I	TrI
	16:30	I	ShE
	17:46	I	TrE
21	1:47	II	EcD
	4:25	II	EcR
	4:30	II	OcD
	6:59	II	OcR
	11:36	I	EcD
	15:08	I	OcR
22	1:51	III	EcD
	4:56	III	EcR
	7:20	III	OcD
	8:45	I	ShI
	9:58	III	OcR
	10:03	I	TrI
	10:58	I	ShE
	12:14	I	TrE
	20:57	II	ShI
	23:33	II	ShE
	23:35	II	TrI
23	2:02	II	TrE
	6:04	I	EcD
	9:35	I	OcR
24	3:13	I	ShI
	4:30	I	TrI
	5:27	I	ShE
	6:42	I	TrE
	15:05	II	EcD
	17:42	II	EcR
	17:44	II	OcD
	20:13	II	OcR
25	0:33	I	EcD
	2:06	IV	EcD
	3:35	IV	EcR
	4:03	I	OcR
	15:56	III	ShI
	18:58	III	ShE
	21:17	III	TrI
	21:42	I	ShI
	22:58	*I*	*TrI*
	23:52	III	TrE
	23:55	I	ShE
26	1:09	I	TrE
26	10:15	II	ShI
	12:49	II	TrI
	12:50	II	ShE
	15:16	II	TrE
	19:01	I	EcD
	22:30	I	OcR
27	16:10	I	ShI
	17:25	I	TrI
	18:24	I	ShE
	19:37	I	TrE
28	4:23	II	EcD
	9:27	II	OcR
	13:30	I	EcD
	16:57	I	OcR
29	5:52	III	EcD
	8:56	III	EcR
	10:39	I	ShI
	11:04	III	OcD
	11:53	I	TrI
	12:52	I	ShE
	13:40	III	OcR
	14:04	I	TrE
	23:33	II	ShI
30	2:02	II	TrI
	2:08	II	ShE
	4:29	II	TrE
	7:58	I	EcD
	11:25	I	OcR
31	5:07	I	ShI
	6:20	I	TrI
	7:21	I	ShE
	8:32	I	TrE
	17:41	II	EcD
	22:40	II	OcR
AUGUST			
1	2:27	I	EcD
	5:52	I	OcR
	19:57	III	ShI
	22:58	III	ShE
	23:36	I	ShI
2	0:47	I	TrI
	0:59	*III*	*TrI*
	1:49	I	ShE
	2:59	I	TrE
	3:32	III	TrE
	11:13	IV	ShI
	12:03	IV	ShE
	12:50	II	ShI
	15:15	II	TrI
	15:25	II	ShE
	17:41	II	TrE
	20:55	I	EcD
3	0:19	I	OcR
	18:04	I	ShI
	19:14	I	TrI
	20:18	I	ShE
	21:26	I	TrE
4	7:00	II	EcD
	11:53	II	OcR
	15:24	I	EcD
5	18:46	I	OcR
	9:54	III	EcD
	12:33	I	ShI
	12:56	III	EcR
	13:42	I	TrI
	14:45	III	OcD
	14:46	I	ShE
	15:53	I	TrE
	17:19	III	OcR
6	2:08	II	ShI
	4:27	II	TrI
	4:43	II	ShE
	6:53	II	TrE
	9:52	I	EcD
	13:13	I	OcR
7	7:01	I	ShI
	8:09	I	TrI
	9:15	I	ShE
	10:20	I	TrE
	20:18	II	EcD
8	1:05	II	OcR
	4:21	I	EcD
	7:40	I	OcR
	23:57	III	ShI
9	**1:30**	**I**	**ShI**
	2:36	I	TrI
	2:57	III	ShE
	3:44	I	ShE
	4:36	*III*	*TrI*
	4:47	I	TrE
	7:08	III	TrE
	15:26	II	ShI
	17:38	II	TrI
	18:00	II	ShE
	20:04	II	TrE
	22:49	I	EcD
10	2:07	I	OcR
	19:58	I	ShI
	20:32	IV	EcD
	21:03	I	TrI
	21:31	IV	EcR
	22:12	I	ShE
	23:14	I	TrE
11	9:37	II	EcD
	14:17	II	OcR
	17:18	I	EcD
	20:34	I	OcR
12	13:55	III	EcD
	14:27	I	ShI
	15:30	I	TrI
	16:41	I	ShE
	16:56	III	EcR
	17:41	I	TrE
	18:19	III	OcD
	20:52	III	OcR
13	4:43	II	ShI
	6:49	II	TrI
	7:18	II	ShE
	9:15	II	TrE
	11:46	I	EcD
	15:00	I	OcR
14	8:55	I	ShI

I = Io; II = Europa; III = Ganymede; IV = Callisto

SATELLITES OF JUPITER, UT OF 2022 GEOCENTRIC PHENOMENA (cont.)

Day	UT	Sat.	Phen.
AUGUST (cont)			
14	9:56	I	TrI
	11:09	I	ShE
	12:08	I	TrE
	22:55	II	EcD
15	3:28	II	OcR
	6:15	I	EcD
	9:27	I	OcR
16	3:24	I	ShI
	3:59	**III**	**ShI**
	4:23	I	TrI
	5:38	I	ShE
	6:35	I	TrE
	6:58	III	ShE
	8:10	III	TrI
	10:40	III	TrE
	18:01	II	ShI
	20:00	II	TrI
	20:35	II	ShE
	22:25	II	TrE
17	0:43	I	EcD
	3:54	I	OcR
	21:52	I	ShI
	22:50	I	TrI
18	0:06	I	ShE
	1:01	I	TrE
	12:14	II	EcD
	16:39	II	OcR
	19:12	I	EcD
	22:20	I	OcR
19	16:21	I	ShI
	17:16	I	TrI
	17:56	III	EcD
	18:35	I	ShE
	19:28	I	TrE
	20:56	III	EcR
	21:49	III	OcD
20	0:21	III	OcR
	7:19	II	ShI
	9:09	II	TrI
	9:53	II	ShE
	11:34	II	TrE
	13:40	I	EcD
	16:47	I	OcR
21	10:50	I	ShI
	11:43	I	TrI
	13:04	I	ShE
	13:55	I	TrE
22	1:32	II	EcD
	5:49	II	OcR
	8:09	I	EcD
	11:13	I	OcR
23	5:18	I	ShI
	6:09	I	TrI
	7:32	I	ShE
	8:00	III	ShI
	8:21	I	TrE
	10:58	III	ShE
	11:38	III	TrI
	14:07	III	TrE
	20:36	II	ShI
	22:18	II	TrI
24	23:10	II	ShE
	0:43	II	TrE
	2:37	I	EcD
	5:39	I	OcR
	23:47	I	ShI
25	0:36	I	TrI
	2:01	I	ShE
	2:48	I	TrE
	14:51	II	EcD
	18:59	II	OcR
	21:06	I	EcD
26	0:06	I	OcR
	18:15	I	ShI
	19:02	I	TrI
	20:29	I	ShE
	21:14	I	TrE
	21:57	III	EcD
27	0:55	III	EcR
	1:14	III	OcD
	3:45	III	OcR
	9:54	II	ShI
	11:27	II	TrI
	12:27	II	ShE
	13:52	II	TrE
	15:35	I	EcD
	18:32	I	OcR
28	12:44	I	ShI
	13:29	I	TrI
	14:58	I	ShE
	15:41	I	TrE
29	4:09	II	EcD
	8:08	II	OcR
	10:03	I	EcD
	12:58	I	OcR
30	7:13	I	ShI
	7:55	I	TrI
	9:27	I	ShE
	10:07	I	TrE
	12:02	III	ShI
	14:59	III	ShE
	15:02	III	TrI
	17:31	III	TrE
	23:11	II	ShI
31	0:35	II	TrI
	1:45	II	ShE
	3:00	II	TrE
	4:32	I	EcD
	7:24	I	OcR
SEPTEMBER			
1	1:41	I	ShI
	2:21	I	TrI
	3:55	I	ShE
	4:33	I	TrE
	17:28	II	EcD
	21:17	II	OcR
	23:00	I	EcD
2	1:50	I	OcR
	20:10	I	ShI
	20:47	I	TrI
	22:24	I	ShE
3	22:59	I	TrE
	1:57	III	EcD
	7:07	III	OcR
	12:29	II	ShI
	13:43	II	TrI
	15:02	II	ShE
	16:08	II	TrE
	17:29	I	EcD
	20:16	I	OcR
4	14:38	I	ShI
	15:13	I	TrI
	16:53	I	ShE
	17:26	I	TrE
5	6:47	II	EcD
	10:25	II	OcR
	11:57	I	EcD
	14:42	I	OcR
6	9:07	I	ShI
	9:40	I	TrI
	11:21	I	ShE
	11:52	I	TrE
	16:04	III	ShI
	18:22	III	TrI
	19:00	III	ShE
	20:52	III	TrE
7	1:46	II	ShI
	2:50	II	TrI
	4:20	II	ShE
	5:16	II	TrE
	6:26	I	EcD
	9:09	I	OcR
8	3:36	I	ShI
	4:06	I	TrI
	5:50	I	ShE
	6:18	I	TrE
	20:06	II	EcD
	23:34	II	OcR
9	0:54	I	EcD
	3:34	I	OcR
	22:05	I	ShI
	22:32	I	TrI
10	0:19	I	ShE
	0:44	I	TrE
	5:59	III	EcD
	10:26	III	OcR
	15:04	II	ShI
	15:57	II	TrI
	17:37	II	ShE
	18:23	II	TrE
	19:23	I	EcD
	22:00	I	OcR
11	16:33	I	ShI
	16:58	I	TrI
	18:47	I	ShE
	19:10	I	TrE
12	9:24	II	EcD
	12:41	II	OcR
	13:52	I	EcD
	16:26	I	OcR
13	11:02	I	ShI
	11:24	I	TrI
13	13:16	I	ShE
	13:36	I	TrE
	20:05	III	ShI
	21:39	III	TrI
	23:00	III	ShE
14	0:10	III	TrE
	4:22	II	ShI
	5:04	II	TrI
	6:55	II	ShE
	7:30	II	TrE
	8:20	I	EcD
	10:52	I	OcR
15	5:31	I	ShI
	5:50	I	TrI
	7:45	I	ShE
	8:02	I	TrE
	22:44	II	EcD
16	1:50	II	OcR
	2:49	I	EcD
	5:18	I	OcR
	23:59	I	ShI
17	0:16	I	TrI
	2:14	I	ShE
	2:28	I	TrE
	10:01	III	EcD
	13:44	III	OcR
	17:39	II	ShI
	18:11	II	TrI
	20:12	II	ShE
	20:36	II	TrE
	21:17	I	EcD
	23:44	I	OcR
18	18:28	I	ShI
	18:42	I	TrI
	20:42	I	ShE
	20:54	I	TrE
19	12:02	II	EcD
	14:57	II	OcR
	15:46	I	EcD
	18:10	I	OcR
20	12:57	I	ShI
	13:08	I	TrI
	15:11	I	ShE
	15:20	I	TrE
21	0:06	III	ShI
	0:54	III	TrI
	3:00	III	ShE
	3:26	III	TrE
	6:57	II	ShI
	7:17	II	TrI
	9:30	II	ShE
	9:43	II	TrE
	10:15	I	EcD
	12:36	I	OcR
22	7:26	I	ShI
	7:33	I	TrI
	9:40	I	ShE
	9:46	I	TrE
23	1:22	II	EcD
	4:05	II	OcR
	4:43	I	EcD
24	7:01	I	OcR
	1:54	I	ShI
	1:59	I	TrI
	4:09	I	ShE
	4:12	I	TrE
	14:03	III	EcD
	17:01	III	OcR
	20:15	II	ShI
	20:23	II	TrI
	22:47	II	ShE
	22:50	II	TrE
	23:12	I	EcD
25	1:27	I	OcR
	20:23	I	ShI
	20:25	I	TrI
	22:37	I	ShE
	22:38	I	TrE
26	14:41	II	EcD
	17:15	II	EcR
	17:41	I	EcD
	19:54	I	EcR
27	14:51	I	TrI
	14:52	I	ShI
	17:04	I	TrE
	17:06	I	ShE
28	4:08	III	ShI
	4:08	III	TrI
	6:42	III	TrE
	7:01	III	ShE
	9:30	II	TrI
	9:32	II	ShI
	11:56	II	TrE
	12:04	II	ShE
	12:07	I	OcD
	14:23	I	EcR
29	9:17	I	TrI
	9:21	I	ShI
	11:30	I	TrE
	11:35	I	ShE
30	3:52	II	OcD
	6:33	I	OcD
	6:34	II	EcR
	8:51	I	EcR
OCTOBER			
1	3:43	I	TrI
	3:50	I	ShI
	5:56	I	TrE
	6:04	I	ShE
	17:40	III	OcD
	20:57	III	EcR
	22:36	II	TrI
	22:50	II	ShI
2	0:59	I	OcD
	1:03	II	TrE
	1:22	II	ShE
	3:20	I	EcR
	22:09	I	TrI
	22:18	I	ShI
3	0:22	I	TrE
	0:32	I	ShE
	16:59	II	OcD

I = Io; II = Europa; III = Ganymede; IV = Callisto

SATELLITES OF JUPITER, UT OF 2022 GEOCENTRIC PHENOMENA (cont.)

Day	UT	Sat.	Phen.
OCTOBER (cont.)			
3	19:25	I	OcD
	19:53	II	EcR
	21:48	I	EcR
4	16:35	I	TrI
	16:47	I	ShI
	18:48	I	TrE
	19:01	I	ShE
5	7:23	III	TrI
	8:11	III	ShI
	9:59	III	TrE
	11:02	III	ShE
	11:43	II	TrI
	12:08	II	ShI
	13:50	I	OcD
	14:10	II	TrE
	14:39	II	ShE
	16:17	I	EcR
6	11:01	I	TrI
	11:16	I	ShI
	13:14	I	TrE
	13:30	I	ShE
7	6:07	II	OcD
	8:16	I	OcD
	9:12	II	EcR
	10:46	I	EcR
8	5:27	I	TrI
	5:45	I	ShI
	7:40	I	TrE
	7:59	I	ShE
	20:55	III	OcD
9	0:49	II	TrI
	0:58	III	EcR
	1:25	II	ShI
	2:42	I	OcD
	3:17	II	TrE
	3:57	II	ShE
	5:14	I	EcR
	23:53	I	TrI
10	0:14	I	ShI
	2:06	I	TrE
	2:28	I	ShE
	19:14	II	OcD
	21:08	I	OcD
	22:31	II	EcR
	23:43	I	EcR
11	18:19	I	TrI
	18:43	I	ShI
	20:32	I	TrE
	20:57	I	ShE
12	10:39	III	TrI
	12:14	III	ShI
	13:18	III	TrE
	13:56	II	TrI
	14:43	**II**	**ShI**
	15:04	III	ShE
	15:34	I	OcD
	16:24	II	TrE
	17:14	II	ShE
	18:12	I	EcR
13	12:45	I	TrI
	13:11	I	ShI
	14:58	I	TrE
	15:25	I	ShE
14	8:22	II	OcD
	10:00	I	OcD
	11:51	II	EcR
	12:40	I	EcR
15	7:12	I	TrI
	7:40	I	ShI
	9:25	I	TrE
	9:54	I	ShE
16	0:11	III	OcD
	3:03	II	TrI
	4:01	II	ShI
	4:26	I	OcD
	4:58	III	EcR
	5:31	II	TrE
	6:32	II	ShE
	7:09	I	EcR
17	1:38	I	TrI
	2:09	I	ShI
	3:51	I	TrE
	4:23	I	ShE
	21:30	II	OcD
	22:53	I	OcD
18	1:09	II	EcR
	1:38	I	EcR
	20:04	I	TrI
	20:38	I	ShI
	22:17	I	TrE
	22:52	I	ShE
19	13:58	III	TrI
	16:11	*II*	*TrI*
	16:17	III	ShI
	16:40	III	TrE
	17:19	I	OcD
	17:19	**II**	**ShI**
	18:39	II	TrE
	19:06	III	ShE
	19:50	II	ShE
	20:07	I	EcR
20	14:31	I	TrI
	15:07	I	ShI
	16:44	I	TrE
	17:21	I	ShE
21	10:40	II	OcD
	11:45	I	OcD
	14:29	II	EcR
	14:35	I	EcR
22	8:57	I	TrI
	9:36	I	ShI
	11:10	I	TrE
	11:50	I	ShE
23	3:31	III	OcD
	5:19	II	TrI
	6:11	I	OcD
	6:37	II	ShI
	7:47	II	TrE
	8:59	III	EcR
	9:04	I	EcR
24	9:07	II	ShE
	3:24	I	TrI
	4:05	I	ShI
	5:37	I	TrE
	6:18	I	ShE
	23:49	II	OcD
25	0:38	I	OcD
	3:33	I	EcR
	3:48	II	EcR
	21:50	I	TrI
	22:34	I	ShI
26	0:03	I	TrE
	0:47	I	ShE
	17:19	III	TrI
	18:27	*II*	*TrI*
	19:04	I	OcD
	19:55	II	ShI
	20:04	III	TrE
	20:20	**III**	**ShI**
	20:56	II	TrE
	22:01	I	EcR
	22:25	II	ShE
	23:07	III	ShE
27	16:17	I	TrI
	17:03	I	ShI
	18:30	I	TrE
	19:16	I	ShE
28	12:59	II	OcD
	13:31	I	OcD
	16:30	I	EcR
	17:07	II	EcR
29	10:44	I	TrI
	11:32	I	ShI
	12:57	I	TrE
	13:45	I	ShE
30	6:54	III	OcD
	7:36	II	TrI
	7:57	I	OcD
	9:12	II	ShI
	9:41	III	OcR
	10:05	II	TrE
	10:12	III	EcD
	10:59	I	EcR
	11:42	II	ShE
	13:00	III	EcR
31	5:10	I	TrI
	6:01	I	ShI
	7:24	I	TrE
	8:14	I	ShE
NOVEMBER			
1	2:09	II	OcD
	2:24	I	OcD
	5:28	I	EcR
	6:26	II	EcR
	23:37	I	TrI
2	0:30	I	ShI
	1:50	I	TrE
	2:43	I	ShE
	20:45	III	TrI
	20:45	*II*	*TrI*
	20:51	I	OcD
	22:30	II	ShI
	23:15	II	TrE
	23:31	III	TrE
	23:56	I	EcR
3	**0:22**	**III**	**ShI**
	1:00	II	ShE
	3:08	III	ShE
	18:04	I	TrI
	18:58	I	ShI
	20:17	I	TrE
	21:12	I	ShE
4	15:17	I	OcD
	15:20	II	OcD
	18:25	I	EcR
	19:46	II	EcR
5	12:31	I	TrI
	13:28	I	ShI
	14:44	I	TrE
	15:41	I	ShE
6	9:44	I	OcD
	9:55	II	TrI
	10:22	III	OcD
	11:48	II	ShI
	12:25	II	TrE
	12:54	I	EcR
	13:11	III	OcR
	14:15	III	EcD
	14:18	II	ShE
	17:01	III	EcR
7	6:58	I	TrI
	7:56	I	ShI
	9:11	I	TrE
	10:09	I	ShE
8	4:11	I	OcD
	4:31	II	OcD
	7:23	I	EcR
	9:05	II	EcR
9	1:25	I	TrI
	2:25	I	ShI
	3:39	I	TrE
	4:38	I	ShE
	22:38	I	OcD
	23:06	II	TrI
10	*0:15*	*III*	*TrI*
	1:06	II	ShI
	1:36	II	TrE
	1:52	I	EcR
	3:04	III	TrE
	3:35	II	ShE
	4:25	III	ShI
	7:09	III	ShE
	19:53	I	TrI
	20:54	I	ShI
	22:06	I	TrE
	23:07	I	ShE
11	17:05	I	OcD
	17:43	II	OcD
	20:20	I	EcR
	22:25	II	EcR
12	14:20	I	TrI
	15:23	I	ShI
	16:33	I	TrE
13	17:36	I	ShE
	11:32	I	OcD
	12:17	II	TrI
	13:55	III	OcD
	14:24	II	ShI
	14:48	II	TrE
	14:49	I	EcR
	16:47	III	OcR
	16:53	II	ShE
	18:18	III	EcD
	21:03	III	EcR
14	8:47	I	TrI
	9:52	I	ShI
	11:00	I	TrE
	12:05	I	ShE
15	6:00	I	OcD
	6:56	II	OcD
	9:18	I	EcR
	11:43	II	EcR
16	3:15	I	TrI
	4:21	I	ShI
	5:28	I	TrE
	6:34	I	ShE
17	0:27	I	OcD
	1:29	II	TrI
	3:42	II	ShI
	3:47	I	EcR
	3:50	*III*	*TrI*
	4:00	II	TrE
	6:11	II	ShE
	6:41	III	TrE
	8:28	III	ShI
	11:10	III	ShE
	21:42	I	TrI
	22:50	I	ShI
	23:55	I	TrE
18	1:03	I	ShE
	18:54	I	OcD
	20:10	II	OcD
	22:16	I	EcR
19	1:03	II	EcR
	16:10	I	TrI
	17:19	I	ShI
	18:23	I	TrE
	19:32	I	ShE
20	13:22	I	OcD
	14:42	II	TrI
	16:44	I	EcR
	17:00	II	ShI
	17:12	II	TrE
	17:33	III	OcD
	19:29	II	ShE
	20:26	III	OcR
	22:21	III	EcD
21	1:04	III	EcR
	10:38	I	TrI
	11:48	I	ShI
	12:51	I	TrE
	14:01	I	ShE
22	7:49	I	OcD
	9:23	II	OcD
	11:13	I	EcR

I = Io; II = Europa; III = Ganymede; IV = Callisto

SATELLITES OF JUPITER, UT OF 2022 GEOCENTRIC PHENOMENA (cont.)

NOVEMBER (cont.)			
22	14:22	II	EcR
23	5:06	I	TrI
	6:17	I	ShI
	7:19	I	TrE
	8:30	I	ShE
24	2:17	I	OcD
	3:55	II	TrI
	5:42	I	EcR
	6:18	II	ShI
	6:26	II	TrE
	7:31	III	TrI
	8:46	II	ShE
	10:23	III	TrE
	12:31	III	ShI
	15:12	III	ShE
	23:33	I	TrI
25	0:46	I	ShI
	1:46	I	TrE
	2:59	I	ShE
	20:45	I	OcD
	22:38	II	OcD
26	0:11	I	EcR
	3:42	II	EcR
	18:01	I	TrI
	19:15	I	ShI
	20:14	I	TrE
	21:28	I	ShE
27	15:13	I	OcD
	17:08	II	TrI
	18:40	I	EcR
	19:36	II	ShI
	19:40	II	TrE
	21:15	III	OcD
	22:04	II	ShE
28	0:10	III	OcR
	2:23	III	EcD
	5:05	III	EcR
	12:29	I	TrI
	13:44	I	ShI
	14:42	I	TrE
	15:57	I	ShE
29	9:40	I	OcD
	11:53	II	OcD
	13:09	I	EcR
	14:28	II	OcR
	14:30	II	EcD
	17:01	II	EcR
30	6:57	I	TrI
	8:13	I	ShI
	9:11	I	TrE
	10:26	I	ShE
DECEMBER			
1	4:08	I	OcD
	6:23	II	TrI
	7:37	I	EcR
	8:54	II	TrE
	8:55	II	ShI
	11:17	III	TrI
	11:22	II	ShE
	14:11	III	TrE
	16:34	III	ShI
	19:14	III	ShE
2	1:26	I	TrI
	2:42	I	ShI
	3:39	I	TrE
	4:55	I	ShE
	22:36	I	OcD
3	1:09	II	OcD
	2:06	I	EcR
	3:45	II	OcR
	3:50	II	EcD
	6:20	II	EcR
	19:54	I	TrI
	21:11	I	ShI
	22:07	I	TrE
	23:24	I	ShE
4	17:05	I	OcD
	19:38	II	TrI
	20:35	I	EcR
	22:09	II	TrE
	22:13	II	ShI
5	0:40	II	ShE
	1:03	III	OcD
	3:59	III	OcR
	6:25	III	EcD
	9:06	III	EcR
	14:22	I	TrI
	15:40	I	ShI
	16:35	I	TrE
	17:52	I	ShE
6	11:33	I	OcD
	14:26	II	OcD
	15:04	I	EcR
	17:01	II	OcR
	17:09	II	EcD
	19:39	II	EcR
7	8:51	I	TrI
	10:10	I	ShI
	11:04	I	TrE
	12:22	I	ShE
8	6:01	I	OcD
	8:53	II	TrI
	9:33	I	EcR
	11:25	II	TrE
	11:31	II	ShI
	13:58	II	ShE
	15:09	III	TrI
	18:04	III	TrE
	20:38	III	ShI
	23:16	III	ShE
9	3:19	I	TrI
	4:38	I	ShI
	5:32	I	TrE
	6:50	I	ShE
10	0:29	I	OcD
	3:43	II	OcD
	4:02	I	EcR
	6:19	II	OcR
	6:28	II	EcD
	8:59	II	EcR
	21:48	I	TrI
	23:08	I	ShI
11	0:01	I	TrE
	1:19	I	ShE
	18:58	I	OcD
	22:10	II	TrI
	22:31	I	EcR
12	0:41	II	TrE
	0:49	II	ShI
	3:16	II	ShE
	4:56	III	OcD
	7:53	III	OcR
	10:28	III	EcD
	13:07	III	EcR
	16:16	I	TrI
	17:37	I	ShI
	18:29	I	TrE
	19:48	I	ShE
13	13:26	I	OcD
	16:59	I	EcR
	17:01	II	OcD
	19:36	II	OcR
	19:48	II	EcD
	22:18	II	EcR
14	10:45	I	TrI
	12:06	I	ShI
	12:58	I	TrE
	14:17	I	ShE
15	7:55	I	OcD
	11:26	II	TrI
	11:28	I	EcR
	13:58	II	TrE
	14:07	II	ShI
	16:34	II	ShE
	19:05	III	TrI
	22:00	III	TrE
16	0:41	III	ShI
	3:18	III	ShE
	5:14	I	TrI
	6:35	I	ShI
	7:27	I	TrE
	8:46	I	ShE
17	2:24	I	OcD
	5:57	I	EcR
	6:19	II	OcD
	8:55	II	OcR
	9:07	II	EcD
	11:37	II	EcR
	23:43	I	TrI
18	1:04	I	ShI
	1:56	I	TrE
	3:15	I	ShE
	20:52	I	OcD
19	0:26	I	EcR
	0:44	II	TrI
	3:16	II	TrE
	3:26	II	ShI
	5:52	II	ShE
	8:54	III	OcD
	11:52	III	OcR
	14:31	III	EcD
	17:09	III	EcR
	18:12	I	TrI
	19:33	I	ShI
	20:25	I	TrE
	21:44	I	ShE
20	15:21	I	OcD
	18:55	I	EcR
	19:38	II	OcD
	22:14	II	OcR
	22:26	II	EcD
21	0:56	II	EcR
	12:41	I	TrI
	14:02	I	ShI
	14:54	I	TrE
	16:13	I	ShE
22	9:50	I	OcD
	13:24	I	EcR
	14:02	II	TrI
	16:34	II	TrE
	16:44	II	ShI
	19:11	II	ShE
	23:06	III	TrI
23	2:01	III	TrE
	4:44	III	ShI
	7:10	I	TrI
	7:20	III	ShE
	8:31	I	ShI
	9:23	I	TrE
	10:42	I	ShE
24	4:19	I	OcD
	7:53	I	EcR
	8:58	II	OcD
	11:34	II	OcR
	11:46	II	EcD
	14:15	II	EcR
25	1:39	I	TrI
	3:00	I	ShI
	3:52	I	TrE
	5:11	I	ShE
	22:48	I	OcD
	2:22	I	EcR
26	3:20	II	TrI
	5:53	II	TrE
	6:02	II	ShI
	8:29	II	ShE
	12:57	III	OcD
	15:55	III	OcR
	18:34	III	EcD
	20:08	I	TrI
	21:11	III	EcR
	21:29	I	ShI
27	22:21	I	TrE
	23:40	I	ShE
	17:17	I	OcD
	20:50	I	EcR
	22:17	II	OcD
28	0:53	II	OcR
	1:05	II	EcD
	3:34	II	EcR
	14:37	I	TrI
	15:58	I	ShI
	16:50	I	TrE
	18:09	I	ShE
29	11:46	I	OcD
	15:19	I	EcR
	16:39	II	TrI
	19:12	II	TrE
	19:21	II	ShI
	21:47	II	ShE
30	3:11	III	TrI
	6:07	III	TrE
	8:47	III	ShI
	9:06	I	TrI
	10:27	**I**	**ShI**
	11:19	I	TrE
	11:21	III	ShE
	12:38	I	ShE
31	6:15	I	OcD
	9:48	I	EcR
	11:38	II	OcD
	14:14	II	OcR
	14:25	II	EcD
	16:54	II	EcR

I = Io; II = Europa; III = Ganymede; IV = Callisto

CONFIGURATIONS OF SATURN'S BRIGHTEST SATELLITES

BY LARRY D. BOGAN

The diagrams on the following three pages give the relative locations of Saturn's five brightest satellites for April through December 2022. Saturn resides in Capricornus this year, is in conjuction with the Sun on Feb. 4 and at opposition on Aug. 15. The names and magnitudes of these satellites, in order of increasing distance from Saturn, are Enceladus 11.8, Tethys 10.3, Dione 10.4, Rhea 9.7, and Titan 8.4.

The curves in the diagrams show the elongations of the satellites from Saturn for each day of the month with 0.0 UT marked with a horizontal line. The dashed curves represent Enceladus and Dione, the first and third out from Saturn. The narrow, central, vertical band represents the disk of Saturn, and the wider band the outer edge of Saturn's A ring.

At the top of each monthly diagram is a scale drawing of Saturn, its rings, and the orbits of the five brightest satellites as seen through an inverting telescope (in the Northern Hemisphere). **South is up.** Due to its faintness and proximity to the bright rings, Enceladus is best seen when near a maximum elongation, but even then good seeing, good optics, and an aperture of at least 200 mm are required.

During 2022, we see Saturn and its satellites from north of the ring plane. The apparent ring tilts for 2022 have a minimum of 12.4° in May and a maximum of 16.9° in January. The direction of motion of the satellites, as viewed with a telescope having an even number (0, 2, 4,…) of reflections in its optics, is counter-clockwise. An arrow has been placed on the orbit of Titan to indicate all satellite orbit revolution directions.

A particular configuration of the satellites may be determined by drawing a horizontal line across the monthly curves at the time (UT) of interest. The intersection of this line with the curves gives the relative elongations of the satellites. Project these elongations onto the drawing of the orbits at the top of the diagram. The east side of the A ring vertical band has been extended up to the drawing to facilitate transfer of each elongation. A millimetre scale, a pair of dividers, or a strip of paper on which to mark enables one to do this quickly and accurately.

The direction of the orbital motion of a satellite determines on which side of its orbit (north or south) a satellite is located. Note the movement of the satellite along the diagram curves past elongation as it revolves around Saturn to determine whether to put the satellite on the north or south side of the orbit. The April diagram shows an example configuration for April 2 at 6 a.m. ADT (April 2nd 9.0 UT).

Greatest Elongations and Conjunctions for Iapetus

The magnitude of Iapetus is comparable to the five plotted satellites, but it varies from 10.2 (western elongation) to 11.9 (eastern elongation). This satellite's orbit is about 2.9 times the size of Titan's and is tilted 15° to Saturn's ring plane; its period is 79.33 days. Iapetus is easiest to find near conjunctions when it is just north or south of Saturn. The table below lists times (UT) of greatest elongations and conjunctions during 2022. This year there are rare transits and occultations at the conjunctions. Use "east is least and west is best" to remember the brightest elongation.

Eastern Elong.	Inferior Conj.	Western Elong.	Superior Conj.
Jan. 18	Feb. 7, 21h	Mar. 01	Mar. 21, 16h occulted
Apr. 10	Apr. 29, 22h transit	May 21	Jun. 9, 20h occulted
Jun. 29	Jul. 18, 04h transit	Aug. 7	Aug. 27, 08h occulted
Sep. 15	Oct. 4, 11h	Oct. 24	Nov. 14, 06h
Dec. 3	Dec. 23, 09h transit	—	—

Note: Stellarium *for Mac, Linux, or Windows, a freeware computer program, displays the configuration of Saturn's satellites on your computer. It can be downloaded at* stellarium.org.

CONFIGURATIONS OF SATURN'S SATELLITES
2022 APRIL–JUNE

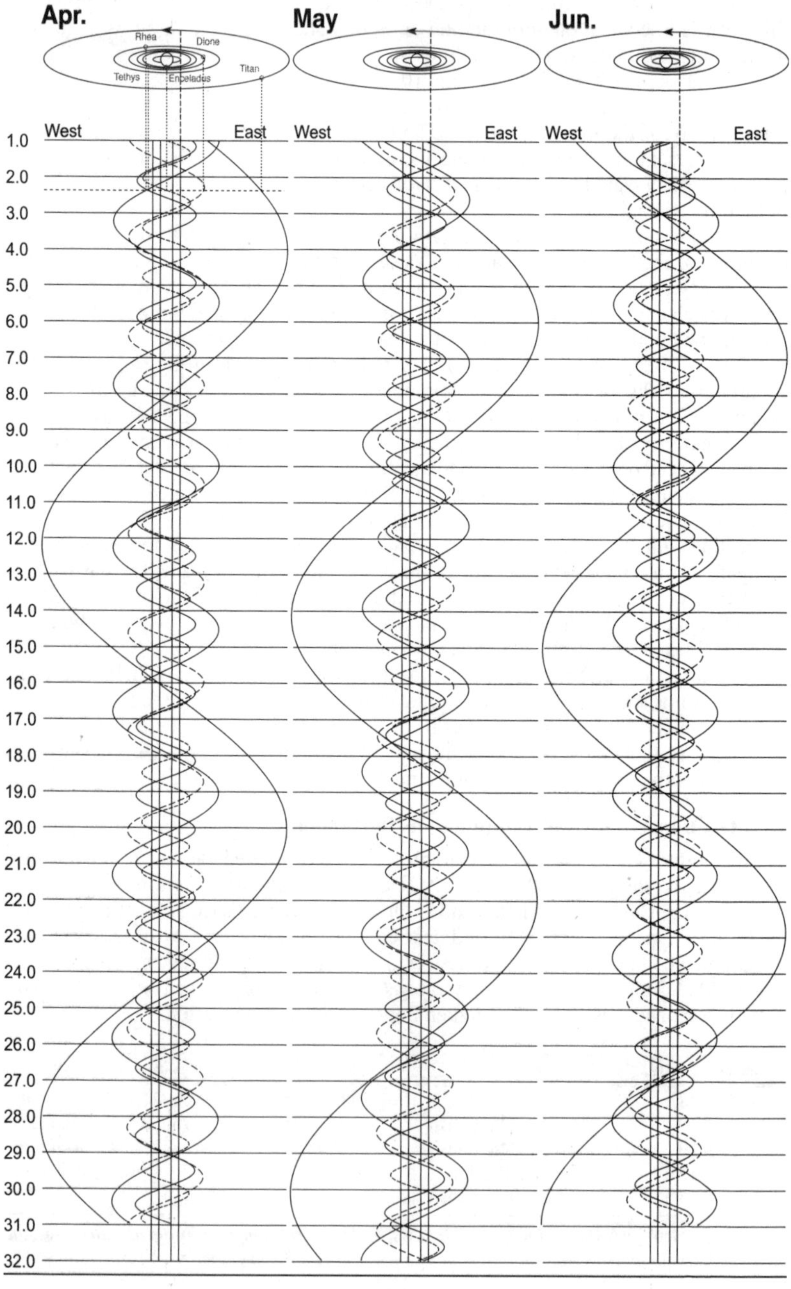

CONFIGURATIONS OF SATURN'S SATELLITES
2022 JULY–SEPTEMBER

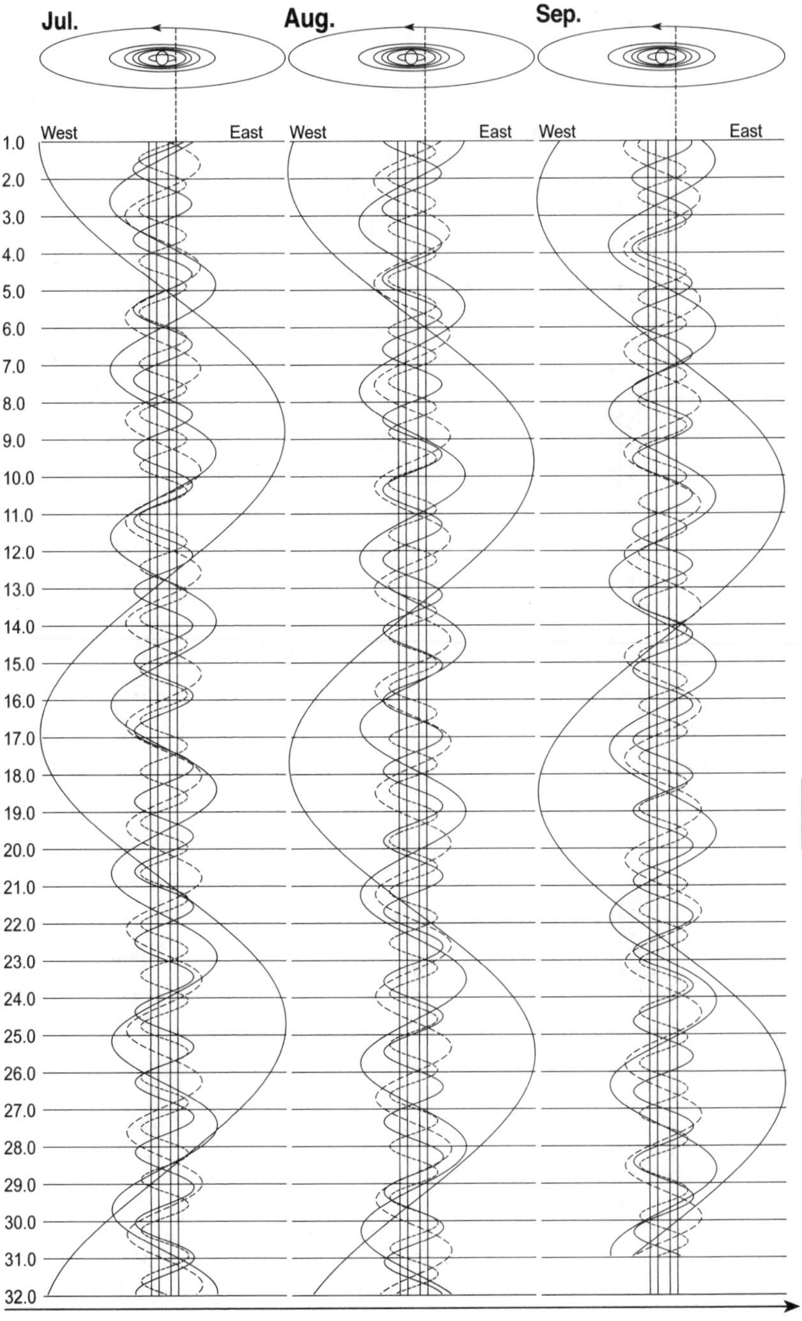

CONFIGURATIONS OF SATURN'S SATELLITES
2022 OCTOBER–DECEMBER

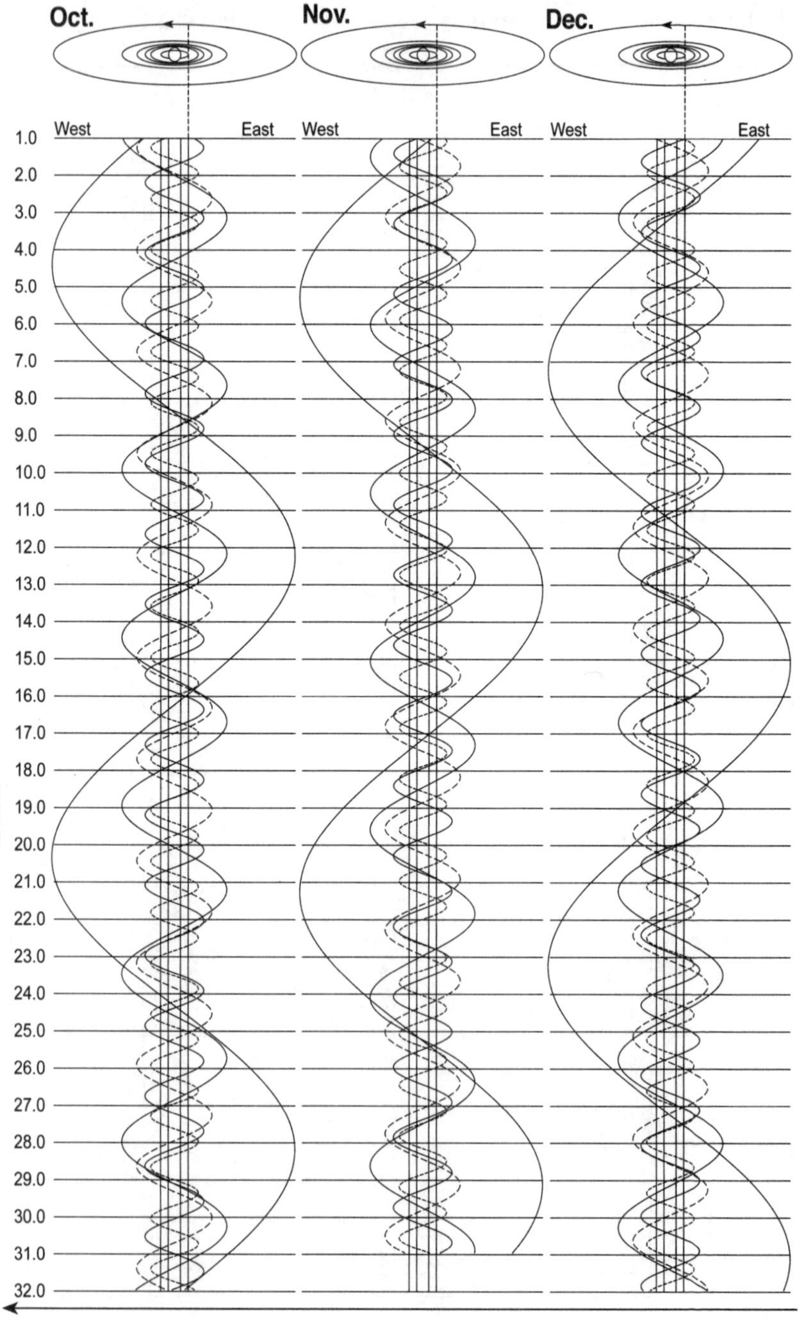

DWARF AND MINOR PLANETS

THE DWARF PLANETS

Classification of Solar System Bodies*

The classification of Solar System bodies has been a rough ride on the pathway of astronomical history, and our destination may still be over the scientific horizon. At the start of the 19th century, the known Solar System included the Sun, the Earth and Moon, the classic five naked-eye planets, the "new" planet Uranus, a handful of natural satellites, and some comets. In quick succession, the "planets" 1 Ceres (1801), 2 Pallas (1802), 3 Juno (1804), and 4 Vesta (1807) were discovered between the orbits of Mars and Jupiter. In 1882, by which time many more small bodies had been discovered, these were reclassified as *asteroids*, numbered serially according to their discovery date. (Today, the designation *minor planet* is preferred over *asteroid*.)

Along the way, the planet Neptune (1846) was discovered and eventually Pluto (1930) became accepted as the ninth planet, even though it has a highly inclined and eccentric orbit relative to the other planets, and is smaller than the Moon and several natural satellites of other planets.

By 2006, the rate of discovery of Pluto-like *trans-Neptunian objects* (TNOs) prompted the International Astronomical Union (IAU) to controversially re-classify Pluto as a *dwarf planet*, numbered 134340 Pluto, followed by 1 Ceres; within two years these two were joined by three more TNOs (see below). The details may be found on the IAU webpage iau.org/public/pluto/ and in Mike Brown's informative book *How I Killed Pluto and Why It Had It Coming* (Random House, 2012).

Currently, the IAU recognizes three principal planetary categories: (1) planets, (2) dwarf planets, and (3) small Solar System bodies. The **planets** are the traditional eight bodies: Mercury, Venus, Earth, Mars, Jupiter, Saturn, Uranus, and Neptune. The **dwarf planets** are 1 Ceres, 134340 Pluto, 136199 Eris, 136108 Haumea, and 136472 Makemake (with 50000 Quaoar, 90377 Sedna, and 9040 Orcus being strongly considered). In plain terms, planets and dwarf planets are round, but dwarf planets are considered too small to have significant gravitational effect on other bodies (other than their satellites, if they have any). **Small Solar System bodies** are everything else, other than satellites: minor planets in the asteroid belt or elsewhere (including most TNOs), and comets. What distinguishes dwarf planets from minor planets is *roundness*: dwarf planets are round, while minor planets are irregular in shape. Such systems of classification are governed by scientific convention, and are subject to change.

* Original text by David M.F. Chapman

1 CERES

Ceres was the first dwarf planet to be discovered, but it is the smallest, and the brightest, only because its orbit lies within the asteroid belt between Mars and Jupiter, while the others are all beyond Neptune. In fact, it is the only dwarf planet in the asteroid belt. This close proximity makes Ceres readily observable, even in binoculars (at opposition). Ceres spends most of the summer well placed for late evening observation in the south. By November, the dwarf planet is lost in the Sun's glare (see the finder chart on the next page and the ephemeris on p. 241). In 2015, the *Dawn* spacecraft orbited Ceres and thoroughly mapped the surface, which appears to be largely water ice above a rocky core and possibly a liquid-water ocean. Interestingly, Ceres was found to be emitting water vapor from several locations, which is quite unusual for a rocky body.

FINDER CHART FOR 1 CERES

BY IAN CAMERON

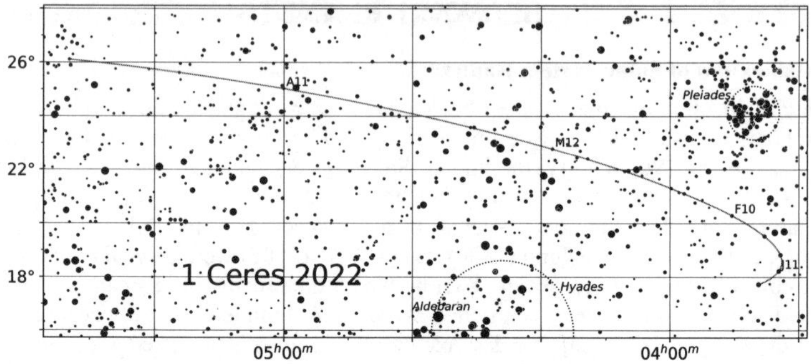

Ceres varies in magnitude from 8 to 9 while it is still observable as it moves toward superior conjunction in July. Stars found on this chart range from 1 (Aldebaran) to mag. 9.5.

(See 134340 Pluto at right for full attribution for all chart generation.)

134340 PLUTO

BY MURRAY PAULSON

Pluto's mean distance from the Sun is 39.3 au, but its highly eccentric orbit currently locates it much closer, about 34.32 au in 2022. At its last perihelion in 1989, Pluto shone at mag. 13.6, a state it will not revisit until the 23rd century. As Pluto moves away from perihelion, it is slowly fading. Clyde Tombaugh discovered Pluto in 1930, when it was 42.3 au distant at mag. 15.3. It will be another 38 years before Pluto becomes this faint again. In July of 2015 we looked in wonder at the first close-up views of Pluto's surface from the *New Horizons* spacecraft. Pluto once again basked in the spotlight and showed there were some interesting surprises out at the edge of the Kuiper belt.

Pluto is 2377 km in diameter, only twice that of its largest moon, Charon (1208 km), which has retrograde rotation of period 6.39 d, synchronous with Charon's revolution. Charon's orbit takes it to only 0.8″ from Pluto and it shines at mag. 16.1. Pluto also has four smaller satellites, Nix, Hydra, Kerberos, and Styx, the last discovered in July 2012. These four satellites are all less than 100 km in diameter and dimmer than mag. 23.

Pluto's year starts off with a conjunction with the Sun on Jan. 15. From this point until the summer observing window, Pluto will be a difficult target. It comes to opposition on Jul. 17 and it will shine at mag. 14.3. Pluto's southerly latitude of –22.4° further complicates the search for northern viewers; it sits low in eastern Sagittarius. Pluto presently is 11° east of the handle of The Teapot and there are only eighth-magnitude stars to guide. A second star hop involves finding M75, then moving 4.5° west to Pluto. Take a look at the finder chart (opposite) and use binoculars to find the field. Then use your favorite star chart software to make your detailed observing chart.

Now, if finding Pluto isn't enough of a challenge, see if you can spot it in a mid-sized refractor. The observation was possible in a 125–130-mm refractor, but the transparency and seeing were both very good. One year, I challenged RASC Edmonton Centre member Alister Ling to find it in his 125-mm APO, and I tackled it with my 94-mm Brandon refractor. Pluto was much higher at that time. Alister achieved the observation with relative ease, but the smaller aperture of 94 mm made it a very tough hunt for me. I found it, but with great difficulty, eyestrain, and over an hour of painstaking star hopping. I welcome any comments or stories of your hunt.

FINDER CHART FOR 134340 PLUTO

BY IAN CAMERON

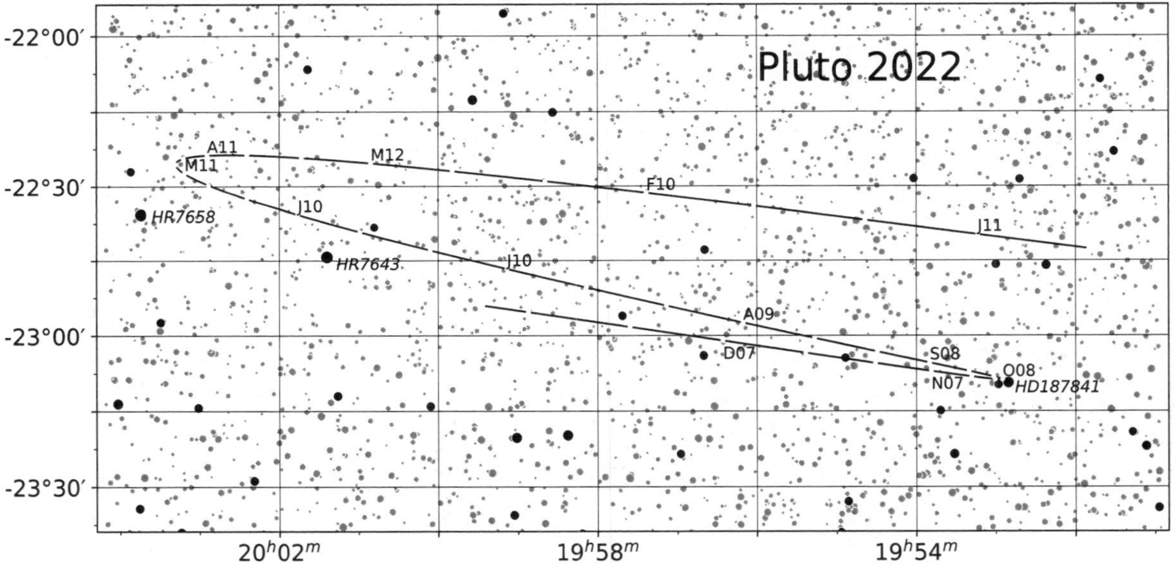

Pluto is typically a mag. 14.5 object found amongst stars ranging from mag. 6 to 14.5 on this chart. Stars brighter than mag. 10.5 are indicated in black. Pluto is at opposition in July at mag. 14.3. The star HD1857841 is a mag. 7.8 double star in Sagittarius.

The charts are produced using the Astropy software package together with the Astroquery package inside an interactive Jupyter Notebook (Anaconda Python distribution). Solar System ephemerides can then be accessed via the JPL Horizons Solar System Dynamics interface and the UCAC4 star catalog via the Strasbourg Observatory VizieR Catalogue Service. Plotting the charts uses the built-in Matplotlib package. The charts were produced with a computer running ver. 10.14.6 of MacOS..

THE BRIGHTEST MINOR PLANETS

The following two pages contain ephemerides for those minor planets (identified by number and name) that reach mag. 9.8 or brighter during 2022 and are positioned more than 60° from the Sun. The table is ordered by opposition date, shown in the headers, along with the opposition magnitude. In the table, **Mag.** is visual magnitude. Opposition dates are given after the minor-planet name; a dash (—) indicates no opposition in 2022.

The ephemeris for the *dwarf planet* 1 Ceres is included here as it is also a minor planet; more information and a finder chart can be found in THE DWARF PLANETS, on p. 237. See p. 23 for the current orbital elements of the 28 brightest minor planets (by absolute magnitude).

Observers can make their own finder charts by plotting the coordinates on a suitable star atlas with equinox J2000.0. Those with computer planetarium software can obtain orbital elements in several popular electronic formats from the Minor Planet Center (minorplanetcenter.net/iau/MPEph/MPEph.html).

FEATURE MINOR PLANET: 10 HYGIEA

Minor planet 10 Hygiea is a major body in the main asteroid belt, having a diameter of 434 km and a mass about 3% of the total mass of the belt. Hygiea is the fourth-largest Minor Planet in the Solar System and is the largest of the dark C-type asteroids with a carbonaceous surface.

Hygiea, nearly spherical, and close to a globe in shape as evidenced by observations made with the Very Large Telescope's SPHERE imager, is not large enough to be designated as a Dwarf Planet.

Discovery was on 1849 Apr. 12 in Naples, Italy, by Annibale de Gasparis, the first of his nine asteroid discoveries. The name "Hygiea," derived from Hygieia, the Greek goddess of health, is in honor of the ruling family of the Kingdom of the Two Sicilies.

FINDER CHART FOR 10 HYGIEA

BY IAN CAMERON

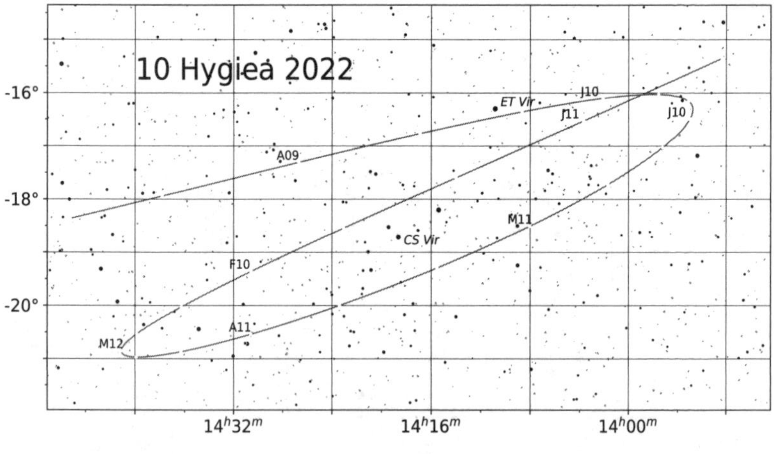

Hygiea varies in magnitude from 11 to 9.3 at opposition (Apr. 29). Stars found on this chart range from mag. 5 (CS Vir and ET Vir) to mag. 11. Stars brighter than mag. 9.5 are indicated in black.

(See 134340 Pluto for full attribution for all chart generation, p. 243.)

EPHEMERIDES FOR THE BRIGHTEST MINOR PLANETS IN 2022

BY DANIEL W.E. GREEN

Date 0h TT	RA (2000) h m	Dec ° ′	Mag.
(1) Ceres*		—	
Jan. 1	03 46.28	+17 43.6	7.7
Jan. 11	03 43.16	+18 13.6	7.9
Jan. 21	03 42.89	+18 49.9	8.1
Jan. 31	03 45.38	+19 31.5	8.3
Feb. 10	03 50.44	+20 17.6	8.4
Feb. 20	03 57.78	+21 06.5	8.5
Mar. 2	04 07.13	+21 56.7	8.6
Mar. 12	04 18.26	+22 46.8	8.7
Mar. 22	04 30.92	+23 35.2	8.8
Apr. 1	04 44.91	+24 20.6	8.8
Nov. 17	11 35.18	+12 26.6	8.7
Nov. 27	11 49.21	+11 32.9	8.6
Dec. 7	12 02.27	+10 48.2	8.5
Dec. 17	12 14.20	+10 14.1	8.4
Dec. 27	12 24.79	+09 52.6	8.3
Jan. 6	12 33.76	+09 45.3	8.2
(2) Pallas		—	
Aug. 9	05 11.39	–04 26.1	9.3
Aug. 19	05 28.79	–05 48.8	9.2
Aug. 29	05 45.64	–07 26.7	9.1
Sep. 8	06 01.76	–09 19.3	9.0
Sep. 18	06 16.95	–11 25.9	8.9
Sep. 28	06 30.99	–13 45.0	8.8
Oct. 8	06 43.60	–16 14.4	8.7
Oct. 18	06 54.52	–18 51.2	8.6
Oct. 28	07 03.40	–21 31.5	8.5
Nov. 7	07 09.89	–24 10.0	8.3
Nov. 17	07 13.69	–26 40.0	8.2
Nov. 27	07 14.49	–28 53.3	8.1
Dec. 7	07 12.23	–30 39.8	8.0
Dec. 17	07 07.11	–31 49.0	7.9
Dec. 27	06 59.75	–32 10.6	7.8
Jan. 6	06 51.24	–31 36.9	7.7
(7) Iris		*Jan. 14, mag. 7.6*	
Jan. 1	07 50.87	+15 48.9	7.8
Jan. 11	07 39.83	+15 42.1	7.6
Jan. 21	07 28.87	+15 42.5	7.8
Jan. 31	07 19.63	+15 47.4	8.2
Feb. 10	07 13.32	+15 54.7	8.5
Feb. 20	07 10.49	+16 02.3	8.8
Mar. 2	07 11.15	+16 08.4	9.1
Mar. 12	07 15.01	+16 11.5	9.4
Mar. 22	07 21.64	+16 09.9	9.6
Apr. 1	07 30.54	+16 02.6	9.8
(20) Massalia		*Feb. 5, mag 8.6*	
Jan. 1	09 37.86	+12 54.3	9.4
Jan. 11	09 34.11	+13 09.6	9.2
Jan. 21	09 27.28	+13 40.8	8.9
Jan. 31	09 18.26	+14 23.0	8.6
Feb. 10	09 08.46	+15 09.1	8.6
Feb. 20	08 59.52	+15 51.3	9.0
Mar. 2	08 52.78	+16 24.3	9.2
Mar. 12	08 49.14	+16 44.8	9.5
(20) Massalia (continued)			
Mar. 22	08 48.91	+16 51.7	9.8
(8) Flora		*Apr. 12, mag. 9.7*	
Apr. 1	13 47.53	–00 49.1	9.9
Apr. 11	13 37.99	+00 14.5	9.7
Apr. 21	13 28.05	+01 09.4	9.8
(15) Eunomia		*Apr. 16, mag. 9.9*	
Apr. 11	13 14.38	–26 24.3	9.9
Apr. 21	13 05.36	–25 31.7	9.8
(10) Hygiea		*Apr. 29, mag. 9.2*	
Apr. 1	14 36.29	–20 52.0	9.8
Apr. 11	14 30.58	–20 32.2	9.6
Apr. 21	14 23.39	–19 59.9	9.3
May 1	14 15.55	–19 17.7	9.2
May 11	14 08.02	–18 30.4	9.4
May 21	14 01.70	–17 43.3	9.6
May 31	13 57.21	–17 01.7	9.8
(29) Amphitrite		*Jun. 7, mag. 9.6*	
May 21	17 10.73	–32 08.0	9.8
May 31	17 00.75	–32 11.6	9.6
Jun. 10	16 49.99	–32 02.5	9.6
Jun. 20	16 39.73	–31 42.0	9.7
Jun. 30	16 31.07	–31 13.3	9.9
(41) Daphne		*Jun. 8, mag. 9.8*	
May 21	17 26.99	+04 49.4	9.9
May 31	17 20.65	+05 57.8	9.8
Jun. 10	17 13.26	+06 30.2	9.8
Jun. 20	17 06.09	+06 24.3	9.9
(14) Irene		*Jul. 6, mag. 9.7*	
Jun. 20	19 19.91	–25 51.2	9.9
Jun. 30	19 10.42	–26 46.9	9.7
Jul. 10	19 00.16	–27 36.7	9.6
Jul. 20	18 50.39	–28 16.9	9.9
(9) Metis		*Jul. 20, mag. 9.6*	
Jul. 10	20 15.27	–26 32.7	9.8
Jul. 20	20 05.13	–27 22.2	9.6
Jul. 30	19 54.54	–28 02.7	9.7
(192) Nausikaa		*Jul. 23, mag. 9.5*	
Jul. 10	20 28.21	–28 45.0	9.8
Jul. 20	20 17.91	–29 02.0	9.5
Jul. 30	20 06.38	–29 05.4	9.5
Aug. 9	19 55.41	–28 51.1	9.7
Aug. 19	19 46.70	–28 19.3	9.9
(4) Vesta		*Aug. 23, mag. 5.9*	
Apr. 1	20 48.34	–18 04.2	7.8
Apr. 11	21 06.37	–17 12.9	7.7
Apr. 21	21 23.37	–16 21.8	7.6
May 1	21 39.22	–15 33.4	7.6
May 11	21 53.79	–14 50.0	7.5
May 21	22 06.92	–14 14.2	7.4
May 31	22 18.40	–13 48.6	7.2
Jun. 10	22 27.97	–13 36.1	7.1
Jun. 20	22 35.38	–13 39.3	6.9
Jun. 30	22 40.30	–14 00.5	6.8
Jul. 10	22 42.44	–14 41.0	6.6
Jul. 20	22 41.60	–15 40.3	6.4
Jul. 30	22 37.76	–16 55.4	6.2

**dwarf planet; see p. 241*

EPHEMERIDES FOR THE BRIGHTEST MINOR PLANETS IN 2022 (cont.)

Date 0h TT	RA (2000) h m	Dec ° ′	Mag.
(4) Vesta *(continued)*			
Aug. 9	22 31.25	−18 19.8	6.0
Aug. 19	22 22.86	−19 44.1	5.8
Aug. 29	22 13.69	−20 58.5	5.9
Sep. 8	22 05.10	−21 54.7	6.1
Sep. 18	21 58.28	−22 28.2	6.4
Sep. 28	21 54.03	−22 38.4	6.6
Oct. 8	21 52.75	−22 27.1	6.8
Oct. 18	21 54.43	−21 57.4	7.1
Oct. 28	21 58.82	−21 12.2	7.2
Nov. 7	22 05.59	−20 14.0	7.4
Nov. 17	22 14.35	−19 04.9	7.6
Nov. 27	22 24.74	−17 46.4	7.7
Dec. 7	22 36.47	−16 20.0	7.9
Dec. 17	22 49.24	−14 46.7	8.0
Dec. 27	23 02.86	−13 07.7	8.1
Jan. 6	23 17.15	−11 23.8	8.1
(3) Juno		***Sept. 8, mag. 7.9***	
Jun. 30	23 09.84	+01 45.4	9.7
Jul. 10	23 14.92	+02 00.1	9.5
Jul. 20	23 18.00	+01 56.2	9.3
Jul. 30	23 18.81	+01 30.2	9.0
Aug. 9	23 17.22	+00 39.7	8.7
Aug. 19	23 13.32	−00 35.9	8.5
Aug. 29	23 07.43	−02 14.4	8.2
Sep. 8	23 00.32	−04 09.2	7.9
Sep. 18	22 53.02	−06 09.9	8.1
Sep. 28	22 46.64	−08 05.2	8.2
Oct. 8	22 42.24	−09 44.7	8.4
Oct. 18	22 40.49	−11 01.6	8.6
Oct. 28	22 41.70	−11 53.1	8.8
Nov. 7	22 45.91	−12 18.7	8.9
Nov. 17	22 52.87	−12 20.4	9.1
Nov. 27	23 02.28	−12 00.2	9.2
Dec. 7	23 13.82	−11 20.7	9.3
Dec. 17	23 27.13	−10 24.5	9.4
Dec. 27	23 41.95	−09 13.9	9.5
Jan. 6	23 58.02	−07 51.1	9.5
(6) Hebe		—	
Nov. 27	08 55.30	+07 50.4	9.8
Dec. 7	08 57.49	+07 56.8	9.7
Dec. 17	08 56.70	+08 22.7	9.5
Dec. 27	08 52.85	+09 10.2	9.3

Date 0h TT	RA (2000) h m	Dec ° ′	Mag.
(6) Hebe (continued			
Jan. 6	08 46.21	+10 18.9	9.1
(27) Euterpe		***Nov. 13, mag. 8.9***	
Oct. 18	03 33.38	+16 47.4	9.7
Oct. 28	03 26.99	+16 24.7	9.3
Nov. 7	03 18.04	+15 55.0	9.0
Nov. 17	03 07.93	+15 22.8	8.9
Nov. 27	02 58.35	+14 54.3	9.2
Dec. 7	02 50.93	+14 36.0	9.5
Dec. 17	02 46.73	+14 32.5	9.7
(115) Thyra		***Nov. 19, mag. 9.6***	
Oct. 28	03 29.03	+41 47.2	9.9
Nov. 7	03 19.37	+41 43.8	9.7
Nov. 17	03 08.37	+40 57.9	9.6
Nov. 27	02 58.34	+39 34.3	9.7
Dec. 7	02 51.34	+37 46.5	9.8
(324) Bamberga		***Nov. 22, mag. 8.9***	
Sep. 18	03 41.37	+35 31.6	9.8
Sep. 28	03 49.55	+37 39.0	9.6
Oct. 8	03 53.49	+39 31.2	9.5
Oct. 18	03 52.72	+41 02.0	9.3
Oct. 28	03 47.23	+42 02.8	9.1
Nov. 7	03 38.01	+42 25.1	9.0
Nov. 17	03 27.04	+42 04.9	8.9
Nov. 27	03 16.70	+41 06.2	9.0
Dec. 7	03 09.14	+39 41.1	9.2
Dec. 17	03 05.51	+38 05.2	9.5
Dec. 27	03 06.07	+36 31.5	9.8
(30) Urania		***Nov. 29, mag. 9.7***	
Nov. 27	04 19.52	+24 57.2	9.7
Dec. 7	04 08.83	+24 21.6	9.9
(44) Nysa		—	
Jan. 1	04 51.35	+17 42.8	9.5
Jan. 11	04 45.66	+18 03.0	9.7
Jan. 21	04 43.58	+18 30.8	9.9
(349) Dembowska		***Dec. 2, mag. 9.6***	
Nov. 7	04 47.90	+28 55.8	9.9
Nov. 17	04 39.62	+29 17.7	9.8
Nov. 27	04 29.74	+29 29.1	9.6
Dec. 7	04 19.44	+29 29.6	9.6
Dec. 17	04 10.01	+29 21.0	9.8
(532) Herculina		***Dec. 3, mag 9.9***	
Dec. 7	04 39.16	+07 10.8	9.9

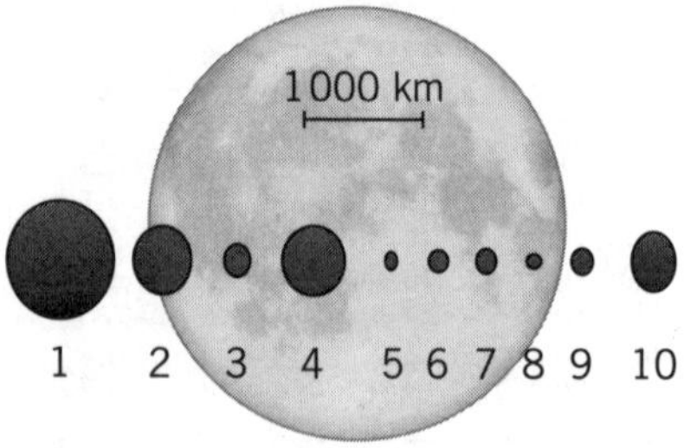

Relative sizes of the Moon and the first 10 subplanets discovered: 1 Ceres, 2 Pallas, 3 Juno, 4 Vesta, 5 Astraea, 6 Hebe, 7 Iris, 8 Flora, 9 Metis, and 10 Hygeia (illustration by Michael Gatto, after Vystrix Nexoth).

PLANETARY OCCULTATIONS

BY DAVID W. DUNHAM, DAVID HERALD, STEVE PRESTON, AND DEREK BREIT

As major, dwarf, and minor planets, and their moons, move across the sky, they occasionally pass directly between an observer and a distant star, producing an occultation. Astronomers have learned much about solar system bodies by carefully monitoring the changing apparent brightness of stars during the immersion and emersion phases of occultations. If the occulting body does not have an atmosphere, the occultation is virtually instantaneous; if there is an atmosphere, it causes the star's disappearance and reappearance to occur gradually. If a planet has rings or other debris in its environs, the extent and degree of transparency of this material can be precisely mapped. The rings of Uranus, the ring arcs of Neptune, and the atmosphere of Pluto were all discovered by occultation observations. If an occultation is observed at several distributed sites, the size and shape of the occulting body can be determined more accurately than by other Earth-based techniques.

Amateur astronomers can make important contributions to occultation observing campaigns. This is particularly true for minor planet occultations, for which the paths across Earth are often very narrow and uncertain in location (due mainly to uncertainties in the ephemeris of the minor planet). By recording the times of the star's disappearance and reappearance as seen from several sites (i.e. by noting the edges of the minor planet's shadow as it sweeps across Earth), the object's profile can be directly determined. Sometimes timings can be made by visual observers with modest telescopes.

When observing an occultation, it is important that an observer know his or her location to within a fraction of a kilometre. Geographic longitude and latitude as well as the altitude of an observing site can be determined with a GPS receiver, from a high-quality topographic map, or from some map websites. If observations are to be of maximum value, the times of immersion and emersion must be determined as accurately as possible—certainly to better than 0.5 s, and better than 0.2 s for the shortest events (those less than about 10 s in duration). Photoelectric equipment with high-speed digital recording systems is well suited for this work. Attaching a low-light-level video camera to a telescope is a less expensive method for accurate timing. Visual observers using smartphones as audio recorders, and another smartphone using an accurate time signal app, can also make useful contributions. Even simple measurements of the duration of an occultation made with a smartphone stopwatch function, can be of value. CCD observers should be aware that most of these systems are incapable of timing accuracies better than about 2 s. But many CCD observers use the trick of turning off the telescope clock drive shortly before the predicted time and let the images trail. The occultation will appear as a break in the trail that can be measured to about a tenth of a second if the moment the exposure is started (just after turning off the clock drive) is accurately timed; see www.asteroidoccultation.com/observations/DriftScan/Index.htm.

Occultation observations are coordinated in North America by the International Occultation Timing Association (IOTA) (www.occultations.org). IOTA member or not, IOTA wants to inform you, and others in your area, able to locate stars to 11th magnitude of prediction updates. IOTA's free *Occult Watcher* software (see below) is best for finding events at your location. Otherwise, you can email the longitude and latitude (or location from the nearest town) of convenient observing sites, telescope size(s), and an indication of whether you are mobile to dunham@starpower.net. Individuals interested in joining IOTA should refer to OCCULTATIONS BY THE MOON, p. 162 in this Handbook, for membership information.

More information is in the Solar System Photometry Handbook (Willmann-

Bell, Inc., 1983), *Sky & Telescope*, and papers in IOTA's *Journal of Occultation Astronomy* (JOA), *Icarus*, *Minor Planet Bulletin*, and other journals.

Observations of occultations by major and minor planets, including negative observations, should be sent to reports@asteroidoccultation.com for analysis, archiving, and publication by IOTA. When reporting timings, describe your geographic longitude, latitude, and altitude (to the nearest arcsecond and 30 m, respectively), telescope size, timing method, the start and end time of observation, an estimate of the observer's reaction time (if applicable) and the accuracy of the timing, and whether the reaction time correction has been applied. IOTA's main website at www.occultations.org, especially the Observing tab, has comprehensive up-to-date information on observing and reporting occultations. The Publications tab includes links to IOTA's free *Journal of Occultation Astronomy* (JOA). In this section, stars are identified by numbers from either the Smithsonian Astrophysical Observatory (SAO) catalog, the *HIPPARCOS* (HIP) catalog, the Tycho (TYC) catalog; or the fourth U.S. Naval Observatory CCD Astrographic (UCAC4) catalog.

Planetary Occultations

Occultations by the major planets are difficult to observe due to the brightness of the occulting body; events involving stars bright enough to observe next to a dazzling planet are rare. The best major planet event that might be observed will be an occultation by Venus of 8.3-mag. SAO 163820 = TYC 6331-00738-1, spectral type K0, a few minutes before 10h UT of Mar. 16, visible from the east coastal areas of North America. The southern limit of the occultation passes a little south of Tampa and Orlando, Florida. With Venus's magnitude of –4.6, the bright-side disappearance can not be observed, but the star might be observed when it reappears on the dark side of Venus's disk, 25.8″ in diameter and 47% sunlit. Predictions for the contacts and circumstances for the event are on a page about the event at occultations.org/publications/rasc/2022/20220316Venus.htm.

Easier to observe are occultations by moons of the planets, but they are not common. There will be an occultation of 8.7-mag. SAO 164648 = HIP 107569, spectral type F0V, by Saturn's large moon Titan visible from much of North America around 9:20 UT of Jul. 9, and an occultation by Uranus's moon Oberon of 7.2-mag. SAO 93185 = HIP 13601, spectral type G5, at 8:51 UT of Nov. 19, visible from much of Mexico, Central America, and the Caribbean. More information about these two events is given in a section on occultations by distant objects on p. 251. A potentially valuable occultation by Neptune's large moon Triton. of an 11.5-mag. star, will be visible from the Aleutian Islands at 14:36 UT of Oct. 6. A few minutes later, the event will occur at high altitude over Japan, China, and India. Occultations by the irregular outer moons of Jupiter are predicted by astronomers working for the Lucky Star project, but usually only a few weeks in advance, based on special astrometric updates; IOTA's *Occult* program found no such events by the larger ones during 2022.

Maps of Asteroidal Occultations

In previous years, we published a two-page table of about 70 of the brighter and/or more valuable or interesting occultations by major and minor planets during the year. We believe that few readers go to the effort to read through those lists, to try to figure out events they might be able to observe. Instead, we are presenting a map of nine of the brightest occultations by main-belt asteroids below. Following it is a table, similar to our previously published tables, but without the long path descriptions we had before, since the path locations can easily be seen on the map. The predictions were generated by Edwin Goffin, Scott Donnell, Steve Preston, Derek Breit, and David Herald. Preston assisted Dunham in the selection for the map and table. IOTA's free *Occult* software (see www.lunar-occultations.com/iota/occult4.htm) was used to create the maps. The orbital elements are all from

FIGURE 1–2022 OCCULTATIONS OF BRIGHT STARS BY MAIN-BELT ASTEROIDS

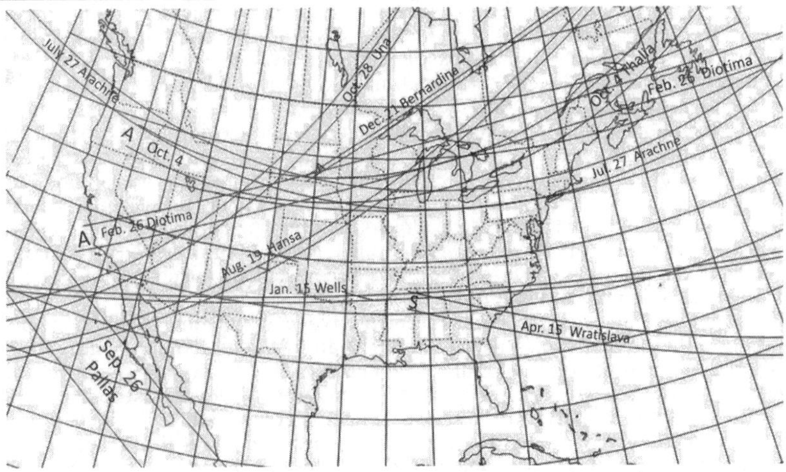

TABLE 1–2022 OCCULTATIONS OF BRIGHT STARS BY MAIN-BELT ASTEROIDS

Date	UT	Occulting Body	Star	Mag.	RA (2000) h m s	Dec ° ′ ″	ΔMag.	Dur. s	Path
Jan. 15	07:06	1721 Wells	HIP 41760	7.8	08 30 56.0	+26 01 22	7.4	3.3	NC-Baja
Feb. 26	01:31	423 Diotima	HIP 53615	7.4	10 58 09.0	+24 22 32	4.5	15.1	NL-CA
Apr. 15	00:29	690 Wratislavia	HIP 22486	8.1	04 50 15.4	+19 55 24	5.9	3.8	MS-SC
Jul. 27	05:35	407 Arachne	TYC 5779-01576-1	11.2	21 10 22.5	-12 32 09	1.6	9.2	OR-MA
Aug. 19	02:53	480 Hansa	TYC 1099-01683-1	11.2	20 30 45.8	+14 42 38	1.6	5.2	Baja-NL
Sep. 26	11:01	2 Pallas	TYC 5376-00624-1	8.6	06 28 54.9	-13 22 48	0.9	20.0	Baja-MX
Oct. 4	02:37	23 Thalia	HIP 4031	6.7	00 51 37.4	-08 49 06	4.4	7.9	OR-NL
Oct. 28	01:50	160 Una	TYC 6351-01171-1	8.7	21 17 44.1	-18 10 22	5.5	7.4	CA-ON
Dec. 21	00:12	629 Bernardina	TYC 1913-02265-1	7.6	07 21 39.7	+25 51 44	6.3	3.7	SD-QC

the NASA JPL Horizons website at **ssd.jpl.nasa.gov/horizons.cgi** and the stellar data are from the Early third release (EDR3) of the European Space Agency's *Gaia* mission, as implemented with UCAC4, Tycho, and *HIPPARCOS* catalog identifiers with Occult.

The successive columns in the table above list: (1) the date and central time of the event; (2) the name of the occulting body; (3) the catalog and number of the occulted star; (4) the star's apparent visual magnitude; (5) the star's right ascension and (6) declination; (7) the expected magnitude change from the combined brightness; (8) the predicted maximum duration of the occultation in seconds; and, (9) the path location specified by the lands crossed by the eastern and western ends of the path shown on the map. The two-letter abbreviations for the US States and Canadian Provinces are given, with the order indicating the direction of motion of the shadow. "Baja" is Baja California, either Norte or Sur, while "Mex" denotes the rest of Mexico. DR is the Dominican Republic. Due to uncertainties mainly in the ephemerides of the minor planets from which these predictions are derived (most star positions are now accurately determined from the European Space Agency's Gaia mission), the region of visibility of an occultation is uncertain, but now by only a few tenths of a path-width for most of these events. Errors remain, so those near but outside the paths should try to observe. It's also useful, especially for the brighter stars that produce high signal-to-noise recordings, to observe even if you are located up to about 10 path-widths from the predicted path, to check for the possibility of an occultation by a previously unknown satellite of the asteroid.

We can only portray the brightest events here. Our searches have found many other occultations, including 113 visible from North America of stars brighter than mag. 11.1. Maps and tables of them are available at occultations.org/publications/rasc/2022/nam22MBoccs.htm. More about all of these events is at www.poyntsource.com/New/RASC_Events.htm.

Note that the times are for the geocentric time of closest approach; for any specific location in North America, the event time can be several minutes earlier or later. A few weeks before each event, improved predictions and the latest path maps, as well as finder charts of different scales to locate the stars, may be obtained from Steve Preston's minor planet occultation website www.asteroidoccultation.com. Much other useful information, including interactive maps to zoom in on the path, circumstances for dozens of stations in and near the path, and lists of stars that can be used to pre-point telescopes to the target stars are at www.poyntsource.com/New/Global.htm. "*Occult Watcher* (OW)" is highly recommended as it will list all of the asteroidal occultations, filtered to a magnitude limit that you specify, visible from your site or region during the next two months; it is a free download from www.hristopavlov.net/OccultWatcher/publish.htm. Since OW, and its companion OW Cloud, works from an interactive website, IOTA uses it to coordinate minor-planet occultation observation plans. It is a valuable tool that all serious observers of these events should use; we provide more information about it at the end of this section.

We attempted to limit the map and table above to stars of magnitude 9.0 or brighter. The magnitudes are *Gaia* "g" magnitudes that are usually close to visual magnitudes, but not always. We had to check the designations of the stars occulted on Jul. 27 and Aug. 19, and in the process, discovered a large discrepancy in their magnitudes relative to other star catalogs. The V magnitudes given by the AAVSO's APASS catalog generally are among closest to visual magnitudes, and for the stars for these two events, it gave V as 11.2, which was confirmed by the Tycho catalog. This is much fainter than our intended 9.0 limit (which was the *Gaia* g mag. for both stars), but still bright enough to observe with most telescopes used by amateur astronomers. Consequently, we didn't go to the considerable effort that would be needed to find other events for the map at that point, and so we kept them, but have used the APASS magnitudes rather than the *Gaia* magnitudes. The Jul. 27 star has a large B–V of 1.3 so it may be a red variable star, but that's not the case for the Aug. 19 star.

Now that the prediction accuracy has improved for most asteroids, thanks to the *Gaia Mission*, we give maps and tables in the next subsections for selected fainter but more scientifically valuable occultations that could be observed by many amateur astronomers.

Occultations by Near-Earth Asteroids

Occultations by Near-Earth Asteroids (NEAs) is an exciting new endeavor that contributes to planetary defense by refining the orbits of these small but possibly dangerous objects. IOTA's first success with NEA events was with (3200) Phaethon in 2019, but more spectacularly with (99942) Apophis last year; much information about the occultations, their value, and how they helped retire the threat of Apophis, is given in a paper presented at the 7th Planetary Defense Conference obtainable at iota.jhuapl.edu/NEOoccultationsDunham.pdf. There are several opportunities in 2022 shown on the map and table below, similar to those described for bright main-belt occultations in the previous subsection. Since the paths for these events are all very narrow, one must travel with mobile equipment to observe them, rather like grazing occultations of stars by the Moon. And like lunar grazes, it is necessary to adjust the location for elevation above sea level. John Irwin in the UK has helped IOTA with this by supplying special *Google Earth* files that take elevation into account.

When an NEA occultation is first observed, it generally must be done by a large team of observers to cover the relatively large uncertainty zone. But after one occultation is observed, that data can refine the orbit to allow more accurate prediction of future events that can then be covered by only a few observers. More about the 2022 NEA occultations, including campaign plans, will be available at occultations.org/publications/rasc/2022/nam22NEAoccs.htm.

FIGURE 2–2022 OCCULTATIONS BY NEAR-EARTH ASTEROIDS

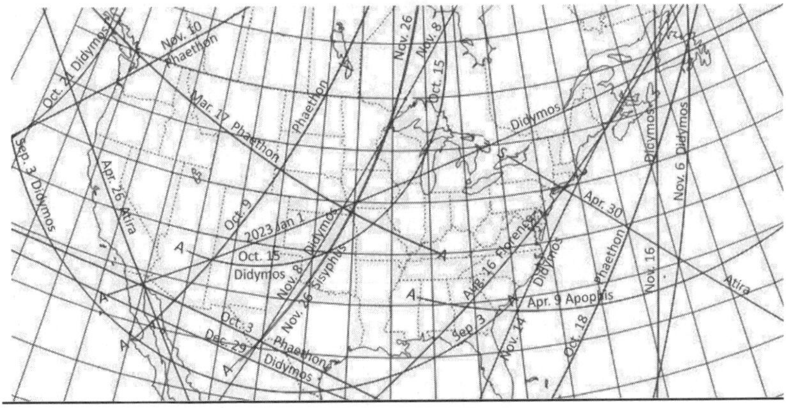

Some information about the occulting NEAs portrayed above and in the table overleaf follows:

(1866) Sisyphus: Observations of occultations by this large NEA would be valuable since Sisyphus is out of radar range for at least the next 20 years. IOTA plans a large campaign for the only event on Nov. 26.

(3122) Florence: 2017 radar observations show that Florence has two moons, one about 200 m across and about 5 km away, while the other is a little more than 300 m across and about 10 km away.

(3200) Phaethon: The paths should be quite accurate, with the orbit well-determined from the 2019 and 2020 occultations. But more observations are desired, to check for variations in Phaethon's non-gravitational forces caused by mass shedding (Geminid meteoroids) from its extreme thermal environment.

(65803) Didymos: The occultations by Didymos have the highest priority since NASA's DART mission plans to impact Dimorphos, Didymos's 160-m moon that is 1.2 km away, on Sep. 30. Once a first occultation is observed, the following ones can be predicted more accurately; then, especially valuable would be any observations of occultations by Dimorphos as well as by Didymos, to help measure the effect of the DART impact. The 6.6-km/sec impact is expected to change the orbital period of Dimorphos around Didymos by several minutes. Besides the events in North America, there is also an occultation of a 12.4-mag. star that will occur over the southern part of Hawaii Island on September 15 at 13:20 UT.

(99942) Apophis: Unfortunately, all of the occultations by Apophis in 2022 are very short, lasting only 0.02s. Thus, the only event that might be observed is the bright one (star mag. 8.5) shown, on April 9. The altitude is low, at best 10° on the Atlantic coast near Savannah, Georgia.

(163693) Atira: Atira has an approximately 1-km moon orbiting perhaps 6 km from the primary.

TABLE 2–2022 OCCULTATIONS BY NEAR-EARTH ASTEROIDS

Date	UT	Occulting Body	Star	Mag.	RA (2000) h m s	Dec ° ′ ″	ΔMag.	Dur. s	Path
Mar.17	03:31	3200 Phaethon	TYC 1219-01612-1	10.1	02 32 41.3	+18 16 41	7.4	0.27	BC-KY
Apr. 9	08:43	99942 Apophis	TYC 5782-01139-1	8.5	21 02 38.3	–14 07 51	11.8	0.02	MS-SC
Apr.26	04:57	163693 Atira	TYC 3769-00890-1	10.8	06 37 06.1	+54 57 57	7.3	0.11	CA-Baja
Apr.30	00:24	163693 Atira	TYC 3771-01267-1	10.3	06 56 27.8	+54 55 53	7.9	0.11	ON-NY
Aug.16	08:36	3122 Florence	TYC 2463-00303-1	9.9	07 12 22.4	+37 22 46	7.4	0.11	FL-NL
Sep. 3	10:44	65803 Didymos	TYC 6989-00024-1	10.4	00 11 53.9	–30 58 01	4.8	0.19	Baja-GA
Oct. 3	10:49	3200 Phaethon	TYC 3312-02354-1	11.4	03 26 00.4	+46 18 30	6.3	0.29	Cuba-Baja
Oct. 9	01:58	3200 Phaethon	TYC 3310-01992-1	10.7	03 10 44.9	+46 16 50	6.8	0.26	MB-Baja
Oct.15	07:05	65803 Didymos	UCAC4 395-013761	10.4	06 28 25.0	–11 02 05	4.9	0.16	AZ-ON
Oct.18	00:30	3200 Phaethon	UCAC4 678-015381	10.8	02 43 32.7	+45 31 21	6.6	0.23	NL-Cuba
Oct.21	10:13	65803 Didymos	TYC 4818-00021-1	9.3	07 04 46.4	–03 41 43	6.3	0.18	BC
Nov. 6	07:14	65803 Didymos	TYC 0780-01085-1	10.4	07 59 40.9	+09 07 48	5.7	0.27	DR-NL
Nov. 8	10:44	65803 Didymos	TYC 0785-01766-1	10.5	08 04 12.1	+10 23 02	5.6	0.28	Mex-ON
Nov.10	05:34	3200 Phaethon	UCAC4 647-005831	11.8	01 35 45.5	+39 21 32	5.6	0.22	AB-WA
Nov.14	10:32	65803 Didymos	TYC 0806-00754-1	10.2	08 14 07.4	+13 30 54	6.0	0.33	FL-NL
Nov.16	07:59	65803 Didymos	HIP 40525	9.3	08 16 30.0	+14 24 43	6.9	0.34	DR-NL
Nov.26	07:39	1866 Sisyphus	TYC 3020-00440-1	11.5	12 29 18.8	+41 51 25	5.8	0.29	Mex-ON
Dec.29	06:46	65803 Didymos	UCAC4 595-042049	10.6	07 48 47.5	+28 55 57	5.8	0.25	Cuba-Baja

FIGURE 3–2022 OCCULTATIONS BY TROJAN ASTEROIDS

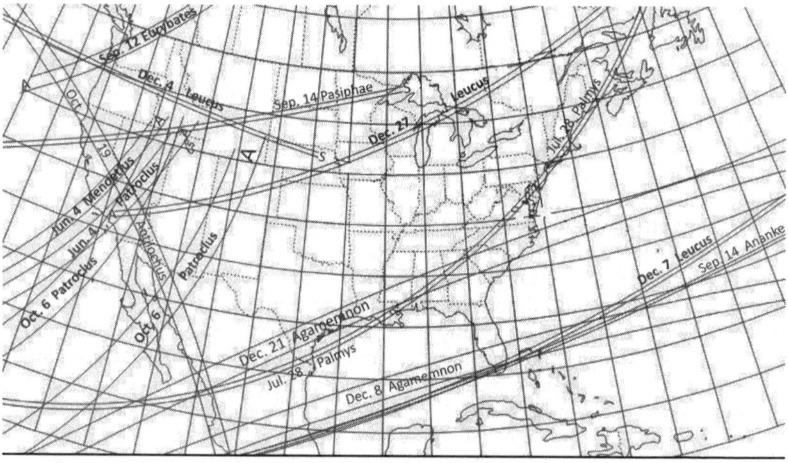

Occultations by Trojan Asteroids

See more about the 2022 Trojan occultations, including predictions for more such events, at occultations.org/publications/rasc/2022/nam22Trojanoccs.htm. Special interactive *Google* maps and other details for the SwRI campaign events is at lucy.swri.edu/occultations.html. Similar information is given for the other occultations at the Lucky Star prediction website at lesia.obspm.fr/lucky-star/predictions.php. It's worth checking these websites a week or two before an occultation that you might observe, since both SwRI and Lucky Star update their predictions with the help of earlier occultation observations, which can shift the paths substantially from what we show on the map.

Information about some of the occulting NEAs portrayed in the foregoing figure and the table below follows:

(617) Patroclus: Patroclus is about 113 km across, but its large (104 km) moon Menoetius is almost as large, so this is a binary pair with a separation of about 680 km in a nearly circular orbit, which is known well enough that we can predict separate paths for the two components.

(911) Agamemnon: This is not a Lucy target, but it is the second- or third-largest Trojan asteroid. A 2012 occultation showed a size of about 160 km, but more well-observed events are sought to better determine its size and shape. The 2021 occultation also revealed a satellite, some 10 km across with a projected separation of 278 km.

(3548) Eurybates: It has a small moon, Queta, only about a kilometre across, discovered by *Hubble Space Telescope* images taken in 2018. Queta orbits about 2310 km from Eurybates in a nearly circular orbit. Eurybates is also the main object of one of the few Trojan asteroid families, with 218 known members of carbonaceous and/or primitive composition.

Ananke and **Pasiphae** are not Trojan asteroids, but are small irregular moons of Jupiter, XII and VIII, respectively. Since they are also at Jupiter's distance, they are included in this section. As part of the Lucky Star Project, astronomers in Brazil are especially interested in these intriguing objects. Their occultation paths are very uncertain, but they may be improved before the events.

TABLE 3–2022 OCCULTATIONS BY TROJAN ASTEROIDS

Date	UT	Occulting Body	Star	Mag.	RA (2000) h m s	Dec ° ′ ″	ΔMag.	Dur. s	Path
Jun. 4	**09:27**	**Menoetius**	**TYC 7927-01558-1**	**9.8**	**18 40 22.5**	**–43 52 22**	**5.4**	**8.6**	**ID-CA**
Jun. 4	**09:27**	**617 Patroclus**	**TYC 7927-01558-1**	**9.8**	**18 40 22.5**	**–43 52 22**	**5.4**	**8.6**	**ID-CA**
Jul. 28	04:24	58931 Palmys	UCAC4 354-171572	12.5	19 14 13.5	–19 12 24	5.9	1.9	NL-Mex.
Sep. 12	**08:21**	**3548 Eurybates**	**UCAC4 593-034505**	**11.7**	**06 40 09.9**	**+28 26 55**	**5.7**	**2.9**	**OR-SK**
Sep. 14	09:28	Ananke	TYC 0002-99865-1	11.9	00 16 45.7	+00 58 28	6.8	1.6	FL-Mex.
Sep. 14	11:10	Pasiphae	TYC 4664-00887-1	12.0	00 16 15.8	–00 10 10	4.8	3.1	MN-CA
Oct. 6	**02:12**	**617 Patroclus**	**UCAC4 238-151066**	**12.7**	**18 10 36.3**	**–42 30 12**	**3.2**	**6.7**	**CA-ID**
Oct. 6	**02:12**	**Menoetius**	**UCAC4 238-151066**	**12.7**	**18 10 36.3**	**–42 30 12**	**3.2**	**6.7**	**Baja-WY**
Oct. 19	09:19	1583 Antilochus	UCAC4 451-019854	12.8	06 35 39.2	+00 00 37	3.4	7.0	CA-Mex.
Dec. 4	**12:57**	**11351 Leucus**	**UCAC4 539-029629**	**13.6**	**06 36 16.2**	**+17 43 01**	**4.4**	**2.5**	**NE-OR**
Dec. 8	05:09	911 Agamemnon	TYC 3352-01794-1	11.0	04 57 05.5	+49 23 42	3.9	9.6	FL-Mex.
Dec. 21	04:44	911 Agamemnon	UCAC4 695-031299	12.5	04 46 47.3	+48 57 21	2.6	9.7	NC-Mex.
Dec. 27	**01:07**	**11351 Leucus**	**UCAC4 537-026171**	**13.2**	**06 24 01.9**	**+17 18 08**	**4.4**	**2.1**	**NL-CA**

On 2021 May 19, Peter Nosworthy and Dave Gault, observing from their observatories west of Sydney, NSW, Australia, both recorded two occultations of a 13.6-mag. star in Sagittarius by the asteroid (4337) Arecibo, discovering a moon of the asteroid. On 2021 Jun. 9, Richard Nolthenius and Kirk Bender observed another occultation, of a 12th-mag. star, by Arecibo with portable telescopes in central California, USA, confirming the satellite and showing that it was 13.5 km across, just over half the size of Arecibo, which Dave Herald's analysis of the observations found to be 24.4 km across. More information about these observations can be found at www.hazelbrookobservatory.com/4337arecibo/?pg=campaigns.

Discovery and confirmation of the satellite of (4337) Arecibo, 2021

Discovery by Peter Nosworthy & Dave Gault, May 19, west of Sydney, NSW, Australia
Confirmation by Richard Nolthenius and Kirk Bender, June 9, central California, USA

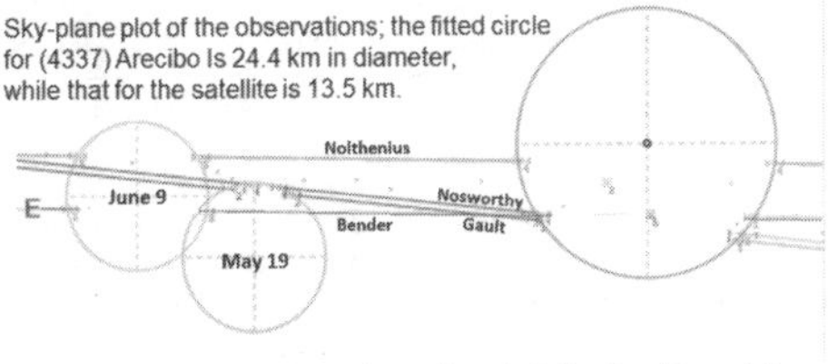

For a good account of these observations, including the videos, visit www.youtube.com/watch?v=w_Cc5Or1FFw
Diagram by Dave Herald using the Occult4 program.

Occultations by Special Main-Belt Asteroids

The map, and the corresponding table below, similar to those of the previous subsections, shows the paths for occultations of a selected group of Main-Belt asteroids that will be occulted in 2022. These are objects that have unusual shapes, or known or suspected significant moons, for which new observations will be valuable to better characterize them. More about these events, including information about the asteroid size, and the elongations of the event from the Sun and Moon, is available at occultations.org/publications/rasc/2022/nam22MBspecialoccs.htm. With fewer objects than considered in the previous section, occultations of fainter stars had to be considered, so these usually require larger telescopes to observe. But three of the stars are relatively bright, one almost reaching the bright Main Belt list. Information about these objects is given below:

(90) Antiope: This is a binary asteroid, with each component just under 90 km across.

(216) Kleopatra: This is the "Dog-bone" asteroid, the 2nd-largest M-class (metallic) asteroid, and has two small moons.

(762) Pulcova: Pulcova is 137 km across and has a 15-km moon orbiting 800 km away with a 4-day period.

(2258) Viipuri: Viipuri, 26 km across, may have a 5+ km moon with events recorded in 2013 and 2018 occultations.

(4552) Nabelek: This was thought to be 6 km across, but a recent paper argues that it is much larger, about 20 km.

(33074) 1997 WP21: This object, 18 km across, may have a 9-km moon with events recorded in a 2021 occultation.

FIGURE 4—OCCULTATIONS BY SPECIAL MAIN-BELT ASTEROIDS

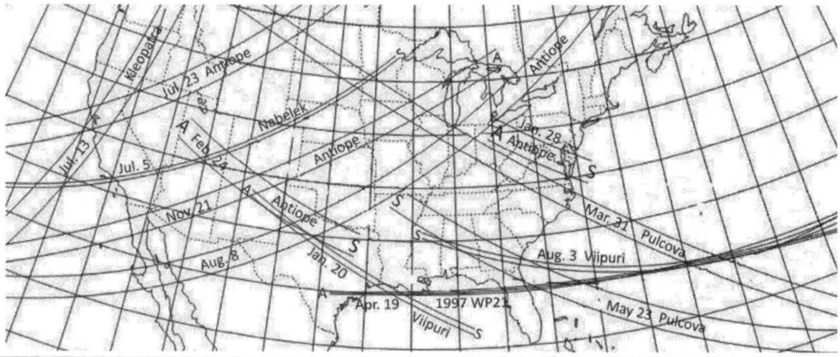

TABLE 4–2022 OCCULTATIONS BY SPECIAL MAIN-BELT ASTEROIDS

Date	UT	Occulting Body	Star	Mag.	RA (2000) h m s	Dec ° ′ ″	ΔMag.	Dur. s	Path
Jan 20	12:12	2258 Viipuri	Gaia 174049.8-241757	13.3	17 40 49.8	-24 17 57	4.5	0.9	NM-LA
Jan 28	11:24	90 Antiope	UCAC4 332-153057	13.4	18 22 39.7	-23 45 24	1.0	2.7	OH-VA
Feb 24	12:12	90 Antiope	UCAC4 335-198707	12.4	19 10 13.1	-23 06 02	1.7	3.1	UT-TX
Mar 31	01:18	762 Pulcova	UCAC4 562-038652	13.3	07 07 47.8	+22 19 58	0.8	9.9	IL-NC
Apr 19	01:46	33074 1997 WP21	UCAC4 467-051017	13.2	15 14 00.3	+03 13 51	4.2	1.4	FL-TX
May23	02:06	762 Pulcova	TYC 1380-01148-1	10.1	08 05 48.2	+17 48 11	3.7	4.3	AR-FL
Jul 5	09:47	4552 Nabelek	TYC 0637-00163-1	11.3	02 21 21.5	+14 47 33	6.8	0.2	CA-MN
Jul 13	09:10	216 Kleopatra	UCAC4 512-137831	14.0	23 09 46.6	+12 22 20	0.1	17.2	CA-AB
Jul 23	09:54	90 Antiope	UCAC4 347-187017	13.9	20 52 47.1	-20 38 05	0.1	13.2	ON-CA
Aug 3	01:34	2258 Viipuri	UCAC4 334-192515	13.3	18 56 14.7	-23 23 06	3.2	2.8	GA-AL
Aug 8	07:22	90 Antiope	TYC 6343-01777-1	9.2	20 40 17.3	-21 34 20	2.6	13.1	NL-Baja
Nov21	03:10	90 Antiope	TYC 6351-01431-1	10.0	21 12 37.3	-18 23 42	3.6	4.6	Baja-ON

Occultations by Distant Solar System Objects

Of special interest are occultations by distant trans-Neptunian and Centaur objects, many of which have moons and some rings. In general, special astrometric observations with large telescopes are needed to predict these occultations well enough for observing campaigns, and these are accomplished usually only a few weeks before the occultation. The few of these events that can be predicted several months in advance are too faint for most amateur telescopes, but an occultation of a 10th-magnitude star by the Centaur object (60558) Echeclus visible from northern Mexico on Jan. 6 is included. The map portrays other events that might be observed with telescope apertures as small as 20 cm and are expected to occur in North America this year. Details of these events will be given on websites of the Paris Observatory Lucky Star Project, the Rio astrometry group, and RECON, the network of observatories in the western USA dedicated to these observations (see tnorecon.net/observation-campaigns).

The map, and the corresponding table, similar to those of the previous subsections, shows the paths for occultations of some of the better distant-object occultations during 2022. More about the occultations, and the objects involved, is available at occultations.org/publications/rasc/2022/nam22distantoccs.htm.

FIGURE 5—OCCULTATIONS BY DISTANT SOLAR SYSTEM OBJECTS

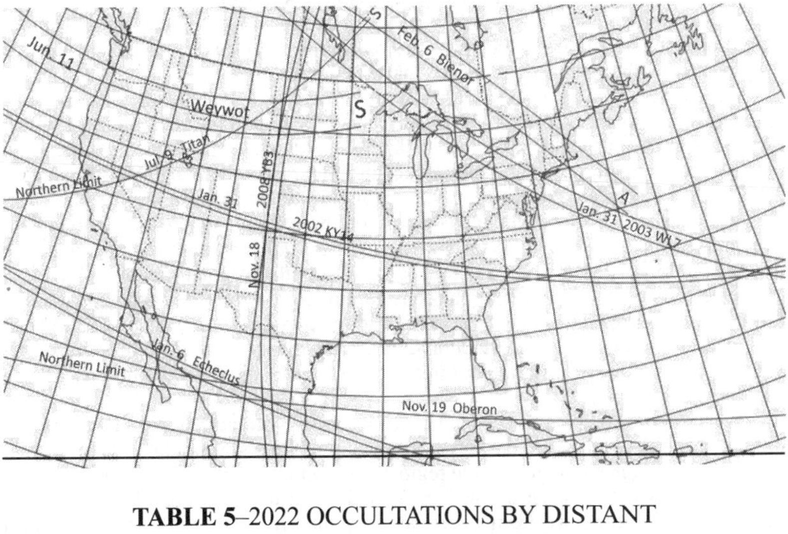

TABLE 5–2022 OCCULTATIONS BY DISTANT SOLAR SYSTEM OBJECTS

Date	UT	Occulting Body	Star	Mag.	RA (2000) h m s	Dec ° ′ ″	ΔMag.	Dur. s	Path
J Jan 6	08:35	60558 Echeclus	TYC 1332-00942-1	9.9	06 29 43.6	+18 39 07	9.7	2.8	Mex-Baja
Jan 31	03:45	250112 2002 KY14	UCAC4 474-035230	13.1	07 38 35.0	+04 44 07	8.2	1.7	SC-CA
Jan 31	09:33	136204 2003 WL7	UCAC4 553-047150	14	10 00 06.4	+20 27 56	7.1	5.4	NJ-AB
Feb 6	08:52	54598 Bienor	UCAC4 670-035234	12.7	05 12 37.6	+43 50 00	6.6	14.6	MA-SK
Jun 11	09:05	Weywot	UCAC4 375-120303	14.4	18 26 06.7	-15 07 47	4.4	6.0	MN-OR
Jul 9	09:22	Titan	HIP 107569	8.7	21 47 10.8	-14 40 59	0.6	326.6	MB-CA
Nov 18	01:58	342842 2008 YB3	UCAC4 651-078239	14.7	19 47 10.1	+40 09 12	6.6	2.2	MB-Mex
Nov 19	08:56	Oberon	HIP 13601	7.2	02 55 17.7	+16 18 32	6.8	75.3	Cuba-BajaN

METEORS, COMETS, AND DUST

METEORS

BY MARGARET CAMPBELL–BROWN AND PETER BROWN

A *meteor* (from the Greek *meteoros*, meaning "high in the air") is the light, heat, ionization, and (occasionally) sound phenomena produced when a solid body (a *meteoroid*) collides with molecules in Earth's upper atmosphere. These collisions heat the surface of the object; then, at a height typically between 120 km and 80 km, the meteoroid begins to ablate, or lose mass. Typically, ablation takes the form of vaporization, although melting and quasicontinuous fragmentation may also contribute. It is these ablated meteoric atoms that collide with air molecules to produce atomic excitations, or ionization, leading to the emission of light we see in the night sky. Typical visual meteors are produced by meteoroids the size of a small pebble, although the relationship between mass, magnitude, and velocity is complex (Figure 1). The faintest meteors visible to the naked eye are due to meteoroids the size of the tip of a ballpoint pen; the brightest meteors are due to meteoroids whose diameters roughly match the thickness of a pen.

Larger and low-velocity meteoroids are favored to pass through Earth's atmosphere, although rarely as a single monolithic body. When these ponderable masses reach the ground, they are called *meteorites*. At the other extreme, very small meteoroids (micrometres in size) efficiently radiate heat from their surface and do not reach ablation temperatures; such particles reach Earth's surface without having been fully ablated, although most are heated many hundreds of degrees.

Meteoroids can be divided broadly into two groups: stream and sporadic meteoroids. *Stream* meteoroids follow similar orbits around the Sun, many of which can be linked to a particular parent object, in most cases a comet. When Earth intersects the orbit of a stream, a meteor shower occurs. Since all the meteoroids in a stream move along nearly identical orbits, their paths in the atmosphere are parallel. This creates a perspective effect: the meteor trails on the celestial sphere appear to radiate from a fixed location, called the meteor *radiant*. *Sporadic* meteoroids, in contrast, are much more loosely associated and are not part of tightly grouped streams.

Meteor showers are named for the constellation from which they appear to radiate. Official rules for naming showers have been adopted by IAU commission #22 and can be found at www.ta3.sk/IAUC22DB/MDC2007/Dokumenty/shower_nomenclature.php. When several showers have radiants in the same constellation, nearby bright stars are used in naming.

The sporadic complex as seen at Earth, however, is structured and shows definite directionalities as well as annual variations in activity levels. Sporadic meteor radiants are concentrated in six major source regions throughout the sky. These sources are in fixed locations with respect to the Sun. Variations in the strengths of these sources throughout the year have been observed; it is the elevation of these sources at a particular location plus the intrinsic strength of each source at a given time of the year that determine the average background sporadic rate. Figure 2 shows the distribution of sporadic radiants in Sun-centered coordinates. The expected sporadic rate varies as a function of the altitude of the apex of Earth's way throughout the year, but is generally in the range of 8–13 meteors per hour for visual observers. The apex is the instantaneous direction of travel of Earth around the Sun; it is the point on the ecliptic that transits at 6:00 local apparent solar time (see p. 40).

In general, meteoroid streams are formed when particles are ejected from comets as they approach the Sun. The parent objects of many showers have been identified from the similarity of the orbits of the object and the stream. Cometary associations include the η-Aquariids and Orionids, which are derived from 1P/Halley; the Leonids, which originate from 55P/Tempel–Tuttle; and the Perseids, from 109P/Swift–Tuttle.

Several minor planets are known to be associated with meteor streams: 3200 Phaethon linked to the Geminid stream and 2003 EH1 linked to the Quadrantid shower are the most prominent examples. All of these particles have orbits that coincide closely with that of the parent object, but their orbits are gradually shifted through radiative effects and planetary perturbations. Such effects lead to a broadening of the stream over time, resulting in an increased duration of the meteor shower as seen from Earth—older streams tend to be more long-lived—and eventually transform stream meteoroids into sporadic meteoroids.

The visual strength of a meteor shower is measured by its Zenithal Hourly Rate (ZHR), defined as the number of meteors a single average observer would see if the radiant were directly overhead and the sky dark and transparent with a limiting stellar magnitude of +6.5 (conditions that are rarely met in reality). A more physical measure is the flux of a meteoroid stream, measured in numbers of meteors of absolute brightness (referenced to a range of 100 km) brighter than +6.5 per square kilometre per second perpendicular to the radiant direction. While an observer will tend to see the largest number of meteors by looking at the shower radiant, the most useful counts are obtained by looking some distance away from the radiant.

Most data on meteor showers are currently gathered visually by amateur observers. It is crucial to observe from a dark-sky location with a clear view of the sky, and to allow at least 20 min before the start of observations to allow dark adaptation of the eyes. One should choose an area of the sky to observe, preferably with an elevation greater than 40°. The limiting magnitude should be carefully recorded for each

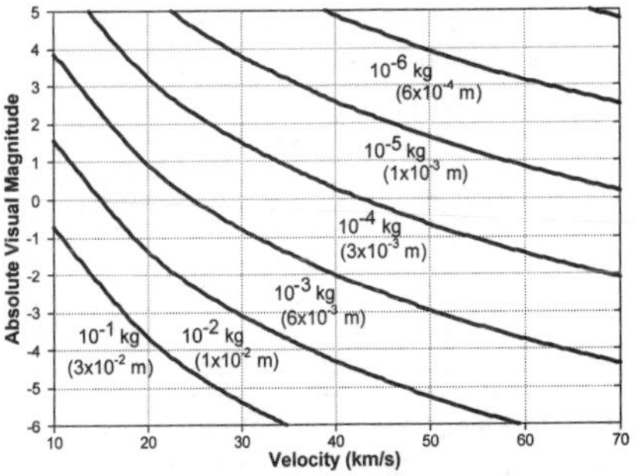

FIGURE 1 *Magnitude as a function of velocity for meteoroids of different sizes. Uncertainties in the mass scale are largest at high velocities and small masses, and may be as large as an order of magnitude in mass at the extremes.*

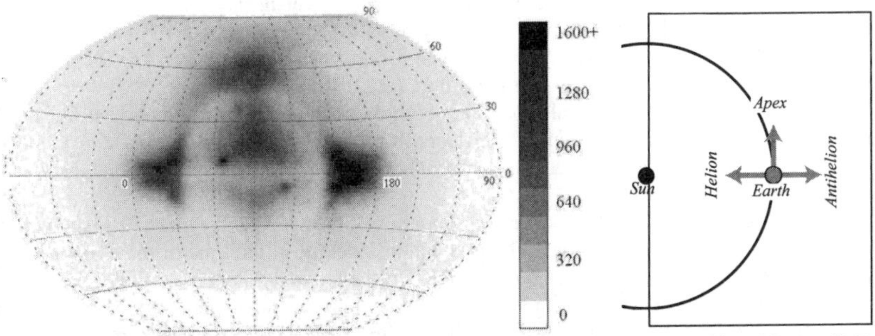

FIGURE 2 *Plot of the radiant distribution of meteors as seen by the Canadian Meteor Orbit Radar throughout the entire year, in Sun-centered ecliptic coordinates. The Sun is at (0,0), the helion, and the Earth's orbital velocity points to the center of the plot, the apex. The antihelion point is at (180,0). The small concentrations visible near the center of the plot are major showers (the Geminids and Eta Aquariids in particular). The intensity of the plot reflects the number of radiants per 2 deg². The rate of sporadic meteors as a function of time depends on which of the sporadic sources are above the horizon at the time of observation. The diagram at right shows the meaning of the coordinate system.*

session, along with the UT and the center of the field of view of the observer. The most basic observations should include an estimate of the brightness of the meteor, the time of observation, and a shower association (based on the radiant and apparent speed of the meteor). Information on collecting and reporting scientifically useful observations can be found at the International Meteor Organization's website, imo.net.

TABLE OF METEOR SHOWERS FOR 2022

The table lists the major visual showers as well as those detectable by radio methods during the day. Of the strongest annual showers, the Moon is favorable for the **Quadrantids**, **η -Aquariids**, **South δ-Aquariids**, and the **Ursids**. A possible outburst of the Tau Herculids (associated with comet 73P/Schwassmann-Wachmann 3) may occur near 5 UT on May 31 and would be visible from central and eastern North America. The Taurid meteor shower may also show enhanced fireball activity between late October and mid-November as the Earth will pass moderately close to the center of the Taurid resonant swarm in 2022.

Shower	Max Date UT	λ 2000	*D*	ZHR	θ $\times10^{-6}$	*R*	Moon %	*r*	RA h m	Dec °	*v* km/s
Quadrantids	Jan. 3 21h	283.16	0.6	120	8.4	✓	2+	2.1	15 20	+49	43
April Lyrids	Apr. 22 18h	32.3	1.3	20	4.6	✓	59–	2.9	18 10	+34	48
η–Aquariids	May 6 8h	45.5	5	60	6.4	>03	25+	2.4	22 30	−2	66
S δ–Aquariids	Jul. 29 10h	126	8	20	6.2	>23	1+	3.2	22 44	−16	43
Perseids	Aug. 13 1h	140.0	2	90	6.0	✓	98–	2.1	3 08	+58	60
Orionids	Oct. 21 18h	208	2	20	2.2	>23	15–	2.4	6 20	+16	67
S Taurids	Nov. 5 18h	223	15	10	1.0	✓	92+	2.3	3 34	+14	31
N Taurids	Nov. 12 18h	230	15	15	1.4	✓	83–	2.3	4 00	+22	30
Leonids	Nov. 18 0h	235.3	1	20	1.9	>00	36–	2.5	10 12	+22	71
Geminids	Dec. 14 13h	262.2	1	120	11.0	✓	68–	2.3	7 28	+33	36
Ursids	Dec. 22 22h	270.7	0.5	10	2.2	✓	1–	3.0	14 36	+75	35
S D ω–Cetids	May 6 21h	46	20	≈20	—	day	—	—	1 24	−6	36
N D ω–Cetids	May 9 23h	49	30	≈20	—	day	—	—	0 47	+19	36
D ζ–Perseids	Jun. 4 23h	74	19	≈25	—	day	—	—	3 47	+23	29
D Arietids	Jun. 9 16h	78.5	16	≈45	—	day	—	2.1	2 52	+26	41
D β–Taurids	Jun. 25 22h	94	9	≈20	—	day	—	—	5 31	+20	29
D Sextantids	Sep. 29 12h	186	12	≈20	—	day	—	—	10 17	−1	33

The column **Max Date** lists the date and hour (in Universal Time) when Earth intersects the densest part of the stream, based on the solar longitude λ (J2000.0) given in the third column.

The fourth column, ***D***, gives the duration of the shower in days, which is the total number of days for which the activity level is over half the maximum activity.

The **ZHR**, or Zenithal Hourly Rate, is given for the peak of the shower. The **θ** column gives the meteoroid flux at the time of maximum (see text for explanation).

The ***R*** column gives the local times for which the radiant is above the horizon for an observer at 45°N latitude (and therefore meteors from the shower are visible); a ✓ symbol indicates that the radiant is up throughout the night hours, while "day" indicates that the shower is not visible at night.

The **Moon** column gives the percent illumination of the Moon at the time of the shower peak (+ for waxing, − for waning). The population index, ***r***, at the time of the maximum is a measure of the size distribution of particles in the stream. A larger *r* value indicates an excess of small particles, while smaller *r* values indicate larger numbers of brighter meteors. A shower with a higher *r* value will therefore suffer more from background light such as moonlight or light pollution. Sporadic meteors at observable visual magnitudes have an *r* value near 3.0.

The **RA** and **Dec** columns show the position in the sky of the radiant at the time of the shower peak. The position of the radiant will vary from these values away from the time of the peak; tables published by IMO in their annual shower calendar provide details of radiant drift. The last column, ***v***, gives the apparent atmospheric speed of the meteors in the shower.

FIREBALLS

BY PHILIP MCCAUSLAND

Fireballs are exceptionally bright meteors (at least mag. −5) that are spectacular enough to light up a wide area and attract public attention. Fireballs can occur as the brightest members of some annual meteor showers, but are more often part of the sporadic meteoroid flux, occurring at any time. The brightest fireballs are sometimes termed bolides, being visible even in daylight.

Fireballs result from the collision of meteoroids ~1 cm or more in diameter with the Earth's atmosphere. Accurate reporting of such events is therefore of great interest for understanding this poorly known impactor population of Solar System material lying in the size range between dust and small asteroids. Fast-moving fireballs are typically destroyed in the upper atmosphere (>50 km altitude). Slower-moving fireballs with initial entry velocities typically <25 km/s can penetrate more deeply into the atmosphere and are capable of delivering meteorites. Reports of these slower type of fireballs are especially useful for assisting meteorite recovery efforts and also critically for understanding the orbit of the object before it arrived on Earth. Excellent recent Canadian examples of meteorite-dropping fireballs with calculated orbits include Tagish Lake (2000), Buzzard Coulee (2008), Grimsby (2009), and Crawford Bay (2017).

Fireball Observation

Systematic observations of fireballs are usually made by instruments in dedicated regional or global networks, using all-sky cameras, radar, and infrasound arrays (see meteor.uwo.ca). More commonly, fireball observations are made by amateur observers and members of the public who are in the right place at the right time! Eyewitness and camera observations (including security cameras or dashcam videos) are valuable and can be reported via the websites given below.

Fireball phenomena may include the development of a trail that persists after the event, the apparent fragmentation of the meteoroid during entry, flaring events, or a terminal burst in brightness, and occasionally reports of simultaneous "sizzling" sound that may be the result of transduced electromagnetic waves from the fireball. Meteorite-dropping fireballs in particular often feature persistence of "embers" after the fireball and a delayed sonic boom. These observations indicate that the meteor likely penetrated into the lower atmosphere (<40 km altitude) and that portions of it may have survived entry to become meteorites. After entry to altitudes <30 km the meteor typically slows down to only 2–3 km/s and fireball phenomena cease; thereafter any surviving fragments drop to the ground on ballistic trajectories over several minutes during a period called dark flight. Such falling objects may sometimes be heard to produce whirring or popping noises by local witnesses within ~1 km of the meteorite fall. Fragments in dark flight can also often be detected in the troposphere by Doppler weather

The brilliant Crawford Bay fireball of 2017 Sep. 5 [UT], widely seen over southern B.C. This dashcam image taken by M. Stevenson shows the fireball and its trail, with the nearly full Moon at right. Meteorites were found beginning 2017 Oct. 29 by researchers from the University of Calgary

radar, which can thus assist in defining the approximate ground locations of the fallen meteorites.

Rapid recovery of freshly fallen meteorites—as well as their careful handling and storage—before they have been exposed much to the terrestrial atmosphere is highly desirable. Fresh recovery allows meteorite researchers to study water-soluble minerals (such as salt), organic phases, and physical properties before terrestrial alteration. Rapid meteorite recovery is also essential for the study of short-lived radioactive isotopes induced by pre-fall exposure to cosmic rays; this information is highly useful for estimating the true pre-fall size of the meteoroid as well as its dynamical history before encountering the Earth.

Fireball reporting

The scientific value of a freshly fallen meteorite is significantly greater when its pre-fall orbit is known. Under favorable circumstances, visual observer data can be used to obtain an atmospheric trajectory, which, coupled with satellite or video observations, can be used to derive a pre-fall orbit.

The main reasons to report the observation of a fireball are: (1) to alert meteor researchers and all-sky camera network operators to the existence of a new event; (2) to add to the global database of observed fireball events; (3) to assist with possible meteorite recovery; (4) to provide trajectory information to help calculate the orbit for a recovered meteorite; (5) to rule out catastrophic events such as airplane crashes and satellite re-entries; and, (6) to help calibrate atmospheric explosions detected by infrasound arrays deployed to monitor the Comprehensive Nuclear Test Ban Treaty.

Sites for reporting fireballs include: United States and Canada (American Meteor Society) fireball.amsmeteors.org/members/imo/report_intro and globally (International Meteor Organization) imo.net/fireball/report. These sites offer smartphone users a fireball reporting app, allowing the user to automatically provide their observing location and indicate their fireball beginning and endpoint observations by phone orientation against the sky. This has proved to be very immediate and useful in recent fireball events and is recommended.

Reports of fireballs seen over Canada can also be sent to the Canadian Fireball Reporting Centre c/o Phil McCausland at pmccausl@uwo.ca. Reports should include the following information (making notes immediately, at least of the precise time, is recommended):

(1) Name and contact information of the observer(s).
(2) Time of occurrence (and uncertainty in this time); an accurate time helps for searching instrumental databases.
(3) Location of the observer at the time the fireball was seen (preferably in precise longitude and latitude).
(4) Beginning and ending points of the fireball, in terms simply of, "Did it pass from right to left, or from left to right?" Ideally, information as either astronomical right ascension and declination or azimuth and degrees elevation above the horizon is useful. Indicate whether the true beginning was observed and whether the ending point was blocked by an object on the horizon.
(5) An estimate of the apparent magnitude; or compare the fireball brightness to that of the Moon. Was the ground lit up? Did the fireball cast shadows?
(6) The duration of the fireball event and the persistent trail (if any).
(7) A qualitative description of the event (e.g. color, flares, fragmentation, dust clouds persisting after the fireball, and sound). If sound was heard, report the time delay between the fireball and the arrival of the sound.
(8) The existence of any video, audio, or photographic records.

METEORITE IDENTIFICATION

BY RICHARD K. HERD AND CHRISTOPHER D.K. HERD

Meteorites are rocks, solid pieces of debris from outer space objects that survive their passage through the atmosphere to reach the surface of a planet or moon. Fossil meteorites are found in ancient Earth strata; others, found at the surface, are recent arrivals or may have lain there for many thousands of years before discovery. Those witnessed to traverse Earth's atmosphere, and recovered based on those observations, are called meteorite *falls*; fewer than 1400 have ever been documented. Those with no record of arrival are meteorite *finds*, when recognized, and are far more numerous. Meteorites are named for where they are found. The Meteoritical Society (Met. Soc.) is the main worldwide organization for meteorite specialists, called *meteoriticists*. It is responsible for approval of new meteorites. Its Nomenclature Committee (meteoritical.org/meteorites/meteorite-names) ensures that new meteorites are named to avoid confusion and ambiguity with existing meteorites, and that type specimens of all new meteorites are preserved in collections accessible to researchers.

Over 75 000 meteorites are known; many more probably exist. Over 45 000 are from Antarctica, over 12 000 are numbered meteorites from the Saharan and Arabian deserts, and about 17 000 (numbered and unnumbered) meteorites worldwide comprise the rest. See: O.R. Norton and L.A. Chitwood, *Field Guide to Meteors and Meteorites*, Springer-Verlag (2008); M. Grady, B. Pratesi, and V.M. Cecchi, *Atlas of Meteorites*, Cambridge University Press (2014); and the *Meteoritical Bulletin* database at: lpi.usra.edu/meteor. The latter allows a rapid search based on meteorite name, country, or any number of qualifiers.

Often there is confusion over when and where meteorites have fallen or have been preserved, and also over what they are and look like, even though websites now provide ready access to meteorite research, photos, and data. All are significantly different from Earth rocks. Samples sent to experts for identification, even by other scientists, are usually "meteorwrongs"—terrestrial rocks or minerals, human-made slag, metals, alloys, or concrete—that rarely resemble meteorites.

Meteorites probably begin as streams of fragments (meteoroids) that are debris from collisions between larger objects. The calculated orbits of several falls intersect the asteroid belt; their ultimate origin in space and time may be elsewhere. Links have been proposed between some types or groups of meteorites and specific asteroids or asteroid types, based on the meteorites' reflectance spectra and density. For example, results from the NASA *Dawn* mission have strengthened a connection between some howardite-eucrite-diogenite (HED) meteorites and minor planet 4 Vesta. New insights into the relationship between meteorites and asteroids are expected once the upcoming NASA *OSIRIS-REx* and JAXA *Hayabusa-2* asteroid sample-return missions are complete. While the exact provenance of most meteorites is uncertain, they are an unparallelled source of information about the Solar System, from its primitive beginnings to its present. Many preserve pre-solar mineral grains made in stars that were part of our local stellar nursery. See: Philipp R. Heck et al., Lifetimes of interstellar dust from cosmic ray exposure ages of presolar silicon carbide, *PNAS 117 (2020), No. 4*, 1884–1889. Decay products of short-lived radionuclides produced in the early Solar System and primordial organic compounds (possibly derived from cold, interstellar, molecular clouds) have been identified, yielding detailed information about the origin of the Solar System and the biological precursors of life.

The diversity of planetary bodies represented by meteorites is unmatched by planetary exploration missions. They are thus invaluable, and represent space exploration "without the commute," providing complementary information to planetary missions, and insights into the overall physical and chemical processes that have acted to form the Sun and its planets and their satellites. With increased space exploration, the current, somewhat arcane, classification schemes will undoubtedly change considerably to realistically reflect planetological contexts, as geological fieldwork provides for Earth rocks. In theory, any rocky Solar System body is a potential source of meteorites already in collections. About 155 meteorites are similar to Apollo samples, and are from the Moon (see curator.jsc.nasa.gov/antmet/lmc/index.cfm and sites.wustl.edu/meteoritesite/lunar-meteorite-information). At least 165 meteorites are derived from Mars (see curator.jsc.nasa.gov/antmet/mmc/index.cfm and imca.cc/mars/martian-meteorites-list.htm). These meteorites, also known as the SNCs (shergottite-nakhlite-chassignite, after their main representatives, Shergotty, Nakhla, and Chassigny), are linked to the Red Planet by trapped gas within them that matches the composition of the unique Martian atmosphere, as measured by the 1976 *Viking* landers. The Martian meteorite of Tissint, Morocco, fell on 2011 Jul. 18, and represents only the 5th Martian meteorite fall and the first one in almost 50 years.

Popular ideas about when and where meteorites fall are connected with the observation of *meteors*, the brief streaks of light produced when high-speed, interplanetary particles enter Earth's upper atmosphere. Sporadic meteors and *meteor showers* do not produce meteorites; their fragile cometary debris fragments are reduced to dust high in the atmosphere. On average, Earth collects over 100 tonnes of cosmic debris per day; about 10% (mainly micrometeorites and sufficiently small and low density dust particles) are infalls without vaporization, without atmospheric excitation, and without alteration to particle interiors. See: Jon Larsen, *In Search of Stardust,* Voyageur Press (2017), and Hope A. Ishii et al., Terrestrial Recovery of Extraterrestrial Materials, NASEM *Planetary Science Decadal Survey* (2020), 2023–2032 (white paper). In contrast, stronger, larger space rocks can survive a fiery passage through the atmosphere and result in meteorites. These first appear as bright *fireballs*, are slowed to terminal speeds by atmospheric friction, and cease to show a bright trail long before they reach Earth's surface. Fireballs, which may seem very close, are usually quite high in the atmosphere, 50 km or more from the observer. Even if an extraterrestrial object does reach the surface, it is likely to plunge into the 70% that is water or to be lost among forests, jungles, or mountainous regions. In only uncommonly recorded cases have meteorites struck or landed within a few metres of humans (see C.E. Spratt, Possible Hazards of Meteorite Falls, *JRASC, 85* (1991), p. 263); the Chelyabinsk event of 2013 Feb. 15 is a rare case where the shock wave from the object's atmospheric entry caused widespread injuries. Rare meteoroids of masses exceeding many thousands of tonnes that are not slowed appreciably by Earth's atmosphere produce impact craters. Large impacts may have dramatically altered the history of life on our planet, but they do not result in meteorites—the kinetic energy is sufficiently high to vaporize the impacting body completely and to deform and melt the target area in seconds. Crater diameters are typically more than ten times the diameter of the impacting body. Glassy *tektites* found scattered over several continents may be evidence of such impacts, but they do not have meteorite compositions or characteristics, instead reflecting the composition of the target materials struck by the meteoroid.

Meteorites are divided into three groups that vary widely both in appearance and properties: *stones* or *stony meteorites*, *stony-irons*, and *irons* or *iron meteorites* (known in the past as *aerolites*, *siderolites*, and *siderites*, respectively). All usually contain metallic nickel-iron compounds (with traces of other metals) and are mildly to strongly magnetic, depending on the amount of nickel-iron relative to other minerals. Those that have lain on Earth's surface for long periods may be rusted almost beyond recognition; some require laboratory tests to confirm their identity. Specimens generally have a quite soft, dull black to brown fusion crust formed by friction during atmospheric passage; more prevalent on stones and stony-irons, the crust may have partially flaked off or been weathered away. Meteorites only rarely contain bubble-like cavities; they are never almost perfectly spherical and smooth. During atmospheric entry, only their surface is affected. Surfaces of irons and stony –irons are dimpled rather than bulbous. They rust easily so there may be no bright metal showing. Stony meteorites do not show protuberances; weathered varieties are rusty, even on broken surfaces. Fresh stony meteorites may have a whitish "concrete –like" rock interior, with bright metal specks. Their crusts are black or smoky grey, varying from quite glassy to dull; telltale lines and bubbled patches orient their flight through the air. More metallic samples may have a shield-like shape, as a result of aerodynamic sculpting, and may therefore also be oriented.

Stones are the most abundant; they resemble some terrestrial rocks but are denser. Most (called *chondrites*) consist mainly of complexly enigmatic spheroids of silicate minerals (*chondrules*), visible on broken, cut, or polished surfaces, agglomerated with matrix, other silicate inclusions, and scattered grains of metal. See *Chondrules* edited by Sara S. Russell et al. Cambridge University Press, 2018. The oldest, most primitive, and least altered meteorites are found among the chondrites. Rare stony meteorites without chondrules are called *achondrites*; these are thought to be melt products from chondrites, or samples of younger volcanic planetary surfaces. In August 1996, NASA scientists announced the discovery of fossil and chemical evidence of bacterial life in the Allan Hills 84001 meteorite—an ancient achondrite from Mars. Most scientists disagree that the weight of evidence points to ancient life on Mars; however, the rock retains evidence of the conditions necessary for life in the form of minerals precipitated by warm water. This controversy has resulted in renewed interest in missions to Mars and in finding water and life on Mars and elsewhere, even in extreme conditions on Earth, and has contributed to current plans to collect samples of Mars with the NASA *Perseverance* rover for eventual return to Earth. Irons and stony-irons are dense, with up to equal amounts of silicates and iron. Most irons are thought to be core material of planetary bodies formed by melting chondrites, whereas stony-irons (in particular the *pallasites*) may be samples of the core-mantle boundary of such planetary bodies.

Rare *carbonaceous chondrites* are grey to black, some resembling charcoal with silicate inclusions. The dark color is from iron oxides and sulphides. They contain a few percent carbon in very fine-grained carbonates, carbides, graphite, diamonds, and primitive organic molecules. They may have had biologically important roles in providing seeds for the origin of life; recent significant insights into this process have come from study of the unique Tagish Lake meteorite. The study of these samples, along with interplanetary dust particles and samples of Comet Wild 2 from the NASA *Stardust* mission, has become important in deciphering the origins of meteorites and, therefore, of the Solar System and everything in it. We are all composed of recycled stardust.

Expertise in meteorite identification and classification exists at several government and university institutions, and museums. If a suspected meteorite passes initial criteria, such as magnetic character, presence of a fusion crust, etc., digital photos are typically requested for follow-up. Further examination and any analysis may be negotiated with the expert, but an expert opinion is usually free of charge. Experts can assist in enabling classification of any new meteorite: anyone who has found a meteorite should consult meteoritical.org/meteorites/meteorite-names for the Met. Soc. guidelines to ensure that the proper name is assigned and that all other requirements are followed. Collectors, meteorite enthusiasts, and experts alike should be aware of local, regional, and national laws regarding meteorite collection and ownership. In some cases (e.g. Canada), meteorites may not be exported from the country without a permit.

METEORITE IMPACT CRATERS OF NORTH AMERICA

BY JOHN SPRAY

Earth has endured the hypervelocity impact of planetary bodies since its inception 4.6 billion years ago, as has every other planet in the Solar System. However, in contrast to the Moon, Mercury, Mars, many minor planets, and some satellites of the gas giants, the Earth shows relatively few impact craters on its surface. Currently, 195 are proven; see the Earth Impact Database (2018) at passc.net/EarthImpactDatabase.

The Moon's surface is saturated with craters, as is Mercury's, and over 42 000 craters have been named on Mars. Our planet's inventory is limited because Earth (like Venus) is an active planet. This means that most craters have been destroyed or buried due to plate tectonics, volcanic activity, or weathering. The interiors of the large gas planets (Jupiter, Saturn, Uranus, Neptune) are obscured, so we see no direct evidence of cratering—if there are indeed stable, solid surfaces on these planets.

Of the 195 known terrestrial craters, 61 occur in North America (see the following table), 31 of which are in Canada, 29 in the United States, and 1 in Mexico (see the map on p. 263). This total represents about one-third of the world inventory. North American craters range in diameter from as small as 36 m for the Whitecourt crater (Alberta), up to ~150 km for Chicxulub (Mexico). The principal criteria for determining if a geological feature is an impact structure formed by the hypervelocity impact of a meteorite or comet are listed below. Criteria are divided into megascopic (a bird's-eye/satellite scale), macroscopic (can be seen with the human eye), and microscopic (requiring a microscope):

1. Presence of *shatter cones* (conical-shaped fracture systems) that are in situ (macroscopic evidence);

2. Presence of multiple *planar deformation features* (PDFs) in minerals within in-situ rocks (microscopic evidence);

3. Presence of *high-pressure mineral polymorphs* within in-situ rocks (microscopic evidence, requiring proof via X-ray diffraction, etc.). Examples include the high-pressure polymorphs of SiO2 (e.g. stishovite);

4. *Morphometry*. On some planetary bodies, such as the Moon and Mars, we rely on the shape of the impact structure to determine its presence and type. This is a megascopic quality (i.e. too big to be seen by the unaided human eye, thus requiring remote sensing). On Earth, recognizing impact structures solely by their morphometry can be complicated by two factors: (a) weathering, erosion, burial processes, and tectonic deformation; and (b) certain terrestrial features having comparable shape (e.g. volcanoes, salt diapirs, glacial landforms), such that a circular structure alone is insufficient to claim impact-structure status;

5. Presence of an impact-generated *melt sheet* and/or *dikes*, and impact-melt *breccias* that were generated by hypervelocity impact (macroscopic). Melt sheets may be overlain by so-called fallback breccias, and material blasted out of the crater may form ejecta blankets around the original central cavity. For large impact events, ejecta can be distributed globally (e.g. Chicxulub);

6. *Pseudotachylyte* is a rock generated by frictional melting at the macroscopic scale. Some pseudotachylytes are associated with seismic faulting (earthquakes, due to isostatic rebound and plate tectonics), so they are not exclusively impact generated; however, in association with features 1–3 above, they can be contributory criteria.

In terms of relative importance, criteria 1–3 above are definitive, with supportive evidence being added by 4–6. For well-preserved buried structures, as revealed by detailed geophysical techniques (especially seismic data), some workers consider this as strong evidence in favor of an impact origin. Normally, buried craters are verified by drilling and sampling rock for evaluation using criteria 1–3 above.

TABLE OF METEORITE IMPACT CRATERS OF NORTH AMERICA

#	Name, Location	Lat. (N) ° ′	Long. (W) ° ′	Diam.* km	Age† My	Surface Expression	Visible Geologic Features
1	Ames, Oklahoma, USA	36 15	98 12	16	470. (30)	buried 3 km	none
2	Avak, Alaska, USA	71 15	156 38	12	3.–95	buried 30 m	none
3	Barringer (Meteor), Arizona, USA	35 02	111 01	1.19	0.049 (0.003)	rimmed polygonal crater	fragments of meteorite, highly shocked sandstone
4	Beaverhead, Montana, USA	44 36	113 00	60	~ 600	oval area of crushed sandstone and shatter cones	shatter cones
5	Brent, Ontario	46 05	78 29	3.8	453. (3)	sediment-filled shallow depression	fracturing
6	Calvin, Michigan, USA	41 50	85 57	8.5	450. (10)	buried 400 m	none
7	Carswell, Saskatchewan	58 27	109 30	39	115. (10)	discontinuous circular ridge	shatter cones, breccia, impact melt
8	Charlevoix, Québec	47 32	70 18	54	450. (20)	semicircular trough, central peak	breccia, shatter cones, impact melt
9	Chesapeake Bay, Virginia, USA	37 17	76 01	90	35.5 (0.3)	buried 400–500 m, ring structure	none
10	Chicxulub, Yucatan, Mexico	21 20	89 30	150	64.98 (0.05)	buried 1 km, ring of sink holes	none (related to the K/T mass-extinction event)
11	Clearwater East, Québec	56 05	74 07	26	284. (3)	circular lake	sedimentary float
12	Clearwater West, Québec	56 13	74 30	36	465.	island ring in circular lake	impact melt, breccias
13	Cloud Creek, Wyoming, USA	43 07	106 45	7	190. (30)	buried 1.1 km	none
14	Couture, Québec	60 08	75 20	8	430. (25)	circular lake	breccia float
15	Crooked Creek, Missouri, USA	37 50	91 23	7	320. (80)	oval area of disturbed rocks,	breccia, shatter cones
16	Decaturville, Missouri, USA	37 54	92 43	6	< 300	slightly oval depression shallow marginal depression	breccia, shatter cones
17	Decorah, Iowa, USA	43 18	91 46	5.6	483.–460	very limited, otherwise buried	limited exposure of basin fill
18	Deep Bay, Saskatchewan	56 24	102 59	13	99 (4)	circular bay	sedimentary float
19	Des Plaines, Illinois, USA	42 03	87 52	8	< 280	buried, 15–100 m	none
20	Eagle Butte, Alberta	49 42	110 30	10	< 65	minor structural disturbance	shatter cones
21	Elbow, Saskatchewan	50 59	106 43	8	395. (25)	buried, small mound	none
22	Flynn Creek, Tennessee, USA	36 17	85 40	3.8	360. (20)	sediment-filled shallow depression with small central peak	breccia, shatter cones
23	Glasford, Illinois, USA	40 36	89 47	4	< 430	buried 350 m	none
24	Glover Bluff, Wisconsin, USA	43 58	89 32	8	< 500	disturbed dolomite exposed	shatter cones
25	Gow, Saskatchewan	56 27	104 29	5	< 250	lake and central island	breccia, impact melt
26	Haughton, Nunavut	75 22	89 41	23	39	shallow circular depression	shatter cones, breccia
27	Haviland, Kansas, USA	37 35	99 10	0.015	< 0.001	excavated depression	fragments of meteorite
28	Holleford, Ontario	44 28	76 38	2.35	550. (100)	sediment-filled shallow depression	sedimentary fill
29	Ile Rouleau, Québec	50 41	73 53	4	< 300	island is central peak of submerged structure	shatter cones, breccia dykes
30	Kentland, Indiana, USA	40 45	87 24	13	< 97	central peak exposed in quarries, rest buried	breccia, shatter cones, disturbed rocks

* Approximate, apparent (post-erosion) rim-to-rim diameter, not including concentric features beyond the rim (e.g. both #32 and #53); also, not all craters are circular.
†Numbers in parentheses are uncertainties.

TABLE OF METEORITE IMPACT CRATERS OF NORTH AMERICA (cont.)

#	Name, Location	Lat. (N) ° ′	Long. (W) ° ′	Diam.* km	Age† My	Surface Expression	Visible Geologic Features
31	La Moinerie, Québec	57 26	66 37	8	453. (5)	lake-filled depression	breccia float
32	Manicouagan, Québec	51 23	68 42	80–90	215. (0.2)	circumferential lake, central peak	impact melt, breccia
33	Manson, Iowa, USA	42 35	94 33	35	73.8 (0.3)	none, central elevation buried 30 m	none
34	Maple Creek, Saskatchewan	49 48	109 6	6	< 75	buried, small mound	disturbed rocks
35	Marquez, Texas, USA	31 17	96 18	12.7	58. (2)	circular area of disturbed rock	shatter cones
36	Middlesboro, Kentucky, USA	36 37	83 44	6	< 300	circular depression	disturbed rocks
37	Mistastin, Newfoundland/Labrador	55 53	63 18	28	36.4 (4)	elliptical lake and central island	breccia, impact melt
38	Montagnais, Nova Scotia	42 53	64 13	45	50.5 (0.8)	none, under water (115 m) and sediment	none
39	Newporte, North Dakota, USA	48 58	101 58	3.2	< 500	none, buried 3 km	none
40	Nicholson, NWT	62 40	102 41	12.5	387. (5)	irregular lake with islands	breccia
41	Odessa, Texas, USA	31 45	102 29	0.168	< 0.0635	sediment-filled depression with very slight rim, 4 others buried & smaller	fragments of meteorite
42	Pilot, NWT	60 17	111 01	6	421. (12)	circular lake	fracturing, breccia float
43	Pingualuit, Québec	61 17	73 40	3.44	1.4 (0.1)	rimmed, circular lake	raised rim, impact melt
44	Presqu'ile, Québec	49 43	74 48	24	< 500	none, heavily eroded	shatter cones
45	Red Wing, North Dakota, USA	47 36	103 33	9	200. (25)	none, buried 1.5 km	none
46	Rock Elm, Wisconsin, USA	44 43	92 14	6	< 505	circular rim depression, central dome	shatter cones, breccia
47	Saint Martin, Manitoba	51 47	98 32	40	220. (32)	none, partially buried	impact melt
48	Santa Fe, New Mexico , USA	35 45	105 56	6–13	<1200	deeply eroded, large and extensive shatter cones	breccia, shatter cones
49	Serpent Mound, Ohio, USA	39 02	83 24	8	< 320	circular area of disturbed rock, slight central peak	breccia, shatter cones
50	Sierra Madera, Texas, USA	30 36	102 55	13	< 100	central hills, annular depression, outer ring of hills	breccia, shatter cones
51	Slate Islands, Ontario	48 40	87 00	30	~ 450	islands are central peak of submerged structure	shatter cones, breccia dykes
52	Steen River, Alberta	59 30	117 38	25	141. (4)	none, buried 200 m	none
53	Sudbury, Ontario	46 36	81 11	130	1850. (3)	deformed elliptical basin	breccia, impact melt, shatter cones, breccia dykes
54	Tunnunik, NWT	72 25	113 58	~ 25	130–450	heavily eroded	shatter cones
55	Upheaval Dome, Utah, USA	38 26	109 54	10	< 170	circular area of disturbed rock	breccia dykes
56	Viewfield, Saskatchewan	49 35	103 04	2.5	190. (20)	buried 1 km	none
57	Wanapitei, Ontario	46 45	80 45	7.5	37.2 (1.2)	lake-filled depression	breccia float
58	Wells Creek, Tennessee, USA	36 23	87 40	12	200. (100)	basin with central hill, inner and outer annular valleys, ridges	breccia, shatter cones
59	West Hawk Lake, Manitoba	49 46	95 11	2.44	351. (20)	circular lake	none
60	Wetumpka, Alabama, USA	32 31	86 10	6.5	81. (1.5)	arcuate outer ridge, central depression	breccia
61	Whitecourt, Alberta	54 00	115 36	0.036	<0.0011	sediment-filled circular depression with raised rim obscured by trees	fragments of meteorite

* Approximate, apparent (post-erosion) rim-to-rim diameter, not including concentric features beyond the rim (e.g. both #32 and #53); also, not all craters are circular.
†Numbers in parentheses are uncertainties.

MAP OF NORTH AMERICAN METEORITE IMPACT STRUCTURES

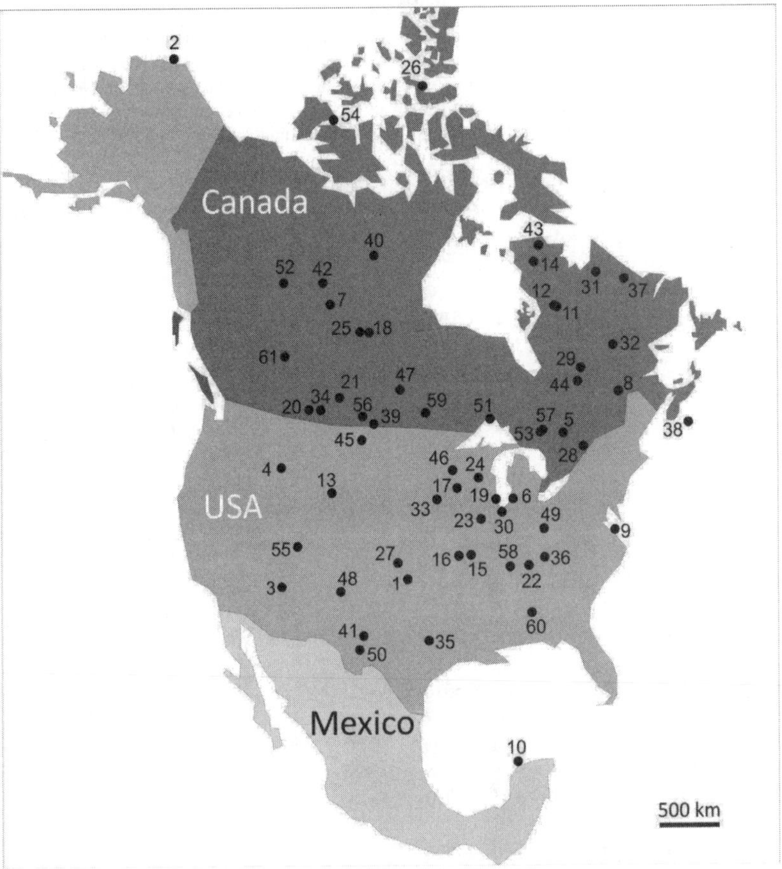

Of the 195 known impact structures identified on Earth, 61 are in North America (31 in Canada, 29 in the United States, and 1 in Mexico). These are shown on the above map; the numbers correspond to the listing in the table on the previous pages. Although the oceans cover ~70% of Earth, only two impact structures have been identified on the seafloor (Mjølnir in the Barents Sea, and #38 off the coast of Nova Scotia). Also, with the exception of structure #53, all were formed within approximately the last 10% of Earth's history. Evidence of many earlier craters has been erased by geological processes. It is possible, however, to calculate a terrestrial cratering rate by focusing only on geologically stable areas of Earth (known as cratons), with low erosion and sedimentation rates. One such area is the North American craton. Calculations indicate that Earth has received at least 10 000 impacts generating craters greater than 20 km in diameter over the last 3.5 billion years. Very early in Earth history, the impactor flux was as high as 100 times the current rate. Some of these impacts had profound influence on the evolution of life on this planet. For example, Chicxulub (#10) is linked to a mass-extinction event 65 million years ago. Some impact craters are the source of considerable economic resources. In North America, hydrocarbons are extracted from #1, 2, 6, 35, 39, 45, 50, 52, 56; #7 produces uranium; #53 is the site of a world-class nickel-copper mining camp.

COMETS IN 2022

BY DANIEL W.E. GREEN AND SYUICHI NAKANO

Listed here are observable periodic comets predicted to return to perihelion in 2022 at about mag. 18 or brighter. In the final column (after the orbital inclination, *i*) is listed a three-letter code based on favorability of the comet's visibility during 2022, with a = favorable, b = ok, c = unfavorable. The precision of the data should allow an ephemeris computation good to about 1′. The angular elements are referred to the ecliptic and mean equinox J2000.0.

Comet	Perihelion Date *T* TT	Perihelion Distance *q* au	Eccen. *e*	Siderial Period *P* a	Arg. Peri. ω °	Asc. Node Ω °	Incl. *i* °	Visi-bility
181P/Shoemaker-Levy	Jan. 8.75	1.1598	0.7006	7.6	336.23	35.41	17.49	c
205P/Giacobini	Jan. 13.46	1.5301	0.5682	6.7	154.19	179.60	15.31	a
152P/Helin-Lawrence	Jan. 13.69	3.0949	0.3086	9.5	163.94	91.86	9.88	a
19P/Borrelly	Feb. 1.83	1.3063	0.6376	6.8	351.92	74.25	29.30	a
P/2015 Q1 (Scotti)	Feb. 13.62	1.8137	0.4777	6.5	199.86	202.85	22.39	a
97P/Metcalf-Brewington	Feb. 15.52	2.5702	0.4599	10.4	229.97	184.08	17.95	a
9P/Tempel	Mar. 4.95	1.5442	0.5091	5.6	179.35	68.71	10.47	a
22P/Kopff	Mar. 18.11	1.5524	0.5488	6.4	163.02	120.83	4.74	a
230P/LINEAR	Mar. 19.33	1.5688	0.5454	6.4	313.43	106.98	15.47	b
P/1997 B1 (Kobayashi)	Mar. 28.81	2.0562	0.7605	25.1	183.32	328.88	12.34	a
325P/Yang-Gao	Mar. 29.18	1.4324	0.5934	6.6	343.70	257.56	16.69	a
135P/Shoemaker-Levy	Apr. 7.35	2.6801	0.2949	7.4	22.32	213.02	6.06	a
274P/Tombaugh-Tenagra	Apr. 8.47	2.4532	0.4393	9.2	38.47	81.34	15.82	a
99P/Kowal	Apr. 12.64	4.7061	0.2292	15.1	174.93	28.10	4.34	a
44P/Reinmuth	Apr. 23.29	2.1127	0.4278	7.1	58.09	286.47	5.90	a
45P/Honda-Mrkos-Pajdusakova	Apr. 26.62	0.5572	0.8175	5.3	327.91	87.70	4.32	c
P/2012 O3 (McNaught)	May 29.71	1.6139	0.6471	9.8	344.75	336.41	16.62	a
117P/Helin-Roman-Alu	Jul. 7.78	3.0396	0.2555	8.2	222.95	58.84	8.70	a
169P/NEAT	Jul. 9.68	0.6028	0.7683	4.2	218.04	176.11	11.30	c
116P/Wild	Jul. 16.93	2.1970	0.3705	6.5	173.29	20.98	3.60	a
119P/Parker-Hartley	Aug. 11.98	2.3275	0.3881	7.4	322.06	104.57	7.39	a
107P/Wilson-Harrington	Aug. 24.66	0.9666	0.6318	4.3	95.44	266.78	2.80	a
73P/Schwassmann-Wachmann	Aug. 25.77	0.9730	0.6853	5.4	199.48	69.61	11.23	a
327P/Van Ness	Sep. 2.41	1.5561	0.5633	6.7	185.03	173.98	36.25	a
157P/Tritton	Sep. 9.82	1.5718	0.5566	6.7	155.06	287.55	12.42	b
51P/Harrington	Oct. 3.89	1.6926	0.5437	7.1	269.25	83.67	5.43	a
408P/Novichonok-Gerke	Oct. 5.04	3.4675	0.2691	10.3	226.45	189.44	19.36	a
P/2007 S1 (Zhao)	Oct. 7.89	2.5246	0.3394	7.5	245.27	141.35	5.96	a
61P/Shajn-Schaldach	Oct. 23.80	2.1258	0.4241	7.1	221.65	162.97	6.00	a
204P/LINEAR-NEAT	Nov. 16.87	1.8344	0.4878	6.8	356.65	108.50	6.60	a
118P/Shoemaker-Levy	Nov. 24.32	1.8290	0.4534	6.1	314.83	142.10	10.09	a
80P/Peters-Hartley	Dec. 8.86	1.6153	0.5986	8.1	339.25	259.80	29.92	c
81P/Wild	Dec. 15.64	1.5984	0.5373	6.4	41.63	136.10	3.24	b

NOTE: For an explanation of these elements, see p. 22; the elements are for an epoch within 20 days of perihelion. Visit the minorplanetcenter.net/iau/Ephemerides/Comets/ site for up-to-date ephemerides. For observers interested in monitoring the brightness of observable comets, visit icq.eps.harvard.edu/CometMags.html for comet magnitude updates. To make personalized finder charts using computer planetarium software, go to minorplanetcenter.net/iau/MPEph/MPEph.html to retrieve downloadable orbital elements in several popular electronic formats.

OBSERVING COMETS

BY DAVID H. LEVY

Each comet has its own unique, changing appearance. Observationally, comets are very much like deep-sky objects. Even in large telescopes, an observer can confuse a comet with a galaxy or a diffuse planetary nebula. Comets near a telescope's limit are virtually impossible to spot without an accurate position extracted from a detailed atlas, such as *Uranometria* or *Millennium*. It is difficult to define a telescope's limiting magnitude for comets, because the more diffuse a comet, the more difficult it is to find. Typically, under a dark sky, a 150-mm telescope will catch a 9th-mag. comet, a 200-mm telescope will see 10th, and a 400-mm should capture a 13th-mag. comet.

If you think you have found a new comet, after confirming the observation, file a *discovery report* according to the procedure in REPORTING OF ASTRONOMICAL DISCOVERIES, p. 7. For more information on comet observing and hunting, read *David Levy's Guide to Observing and Discovering Comets* (Cambridge, 2003).

Magnitude Estimates

The brightness of the coma can be estimated using a variety of methods, the most common of which is the "In-Out" method:

(1) Study the coma until you are familiar with its "average" brightness, an easy process if the coma is of uniform brightness, but rather difficult if there is a strong central condensation.

(2) With the help of a variable-star chart or some source in which star magnitudes are listed, find a comparison star at approximately the same altitude as the comet.

(3) Defocus the star to the size of the in-focus coma.

(4) Compare the star's out-of-focus brightness with that of the coma.

Repeat the last three steps with a second star, or more if needed, until an interpolation can be made.

Physical Characteristics

An estimate of a comet's magnitude is more useful if an estimate of the coma diameter is made at the same time. An observer seeing a $3'$ coma, for example, will estimate much brighter than one who sees only a $1'$ coma at the same time. The simplest way of estimating coma size is to draw the coma with the embedded and surrounding field stars, and then compare the drawing to an atlas, using its scale to determine the size.

A nightly measurement of a comet's degree of condensation is a good way of studying its changing behavior. A comet undergoing an outburst of dust from its nucleus might begin its display by showing almost overnight the development of an increased condensation. Use an integer scale from 0 to 9, where 0 means a diffuse coma with absolutely uniform brightness, 3 means a diffuse coma with gradually increasing brightness toward the center, 6 involves a definite central condensation, and 9 refers to an almost stellar image.

Because of the changing Earth–Sun–comet geometry and the changing activity in a comet, the length and position angle of a tail should be measured. A rough way to measure the length of a tail is to sketch it and compare with a detailed atlas, as with the coma. Observers can also measure the position angle using an atlas and a protractor.

Visual Comet Hunting

The key ingredient to a successful comet search is perseverance, especially in this time of automated searches. The chances for a visual discovery have plummeted in the last few years. Although there are stories of people finding comets very quickly

(Mark Whitaker discovered Comet Whitaker–Thomas 1968 V after three nights of comet hunting), these are the exception. Don Machholz searched for some 1700 hours for each of his first two comets, and I spent more than 917 hours before my first discovery. In contrast, neither Alan Hale nor Tom Bopp was comet hunting when they independently discovered what later became the Great Comet of 1997.

It is important to know the sky well before beginning a comet search program, but it is more important to know the difference between the fuzzy appearances of comets compared to galaxies, nebulae, and clusters. Observing all the objects in THE MESSIER CATALOGUE (see p. 314) provides an excellent education in what these distant objects look like, and observing as many known comets as possible is good preparation for recognizing an interloper. Generally, comets lack the bilateral symmetry of spiral galaxies and the mottled appearance of globular clusters. More important, they usually have unsharp edges, fading off into space so that it is often difficult to tell where the comet ends and the sky begins.

Although most comet hunters still use traditional star atlases to check their suspects, some are moving into a new mode of comet hunting. These hunters have attached encoders to their telescopes that allow an instant reading of the suspect's position in RA and Dec. If the telescope has been properly set up, this approach is faster. However, a sense of the nature of the fuzzy object in the field of view is still important since thousands of nonstellar objects dot the sky.

Comets may appear at any time, but they are usually found within 90° of the Sun. Good areas to search are in the evening western sky during the week after full Moon and in the morning eastern sky before dawn around new Moon. Although comet hunters differ in their approaches to searching, one way is to use an altazimuth mount and make horizontal sweeps. In the western sky, begin near the end of evening twilight at the horizon, sweep across, then return to the point of origin, move upward about half a field of view and sweep again, etc. In the morning, reverse the process.

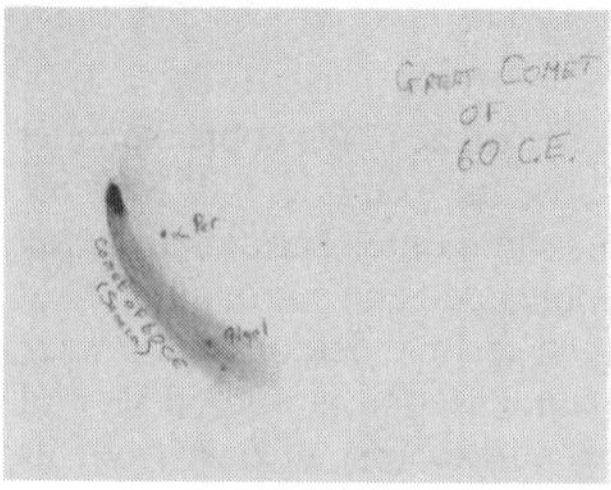

This is a hand-drawn sketch I did of the Comet of 60 CE. This bright comet, which was visible for many weeks that year, appeared some two millennia before the current practice of naming comets was instituted. It is one of the comets that appeared during the reign of Nero. Using a rough orbit, I have sketched how it might have appeared that year as it cruised through Perseus. I have informally named it Comet Seneca or Seneca's comet since he studied it so thoroughly and even suggested that it was responsible for Nero's good fortune. The comet might have been good for Nero but it was not for Seneca, who was forced to commit suicide five years later.

Photographic and Electronic Comet Hunting

While still possible, it is now very difficult to discover comets photographically because the sky is so well covered by the professional surveys. With film and a wide-angle camera like a Schmidt camera, take photographs of selected areas of sky, then repeat these exposures after at least 45 min. Using a stereomicroscope or a blink microscope, it is then possible to spot moving objects. Through a stereomicroscope, the comet will appear to "float" above or "sink" below the stellar background. If a blink microscope is used, the comet will appear to jump back and forth.

Using a CCD, take at least three images of each field, then examine either visually or using a moving-object detection program. Visual inspection is like blinking, so moving objects appear to move steadily through the three pictures, then jump back and begin moving again.

Finally, it is possible to discover comets over the internet. Since images from the *SOHO* spacecraft are made available soon after they are taken, amateur astronomers can scan these images for Sun-grazing comets. RASC member Michael Boschat won the 2001 Ken Chilton Prize for his discoveries of over 50 *SOHO* comets in this way.

Designation of Comets

The International Astronomical Union assigns each comet a unique designation that is similar to, although not identical to, the provisional designation system for minor planets (see minorplanetcenter.net/iau/lists/CometResolution).

The first component of the designation is a letter indicating the comet's status: C/ for a long-period comet, P/ for a periodic comet (defined as having a period of less than 200 years), X/ for a comet for which a reasonable orbit cannot be computed, and D/ for a disappeared comet. Then the year is stated, followed by the *half-month* letter. (The year is sub-divided into half-month intervals beginning with A (the first half of January) and concluding with Y (the last half of December), omitting the letter I.) Thus Comet Hale–Bopp, the first comet to be found in the second part of July 1995, is labeled C/1995 O1. Once the orbit of a periodic comet is well known, that comet receives a permanent number according to the order in which the comet's periodicity was recognized. Comet Halley—the first comet ever recognized to be periodic—is 1P/Halley. Comet Shoemaker–Levy 9, now disappeared, has the designation D/1993 F2, as it was discovered in the second half of March 1993.

Under a previous system, a comet was designated according to its order of discovery or recovery in a given year (e.g. 1982i, Comet Halley, was the ninth comet to appear in 1982). After cometary information was complete for a given year, each comet also received a Roman numeral designation based on the order of perihelion passage (e.g. Halley at its last return was also known as 1986 III). The current designation went into effect in January 1995, but it is retroactive to every previously discovered comet for which a reasonable orbit is available.

When a comet becomes well known, the vast majority of scientists, press, and public ignore the official designation, preferring instead to use more easily remembered names. Our experience with comets Hale–Bopp and Hyakutake (C/1996 B2) shows clearly that people are more comfortable with proper names. However, with two comets named Hyakutake, almost 1500 named *SOHO*, and well over 100 named LINEAR, we need to become familiar with the official designation in order to separate one comet from another (see cbat.eps.harvard.edu/cometnameg).

A handful of comets are named not for their discoverers, but for the persons who computed their orbits. The most famous of these is 1P/Halley, which has been well observed since at least 240 BCE. It was finally identified as a comet appearing every 76 years or so by Edmund Halley in 1705. Two others are 2P/Encke and 27P/Crommelin.

In the event that the cometary nature of an object is established after it was originally given an minor planet designation, the original designation remains. When Gene and Carolyn Shoemaker and I discovered asteroid 1990 UL3 using the Palomar 18-in. telescope, for example, its orbit appeared to be more cometary than asteroidal. A few weeks after discovery, Steve Larson and I took a series of images through the Kuiper 61-in. telescope that clearly showed a tail, and the identification was changed to periodic comet Shoemaker–Levy 2. The mixed designation C/1990 UL3 applies.

Editor's Note: David Levy has discovered 23 comets: 9 by visual searches, 13 photographically at Palomar Observatory under the combined name Shoemaker–Levy, and the latest, co-discovered with Wendee Levy and Tom Glinos, by Hyperion, an automated telescope at Jarnac Observatory (at his home in Arizona): P/2010 E2 (Jarnac).

INTERPLANETARY DUST

BY ROY BISHOP

Outside of the astronomical community it is not generally realized that the inner Solar System contains a vast cloud of dust. As viewed from Earth, the cloud is concentrated within approximately ±10 degrees of the ecliptic. Measurements from spacecraft indicate that the cloud extends well beyond the orbit of Mars, but is negligible in the vicinity of Jupiter's orbit and beyond.

The particles composing the cloud have a continuum of sizes, from pebble-sized clumps down to specks with diameters comparable to the wavelength of visible light and smaller. The smaller particles are the more numerous, although the mass distribution appears to peak near 10^{-8} kg, corresponding to a particle diameter of a few tenths of a millimetre. The total mass of the cloud is small, amounting to perhaps 10^{-14} of the mass of the Solar System. It is as if the satellites of Mars had been pulverized and spread throughout the inner Solar System.

Like the planetary system, the interplanetary dust cloud is not static; its particles generally move in orbits about the Sun. In addition, the particles undergo continual fragmentation due to collisions, sputtering associated with bombardment by the solar wind, electrostatic bursting, and sublimation. This progression toward smaller and smaller sizes is of crucial significance for the cloud, since particles with diameters appreciably less than a tenth of a millimetre have a sufficiently large surface-to-volume ratio that the radiation pressure of sunlight has a significant effect upon their motion—aberration of sunlight results in a small backward force, causing them to slowly spiral inward toward the Sun (the Poynting–Robertson Effect). During a total solar eclipse in 1983, instruments carried by a balloon detected a ringlike concentration of dust only a couple of solar diameters from the Sun. Its inner edge apparently marks the point at which solar heat vaporizes the infalling particles. The resulting tiny gas molecules, like the smallest particles of dust, are blown out of the Solar System by the dominant radiation pressure and interactions with the solar wind.

Because of the above-mentioned influences on the sizes and motions of the dust particles, the estimated mean life of a cloud particle is about 10^4 years. Since that is much less than the age of the Solar System, the cloud must be in a dynamic equilibrium—that is, it must be gaining new material as it loses the old. Both short-period comets and asteroid collisions have been conjectured as supplying the new material, but data from NASA's *Juno* spacecraft obtained during its voyage to Jupiter during 2011–2016 indicate that Mars (!) may be the main source of dust. Mars is subject to planet-wide dust storms, but how that dust might escape Martian gravity is not yet understood (see Jorgensen et al., *J. of Geophysical Research:Planets, 10.1029/2020JE006509*).

To an observer on Earth the most noticeable aspect of the dust cloud is meteors—larger particles of the cloud that encounter Earth at high speeds and vaporize in the upper atmosphere. In addition, sunlight scattered by the dust cloud appears as a faint (fortunately!) glow in the vicinity of the ecliptic. The glow is brightest toward the Sun, is due primarily to particles with diameters between a few micrometres and a millimetre, and is referred to as the *zodiacal light*. A slight brightening in the sky opposite the Sun, called the *gegenschein* (German for "counterglow"), is due to a phase effect (analogous to full Moon) and also, possibly, to a concentration of dust at the L3 Lagrangian point of the Earth–Sun system. The integrated visual magnitude of the dust is about −8.5, making it the brightest Solar System object in the sky after the Sun and Moon. As astronomical objects the zodiacal light and the gegenschein are unusual in that they can be seen only with the unaided eye. Because of their large angular sizes and indistinct borders, both are invisible in binoculars or a telescope.

The Zodiacal Light

Poetic references to the zodiacal light go back several centuries (e.g. see *The Observatory, 108* (1988), p. 181). The 19th-century poet Edward FitzGerald is noted for his translation of the famous poem "Rubaiyat" by the Persian Omar Khayyam. In one of the stanzas Khayyam's reference to the morning was altered by FitzGerald into haunting references to the zodiacal light: "Dreaming when Dawn's Left Hand was in the Sky" (in mid-northern latitudes the zodiacal light and the first glow of the early autumn dawn combine to produce a large, glowing, recumbent, ghostly figure having an upraised left arm); and "Before the phantom of False morning died" (the zodiacal light soon vanishes in the glow of the true dawn).

When conditions are favorable, the zodiacal light is indeed a mysterious and beautiful sight. Because the zodiacal light is brightest nearest the Sun, it is best seen within half an hour following the end of evening twilight and in the half hour prior to the beginning of morning twilight (for times of twilight, see p. 208), and when the ecliptic is at a steep angle relative to the horizon. In the tropics the ecliptic is always at a steep angle to the horizon. In mid-northern latitudes the optimum geometry occurs in the evening western sky in February and March, and in the morning eastern sky in September and October. The zodiacal light appears as a huge, softly radiant pyramid of white light with its base near the horizon and its axis centered on the zodiac (or better, the ecliptic). In its brightest parts it exceeds the luminance of the central Milky Way.

Despite its brightness, most people have not seen the zodiacal light. As mentioned above, certain times of night and year are more favorable than others. In addition, moonlight, haze, or light pollution rule out any chance of seeing this phenomenon. Even with a dark, transparent sky the inexperienced observer may confuse the zodiacal light with twilight and thus ignore it, or may not notice it because he or she is expecting a much smaller object.

The Gegenschein

The zodiacal light extends all around the zodiac with a shallow minimum in brightness some 120° to 150° from the Sun; nevertheless, this "zodiacal band" or "light bridge" is exceedingly faint and is visible only from high-altitude sites having very dark, transparent skies. However, the slight brightening in the vicinity of the antisolar point can be seen from most dark observing sites, provided the air is transparent.

The gegenschein is very faint. Haze, moonlight, bright nearby stars, planets, or light pollution will hide it completely. Most observers, including experienced ones, have not seen it. The gegenschein is sufficiently faint that, except from high-altitude sites with very dark skies, a person will not notice it without making a special effort to *look* for it. It is a ghostly apparition best seen near midnight, and in mid-northern latitudes, in the autumn or winter when the antisolar point is nearest the zenith. To avoid interference from bright stars or the Milky Way, the periods late September to early November and late January to early February are best. At these times the gegenschein is in Pisces and Cancer, respectively. It appears as a faint yet distinct, somewhat elliptical glow perhaps 10° in diameter. The luminance of the gegenschein is about 10^{-4} cd/m^2, some 10 orders of magnitude dimmer than the brightest light the human eye can tolerate.

Don't determine the antisolar point before you look—imagination is too powerful. Find the antisolar point by locating the gegenschein, and *then* check your star charts!

STARS

CONSTELLATIONS—NAMES AND ABBREVIATIONS

Nominative & Pronunciation	Genitive & Pronunciation	Abbr.	Meaning
Andromeda, ăn-drŏm′ē-dȧ	Andromedae, ăn-drŏm′ē-dē′	And	Daughter of Cassiopeia
Antlia, ănt′lĭ-ȧ	Antliae, ănt′lē-ē′	Ant	The Air Pump
Apus, ā′pŭs	Apodis, ăp′ă-dĭs	Aps	Bird of Paradise
Aquarius, ȧ-kwâr′ē-ŭs	Aquarii, ȧ-kwâr′ē-ī′	Aqr	The Water Bearer
Aquila, ȧ-kwĭl′ȧ	Aquilae, ȧ-kwĭl′e	Aql	The Eagle
Ara, ā′rȧ	Arae, ā′rē	Ara	The Altar
Aries, âr′ēz	Arietis, ȧ-rī′ē-tĭs	Ari	The Ram
Auriga, ô-rī′gȧ	Aurigae, ô-rī′jē	Aur	The Charioteer
Boötes, bō-ō′tēz	Boötis, bō-ō′tĭs	Boo	The Herdsman
Caelum, sē′lŭm	Caeli, sē′lī	Cae	The Chisel
Camelopardalis kȧ-mĕl′ō-pȧr′dȧ-lĭs	Camelopardalis kȧ-mĕl′ō-pȧr′dȧ-lĭs	Cam	The Giraffe
Cancer, kăn′sẽr	Cancri, kăn′krē	Cnc	The Crab
Canes Venatici kā′nēz vē-năt′ĭ-chī	Canum Venaticorum kā′nŭm vē-năt′ĭ-kôr′ŭm	CVn	The Hunting Dogs
Canis Major, kā′nĭs mā′jẽr	Canis Majoris, kā′nĭs mā-jôr′ĭs	CMa	The Big Dog
Canis Minor, kā′nĭs mī′nẽr	Canis Minoris, kā′nĭs mī-ñôr′ĭs	CMi	The Little Dog
Capricornus, kăp′rĭ-kôr-nŭs	Capricorni, kăp′rĭ-kôr-nī	Cap	The Goat
Carina, kȧ-rī′-nȧ	Carinae, kȧ-rī′-nē	Car	The Keel
Cassiopeia, kăs′ĭ-ō-pē′yȧ	Cassiopeiae, kăs′ĭ-ō-pē′yē	Cas	The Queen
Centaurus, sĕn-tôr′ŭs	Centauri, sĕn-tôr′ī	Cen	The Centaur
Cepheus, sē′fē-ŭs	Cephei, sē′fē-ī′	Cep	The King
Cetus, sē′tŭs	Ceti, sē′tī	Cet	The Whale
Chamaeleon, kȧ-mē′lē-ŭn	Chamaeleontis, kȧ-mē′lē-ŏn′tĭs	Cha	The Chameleon
Circinus, sûr′sĭ-nŭs	Circini, sûr′sĭ-nī	Cir	The Compasses
Columba, kō-lŭm′bȧ	Columbae, kō-lŭm′bē	Col	The Dove
Coma Berenices kō′mȧ bĕr′ĕ-nī′sēz	Comae Berenices kō′mē bĕr′ĕ-nī′sēz	Com	Berenice's Hair
Corona Australis kō-rō′nȧ ôs-trā′lĭs	Coronae Australis kō-rō′nē ôs-trā′lĭs	CrA	The Southern Crown
Corona Borealis kō-rō′nȧ bôr′ē-ăl′ĭs	Coronae Borealis kō-rō′nē bôr′ē-ăl′ĭs	CrB	The Northern Crown
Corvus, kôr′vŭs	Corvi, kôr′vī	Crv	The Crow
Crater, krā′tẽr	Crateris, krā-tẽr′ĭs	Crt	The Cup
Crux, krŭks	Crucis, kro͞o′sĭs	Cru	The Cross
Cygnus, sĭg′nŭs	Cygni, sĭg′nī	Cyg	The Swan
Delphinus, dĕl-fī′nŭs	Delphini, dĕl-fī′nī	Del	The Dolphin
Dorado, dō-rȧ′dō	Doradus, dō-rȧ′dŭs	Dor	The Swordfish
Draco, drā′kō	Draconis, drā′kō′nĭs	Dra	The Dragon
Equuleus, ē-kwo͞o′lē-ŭs	Equulei, ē-kwo͞o′lē-ī′	Equ	The Little Horse
Eridanus, ē-rĭd′ȧ-nŭs	Eridani, ē-rĭd′ȧ-nī′	Eri	The River
Fornax, fôr′năks	Fornacis, fôr-nās′ĭs	For	The Furnace
Gemini, jĕm′ĭ-nī	Geminorum, jĕm′ĭ-nôr′ŭm	Gem	The Twins
Grus, grŭs	Gruis, gro͞o′ĭs	Gru	The Crane (bird)
Hercules, hûr′kū-lēz	Herculis, hûr′kū-lĭs	Her	The Son of Zeus
Horologium, hŏr′ō-lō′jĭ-ŭm	Horologii, hŏr′ō-lō′jĭ-ī	Hor	The Clock
Hydra, hī′drȧ	Hydrae, hī′drē	Hya	The Water Snake (□)
Hydrus, hī′drŭs	Hydri, hī′drī	Hyi	The Water Snake (□)
Indus, ĭn′dŭs	Indi, ĭn′dī	Ind	The Indian

CONSTELLATIONS—NAMES AND ABBREVIATIONS (continued)

Nominative & Pronunciation	Genitive & Pronunciation	Abbr.	Meaning
Lacerta, lȧ-sûr′tȧ	Lacertae, lȧ-sûr′tē	Lac	The Lizard
Leo, lē′ō	Leonis, lē′ō′nĭs	Leo	The Lion
Leo Minor, lē′ō mī′nẽr	Leonis Minoris lē′ō′nĭs mī-nôr′ĭs	LMi	The Little Lion
Lepus, lē′pŭs	Leporis, lĕp′ôr-ĭs	Lep	The Hare
Libra, lē′brȧ	Librae, lē′brē	Lib	The Balance
Lupus, lo͞o′pŭs	Lupi, lo͞o′pī	Lup	The Wolf
Lynx, lĭnks	Lyncis, lĭn′sĭs	Lyn	The Lynx
Lyra, lī′rȧ	Lyrae, lī′rē	Lyr	The Lyre
Mensa, mĕn′sȧ	Mensae, mĕn′sē	Men	The Table
Microscopium mī′krō-skō′pē-ŭm	Microscopii mī′krō-skō′pē-ī′	Mic	The Microscope
Monoceros, mō-nŏs′ẽr-ŏs	Monocerotis, mō-nŏs′ẽr-ō′tĭs	Mon	The Unicorn
Musca, mŭs′kȧ	Muscae, mŭs′ē	Mus	The Fly
Norma, nôr′mȧ	Normae, nôr′mē	Nor	The Square
Octans, ŏk′tănz	Octantis, ŏk′tăn′tĭs	Oct	The Octant
Ophiuchus, ō′fē-ū′kŭs	Ophiuchi, ō′fē-ū′kī	Oph	The Serpent Bearer
Orion, ō-rī′ŏn	Orionis, ôr′ē-ō′nĭs	Ori	The Hunter
Pavo, pā′vō	Pavonis, pȧ-vō′nĭs	Pav	The Peacock
Pegasus, pĕg′ȧ-sŭs	Pegasi, pĕg′ȧ-sī	Peg	The Winged Horse
Perseus, pûr′sē-ŭs	Persei, pûr′sē-ī′	Per	Rescuer of Andromeda
Phoenix, fē′nĭks	Phoenicis, fē-nī′cĭs	Phe	The Phoenix
Pictor, pĭk′tẽr	Pictoris, pĭk-tor′ĭs	Pic	The Painter
Pisces, pī′sēz	Piscium, pĭsh′ē-ŭm	Psc	The Fishes
Piscis Austrinus, pī′sĭs ôs-trī′nŭs	Piscis Austrini, pī′sĭs ôs-trī′nī	PsA	The Southern Fish
Puppis, pŭp′ĭs	Puppis, pŭp′ĭs	Pup	The Stern
Pyxis, pĭk′sĭs	Pyxidis, pĭk′sĭ-dĭs	Pyx	The Compass
Reticulum, rē-tĭk′-ū-lŭm	Reticuli, rē-tĭk′-ū-lī	Ret	The Reticle
Sagitta, sȧ-jĭt′ȧ	Sagittae, sȧ-jĭt′ē	Sge	The Arrow
Sagittarius, săj′ĭ-târ′ē-ŭs	Sagittarii, săj′ĭ-târ′ē-ī′	Sgr	The Archer
Scorpius, skôr′pē-ŭs	Scorpii, skôr′pē-ī	Sco	The Scorpion
Sculptor, skŭlp′tẽr	Sculptoris, skŭlp′tôr′ĭs	Scl	The Sculptor
Scutum, skū′tŭm	Scuti, sko͞o′tī	Sct	The Shield
Serpens, sûr′pĕnz	Serpentis, sûr-pĕn′tĭs	Ser	The Serpent
Sextans, sĕks′tănz	Sextantis, sĕks-tăn′tĭs	Sex	The Sextant
Taurus, tôr′ŭs	Tauri, tôr′ī	Tau	The Bull
Telescopium tĕl′ȧ-skō′pē-ŭm	Telescopii, tĕl′ȧ-skō′pē-ī	Tel	The Telescope
Triangulum, trī-ăng′gū-lŭm	Trianguli, trī-ăng′gū-lī′	Tri	The Triangle
Triangulum Australe trī-ăng′gū-lŭm ôs-trā′lē	Trianguli Australis trī-ăng′gū-lī′ ôs-trā′lĭs	TrA	The Southern Triangle
Tucana, to͞o-kăn′ȧ	Tucanae, to͞o-kăn′ē	Tuc	The Toucan
Ursa Major, ûr′să mā′jẽr	Ursae Majoris, ûr′sē mȧ-jôr′ĭs	UMa	The Great Bear
Ursa Minor, ûr′să mī′nẽr	Ursae Minoris, ûr′sē mī-nôr′ĭs	UMi	The Little Bear
Vela, vē′lȧ	Velorum, vē-lôr′ŭm	Vel	The Sails
Virgo, vûr′gō	Virginis, vûr′jĭn-ĭs	Vir	The Maiden
Volans, vō′lănz	Volantis, vō-lăn′tĭs	Vol	The Flying Fish
Vulpecula, vŭl-pĕk′ū-lȧ	Vulpeculae, vŭl-pĕk′ū-lē′	Vul	The Fox

ā dāte; ă tăp; â câre; ȧ gȧgȧ; ē wē; ĕ mĕt; ẽ makẽr; ī īce; ĭ bĭt; ō gō; ŏ hŏt; ô ôrb; o͞o mo͞on; ū ūnite; ŭ sŭn; û ûrn.

In terms of area (based on the official IAU boundaries), of the 88 constellations the 3 largest are Hydra (1303 square degrees), Virgo (1294), and Ursa Major (1280); the 3 smallest: Sagitta (80), Equuleus (72), and Crux (68). A complete list of the areas of the constellations appears in the 1972 edition of *The Handbook of the British Astronomical Association*, and was reproduced in the June 1976 issue of *Sky & Telescope* (p. 408).

OPHIUCHUS, THE SERPENT BEARER

BY CHRIS BECKETT & RANDALL ROSENFELD

To the Phantom's back the Crown is near, but by his head mark near at hand the head of Ophiuchus, and then from it you can trace the starlit Ophiuchus himself...but his hands are not at all so bright; for faint runs the gleam of stars along on this side and on that....Both firmly clutch the Serpent, which encircles the waist of Ophiuchus, but he, steadfast with both his feet well set, tramples a huge monster. — Aratus

Southern Ophiuchus is the best Milky Way region for exploring on late spring nights. One of the 48 constellations listed in Ptolemy's Almagest, in classical mythology the Centaur raised Ophiuchus, teaching him to heal, but the snakes on his staff taught him to raise the dead. Rasalhague, α Oph, the "Head of the Serpent Collector," is among the brighter stars in the summer sky. On Ophiuchus's shoulder, Ptolemy lists 66, 67, 68, 70, and 72 Ophiuchi as a distinct pattern, eventually known as Taurus Poniatovii; this defunct summer bull is framed perfectly in binoculars. Small telescopes split 4th-mag. 70 Oph, one of the finest colorful double stars, and a short star hop from 66 Oph is Barnard's Star, discovered by E.E. Barnard as the second-nearest star and one of the fastest moving, but at mag. 9.5 requires patience and a good finder. Barnard's motion against the stars is evident over the 41 years of observation by Rick Huziak. A binocular field northwest is IC 4665, the Summer Beehive, appearing as the terminus of an off-piste branch of the Milky Way and among the best open clusters for wide-field instruments. Farther east in this branch is NGC 6633, discovered by de Chéseaux. This naked-eye cluster curls around a 6th-mag. star in small telescopes and binoculars. Nearby NGC 6572 is one of the best planetary nebulae, shining as an emerald-green 8th-mag. diamond. Large instruments show a couple of nearby 11th-mag. gems in the globular cluster NGC 6426, which appears as a ghost in a 12-inch telescope, while NGC 6384, a rare summer galaxy, requires dark, transparent nights.

Stay up late and observe the "dueling clusters" M14, M10, and M12, which run across the middle of Ophiuchus and combine with M9, M19, M62, and M107 to create a grapevine of globular clusters, all easy targets and showpiece objects in a 12-inch reflector. M10 is a favorite for small scopes, easy to find with well-defined extensions; for larger reflectors, M107 pairs well in the same field with V Oph, a brilliant crimson-red pulsating Mira-type carbon star 1.5° east. Locate this field by star hopping south of ζ Oph, the nearest O-type star, and one of the most famous "runaway stars," having likely been expelled from a double-star system when its more-massive companion exploded. Near ζ Oph is Sharpless 2-27; use a broadband nebular filter in a rich-field telescope to see this huge horseshoe-shaped nebula extending as far as V Oph and looping back up to υ Oph. For an easier challenge, center δ Oph in a low-power field to view a beautiful symmetrical scattering of stars flanking δ Oph.

The most well-known Barnard discoveries are dark nebulae and Ophiuchus is home to many: the Dark Horse Nebula, visible to the unaided eye from dark skies; with binoculars, B59, B78, and B77 form the Pipe Bowl and Stem, while B262, B63, B64, and B268 help fill out the horse. The easiest way to see them is to center θ Oph in your binoculars and sweep southeast. From the best sites, B72, the Snake Nebula, is visible in telescopes as a broken "S" with B44 extending from the forelegs of the horse. B44 is a long, dark filament terminating at 22 Sco. Nearby Rho Ophiuchi is among the best multiple stars, while the ethereal Rho Ophiuchi Nebula, made famous in long-exposure images, is elusive, requiring perfect skies but just 50-mm binoculars to detect. From more southern latitudes, telescopes of all sizes can ferret out many ethereal nebulae in this region.

The above is a selection from this *Observer's Handbook*, which details at least 49 objects worth seeking out in Ophiuchus during 2022.

OPHIUCHUS, THE SERPENT BEARER

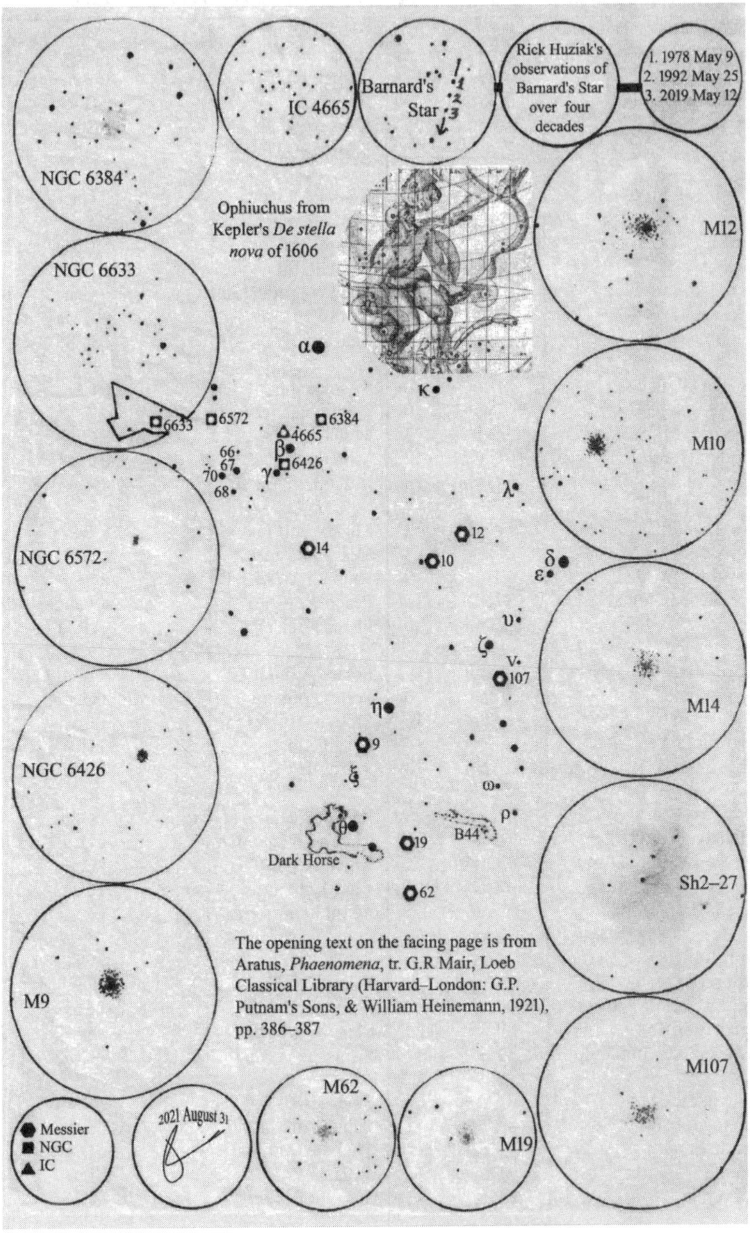

Diagram by Randall Rosenfeld

FINDING LIST OF SOME NAMED STARS

Name & Pronunciation	Con.	RA
Acamar, ā′kȧ-mȧr	θ Eri	2
Achernar, ā′kẽr-nȧr	α Eri	1
Acrux, ā′krŭks	α Cru	12
Adhara, ȧ-dā′rȧ	ε CMa	6
Alnair, ăl-nâr′	α Gru	22
Albireo, ăl-bĭr′ē-ō	β Cyg	19
Alcor, ăl-kôr′	80 UMa	13
Alcyone, ăl-sī′ō-nē	η Tau	3
Aldebaran, ăl-dĕb′ȧ-rȧn	α Tau	4
Alderamin, ăl-dĕr′ȧ-mĭn	α Cep	21
Algieba, ăl-jē′bȧ	γ Leo	10
Algenib, ăl-jē′nĭb	γ Peg	0
Algol, ăl′gŏl	β Per	3
Alioth, ăl′ĭ-ŏth	ε UMa	12
Alkaid, ăl-kād′	η UMa	13
Almach, ăl′măk	γ And	2
Alnilam, ăl-nī′lăm	ε Ori	5
Alphard, ăl′fȧrd	α Hya	9
Alphecca, ăl-fĕk′ȧ	α CrB	15
Alpheratz, ăl-fē′răts	α And	0
Altair, ăl-târ′	α Aql	19
Ankaa, ăn′kȧ	α Phe	0
Antares, ăn-tā′rēs	α Sco	16
Arcturus, ark-tū′rŭs	α Boo	14
Atria, ā′trē-a	α TrA	16
Avior, ă-vē-ôr′	ε Car	8
Bellatrix, bĕ-lā′trĭks	γ Ori	5
Betelgeuse, bĕt′ĕl-jūz	α Ori	5
Canopus, kȧ-nō′pŭs	α Car	6
Capella, kȧp-pĕl′ȧ	α Aur	5
Caph, kăf	β Cas	0
Castor, kȧs′tẽr	α Gem	7
Cor Caroli, kôr kăr′ŏ-lē	α CVn	12
Deneb, dĕn′ĕb	α Cyg	20
Denebola, dĕ-nĕb′ō-la	β Leo	11
Diphda, dĭf′dȧ	β Cet	0
Dubhe, dŭb′ē	α UMa	11
Elnath, ĕl′năth	β Tau	5
Eltanin, ĕl-tā′nĭn	γ Dra	17
Enif, ĕn′ĭf	ε Peg	21
Fomalhaut, fō′măl-ôt	α PsA	22
Gacrux, gȧ′krŭks	γ Cru	12
Gienah, jē′nȧ	γ Crv	12
Hadar, hăd′ar	β Cen	14
Hamal, hăm′al	α Ari	2
Izar, ē′zar	ε Boo	14
Kaus Australis, kôs ôs-trā′lĭs	ε Sgr	18
Kochab, kō′kăb	β UMi	14
Markab, mȧr′kăb	α Peg	23
Megrez, me′grĕz	δ UMa	12
Menkar, mĕn′kȧr	α Cet	3
Menkent, mĕn′kĕnt	θ Cen	14
Merak, mē′răk	β UMa	11
Merope, mĕr′ō-pē	23 Tau	3
Miaplacidus, mē′ȧ-plăs′ĭ-dŭs	β Car	9
Mintaka, mĭn-tȧ′kȧ	δ Ori	5
Mira, mē′rȧ	ο Cet	2
Mirach, mī′răk	β And	1
Mirfak, mir′făk	α Per	3
Mizar, mē′zȧr	ζ UMa	13
Nunki, nŭn′kē	σ Sgr	18
Peacock, pē′kŏk	α Pav	20
Phecda, fĕk′dȧ	γ UMa	11
Polaris, pō-lâr′ĭs	α UMi	2
Pollux, pŏl′ŭks	β Gem	7
Procyon, prō′sĭ-ŏn	α CMi	7
Rasalgethi, rȧs′ăl-jē′thē	α Her	17
Rasalhague, rȧs′ăl-hāg	α Oph	17
Regulus, rĕg′ū-lŭs	α Leo	10
Rigel, rē′gĕl	β Ori	5
Rigil Kentaurus, rē′gĭl kĕn-tô′rŭs	α Cen	14
Sabik, sā′bĭk	η Oph	17
Scheat, shē′ăt	β Peg	23
Schedar, shĕd′ȧr	α Cas	0
Shaula, shô′lȧ	λ Sco	17
Sirius, sĭr′ē-ŭs	α CMa	6
Spica, spē′kȧ	α Vir	13
Suhail, sŭ-hāl′	λ Vel	9
Thuban, tho͞o′ban	α Dra	14
Vega, vey′gȧ	α Lyr	18
Zubenelgenubi, zo͞o-bĕn′ĕl-jĕ-nū′bē	α Lib	14

Key to pronunciation at the foot of p. 271.

THE BRIGHTEST STARS

BY TOOMAS KARMO, CHRIS CORBALLY, AND RICHARD GRAY

This table has the 288 brightest stars (allowing for variability). An extended table-with-essay is in rasc.ca/handbook/supplements. The † symbol flags data further discussed (e.g. with context or caveat) in "Remarks", in most cases only in the extended (online) table. We apply the *Washington Double Star Catalog* naming scheme for multiplicity, both in the case of true binarity and in the case of mere optical doubles. We try to supply a few details, at any rate in the extended table, for binary and mere-optical companions brighter than mag. 10.

Apparent Visual Magnitude (***mV*** **=** ***V***): Apparent magnitudes, with "v" appended for variations ≥ 0.1 mag., are from *HIPPARCOS*. (For variables, these data are occasionally in mild conflict with published magnitude ranges.) Our photometry system follows Johnson and Morgan, *ApJ., 117* (1953), with V corresponding roughly to the response of the eye. The probable error of a V value is at most 0.03.

Color Index (***B*** **–** ***V***): Since B on this system is the brightness of a star through a blue filter, the difference B – V, here taken from *HIPPARCOS*, measures apparent color (as possibly reddened by interstellar dust; although, in general, B – V and spectral type are well correlated). The probable error of a B – V value is at most 0.02.

Spectral Classification (**MK Type**): The "temperature type" (O, B, A, F, G, K, M) is given first, followed by a finer subtype (0–9) and a "luminosity class" (Roman numerals I–V, with "a" or "b" added occasionally to indicate slightly brighter or fainter stars within the class). O stars are hottest, M stars coolest; Ia stars are the most luminous supergiants, III stars are giants, and V stars are dwarfs. (V stars form the largest class in the cosmos, comprising the main sequence.) Other MK symbols include "e" for hydrogen emission; "f " for broad, non-hydrogen emission in hot stars; "m" for strong metallic absorption; "n" or "nn" for unusually broad absorption (a signature of rotation); "p" for peculiarities; "s" for a mixture of broad and sharp lines; and ":" for a minor uncertainty. The types are the best available from Garrison's unpublished spectrograms and the literature. Where a single star (e.g. α CMa A) is given two types (e.g. A0 and A1), with the second type flagged "m", the first is the type that best characterizes the hydrogen lines, the second the type that best characterizes the metal lines.

Parallax (**π**), *Proper Motion* (**μ**), and *Position Angle* (**PA**): Parallaxes, in milliarcseconds (mas), proper-motion vector norms ("/y), and vector position angles (degrees, from N through E) are derived from the *HIPPARCOS* 2007 data reduction, with a few exceptions discussed in the extended table.

Absolute Visual Magnitude (***MV***) and *Distance in Light-Years* (***D***): Absolute magnitudes and distances are determined from parallaxes, except where a colon follows the absolute magnitude; in these cases, both quantities are determined from a calibration of the spectral classification. The absolute magnitude is left uncorrected for interstellar absorption. The appropriate correction is typically ~–0.06 mag. per 100 ly outside the Local Bubble, i.e. beyond ~100 ly.

Radial Velocity (**Vrad**): Radial velocities are from BSC5. "SB" indicates a spectroscopic binary, an unresolved system whose duplicity is revealed by periodic Doppler oscillations in its spectrum and for which an orbit is possibly known. If the lines of both stars are detectable, "SB2" is used; "+" and "–" indicate, respectively, motion away from and toward the observer. "V" indicates a variable velocity in a star not observable as a spectroscopic binary. (In most "V" cases, the orbit is unknown.)

Remarks: Remarks include data on variability and spectra, and particulars on companions which are stars. Our principal source for variability ranges is the AAVSO online database aavso.org/vsx. We follow the IAU rules, as promulgated from 2016 onward, for star names, but adding **boldface** for navigation-star names.

We thank the late Professor Emeritus R.F. Garrison (University of Toronto), lead author of this article for editions 1984 through 2015, for the guidance and encouragement he generously gave to us and the wider RASC family.

TABLE OF BRIGHTEST STARS

Star Name	RA (2022.5) h m	Dec ° ′	m_V	$B-V$	MK Type	π mas	M_V	D ly	μ ″/y	PA °	V_{rad} km/s	Remarks
Sun			−26.75	0.63	G2 V		4.8	8 lm				
α And Aa	0 09.6	+29 13	2.07	−0.04	B9p IV: (HgMn)	34	−0.3	97	0.214	140	−12 SB	Aa,Ab < 0.001″ **Alpheratz**
β Cas A	0 10.4	+59 16	2.28†	0.38	F2 III	60	1.2	55	0.554	109	+12	slight var.: 2.25–2.29 in V, 0.1010 d Caph
γ Peg A	0 14.4	+15 19	2.83†	−0.19	B2 IV	8	−2.6	400	0.009	168	+4 SB	slight var., β Cep type, 2.82–2.86 in V, 0.1518 d Algenib
β Hyi†	0 26.9	−77 08	2.82	0.62	G1 IV	134.1	3.5	24.3	2.243†	82	+23†	possible exoplanet
α Phe	0 27.4	−42 11	2.40	1.08	K0 IIIb	38.5	0.3	~85	0.426	147	+75 SB	**Ankaa**
δ And Aa	0 40.5	+30 59	3.27	1.27	K3 III	~30.9	0.7	106	0.142	126	−7 SB	
α Cas A	0 41.8	+56 40	2.24†	1.17	K0 IIIa	~14.3	−2.0	230	0.060	122	−4 V?	**Schedar**
β Cet	0 44.7	−17 52	2.04	1.02	K0 III†	~33.9	−0.3	96	0.235	82	+13 V?	**Diphda**
η Cas A†	0 50.5	+57 56	3.46	0.59	G0 V†	168	4.6	19.4	1.222	117	+9 SB	B:7.51, K4 Ve, 13.4″, PA:62°→326°, 1779→2019 Achird
γ Cas A†	0 58.1	+60 50	2.15v†	−0.05	B0 IVnpe (shell) †	5	−4.2	600	0.026	98	−7 SB	var.:1.6–3.0 (V); B:10.9, 2.1″, PA:255°→259°, 1888→2002
β Phe AB†	1 07.1	−46 36	3.32	0.88	G8 III + G8 III	16	0.3:	~180	0.088	293	−1	AB similar, 0.6″, PA: 26°→76°, 1891→2018
η Cet A+2P	1 09.7	−10 04	3.46	1.16	K1.5 III CN1†	26.3	0.6	124	0.257	123	+12V	
β And A	1 11.0	+35 44	2.07†	1.58	M0 IIIa†	17	−1.8	200	0.209	123	+3 V	slight var.? (AAVSO(VSX): 2.01–2.10 in V) Mirach
δ Cas A	1 27.3	+60 21	2.66	0.16	A5 IV	32.8	0.2	99	0.301	99	+7 SB	slight var. 2.68–2.76 in V (as ecl.) now discounted? Ruchbah
γ Phe	1 29.3	−43 12	3.41v	1.54	K7 IIIa†	14	−0.9	230	0.209	185	+26 SB	SB period 193.85 d; also var.: 3.39–3.49 in V, 194.1 d
α Eri	1 38.5	−57 07	0.45†	−0.16	B3 Vnpe (shell?) †	23	−2.7	140	0.095	114	+16 V	ecl. slight var.: 0.40–0.46 in Hp, 1.263 d **Achernar**
α Tri A	1 54.4	+29 41	3.42	0.49	F6 IV	52	2.0	63	0.234	177	−13 SB	Mothallah
β Ari A†	1 55.9	+20 55	2.64	0.16	A4 or A5 Va†	56	1.4	59	0.148	138	−2 SB†	β Ari B (mag. 5.2) is SB companion of β Ari A Sheratan
ε Cas	1 56.0	+63 47	3.35	−0.15	B3 IV:pe (shell?) †	8	−2.2	400	0.037	121	−8 V	Segin
α Hyi	1 59.5	−61 28	2.86	0.29	F0n III–IV†	45	1.1	72	0.265	84	+1 V	
γ And A	2 05.3	+42 26	2.10	1.37	K3 IIb†	9	−3.1	400	~0.065	~139	−12 SB	B: 5.0, B9 V, 9.6″ (2019); C: 6.5, A0 V; BC 0.2″ Almach
α Ari +1P	2 08.4	+23 34	2.01†	1.15	K2 IIIab	~49.6	0.5	66	0.240	128	−14 SB	slight slow irreg. variability, 2.00–2.03 in V **Hamal**
β Tri	2 10.9	+35 06	3.00	0.14	A5 IV	26	0.1	130	0.154	105	+10 SB2†	
ο Cet Aa†	2 20.5	−2 53	6.47v†	0.97	M5–10 IIIe†	11†	1.7	300†	0.238	178	+64 V	LPV, 2-10.1; Ab (VZ Cet)WD, 10.4, 0.5″, ~500–600 y Mira†
γ Cet A†	2 44.5	+3 20	3.54	0.09	A2 Va	41	1.5	80	0.207	225	−5 V	B: 6.23, 2.0″, PA:283°→299°, 1825→2015 Kaffaljidhma
θ Eri A	2 59.1	−40 13	3.28	0.17	A5 IV	30	0.5	100	0.057	293	+12 SB2	B: 4.35, A1 Va, 8.2″, PA:82°→90°, 1835→2020 **Acamar**
α UMi Aa†	3 00.7	+89 21	1.97†	0.64	F5–8 Ib	7.5†	−3.6	430†	~0.046	~105?	−17 SB	slight Cep. var, 4.0 d; B: 9.1, F3 V, 18.4″ (2016) **Polaris**
α Cet	3 03.5	+4 11	2.54†	1.63	M2 III†	13	−1.9	250	0.078	188	−26 V	slight var., 2.45–2.54 in V **Menkar**
γ Per Aa,Ab†	3 06.4	+53 36	2.91v†	0.72	G8 III† + A2? V?	13	−1.5	240	0.006	175	+3 SB2†	composite spectrum; orbit 14.6 y, next eclipse 2035
ρ Per	3 06.6	+38 56	3.32v†	1.53	M4 II	11	−1.6	310	0.167	129	+28	semiregular variable: 3.3–4.0 in V, ~50 d, ~120 d, ~250 d
β PerAa1†	3 09.6	+41 02	2.09v†	0.00	B8 V †	36	−0.1	90	0.003	119	+4 SB	Aa=compos. spectrum Aa1,2 ecl,;2.09-3.30 in V, 2.9 d Algol
α Per A	3 25.9	+49 56	1.79†	0.48	F5 Ib	~6.4	−4.2	510	0.035	138	−2 V	in open cluster Melotte 20, a.k.a. Collinder 39 **Mirfak**
δ Per Aa	3 44.5	+47 51	3.01†	−0.12	B5 IIIn†	6	−3.0	500	0.050	149	+4 SB	slight var., γ Cas type, 2.99–3.04 in V
γ Hyi	3 46.9	−74 10	3.26	1.59	M2 III	15.2	−0.8	~214	0.126	24	+16	
η Tau Aa	3 48.8	+24 10	2.85	−0.09	B7 IIIne†	8	−2.6	400	0.048	156	+10 V?	brightest member of Pleiades Alcyone

TABLE OF BRIGHTEST STARS (continued)

Star Name	RA (2022.5) h m	Dec ° ′	m_V	$B-V$	MK Type	π mas	M_V	D ly	μ ″/y	PA °	V_{rad} km/s	Remarks	
ζ Per A†	3 55.6	+31 57	2.84	0.27	B1 Ib	4	−4.0	800	0.011	150	+20 SB	B: 9.16, B8 V, 12.8″, PA:205°→208°, 1824→2020	
γ Eri A	3 59.1	−13 27	2.97	1.59	M1 IIIb†	16	−1.0	200	0.129	151	+62	Ca, Cr weak	Zaurak
ε Per A†	3 59.4	+40 04	2.90†	−0.20	B0.5 IV†	5	−3.6	600	0.028	149	+1 SB2	B: 8.9, B9.5 V, 9.1″, PA:10°→10°, 1821→2015	
λ Tau	4 01.9	+12 33	3.41v†	−0.10	B3 V	7	−2.4	480	0.017	209	+18 SB2†	ecl.: 3.37–3.91 in V, 3.953 d; secondary is A4 IV	
α Ret A	4 14.7	−62 25	3.33	0.92	G8 II–III	20.2	−0.1	162	0.065	40	+36 SB?		
θ Tau Aa†	4 30.0	+15 55	3.40†	0.18	A7 III	22	0.1	150	0.112	104	+40 SB†	in Hyades, system Aa-plus-Ab is a.k.a. θ^2 Tau	Chamukuy
α Dor A†	4 34.5	−55 00	3.30	−0.08	A0p V: (Si) †	19	−0.3	169	~0.059	~79?	+26	A: 3.8; B: 4.3, B9 IV; 0.2″ (2019); orbit 12 y	
α Tau A +1P†	4 37.2	+16 33	0.87	1.54	K5 III†	49	−0.7	67	0.199	161	+54 SB	slight irregular var., 0.86–0.89 in V	**Aldebaran**
π^3 Ori A	4 51.1	+7 00	3.19	0.48	F6 V	124	3.7	26.3	0.464	89	+24 SB2		Tabit
ι Aur	4 58.5	+33 12	2.69v	1.49	K3 II	7	−3.2	500	0.016	155	+18V	var.: 2.63–2.78 in V; maybe "+2P" (brown dwrfs?)	Hassaleh
ε Aur A	5 03.6	+43 51	3.03v†	0.54	F0Iab?†	~2†	−8.0:	~1450†	~0.003	n.a.	−3 SB†	ecl.: 2.92–3.83 in V, ~27.1 y (dim ~700 d)	Almaaz
ε Lep	5 06.4	−22 21	3.19	1.46	K4 III	15	−0.9	210	0.076	164	+1		
η Aur	5 08.1	+41 16	3.18	−0.15	B3 V†	13	−1.2	240	0.075	155	+7 V?	slight rotating ellips. var?: 3.16–3.18 in V, 2.5617 d	Haedus
β Eri A	5 09.0	−5 04	2.78†	0.16	A3 IVn	36	0.6	89	0.112	228	−9		Cursa
μ Lep	5 13.9	−16 11	3.29v?†	−0.11	B9p IV: (HgMn) †	18	−0.5	190	0.050	109	+28	var?.: 2.97–3.41 in V?, 2 d?	
β Ori A†	5 15.6	−8 11	0.18†	−0.03	B8 Ia	4	−6.9	900	0.001	69	+21 SB	B: 6.8, B5 V, 9.7″ (2017); C: 7.6; BC: 0.1″	**Rigel**
α Aur Aa,Ab†	5 18.4	+46 01	0.08	0.80	G6:III + G2:III	76	−0.5	43	0.433	170	+30 SB2	composite; Aa: 0.7, Ab: 0.9; Aa,Ab < 0.1″	**Capella**
η Ori Aa†	5 25.6	−2 23	3.35v†	−0.24	B0.5 Ve†	3	−4.0	1000	~0.004?	n.a.	+20 SB2	ecl.: 3.31–3.60 in V, 8.0 d; A: 3.6; B: 4.9, 1.8″ (2019)	
γ Ori A	5 26.3	+6 22	1.64	−0.22	B2 III†	13	−2.8	250	0.015	212	+18 SB?		**Bellatrix**
β Tau	5 27.7	+28 37	1.65	−0.13	B7 III†	24	−1.4	130	0.175	173	+9 V SB		**Elnath**
β Lep A†	5 29.2	−20 45	2.81	0.81	G5 II	~20.3	−0.6	160	0.086	183	−14 V?	B: 7.5, 2.7″, PA:268°→10°, 1875→2017	Nihal
δ Ori Aa†	5 33.2	−0 17	2.25v†	−0.18	O9.5 II	5	−4.4	700	0.001	137	+16 SB	a good marker of celestial equator	Mintaka
α Lep A	5 33.7	−17 48	2.58	0.21	F0 Ib†	1.5	−6.6	2000	0.004	72	+24		Arneb
λ Ori A†	5 36.4	+9 57	3.39	−0.16	O8 IIIf	3	−4.2	~1100	0.004	216	+34	B: 5.45, B0 V, 4.3″, PA:45°→44°, 1779→2019	Meissa
ι Ori Aa†	5 36.5	−5 54	2.75	−0.21	O9 III	~1.4	−6.5	2000	0.001	108	+22 SB2	Aa,Ab 0.1″ (2016), mags. 3.0, 6.3	Hatysa
ε Ori A	5 37.4	−1 11	1.69v	−0.18	B0 Ia	2	−7.2	2000	0.002	118	+26 SB	var. of α Cyg type, 1.64–1.74 in V	**Alnilam**
ζ Tau	5 39.0	+21 09	2.97v†	−0.15	B2 IIIpe (shell) †	7	−2.7	400	0.020	175	+20 SB†	var., eclips. (and γ Cas?), 2.80–3.17 in V, 133.0 d	Tianguan
α Col A	5 40.5	−34 04	2.65†	−0.12	B7 IVe†	12	−1.9	260	0.025	176	+35 V?	slight var. of γ Cas type, 2.62–2.66 in V	Phact
ζ Ori Aa	5 41.9	−1 56	1.74	−0.20	O9.5 Ib	4	−5.0	700	0.005	58	+18 SB†	B: 4.2, B0 III, 2.4″, PA:152°→167°, 1822→2017	Alnitak
κ Ori	5 48.8	−9 40	2.07†	−0.17	B0.5 Ia†	5	−4.4	600	0.002	131	+21 V?	slight var. of α Cyg type, 2.04–2.09 in V	Saiph
β Col	5 51.8	−35 46	3.12	1.15	K1.5 III†	37.4	1.0	87	0.408†	8	+89† V		Wazn
α Ori Aa†	5 56.4	+7 25	0.45v†	1.50	M2 Iab†	7†	−5.5	500†	0.030†	68	+21† SB	semireg., late-type supergiant var.: ~0–1.7 in V	**Betelgeuse**
β Aur Aa,Ab	6 01.2	+44 57	1.90†	0.08	A1 IV + A1 IV	~40.2	−0.1	81	0.056	269	−18 SB2	slight ecl.: 1.89–1.98 in V, 3.96 d (mags. equal)	Menkalinan
θ Aur A	6 01.3	+37 13	2.65	−0.08	A0p II: (Si)†	~19.7	−0.9	166	~0.086	~149	+30 SB	B: 7.2, G2 V, 4.2″, PA:7°→304°, 1871→2019	Mahasim
η Gem A†	6 16.2	+22 30	3.31v†	1.60	M3 III	8	−2.0	400	~0.064	~259	+19 SB	var.: 3.15–3.9 in V, 233 d; B: 6.2, 1.7″ (2018)	Propus
ζ CMa A	6 21.2	−30 04	3.02†	−0.16	B2.5 V	9.0	−2.2	360	0.008	61	+32 SB†		Furud
β CMa A	6 23.7	−17 58	1.98†	−0.24	B1 II–III	7	−3.9	~490	0.003	256	+34 SB	slight var., β Cep type, 1.97–2.00 in V, 0.25130 d	Mirzam

TABLE OF BRIGHTEST STARS (continued)

Star Name	RA (2022.5) h m	Dec ° ′	m_V	$B-V$	MK Type	π mas	M_V	D ly	μ ″/y	PA °	V_{rad} km/s	Remarks	
β CMa A	6 23.7	−17 58	1.98†	−0.24	B1 II–III	7	−3.9	~490	0.003	256	+34 SB	slight var., β Cep type, 1.97–2.00 in V, 0.25130 d	Mirzam
μ Gem A	6 24.3	+22 30	2.87v	1.62	M3 IIIab	14	−1.4	230	0.124	153	+55 V?	semiregular variable: 2.75–3.02 in V	Tejat
α Car	6 24.5	−52 43	−0.62	0.16†	A9 Ib†	11	−5.5	~310	0.031	41	+21		**Canopus**
ν Pup	6 38.4	−43 13	3.17	−0.10	B8 IIIn†	9	−2.1	370	0.004	186	+28 SB	rapid rotator, with period < 1.7 d	
γ Gem Aa	6 39.0	+16 23	1.93	0.00	A1 IVs	30	−0.7	110	0.057	166	−13 SB†		Alhena
ε Gem A	6 45.3	+25 06	3.06	1.38†	G8 Ib	4	−4.0	800	0.014	204	+10 SB		Mebsuta
α CMa A†	6 46.1	−16 45	−1.44	0.01	A0mA1 Va†	~379	1.5	8.6	~1.339	~204	−8 SB	B: 8.5, WDA; 10.7″ (2016); orbit 50.1 y	**Sirius**
ξ Gem	6 46.6	+12 52	3.35	0.44	F5 IV	56	2.1	58.7	0.223	211	+25 V? †		Alzirr
α Pic	6 48.4	−61 58	3.24	0.22	A6 Vn kA6†	~34	0.9	100	0.252	345	+21		
τ Pup	6 50.5	−50 39	2.94	1.21	K1 III	18	−0.8	180	0.077	154	+36 SB†		
κ CMa	6 50.7	−32 32	3.50v†	−0.12	B1.5 IVne†	4.9	−3.0	700	0.010	293	+14	var., γ Cas type, 3.40–3.97 in V	
ε CMa A†	6 59.5	−29 00	1.50	−0.21	B2 II	8.0	−4.0	410	0.004	68	+27	B:7.5, 7.9″, PA: 161°→162°, 1850→2008	**Adhara**
o^2 CMa	7 04.0	−23 52	3.02†	−0.08	B3 Ia	1	−6.6	3000	0.004	329	+48 SB	slight var., α Cyg type, 2.98–3.04 in Hp, 24.44 d	
δ CMa	7 09.3	−26 26	1.83	0.67	F8 Ia†	2	−6.6	2000	0.005	317	+34 SB		Wezen
L$_2$ Pup A	7 14.2	−44 41	~7.70v†	1.33	M5 IIIe	16	0.4	210	0.342	18	+53 V?	semireg., 2.6–8.0 in V, since ~1995 never bright	HR2748
π Pup Aa	7 17.9	−37 08	2.71v†	1.62	K3 Ib	4	−4.3	800	0.012	303	+16	B: 7.9, 66″, PA:214°→213°, 1826→2009	
η CMa A	7 25.0	−29 21	2.45v†	−0.08	B5 Ia	2	−6.5	2000	0.007	325	+41 V	B: 6.8, 178″ (2010) is mere optical companion	Aludra
β CMi A	7 28.4	+8 15	2.89†	−0.10	B8 Ve†	~20.2	−0.6	~162	0.064	234	+22 SB		Gomeisa
σ Pup A	7 29.9	−43 21	3.25†	1.51	K5 III	17	−0.6	190	0.198	342	+88 SB†	B: 8.8, G5: V, 22.1″, PA:90°→74°, 1826→2015	
α Gem A†	7 36.0	+31 50	1.93	0.03	A1mA2 Va	63	0.9	52	~0.254	~234	+6 SB	orbit 445 y; max = 6.5″, in 1880;	
α Gem B†	7 36.0	+31 50	2.97	0.03	A2mA5 V:	63	2.0	52	~0.254	~234	−1 SB	min = 1.8″, in 1965; 5.5″ (2019)	Castor
α CMi A†	7 40.5	+5 10	0.40†	0.43	F5 IV-V	285	2.7	11.5	~1.259	~215	−3 SB	B: 10.8, WD; 3.8″ (2014); orbit 41 y	**Procyon**
β Gem A+1P†	7 46.7	+27 58	1.16	0.99	K0 IIIb	97	1.1	33.8	0.628	266	+3 V		**Pollux**
ξ Pup A†	7 50.2	−24 55	3.34	1.22	G6 Iab–Ib†	3	−4.5	1200	0.005	260	+3 SB†		Azmidi
χ Car	7 57.4	−53 03	3.46†	−0.18	B3 IV(p?)†	7	−2.3	500	0.035	304	+19 V		
ζ Pup	8 04.4	−40 04	2.21†	−0.27†	O5 Iafn†	3.0†	−5.4	1080†	0.034†	299	−24† V?	blue supergiant	Naos
ρ Pup A	8 08.5	−24 22	2.83v†	0.46	F2mF5 II: (var)†	51.3	1.4	64	0.095	299	+46 SB	var.: 2.68–2.87 in V, 0.14 d	Tureis
γ Vel Aa†	8 10.2	−47 24	1.75	−0.14	O7.5 III-I†	3†	−5.9	~1100†	0.012	330	+35 SB2†	slightly eruptive, 1.81–1.87 in V; Aa,Ab pair is a.k.a. γ^2 Vel	
ε Car A	8 23.0	−59 35	1.86v†	1.20	K3:III	5	−4.5	600	0.034	311	+2	ecl.: 1.82–1.94 in V	**Avior**
o UMa A+1P	8 32.1	+60 38	3.35†	0.86	G5 III	~18.2	−0.3	~179	0.172†	231	+20†	slight var.?: 3.30?–3.36 in V?	Muscida
δ Vel Aa†	8 45.3	−54 48	1.95v†	0.04	A1 Va	40	0.0	81	~0.107	~164	+ 2 V?	Aa,Ab is brightest ecl. binary (1.95–2.43 in V)	Alsephina
ε Hya A†	8 48.0	+6 20	3.38	0.68	G5:III	25	0.4	130	~0.232	259	+36 SB†		Ashlesha
ζ Hya	8 56.6	+5 52	3.11	0.98	G9 II–III	~21†	−0.4	~157	0.101	279	+23		
ι UMa A†	9 00.7	+47 57	3.12	0.22	A7 IVn	~68.9	2.3	47.3	~0.491	~244	+9 SB†	A+BC 2.4″, PA: 349°→90°, 1831→2017	Talitha
λ Vel A	9 08.8	−43 31	2.23v†	1.66	K4 Ib–IIa†	6.0	−3.9	540	0.028	299	+18	semireg. var.: 2.14–2.30 in V	**Suhail**
a† Car	9 11.6	−59 04	3.43†	−0.19	B2 IV–V	7	−2.3	500	0.022	312	+23 SB2†	slight ecl.: 3.41–3.44 in V	HR 3659

TABLE OF BRIGHTEST STARS (continued)

	Star Name	RA (2022.5) h m	Dec ° ′	m_V	$B-V$	MK Type	π mas	M_V	D ly	μ ″/y	PA °	V_{rad} km/s	Remarks	
β	Car	9 13.4	−69 49	1.67	0.07	A1 III	28.8†	−1.0	113	0.191	305	−5 V?		**Miaplacidus**
ι†	Car	9 17.7	−59 22	2.21†	0.19	A7 Ib	4.3	−4.6	800	0.022	302	+13	slight var.: 2.23–2.28 in V	Aspidiske
α	Lyn A	9 22.4	+34 18	3.14†	1.55	K7 IIIab	16	−0.8	~203	0.224	274	+38	B: 8.8, 223″, PA: 33°→43°, 1823→2016	
κ	Vel	9 22.8	−55 06	2.47	−0.14	B2 IV–V	6	−3.8	600	0.016	315	+22 SB†		Markeb†
α	Hya A†	9 28.7	−8 45	1.99†	1.44	K3 II–III†	18	−1.7	180	0.038	336	−4 V?	poss. slight var., underobserved (1.93–2.01 in V?)	**Alphard**
N	Vel	9 31.9	−57 08	3.16†	1.54	K5 III	13.6	−1.2	240	0.033	280	−14	slight semiregular var., 3.12–3.18 in V, 82.0 d	HR 3803
θ	UMa A	9 34.4	+51 34	3.17	0.48	F6 IV†	74.2	2.5	44.0	1.088	241	+15 SB†		
ε	Leo	9 47.1	+23 40	2.97†	0.81	G1 II	13.2	−1.4	250	0.047	259	+4 V?	poss. slight var., underobserved (2.95–3.04 in V?)	
υ	Car A	9 47.7	−65 11	2.92	0.29	A6 II	2.3†	−5.3	~1400†	0.028	307	+14	A: 3.01; B: 5.99, B7 III, 5.1″, PA:126°→128°, 1836→2015	
η	Leo A	10 08.6	+16 39	3.48	−0.03	A0 Ib†	3	−4.5	1300	~0.003	n.a.	+3 V	B: 8.4, 0.4″, PA:84°→239°, 1937→2015	
α	Leo A†	10 09.6	+11 51	1.36	−0.09	B8 IVn†	41	−0.6	79	0.249	271	+6 SB†		**Regulus**
ω	Car	10 14.3	−70 09	3.29†	−0.07	B8 IIIn†	9.5	−1.8	340	0.037	281	+7 V	or "IIIne"; shell star	
q	Car A	10 17.8	−61 27	3.39†	1.54	K3 IIa†	5.0	−3.1	660	0.026	286	+8	slight irregular variable: 3.36–3.44 in V	HR 4050
ζ	Leo A	10 17.9	+23 18	3.43	0.31	F0 IIIa†	12	−1.2	270	0.020	110	−16 SB	B (6.0, 331″ in 2015) is mere optical companion	Adhafera
λ	UMa	10 18.4	+42 48	3.45	0.03	A1 IV†	24	0.3	140	0.186	256	+18 V		Tania Borealis
γ	Leo A +1P†	10 21.2	+19 44	2.61†	1.13	K1 IIIb Fe–0.5†	26	−0.3	130	~0.333†	~118	−37† SB	4.7″ (2020), PA:99°→127°, 1820→2020 (510.3 y);	Algieba
γ	Leo B	10 21.2	+19 44	3.16†	1.42	G7 III Fe–1†	26	0.2	130	~0.346†	~118	−36† V	max = ~5″, around 2100	
μ	UMa	10 23.7	+41 23	3.06 †	1.60	M0 IIIp†	14	−1.2	230	0.089	293	−21 SB†	slight var., 3.03–3.10 in V	Tania Australis
p	Car	10 32.8	−61 48	3.30v	−0.09	B4 Vne†	7	−2.6	500	0.021	304	+26	variable of γ Cas type, 3.22–3.55 in V	HR 4140
θ	Car	10 43.8	−64 31	2.74	−0.22	B0.5 Vp	7	−3.0	460	0.022	303	+24 SB†		
μ	Vel A†	10 47.7	−49 32	2.82	1.07	G5 III†	28	−0.1	~117	0.083	131	+6 SB	A: 2.82; B: 5.65, 2.3″, PA:55°→58°, 1880→2019	
ν	Hya	10 50.7	−16 19	3.11	1.23	K2 III†	23	−0.1	144	0.220†	25	−1†		
β	UMa	11 03.2	+56 16	2.34	0.03	A0mA1 IV–V	~40.9	0.4	80	0.088	68	−12 SB		Merak
α	UMa A†	11 05.1	+61 38	1.81†	1.06	K0 IIIa	27	−1.1	120	0.139	255	−9 SB	A: 1.86; B: 5.0, A8 V, 0.8″ (2017), PA 342°	**Dubhe**
ψ	UMa	11 10.9	+44 23	3.00	1.14	K1 III	22.6	−0.2	145	0.068	246	−4 V?		
δ	Leo A	11 15.3	+20 24	2.56†	0.13	A4 IV	56	1.3	58	0.193	132	−20 V	possibly slight (δ Sct type?) var., 2.54–2.57 in V	Zosma
θ	Leo	11 15.4	+15 18	3.33	0.00	A2 IV†	~19.8	−0.2	165	0.099	217	+8 V		Chertan
λ	Cen Aa†	11 36.8	−63 09	3.11	−0.04	B9.5 IIn†	8	−2.4	400	0.034	258	−1 V		
β	Leo A	11 50.2	+14 27	2.14†	0.09	A3 Va	91	1.9	36	0.511	257	0 V		**Denebola**
γ	UMa A	11 55.0	+53 34	2.41	0.04	A0 Van†	39	0.4	83	0.108	84	−13 SB		Phecda
δ	Cen Aa†	12 09.5	−50 51	2.58v	−0.13	B2 IVne†	8	−2.9	400	0.050	262	+11 V	var. of γ Cas type, 2.51–2.65 in V	
ε	Crv	12 11.3	−22 45	3.02	1.33	K2 III†	~10.3	−1.9	320	0.072	278	+5		
δ	Cru	12 16.4	−58 52	2.79†	−0.19	B2 IV†	9.4	−2.3	350	0.037	254	+22 V?	slight var., β Cep type, 2.78–2.84 in V, 0.15 d	Imai
δ	UMa A	12 16.5	+56 54	3.32	0.08	A2 Van	40.5	1.4	81	0.104	86	−13 V		Megrez
γ	Crv	12 17.0	−17 40	2.58†	−0.11	B8 III†	21	−0.8	154	0.160	278	−4 SB	slight var., 2.56–2.60 in V, of unknown type	**Gienah**
α	Cru A†	12 27.9	−63 13	1.25†	−0.20	B0.5 IV	10	−3.7	~320	0.037	251	−11 SB	5.4″ (1826); 3..5″ (2020)	**Acrux**
α	Cru B†	12 27.9	−63 13	1.64†	−0.18	B1 Vn	10	−3.3	~320	0.037?	251?	−1	PA: 114°→111°, 1826→2020	
δ	Crv A†	12 31.0	−16 38	2.94	−0.01	B9.5 IVn	~37.6	0.8	87	0.252	237	+9 V	B:8.26, K2 V, 24.2″, PA: 216°→216°,1782→2020	Algorab

TABLE OF BRIGHTEST STARS (continued)

Star Name	RA (2022.5) h m	Dec ° ′	m_V	B − V	MK Type	π mas	M_V	D ly	μ ″/y	PA °	V_{rad} km/s	Remarks
γ Cru A	12 32.4	−57 14	1.59†	1.60	M3.5 III†	37	−0.6	89	0.267	174	+21	slight semiregular var., 1.60–1.67 in V **Gacrux**
β Crv	12 35.6	−23 31	2.65†	0.89	G5 II†	22	−0.6	146	0.057	179	−8 V	slight var. (2.60–2.66 in V) reported or suspected Kraz
α Mus Aa	12 38.6	−69 16	2.69†	−0.18	B2 IV–V	10.3	−2.2	320	0.042	252	+13 V	slight var., β Cep type?, 2.68–2.73 in V, 0.090 d
γ Cen A†	12 42.8	−49 05	2.95	−0.02	A1 IV	25	−0.1	130	~0.194	~267	−6	[orbit 84 y; 0.4″ (2010),
γ Cen B†	12 42.8	−49 05	2.85	−0.02	A0 IV	25	−0.2	130	~0.194	~267	−6	0.3″ (2019); max = 1.7″
γ Vir AB†	12 42.8	−1 34	2.74	0.37	F1 V + F0mF2 V	85	2.4	39	~0.619	~276	−20	A: 3.48; B: 3.53; 0.8″ (2007); 3.0″ (2020) Porrima
β Mus Aa	12 47.7	−68 14	3.04	−0.18	B2 V†	~9.6	−2.1	340	~0.043†	~258	+42† V	A: 3.52; B: 3.98, 1.0″, PA:317°→58°, 1880→2019
β Cru A	12 49.1	−59 49	1.25†	−0.24	B0.5 III†	12	−3.4	300	0.046	249	+16 SB†	slight var., β Cep type, 1.23–1.31 in V, 0.24 d Mimosa
ε UMa A	12 55.0	+55 50	1.76†	−0.02	A0p IV: (CrEu)	~39.5	−0.3	83	0.112	94	−9 SB?	slight var., α^2 CVn type, 1.76–1.78 in V, 5.1 d **Alioth**
δ Vir A	12 56.7	+3 17	3.39†	1.57	M3 III†	16	−0.5	~198	0.473†	264	−18† V?	slight var., semiregular, 3.32–3.40 in V Minelauva
α CVn A†	12 57.1	+38 12	2.85v†	−0.06	A0 Vp (SiEu)	28	0.1	110	0.241	283	−3 V	B:5.5, F0 V, 19.5″, PA:234°→230°, 1777→2018 Cor Caroli
ε Vir A	13 03.3	+10 50	2.85	0.93	G9 IIIab†	29.8	0.2	110	0.275	274	−14 V?	Vindemiatrix
γ Hya A	13 20.2	−23 17	2.99	0.92	G8 IIIa	~24.4	−0.1	134	0.081	121	−5 V?	
ι Cen	13 21.9	−36 50	2.75	0.07	A2 Va†	55	1.5	59	0.352	256	0	
ζ UMa Aa†	13 24.8	+54 48	2.23	0.06	A1 Va†	40	0.1	90	0.123	100	−6 SB2†	B:3.88, A1mA7 IV–V, 14.6″ (2019); period >5000 y? Mizar
α Vir Aa†	13 26.4	−11 17	0.98†	−0.24	B1 V†	13	−3.4	250	0.052	234	+1 SB2†	slight var., 0.96–1.00 in V, 4.0 d; mags 3.1, 4.5, 7.5 **Spica**
ζ Vir A	13 35.8	−0 43	3.38	0.11	A2 IV†	44	1.6	74	0.285	280	−13	a good marker of celestial equator Heze
ε Cen Aa	13 41.3	−53 35	2.29†	−0.17	B1 III†	8	−3.3	400	0.019	233	+3	slight var., β Cep type, 2.29–2.31 in V
η UMa	13 48.4	+49 12	1.85	−0.10†	B3 V†	31	−0.7	104	0.122	263	−11 SB?	**Alkaid**
ν Cen	13 50.9	−41 48	3.41†	−0.22	B2 IV†	~7.5	−2.2	440	0.034	233	+9 SB†	
μ Cen Aa	13 51.0	−42 35	3.47v†	−0.17	B2 IV–V pne†	~6.4	−2.5	510	0.031	232	+9 SB	variable of γ Cas type,: 2.92–3.47 in V
η Boo A	13 55.8	+18 17	2.68	0.58	G0 IV†	88	2.4	37	0.361	190	0 SB	Muphrid
ζ Cen	13 57.0	−47 24	2.55	−0.18	B2.5 IV†	8.5	−2.8	380	0.073	232	+7 SB2	
β Cen Aa,Ab	14 05.4	−60 29	0.58†	−0.23	B1 III + B1 III	8†	−4.8	400†	0.041	235	+6 SB†	B:3.94, A1mA7 IV–V, 0.3″ (2019) **Hadar**
π Hya	14 07.7	−26 47	3.25	1.09	K2 IIIb†	~32.3†	0.8	~101†	0.148†	163	+27† V	
θ Cen A	14 08.0	−36 29	2.06	1.01	K0 IIIb†	55	0.8	59	0.734†	225	+1†	**Menkent**
α Boo A	14 16.7	+19 04	−0.05	1.24	K1.5 III Fe–0.5†	89	−0.3	37	2.279†	209	−5† V	high space velocity **Arcturus**
γ Boo Aa†	14 33.0	+38 13	3.04†	0.19	A7 IV+	37.6	0.9	87	0.190	323	−37 V	slight var. of δ Sct type, 3.02–3.07 in V, 0.2903 d Seginus
η Cen	14 36.9	−42 15	2.33v†	−0.16	B1.5 IV pne†	11	−2.5	310	0.048	227	0 SB	var. of γ Cas and λ Eri types, possibly shell, 2.29–2.47 in V
α Cen B†	14 41.1	−60 56	1.35	0.9	K1 V†	750	5.7	4.3	~3.703	~283	−21 V?	[AB 5.2″ (2019) orbit 79.9y Toliman
α Cen A†	14 41.1	−60 56	−0.01	0.71	G2 V†	750	4.4	4.3	~3.710	~277	−22 SB	Ca (Proxima), 11.1, M5e, 212°, Cb (exopl) **Rigil Kentaurus**
α Lup A	14 43.4	−47 29	2.30†	−0.15	B1.5 III	7	−3.5	460	0.032	221	+5 SB	slight var. of β Cep type, 2.29–2.34 in V, 0.26 d
α Cir A†	14 44.4	−65 04	3.18†	0.26	A7 Vp (Sr)	60.4	2.1	54.1	0.303	220	+7 SB?	B: 8.5, K5 V, 15.7″, PA:263°→224°, 1826→2016
ε Boo A	14 46.0	+26 59	2.58	1.34	K0 II–III†	16†	−1.6	200†	0.044	288	−17 V	B:4.81, 2.8″, PA:318°→347°, 1822→2018 Izar
β UMi A+1P†	14 50.7	+74 04	2.07	1.46	K4 III†	24.9	−0.9	131	0.035	289	+17 V	useful for aligning small equatorial mount **Kochab**

TABLE OF BRIGHTEST STARS (continued)

	Star Name	RA (2022.5) h m	Dec ° ′	m_V	$B-V$	MK Type	π mas	M_V	D ly	μ ″/y	PA °	V_{rad} km/s	Remarks	
α	Lib Aa†	14 52.1	−16 08	2.75	0.15	A3 III–IV†	43	0.9	76	0.126	237	−10 SB†	B. 5.2, 231″ (2012)	**Zubenelgenubi**
β	Lup	15 00.0	−43 13	2.68†	−0.18	B2 IV†	9	−2.7	380	0.054	222	0 SB		
κ	Cen Aa†	15 00.6	−42 12	3.13†	−0.21	B2 V	9	−2.2	400	0.029	218	+8 SB		
σ	Lib	15 05.4	−25 22	3.25v†	1.67	M2.5 III	11	−1.5	290	0.083	239	−4	semireg. var.: 3.20–3.46 in V, mean period 20 d	Brachium
ζ	Lup A†	15 13.9	−52 11	3.50	0.92	G8 III	~27.8	0.6	117	0.133	238	−10	B: 6.74; 71.7″ (2020), PA: 249°→249°, 1826→2020	
δ	Boo A†	15 16.4	+33 14	3.46	0.96	G8 III Fe–1†	~26.8	0.6	122	0.140	143	−12 SB	a very wide true binary: B is mag. 7.89, 105″ (2017)	
β	Lib	15 18.2	−9 28	2.61†	−0.07	B8 IIIn	~17.6	−1.2	190	0.100	259	−35 SB		Zubeneschamali
γ	UMi	15 20.7	+71 45	3.00†	0.06	A3 III†	6.7	−2.9	490	0.025	315	−4 V		Pherkad
γ	TrA	15 21.0	−68 46	2.87	0.01	A1 IIIn†	17.7	−0.9	184	0.074	244	−3 V		
δ	Lup	15 22.9	−40 44	3.22†	−0.23	B1.5 IVn	4	−3.9	900	0.032	218	0 V?		
ε	Lup Aa†	15 24.2	−44 46	3.37†	−0.19	B2 IV–V	6	−2.6	500	~0.030	~230	+8 SB2	A: 3.56; B: 5.04, 0.1″, PA:285°→53°, 1883→2019	
ι	Dra A+1P†	15 25.4	+58 53	3.29	1.17	K2 III†	32.2	0.8	101	0.019	334	−11		Edasich
α	CrB	15 35.6	+26 38	2.22v†	0.03	A0 IV (composite) †	43	0.4	75	0.150	127	+2 SB†	ecl.: 2.21–2.32 in B band, 17 d	**Alphecca**
γ	Lup A†	15 36.6	−41 14	2.80	−0.22	B2 IVn†	8	−2.8	400	~0.030	~212	+2 V	A: 3.0; B: 4.4; similar spectra 0.8″ (2019)	
α	Ser A	15 45.4	+6 21	2.63? †	1.17	K2 IIIb CN1†	44	0.9	74	0.141	71	+3 V?	semiregular variable? (range ~0.2 in V?)	Unukalhai
β	TrA A	15 57.1	−63 30	2.83	0.32	F0 IV†	~80.8	2.4	40.4	0.444	205	0		
π	Sco A	16 00.2	−26 11	2.89†	−0.18	B1 V†	6	−3.4	600	0.029	203	−3 SB2	A: slight ecl. binary.: 3.4 & 4.5, 1.57 d, 2.88–2.91 in V	Fang
T	CrB A	16 00.4	+25 51	9.8v†	1.34	M3 III†	—	0.6	2500?	0.011	329	−29 SB	recurrent nova 1866&1946 mags 3&2; V~9.8 2021 Aug. 06	
η	Lup A†	16 01.6	−38 28	3.37	−0.21	B2.5 IVn†	7	−2.2	440	0.033	211	+8 V	B: 7.50, 14.8″, PA:22°→19°, 1834→2020	
δ	Sco A†	16 01.7	−22 41	2.29v†	−0.12	B0.3 IVe†	7	−3.6	500	~0.037	~196	−7	var. of γ Cas type, 1.59–2.32 in V, bright in 2011	Dschubba
β	Sco Aa†	16 06.7	−19 52	2.56	−0.06	B0.5 V	8	−2.9	400	0.025	192	−1 SB	Aa: 2.62; B: 10.6, 0.3″ (2019); C: 4.52, 13″	Acrab
δ	Oph A	16 15.5	−3 45	2.73†	1.58	M1 III†	~19.1	−0.9	171	0.150	198	−20 V	slight var.? (2.72–2.75 in V?)	Yed Prior†
ε	Oph A	16 19.5	−4 45	3.23	0.97	G9.5 IIIb†	31	0.7	106	0.093	64	−10 V		Yed Posterior
σ	Sco Aa1†	16 22.6	−25 39	2.91†	0.13	B1 III†	5	−3.7	700	0.019	213	+3 SB†	slight var.: 2.86–2.94, 0.25 d; B: 8.4, B9 V, 20.5″ (2019)	Alniyat
η	Dra A	16 24.3	+61 28	2.73†	0.91	G8 IIIab	35.4	0.5	92	0.059	343	−14 SB?	B: 8.2, 4.4″, PA: 150°→143°, 1843→2015	Athebyne
α	Sco A†	16 30.8	−26 29	1.06v†	1.86	M1.5 Iab†	6	−5.1	600	0.026	207	−26 SB	semireg. var.: 0.75–1.21, 5.97 y; B: 5.40, 2.8″ (2019)	**Antares**†
β	Her Aa	16 31.2	+21 27	2.78†	0.95	G7 IIIa†	23	−0.4	140	0.100	261	−26 SB†		Kornephoros†
τ	Sco	16 37.3	−28 16	2.82	−0.21	B0 V†	7	−3.0	500	0.025	203	+2 V		Paikauhale†
ζ	Oph	16 38.4	−10 37	2.54†	0.04	O9.5 Vne†	9	−2.7	370	0.029†	32	−15 V†	the nearest O-type star	
ζ	Her A†	16 42.1	+31 34	2.62	0.65	G1 IV†	93	2.7	35	~0.575	~307	−70† SB	B: 5.40, G7 V, 1.6″ (2019), orbit 34.45 y	
η	Her A	16 43.7	+38 53	3.48	0.92	G7.5 IIIb Fe–1†	30.0	0.9	109	0.092	157	+8 V?		
α	TrA A	16 51.1	−69 04	1.91	1.45	K2 IIb–IIIa†	~8.4	−3.5	390	0.036	150	−3		**Atria**
ε	Sco	16 51.6	−34 20	2.29	1.14	K2 III	51	0.8	64	0.666†	247	−3†		Larawag
μ[1]	Sco A	16 53.4	−38 05	3.00v†	−0.20	B1.5 IVn	7	−2.9	500	0.024†	206	−25† SB2†	eclipsing binary: 2.94–3.22 in V, 1.4 d	Xamidimura
κ	Oph	16 58.7	+9 20	3.19†	1.16	K2 III	36	1.0	91	0.292†	268	−56 V†		
ζ	Ara	17 00.5	−56 01	3.12	1.55	K4 III	7	−2.7	490	0.041	206	−6		
ζ	Dra A	17 08.9	+65 41	3.17	−0.12	B6 III†	10	−1.8	330	0.028	314	−17 V	A,B: mags 3.2, 4.2, respectively; 0.10″ (1994)	Aldhibah

TABLE OF BRIGHTEST STARS (continued)

Star Name	RA (2022.5) h m	Dec ° ′	m_V	$B-V$	MK Type	π mas	M_V	D ly	μ ″/y	PA °	V_{rad} km/s	Remarks	
η Oph AB†	17 11.7	−15 45	2.43	0.06	A1 IV + A1 IV?†	37	0.3	90	~0.107	~22	−1 SB	A: 3.0; B: 3.3, A3 V, 0.5″ (2019), orbit 87.6 y	**Sabik†**
η Sco	17 13.8	−43 16	3.32	0.44	F5 IV†	~44.4	1.6	73	0.290	175	−28		
α Her Aa†	17 15.7	+14 22	2.78†	1.16	M5 Ib–II	9	−2.4	400	0.032	347	−33 V	slight semireg. var.: 2.73–3.60 in V; B: 5.4, 4.9″ (2020)	Rasalgethi†
π Her	17 15.8	+36 47	3.16†	1.44	K3 IIab†	8.7	−2.2	380	0.027	276	−26 V?		
δ Her Aa†	17 16.0	+24 49	3.12	0.08	A1 Vann	43.4	1.3	75	~0.158	~188	−40 SB†	B: 8.3, 13.7″ (2019) is mere optical companion	Sarin
θ Oph A†	17 23.4	−25 01	3.27†	−0.19	B2 IV	~7.5	−2.4	440	0.025	197	−2 SB†	slight var., β Cep type, 3.25–3.31 in V, 0.14 d	
β Ara	17 27.2	−55 33	2.84	1.48	K3 Ib–IIa†	5	−3.6	600	0.027	199	0		
γ Ara A	17 27.3	−56 24	3.31	−0.15	B1 Ib	~2.9	−4.4	1100	0.016	182	−3 V		
β Dra A	17 30.9	+52 17	2.79†	0.95†	G2 Ib–IIa	8.6	−2.5	380	0.020	308	−20 V		Rastaban
υ Sco	17 32.3	−37 19	2.70	−0.18	B2 IV†	6	−3.5	600	0.030	185	+8 SB		Lesath
α Ara A	17 33.6	−49 53	2.84	−0.14	B2 Vne†	12†	−1.7	300†	0.075	206	0 SB		
λ Sco Aa,Ab†	17 35.1	−37 07	1.62†	−0.23	B1.5 IV + n.a.	>6†	−4.6	400†	0.032	195	−3 SB2	slight ecl. and slight β Cep var., 1.59–1.65 in V	**Shaula**
α Oph A†	17 36.0	+12 33	2.08†	0.16	A5 Vnn	67	1.2	49	0.247	154	+13 SB?	slight var., δ Sct type & γ Dor type, ~0.006 in V	**Rasalhague**
θ Sco A†	17 38.9	−43 01	2.0	0.41	F1 III	~11	−3.0	300	0.006	119	+1		Sargas†
κ Sco†	17 44.0	−39 02	2.41†	−0.17	B1.5 III	7	−3.5	480	0.026	193	−14 SB2	slight var., β Cep type, 2.41–2.42 in V, ~0.2 d	
β Oph	17 44.6	+4 34	2.76†	1.17	K2 III†	~39.8	0.8	82	0.165	345	−12 V		Cebalrai
μ Her Aa†	17 47.3	+27 43	3.42	0.75	G5 IV	~120.3	3.8	27.1	0.804	201	−16 V	BC: 9.78, 35.5″, PA:240°→249°, 1781→2015	
$ι^1$ Sco A	17 49.2	−40 08	2.99	0.51†	F2 Ia	2†	−5.9	2000†	0.006	180	−28 SB	B: mag.13, 38″ (2000)	
G Sco A	17 51.4	−37 03	3.19	1.19	K2 III	25.9	0.3	126	0.049	56	+25		HR6630, Fuyue
γ Dra A	17 57.1	+51 29	2.24	1.52	K5 III†	21.1	−1.1	154	0.024	200	−28		**Eltanin**
ν Oph +2P†	18 00.3	−9 46	3.32	0.99	G9.5 IIIa†	22	0.0	150	0.117	185	+13	brown-dwarf companions	
$γ^2$ Sgr	18 07.3	−30 25	2.98	0.98	K0 III†	34	0.6	97	0.189	197	+22 SB		Alnasl
η Sgr A†	18 19.2	−36 45	3.10†	1.5	M3.5 IIIab	22	−0.2	~146	0.211	218	+1 V?	slight irreg. var.: 3.05–3.12; B: 8.00, G8: IV:, 3.5″ (2016)	
δ Sgr A	18 22.4	−29 49	2.72	1.38	K2.5 IIIa†	9	−2.4	350	0.041	128	−20 V?		Kaus Media†
η Ser A	18 22.5	−2 53	3.23	0.94	K0 III–IV†	54	1.9	~60.5	0.890	218	+9 V?		
ε Sgr A	18 25.7	−34 22	1.79	−0.03	A0 IIn (shell?) †	23	−1.4	~143	0.130	198	−15		**Kaus Australis†**
λ Sgr A	18 29.4	−25 24	2.82	1.02	K1 IIIb	~41.7	0.9	78	0.191	194	−43 V?		Kaus Borealis†
α Lyr A	18 37.7	+38 48	0.03†	0.00	A0 Va†	130	0.6	25.0	0.350	35	−14 V	pole-on rapid rotator with circumstellar disk	**Vega**
φ Sgr†	18 47.1	−26 58	3.17	−0.11	B8 III	14	−1.2	240	0.051	89	+22	apparent duplicity now discounted	
σ Sgr Aa	18 56.7	−26 16	2.05	−0.13	B3 IV	14	−2.2	230	0.056	164	−11V		**Nunki**
γ Lyr A	18 59.8	+32 43	3.25	−0.05	B9 II†	5	−3.1	600	0.003	290	−21 V†		Sulafat
ζ Sgr AB†	19 04.0	−29 51	2.60	0.06	A2 IV–V + A4:V:	37	0.4	90	n.a.	n.a.	+22 SB	A: 3.2; B: 3.5, 0.5″ (2019), orbit 21.1 y	Ascella
ζ Aql A†	19 06.4	+13 54	2.99	0.01	A0 Vann	~39.3	1.0	83	0.096	184	−25 SB		Okab
λ Aql	19 07.4	−4 51	3.43	−0.10	B9 Vnp (kB7HeA0) †	26	0.5	120	0.093	192	−12 V†	possibly SB	
τ Sgr	19 08.3	−27 38	3.32	1.17	K1.5 IIIb†	27	0.5	120	0.255†	191	+45†	possibly SB	

TABLE OF BRIGHTEST STARS (continued)

Star Name	RA (2022.5) h m	Dec ° ′	m_V	$B-V$	MK Type	π mas	M_V	D ly	μ ″/y	PA °	V_{rad} km/s	Remarks	
π Sgr AB†	19 11.1	−20 59	2.88†	0.38	F2 II–III + n.a.	6	−3.1	500	0.036	182	−10	triple system, with AB–C poorly measured	Albaldah
δ Dra A	19 12.6	+67 42	3.07	0.99	G9 III	33.5	0.7	97	0.133	46	+25 V		Altais
δ Aql Aa	19 26.6	+3 10	3.36†	0.32	F2 IV†	64	2.4	51	0.268	72	−30 SB†		
β Cyg Aa†	19 31.6	+28 00	3.36	1.09	K3 II†	10†	−2.3	330†	0.009	229	−24 V	B: 4.68, 35″; Aa, Ab, Ac ≤ 0.3″ (2020)	Albireo
δ Cyg A†	19 45.7	+45 11	2.89†	0.00	B9.5 III	20	−0.7	160	~0.066	~42	−20 SB	B. 6.4, F1 V; 2.7″, PA:41°→215°, 1826→2017	Fawaris
γ Aql A	19 47.3	+10 40	2.72†	1.51	K3 II†	~8.3	−2.7	390	0.017	100	−2 V		Tarazed
α Aql A	19 51.9	+8 56	0.76†	0.22	A7 Vnn	195	2.2	16.7	0.660	54	−26	rapid rotator (~7 h or ~8 h, latitude-dependent)	**Altair**
θ Aql Aa	20 12.5	−0 45	3.24	−0.07	B9.5 III†	11	−1.5	290	0.036	81	−27 SB2†	a good marker of celestial equator	
β Cap Aa†	20 22.3	−14 43	3.05	0.79	K0: II:†	10	−2.0	300	0.046	81	−19 SB	hierarchical quintuplet (or greater)	Dabih
γ Cyg A†	20 23.0	+40 20	2.23†	0.67	F8 Ib†	2	−6.5	2000	0.003	111	−8 V		Sadr
α Pav A	20 27.4	−56 40	1.94	−0.12	B2.5 V	18	−1.8	180	0.086	175	+2 SB†		**Peacock†**
α Ind A	20 39.1	−47 13	3.11	1.00	K0 III CN−1†	33	0.7	98	0.083	37	−1		
α Cyg A	20 42.2	+45 22	1.25†	0.09†	A2 Ia	2†	−6.9	~1400†	0.003	47	−5	blue supergiant, of radius ~0.5 AU or ~1 AU	**Deneb**
η Cep A	20 45.7	+61 56	3.41	0.91	K0 IV†	70.1	2.6	46.5	0.823†	6	−87†		
β Pav	20 47.0	−66 07	3.42	0.16	A6 IV†	~24.1	0.3	135	0.044	283	+10		
ε Cyg Aa†	20 47.1	+34 03	2.48	1.02	K0 III	44.9	0.7	73	0.486†	47	−11† SB†		Aljanah
ζ Cyg Aa†	21 13.9	+30 19	3.21	0.99	G8 IIIa Ba† 0.5	23	0.0	140	0.069	175	+17 SB		
α Cep A	21 19.1	+62 41	2.45†	0.26	A7 Van†	66.5	1.6	49.1	0.158	72	−10 V		Alderamin
β Cep Aa†	21 28.9	+70 40	3.23v†	−0.20	B1 III†	5	−3.4	700	0.015	56	−8 SB	variable: 3.16–3.27 in V, 0.19 d; B: 8.6; 13.5″ (2016)	Alfirk
β Aqr A	21 32.7	−5 28	2.9†	0.83†	G0 Ib†	6	−3.2	500	0.020	114	+7 V?		Sadalsuud
ε Peg A	21 45.3	+9 59	2.38†	1.52†	K2 Ib†	5	−4.2	700	0.027	89	+5 V	slight irregular var.: 2.37–2.45 in V (flare in 1972)	**Enif**
δ Cap A	21 48.3	−16 01	2.85v†	0.18	A3mF2 IV: †	84	2.5	38.7	0.396	139	−6 SB†	eclipsing binary: V 2.81–3.05, 1.0 d, 3.2 + 5.2	Deneb Algedi
γ Gru	21 55.3	−37 15	3.00	−0.08	B8 IV–Vs	15	−1.1	210	0.099	98	−2 V?		Aldhanab
α Aqr A	22 06.9	−0 13	2.95†	0.97†	G2 Ib†	6	−3.1	~520	0.021	117	+8 V?	a good marker of celestial equator	Sadalmelik
α Gru A	22 09.6	−46 51	1.73	−0.07	B7 Vn	32	−0.7	101	0.194	139	+12		**Alnair**
ζ Cep	22 11.6	+58 19	3.39†	1.56†	K1.5 Ib†	3.9	−3.7	800	0.014	69	−18 SB	orange supergiant	
α Tuc	22 20.0	−60 09	2.87	1.39	K3 III†	16	−1.1	200	0.081	241	+42 SB†		
ζ Peg A	22 42.6	+10 57	3.41†	−0.09	B8.5 III†	16	−0.6	210	0.078	98	+7 V?		Homam
β Gru	22 44.0	−46 46	2.07v†	1.61†	M5 III†	18	−1.6	180	0.135	92	+2	semregular variable, 1.90–2.3 in V, 37d	Tiaki
η Peg Aa†	22 44.1	+30 20	2.93†	0.85	G8 II	15	−1.2	210	0.029	153	+4 SB		Matar
δ Aqr	22 55.8	−15 42	3.27	0.07	A3 IV–V	20	−0.2	160	0.051	237	+18 V		Skat
α PsA Aa†	22 58.9	−29 30†	1.17	0.14	A3 Va†	130	1.7	25.1	0.368	1 17	+7	2008 (HST) image was debris cloud, not exoplnt	**Fomalhaut**
β Peg A	23 04.9	+28 12	2.44v†	1.66	M2 II–III†	16.6	−1.5	~196	0.232	54	+9 V	semiregular variable, mag. 2.31–2.74 in V, 43.3 d	Scheat
α Peg	23 05.9	+15 20	2.49	0.00	A0 III–IV	24	−0.6	133	0.073	124	−4 SB		**Markab**
γ Cep A†+1P†	23 40.3	+77 45	3.21	1.03	K1 III–IV†	71	2.5	46	0.135	339	−42 V?	B: 7.30, 0.9 ″, PA: 257°→256°, 2006→2006	Errai

SPECTROSCOPY OF STARS

BY CHRIS CORBALLY, RICHARD GRAY, AND TOOMAS KARMO

An important column is included in the table of Brightest Stars. This is the classification of the star's spectrum in terms of MK Type, after Morgan and Keenan who first developed this primary system in 1943. Its symbols are explained in the introduction to the table. The MK type is really a compact description of the star's spectrum in relation to a grid of standard stars, first covering the two dimensions of temperature type and luminosity, and then including common peculiarities that stars may show.

The MK types are useful in estimating the physical parameters of stars, along with their ages, distances, and reddenings (the amount of dust in their line of sight), which are important for galactic astronomy. The classifications identify the more astrophysically interesting stars.

Classifying spectra: The classification process for normal stars is straightforward, matching as close as possible the "look" of a star's spectrum with how it fits into a "library of standard spectra." You can either build up that library through your own spectra, which is the best way eventually, or find a library that suits the resolution of your spectra on the internet.[1] For precise work, be careful that the stars you are using as standards are genuine MK system standards. The matching of unknown to standard spectra is made easier and more precise by using ratios of spectral features, traditionally called "absorption lines." The best features to use change, depending on the temperature type of the star. Richard Gray's Digital Spectral Classification Atlas[2] points out these features in the blue-green region of the spectrum, where the criteria are the most sensitive, while *winmk* and *xmk* are programs for comparing digital spectra on screen.[3]

Observing spectra: Slitless spectroscopy is a simple way to start obtaining one's own spectra. This involves putting a prism or diffraction grating in front of a DSLR lens or the digital imager on a telescope.[4] The spectra are of low resolution, but are sufficient to distinguish the broad MK "letter classes" of stars, to monitor variable stars, and get novae and supernovae, emission nebulae, and comets.[5] There are plenty of bright examples of these. For more detailed spectra, a spectrograph matching your telescope needs to be bought or made.[6]

Processing spectra: While a picture of a spectrum, or group of them in a crowded field, is beautiful, the science comes alive when one displays the intensity of the signal against wavelength. Extracting a 1-D digital spectrum from the 2-D image on the detector is both a science and an art, but there is abundant help on the internet.[7] The other step for science is calibrating the pixel position against actual wavelength along the spectrum. Again look to the internet for help in this.

What to observe: Examples of spectral interest are given under Resources 5 and 6 below. The AAVSO posts campaigns for observing objects, which often include the need for spectral data.[8] There are also interesting, bright variable stars, like Miras and B-type shell stars, that repay long-term spectroscopic observing. As John Martin remarks, "interesting" is a matter of individual taste and scientific curiosity. As these develop, you will surely become delighted with looking at your spectra and very knowledgeable about them.

A Few Resources

1 phys.unm.edu/~tw/spectra/mk.html
2 ned.ipac.caltech.edu/level5/Gray/frames.html
3 appstate.edu/~grayro/MK/winmk.htm (for MS Windows)
appstate.edu/~grayro/spectrum/ftp/download.html
(see Auxiliary X-Windows programs for Linux and iOS versions)
4 The Star Analyser is one such grating rspec-astro.com/star-analyser
John Martin's page comprehensively describes slitless spectroscopy, go.uis.edu/gratingspectra
5 Examples are at rspec-astro.com/sample-projects
6 Modest off-the-shelf spectrographs include the Shelyak ALPY-600, while both Christian Buil's and John Menke's websites offer advice on building your own and show their inspiring images astrosurf.com/buil/index.html and menkescientific.com/johnspage.html
7 Start at go.uis.edu/gratingspectra
8 aavso.org/observing-campaigns#current

★

THE 50 BRIGHTEST STARS BY MAGNITUDE

This table contains the Sun and 50 other stars with an apparent magnitude brighter than mag. 2.0 that appear in the previous table. A subset of data from that table is included, although the spectral classifications have been simplified. As in the previous table, the components of visual binary stars are listed separately; their combined magnitudes appear in footnotes. Where more than one star has the same apparent magnitude, they have been sorted by right ascension. Navigation star names are **bold**.

Rank	Star Name	RA (2022.5) h m	Dec ° ′	m_V	$B-V$	MK Type	M_V	*D* ly	
	Sun			−26.75	0.63	G2 V	4.8	8 lm	
1	α CMa A	6 46.1	−16 45	−1.44	0.01	A0mA1 Va†	1.5	8.6	**Sirius**
2	α Car	6 24.4	−52 43	−0.62	0.16	A9 Ib†	−5.5	~310	**Canopus**
3	α Boo	14 16.7	+19 04	−0.05	1.24	K1.5 III Fe–0.5†	−0.3	37	**Arcturus**
4	α Cen A	14 41.1	−60 56	−0.01	0.71	G2 V†	4.4	4.3	**Rigil Kentaurus**[1]
5	α Lyr	18 37.7	+38 48	0.03	0.00	A0 Va†	0.6	25.0	**Vega**
6	α Aur Aa,Ab	5 18.3	+46 01	0.08	0.80	G6:III + G2:III	−0.5	43	**Capella**
7	β Ori A	5 15.6	−8 11	0.18	−0.03	B8	−6.9	900	**Rigel**
8	α CMi A	7 40.5	+5 10	0.40	0.43	F5 IV-V	2.7	11.5	**Procyon**
9	α Eri	1 38.5	−57 07	0.45	−0.16	B3 Vnpe (shell?) †	−2.7	140	**Achernar**
10	α Ori A	5 56.4	+7 25	0.45v	1.50	M2 Iab†	−5.5	500	**Betelgeuse**
11	β Cen Aa,Ab	14 05.4	−60 29	0.58v	−0.23	B1 III + B1 III	−4.8	400	**Hadar**
12	α Aql A	19 51.8	+8 56	0.76	0.22	A7 Vnn	2.2	16.7	**Altair**
13	α Tau A	4 37.2	+16 33	0.87v	1.54	K5 III†	−0.7	67	**Aldebaran**
14	α Vir Aa†	13 26.4	−11 16	0.98v	−0.24	B1 V†	−3.4	250	**Spica**
15	α Sco A	16 30.8	−26 29	1.06v	1.86	M1.5 Iab†	−5.1	600	**Antares**
16	β Gem A	7 46.7	+27 58	1.16	0.99	K0 IIIb	1.1	33.8	**Pollux**
17	α PsA A	22 58.9	−29 30	1.17	0.14	A3 Va†	1.7	25.1	**Fomalhaut**
18	α Cru A	12 27.9	−63 13	1.25	−0.20	B0.5 IV	−3.7	~320	**Acrux**[2]
19	β Cru A	12 49.1	−59 49	1.25v	−0.24	B0.5 III†	−3.4	300	Mimosa
20	α Cyg A	20 42.2	+45 21	1.25	0.09	A2 Ia	−6.9	~1400	**Deneb**
21	α Cen A	14 41.1	−60 56	1.35	0.88	G2 V†	4.4	4.3	**Rigil Kentaurus**[1]
22	α Leo A	10 09.6	+11 51	1.36	−0.09	B8 IVn†	−0.6	79	**Regulus**
23	ε CMa A	6 59.5	−29 00	1.50	−0.21	B2 II	−4.0	410	**Adhara**
24	γ Cru A	12 32.4	−57 14	1.59v	1.60	M3.5 III†	−0.6	89	**Gacrux**
25	λ Sco Aa,Ab	17 35.1	−37 07	1.62v	−0.23	B1.5 IV + n.a.	−4.6	400	**Shaula**
26	γ Ori A	5 26.3	+6 22	1.64	−0.22	B2 III†	−2.8	250	**Bellatrix**
27	α Cru B	12 27.9	−63 13	1.64	−0.20	B0.5 IV	−3.7	~320	**Acrux**[2]
28	β Tau	5 27.7	+28 37	1.65	−0.13	B7 III	−1.4	130	**Elnath**
29	β Car	9 13.4	−69 49	1.67	0.07	A1 III	−1.0	113	**Miaplacidus**
30	ε Ori A	5 37.4	−1 11	1.69	−0.18	B0 Ia	−7.2	2000	**Alnilam**
31	α Gru A	22 09.6	−46 51	1.73	−0.07	B7 Vn	−0.7	101	**Alnair**
32	ζ Ori Aa,Ab	5 41.9	−1 56	1.74	−0.20	O9.5 Ib	−5.0	700	Alnitak
33	γ Vel Aa	8 10.2	−47 24	1.75v	−0.14	O7.5 III-I†	−5.9	1100	[no IAU name]
34	ε UMa AB	12 55.0	+55 50	1.76v	−0.02	A0p IV: (CrEu)	−0.3	83	**Alioth**
35	α Per A	3 25.9	+49 56	1.79	0.48	F5 Ib	−4.2	510	**Mirfak**
36	ε Sgr A	18 25.7	−34 22	1.79	−0.03	A0 IIn (shell?) †	−1.4	~143	**Kaus Australis**
37	α UMa AB	11 05.1	+61 38	1.81	1.06	K0 IIIa	−1.1	120	**Dubhe**
38	δ CMa	7 09.3	−26 26	1.83	0.67	F8 Ia†	−6.6	2000	Wezen
39	η UMa	13 48.4	+49 12	1.85	−0.10	B3 V†	−0.7	104	**Alkaid**
40	θ Sco AB	17 38.9	−43 01	1.86	0.41	F1 III	−3.0	300	Sargas
41	ε Car AB	8 23.0	−59 35	1.86v	1.20	K3:III	−4.5	600	**Avior**
42	β Aur Aa,Ab	6 01.2	+44 57	1.90v	0.08	A1 IV + A1 IV	−0.1	81	Menkalinan
43	α TrA A	16 51.1	−69 04	1.91	1.45	K2 IIb–IIIa†	−3.5	390	**Atria**
44	γ Gem Aa	6 39.0	+16 23	1.93	0.00	A1 IVs	−0.7	110	Alhena
45	α Gem B	7 36.0	+31 50	1.93	0.03	A2mA5 V:	0.9	52	Castor
46	δ Vel AB	8 45.3	−54 48	1.93	0.04	A1 Va	0.0	81	Alsephina
47	α Pav A	20 27.4	−56 40	1.94	−0.12	B2.5 V	−1.8	180	**Peacock**
48	α UMi Aa,Ab	3 00.7	+89 21	1.97v	0.64	F5–8 Ib	−3.6	450	**Polaris**
49	β CMa	6 23.7	−17 58	1.98v	−0.24	B1 II–III	−3.9	~490	Mirzam
50	α Hya A	9 28.7	−8 45	1.99	1.44	K3 II–III†	−1.7	180	**Alphard**

[1] To the unaided eye, the combined visual magnitude of Rigil Kentaurus A and B is –0.28.
[2] To the unaided eye, the combined visual magnitude of Acrux A and B is 0.68.

THE NEAREST STARS

BY TODD J. HENRY

The nearest stars hold a special fascination for any of us who have gazed skyward. Astronomers study the Sun's neighbors because they are the nearest, and therefore brightest, examples of their types. For many kinds of stars, the fundamental framework of stellar astronomy is built upon direct measurements of luminosities, colors, temperatures, and masses of nearby stars. Their surrounding environments are remote destinations to explore from Earth, and any planets orbiting them could someday become outposts of humankind because the nearest stars are the first step beyond our own Solar System.

The definition of a "nearby" star system is that its distance is accurately known to be within a designated horizon. Distances may be measured geometrically, via astrometry using the technique of trigonometric parallax, or estimated using myriad combinations of photometric and spectroscopic data. Here we adopt distances based on trigonometric parallaxes only, as they are the most reliable and are independent of assumptions about the type of star under scrutiny. With results from the *Gaia* spacecraft, we now know the distances to millions of stars to better than 1% accuracy.

The list presented here includes the Sun's 52 nearest stellar neighbors and their companions within the astronomically convenient horizon of 5.0 parsecs, or 16.3 light-years (ly). The definition of a parsec, which is equivalent to 3.26 ly, is based upon the radius of the Earth's orbit: as the Earth swings around the Sun, nearby stars shift back and forth relative to more distant, background objects because of our changing perspective, much as a thumb held at arm's length will seem to shift relative to a distant background when you close one eye, then the other. This shift is called parallax. The size of the shift depends entirely upon the star's distance, and astronomers have defined the distance at which a star's parallax is 1.00″ to be 1.00 parallax-second (parsec). As the distance increases, the shift decreases inversely, i.e. parallax = 1/distance. Thus, a star at 5.00 parsecs will exhibit a trigonometric parallax of 0.200 arcseconds, or 200 milliarcseconds (mas). The shifts are slight—the parallax of the nearest star, Proxima Centauri, is 769 mas and is only about 1/2300th the width of the full Moon.

To be included in the list, a stellar system must have a trigonometric parallax of at least 200 mas with an error of less than 10 mas published in the refereed literature, meaning that the distance is known to 5% or better. There are, effectively, five broad categories of nearby star parallaxes: (1) A wonderful compendium of ground-based parallax efforts through 1995 is *The General Catalogue of Trigonometric Stellar Parallaxes* (a.k.a. the *Yale Parallax Catalog*, or *YPC*) by van Altena et al. The *YPC* includes nearly 16 000 parallax measurements of more than 8 000 stars. Stars as bright as Sirius and as faint as mag. 20 can be found in the *YPC*, with most parallaxes accurate to 3–13 mas. (2) ESA's *HIPPARCOS* space astrometry mission targeted nearly 120 000 relatively bright stars at a precision of typically 0.5–4 mas, with a compendium of results published in 1997. In 2007, van Leeuwen published a new reduction of the *HIPPARCOS* data, and those results have been used to generate the parallaxes given here. (3) Since then, several teams have continued using traditional telescopes on the ground to measure parallaxes for both new and known stars within 5 parsecs, primarily by the Allegheny, Dartmouth, RECONS, Torino, and USNO groups. (4) In space, the *Hubble Space Telescope* has been used to determine parallaxes of several of the Sun's neighbors, while measuring stellar masses or searching for exoplanets (primarily by the U. Texas group). (5) ESA's *Gaia* spacecraft released results for 1.7

billion sources in April 2018, many of which have errors less than 1 milliarcsecond. The list presented here uses a comprehensive combination of trigonometric parallaxes from various sources to arrive at a weighted mean parallax for each system, which simply means that higher-quality parallaxes are mathematically given more weight in the averaging process. Individual component parallaxes have been combined for all systems except for the nearest one, which is, in fact, a triple including Proxima and the two components of α Centauri, A and B. The *YPC* includes 43 of the 52 extrasolar systems, while *HIPPARCOS* improved upon many of those, but added no new systems. RECONS added five of the nine remaining systems, with the latest four additions having parallaxes measured by other teams. In total, 185 different parallaxes have been used to generate the distances given. The RECONS group (recons.org) is keeping a tally of all trigonometric parallax efforts since the *YPC* and *HIPPARCOS*, and the reader is encouraged to contact the author about any overlooked publications (thenry@astro.gsu.edu).

Including the Sun, there are 53 known systems in the 5-parsec sphere, made up of 66 stars, 9 brown dwarfs, and at least 13 extrasolar planets (plus, of course, the 8 planets in the Solar System). Curiously, there are one-third more systems in the southern sky (31) than in the north (21), even though historically far more astronomical observations have been made in the northern sky. Seventeen of the systems include stellar or brown-dwarf companions, while nine (including the Solar System) have planets. The smallest type of star, known as red dwarfs of spectral type M, dominate our galaxy, accounting for 73% of the 5-parsec sample (48 of 66 stars—all stars without types in the list are type M, but individual spectral types are not available because of close separations in multiple systems, hence the "J" for joint in some spectral types). None of these red dwarfs is visible with the unaided eye. In some ways, our galaxy mimics an ocean full of creatures, large and small, but it is the smallest fish that dominate the population. Missing from the nearby waters are the largest whales, the most massive stars of spectral types O and B. Such stars are exceedingly rare and have lifetimes of only a few million years. The visually brightest star in the night sky is Sirius, which is the brighter star in the seventh-nearest system, and the only A-type star listed. Near Sirius in the sky is Procyon (the 16th-nearest system), nearly as bright and the only F-type star listed. Both Sirius and Procyon have white-dwarf companions that are the leftover embers of more-massive counterparts. These stars have already reinvented themselves, having changed from stars larger than Sirius and Procyon to reveal only their cores as white dwarfs by sloughing off their outer layers long ago. In the past, the light of Sirius and Procyon would be lost in the glare of their much larger, and brighter, components. In all, there are five white dwarfs, denoted by "D" in the list, nearer than 5 parsecs. The two stars most similar to our Sun are the only other two G dwarfs, α Centauri A and τ Ceti. Finally, eight stars are of K type, including α Centauri B, 61 Cygni A and B, and the naked-eye stars ε Indi, o^2 Eridani A, and ε Eridani. The latter star is particularly interesting because it is circled by a band of cold dust and at least one planet, with reports of two additional planets inferred because of gaps in the dusty disk. Also worthy of note is Kapteyn's Star, which is a rare subdwarf—an ancient, subluminous star of spectral luminosity class VI—that is moving quickly through the solar neighborhood. It has the largest radial velocity of the systems in the list, and has the second-fastest proper motion, only surpassed by Barnard's Star, the second-nearest system.

We continue to find more of the Sun's neighbors, even so close to home. Recent and ongoing sky surveys provide a wealth of solar neighborhood candidates for those who cleverly dig through the databases for gems. DENIS (DEep Near-Infrared Survey) has provided two recent additions, the red dwarf DENIS 1048–3956 and the brown dwarf DENIS 0255–4700. Following in the footsteps of Giclas and Luyten, who both did breakthrough work in studies of nearby stars via proper-motion searches, the SCR (SuperCOSMOS–RECONS) effort trawls an electronic database generated by scanning glass plates of the entire sky. The 28th-nearest system, an M/T dwarf pair known as SCR 1845–6357, was found during an early SCR search.

In the following table, names are given in the first column with emphasis on discovery names or variable-star names, the latter if for no other reason than it gives some idea as to the system's location in the sky. Component designations within a single system are listed as A, B, or C, and are enclosed by parentheses if there are different names for individual members. Presumed planets are listed as "+nP" in the companion column, where n is the number of planets. Astrometric information is given next, including **RA** and **Dec** for equinox J2000.0, the weighted mean parallax (**π**) and its estimated error (***err***) in mas, the derived distance (**D**) in light-years, and the proper motion (**μ**) in mas/y with the position angle of the motion (**PA**) (north is 0°, east is 90°). Spectroscopic information is then listed, including the systemic radial velocity (**V_{rad}**) and spectral type (**Sp.**) for each component, when known. Photometric information is provided in the form of the visual magnitude (**m_V**), where it may be useful to know that the human eye can see to about mag. 6. The list closes with the derived absolute magnitude (**M_V**), which is a valuable measurement of an object's intrinsic brightness, and reflects how bright an object would appear if it were at a standard distance of 10 parsecs.

In the past few years, brown dwarfs very near the Sun have been found, including WISE 1049–5319AB and WISE 0855-0714, which currently rank as the third – and fourth-nearest systems. Nine brown dwarfs are now known within 5 parsecs. Nonetheless, the stars still outnumber the brown dwarfs by 7:1, and there are more extrasolar planets known than brown dwarfs. GJ 1061, now ranked as the 22nd-nearest system, remains the closest new star found to the Sun since the *YPC* and *HIPPARCOS* compendia. There is a new entry to the 5-parsec list, WISE 0855-0714, for which the first high-quality parallax has now been published. The Gaia spacecraft has delivered its first full set of parallaxes, of which 49 measurements are included for 42 of the 52 systems. No new systems were added by *Gaia*, but the average error for the systems it did observe has now been reduced to only 0.12 milliarcseconds.

In 1999, the first planet around Ross 780 was announced, and thus the first reliable exoplanet discovery within 5 parsecs made it into the *Observer's Handbook* in 2000. Other than the Sun, there are now 8 systems within 5 parsecs that are *reported* to have planets. Research on individual nearby stars has recently been reinvigorated because the nearest stellar systems are prime targets for more-sensitive exoplanet searches and, ultimately, life. The population of nearby stars remains a compelling area of research because we have yet to answer the fundamental questions, what types of stars form at what rates? and, how much mass in our galaxy can be found in stars? That so many faint, yet nearby, objects have slipped through previous surveys of our neighborhood hints at more to come. Undoubtedly, the more complete our reconnaissance of the solar neighborhood, the better we will understand the nature of stars that make up our galaxy, and our Sun's place among them.

*(See entry 2 at right.) For the fastest-moving star in the sky, Barnard's Star, the 2022.0 coordinates are RA 17h 57m 48s, Dec +4° 41′ 36″, moving steadily southward in eastern Ophiuchus at 10.326 mas/y.

TABLE OF NEAREST STARS

Name		RA (2000) h m	Dec ° ′	π mas	*err* mas	*D* ly	μ mas/y	PA °	V_{rad} km/s	Sp.	m_V	M_V
Sun	+8P									G2V	–26.71	4.84
Proxima Cen	(C)+1P	14 30	–62 41	768.62	0.16	4.24	3853	281.5	–16	M5.0V	11.13	15.56
α Cen	A	14 40	–60 50	747.23	1.17	4.36	3710	277.5	–26	G2V	0.01	4.38
	B	14 40	–60 50				3724	284.8	–18	K0.0V	1.34	5.71
Barnard's		17 58	+04 42*	546.47	0.20	5.97	10352	355.6	–111	M3.5V	9.54	13.23
WISE 1049–5319	A	10 49	–53 19	495.02	4.56	6.59	2787	277.5		L8	23.25	26.72
	B	10 49	–53 19							T1	24.07	27.54
WISE 0855–0714		8 55	–07 14	449.00	8.00	7.26	8130	274.6		brown dwarf		
Wolf 359		10 56	+07 01	414.37	0.87	7.87	4696	234.6	+19	M5.5V	13.61	16.70
Lalande 21185		11 03	+35 58	393.25	0.57	8.29	4802	186.9	–85	M2.0V	7.46	10.43
Sirius	A	6 45	–16 43	377.05	0.43	8.65	1339	204.1	–9	A1V	–1.43	1.45
	B	6 45	–16 42							DA2	8.44	11.32
BL Cet	(A)	1 39	–17 57	371.01	0.19	8.79	3368	80.4	+29	M5.5V	12.63	15.48
UV Cet	(B)	1 39	–17 57						+32	M6.0V	13.08	15.93
Ross 154		18 50	–23 50	336.12	0.06	9.70	666	106.8	–10	M3.5V	10.50	13.13
Ross 248		23 42	+44 11	316.91	0.12	10.29	1617	177.0	–78	M5.5V	12.29	14.79
ε Eri	+1P	3 33	–09 27	311.26	0.09	10.48	977	271.1	+16	K2.0V	3.73	6.20
CD –36 15693		23 06	–35 51	304.22	0.05	10.72	6896	78.9	+9	M1.0V	7.34	9.76
Ross 128		11 48	+00 48	296.31	0.07	11.01	1361	153.6	–31	M4.0V	11.15	13.51
EZ Aqr	A	22 39	–15 18	289.50	4.40	11.27	3254	46.6	–50	M5.0VJ	13.03	15.34
	B	22 39	–15 18								13.27	15.58
	C	22 39	–15 18								15.07	17.38
61 Cyg	A	21 07	+38 45	286.09	0.05	11.40	5281	51.9	–66	K5.0V	5.21	7.49
	B	21 07	+38 45				5172	52.6	–64	K7.0V	6.03	8.31
Procyon	A	7 39	+05 13	285.17	0.64	11.44	1259	214.7	–4	F5 IV–V	0.37	2.65
	B	7 39	+05 13							DQZ	10.70	12.98
BD +59 1915	A	18 43	+59 38	283.83	0.05	11.49	2238	323.6	–1	M3.0V	8.90	11.17
	B	18 43	+59 38				2313	323.0	+1	M3.5V	9.69	11.96
GX And	(A)+1P	0 18	+44 01	280.73	0.03	11.62	2918	81.9	+12	M1.5V	8.09	10.33
GQ And	(B)	0 18	+44 02						+11	M3.5V	11.07	13.31
DX Can		8 30	+26 47	279.28	0.13	11.68	1290	242.2	–5	M6.0V	14.96	17.19
ε Ind	A	22 03	–56 47	276.07	0.28	11.81	4704	122.7	–40	K4.0V	4.68	6.89
	B	22 04	–56 47				4698	122.3		T1		
	C	22 04	–56 47							T6		
τ Cet		1 44	–15 56	274.32	0.16	11.89	1922	296.4	–17	G8.5V	3.49	5.68
GJ 1061		3 36	–44 31	272.20	0.07	11.98	831	118.8	–20	M5.0V	13.09	15.26
YZ Cet		1 13	–17 00	269.36	0.08	12.11	1372	61.9	+28	M4.0V	12.16	14.31
Luyten's		7 27	+05 14	266.23	0.66	12.25	3738	171.2	+18	M3.5V	9.88	12.01
SO 0253+1652		2 53	+16 53	260.86	0.24	12.50	5103	138.1		M6.5V	15.14	17.22
Kapteyn's		5 12	–45 01	254.23	0.03	12.83	8670	131.4	+245	M2.0VI	8.85	10.88
AX Mic		21 17	–38 52	251.84	0.06	12.95	3455	250.6	+28	K9.0V	6.67	8.68
SCR 1845–6357	A	18 45	–63 58	249.98	0.15	13.05	2661	77.0		M8.5V	17.40	19.39
	B	18 45	–63 58							T6		
Kruger 60	A	22 28	+57 42	249.40	0.16	13.08	782	246.1	–34	M3.0V	9.79	11.77
	B	22 28	+57 41							M4.0V	11.41	13.39
DENIS 1048–3956		10 48	–39 56	247.21	0.12	13.19	1532	229.9		M8.5V	17.39	19.36
UGP 0722–0540		7 22	–05 40	242.80	2.40	13.43	970	291.3		T9		
Ross 614	A	6 29	–02 49	241.75	0.34	13.49	930	131.7	+17	M4.0V	11.18	13.12
	B	6 29	–02 49							M5.5V	14.26	16.20
Wolf 424	A	12 33	+09 01	233.34	2.45	13.98	1755	276.6		M5.0VJ	13.23	15.07
	B	12 33	+09 01								13.22	15.06
Wolf 1061	+2P	16 30	–12 40	232.21	0.06	14.05	1189	184.5	–21	M3.5V	10.07	11.90
van Maanen's		0 49	+05 23	231.74	0.04	14.07	2971	156.9	+54	DZ7	12.40	14.23
CD –37 15492		0 05	–37 21	230.13	0.06	14.17	6100	112.5	+23	M1.5V	8.54	10.35
TZ Ari		2 00	+13 03	223.59	0.11	14.59	2097	147.8	–29	M4.0V	12.35	14.10

TABLE OF NEAREST STARS (continued)

#	Name		RA (2000) h m	Dec ° ′	π mas	err mas	D ly	μ mas/y	PA °	V_{rad} km/s	Sp.	m_V	M_V
38	CD –46 11540	+1P	17 29	–46 54	219.80	0.05	14.84	1050	146.9	–10	M2.5V	9.39	11.10
39	BD +68 946	+1P	17 36	+68 20	219.78	0.03	14.84	1309	194.2	–29	M3.0V	9.17	10.88
40	LHS 292		10 48	–11 20	218.96	0.15	14.90	1644	158.5	–7	M6.5V	15.78	17.48
41	L 145–141		11 46	–64 50	215.74	0.03	15.12	2692	97.5		DQ6	11.50	13.17
42	G 208–44	(A)	19 54	+44 25	214.69	0.08	15.19	731	143.1		M5.5VJ	13.46	15.12
	G 208–45	(B)	19 54	+44 25							M6.0V	14.01	15.67
	G 208–44	(C)	19 54	+44 25								16.75	18.41
43	Ross 780	+4P	22 53	–14 16	213.88	0.08	15.25	1174	125.1	–2	M3.5V	10.18	11.83
44	LHS 288		10 44	–61 13	206.83	0.07	15.77	1657	348.1		M5.5V	13.90	15.48
45	G 158–27		0 07	–07 32	206.23	0.13	15.82	2041	203.6	–42	M5.0V	13.84	15.41
46	DENIS 0255–4700		2 55	–47 01	205.41	0.23	15.88	1149	119.5		L8	22.92	24.48
47	BD +50 1725		10 11	+49 27	205.39	0.03	15.88	1452	249.7	–26	K7.0V	6.59	8.15
48	BD +44 2051	(A)	11 05	+43 32	204.11	0.17	15.98	4511	282.1	+69	M1.0V	8.77	10.32
	WX UMa	(B)	11 06	+43 31				4531	281.9		M5.5V	14.44	15.99
49	WISE 1639–6847		16 40	–68 48	202.30	3.10	16.12	3156	169.3		brown dwarf		
50	CD –49 13515	+2P	21 34	–49 01	201.41	0.04	16.19	819	183.2	+4	M1.5V	8.66	10.18
51	BD +20 2465		10 20	+19 52	201.37	0.07	16.20	506	264.0	+12	M2.5V	9.29	10.81
52	o^2 Eri	A	4 15	–07 39	200.05	0.17	16.30	4088	213.2	–42	K0.5V	4.43	5.94
		B	4 15	–07 39				4073	212.4		DA4	9.52	11.03
		C	4 15	–07 39							M4.0V	11.24	12.75

SOME EASILY OBSERVABLE NEARBY STARS

BY DAVID M.F. CHAPMAN

This table lists some of the nearby stars from the main table that may be of interest to the observer, including all those of mag. 6 and brighter, plus three of historical interest (all red dwarfs). The stars have been reordered by magnitude of the primary component. The table data have been simplified—consult the original table for details.

Name		RA (2000) h m	Dec ° ′	π mas	D ly	μ ″/y	PA °	Sp.	m_V
Sun	+8P							G2	–26.7
Sirius[1]	A	6 45	–16 43	377	8.7	1.3	204	A1	–1.4
α Cen[2, 3]	A	14 41	–60 55	747	4.4	3.7	278	G2	0.0
	B	14 41	–60 55			3.7	285	K0.0	1.3
Procyon[4]	A	7 39	+5 13	285	11.4	1.3	215	F5	0.4
τ Cet[5]		1 44	–15 56	274	11.5	1.9	296	G8.5	3.5
ε Eri[5]	+1P	3 33	–09 27	311	10.5	1.0	271	K2.0	3.7
o^2 Eri[6]	A	4 15	–07 39	200	16.3	4.1	213	K0.5	4.4
	B	4 15	–07 39			4.1	212	DA4	9.5
ε Ind	A	22 03	–56 47	275	11.8	4.7	123	K4.0	4.7
61 Cyg[7]	A	21 07	+38 45	285	11.4	5.3	52	K5.0	5.2
	B	21 07	+38 45			5.2	53	K7.0	6.0
Kapteyn's		5 12	–45 01	255	12.8	8.7	131	M2.0	8.9
Barnard's[8]		17 58	+4 45	546	6.0	10.4	356	M3.5	9.5
Luyten's[9]		7 27	+5 14	266	12.3	3.7	171	M3.5	9.9

[1] α CMa, see note on facing page.
[2] Rigil Kentaurus, similar to Sun, see note on p. 292.
[3] The star system nearest to Sun reported to have at least one planet (Proxima Centauri, α Cen C.
[4] α CMi, see note on p. 292
[5] Similar to Sun, the nearest such star visible to observers at north-temperate latitudes.
[6] B is the nearest white-dwarf star that is easily observable, see p. 304.
[7] First star to have its stellar parallax measured (Bessel, 1838).
[8] Star with the largest proper motion; second-closest star system to Sun (Barnard, 1916).
[9] Only 1.2 ly from Procyon.

DOUBLE AND MULTIPLE STARS

BY BRIAN D. MASON AND RACHEL MATSON

Approximately 85% of stars are found in double or multiple systems consisting of two or more stars. While the first detections of double stars date back to the 17th century, systematic observations with large-aperture telescopes (notably by William Herschel) in the early 18th century determined that many double stars are gravitationally bound. Such physically associated double stars are referred to as binaries, while stars that merely appear nearby on the sky are known as optical doubles. The components of binary stars can be as close as 1–20 times the sum of their radii and cannot be visually resolved into two separate stars, or as wide as a few degrees apart, allowing the components to be clearly separated and their apparent motions in the sky measured. Close binaries may be detected by their brightness variations if the two components pass in front of one another (see Binary Systems in the Variable Star section) or by the superposition of spectral lines from both components. For visual binaries, resolving the individual stars depends on their separation, magnitude difference (Δm), and the aperture of the telescope. The resolving power of a telescope can be estimated as 120/D, where D is the diameter of the telescope objective in millimetres. Astronomers using long-baseline optical interferometry have measured double-star separations less than a milliarcsecond (0.001″).

A good source of information on double and multiple stars is *The Journal of Double Star Observations* (JDSO; **jdso.org**), which publishes the work of professionals, amateurs, and students. Sissy Haas (*Sky & Telescope*, September 2012) also produced a book titled *Double Stars for Small Telescopes* that provides targets and descriptions as well as test objects for determining your Δm limit at a range of separations. A Double Stars observing certificate program was also recently instituted by the RASC (**rasc.ca/double-stars**).

The following table provides the position angles (PA) and separation (Sep) of 138 double and multiple stars. PA is the angular direction of the fainter star (2) from the brighter (1), measured from north through east, then south, and so on. Since some of the stars exhibit significant motion, the predicted position angles and separations are given for both 2022.0 and 2023.0. Note that data for 2022.0 have been changed for some systems due to improvements in orbit calculations or more recent measurements. If no 2023.0 data are provided, there is no calculation (orbital or linear) of the motion (if any) of the double and the predicted PA and Sep are the most recent measurements.

The systems were selected to cover a wide variety of interests. Wide or slowly moving pairs are good for evaluating optical performance or estimating seeing. With the preponderance of inexpensive, large-aperture telescopes, the availability of interferometry for the amateur (see R. Caloi, JDSO 4, 111, 2008), and access to systems with larger magnitude differences (see J. Daley, JDSO 3, 159, 2007), closer systems have also been included. The list is well distributed in RA and covers a range of separations with small and large Δm. Of the 138 listed systems, 20 have separations of 1″ or less and 19 between 1″ and 2″. At more moderate separations, there are 19 between 2″ and 3″, 23 between 3″ and 5″, 22 between 5″ and 7″, 21 between 7″ and 10″, and 14 with separations greater than 10″.

Notes on some double and multiple stars in the table (marked with *); a dagger (†) in the orbital period indicates the orbit was recently improved.

κ **Tuc:** This pair is part of a quintuple star system of solar-type stars approximately 70 light-years from Earth. From the AB pair listed in the table, a bright, common proper-motion companion can be seen 5.3′ to the northwest, which consists of two closely separated stars (1″) with a period of 86 years. The A component is also a binary, with an invisible companion detected through precise astrometry and a tentative period of 22 years.

γ **And:** Also known as Almaak or Almach, the AB system is striking in color with the brighter star a K-type giant that appears yellow-gold, while its companion is a hot blue main-sequence star. The B component is itself a triple system consisting of a close (2.7 day) spectroscopic binary and the wider BC pair also listed in the table.

ι **Tri:** This attractive pair consists of yellow and blue stars that form a very slow binary that has moved by only 12 degrees in over 200 years. Two preliminary orbits were proposed in

2020 with periods of 2600 and 5200 years. Both stars are also spectroscopic binaries with periods of 14.7 days (brighter) and 2.2 days (fainter).

94 Cet: The binary nature of 94 Cet was first discovered by Admiral Smyth in 1836. More recently, astrometric measurements determined the B component was itself a binary consisting of two M-dwarfs with an orbital period of 2 years. Not to be left out, the A component hosts a planet in a 450 day orbit at a distance of 1.3 AU from the star and a mass roughly 1.2 times the mass of Jupiter.

α **Gem:** Castor actually has six components associated with it! In addition to AB listed here, the fainter C & D are at 72.5″ and 164.0°, and 204.4″ and 222.0°, respectively. Both A & B also have spectroscopic companions with periods of a few days.

ζ **Cnc:** A gorgeous and easily seen triple system, the wide component is quite bright (Mv = 6.3) and is well separated (6″) with a preliminary orbit of 735 years. In 2000, a long-suspected companion to the C component was resolved at 0.3″ with a period of about 17 years. There is also tentative evidence that this D component may itself be a pair of M stars.

44 Boo: This close pair was first discovered by William Herschel in 1781. The eccentricity of the system results in large changes in the separation of the two stars, as they were nearly 5″ apart in the 1800s but only 0.2″ apart in 2021. Due to the tilt of the orbit against the plane of the sky, however, the stars were physically closest in 2012 despite appearing closer in the sky in 2021. The B component is a contact variable star known as a W UMa type eclipsing binary with a period of 6.4 hours.

η **CrB:** One of the shortest-period visual binaries visible in a small telescope, this binary has a very well-determined orbit. It reached its most recent closest separation in 2020 and its position will be changing rapidly over the next dozen years. Both components are similar to the Sun.

70 Oph: At a distance of 16 light-years, 70 Oph is a wide system that moves quickly due to its proximity. Both components are small, orange main-sequence stars, with the brighter star appearing yellow-gold, while the fainter star looks more orange-red. Claims of an additional astrometric companion date back to 1855 when Captain W.S. Jacob proposed the existence of a planet with a 26-year orbit around the B component, but high-resolution spectroscopy has since disproven its existence.

μ **Cyg:** Discovered at a separation of 6″ in the late 1700s, this system closed to about one-half arcsecond in the 1930s has now opened up to 1.5″. Observations cover about a third of the preliminary 700-year orbit.

TABLE OF DOUBLE AND MULTIPLE STARS

	RA (2000) Dec				Magnitudes			2022.0		2023.0		
Star	h	m	°	′	comb.	1	2	PA °	Sep. ″	PA °	Sep. ″	Period y
36 And AB	00	55.0	+23	38	5.6	6.1	6.5	337	1.19	338	1.20	168
ζ Phe AB,C	01	08.4	−55	15	4.0	4.0	8.2	239	6.76			
φ Psc AB	01	13.7	+24	35	4.6	4.7	9.1	226	7.59			
κ Tuc AB*	01	15.8	−68	53	4.9	5.0	7.7	314	4.53	313	4.51	1200†
γ Ari AB	01	53.5	+19	18	3.8	4.5	4.6	1	7.38			
α Psc AB	02	02.0	+02	46	3.8	4.1	5.2	260	1.86	259	1.86	1947
γ And A,BC*	02	03.9	+42	20	2.2	2.3	5.0	63	9.63			
γ And BC*	02	03.9	+42	20	4.8	5.1	6.3	117	0.24	116	0.27	63
ι Tri*	02	12.4	+30	18	5.0	5.3	6.7	68	3.92	68	3.92	2647†
ι Cas AB	02	29.1	+67	24	4.5	4.6	6.9	228	3.04	228	3.05	2400†
ι Cas AC	02	29.1	+67	24	4.5	4.6	9.1	117	6.67			
α UMi AB	02	31.8	+89	16	2.1	2.1	9.1	236	18.39			
ν Cet	02	35.9	+05	36	4.3	5.0	9.1	80	8.41			
84 Cet	02	41.2	−00	42	5.8	5.8	9.7	301	3.85	301	3.85	3194
γ Cet AB	02	43.3	+03	14	3.4	3.5	6.2	299	2.03			
τ Per Aa,Ab	02	54.3	+52	46	4.0	4.2	5.9	104	0.02	279	0.06	4
ε Ari AB	02	59.2	+21	20	4.6	5.2	5.6	210	1.31	210	1.30	710
γ Per Aa,Ab	03	04.8	+53	30	2.7	2.9	4.4	245	0.09	245	0.15	15

* and † See note in text.

TABLE OF DOUBLE AND MULTIPLE STARS (continued)

Star	RA (2000) h	m	Dec °	′	Magnitudes comb.	1	2	2022.0 PA °	Sep. ″	2023.0 PA °	Sep. ″	Period y
α For	03	12.1	−28	59	3.9	4.0	7.2	301	5.44	301	5.45	268
94 Cet AB*	03	12.8	−01	12	5.1	5.1	11.0	185	2.10	184	2.09	1420
HR 997	03	18.7	−18	34	5.8	5.9	8.2	122	7.96			
32 Eri AB	03	54.3	−02	57	4.5	4.8	5.9	349	6.93			
HR 1230	04	10.0	+80	42	5.2	5.6	6.3	161	0.67	162	0.66	372
40 Eri A,BC	04	15.3	−07	39	4.4	4.4	9.8	102	82.69			
40 Eri BC	04	15.3	−07	39	9.8	10.0	11.5	329	7.72	329	7.63	223
ε Aur AB	05	02.0	+43	49	3.0	3.0	14.0	226	29.84			
14 Ori	05	07.9	+08	30	5.4	5.8	6.7	280	0.99	278	1.00	198
β Ori A,BC	05	14.5	−08	12	0.3	0.3	6.8	203	10.30			
14 Aur AB	05	15.4	+32	41	5.0	5.0	10.9	11	9.75			
16 Aur	05	18.2	+33	22	4.8	4.8	10.6	55	4.14			
HR 1771 AB	05	21.8	−24	46	5.1	5.4	6.6	91	3.52			
118 Tau AB	05	29.3	+25	09	5.4	5.8	6.7	209	4.93			
33 Ori AB	05	31.2	+03	18	5.4	5.7	6.7	26	1.85			
λ Ori AB	05	35.1	+09	56	3.3	3.5	5.5	44	4.33			
ζ Ori AB	05	40.7	−01	57	1.7	1.9	3.7	167	2.15	167	2.15	1509
52 Ori	05	48.0	+06	27	5.3	6.0	6.0	221	0.98	221	0.97	1260
β Mon AB	06	28.8	−07	02	4.0	4.6	5.0	133	7.10			
β Mon AC	06	28.8	−07	02	4.2	4.6	5.4	126	9.90			
HR 2384 AB	06	29.8	−50	14	5.3	6.0	6.2	210	0.08	304	0.11	53
α CMa AB	06	45.1	−16	43	−1.5	−1.5	8.5	64	11.30	63	11.33	50
12 Lyn AB	06	46.2	+59	27	4.8	5.4	6.0	64	1.91	64	1.92	733
12 Lyn AC	06	46.2	+59	27	4.8	5.4	7.1	309	8.89			
38 Gem AB	06	54.6	+13	11	4.7	4.8	7.8	142	7.41	142	7.41	1750
HR 2674	07	03.3	−59	11	5.5	5.8	6.8	88	1.30			
δ Gem	07	20.1	+21	59	3.5	3.6	8.2	230	5.46	230	5.44	1418
α Gem*	07	34.6	+31	53	1.6	1.9	3.0	51	5.50	51	5.57	460
HR 2949 AB	07	38.8	−26	48	3.8	4.4	4.6	318	9.93			
α CMi AB	07	39.3	+05	14	0.4	0.4	10.8	333	4.90	338	4.96	41
κ Gem	07	44.4	+24	24	3.7	3.7	8.2	243	7.18			
ζ Cnc AB*	08	12.2	+17	39	4.9	5.3	6.3	357	1.10	354	1.10	59
ζ Cnc AB,C*	08	12.2	+17	39	4.6	4.9	5.9	64	6.28	63	6.30	735
HR 3432	08	37.3	−62	51	5.5	5.5	11.0	237	6.15			
ι Cnc	08	46.7	+28	46	4.0	4.1	6.0	308	30.70			
ε Hya AB,C	08	46.8	+06	25	3.4	3.5	6.7	312	2.70	313	2.70	372
ι UMa A,BC	08	59.2	+48	03	3.1	3.1	9.2	109	2.36	111	2.39	486
$σ^2$ UMa AB	09	10.4	+67	08	4.8	4.9	8.9	346	4.61	345	4.64	921
38 Lyn AB	09	18.8	+36	48	3.8	3.9	6.1	222	2.61	222	2.61	2783
HR 3752	09	25.5	−61	57	5.8	5.8	9.6	330	8.82			
ψ Vel	09	30.7	−40	28	3.6	3.9	5.1	143	0.88	147	0.83	34
11 LMi	09	35.7	+35	49	4.8	4.8	12.5	50	6.11	50	6.14	241
γ Sex AB	09	52.5	−08	06	5.1	5.4	6.4	33	0.45	31	0.43	78
γ Leo AB	10	20.0	+19	50	2.1	2.4	3.6	128	4.76	128	4.76	554
μ Vel	10	46.8	−49	25	2.7	2.8	5.7	58	2.32	59	2.32	143
54 Leo	10	55.6	+24	45	4.3	4.5	6.3	112	6.76			
ξ UMa AB	11	18.2	+31	32	3.8	4.3	4.8	145	2.34	142	2.42	60
ν UMa AB	11	18.5	+33	06	3.5	3.5	10.1	149	7.45			
57 UMa AB	11	29.1	+39	020	5.3	5.4	10.7	354	5.46			
$α^1$ Cru AB	12	26.6	−63	6	0.6	1.3	1.6	111	3.52			
24 Com	12	35.1	+18	023	4.8	5.1	6.3	272	20.20			
γ Vir AB	12	41.7	−01	27	2.8	3.5	3.5	355	3.16	354	3.27	169
β Mus AB	12	46.3	−68	06	3.0	3.5	4.0	61	0.92	62	0.91	459
θ Vir AB	13	09.9	−05	32	4.4	4.4	9.4	342	6.82			
α Com AB	13	10.0	+17	32	4.4	4.9	5.5	192	0.36	192	0.28	26
ζ UMa AB	13	23.9	+54	56	2.0	2.2	3.9	154	14.58			
84 Vir	13	43.1	+03	32	5.5	5.6	8.3	227	2.73			
τ Boo	13	47.3	+17	27	4.5	4.5	11.1	96	1.23	102	1.20	964
HR 5386 A,BC	14	23.4	+08	27	4.8	5.0	6.8	196	6.23			
ϕ Vir AB	14	28.2	−02	14	4.9	4.9	10.0	113	4.81			
α Cen AB	14	39.6	−60	50	−0.2	0.1	1.2	357	6.78	2	7.45	80

* and † See note in text.

TABLE OF DOUBLE AND MULTIPLE STARS (continued)

	RA (2000)		Dec		Magnitudes			2022.0		2023.0		
Star	h	m	°	′	comb.	1	2	PA °	Sep. ″	PA °	Sep. ″	Period y
π[1] Boo	14	40.7	+16	25	4.5	4.9	5.8	113	5.36			
ζ Boo AB	14	41.1	+13	44	3.8	4.5	4.6	268	0.15	250	0.09	125
ε Boo AB	14	45.0	+27	04	2.4	2.6	4.8	347	2.83			
ξ Boo AB	14	51.4	+19	06	4.6	4.8	7.0	294	5.17	293	5.08	153
44 Boo*	15	03.8	+47	39	4.8	5.2	6.1	179	0.27	200	0.39	214
π Lup	15	05.1	−47	30	3.8	4.6	4.6	64	1.64			
η CrB AB*	15	23.2	+30	17	5.0	5.6	6.0	326	0.43	341	0.52	42
δ Ser AB	15	34.8	+10	32	3.8	4.2	5.2	171	4.04	171	4.03	1150
ζ[2] CrB	15	39.4	+36	38	4.6	5.0	5.9	306	6.25			
ι[1] Nor AB	16	03.5	−57	47	4.7	5.2	5.8	324	0.31	313	0.35	27
ξ Sco AB	16	04.4	−11	22	4.1	4.8	4.9	15	1.13	16	1.12	46
ξ Sco AC	16	04.4	−11	22	4.7	4.8	7.3	43	7.52	42	7.52	1514
11 Sco AB	16	07.6	−12	45	5.7	5.8	9.8	263	3.34			
κ Her AB	16	08.1	+17	03	4.8	5.1	6.2	14	27.03			
σ CrB AB	16	14.7	+33	52	5.2	5.6	6.5	239	7.31	240	7.33	657
ρ Oph AB	16	25.6	−23	27	4.6	5.1	5.7	333	3.00	333	3.00	4193
α Sco	16	29.4	−26	26	0.9	1.0	5.4	277	2.61	277	2.61	2666
λ Oph AB	16	30.9	+01	59	3.8	4.2	5.2	47	1.36	48	1.35	129
HR 6246 AB	16	49.6	+13	16	5.7	5.7	10.0	43	4.87			
μ Dra AB	17	05.3	+54	28	4.9	5.7	5.7	356	2.59	355	2.61	424
η Oph AB	17	10.4	−15	44	2.4	3.1	3.3	225	0.41	224	0.34	88
α Her AB	17	14.6	+14	23	3.3	3.5	5.4	102	4.64	102	4.64	3600
36 Oph AB	17	15.3	−26	36	3.9	4.3	5.1	139	5.11	138	5.12	471
HR 6426 AB	17	19.0	−34	59	6.0	6.4	7.4	322	1.28	315	1.49	42
41 Ara AB	17	19.1	−46	38	5.6	5.6	8.9	259	10.82	260	10.89	609
95 Her	18	01.5	+21	36	4.3	4.9	5.2	257	6.38			
τ Oph AB	18	03.1	−08	11	4.8	5.3	5.9	290	1.44	291	1.43	257
70 Oph AB*	18	05.5	+02	30	4.1	4.2	6.2	120	6.70	119	6.72	88
HR 6749–50	18	06.8	−43	25	4.9	5.7	5.7	357	1.75	356	1.75	450
HR 6997 AB	18	36.6	+33	28	5.4	5.4	9.4	204	7.15			
ε[1] Lyr AB	18	44.3	+39	40	4.8	5.2	6.1	357	1.75	356	1.75	2803†
ε[2] Lyr CD	18	44.3	+39	40	4.6	5.3	5.4	74	2.41	73	2.41	724†
HR 7048 AB	18	45.5	+05	30	5.8	6.3	6.7	120	2.59			
β Cyg AB	19	30.7	+27	58	2.9	3.2	4.7	54	34.59			
16 Cyg AB	19	41.8	+50	32	5.4	6.9	6.2	133	39.83	133	39.84	13513
δ Cyg AB	19	45.0	+45	08	2.8	2.9	6.3	214	2.79	214	2.80	657
ε Dra	19	48.2	+70	16	3.9	4.0	6.9	22	3.20	22	3.21	2753
π Aql AB	19	48.7	+11	49	5.8	6.3	6.8	105	1.43			
ζ Sge AB,C	19	49.0	+19	09	5.0	5.0	9.0	311	8.26			
ψ Cyg AB	19	55.6	+52	26	4.9	5.0	7.5	175	2.80			
16 Vul	20	02.0	+24	56	5.2	5.8	6.2	128	0.85	128	0.85	1201
κ Cep AB	20	08.9	+77	43	4.4	4.4	8.3	120	7.34			
β Cap AB	20	21.0	−14	47	3.1	3.2	6.1	267	205.40			
β Del AB	20	37.5	+14	36	3.7	4.1	5.0	301	0.25	315	0.31	27
52 Cyg	20	45.6	+30	43	4.2	4.2	8.7	72	5.90			
γ Del	20	46.7	+16	07	3.9	4.4	5.0	265	8.84	265	8.82	3249
HR 8040 AB	20	58.5	+50	28	5.5	5.9	6.8	25	1.97			
ε Equ AB	20	59.1	+04	18	5.4	6.0	6.3	116	0.05	109	0.11	104
12 Aqr AB	21	04.1	−05	49	5.6	5.8	7.5	197	2.46			
τ Cyg AB	21	14.8	+38	03	3.7	3.8	6.6	176	1.02	173	1.02	50
μ Cyg AB*	21	44.1	+28	45	4.5	4.8	6.2	324	1.49	325	1.47	692
λ Oct	21	50.9	−82	43	5.4	5.6	7.3	63	3.48			
30 Peg AB	22	20.5	+05	47	5.4	5.4	11.5	17	6.37			
Kruger 60 AB	22	28.0	+57	42	9.7	9.9	11.4	197	2.21	189	2.36	45
ζ[2] Aqr AB	22	28.8	−00	01	3.7	4.3	4.5	155	2.39	154	2.41	427
δ Cep AC	22	29.2	+58	25	4.0	4.2	6.1	191	40.96			
ο Cep AB	23	18.6	+68	07	4.8	5.0	7.3	224	3.45	224	3.45	2199
72 Peg	23	34.0	+31	20	5.1	5.7	6.1	108	0.58	109	0.58	492
σ Cas AB	23	59.0	+55	45	4.9	5.0	7.2	326	3.11			

* and † See note in text.

CARBON STARS

BY RON OSTROMECKI AND RICHARD HUZIAK

Carbon stars are variable, late-stage red giants with periodicities ranging from around 70 days to over 400 days. Carbon in the outer atmosphere of the star absorbs blue light, resulting in the red appearance. Magnitude estimation can be tricky because of a phenomenon called the Purkinje effect, which can lead to overstating the brightness of the star. The newer spectral classification C encompasses the older classifications J, N, and R.

	RA (2000)	Dec	Tycho 2		
Star	h m	° ′	Δm_V	*B–V*	Spec.
WZ Cas	0 01.3	+60 21	6.8–7.7	2.8	C9,2JLi
SU And	0 04.6	+43 33	8.0–8.5	2.81	C6,4
ST Cas	0 17.5	+50 17	9.0–10.0	2.48	C4,4
VX And	0 19.9	+44 43	7.5–9.7	5.59	C4,5J
NQ Cas	0 24.6	+54 18	9.1–9.8	1.83	C4,5J
AQ And	0 27.5	+35 35	7.7–9.5	3.65	C5,4
W Cas	0 54.9	+58 34	7.8–12.5	3.6	C7,1e
Z Psc	1 16.1	+25 46	6.4–7.5	2.86	C7,2
WW Cas	1 33.5	+57 45	9.1–11.7	2.1	C5,5
R Scl	1 27.0	–32 33	5.7–8.1	4.4	C6,5ea
V Ari	2 15.0	+12 14	8.2–8.9	2.15	C5p,5
R For	2 29.3	–26 06	7.5–13.0	2.21	C4,3e
HD 16115	2 35.1	–9 27	8.15	1.21	C2,3
DY Per	2 35.3	+56 09	10.5–16.0	2.0	C4,5
V623 Cas	3 11.4	+57 54	7–3–8.0	2.3	C4,5J
Y Per	3 27.7	+44 11	8.1–11.3	2.52	C4,3e
V466 Per	3 41.5	+51 30	7.6–9.1	4.25	C5,5
U Cam	3 41.8	+62 39	7.5–9.0	3.95	C5.5e
AC Per	3 45.1	+44 47	9.0–9.6:	3.09	C6,3
UV Cam	4 05.9	+61 48	7.5–7.7	2.26	C5,3
T Cae	4 47.3	–36 13	7.7–8.7	2.59	C6,4
ST Cam	4 51.2	+68 10	6.7–8.0	3.38	C5,4
TT Tau	4 51.5	+28 32	7.9–9.0	2.3	C7,4
SU Tau	5 49.1	+19 04	9.1–18.0	1.1	C1,0
V346 Aur	4 52.6	+38 30	9.3–9.8	3.56	C8,1J
R Lep	4 59.6	–14 48	5.5–11.7	4.93	C7,6e
EL Aur	5 03.4	+50 38	8.7–9.2	3.4	C5,4
W Ori	5 05.4	+1 11	5.5–6.9	3.81	C5,4
TX Aur	5 09.1	+39 0	8.5–9.2	3.71	C5,4
SY Eri	5 09.8	–5 31	7.8–9.1	2.62	C6,3
UV Aur	5 21.8	+32 31	7.3–10.9	2.1	C7,2Jep
S Aur	5 27.1	+34 09	8.2–13.3	1.81	C4–5
RT Ori	5 33.2	+7 09	7.6–8.6	2.97	C6,4
SZ Lep	5 35.8	–25 44	7.4–7.9	2.4	C7,3
S Cam	5 41.0	+68 48	8.1–10.9	2.95	C7,3e
TU Tau	5 45.2	+24 25	7.7–8.8	2.75	C5,4
Y Tau	5 45.7	+20 42	6.4–7.3	3.44	C6.5,4e
FU Aur	5 48.1	+30 38	8.5–9.2	2.77	C7,2
TU Gem	6 10.9	+26 01	6.9–8.0	3.36	C6,4
GK Ori	6 17.7	+8 31	9.5–11	2.0	C4–5
V Aur	6 24.0	+47 42	8.5–13	3.87	C6,2e
BL Ori	6 25.5	+14 43	5.9–6.6	2.55	C6,3
RV Aur	6 34.7	+42 30	9.9–10.4:	3.47	C4,5
UU Aur	6 36.5	+38 27	5.1–6.6	3.1	C6,3
VW Gem	6 42.1	+31 27	8.1–8.5	2.68	C5,4
GY Mon	6 53.2	–4 35	8.1–9.1:	2.64	C6,3
NP Pup	6 54.4	–42 22	6.2–6.5	2.5	C–R3
RV Mon	6 58.4	+6 10	6.9–7.7	3.2	C5,3
V614 Mon	7 01.0	–3 15	7.0–7.4	1.96	C4,5J
RY Mon	7 06.9	–7 33	7.5–9.2	4.38	C6,5:
W CMa	7 08.1	–11 55	6.3–7.1	2.66	C6,3
R CMi	7 08.7	+10 01	7.5–11.6	2.55	C7,1Je
BM Gem	7 21.0	+24 60	8.9–10.0:	2.8	C5,4J
RU Cam	7 21.7	+69 40	8.1–9.8	1.16	C2,2e
BE CMa	7 23.6	–22 58	9.3–9.8:	2.46	C5,5J
NQ Gem	7 31.9	+24 30	7.4–8.2:	2.27	C6,2e
W CMi	7 48.8	+5 24	8.7–9.0	3.23	C7,2
RT Pup	8 05.3	–38 47	8.2–9.1	2.43	C6,2
RU Pup	8 07.5	–22 55	8.3–8.5:	3.61	C5,4
RY Hya	8 20.1	+2 46	8.3–11.1	3.77	C6,4e
AC Pup	8 22.7	–15 55	8.9–10.1	3.04	C5,4
YY Pyx	8 28.2	–27 15	9.0–9.7	4.52	C
UZ Pyx	8 46.6	–29 44	7.0–7.6	2.39	C5,5J
X Cnc	8 55.4	+17 14	5.7–6.9	3.37	C5,4
T Cnc	8 56.7	+19 51	7.6–10.5	4.32	C4,7
RT UMa	9 18.4	+51 24	8.6–9.6	3.69	C4,4
Y Hya	9 51.1	–23 01	6.2–7.4	4.17	C5,4
SZ Car	9 59.9	–60 13	7.2–7.8	2.81	C
AB Ant	10 11.9	–35 19	6.6–7.1	2.47	C6,3
U Hya	10 37.6	–13 23	4.6–5.4	2.8	C6.5,3
VY UMa	10 45.1	+67 25	5.7–6.3	2.59	C6,3
TZ Car	10 46.1	–65 37	8.7–9.1	2.43	C
V Hya	10 51.6	–21 15	6.0–12.3	5.55	C6,3e
SY Car	11 15.6	–57 56	8.8–9.0	2.48	C
S Cen	12 24.6	–49 26	8.1–8.6	2.04	C4,5
SS Vir	12 25.2	+0 46	6.0–9.6	4.2	C6,3e
Y CVn	12 45.1	+45 26	4.9–5.9	3.4	C5,4J
RU Vir	12 47.3	+4 09	8.1–14.2	4.5	C8,1e
RY Dra	12 56.4	+65 60	5.9–8.0	3.7	C4,5J
TT CVn	12 59.4	+37 49	8.0–8.6	1.99	C3,5CH
R CrB	15 48.6	+28 09	5.7–15.2	1.9	C0,0
V CrB	15 49.5	+39 34	6.9–12.6	3.12	C6,2e
RR Her	16 04.2	+50 30	8.1–9.4	3.0	C6.5e
V Oph	16 26.7	–12 26	7.3–11.6	4.38	C6,3e
SU Sco	16 40.6	–32 23	8.6–<13.0:	3.36	C5,5
TW Oph	17 29.7	–19 28	8.5–9.4	4.34	C5,5
SZ Sgr	17 44.9	–18 39	8.4–8.8	2.89	C7,3
SX Sco	17 47.5	–35 42	8.7–9.8	3.82	C5,4
T Dra	17 56.4	+58 13	7.2–13.5	2.7	C7,2e
FO Ser	18 19.4	–15 37	8.4–8.7	2.03	C4,5
SS Sgr	18 30.4	–16 54	9.6–10.2	3.82	C3,4
T Lyr	18 32.3	+36 60	7.5–9.2	5.46	C6,5
HK Lyr	18 42.8	+36 58	7.5–8.4	3.5	C7,4
RV Sct	18 44.4	–13 13	8.7–9.1	2.63	C4,4
S Sct	18 50.3	–7 54	6.6–7.3	3.32	C6,4
UV Aql	18 58.5	+14 22	8.6–9.8:	4.39	C5,4–5
V Aql	19 04.4	–5 41	6.7–7.2	4.0	C5,4
V1942 Sgr	19 19.2	–15 55	6.7–7.2	2.73	C6,4
UX Dra	19 21.6	+76 34	5.9–7.1	2.91	C7,3
AW Cyg	19 28.8	+46 03	8.2–9.2	3.87	C4,5
AQ Sgr	19 34.3	–16 22	7.0–7.4	3.26	C7,4
TT Cyg	19 41.0	+32 37	7.2–8.0	2.6	C5,4e
AX Cyg	19 57.2	+44 16	7.7–8.9	4.4	C4,5
V1469 Aql	20 01.1	+9 31	8.4–8.5:	2.04	C
SV Cyg	20 09.5	+47 52	8.5–9.8	3.15	C7.4
RY Cyg	20 10.4	+35 57	8.5–10.3	2.82	C5,5
RS Cyg	20 13.4	+38 44	6.5–9.5	2.8	C8,2e
RT Cap	20 17.1	–21 19	6.8–8.0	4.42	C6,4
WX Cyg	20 18.6	+37 27	8.8–13.2	2.59	C8,2JLi
U Cyg	20 19.6	+47 54	5.9–12.1	2.81	C8,2e
V778 Cyg	20 36.1	+60 05	10.2–11.4	3.2	C4,5J
BD Vul	20 37.3	+26 29	9.3–12.7	3.74	C7,3e
V Cyg	20 41.3	+48 08	7.7–13.9	4.04	C6,3e
S Cep	21 35.2	+78 37	7.4–12.9	4.45	C7,4e
V460 Cyg	21 42.0	+35 31	5.6–6.5	2.75	C6,4
RV Cyg	21 43.3	+38 01	7.8–8.4	4.52	C6,4e
RX Peg	21 56.4	+22 52	8.6–9.8	3.18	C4,4J
RZ Peg	22 05.9	+33 30	7.6–13.6	2.65	C9,1e
DG Cep	22 44.2	+61 44	8.7–9.7	3.17	C6,4
TV Lac	22 56.1	+54 14	8.7–9.5:	2.94	C4,5
VY And	23 01.8	+45 53	9.6–11.8	3.81	C4,4J
EW And	23 27.0	+49 31	8.8–9.4	3.33	C7,3
ST And	23 38.8	+35 46	7.7–11.8	3.53	C5,3e
TX Psc	23 46.4	+3 29	4.8–5.2	2.78	C7,2

COLORED DOUBLE STARS

BY MICHEL DUVAL

The list of *colored* double stars in the following table is limited to the most beautiful pairs and those pairs most easily viewed by beginning observers in small instruments (75-mm to 150-mm objective diameter).

Subjective appreciations are suggested regarding beauty (!!!—very beautiful, !!—beautiful, !—nice) and the difficulty of visually separating the pairs in the telescope (T—tight, VT—very tight, F—faint).

The abbreviations used for colors are: B—Blue, E—Emerald, G—Green, Gd—Gold, L—Lilac, O—Orange, R—Red, T—Topaz, V—Violet, W—White, and Y—Yellow. Different observers may perceive colors differently depending on their eye physiology, telescope optics, and local seeing conditions.

The colored double stars β Cyg, α CVn, and ε Boo are better known as Albireo, Cor Caroli ("Heart of Charles"), and Izar, respectively.

An online supplement to this table at rasc.ca/handbook/supplements contains pairs that may be easier to observe with higher magnifications and/or with larger instruments. Four new colored double stars observed recently with a 16-inch instrument have been added to this supplement. François Chevrefils of the Centre francophone de Montréal de la SRAC is thanked for revising and correcting this table and its supplement; "(AC)" in the last column means the colored pair is AC, not AB.

TABLE OF COLORED DOUBLE STARS

Star	SAO	RA (2000) Dec h	m	°	′	Magnitudes A	B	Sep. ″	Color A	B	Notes Beau.	Diff.
WINTER												
Σ 163 Cas	12006	1	51	+64	51	6.8	9.1	34	O	B	!!	F
λ Ari	75051	1	58	+23	36	5.0	6.7	37	Y	B	!!	
γ And	37734	2	04	+42	20	2.3	5.4	10	O	B	!!!	
59 And	55330	2	11	+39	02	6.0	6.7	17	Y	B	!!	
66 Cet	129752	2	13	−2	24	5.7	7.7	16	O	B	!	F
η Per	23655	2	51	+55	53	3.8	8.5	28	O	B	!!	F
32 Eri	130806	3	54	−2	57	4.8	5.9	7	T	B	!!!	T
ε Per	56840	3	58	+40	01	3.0	9.0	9	Y	G		VT
φ Tau	76558	4	20	+27	21	5.1	7.5	49	Y	B		F
χ Tau	76573	4	22	+25	38	5.4	8.5	19	Y	G		F
Σ 627 Ori	112305	5	00	+3	37	6.6	7.0	21	Y	G	!!	
ρ Ori	112528	5	13	+2	52	4.6	8.5	7	O	B	!	F
Σ 680 Tau	77098	5	19	+20	08	6.2	9.7	9	Y	B		F
σ Ori	132406	5	39	−2	36	3.9	6.5	42	O	B	!!	
26 Aur	58280	5	39	+30	30	6.0	8.4	12	Y	B	!	F (AC)
8 Mon	113810	6	24	+4	36	4.5	6.5	12	Y	B	!	F
5 Lyn	25733	6	27	+58	25	5.2	9.8	32	Y	B	!	F
20 Gem	95795	6	32	+17	47	6.3	6.9	20	Y	B	!	
38 Gem	96265	6	54	+13	11	5.0	7.8	7	Y	B	!!	T
h 3945 CMa	173349	7	17	−23	19	4.8	5.8	27	Y	B	!!!	
δ Gem	79294	7	20	+21	59	3.5	8.2	6	Y	R	!!	T
κ Gem	79653	7	44	+24	24	3.6	8.1	7	O	B		F, VT
Σ 1149 CMi	115981	7	49	+3	13	7.8	9.2	22	Y	B	!	F
Σ 1183 Mon	135505	8	06	−9	14	6.2	7.8	31	Y	G	!	F
ι Cnc	80416	8	47	+28	46	4.0	6.0	31	Y	B	!!	

Note1: The Smithsonian Astrophysical Observatory (SAO) numbers in column 2 are provided for use with Go To telescope databases. The SAO Star Catalog contains details on 258 996 stars, see tdc-harvard.edu/catalogs/sao.html. The SAO and Harvard College Observatory are joined as the Harvard–Smithsonian Center for Astrophysics (CfA).
Note 2: Σ 163 Cas is better seen in WINTER, even though Cassiopeia is normally considered an AUTUMN constellation.

TABLE OF COLORED DOUBLE STARS (continued)

Star	SAO	RA (2000) h	m	Dec °	′	Magnitudes A	B	Sep. ″	Color A	B	Notes Beau.	Diff.
SPRING												
Σ 1321 UMa	27178	9	14	+52	41	8.0	8.0	18	Y	B		
Σ 1360 Leo	98615	9	30	+10	36	8.3	8.6	14	B	G		
6 Leo	117751	9	32	+9	43	5.4	9.3	37	O	G		
γ Leo	81298	10	20	+19	50	2.4	3.6	5	O	Y	!	VT
35 Sex	118449	10	43	+04	45	6.2	7.1	7	O	B		
54 Leo	81583	10	56	+24	45	4.3	6.3	6	Y	B	!	T
88 Leo	99648	11	32	+14	22	6.4	9.1	15	Y	B	!	F
2 CVn	44097	12	16	+40	40	5.9	8.7	11	Gd	B		
17 Vir	119360	12	22	+05	18	6.6	10.0	21	B	O		
24 Com	100160	12	35	+18	23	5.1	6.3	20	Gd	B	!!	
32 Cam	2102	12	49	+83	25	5.3	5.8	21	Y	B		
35 Com	82550	12	53	+21	15	5.2	9.8	28	Y	B		(AC)
α CVn	63257	12	56	+38	19	2.9	5.6	19	B	G	!!!	
ε Boo	83500	14	45	+27	04	2.6	4.8	3	O	B		VT
ξ Boo	101250	14	51	+19	06	4.8	7.0	5	Y	O		VT
ζ CrB	64834	15	39	+36	38	5.0	6.0	6	Y	B	!!!	
SUMMER												
β Sco	159682	16	05	−19	48	2.6	4.9	14	B	O	!	(AC)
κ Her	101951	16	08	+17	03	5.0	6.0	27	Y	R	!	
α Her	102680	17	15	+14	23	2.7–3.6	5.4	5	Ry	G	!	VT
ψ Dra	8890	17	42	+72	09	4.6	5.6	30	Y	L	!	
95 Her	85648	18	01	+21	36	5.0	5.1	6	G	B	!!	T
59 Ser	123497	18	27	+0	12	5.4	7.7	4	Y	G	!!	VT
ζ Lyr	67321	18	45	+37	36	4.3	5.6	44	Y	G	!!	(AD)
ο Dra	31219	18	51	+59	23	4.8	7.8	36	Gd	L	!!	F
11 Aql	104308	18	59	+13	37	5.3	9.3	19	Y	B	!!	
β Cyg	87301	19	31	+27	58	3.1	5.1	35	Y	B	!!!	
17 Cyg	68827	19	46	+33	44	5.0	9.0	26	R	B	!	F
57 Aql	143898	19	54	−8	14	6.0	6.0	36	Y	G	!!	
ΟΣ 394 Cyg	69238	20	00	+36	25	7.0	10.0	11	O	B	!	
26 Cyg	49098	20	01	+50	06	5.0	9.0	41	Y	B		F
31 Cyg	49337	20	13	+46	44	3.8	7.0	107	O	B	!!	(AC)
σ Cap	163445	20	19	−19	07	5.4	9.4	56	O	B	!	F
52 Cyg	70467	20	45	+30	43	4.0	9.0	6	Y	B		
AUTUMN												
γ Del	106476	20	47	+16	07	4.4	5.0	9	O	G	!	T
1 Peg	107073	21	22	+19	48	4.2	7.6	36	O	V		
h 1647 Peg	89737	21	29	+22	11	6.1	10.2	41	O	B		
β Cep	10057	21	29	+70	34	3.2	8.6	13	W	B	!	T
41 Aqr	190986	22	14	−21	04	5.6	6.7	5	Y	B	!	VT
δ Cep	34508	22	29	+58	25	4.2v	6.1	41	Y	B	!!	(AC)
Σ 2978 Peg	73010	23	07	+32	50	6.4	7.5	8	Y	B	!	
57 Peg	128001	23	10	+8	41	5.1	9.7	32	Y	B		F
Σ 2991 Peg	108463	23	13	+11	04	6.0	10.0	33	Y	B	!	F
Ψ^1 Aqr	146598	23	16	−9	05	4.5	10.0	49	Y	B	!	
94 Aqr	165625	23	19	−13	27	5.3	7.0	12	Y	G	!!	
ΟΣΣ 254 Cas	21002	00	01	+60	21	7.6v	8.7	57	R	B	!!	WZCas
Σ 3053 Cas	10937	00	02	+66	06	5.9	7.3	15	O	B	!!	
42 Psc	91866	00	22	+13	29	6.4	10.3	29	T	E		
12 Cet	128791	00	30	−3	57	6.0	10.8	12	Y	B		
55 Psc	74182	00	40	+21	26	5.6	8.5	7	O	B	!!	F
η Cas	21732	00	49	+57	49	3.5	7.2	13	W	G	!	
Σ 80 Cet	109577	00	59	+0	47	7.8	9.0	28	Y	B		

VARIABLE STARS

BY STELLA KAFKA AND ELIZABETH O. WAAGEN

Variable stars are stars whose brightness changes on timescales from minutes to years. They reveal many stellar properties. Depending upon their type, variables can tell us their age, mass, radius, temperature, luminosity, internal and external structure, composition, and evolutionary history. Systematic observation of variable stars is an area in which amateur astronomers can make a valuable contribution to astronomy.

For beginning observers, simplified charts of the fields of four different types of bright variable stars are shown below (see aavso.org for authoritative versions). On each chart the magnitudes (with decimal point omitted) of several suitable comparison stars are shown. A brightness estimate of the variable is made using two comparison stars, one brighter, one fainter than the variable. The magnitude, date, and time of each observation are recorded. When a number of observations have been made, a graph of magnitude versus date can be plotted. The shape of this *light curve* depends upon the type of variable. Further information about variable-star observing is available from the American Association of Variable Star Observers (AAVSO), 49 Bay State Road, Cambridge MA 02138, USA (email: aavso@aavso.org).

Table 1 is a list of long-period variables, brighter than mag. 8.0 at maximum and north of –20°. The first column (the Harvard designation of the star) gives the position for the year 1900: the first four characters give the hours and minutes of right ascension, the next three the declination in degrees. The **Max.** column gives the mean maximum magnitude. The **Min.** column gives the mean minimum magnitude. The period (**Per.**) is in days. **Epoch** gives the predicted date of the earliest maximum occurring this year; by adding multiples of the period to this epoch, the dates of subsequent maxima can be found. These variables

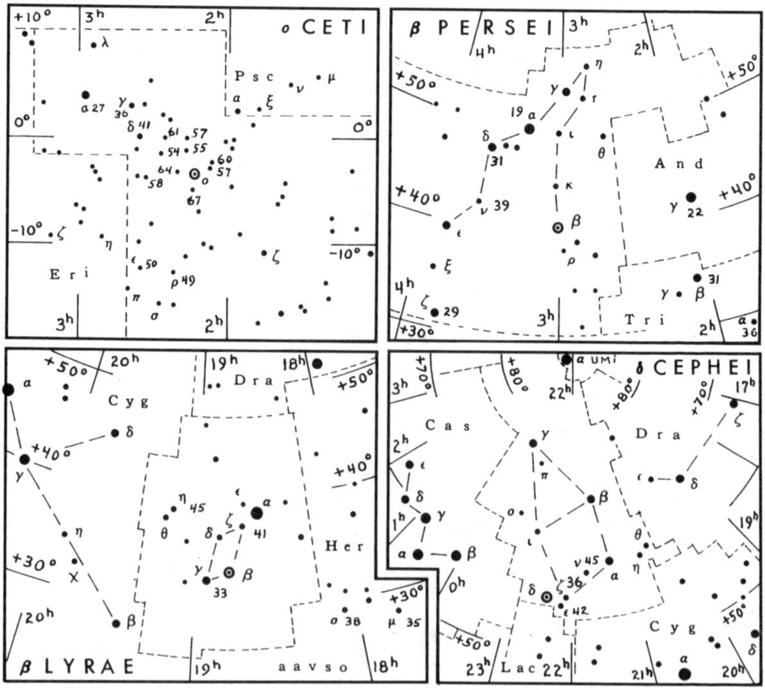

TABLE 1—LONG–PERIOD VARIABLE STARS NORTH OF −20°

Variable		Max. m_V	Min. m_V	Per. d	Epoch 2022	Variable		Max. m_V	Min. m_V	Per. d	Epoch 2022
0017+55	T Cas	7.9	11.9	445	no max	1425+39	V Boo	7.0	11.3	260	Aug. 28
0018+38	R And	6.9	14.3	409	Dec. 31	1432+27	R Boo	7.2	12.3	223	Jun. 8
0211+43	W And	7.4	13.7	396	Jul. 31	1517+31	S Crb	7.3	12.9	361	Jul. 12
0214-03A	o Cet	3.4	9.3	332	Jul. 13	1546+39	V CrB	7.5	11.0	358	Sep. 10
0228-13	U Cet	7.5	12.6	235	May 23	1546+15	R Ser	6.9	13.4	356	Apr. 27
0231+33	R Tri	6.2	11.7	267	Jan. 2	1606+25	RU Her	8.0	13.7	485	Dec. 26
0430+65	T Cam	8.0	13.8	373	Dec. 24	1621+19	U Her	7.5	12.5	406	no max
0455-14	R Lep	6.8	9.6	427	Feb. 1	1621-12	V Oph	7.5	10.2	297	Mar. 24
0509+53	R Aur	7.7	13.3	458	no max	1632+66	R Dra	7.6	12.4	246	Jan. 5
0549+20A	U Ori	6.3	12.0	368	May 8	1647+15	S Her	7.6	12.6	307	Jun. 19
0617-02	V Mon	7.0	13.1	340	Jan. 22	1702-15	R Oph	7.6	13.3	306	Jul. 12:
0653+55	R Lyn	7.9	13.8	365	Sep. 17	1717+23	RS Her	7.9	12.5	220	Mar. 3
0701+22A	R Gem	7.1	13.5	370	Mar. 12	1805+31	T Her	8.0	12.8	165	Feb. 17
0703+10	R Cmi	8.0	11.0	338	Nov. 1	1811+36	W Lyr	7.9	12.2	198	Feb. 14
0727+08	S Cmi	7.5	12.6	333	Oct. 13	1833+08	X Oph	6.8	8.8	338	Sep. 27
0811+12	R Cnc	6.8	11.2	362	Jul. 12	1901+08	R Aql	6.1	11.5	269	Apr. 7
0816+17	V Cnc	7.9	12.8	272	Aug. 17	1910-17	T Sgr	8.0	12.6	395	Aug. 1
0848+03	S Hya	7.8	12.7	257	Apr. 3	1910-19	R Sgr	7.3	12.5	270	Jun. 19
0850-08	T Hya	7.8	12.6	289	Aug. 17	1934+49	R Cyg	7.5	13.9	426	no max
0939+34	R LMi	7.1	12.6	372	Jun. 13	1940+48	RT Cyg	7.3	11.8	190	Jan. 28
0942+11	R Leo	5.8	10.0	310	Jul. 10	1946+32	χ Cyg	5.2	13.4	408	May 2
1037+69	R UMa	7.5	13.0	302	Jun. 3	2016+47	U Cyg	7.2	10.7	463	Dec. 31
1214-18	R Crv	7.5	13.8	317	Feb. 24	2044-05	T Aqr	7.7	13.1	202	May 25
1220+01	SS Vir	6.8	8.9	364	Jan. 22:	2108+68	T Cep	6.0	10.3	388	Jun. 19
1231+60	T UMa	7.7	12.9	257	May 7	2137+53	RU Cyg	8.0	9.4	233	Apr. 24::
1233+07	R Vir	6.9	11.5	146	May 3	2301+10	R Peg	7.8	13.2	378	Jun. 23
1239+61	S UMa	7.8	11.7	226	Aug. 5	2307+59	V Cas	7.9	12.2	229	May 9
1315+46	V Cvn	6.8	8.8	192	Mar. 15	2315+08	S Peg	8.0	13.0	319	Jan. 14:
1327+06	S Vir	7.0	12.7	375	Jun. 19	2338-15	R Aqr	6.5	10.3	387	Aug. 15
1344+40	R Cvn	7.7	11.9	329	Apr. 15	2353+50	R Cas	7.0	12.6	430	Jan. 9
1425+84	R Cam	8.3	13.2	270	Jan. 24	2357-15	W Cet	7.6	14.4	351	Feb. 17

may reach maximum two or three weeks before or after the epoch and may remain at maximum for several weeks. This table has been prepared with AAVSO observations.

Table 2 lists stars that are representative of some other types of variables. Elements for preparation of predicted maxima of Cepheids and minima of eclipsing binaries are from aavso.org/vsx, the International Variable Star Index (VSX). Data and elements for the predicted maximum of RR Lyr are from the GEOS RR Lyr Database (rr-lyr.irap.omp.eu/dbrr/index.php), using the Le Bourne et al. 2014 elements therein.

DESCRIPTION OF VARIABLE-STAR TYPES

Variable stars can be divided into two main classes: intrinsic variables, in which the variation is due to changes of a single star, and extrinsic variables, in which the variation is due to interaction of multiple stars or objects within a stellar system. There are many cases of overlapping variability types, such as a Mira pulsating variable as part of an eclipsing binary system. Intrinsic variables fall into three main classes: (1) pulsating stars, in which periodic expansion and contraction of the stellar surface occur; (2) eruptive variables, in which solarlike flares occur; and (3) rotating stars, in which shape distortion or star spots cause variation. Extrinsic variables consist of two main classes: (4) binary systems, in which variability is caused by orbital motion or mass transfer; and (5) cataclysmic variables, in which accretion onto a compact object can cause it to go into outburst. With modern detectors, about 1% of all stars are found to be variable. Brief and general descriptions of the major types in each class are given below.

TABLE 2—OTHER TYPES OF VARIABLE STARS

Variable		Max. m_V	Min. m_V	Type	Spectral Class	Period d	Epoch 2022 UT
0053+81	U Cep	6.8	9.3	Ecl.	B7Ve + G8III-IV	2.493087	Jan 3.42*
0301+40	β Per	2.1	3.3	Ecl.	B8V + G8III	2.86734#	†
0355+12	λ Tau	3.4	3.9	Ecl.	B3V + A4IV	3.9529478	Jan. 3.20*
0416+19	T Tau	9.3	13.5	CTTS/ROT	K0		
0530-05	T Ori	9.5	12.6	UXOR	B8-A3eap		
0539+09	FU Ori	8.7	10.6	FUOR	F2I-IIpeaq		
0619+07	T Mon	5.6	6.6	Cep	F7Iab-K1Iab + A0V	27.024649	Jan. 14.53
0658+20	ζ Gem	3.6	4.2	Cep	F7Ib-G3Ib	10.149806	Jan. 9.36
0749+22	U Gem	8.6	15.5	UGSS	Pec(UG) + M4.5V		
1846+33	β Lyr	3.4	4.4	Ecl.	B8II-IIIep	12.944#	Jan. 9.49*
1922+42	RR Lyr	6.9	8.0	RR Lyr	A5.0-F7.0	0.5669#	Jan. 1.26
1946+35	CI Cyg	9.0	12.3	ZAND	Bep + M5III		
1947+00	η Aql	3.5	4.3	Cep	F6Ib-G4Ib + B9.8V	7.17679	Jan. 1.97
2138+43	SS Cyg	8.0	12.5	UGSS	K5V + (Pec)UG		
2225+57	δ Cep	3.5	4.4	Cep	F5Ib-G1Ib	5.36627	Jan. 5.56

*Minimum # Changing period; revised for 2022.

†Algol; predictions for all minima in 2022 are given in THE SKY MONTH BY MONTH section (p. 98).

(1) Pulsating Variables

δ Scuti stars are variables that have both radial and nonradial pulsation modes with periods of 0.01–0.2 day and amplitudes from barely measurable to nearly a full magnitude. They are of A–F spectral types. Typical representative: CY Aquarii.

Cepheids are variables that pulsate with periods of 1–70 days. They have high luminosity, and the amplitude of light variation ranges from 0.1 to 2 magnitudes. The prototypes of the group, classical Cepheids, are located in open clusters and obey the well-known period-luminosity relation. They are of late F spectral class at maximum and G to K at minimum. The later (cooler) the spectral class of a classical Cepheid at minimum, the longer is its period. Typical representative of classical Cepheids: δ Cephei.

RR Lyrae stars are giant variables with periods of 0.2–1.2 days and amplitude of light variation between 0.5 and 2 magnitudes. They are usually of spectral class A. About 20% of RR Lyrae stars exhibit the Blazhko effect (a long-term variation in period and amplitude), including the prototype of the class itself, RR Lyrae.

RV Tauri stars are supergiant variables with a characteristic light curve of alternating deep and shallow minima. The periods, defined as the interval between two deep minima, range from 30 to 150 days. The amplitude of light variation may be as much as 3 magnitudes. Many show long-term cyclic variation of 500 to 9000 days. Generally, the spectral classes range from F–G at maximum to K–M at minimum light. Typical representative: R Scuti.

Long-period (Mira Ceti) variables are giants that vary with visual amplitudes from 2.5 to 5 magnitudes or more. They have well-defined periodicity, ranging from 80 to 1000 days. They show characteristic emission spectra of late spectral classes M, C, and S. Typical representative: o Ceti (Mira).

Semiregular variables are giants or supergiants showing appreciable periodicity accompanied by intervals of irregularities in light variation. The periods range from 30 to 1000 days with visual amplitudes not more than 1 to 2 magnitudes in general. Typical representative: R Ursae Minoris.

(2) Eruptive Variables

Eruptive variables are those with flares occurring in their chromospheres, along with shell mass ejections and other stellar-wind phenomena. The ejected matter can cause brightness increases or drops.

FU Orionis variables are young stars embedded in nebulae. Usually they have large-amplitude fluctuations that may take years to complete. Typical representative: FU Orionis.

T Tauri variables are young stars that have not yet reached the Zero Age Main Sequence. They are characterized by irregular variations of several magnitudes, often accompanied by emission lines and brightness fadings, probably due to dust. Typical representative: T Tauri.

UV Ceti stars are late-type dwarfs that display flare activity. The flares can range from several tenths of a magnitude to many magnitudes in size, lasting a few minutes. Typical representative: UV Ceti.

R Coronae Borealis stars are highly luminous variables that have nonperiodic drops in brightness from 1 to 9 magnitudes due to the formation of "carbon soot" in the star's atmosphere. The duration of minima varies from a few months to years. Members of this group fall into the F–K and R spectral classes. Typical representative: R Coronae Borealis.

Irregular variables are stars that at times show only a trace of periodicity or none at all. Often, poorly studied stars are placed in this category. Typical representative: RX Leporis.

(3) Rotating Variables

Rotating variables are stars with nonuniform surface brightness, caused by star spots, mass outflow, or even shape distortion.

γ Cassiopeiae variables are rapidly rotating B stars with mass outflow, forming equatorial rings or disks that can cause temporary fading episodes. Typical representative: γ Cassiopeiae.

RS Canum Venaticorum variables are rapidly rotating stars, usually close binary systems that undergo small amplitude changes in light that may be due to dark or bright spots on their surface. Eclipses may also be present in such systems (due to binarity). Typical representative: RS Canum Venaticorum.

(4) Binary Systems

Binary systems are composed of two stars or a planet around a star, in which the orbital plane is oriented such that one object crosses the disk of another object. These are usually divided into four main classes: detached, semi-detached, contact, and transitting. The first three relate to whether two stars overfill their Roche lobes or are completely isolated from one another.

Detached systems are those in which the two stars are completely isolated from one another. Light curves usually show constant light between eclipses; eclipse depth can be quite large, depending on the relative brightness of the stellar pair. Typical representative: β Persei (Algol).

Semi-detached systems have one member (the donor) overflowing its Roche lobe, with mass accreting onto the other star. Typical representative: U Cephei.

Contact binaries have both members within a common envelope. These stars often exhibit ellipsoidal variations, with the light curves continuously varying throughout the orbit. Typical representative: β Lyrae.

Transiting systems are a new class of binary, in which a planet crosses the disk of the parent star. These variations are quite small (a few hundredths of a magnitude at best), but give a great deal of information about the host star and about the transitting planet. Typical representative: HD 209458.

(5) Cataclysmic Variables

These are semi-detached binaries that typically show outbursts caused by thermonuclear runaway on either the star surface or on an accretion disk. They are a product of accretion from one star of a binary system onto the other star, usually a compact object such as a white dwarf or neutron star.

Novae consist of a normal star and a white dwarf, whose combined magnitude increases 7 to 16 magnitudes in brightness in one to several hundred days. After the outburst, the star fades slowly, returning to initial brightness in several years or decades. Near maximum brightness, the spectrum is generally similar to A or F giants. Typical representative: CP Puppis (Nova 1942).

Supernovae increase in brightness by 20 or more magnitudes due to a gigantic stellar explosion that destroys the system. The general appearance of the light curve is similar to novae. Typical representative: CM Tauri (supernova of 1054 CE, and now the central star of the Crab Nebula).

U Geminorum types are dwarf novae that have long intervals of quiescence at minimum with sudden rises to maximum. Depending upon the star, the amplitude of eruptions ranges from 2 to 6 magnitudes, and the duration between outbursts can be tens to thousands of days. Most of these stars are spectroscopic binaries with periods of a few hours. Typical representative: SS Cygni.

SU Ursae Majoris types are dwarf novae similar to U Gem and Z Cam stars in their physical and spectroscopic properties. They have frequent, faint, and narrow eruptions that last from one to a few days, along with infrequent, bright, and long eruptions—superoutbursts—that last 10 to 20 days. During superoutbursts, there are small-amplitude, periodic variations—superhumps—that are 2% to 3% longer than the orbital period of the system. Typical representative: SU Ursae Majoris.

Z Camelopardalis types are variables similar to U Gem stars in their physical and spectroscopic properties. They show brightness variations interrupted by intervals of constant brightness—standstills—lasting for several cycles, approximately one-third of the way from maximum to minimum. Typical representative: Z Camelopardalis.

VARIABLE STAR OF THE YEAR: V CORONAE BOREALIS

BY RICHARD ROBERTS

V CrB (15 49 31.31 +39 34 17.9, J2000) is a peculiar orange-red carbon star (C6,2e (N2e)) with a long history of AAVSO coverage. V CrB recently became an asymptotic giant branch (AGB) star and is currently in its hydrogen –and helium-shell burning stage of life. V CrB is in the AAVSO's legacy LPV program and Dr. John Percy's list of pulsating red giants (PRGs) exhibiting unusual behavior. V CrB is almost 14° north of Alphecca and thus placed well outside the Northern Crown at the border regions of Hercules, Bootës, and Corona Borealis. It can be found by following a line from Arcturus, to Izar, to Delta Boo, to V CrB. The star's magnitude range is 6.9–12.6 V and since it is located in a sparse star field, making accurate estimates can be a challenge when it is near maximum.

Marsakova (1999) studied the mean brightness variation of 16 carbon Miras and found they are cyclic with a super-period of 10 times the normal period. Marsakova noted that V CrB exhibited a decreasing minimum and maximum in all bands and found that V CrB had the strongest variations and was the only Mira to exhibit both cyclic and decreasing brightness in the study. However, if you analyze all available data, you see that the Marsakova (1999) data started at a peak. Around JD 2450000 (1995), shortly after this paper was published, the mean brightness of V CrB rises and then steadies back out, demonstrating the importance of continued monitoring of LPVs as they exhibit changes in behavior over long time scales.

Kipper (1998) analyzed the chemical composition of V CrB and found it similar to other late-type CH stars, moderately aged halo population II (first generation, metal deficient) stars with strong methylidyne (CH) absorption lines. He also found V CrB to undergo very mild shock waves and to have a low mass-loss rate for a carbon star. Libert et al. (2010) further determined V CrB has only been losing mass for about 3 000 years and that the mass-loss rate is changing with time. The integrated mass loss was determined to be 6.5×10^{-3} solar masses of material, most of which was molecular compounds. Hoffman et al. (2002) used interferometry to study the disks of several Miras, and found V CrB to have a very small disk relative to the other stars in the study, which agrees with the other results. This may indicate V CrB is new to the AG branch since mass-loss rates increase toward the end of the AGB stage.

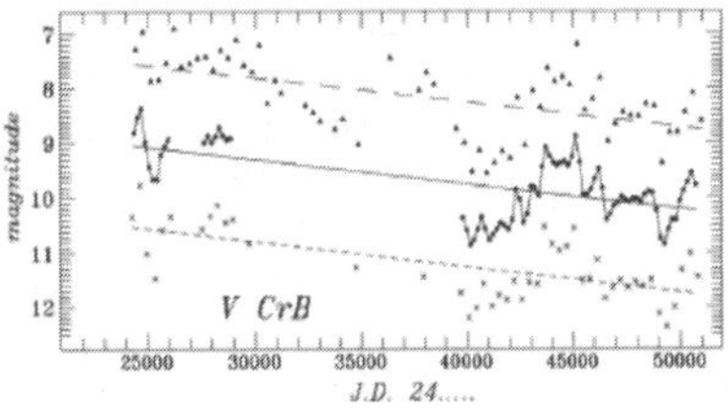

Figure 1. Variations of mean brightness (points) or magnitude of maxima (triangles) and minima (crosses) for V CrB. from Marsakova (1999)

Another peculiarity of V CrB is that it exhibits a phase shift between the maximum brightness in the infrared and the visual. Smith, Price, and Moffett (2005) found this lag to be almost 10% of the period length. This phase shift is common in oxygen-rich Miras, but V CrB is the only carbon-rich Mira known to exhibit this behavior. The phase lag in oxygen Miras is attributed to the TiO and VO absorptions, but these molecules can't explain the lag in carbon Miras. Smith, Price, and Moffett (2005) believe the phase lag in V CrB is likely due to C_2H_2 absorptions at maximum and C_2, CN absorptions at minimum. Other contributing factors believed to play a role in V CrB's phase lag are its low temperature (2100–2200 K) and large amplitude in brightness. Finder charts and comparison stars may be obtained using the AAVSO Variable Star Plotter (www.aavso.org/vsp).

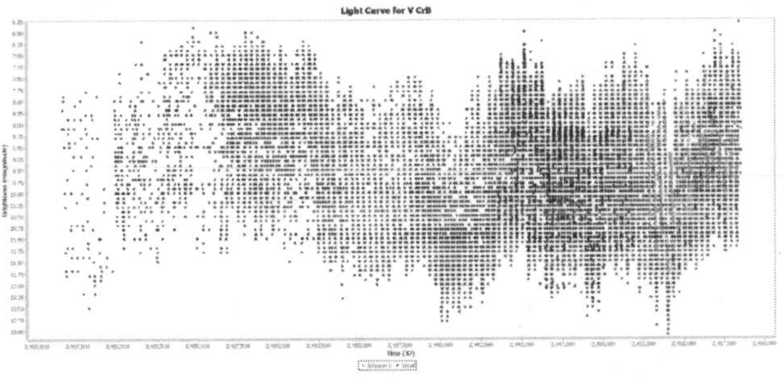

Figure 2. V CrB visual and Johnson V data from the AAVSO International Database from April 1904 – April 2019 (JD 2416571 – 2458574).

In conclusion, V CrB is a star that needs continued monitoring. The study of AGB stars is vital to our understanding of the life cycle of the galaxy as a whole, since they significantly contribute to the enrichment of the interstellar medium (Busso, Gallino, & Wasserburg 1999) and V CrB is in the initial stages of this process. The long history of AAVSO coverage and over 100 years of complete cycles gives us a great history to build on, as researchers continue to answer the several unresolved questions surrounding this star. Everyone has a chance to contribute since this star requires a telescope when dim and is best observed with binoculars when bright. For more information on observing variable stars, contact the AAVSO (see contact information on page 298).

References:

Busso M., Gallino R., & Wasserburg G.J. 1999, *ARA&A, 37*, 239.
Hoffman K. et al. arXiv:astro-ph/0206406v1 2002 Jun. 24
Kipper T. (1998) *Baltic Astronomy, Vol. 7*, pp. 435–450.
Libert, Y., Gerard, C., Thum, C., Winters, J.M., Mathews, L.D., and LeBerte, T. 2010, *A&A, 510*, A14.
Marsakova V.I. (1999) *Odessa Astronomical Publications, Vol 12*, 205.
Smith B.J., Price S.D., & Moffett A.J. arXiv:astro-ph/0509204v1. 2005 Sep. 7.

EXPIRED STARS

BY ROY BISHOP

Stars are where the action is, and the action is fueled by gravitation and thermonuclear fusion. Gravitation, the midwife and undertaker, forms a star, heats it to the temperatures necessary to ignite successive stages of fusion reactions, and when nuclear fuel runs out, crushes the ashes of the star into one of three final states: white dwarf, neutron star, or black hole. Thermonuclear fusion, powered by the strong nuclear interaction between protons and neutrons, merely delays the onset of further collapse and higher temperatures. In the case of our Sun, the first and by far the longest delay, the "hang-up" provided by hydrogen-to-helium fusion, is already half over.

White Dwarfs

Stars comparable to our Sun have insufficient gravity to reach the temperatures necessary to form nuclei heavier than carbon or oxygen. When the thermal support pressure generated by fusion wanes, gravity gradually crushes the central portion of the star. If the mass of this core is less than 1.4 solar masses (a limit discovered by a leading astrophysicist of the 20th century, Subramanyan Chandrasekhar), the collapse halts at a very hot, Earth-sized remnant known as a white dwarf. At this point, the squeeze of gravity is offset by *electron degeneracy pressure*, an intrinsic aspect of the wave–particle nature of matter and the same pressure responsible for the stability and size of an atom. However, in the case of a white dwarf, the temperature is such that the electrons are not tied to individual atomic nuclei but occupy the whole star. In this sense, the star has become a giant atom. In physics jargon: electrons are fermions (i.e. they obey Fermi–Dirac quantum statistics) and hence abide by the Pauli Exclusion Principle, which dictates that no two electrons can occupy the same quantum state. That results in an immense pressure, sufficient to prevent further collapse, provided the mass is less than the Chandrasekhar limit. White-dwarf diameters are about 1% that of our Sun, which has a nearly water-like average density (1 g/cm^3). Thus a cubic centimetre of white-dwarf material has a mass near 100^3 g or one tonne (like a Honda Fit crushed into a sugar cube).

Because of their immense thermal energy and small surface area, white dwarfs cool extremely slowly. The Universe is not yet old enough for any white dwarf to have cooled sufficiently to become a "black dwarf." Also, white dwarfs are intrinsically very faint; thus only those close to the Solar System can be seen.

Five white dwarfs are within 16.3 ly of Earth (see pp. 286–290), but only the furthest one is easily visible with a small telescope: **Omicron 2 Eridani B** (also designated **40 Eridani B**). Omicron 2 Eridani A, the bright (mag. 4.4) companion to the dim (mag. 9.5) white dwarf, is shown on the JANUARY ALL-SKY MAP on p. 340: o^2 Eri A is the eastern (left-hand) member of the close pair of stars located due west of the word "Rigel." Omicron 2 Eridani B, the white dwarf, is located only 84″ east-southeast of o^2 Eri A (position angle ≈102°). Remarkably, stars A and B are accompanied by a third star, a faint (mag. 11.2) red-dwarf star, o^2 Eri C, which resides only 8″ north of B. (There is a brighter and closer white dwarf, the companion of Sirius, α CMa B, but it is usually lost in the glare of Sirius. See pp. 291 and 293 for more information on both of these stellar systems). For information of a different kind see earthsky.org/space/star-trek-planet-vulcan-40-eridani-a, and google: 40 Eridani A, Spock's star.

The white dwarf Omicron 2 Eridani B (40 Eridani B) is the easiest to see: Earth-sized object in the depths of interstellar space; object with a mass density far exceeding that of ordinary matter; star that is no longer powered by nuclear reactions; star that has expired and can still be seen.

Neutron Stars

For a large star of about eight or more solar masses, energy-releasing reactions end in its center with the fusion of silicon nuclei into iron. Iron has the most tightly bound nucleus (per nuclear particle) and hence is no good as a fuel for further fusion. Electron degeneracy pressure supports the inert iron core until silicon fusion in a surrounding shell supplies enough additional iron to push the inert core over the Chandrasekhar limit. Gravity then overwhelms electron degeneracy pressure, and the core collapses in less than a second, so quickly that, momentarily, the outer layers of the star stay where they were. Gravitation-induced temperatures in the core rise past 10^{10} K, sufficient to disassemble heavy nuclei synthesized over the life of the star. That absorbs energy, accelerating the collapse. Also, electrons attain sufficient energy to combine with protons to form neutrons and neutrinos, another energy-absorbing reaction that also removes electrons, further hastening the collapse.

Provided the infalling mass is less than about three solar masses, like a hammer striking an anvil, when the core reaches a diameter of about 20 km, the infall is violently arrested by *neutron degeneracy pressure*, the same pressure that, in the case of both neutrons and protons, governs the size and structure of the nuclei of atoms of ordinary matter. With a diameter 500 times smaller than that of a white dwarf, the density at this stage is 500^3 larger, 100 million tonnes per cubic centimetre (like an aircraft carrier crushed to the size of the ball of a ballpoint pen). That is the density of ordinary atomic nuclei. The star's core has effectively become a gigantic nucleus, composed primarily of neutrons.

The abrupt rebound of the nearly rigid central core reverses the infall of the adjacent layers, turning the implosion into a spectacular explosion, a Type II supernova. The explosion mechanism is complex and not yet well understood, but appears to involve interactions with the immense numbers of neutrinos generated in the neutron production, and possibly acoustic waves generated by vibrations of the core as it is pummeled by infalling material within a second of its formation. The gravitational energy released in the sudden collapse of the couple of solar masses now locked in the central neutron star is about 10^{46} J. That is far more energy than our Sun will produce in its entire 10-billion-year lifetime.

Over the next several thousand years, the remnants of the outer layers of the star form an expanding, glowing cloud of gas and dust, seeding interstellar space with the heavy chemical elements (oxygen, silicon, iron, uranium, etc.) synthesized in its outer layers both before and during the supernova explosion. The potassium ions moving in the neurons of your brain as you read these words emerged from such a conflagration some 5 billion years ago.

No neutron stars are visible in a small telescope, although one is *indirectly* visible in the **Crab Nebula**, M1. The Crab supernova was a bright, naked-eye star in the skies of Earth in the year 1054 CE, although it had taken 6000 years for the light of the explosion to reach our planet. The nebula we see today is the expanding debris cloud as it was nearly 1000 years after the initial explosion.

The Crab Nebula glows across the electromagnetic spectrum, from radio waves to gamma rays, powered by the rapid but decreasing spin of the neutron star at its center. The glow of the debris cloud is like the glow of a red-hot disk brake slowing the spin of a wheel. The visible light from the cloud is *synchrotron radiation* emitted by electrons as they spiral in the tangled magnetic field of the neutron star. Nowhere else in the heavens is such an exotic light visible in a small telescope, polarized light with the brilliance of a thousand suns, emitted not by atoms but by free electrons being flung about by a spinning neutron star. The neutron star itself is known as a *pulsar* because it flashes (30 times per second!) in step with its spin. Even if the Crab pulsar were bright enough to be visible in a small telescope, the flashing would not be apparent because, as in a motion picture or cathode-ray-tube monitor, the flicker is too rapid for the eye to follow.

Color photographs of the Crab Nebula reveal a celestial gift: a package of bluish synchrotron radiation wrapped in the loops of a tattered red ribbon—fragments of the shattered star, fluorescing in hydrogen-alpha light. Unfortunately, the luminance of the fluorescence is below the threshold for vision in the red part of the spectrum. Thus all we see is the ghostly cloud of synchrotron radiation.

The Crab Nebula is located 1° northwest of the star ζ Tau, at the tip of the east horn of Taurus. In the JANUARY ALL-SKY MAP on p. 340, the nebula is the tiny circle of dots 5 mm to the right of the cross marking the summer solstice (SS). In a telescope, the nebula appears merely as a small glowing cloud, but to the knowledgeable observer, this synchrotron radiation brake of a spinning neutron star is an object for profound contemplation.

Black Holes

Stars whose masses are greater than about 20 solar masses likely retain more than 3 solar masses in their imploding cores. This is sufficient that gravitation will overwhelm not only the degeneracy pressure of electrons, but also the highly incompressible nature of nuclear matter. Within seconds, spacetime itself closes around the imploding stellar core, removing all but the core's gravitational field from the observable Universe. The star has become a black hole.

The earliest and best candidate for a stellar black hole is **Cygnus X-1**. Discovered by Dr. Tom Bolton (1941–2021) of the University of Toronto, using the 1.88-m telescope at the David Dunlap Observatory (see p. 11), it is one of the strongest galactic X-ray sources in the sky. Cygnus X-1 is the invisible companion of a star that can be seen in a small telescope: HDE 226868, an O9.7Iab star, a very luminous, very hot supergiant located about 8000 ly from the Sun. It orbits its nearby, unseen companion with a 5.6-day period. The mass of the companion is between 10 and 16 solar masses, far too large for it to be a white dwarf or neutron star. X-rays are generated as material from the supergiant falls toward the invisible companion. The X-rays extend to energies of 100 keV and vary on time scales as short as milliseconds, indicative of a very compact companion.

At 9th magnitude, the supergiant HDE 226868 is visible in any small telescope. It is less than half a degree from the 4th-magnitude star η Cygni, which is the star in the neck of the swan, next to the "C" in CYGNUS on the SEPTEMBER ALL-SKY MAP on p. 344. Any low magnification will more than encompass the field shown in the **finder chart** at left. North is upward, η Cygni is at the lower right, and HDE 226868 is indicated by the small arrow. The chart magnitude limit is about 13. Although HDE 226868 is a blue supergiant, in telescopes of sufficient aperture this star appears orange because of interstellar dust between us and the star.

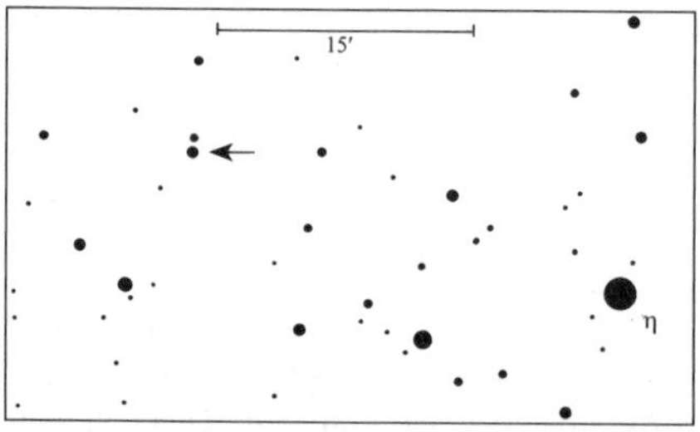

All that is to be seen is the hot supergiant, but the view will be worth the search if you know that at this same location in the field of your telescope lurks one of the most likely candidates for a black hole, a knot in the fabric of spacetime where a giant star has vanished. No painting, computer simulation, or Hollywood movie can match this observation.

For a discussion on visually observing quasars by Ian Wheelband and Blake Nancarrow of Toronto, go to rasc.ca/supplements.

Go to snews.bnl.gov/amateur.html to find out about early alert network for nearby supernovae.

THE DEEP SKY

THE DEEP SKY—FROM NEAR TO FAR

BY LOUISE O.V. EDWARDS

From the blinding light of city streets, obscuring our view, we barely make out the brightest stars; however, the view of the sky from a dark park or an isolated campsite is truly striking and awe-inspiring. From there, we see the swath of the Milky Way and—from the corners of our eyes—we begin to notice fainter stars, including a few "fuzzy" objects. These celestial wonders were familiar to ancient astronomers the world over: every clear, moonless night, naked eyes gazed into the dark night, unpolluted by artificial light. As part of many Australian aboriginal oral traditions, the diffuse glow from the impressive Magellanic Clouds was seen as distant campfires; dark patches in the Milky Way traced outlines of animals known to the Inca, who imagined "dark-cloud constellations"; Inuit skygazers tell stories interpreting the "fuzzy star" in Orion as fur carried by children of the Hunters (Orion's three belt stars, *Ullaktut*). Greek and Arab astronomers called these diffuse celestial objects "clouds," a concept passed down to us as we use the Latin word *nebula*, meaning mist or cloud.

Since the advent of the telescope (c. 1610), astronomers have been able to peer deeper into the Universe, and thousands of nebulae were soon counted and cataloged (c. 1750–1800). As telescopes and instrumentation continued to improve, astronomers began to distinguish one type of nebulosity from another. Some nebulae resolved into clusters of stars, while others remained truly cloud-like in nature, being composed of gas and dust. Many turned out to be galaxies in their own right, separate and quite outside the Milky Way (c. 1920). Today, amateur astronomers loosely gather these disparate and often far-flung nebulae into the category "deep-sky objects," a term popularized by *Sky & Telescope* magazine since the 1940s.

But why is the nebular glow so diffuse? The reasons vary, and a key factor is the vast range of distances involved. Looking up into the sky from the Earth, the three-dimensional Universe is projected onto the two-dimensional celestial sphere: we specify sky positions with just two directional coordinates, RA and Dec. Although the third dimension—distance—can be difficult to establish, it is critical to our understanding of the physical nature of the objects we observe. Specifically, without knowing the distance to an object, its linear dimensions become impossible to determine from its angular size, since it may be intrinsically large and far away, or intrinsically small and relatively close. The deep-sky selection tabled overleaf is sorted by increasing distance from Earth, which roughly correlates with physical size; the smallest objects, normally giving off less light, are only visible if they are close.

Let's classify the astrophysics of nebulae into three categories: (1) those associated with the birth of stars, (2) those displaying the late evolutionary stages and deaths of stars, and (3) those so distant that their intrinsic morphology is difficult to determine, as they truly appear to be diffuse clouds. In reality, these last are the combined light from thousands to billions of distant individual stars and associated nebulae belonging to the previous categories. In the table, note that the nearest objects (those within a few thousand light-years) are mostly open clusters (**OC**), reflection nebulae (**RN**), emission nebulae (**EN**), giant molecular clouds (**GMC**), or dark nebulae (**DN**). Observing these objects, we see giant clouds of gas and dust (GMC) from which hot, young individual stars or open clusters of stars (OC) are just forming. We are witnessing sites of stellar birth—this starlight reflects from clouds of dust (RN) and can activate the clouds of gas (EN) to emit radiation. Occasionally, cold, dark nebulae (DN) are seen in silhouette against bright backgrounds.

As our Sun is located in a region of the Milky Way with an abundance of the gas and dust necessary to form new stars, the above category of objects can be seen very close by. On the other hand, globular clusters (**GC**) of very old stars are found all the way out to the stellar halo of the galaxy, beyond the dusty disk. (For more about GCs and OCs, see STAR CLUSTERS, p. 310.) Note how GCs are found much further down in the table, out to almost 100 kly. These groups of aging stars appear fuzzy because they are too far away for our eyes—even when aided by small telescopes—to resolve the stars as individual objects; everything gets blurred together. However, when observed in larger telescopes, the individual stars of a globular cluster can be discerned and the "nebula" is revealed to be a dense clump of point sources, not a diffuse cloud.

Other systems associated with the end stages of stellar life are the planetary nebulae and supernova remnants, typically observed up to thousands of light-years distant (see EXPIRED STARS, p. 304). We are no longer seeing star formation or star clusters, but observing the remains of a single star once it has finished its main-sequence life. After a *low-mass* star (like the Sun) enlarges into a red giant, and before it becomes a white dwarf, it goes through a phase where it blows off its outer layers into a surrounding sphere of gas and dust that appears to us as a cloud with a gorgeous symmetric shape: a planetary nebula (**PN**). A supernova remnant (**SNR**) is also the end product of a star, but in this case a massive star. Again, the outer gaseous layers of the ex-star have been blown into a shell around the center. The SNRs within our galaxy stay visible for millennia, and recent ones are more compact and spherical than those formed long ago, which eventually extend, twist, and fade into the background interstellar medium.

The final category of deep-sky objects is very different. Many nebulae thought to lie within our own galaxy were discovered to be in fact distinct and distant galaxies (**G**) (see GALAXIES: BRIGHTEST AND NEAREST, p. 332). All galaxies contain old and young stars (alone or in clusters), the ingredients for stellar birth, and the remnants of stellar death. Notice that the galaxies in the table are vastly more distant than the other deep-sky objects: millions to hundreds of millions of light-years. Like globular clusters, galaxies appear diffuse because of their incredible distance; even the largest telescopes on Earth and in orbit cannot resolve all the individual stars and contained nebulae! (Some bright galaxies, including the Large and Small Magellanic Clouds, M33, and M101, contain nebulae that are included in the classic deep-sky catalogs.) Finally, the one tabled quasar (**Q**) is the bright core of a galaxy discovered using radio telescopes, yet so distant that its appearance is quasi-stellar in visible light.

RASC OBSERVING PROGRAMS AND CERTIFICATES

The RASC offers four observing certificates for **members** who observe all objects in each of the following observing lists in this chapter:

THE MESSIER CATALOGUE (p. 314)
THE FINEST NGC OBJECTS (p. 318),
THE DEEP-SKY CHALLENGE OBJECTS (p. 322),
DEEP-SKY GEMS (p. 324).

See rasc.ca/certificate-programs for details and contact the RASC Observing Committee Chair at rasc.ca/contact/observing for further information.

The RASC also offers the **Explore the Universe Certificate** for novice observers (who do not have to be RASC members), the **Explore the Moon Certificate** for beginning members, and the **Isabel Williamson Lunar Observing Certificate** and the **Double Stars Observing Certificate** for intermediate to advanced members.In addition, **Astroimaging certificates** are available for those members with a photographic bent. See rasc.ca/astro-imaging-certificate

A DEEP-SKY SELECTION—FROM NEAR TO FAR

NGC	M	Type[A]	Con	RA h	OH List[B]	Size[C] ′	S[C] mag/arcsec²	m[D]	Distance	Remarks
	45	OC	Tau	3	M, OC	100	20	(1.4)	0.44 kly	Pleiades Cluster
1435		RN	Tau	3	DSCO	20 × 15	21.6	4	0.44	Merope Nebula in above
ρ Oph area		GMC	Oph	16	WFW[E]	5.5°			0.46	EN+DN complex
6726–7		E/RN	CrA	19	SHS	2		11v	0.5	complex region
		DN	Cru	12	SHS	7° × 5°	—	—	0.6	Coalsack
7293		PN	Aqr	22	FNGC	16 × 12	20.8	14.6	0.7	Helix Nebula
ζ Ori		GMC	Ori	5	various[F]	2°		2	1.2	Flame, Horsehead, etc.
6853	27	PN	Vul	19	M	8 × 6	20.8	13	~1.2	Dumbbell Nebula
1976	42	EN	Ori	5	M	65	15–22	4	1.34	Orion Nebula
6960		SNR	Cyg	20	FNGC	70 × 6	23.2		1.5	Veil Nebula (west)
2068	78	RN	Ori	5	M	8 × 6	20.8	10	1.6	many young var. stars
7000		EN	Cyg	20	FNGC	100	23.6		~1.9	North America Nebula
3132		PN	Vel	10	SHS	1.4	17.6	10	2.0	Eight-Burst Nebula
B142–3		DN	Aql	19	DN	80 × 50	—	—	2	Barnard's "E"
6720	57	PN	Lyr	18	M	1.5 × 1	17.9	14.8	2.3	Ring Nebula
2261		E/RN	Mon	6	FNGC	2	20.1	11v	2.5	Hubble's Variable Nebula
3587	97	PN	UMa	11	M	2.5	21.6	13	~2.8	Owl Nebula
2392		PN	Gem	7	FNGC	0.7	16.2	10	2.9	Clown Face
7009		PN	Aqr	21	FNGC	0.4	14.6	12	3.0	Saturn Nebula
7129		RN	Cep	21	FNGC	7	22.5	10	3.3	small OC imbedded
6514	20	EN	Sgr	18	M	28	24.4		~4.7	Trifid Nebula
188		OC	Cep	0	OC	15	24.5	(10)	5.0	oldest OC
IC 443		SNR	Gem	6	DSCO	50 × 40			5	Jellyfish Nebula
2237–9		EN	Mon	6	FNGC	80 × 60	26.8	5	5.2	Rosette Nebula
2244		OC	Mon	6	OC	40	22.1	(4.8)	5.2	OC in above
1952	1	SNR	Tau	5	M, RS	5 × 3	20.6	16v	6.5	Crab and central pulsar
4755		OC	Cru	12	SHS, OC	10	17.8	(4.2)	6.8	Jewel Box
3372		EN	Car	10	SHS	85 × 80		4.5v	8	Carina Nebula
6838	71	GC	Sge	19	M	6	21.5	(9)	13	looks like OC
5139		GC	Cen	13	SHS, GC	30	19.6	(3.6)	17	ω Centauri GC
6205	13	GC	Her	16	M, GC	23	21.1	(5.7)	21	Hercules Cluster
6715	54	GC	Sgr	18	M, GC	6	21.5	(9)	89	core of Sgr Dwarf Gal.?
2070		EN	Dor	5	SHS	20	20	13	160	Tarantula Nebula in LMC
		G	Dor	5	SHS, G	6° × 5°	22.4	(1)	163	Large Magellanic Cloud
224	31	G	And	0	M, G	150 × 50	22.3	(4)	2.6 Mly	Andromeda Galaxy
598	33	G	Tri	1	M, G	60	22.8	(5.3)	2.8	Triangulum Galaxy
3031	81	G	UMa	9	M, G	18 × 10	22.3	(8)	12	paired with M82
5128		G	Cen	13	SHS, RS	10 × 8	20.6	(7.2)	12	Centaurus A radio source
5236	83	G	Hya	13	M, G	10 × 8	21.4	(8)	15	Southern Pinwheel
5427		G	Vir	14	DSG	2.0 × 1.7	22.0	(12.0)	110	interacting with 5426
Abell 1367		G	Leo	11	DSCO	1°		(13–16)	380	Leo Galaxy Cluster
3C 273		Q	Vir	12	DSCO, RS	stellar		(12.8)	2440	brightest quasar

[A] **DN**–dark nebula, **EN**–emission nebula (HII), **G**–galaxy, **GC**–globular cluster, **GMC**–giant molecular cloud, **OC**–open cluster, **PN**–planetary nebula, **Q**–quasar, **RN**–reflection nebula, **SNR**–supernova remnant

[B] **DN**–DARK NEBULAE, **DSG**–DEEP SKY GEMS, **DSCO**–DEEP-SKY CHALLENGE OBJECTS, **FNGC**–THE FINEST NGC OBJECTS, **G**–GALAXIES: BRIGHTEST AND NEAREST, **GC**–GLOBULAR CLUSTERS, **M**–THE MESSIER CATALOGUE, **OC**–OPEN CLUSTERS, **RS**–RADIO SOURCES, **SHS**–SOUTHERN HEMISPHERE SPLENDORS, **WFW**–WIDE-FIELD WONDERS (*Use a combination of* **NGC** *or* **M** *catalog number,* **Con**, *and* **RA** *hour to locate an object in one of the lists in this chapter.*)

[C] Approximate observable **Size** and surface brightness (***S***) from R.N. Clark, *Visual Astronomy of the Deep Sky* (Sky Publishing, 1990) available online at **clarkvision.com**. These values are not definitive!

[D] ***m*** is the mag. of the associated star for nebulae; v = variable; (***m***) is the total mag. for G, GC, OC, and Q.

[E] 1° south of ρ Oph, RA 16h 28m, Dec –24° 3.3′, star cloud and several ICs, see WIDE-FIELD WONDERS

[F] See FNGC (2024), DSG (2023), DSCO (IC 434), WFW, and DN (B33)

STAR CLUSTERS

BY PETER JEDICKE AND ANTHONY MOFFAT

The study of star clusters is crucial to the understanding of stellar structure and evolution. For most purposes, it can be assumed that the stars in a given cluster formed nearly simultaneously from the same parent cloud of gas and dust. Thus the basic factor that distinguishes one star in a cluster from another is the quantity of matter each contains. When comparing clusters, it is essentially only the age and the chemical composition of their stars that differ. But what makes one cluster *appear* different from another is mainly the degree of concentration and regularity, the spread in magnitude and color of the member stars (all of which vary mainly with age), and the total number of stars. Extremely young clusters are often irregular in shape, with clumps of newly formed stars pervaded by lanes of obscuring dust and bright nebulosity (e.g. the Orion Nebula around the Trapezium Cluster). The oldest clusters, which have not yet dissipated, and those that have not been torn apart by external forces, tend to be symmetrical in shape, with only the slower-burning, low-mass stars remaining visible; the massive stars will have spent their nuclear fuel and passed to the degenerate graveyard of white dwarfs, neutron stars, or black holes, depending upon their original mass.

The star clusters in the following tables were selected as the most conspicuous. Two types can be recognized: *open* and *globular*. Open clusters often appear as irregular aggregates of tens to thousands of stars, sometimes barely distinguishable from random fluctuations of the general field. Ranging in age from very young to very old, open clusters are concentrated toward the disk of the Milky Way and generally contain stars of chemical abundance similar to the Sun.

Sometimes we observe loose, extended groups of very young stars. Using precise methods of photometry, spectroscopy, and kinematics, we see that these stars often have a common, but not necessarily strictly coeval, origin. Such loose concentrations are called *associations*. Dynamically, both open clusters and associations are generally unbound over time scales of the order of 10 million years, being subject to the strong tidal forces of passing clouds and the background Milky Way Galaxy. Often, associations contain subconcentrations of young open clusters (e.g. The Double Cluster h and χ Persei of slightly different ages despite their proximity, in the association Per OB1, which stretches over 6° of the sky), with a strong gradient in age as the star-formation process rips through them from one edge to another. In view of their sparse nature, we do not include any of the 100-plus cataloged Milky Way associations.

Globular clusters, on the other hand, are highly symmetric, extremely old and rich agglomerations of up to several million stars, distributed throughout the galactic halo but concentrated toward the center of the galaxy. Compared to the Sun and other disk stars, they tend to be much less abundant in elements heavier than hydrogen and helium. For the larger and brighter globular clusters, the observer's goal is to see them well enough to distinguish a generous sprinkling of individual stars against a diffuse glowing background. Large telescope apertures and good skies will help resolve globular clusters. Higher powers are helpful for identification of smaller, more distant globular clusters.

The following table lists all well-defined open clusters in the Milky Way Galaxy with angular diameters* greater than 40′ and/or integrated magnitudes brighter than 5.0, as well as the richest clusters and some of special interest. The apparent integrated photographic magnitude (**m_{pg}**) is from Collinder, the angular diameter (**Diam.**) is generally from Trumpler, and the photographic magnitude of the fifth-brightest star (**m_5**) is from Shapley, except where in *italics*, which are new data. The distance (**Dist.**) is mainly from Becker and Fenkart (*Astr. Astrophys. Suppl. 4* (1971), p. 241). The earliest

* Note that the apparent angular diameter of a cluster may underestimate the full cluster diameter and may be closer to the nuclear diameter, excluding the corona (see David Turner, tinyurl.com/3uaulcb).

spectral type of cluster stars (**Sp**) is a measure of the age as follows: expressed in millions of years, O5 = 2, B0 = 8, B5 = 70, A0 = 400, A5 = 1000, F0 = 3000, and F5 = 10 000. Complete source lists of open clusters can be found at univie.ac.at/webda/navigation.html.

OPEN CLUSTERS

NGC/ other†	**RA** (2000) h m	**Dec** ° ′	**Mag.** m_{pg}	**Diam.** ′	m_5	**Dist.** 10^3 ly	**Sp**	**Remarks**
188	0 44.0	+85 21	9.3	14	14.6	5.0	F2	Oldest known
752	1 57.8	+37 41	6.6	45	9.6	1.2	A5	
869	2 19.0	+57 10	4.3	30	9.5	7.0	B1	h Per
884	2 22.4	+57 07	4.4	30	9.5	8.1	B0	χ Per, M supergiants
Perseus	3 22	+48 36	2.3	240	5	0.6	B1	Moving cl.; α Per
Pleiades	3 47.1	+24 08	1.6	120	4.2	0.41	B6	M45, best known
Hyades	4 20	+15 38	0.8	400	*3.9*	0.15	A2	Moving cl. *, in Taurus
1912	5 28.6	+35 50	7.0	18	9.7	4.6	B5	M38
1976/80	5 35.4	−5 23	2.5	50	*5.5*	1.3	O5	Trapezium, very young
2099	5 52.4	+32 32	6.2	24	9.7	4.2	B8	M37
2168	6 08.8	+24 21	5.6	29	9.0	2.8	B5	M35
2232	6 26.5	−4 45	4.1	20	*7*	1.6	B1	
2244	6 32.4	+4 52	5.2	27	*8.0*	5.3	O5	Rosette, very young
2264	6 41.0	+9 53	4.1	30	*8.0*	2.4	O8	S Mon
2287	6 47.1	−20 44	5.0	32	*8.8*	2.2	B4	M41
2362	7 18.8	−24 56	3.8	7	9.4	5.4	O9	τ CMa
2422	7 35.6	−14 30	4.3	30	9.8	1.6	B3	
2437	7 41.8	−14 49	6.6	27	10.8	5.4	B8	M46**
2451	7 45.4	−37 58	3.7	37	6	1.0	B5	
2516	7 58.3	−60 54	3.3	50	10.1	1.2	B8	
2546	8 12.5	−37 39	5.0	45	7	2.7	B0	
2632	8 40.1	+20 00	3.9	90	7.5	0.59	A0	Praesepe, M44
IC 2391	8 40.3	−53 03	2.6	45	3.5	0.5	B4	
IC 2395	8 41.0	−48 11	4.6	20	10.1	2.9	B2	
2682	8 50.4	+11 50	7.4	18	10.8	2.7	F2	M67, very old
3114	10 02.6	−60 07	4.5	37	7	2.8	B5	
IC 2602	10 43.3	−64 23	1.6	65	6	0.5	B1	θ Car
Tr 16	10 45.2	−59 42	6.7	10	10	9.6	O3	η Car and Nebula
3532	11 06.4	−58 39	3.4	55	8.1	1.4	B8	
3766	11 36.1	−61 37	4.4	12	8.1	5.8	B1	
Coma	12 25.1	+26 06	2.9	300	5.5	0.3	A1	Very sparse
4755	12 53.6	−60 20	5.2	12	7	6.8	B3	κ Cru, “Jewel Box”
6067	16 13.3	−54 13	6.5	16	10.9	4.7	B3	Classic Cepheids
6231	16 54.0	−41 48	3.5	16	7.5	5.8	O9	O supergiants, WR stars
Tr 24	16 57.0	−40 40	3.5	60	*7.3*	5.2	O5	
6405	17 40.1	−32 13	4.6	26	8.3	1.5	B4	M6
IC 4665	17 46.7	+5 44	5.4	50	7	1.1	B8	
6475	17 53.9	−34 48	3.3	50	7.4	0.8	B5	M7
6494	17 56.9	−19 01	5.9	27	10.2	1.4	B8	M23
6523	18 03.1	−24 23	5.2	45	7	5.1	O5	M8, Lagoon Nebula
6611	18 18.9	−13 47	6.6	8	10.6	5.5	O7	M16, nebula
IC 4725	18 31.7	−19 15	6.2	35	9.3	2.0	B3	M25, Cepheid U Sgr
IC 4756	18 39.3	+5 27	5.4	50	8.5	1.4	A3	
6705	18 51.1	−6 17	6.8	12.5	12	5.6	B8	M11, very rich
Mel 227	20 11.2	−79 19	5.2	60	*9*	0.8	B9	
IC 1396	21 38.9	+57 30	5.1	60	*8.5*	2.3	O6	Tr 37
7790	23 58.4	+61 13	7.1	4.5	11.7	10.3	B1	Cepheids CEa, CEb, and CF Cas

†IC = Index Catalogue, Tr = Trumpler, Mel = Melotte. *Basic for distance determination.
**Appears to contain planetary nebula NGC 2438, but this is not a cluster member.

The table below lists all the globular clusters in the Messier list and most of the globular clusters with a total apparent visual magnitude brighter than about 8.0. A table of Milky Way Galaxy globular-cluster data is available on W.E. Harris's website physics.mcmaster.ca/~harris/mwgc.dat. The apparent diameter (**Diam.**) is from Cragin, Lucyk, and Rappaport (*Deep Sky Field Guide To Uranometria 2000.0*, Willmann-Bell, 1993). The concentration class (**CC**) is from I to XII, where I is the most compact and XII the least. The integrated spectral type (**Int. Sp. T.**) varies mainly with the abundances. An observer who can see stars down to the magnitude given in the ***V*(HB)** ("horizontal-branch" magnitude) column has a good chance of being able to resolve the globular cluster; this information is from Djorgovski and Meylan (*Structure and Dynamics of Globular Clusters*, Astronomical Society of the Pacific, 1993, p. 341).

GLOBULAR CLUSTERS

NGC	M/ other	RA (2000) h m	Dec ° ′	Mag. m_V	Diam. ′	CC	Int. Sp. T.	Dist. 10^3 ly	*V*(HB)
104	47 Tuc	0 24.0	−72 04	3.95	30.9	III	G4	13	14.06
288		0 52.8	−25 35	8.09	13.8	X		29	15.44
362		1 03.2	−70 50	6.40	12.9	III	F9	28	15.40
1851		5 14.0	−40 02	7.14	11.0	II	F7	46	16.10
1904	79	5 24.1	−24 31	7.73	8.7	V	F5	42	16.20
2808		9 11.9	−64 51	6.20	13.8	I	F7	30	16.19
3201		10 17.6	−46 24	6.75	18.2	X	F6	17	14.75
4590	68	12 39.5	−26 44	7.84	12.0	X	F2	33	15.60
4833		12 59.5	−70 52	6.91	13.5	VIII	F3	20	15.45
5024	53	13 12.9	+18 10	7.61	12.6	V	F6	60	16.94
5139	ω Cen	13 26.8	−47 28	3.68	36.3	VIII	F5	17	14.52
5272	3	13 42.2	+28 22	6.19	16.2	VI	F6	35	15.65
5904	5	15 18.5	+2 04	5.65	17.4	V	F7	26	15.11
6093	80	16 17.0	−22 58	7.33	8.9	II	F6	33	15.86
6121	4	16 23.6	−26 31	5.63	26.3	IX	F8	14	13.35
6171	107	16 32.5	−13 03	7.93	10.0	X	G0	21	15.70
6205	13	16 41.7	+36 27	5.78	16.6	V	F6	21	14.95
6218	12	16 47.1	−1 56	6.70	14.5	IX	F8	24	14.90
6254	10	16 57.1	−4 05	6.60	15.1	VII	F3	20	14.65
6266	62	17 01.2	−30 06	6.45	14.1	IV	F9	22	15.90
6273	19	17 02.6	−26 16	6.77	13.5	VIII	F7	28	16.95
6333	9	17 19.2	−18 30	7.72	9.3	VIII	F5	27	16.10
6341	92	17 17.1	+43 08	6.44	11.2	IV	F2	26	15.05
6356		17 23.6	−17 49	8.25	7.2	III	G4	50	17.50
6388		17 36.3	−44 44	6.72	8.7	III	G2	37	16.90
6397		17 40.7	−53 40	5.73	25.7	IX	F4	9	12.90
6402	14	17 37.6	−3 14	7.59	11.7	VIII	F4	29	17.50
6541		18 08.0	−43 42	6.30	13.1	III	F6	13	15.10
6626	28	18 24.5	−24 52	6.79	11.2	IV	F8	19	15.68
6637	69	18 31.4	−32 20	7.64	7.1	V	G2	28	16.20
6656	22	18 36.3	−23 54	5.10	24.0	VII	F5	10	14.15
6681	70	18 43.2	−32 17	7.87	7.8	V	F5	29	15.60
6715	54	18 55.0	−30 28	7.60	9.1	III	F7	89	17.71
6752		19 10.9	−59 58	5.40	20.4	VI	F4	17	13.85
6779	56	19 16.6	+30 11	8.27	7.1	X	F5	33	16.20
6809	55	19 40.1	−30 57	6.32	19.0	XI	F4	20	14.35
6838	71	19 53.8	+18 46	8.19	7.2	†	G1	13	14.44
6864	75	20 06.0	−21 55	8.52	6.0	I	F9	61	17.45
6981	72	20 53.5	−12 32	9.27	5.9	IX	F7	55	16.99
7078	15	21 30.1	+12 10	6.20	12.3	IV	F3	34	15.86
7089	2	21 33.5	−0 50	6.47	12.9	II	F4	40	16.05
7099	30	21 40.4	−23 10	7.19	11.0	V	F3	26	15.10

† Originally thought to be an open cluster; never assigned a concentration class

FEATURED CLUSTER—WHITE-DWARF STARS IN THE COLLAPSED CORE OF NGC 6397

Early in 2021, researchers reported that the globular cluster NGC 6397 probably includes a significant number of stellar-mass black holes (*Vitral & Mamon A&A 646*, A63). But within a few months, this was refuted by another analysis that showed how the motion and energy of compact objects in a globular cluster favors fewer and fewer such black holes as time goes by. It's worth taking a look at what is going on inside a globular cluster.

With all the superlatives involved with modern astronomy, it's easy to be glib about the random motions of astronomical objects in star clusters. Of course, they are dominated by gravity, an exclusively attractive phenomenon and the only one that reaches effectively across distances appropriate to the scale of astronomy. But there is an elusive point about the motions of stars in a globular cluster: although direct collisions are unlikely because the sizes of even such impressive objects as stars are miniscule compared to the distances between them, the deflection of stars due to gravity as they approach and recede from one another is quite similar to the electromagnetic scattering of molecules off each other in an ideal gas. Always eager to leverage their understanding of more-easily accessible phenomena, scientists in the 20th century were quick to pursue this similarity, and apply concepts like pressure and heat capacity, which seem so sensible for an ideal gas, to globular clusters.

So, whereas we commonly think of objects like planets moving in well-behaved elliptical orbits according to Kepler's Laws, the effect of gravity on a three-dimensional affiliation of objects arranged in a sphere is to scramble their motions: stars do not simply orbit around the center of a globular cluster. Instead, they migrate back and forth, in and out in curving loops, which gives rise to the appealing analogy of a swarm of bees. Statistical principles can then be applied, and one process that occurs is the tendency for stars of different masses to share their kinetic energy of motion, such that massive stars eventually give up their kinetic energy to less-massive stars. The more-massive stars gravitate (pun intended) to the middle of the community.

Then what? You might expect the process to be inexorable, and a globular cluster to turn into a single lump of smashed stars eventually, the way snowflakes get rolled into a snowball. If this were true, the globular clusters would not have survived since almost the very beginning of the Universe. What happens instead is that, as more stars are concentrated in the central region, the likelihood increases that gravity will nudge some stars into a specific, but unstable, orbit around each other. We think of stars orbiting each other at large distances compared to the size of the Earth's orbit around the Sun, but these orbital pair (or triple) systems are still tiny relative to the overall dimensions of a globular cluster. The subsequent dynamics of this post-collapse phase lets a globular cluster "relax" over a few more billion years. Here's how: the smaller a randomly moving individual object is, the closer it can pass to the center of a multiple system. It is then more likely to pick up enough kinetic energy from the multiple system to be ejected from the globular cluster altogether. The aforementioned analysis (Kremer et al. 2021, arxiv.org/abs/2104.11751) of models simulating globular clusters with either collapsed cores, like NGC 6397, or not, such as NGC 5897 (our Featured Cluster in 2016) concluded that very few stellar-mass black holes would remain in a globular cluster, and that a grouping of white-dwarf stars that remains is a better explanation for the dynamics of a core-collapsed globular cluster.

When we look through the eyepiece, there is no way to see this complex activity, unfortunately. NGC 6397 happens to be the second-closest globular cluster to our Solar System; this was established by observations in the 1960s and recently confirmed by parallax measurements made with the *Hubble Space Telescope* (Brown et al. 2018, *ApJ Letters, 856*, L6). From our vantage point in the Northern Hemisphere, we can see Messier 4, the one globular cluster that is closer, but NGC 6397 is permanently below our horizon. So Alan Whitman includes NGC 6397 on the list of Southern Hemisphere Splendors, rating it with two exclamation marks and describing it as "easily resolved" (page 331). Like 47 Tucanae, this year's featured cluster was first observed by Nicolas-Louis de Lacaille at Cape of Good Hope in 1755; a modern observer can only imagine what it must have been like for the first astronomers from the Northern Hemisphere who had the opportunity to turn a decent telescope on the rich southern sky!

THE MESSIER CATALOGUE

BY ALAN DYER

Charles Messier's Catalogue provides a selection of the best and brightest deep-sky wonders for Northern Hemisphere viewers. Messier compiled his list in the late 1700s to aid prospective comet hunters. Some of these objects he discovered himself, some were first seen by other astronomers of the day, while a few (the Pleiades and the Beehive) were known since antiquity. The Messier numbers do not follow an ordered sequence across the sky. Rather, they are numbered in the order he discovered and cataloged them. Although he intended to, Messier never did publish a list with entries renumbered in order of right ascension.

In our version of THE MESSIER CATALOGUE, we've listed the objects by season *for the evening observer*, grouping the objects within their respective constellations. The constellations are then listed roughly in order of increasing right ascension, that is, constellations farther to the east and that rise later in the night are farther down the list. This is to help plan the sequence of an evening's Messier hunt.

The identity of some Messier objects is controversial. There is evidence that M91 and M102 are mistaken observations of M58 and M101, respectively. M104 and M109 were found by a colleague, Pierre Mechain, and reported to Messier for inclusion in his Catalogue. NGC 205, one of the companion galaxies to M31, the Andromeda Galaxy, was apparently found by Messier but never included in his catalog. Modern-day observers have dubbed this object M110. In our list, we have included 110 entries, including two objects that some have suggested as alternative candidates for M91 and M102.

Modern-day Messier hunters often wonder what telescopes Messier used. The largest were 190-mm and 200-mm reflectors. However, their speculum metal mirrors would have had the equivalent light-gathering power of a modern 80-mm to 100-mm reflector. He also used a number of 90-mm refractors. Today, a dark site and a good 80-mm refractor or 100-mm reflector should be sufficient for completing the entire list. Objects M6 and M7 are the most southerly, while M74 and M76 are often considered the faintest and most difficult. M83's low altitude and diffuse appearance make it a challenge for Canadian observers north of 50° latitude.

The columns contain the Messier number, the equivalent NGC (New General Catalogue) number, the constellation, the type (see below), the equinox J2000.0 coordinates, the visual magnitude m_V, the angular size in arcminutes (arcseconds for planetary nebula), and observing remarks. Entries marked "!!" are showpiece objects. Data are taken from *The Deep Sky Field Guide to Uranometria 2000.0* (Willmann-Bell, Inc., 1993), compiled by Murray Cragin, James Lucyk, and Barry Rappaport from a variety of contemporary catalogs. Some sizes have been rounded to two significant figures. Also recommended as an excellent guide is *The Messier Objects*, by Stephen James O'Meara (Cambridge University Press, 1998).

MESSIER AND NGC OBJECT TYPES

OC = open cluster	GC = globular cluster
EN = emission nebula	RN = reflection nebula
E/RN = EN + RN	
PN = planetary nebula	SNR = supernova remnant
G-SA *or* G-S = spiral galaxy	G-SB = barred spiral galaxy
G-E = elliptical galaxy	G-S0 = lenticular galaxy
G-I = irregular galaxy	(alphanumeric suffixes denote galaxy sub-types)

NUMERICAL LISTING OF MESSIER OBJECTS

M#	Sky	Con	M#	Sky	Con	M#	Sky	Con	M#	Sky	Con	M#	Sky	Con
1	Win	Tau	23	Sum	Sgr	45	Win	Tau	67	Spr	Cnc	89	Spr	Vir
2	Aut	Aqr	24	Sum	Sgr	46	Win	Pup	68	Spr	Hya	90	Spr	Vir
3	Spr	CVn	25	Sum	Sgr	47	Win	Pup	69	Sum	Sgr	91	Spr	Com
4	Sum	Sco	26	Sum	Sct	48	Win	Hya	70	Sum	Sgr	92	Sum	Her
5	Spr	Ser	27	Sum	Vul	49	Spr	Vir	71	Sum	Sge	93	Win	Pup
6	Sum	Sco	28	Sum	Sgr	50	Win	Mon	72	Aut	Aqr	94	Spr	CVn
7	Sum	Sco	29	Sum	Cyg	51	Spr	CVn	73	Aut	Aqr	95	Spr	Leo
8	Sum	Sgr	30	Aut	Cap	52	Aut	Cas	74	Aut	Psc	96	Spr	Leo
9	Sum	Oph	31	Aut	And	53	Spr	Com	75	Sum	Sgr	97	Spr	UMa
10	Sum	Oph	32	Aut	And	54	Sum	Sgr	76	Aut	Per	98	Spr	Com
11	Sum	Sct	33	Aut	Tri	55	Sum	Sgr	77	Aut	Cet	99	Spr	Com
12	Sum	Oph	34	Aut	Per	56	Sum	Lyr	78	Win	Ori	100	Spr	Com
13	Sum	Her	35	Win	Gem	57	Sum	Lyr	79	Win	Lep	101	Spr	UMa
14	Sum	Oph	36	Win	Aur	58	Spr	Vir	80	Sum	Sco	102	Spr	Dra?
15	Aut	Peg	37	Win	Aur	59	Spr	Vir	81	Spr	UMa	103	Aut	Cas
16	Sum	Ser	38	Win	Aur	60	Spr	Vir	82	Spr	UMa	104	Spr	Vir
17	Sum	Sgr	39	Sum	Cyg	61	Spr	Vir	83	Spr	Hya	105	Spr	Leo
18	Sum	Sgr	40	Spr	UMa	62	Sum	Oph	84	Spr	Vir	106	Spr	CVn
19	Sum	Oph	41	Win	CMa	63	Spr	CVn	85	Spr	Com	107	Sum	Oph
20	Sum	Sgr	42	Win	Ori	64	Spr	Com	86	Spr	Vir	108	Spr	UMa
21	Sum	Sgr	43	Win	Ori	65	Spr	Leo	87	Spr	Vir	109	Spr	UMa
22	Sum	Sgr	44	Spr	Cnc	66	Spr	Leo	88	Spr	Com	110	Aut	And

SEASONAL LISTING OF MESSIER OBJECTS

M#	NGC	Con	Type	RA (2000) h m	Dec ° ′	m_v	Size ′	Remarks
The Winter Sky								
1	1952	Tau	SNR	5 34.5	+22 01	8.4	6×4	!! famous Crab Neb. supernova remnant
45	—	Tau	OC	3 47.0	+24 07	1.2	110	!! Pleiades; look for subtle nebulosity
36	1960	Aur	OC	5 36.1	+34 08	6.0	12	bright but scattered group; use low pow.
37	2099	Aur	OC	5 52.4	+32 33	5.6	20	!! finest of three Auriga clusters; very rich
38	1912	Aur	OC	5 28.7	+35 50	6.4	21	look for small cluster NGC 1907 0.5° S
42	1976	Ori	E/RN	5 35.4	−5 27	—	65×60	!! Orion Nebula; finest in northern sky
43	1982	Ori	E/RN	5 35.6	−5 16	—	20×15	detached part of Orion Nebula
78	2068	Ori	RN	5 46.7	+0 03	—	8×6	bright featureless reflection nebula
79	1904	Lep	GC	5 24.5	−24 33	7.8	8.7	200-mm telescope needed to resolve
35	2168	Gem	OC	6 08.9	+24 20	5.1	28	!! look for sm. cluster NGC 2158 0.25° S
41	2287	CMa	OC	6 47.0	−20 44	4.5	38	4° south of Sirius; bright but coarse
50	2323	Mon	OC	7 03.2	−8 20	5.9	16	between Sirius & Procyon; use low mag
46	2437	Pup	OC	7 41.8	−14 49	6.1	27	!! contains planetary nebula NGC 2438
47	2422	Pup	OC	7 36.6	−14 30	4.4	29	coarse cluster 1.5° west of M46
93	2447	Pup	OC	7 44.6	−23 52	≈6.2	22	compact, bright cluster; fairly rich
48	2548	Hya	OC	8 13.8	−5 48	5.8	54	former “lost” Messier; large, sparse cl.

SEASONAL LISTING OF MESSIER OBJECTS (continued)

M#	NGC	Con	Type	RA (2000) h m	Dec ° ′	m_v	Size ′	Remarks
The Spring Sky								
44	2632	Cnc	OC	8 40.1	+19 59	3.1	95	!! Beehive or Praesepe; use low power
67	2682	Cnc	OC	8 50.4	+11 49	6.9	29	one of the oldest star clusters known
40	—	UMa	2 stars	12 22.4	+58 05	8.0	—	double star Winnecke 4; separation 50″
81	3031	UMa	G-SAab	9 55.6	+69 04	6.9	24×13	!! bright spiral visible in binoculars
82	3034	UMa	G-I0	9 55.8	+69 41	8.4	12×6	!! the "exploding" galaxy; M81 0.5° S
97	3587	UMa	PN	11 14.8	+55 01	9.9	194″	!! Owl Nebula; distinct grey oval
101	5457	UMa	G-SABcd	14 03.2	+54 21	7.9	26×26	!! Pinwheel Gal.; diffuse face-on spiral
108	3556	UMa	G-SBcd	11 11.5	+55 40	10.0	8.1×2.1	nearly edge-on; paired with M97 0.75° SE
109	3992	UMa	G-SBbc	11 57.6	+53 23	9.8	7.6×4.3	barred spiral near γ UMa
65	3623	Leo	G-SABa	11 18.9	+13 05	9.3	8.7×2.2	!! bright elongated spiral
66	3627	Leo	G-SABb	11 20.2	+12 59	8.9	8.2×3.9	!! M65 and NGC 3628 in same field
95	3351	Leo	G-SBb	10 44.0	+11 42	9.7	7.8×4.6	bright barred spiral
96	3368	Leo	G-SABab	10 46.8	+11 49	9.2	6.9×4.6	M95 in same field
105	3379	Leo	G-E1	10 47.8	+12 35	9.3	3.9×3.9	bright elliptical near M95 and M96
53	5024	Com	GC	13 12.9	+18 10	7.5	12.6	150-mm telescope needed to resolve
64	4826	Com	G-SAab	12 56.7	+21 41	8.5	9.2×4.6	!! Black Eye Gal.; eye needs big scope
85	4382	Com	G-SA0$^+$	12 25.4	+18 11	9.1	7.5×5.7	bright elliptical shape
88	4501	Com	G-SAb	12 32.0	+14 25	9.6	6.1×2.8	bright multiple-arm spiral
91	4548	Com	G-SBb	12 35.4	+14 30	10.2	5.0×4.1	some lists say M91 = M58, not NGC 4548
98	4192	Com	G-SABab	12 13.8	+14 54	10.1	9.1×2.1	nearly edge-on spiral near star 6 Com. B.
99	4254	Com	G-SAc	12 18.8	+14 25	9.9	4.6×4.3	nearly face-on spiral near M98
100	4321	Com	G-SABbc	12 22.9	+15 49	9.3	6.2×5.3	face-on spiral with starlike nucleus
49	4472	Vir	G-E2	12 29.8	+8 00	8.4	8.1×7.1	very bright elliptical
58	4579	Vir	G-SABb	12 37.7	+11 49	9.7	5.5×4.6	bright barred spiral; M59 and M60 1° E
59	4621	Vir	G-E5	12 42.0	+11 39	9.6	4.6×3.6	bright elliptical paired with M60
60	4649	Vir	G-E2	12 43.7	+11 33	8.8	7.1×6.1	bright elliptical with M59 and NGC 4647
61	4303	Vir	G-SABbc	12 21.9	+4 28	9.7	6.0×5.9	face-on two-armed spiral
84	4374	Vir	G-E1	12 25.1	+12 53	9.1	5.1×4.1	!! w/ M86 in Markarian's Chain
86	4406	Vir	G-E3	12 26.2	+12 57	8.9	12×9	!! w/ many NGC galaxies in Chain
87	4486	Vir	G-E0-1	12 30.8	+12 24	8.6	7.1×7.1	the one with famous jet and black hole
89	4552	Vir	G-E	12 35.7	+12 33	9.8	3.4×3.4	elliptical; resembles M87 but smaller
90	4569	Vir	G-SABab	12 36.8	+13 10	9.5	10×4	bright barred spiral near M89
104	4594	Vir	G-SA	12 40.0	−11 37	8.0	7.1×4.4	!! Sombrero Galaxy; look for dust lane
3	5272	CVn	GC	13 42.2	+28 23	5.9	16.2	!! contains many variable stars
51	5194/5	CVn	G-SAbc	13 29.9	+47 12	8.4	8×7	!! Whirlpool Galaxy; superb in big scope
63	5055	CVn	G-SAbc	13 15.8	+42 02	8.6	14×8	!! Sunflower Galaxy; bright, elongated
94	4736	CVn	G-SAab	12 50.9	+41 07	8.2	13×11	very bright and comet-like
106	4258	CVn	G-SABbc	12 19.0	+47 18	8.4	20×8	!! superb large, bright spiral
68	4590	Hya	GC	12 39.5	−26 45	7.7	12	150-mm telescope needed to resolve
83	5236	Hya	G-SABc	13 37.0	−29 52	7.6	16×13	large and diffuse; superb from far south
102	5866?	Dra	G-SA0$^+$	15 06.5	+55 46	9.9	6.6×3.2	or is M102 = M101? (look for 5907)
5	5904	Ser	GC	15 18.6	+2 05	5.7	17.4	!! one of the sky's finest globulars
The Summer Sky								
13	6205	Her	GC	16 41.7	+36 28	5.7	16.6	!! Hercules Cluster; NGC 6207 0.5° NE
92	6341	Her	GC	17 17.1	+43 08	6.4	11.2	9° NE of M13; fine but often overlooked
9	6333	Oph	GC	17 19.2	−18 31	7.6	9.3	smallest of Ophiuchus globulars
10	6254	Oph	GC	16 57.1	−4 06	6.6	15.1	rich globular cluster; M12 is 3° NW
12	6218	Oph	GC	16 47.2	−1 57	6.8	14.5	loose globular cluster near M10
14	6402	Oph	GC	17 37.6	−3 15	7.6	11.7	200-mm telescope needed to resolve
19	6273	Oph	GC	17 02.6	−26 16	6.7	13.5	oblate globular; M62 4° S
62	6266	Oph	GC	17 01.2	−30 07	6.7	14.1	asymmetrical; in rich field

SEASONAL LISTING OF MESSIER OBJECTS (continued)

M#	NGC	Con	Type	RA (2000) h m	Dec ° ′	m_v	Size ′	Remarks
Summer Sky (cont.)								
107	6171	Oph	GC	16 32.5	−13 03	8.1	10.0	small, faint globular
4	6121	Sco	GC	16 23.6	−26 32	5.8	26.3	bright globular near Antares
6	6405	Sco	OC	17 40.1	−32 13	4.2	33	!! Butterfly Cluster; best at low power
7	6475	Sco	OC	17 53.9	−34 49	3.3	80	!! excellent in binocs or rich-field scope
80	6093	Sco	GC	16 17.0	−22 59	7.3	8.9	very compressed globular
16	6611	Ser	EN + OC	18 18.6	−13 58	—	35×28	Eagle Neb. w/ open cl.; use neb. filter
8	6523	Sgr	EN	18 03.8	−24 23	—	45×30	!! Lagoon Nebula w/ open cl. NGC 6530
17	6618	Sgr	EN	18 20.8	−16 11	—	20×15	!! Swan or Omega Nebula; use neb. filter
18	6613	Sgr	OC	18 19.9	−17 08	6.9	10	sparse cluster; 1° south of M17
20	6514	Sgr	E/RN	18 02.3	−23 02	—	20×20	!! Trifid Nebula; look for dark lanes
21	6531	Sgr	OC	18 04.6	−22 30	5.9	13	0.7° NE of M20; sparse cluster
22	6656	Sgr	GC	18 36.4	−23 54	5.1	24	spectacular from southern latitude
23	6494	Sgr	OC	17 56.8	−19 01	5.5	27	bright, loose open cluster
24	—	Sgr	starcloud	18 16.5	−18 50	4.6	95×35	rich star cloud; best in big binoculars
25	IC 4725	Sgr	OC	18 31.6	−19 15	4.6	32	bright but sparse open cluster
28	6626	Sgr	GC	18 24.5	−24 52	6.8	11.2	compact globular near M22
54	6715	Sgr	GC	18 55.1	−30 29	7.6	9.1	not easily resolved
55	6809	Sgr	GC	19 40.0	−30 58	6.4	19.0	bright, loose globular cluster
69	6637	Sgr	GC	18 31.4	−32 21	7.6	7.1	small, poor globular cluster
70	6681	Sgr	GC	18 43.2	−32 18	8.0	7.8	small globular 2° east of M69
75	6864	Sgr	GC	20 06.1	−21 55	8.5	6	small and distant; 59 000 ly away
11	6705	Sct	OC	18 51.1	−6 16	5.8	13	!! Wild Duck Cl.; the best open cluster?
26	6694	Sct	OC	18 45.2	−9 24	8.0	14	bright, coarse cluster
56	6779	Lyr	GC	19 16.6	+30 11	8.3	7.1	within a rich starfield
57	6720	Lyr	PN	18 53.6	+33 02	8.8	>71″	!! Ring Nebula; an amazing smoke ring
71	6838	Sge	GC	19 53.8	+18 47	8.0	7.2	loose globular; looks like an open cluster
27	6853	Vul	PN	19 59.6	+22 43	7.3	>348″	!! Dumbbell Nebula; a superb object
29	6913	Cyg	OC	20 23.9	+38 32	6.6	6	small, poor open cluster 2° S of γ Cygni
39	7092	Cyg	OC	21 32.2	+48 26	4.6	31	very sparse cluster; use low power
The Autumn Sky								
2	7089	Aqr	GC	21 33.5	−0 49	6.4	12.9	200-mm telescope needed to resolve
72	6981	Aqr	GC	20 53.5	−12 32	9.3	5.9	near the Saturn Nebula, NGC 7009
73	6994	Aqr	OC	20 59.0	−12 38	8.9p	2.8	group of four stars only; an “asterism”
15	7078	Peg	GC	21 30.0	+12 10	6.0	12.3	rich, compact globular
30	7099	Cap	GC	21 40.4	−23 11	7.3	11	toughest in one-night Messier marathon
52	7654	Cas	OC	23 24.2	+61 35	6.9	12	young, rich cl.; faint Bubble Neb. nearby
103	581	Cas	OC	1 33.2	+60 42	7.4	6	three NGC open clusters nearby
31	224	And	G-SAb	0 42.7	+41 16	3.4	185×75	!! Andromeda Gal.; look for dust lanes
32	221	And	G-E2	0 42.7	+40 52	8.1	9×7	closest companion to M31
110	205	And	G-S0/E5 pec	0 40.4	+41 41	8.1	22×11	more distant companion to M31
33	598	Tri	G-SAcd	1 33.9	+30 39	5.7	67×42	large, diffuse spiral; requires dark sky
74	628	Psc	G-SAc	1 36.7	+15 47	9.4	11×11	faint, elusive spiral; tough in small scope
77	1068	Cet	G-SABab	2 42.7	−0 01	8.9	8.2×7.3	a Seyfert galaxy; with starlike nucleus
34	1039	Per	OC	2 42.0	+42 47	5.2	35	best at low power
76	650/51	Per	PN	1 42.4	+51 34	10.1	>65″	Little Dumbbell; faint but distinct

THE FINEST NGC OBJECTS

BY ALAN DYER

Those looking for an observing project beyond THE MESSIER CATALOGUE turn to the New General Catalogue (NGC). The NGC contains 7840 entries and forms the core database of today's computerized backyard telescopes. To match THE MESSIER CATALOGUE, this list contains 110 of the finest NGC objects visible from mid-northern latitudes. The seasonal order is similar to that used in THE MESSIER CATALOGUE, and there is no overlap. While the brightness of the best NGCs rivals many Messier targets, at least a 200-mm telescope is required to see all 110 objects on this list. Most are easy; a few are challenging.

The NGC was originally published by J.L.E. Dreyer in 1888, a work that expanded upon Sir John Herschel's 1864 "General Catalogue." Supplementary "Index Catalogues" were published by Dreyer in 1895 and 1908. The first IC extends the NGC with another 1529 objects discovered visually between 1888 and 1894. Most are faint, elusive targets. (To provide a flavor of this extension to the NGC, one entry from the first IC is included on this list, IC 289.) The Second Index Catalogue contains 3857 entries, most discovered photographically between 1895 and 1907.

The *Sky Atlas 2000.0*, the sets of index card charts called *AstroCards*, *The Night Sky Observer's Guide Vols. 1 and 2* by Kepple and Sanner, and the *Uranometria 2000.0 Deep Sky Atlas* are recommended finder aids. Most planetarium and deep-sky charting computer programs, as well as computerized telescopes, include all the objects on this list and many more.

Notation below is as in THE MESSIER CATALOGUE, p. 314. Magnitudes (m_V) are visual, with the exception of those marked "p," which are photographic, or blue, magnitudes. Most galaxies appear smaller than the sizes listed. For open clusters, the number of stars (*) is also given. Data are taken from *The Deep Sky Field Guide to Uranometria 2000.0* (see the introduction to THE MESSIER CATALOGUE), with some sizes rounded to two significant figures.

SEASONAL LISTING OF FINEST NGC OBJECTS

#	NGC	Con	Type	RA (2000) h m	Dec ° ′	m_V	Size ′	Remarks
The Autumn Sky								
1	7009	Aqr	PN	21 04.2	−11 22	8.3p	>25″	!! Saturn Nebula; small bright oval
2	7293	Aqr	PN	22 29.6	−20 48	7.3	>769″	!! Helix Nebula; large, diffuse; use filter
3	7331	Peg	G-SAb	22 37.1	+34 25	9.5	10×4	!! large, bright spiral galaxy
4	7635	Cas	EN	23 20.7	+61 12	—	15×8	Bubble Neb.; very faint; 0.5° SW of M52
5	7789	Cas	OC	23 57.0	+56 44	6.7	15	!! 300*; faint but very rich cluster
6	185	Cas	G-E3	0 39.0	+48 20	9.2	14×12	companion to M31; small and faint
7	281	Cas	EN	0 52.8	+56 37	—	35×30	!! large faint nebulosity near η Cas
8	457	Cas	OC	1 19.1	+58 20	6.4	13	80*; rich; one of the best Cas. clusters
9	663	Cas	OC	1 46.0	+61 15	7.1	16	80*; look for NGCs 654 and 659 nearby
10	IC 289	Cas	PN	3 10.3	+61 19	13.3	>34″	dim oval smudge; use a nebular filter!
11	7662	And	PN	23 25.9	+42 33	8.3	>12″	!! Blue Snowball; annular at high power
12	891	And	G-SAb	2 22.6	+42 21	9.9	13×3	!! faint, classic edge-on with dust lane
13	253	Scl	G-SABc	0 47.6	−25 17	7.6	30×7	!! very large and bright but at low altitude
14	772	Ari	G-SAb	1 59.3	+19 01	10.3	7.3×4.6	diffuse spiral galaxy
15	246	Cet	PN	0 47.0	−11 53	10.9	225″	large and faint with mottled structure
16	936	Cet	G-SB	2 27.6	−1 09	10.2	5.7×4.6	near M77; NGC 941 in the same field

SEASONAL LISTING OF FINEST NGC OBJECTS (continued)

#	NGC	Con	Type	RA (2000) h m	Dec ° ′	m_V	Size ′	Remarks
Autumn Sky (continued)								
17	869/884	Per	OC	2 21.0	+57 08	≈5	30/30	!! Double Cluster; 315*; use low power
18	1023	Per	G-SB0$^-$	2 40.4	+39 04	9.3	8.6×4.2	bright lens-shaped galaxy near M34
19	1491	Per	EN	4 03.4	+51 19	—	25×25	visually small and faint emission nebula
20	1501	Cam	PN	4 07.0	+60 55	11.5	52″	faint; dark center; look for NGC 1502
21	1232	Eri	G-SABc	3 09.8	−20 35	10.0	6.8×5.6	face-on spiral; look for NGC 1300 nearby
22	1535	Eri	PN	4 14.2	−12 44	9.6p	>18″	bright planetary with blue-grey disk
The Winter Sky								
23	1514	Tau	PN	4 09.2	+30 47	10.9	>114″	faint glow around 9.4^m central star
24	1931	Aur	E/RN	5 31.4	+34 15	—	4×4	haze surrounding four close stars
25	1788	Ori	RN	5 06.9	−3 21	—	5×3	fairly bright but diffuse reflection nebula
26	1973+	Ori	E/RN	5 35.1	−4 44	—	≈20×10	NGC 1973-5-7 just N. of M42 and M43
27	2022	Ori	PN	5 42.1	+9 05	11.9	>18″	small, faint & distinct with annular form
28	2024	Ori	EN	5 41.9	−1 51	—	30×30	bright but masked by glow from ζ Ori
29	2194	Ori	OC	6 13.8	+12 48	8.5	8	80*, fairly rich; look for 2169 nearby
30	2371/2	Gem	PN	7 25.6	+29 29	11.3	>55″	faint double-lobed planetary; use filter
31	2392	Gem	PN	7 29.2	+20 55	9.2	>15″	!! Clown Face Nebula
32	2237+	Mon	EN	6 32.3	+5 03	—	80×60	!! Rosette Nebula; very large; use filter
33	2261	Mon	E/RN	6 39.2	+8 44	var	3.5×1.5	Hubble's Variable Nebula; comet-shaped
34	2359	CMa	EN	7 18.6	−13 12	—	9×6	bright; look for 2360 & 2362 nearby
35	2440	Pup	PN	7 41.9	−18 13	9.4	>14″	almost starlike; irregular at high power
36	2539	Pup	OC	8 10.7	−12 50	6.5	21	50*; rich cluster; near M46 and M47
37	2403	Cam	G-SABc	7 36.9	+65 36	8.5	26×13	!! very large & bright; visible in binocs.
38	2655	Cam	G-SAB0	8 55.6	+78 13	10.1	6.0×5.3	bright ellipse with starlike nucleus
The Spring Sky								
39	2683	Lyn	G-SAb	8 52.7	+33 25	9.8	8.4×2.4	nearly edge-on spiral; very bright
40	2841	UMa	G-SAb	9 22.0	+50 58	9.2	6.8×3.3	!! classic elongated spiral; very bright
41	3079	UMa	G-SBc	10 02.2	+55 41	10.9	8.0×1.5	edge-on spiral; NGC 2950 nearby
42	3184	UMa	G-SABc	10 18.3	+41 25	9.8	7.8×7.2	large, diffuse face-on spiral
43	3877	UMa	G-SAc	11 46.1	+47 30	11.0	5.1×1.1	edge-on; same field as χ UMa
44	3941	UMa	G-SB0°	11 52.9	+36 59	10.3	3.7×2.6	small, bright. and elliptical
45	4026	UMa	G-S0	11 59.4	+50 58	10.8	4.6×1.2	lens-shaped edge-on near γ UMa
46	4088	UMa	G-SABbc	12 05.6	+50 33	10.6	5.4×2.1	nearly edge-on; NGC 4085 in same field
47	4157	UMa	G-SABb	12 11.1	+50 29	11.3	7.1×1.2	a thin sliver; NGC 4026 and 4088 nearby
48	4605	UMa	G-SBcp	12 40.0	+61 37	10.3	6.4×2.3	bright, distinct edge-on spiral
49	3115	Sex	G-S0$^-$	10 05.2	−7 43	8.9	8.1×2.8	Spindle Galaxy; bright and elongated
50	3242	Hya	PN	10 24.8	−18 38	7.8	>16″	!! Ghost of Jupiter; small but bright
51	3003	LMi	G-Sbc?	9 48.6	+33 25	11.9	5.2×1.6	faint elongated streak
52	3344	LMi	G-SABbc	10 43.5	+24 55	9.9	6.9×6.4	diffuse face-on barred spiral
53	3432	LMi	G-SBm	10 52.5	+36 37	11.2	6.9×1.9	nearly edge-on; faint flat streak
54	2903	Leo	G-SABbc	9 32.2	+21 30	9.0	12×6	!! very large, bright elongated spiral
55	3384	Leo	G-SB0$^-$	10 48.3	+12 38	9.9	5.5×2.9	same field as M105 and NGC 3389
56	3521	Leo	G-SAb	11 05.8	−0 02	9.0	12×6	very large, bright spiral
57	3607	Leo	G-SA0°	11 16.9	+18 03	9.9	4.6×4.1	NGC 3605 & 3608 in same field
58	3628	Leo	G-Sb pec	11 20.3	+13 36	9.5	14×4	large edge-on; same field as M65 & M66
59	4111	CVn	G-SA0$^+$	12 07.1	+43 04	10.7	4.4×0.9	bright lens-shaped edge-on spiral
60	4214	CVn	G-I AB	12 15.6	+36 20	9.8	10×8	large irregular galaxy
61	4244	CVn	G-SAcd	12 17.5	+37 49	10.4	17×2	!! large distinct edge-on spiral

SEASONAL LISTING OF FINEST NGC OBJECTS (continued)

#	NGC	Con	Type	RA (2000)	Dec	m_V	Size	Remarks
Spring Sky (continued)				h m	° ′		′	
62	4449	CVn	G-I Bm	12 28.2	+44 06	9.6	5.5×4.1	bright with odd rectangular shape
63	4490	CVn	G-SBd p	12 30.6	+41 38	9.8	6.4×3.3	Cocoon Gal.; bright spiral; 4485 in field
64	4631	CVn	G-SBd	12 42.1	+32 32	9.2	16×3	!! large edge-on; with companion 4627
65	4656/7	CVn	G-SBm p	12 44.0	+32 10	10.5	20×3	!! in field with 4631; NE end curves up
66	5005	CVn	G-SABbc	13 10.9	+37 03	9.8	5.8×2.8	bright elongated spiral near α CVn
67	5033	CVn	G-SAc	13 13.4	+36 36	10.2	10×5	large bright spiral near NGC 5005
68	4274	Com	G-SBab	12 19.8	+29 37	10.4	6.7×2.5	NGCs 4278/83/86 in same field
69	4414	Com	G-SAc	12 26.4	+31 13	10.1	4.4×3.0	bright spiral with starlike nucleus
70	4494	Com	G-E1-2	12 31.4	+25 47	9.8	4.6×4.4	small bright elliptical
71	4559	Com	G-SABc	12 36.0	+27 58	10.0	12×5	large spiral with coarse structure
72	4565	Com	G-SAb	12 36.3	+25 59	9.6	14×2	!! superb edge-on spiral with dust lane
73	4725	Com	G-SABab	12 50.4	+25 30	9.4	10×8	very bright, large spiral
74	4038/9	Crv	G-SB/IB	12 01.9	−18 52	≈10.4	≈5×3 ea.	"Antennae" interacting galaxies
75	4361	Crv	PN	12 24.5	−18 48	10.9	>45″	small and bright; with 13^m central star
76	4216	Vir	G-SABb	12 15.9	+13 09	10.0	7.8×1.6	nearly edge-on; with NGC 4206 and 4222
77	4388	Vir	G-SAb	12 25.8	+12 40	11.0	5.7×1.6	with M84 and M86 in Markarian's Chain
78	4438	Vir	G-SA0/a	12 27.8	+13 01	10.2	8.9×3.6	paired w/ NGC 4435 to form the "Eyes"
79	4517	Vir	G-Scd	12 32.8	+0 07	10.4	9.9×1.4	edge-on spiral; often mislabeled NGC 4437
80	4526	Vir	G-SAB0°	12 34.0	+7 42	9.7	7.1×2.9	between two 7^m stars
81	4535	Vir	G-SABc	12 34.3	+8 12	10.0	7.1×6.4	near M49 and 0.75° N of NGC 4526
82	4567/8	Vir	G-SAbc	12 36.5	+11 15	≈11	≈3×2 ea.	pair of interacting galaxies
83	4699	Vir	G-Sab	12 49.0	−8 40	9.5	4.4×3.2	small & bright; look for NGC 4697 3°N
84	4762	Vir	G-SB0°?	12 52.9	+11 14	10.3	9.1×2.2	flattest galaxy known; 4754 in same field
85	5746	Vir	G-SA?b	14 44.9	+1 57	10.3	6.8×1.0	fine edge-on near 109 Virginis
86	5466	Boo	GC	14 05.5	+28 32	9.0	11	loose class XII; like rich open cl.; faint
87	5907	Dra	G-SAc	15 15.9	+56 20	10.3	12×2	!! fine edge-on with dust lane; near 5866
88	6503	Dra	G-SAcd	17 49.4	+70 09	10.2	7.3×2.4	bright elongated spiral
89	6543	Dra	PN	17 58.6	+66 38	8.1	>18″	Cat's Eye Nebula; with 10.9^m central star
The Summer Sky								
90	6210	Her	PN	16 44.5	+23 49	8.8	>14″	blue starlike planetary
91	6369	Oph	PN	17 29.3	−23 46	11.4	>30″	"Little Ghost"; look for 6309 nearby
92	6572	Oph	PN	18 12.1	+6 51	8.1	8″	tiny bright blue oval
93	6633	Oph	OC	18 27.7	+6 34	4.6	27	sparse wide field cluster; IC 4756 nearby
94	6712	Sct	GC	18 53.1	−8 42	8.2	7.2	small globular; look for IC 1295 in field
95	6781	Aql	PN	19 18.4	+6 33	11.4	>109″	pale version of the Owl Nebula, M97
96	6819	Cyg	OC	19 41.3	+40 11	7.3	9.5	150*; faint but rich cluster in Milky Way
97	6826	Cyg	PN	19 44.8	+50 31	8.8	>25″	!! Blinking Planetary; 10.6^m central star
98	6888	Cyg	EN	20 12.0	+38 21	—	18×13	Crescent Nebula; faint; use nebular filter
99a	6960	Cyg	SNR	20 45.7	+30 43	—	70×6	!! Veil Nebula west half; use filter!
99b	6992/5	Cyg	SNR	20 56.4	+31 43	—	72×8	!! Veil Nebula east half; use filter!
100	7000	Cyg	EN	20 58.8	+44 20	—	120×100	!! North America; use filter & low power
101	7027	Cyg	PN	21 07.1	+42 14	8.5	15″	unusual protoplanetary nebula
102	6445	Sgr	PN	17 49.2	−20 01	11.2	>34″	small, bright and annular; near M23
103	6520	Sgr	OC	18 03.4	−27 54	7.6p	6	60*; small; dark nebula B86 in same field
104	6818	Sgr	PN	19 44.0	−14 09	9.3	>17″	"Little Gem"; annular; NGC 6822 0.75°S
105	6802	Vul	OC	19 30.6	+20 16	8.8	3.2	50*, at east end of Brocchi's Cluster
106	6940	Vul	OC	20 34.6	+28 18	6.3	31	60*; fairly rich cluster in Milky Way
107	6939	Cep	OC	20 31.4	+60 38	7.8	7	80*; very rich; NGC 6946 in same field
108	6946	Cep	G-SABcd	20 34.8	+60 09	8.8	13×13	faint, diffuse face-on spiral near 6939
109	7129	Cep	RN	21 42.8	+66 06	—	7×7	faint reflection neb. around sparse cluster
110	40	Cep	PN	0 13.0	+72 32	12.4	>37″	unusual red planetary; 11.6^m central star

DARK NEBULAE

BY PAUL GRAY

Dark nebulae, often appearing as "holes in the sky," are fascinating to observe. The following is a representative selection of visually observable dark nebulae. The **minimum aperture** in millimetres is what observers have found to be necessary to see each nebula; however, many may be observable with smaller apertures under excellent skies. Quality of optics, the observer's experience, and full dark adaptation are often more important than the aperture. Some objects will also benefit from the use of a filter because they are superimposed upon a bright nebula.

Nebulae are listed in order of RA. Column **B** lists the *Barnard Catalogue* number; two objects (L 889 and L 906) are from the *Lynds Catalogue*, one (LG 3) is from the *Le Gentil Catalogue*, and one is uncataloged. The column **Chart #** lists the chart in *Uranometria 2000.0 Deep Sky Atlas* (2nd Ed., 2001) that contains the object; *italic* numbers indicate that the object is not actually marked on the given chart. The **opacity** is based on a scale of 1 to 6, with 6 being the easiest to observe; no objects of opacity 1 or 2 are listed, since these objects are very difficult to observe visually. Showpiece objects are marked "!!". For further information, including finder charts, images, and observation reports, visit rasc.ca/handbook/supplements.

#	B	Con	RA (2000) h m	Dec ° ′	Chart #	Size ′	Opa-city	Min. Aper. mm	Remarks
1	5	Per	3 48	+32 54	60	22×9	5	200	1° NE of o Per
2	211/3	Tau	4 17.2	+27 48	78	12×110	3	200–250	narrow NW–SE lanes, faint bkgd starfield
3	33	Ori	5 40.9	−2 28	116	6×4	4	100–150	Horsehead Nebula; use Hβ filter
4	34	Aur	5 43.5	+32 39	59	20	4	200	2° W of M37; spider-like appearance
5	35	Ori	5 45.5	+9 03	96	20×10	5	150–200	near FU Ori and bright nebula Ced 59
6	37	Mon	6 33	+11 00	96	3°	5	150 RFT	near NGC 2245, 2247; try binoculars
7	40	Sco	16 14.7	−18 59	147	15	3	250	in bright nebula IC 4592; 50′ NE of ν Sco
8	44	Oph	16 40	−24 04	146	35×300	6	10×70	large dark rift; naked-eye in superb sky
9	59	Oph	17 11.4	−27 29	146	60	6	10×70	3° SW of θ Oph; part of stem of Pipe Nebula
10	64	Oph	17 17.2	−18 32	146	20	6	150–200	30′ W of M9; causes darkening of M9
11	68	Oph	17 22.6	−23 44	146	3	6	200	small; near B72; region rich in dark nebulae
12	70	Oph	17 23.6	−23 58	146	4	4	200	small; near B72; region rich in dark nebulae
13	72	Oph	17 23.6	−23 38	146	30	6	80–125	!! the Snake; "S" shape; 1.5° N of θ Oph
14	78	Oph	17 33	−26 00	146	3°	6	eye	!! Pipe bowl, "Prancing Horse" hindquarters
15	84A	Sgr	17 57.5	−17 40	146	16	5	150–200	1.5° N of M23; try for extensions to S
16	85	Sgr	18 02.6	−23 02	145	5	4	100	!! dark lanes inside Trifid Nebula (M20)
17	86	Sgr	18 02.7	−27 50	145	4	5	200	!! Ink Spot; nice pair with NGC 6520 5′ E
18	87	Sgr	18 04.3	−32 30	163	12	4	200	Parrot's Head; 2° S of γ Sgr
19	88	Sgr	18 04.4	−24 07	145	2	4	200	on edge of M8; *not* Burnham's "Dark Comet"
20		Sgr	18 04.5	−24 14	*145*	2×1	4	200	Burnham's "Dark Comet"; use filter
21	303	Sgr	18 09.5	−24 00	145	1	5	200–250	inside IC 4685; use filter; challenging
22	92/3	Sgr	18 15.5	−18 11	145	12×6	6	7×50	!! on NW edge of Small Sgr Star Cloud, M24
23	103	Sct	18 39.2	−6 37	126	40×40	6	10×70	on NW side of Scutum star cloud
24	104	Sct	18 47.3	−4 32	105	16×1	5	150–200	20′ N of β Sct; a checkmark shape
25	108	Sct	18 49.6	−6 19	125	3	3	200	30′ W of M11; rich region
26	112	Sct	18 51.2	−6 40	125	20	4	200	30′ S of M11; also look for B114, B118
27	133	Aql	19 06.1	−6 50	125	10×3	6	100	on Scutum star cloud; very dark spot!
28	142/3	Aql	19 40.7	+10 57	85	80×50	6	10×50	!! Barnard's famous "E" cloud
29	145	Cyg	20 02.8	+37 40	48	6×35	4	200	triangular shape
30	L 889	Cyg	20 24.8	+40 10	48	100×20	–	7×50	within γ Cygni Nebula, IC 1318
31	L 906	Cyg	20 37	+42 00	48	6°	–	eye	"Northern Coalsack"
32	150	Cep	20 00.6	+60 18	20	60×3	5	250	curved filament 1.6° S of η Cep
33	353	Cyg	20 57.1	+45 32	32	20×10	5	100	in N of North America Nebula; B352 in field
34	LG 3	Cyg	21 00	+53 00	*32*	12°	–	eye	!! "Funnel Cloud Nebula"; best after Coalsack
35	361	Cyg	21 12.9	+47 22	32	20	4	100	cluster IC 1369 to N; try for 1° tendril to W
36	365	Cep	21 34.9	+56 43	19	22×3	4	200	in IC 1396; indistinct "S" shape; use filter
37	163	Cep	21 42.2	+56 42	19	4	4	200	in IC 1396; use filter
38	168	Cyg	21 49	+47 29	31	100×20	5	7×50	large E–W lane; Cocoon Nebula at E end

DEEP-SKY CHALLENGE OBJECTS

BY ALAN DYER AND ALISTER LING

The beauty of the deep sky extends well past the best and brightest objects. The attraction of observing is not the sight of an object itself but our intellectual contact with what it *is*. A faint, stellar point in Virgo evokes wonder when you try to fathom the depths of this quasar billions of light-years away. The eclectic collection of objects below is designed to introduce some "fringe" catalogs while providing challenging targets for a wide range of apertures. Often more important than sheer aperture are factors such as the quality of sky, quality of the optics, use of an appropriate filter, and the observer's experience. Don't be afraid to tackle some of these with a smaller telescope.

Objects are listed in order of right ascension. Abbreviations are the same as in THE MESSIER CATALOGUE and THE FINEST NGC OBJECTS, with the addition of DN = dark nebula and Q = quasar. **Chart #** indicates the chart in which the object can be found in *Uranometria 2000.0 Deep Sky Atlas* (2nd Ed., 2001). The last column suggests the minimum aperture, in millimetres, needed to see that object. Most data are taken from *Sky Catalogue 2000.0, Vol. 2*. Some visual magnitudes are from other sources.

#	Object	Con	Type	RA (2000) h m	Dec ° ′	m_V	Size ′	Chart #	Minimum Aperture mm
1	**NGC 7822**	Cep	E/RN	0 03.6	+68 37	—	60 × 30	8	300
	large, faint emission nebula; rated "eeF"; also look for E/R nebula Ced 214 (associated w/ star cluster Berkeley 59) 1° S								
2	**IC 59**	Cas	E/RN	0 56.7	+61 04	—	10 × 5	18	200–250
	faint emission/reflection nebula paired with IC 63 very close to γ Cas.; requires clean optics; rated as "pF"								
3	**NGC 609**	Cas	OC	1 37.2	+64 33	11.0	3.0	17	250–300
	faint patch at low power; high power needed to resolve this rich cluster (also look for Trumpler 1 cluster 3° S)								
4	**IC 1795**	Cas	EN	2 24.7	+61 54	—	27 × 13	29	200
	brightest part of a complex of nebulosity that includes IC 1805 and IC 1848; use a nebular filter								
5	**Maffei I**	Cas	G-E3	2 36.3	+59 39	≈14	5 × 3	29	300
	heavily reddened galaxy; very faint; requires large aperture and black skies; nearby Maffei II for extremists								
6	**NGC 1049**	For	GC	2 39.7	−34 29	11.0	0.6	175	250–300
	Class V globular in dwarf "Fornax System" Local Group galaxy 630 000 ly away; galaxy itself invisible?								
7	**Abell 426**	Per	G cl.	3 19.8	+41 31	12–16	≈30	43, A4	200–400
	Perseus galaxy cluster 300 million ly away; mag. 11.6 NGC 1275 Perseus A at center; see close-up chart A4								
8	**NGC 1432/35**	Tau	RN	3 46.1	+23 47	—	30 × 30	78, A12	100–150
	Pleiades nebulosity (also includes IC 349); brightest around Merope; requires transparent skies and clean optics								
9	**IC 342**	Cam	G-SBc	3 46.8	+68 06	≈12	17 × 17	16	200–300
	large and diffuse face-on spiral; member of UMa–Cam cloud (Kemble's Cascade of stars also on this chart)								
10	**NGC 1499**	Per	EN	4 00.7	+36 37	—	145 × 40	60	80–125 RFT
	California Nebula; very large and faint; use a wide-field telescope or big binoculars plus Hβ filter								
11	**IC 405**	Aur	E/RN	5 16.2	+34 16	—	30 × 19	59	200
	Flaming Star Nebula associated with runaway star AE Aurigae; see Burnham's Handbook p. 285 (also look for IC 410)								
12	**HH 1**	Ori	E	5 36.3	−06 45	≈14.5	8″	136	250
	Herbig–Haro 1; best with no filter at 250× or more; bipolar jets from forming star; not plotted; 2.5′ SW NGC 1999								
13	**IC 434 / B 33**	Ori	E/DN	5 40.9	−2 28	—	60 × 10	116	100–150 in dark sky!
	B 33 is the Horsehead Nebula, a dark nebula superimposed on a very faint emission nebula IC 434; use Hβ filter								
14	**Sh 2-276**	Ori	EN	5 48.0	+1 —	—	600 × 30!	116	100–150 RFT
	Barnard's Loop; SNR or interstellar bubble? difficult to detect due to size; use filter and sweep with wide field								
15	**Abell 12**	Ori	PN	6 02.4	+9 39	≈13	37″	96	250–300
	plotted in *Uranometria* as PK 198.6–6.3; on NW edge of μ Orionis; OIII filter required								
16	**IC 443**	Gem	SNR	6 16.9	+22 47	—	50 × 40	76	250–300
	faint supernova remnant very close to η Gem.; use filter (also look for NGC 2174 and Sh 2–247 on this chart)								
17	**J 900**	Gem	PN	6 25.9	+17 47	12.2	8″	76	200
	Jonckheere 900; bright starlike planetary; plotted as PK 194.2+2.5 in *Uranometria*; use OIII filter & high power								
18	**IC 2177**	Mon	E/RN	7 05.1	−10 42	—	120 × 40	135	200–300
	Seagull Nebula; large, faint; contains bright patches Gum 1 (−10°28′), NGC 2327 (−11°18′) & Ced 90 (−12°20′)								

DEEP-SKY CHALLENGE OBJECTS (continued)

#	Object	Con	Type	RA (2000) Dec		m_v	Size	Chart #	Minimum Aperture
				h m	° ′		′		mm
19	**PK 205 +14.2**	Gem	PN	7 29.0	+13 15	≈13	≈700″	95	200–250
	Medusa Nebula or Abell 21; impressive in large aperture w/ OIII filter								
20	**PK 164 +31.1**	Lyn	PN	7 57.8	+53 25	≈14	400″	26	250
	Jones–Emberson 1; faint with two small components; use OIII filter; sometimes confused with nearby NGC 2474–75								
21	**Leo I**	Leo	G-E3	10 08.4	+12 18	9.8	10.7 × 8.3	93	300
	dwarf elliptical; satellite of Milky Way; very low surface brightness; 0.3° N of Regulus! requires clean optics								
22	**Abell 1367**	Leo	G cl.	11 44.0	+19 57	13–16	≈60	72, A11	300–400
	cluster of some 30 or more galaxies within a 1° field near 93 Leonis; Copeland's Septet nearby								
23	**NGC 3172**	UMi	G-Sb	11 50.2	+89 07	13.6	0.7 × 0.7	1	250
	"Polarissima Borealis"—closest galaxy to the north celestial pole; small, faint, and otherwise unremarkable								
24	**NGC 4236**	Dra	G-SBb	12 16.7	+69 28	9.6	18.6 × 6.9	13	200–250
	very large, dim barred spiral; a diffuse glow (NGC 4395 on Chart #54 a similar large diffuse face-on)								
25	**Mrk 205**	Dra	Q	12 21.6	+75 18	14.5	stellar	5	300
	Markarian 205; a faint star on SW edge of NGC 4319; center of redshift controversy								
26	**3C 273**	Vir	Q	12 29.1	+2 03	12–13	stellar	111	250–300
	at 2–3 billon ly away, one of the most distant objects visible in amateur telescopes; magnitude variable								
27	**NGC 4676**	Com	G cl.	12 46.2	+30 44	14.lp	2 × 1	53	250
	"The Mice" or VV 224—two classic interacting galaxies; very faint double nature detectable at high power								
28	**Abell 1656**	Com	G cl.	13 00.1	+27 58	12–16	≈60	71, A8	250–300
	Coma Berenices galaxy cluster; very rich; 400 million ly away; brightest member NGC 4889; see close-up chart A8								
29	**NGC 5053**	Com	GC	13 16.4	+17 42	9.8	10.5	71	100–200
	faint and very loose globular 1° SE of M53; requires large aperture to resolve; difficult in hazy skies; class XI								
30	**NGC 5897**	Lib	GC	15 17.4	−21 01	8.6	12.6	148	150–200
	large and loose; easily hidden in hazy skies at higher latitude; brightest stars mag. 13.3, main branch mag. 16.3								
31	**Abell 2065**	CrB	G cl.	15 22.7	+27 43	≈16	≈30	69	500 in superb sky!
	Corona Borealis galaxy cluster; perhaps the most difficult object for amateur telescopes; 1.5 billion ly away								
32	**NGC 6027**	Ser	G cl.	15 59.2	+20 45	≈15	2 × 1	69	400
	Seyfert's Sextet (6027 A–F); compact group of 6 small and very faint galaxies; see Burnham's Handbook p. 1793								
33	**B 72**	Oph	DN	17 23.5	−23 38	—	30	146	80–125 RFT
	Barnard's dark S-Nebula or "The Snake"; opacity of 6/6; 1.5° NNE of θ Ophiuchi; area rich in dark nebulae								
34	**NGC 6791**	Lyr	OC	19 20.7	+37 51	9.5	16	48	200–250
	large, faint but very rich open cluster with 300 stars; a faint smear in smaller instruments; Type II 3 r								
35	**PK 64 +5.1**	Cyg	PN	19 34.8	+30 31	9.6	8″	48	200
	Campbell's Hydrogen Star; very bright but very starlike; also cataloged as star BD +30°3639								
36	**M 1-92**	Cyg	RN	19 36.3	+29 33	11.0	12″ × 6″	48	250–300
	Minkowski 1-92 or Footprint Nebula; bright, starlike reflection nebula; double at high mag; associated star invisible								
37	**NGC 6822**	Sgr	G-I	19 44.9	−14 48	≈11	10.2 × 9.5	125	100–150
	Barnard's Galaxy; member of the Local Group; large but very low surface brightness; requires transparent skies								
38	**Palomar 11**	Aql	GC	19 45.2	−8 00	9.8	3.2	125	200–300
	brightest of 15 heavily reddened GCs found on Sky Survey; magnitude is misleading; 11 Terzan GCs more challenging								
39	**IC 4997**	Sge	PN	20 20.2	+16 45	10.9	2″	84	200
	bright but starlike planetary; the challenge is to see the disk! blink the field with and without a nebular filter								
40	**IC 1318**	Cyg	EN	20 26.2	+40 30	—	large	32, A2	80–150 RFT
	complex of nebulosity around γ Cygni; multitude of patches in rich starfield; use a very wide field plus filter								
41	**PK 80 −6.1**	Cyg	PN?	21 02.3	+36 42	13.5	16″	47	250
	the "Egg Nebula"; a very small proto-planetary nebula; can owners of large telescopes detect polarization?								
42	**IC 1396**	Cep	EN	21 39.1	+57 30	—	170 × 140	19	100–125 RFT
	extremely large and diffuse area of emission nebulosity; use nebular filter and very wide-field optics in dark sky								
43	**IC 5146**	Cyg	E/RN	21 53.5	+47 16	—	12 × 12	31	200–250
	Cocoon Nebula; faint and diffuse; use Hβ filter; at the end of the long filamentary dark nebula Barnard 168								
44	**NGC 7317–20**	Peg	G cl.	22 36.1	+33 57	13–14	≈1 ea.	46	250–300
	Stephan's Quintet; 0.5° SSW of NGC 7331; easy to pick out 3 or 4 (also look for "companions" to 7331)								
45	**Jones 1**	Peg	PN	23 35.9	+30 28	12.1	332″	45	250–300
	plotted as PK 104.2 −29.6 in *Uranometria*; large dim glow; OIII filter required								

DEEP-SKY GEMS
BY DAVID H. LEVY

The 154 objects in this personal list are selected from more than 400 deep-sky objects that I assembled over 55-plus years of comet-hunting. My observing program, called CN-3, began on 1965 Dec. 17 and has continued without interruption since then (see rasc.ca/david-h-levy-logbooks). The objects are numbered chronologically (**L#**) in the order I first located them in the night sky, and these numbers match those in my book, *Deep Sky Objects: The best and brightest from four decades of comet chasing* (Prometheus Books, New York, 2005). **UI** refers to the charts in *Uranometria 2000.0*. **UII** refers to charts in *Uranometria 2000.0 Deep Sky Atlas* (the 2nd edition of **UI**).

This selection complements the other Handbook deep-sky observing lists. Specifically, the following objects are not included here: all objects that appear in THE MESSIER CATALOGUE, THE FINEST NGC OBJECTS, and THE DEEP-SKY CHALLENGE OBJECTS; also, several double stars and variable stars, a few asterisms, some photographic objects, and the gegenschein are not included, though observing them is strongly encouraged; finally, several objects with southern declinations are left out to ensure that the Deep-Sky Gems observing certificate can be earned without travel by the typical RASC member. Levy 384 deserves special note: Just as the terms "Plaskett's Star" and "Kemble's Cascade" recognize Canadian astronomers from the past, "Levy 384" has become the recognized name for a previously unnamed asterism.

On a final, personal note, the late Leo Enright deserves great credit and thanks for the amount of time and effort he invested since he originated this project in 2007. A dear and special friend, Leo devoted his life to inspiring people to take up skywatching. He was one of my closest friends and I miss him deeply.

The main list is grouped by season and ordered by RA. The list below is a cross-reference aid.

NUMERICAL LISTING OF DEEP-SKY GEMS

L#	Sky RA	L#	Sky RA	L#	Sky RA	L#	Sky RA	L#	Sky RA	L#	Sky RA	L#	Sky RA
5	Spr 14	**59**	Aut 1	**133**	Spr 9	**172**	Spr 12	**207**	Sum 17	**247**	Aut 22	**282**	Aut 22
6	Sum 16	**62**	Aut 2	**134**	Spr 12	**178**	Spr 12	**208**	Sum 17	**249**	Aut 23	**284**	Aut 1
8	Win 4	**64**	Aut 1	**135**	Spr 12	**181**	Spr 11	**209**	Spr 9	**255**	Spr 13	**286**	Win 3
19	Sum 16	**81**	Aut 0	**136**	Spr 11	**182**	Spr 12	**210**	Spr 12	**256**	Win 8	**296**	Win 7
27	Spr 13	**82**	Spr 14	**137**	Spr 11	**183**	Spr 12	**211**	Spr 12	**257**	Spr 12	**300**	Spr 10
28	Spr 14	**83**	Spr 14	**138**	Spr 11	**184**	Spr 13	**212**	Spr 12	**259**	Spr 12	**315**	Spr 13
29	Spr 14	**95**	Win 5	**140**	Spr 12	**185**	Spr 13	**213**	Spr 12	**260**	Spr 12	**317**	Spr 15
31	Aut 1	**96**	Win 8	**145**	Spr 12	**186**	Spr 13	**214**	Spr 12	**261**	Spr 13	**324**	Win 3
34	Aut 1	**98**	Sum 18	**147**	Sum 18	**187**	Spr 13	**215**	Spr 12	**262**	Sum 19	**326**	Spr 12
35	Win 7	**99**	Aut 2	**149**	Sum 18	**188**	Spr 12	**217**	Spr 11	**263**	Aut 21	**331**	Spr 10
36	Sum 17	**110**	Sum 19	**156**	Sum 20	**189**	Spr 13	**219**	Spr 10	**266**	Spr 15	**334**	Sum 17
37	Spr 9	**112**	Aut 21	**158**	Win 7	**190**	Spr 13	**220**	Sum 20	**267**	Spr 13	**337**	Spr 10
38	Aut 23	**114**	Win 4	**159**	Win 6	**191**	Spr 12	**223**	Aut 0	**268**	Spr 14	**338**	Aut 2
41	Spr 11	**116**	Win 6	**160**	Win 6	**192**	Spr 12	**224**	Aut 2	**270**	Sum 18	**340**	Aut 2
42	Spr 12	**120**	Sum 17	**161**	Win 6	**193**	Spr 12	**226**	Win 8	**271**	Sum 17	**341**	Aut 2
44	Win 3	**121**	Spr 15	**162**	Win 6	**195**	Win 7	**231**	Spr 13	**273**	Win 5	**342**	Aut 0
50	Win 4	**123**	Win 4	**164**	Spr 11	**196**	Spr 14	**232**	Spr 13	**276**	Aut 0	**367**	Aut 1
51	Spr 9	**124**	Win 6	**165**	Spr 10	**201**	Spr 11	**236**	Sum 16	**277**	Aut 22	**382**	Spr 11
53	Aut 1	**125**	Win 5	**167**	Spr 10	**202**	Spr 14	**238**	Aut 1	**278**	Aut 1	**384**	Win 8
55	Aut 23	**129**	Spr 10	**169**	Spr 9	**203**	Spr 14	**239**	Aut 0	**279**	Sum 18	**401**	Spr 9
56	Aut 0	**130**	Spr 10	**170**	Spr 12	**204**	Spr 15	**240**	Aut 0	**280**	Aut 23	***402***	*Win 6*
57	Aut 23	**131**	Spr 9	**171**	Spr 12	**205**	Sum 16	**243**	Sum 17	**281**	Aut 23	***403***	*Aut 21*

Editor's note: For certificate purposes, this list was revised in summer 2020 by introducing Levy 402 (in italics) in place of previous entry Levy 226, and Levy 403 in place of Levy 206.

DEEP-SKY GEMS (continued)

L#	NGC	RA (2000) h m	Dec ° ′	m_V	Size (′)	UI	UII	Remarks
The Autumn Sky								
112	7023	21 00.5	+68 10	7.0	10×8	32	9	Unusual-looking nebula in Cepheus
263	7006	21 01.5	+16 11	10.5	2.8	209	83	Globular cluster in Delphinus
403	—	21 08.0	+46 10	5.9	7			*"Daffy Duck" nebula †*
277	7184	22 02.7	−20 49	11.2	6.5×1.4	346	142	Very elongated galaxy in Aquarius
247	7217	22 07.9	+31 22	10.1	3.5×3.0	122	46	Round galaxy in Pegasus
282	7314	22 35.8	−26 03	10.9	4.2×1.7	347	142	Elongated galaxy in Piscis Austrinus
249	7457	23 01.0	+30 09	11.2	4.1×2.5	124	46	Elongated galaxy in Pegasus
55	7664	23 26.6	+25 04	12.7	3.0×1.7	169	63	Galaxy in Pegasus
57	7723	23 38.8	−12 58	11.2	2.8×1.9	304	121	Galaxy in Aquarius
280	7721	23 38.8	−06 31	11.6	3.3×1.3	304	121	Elongated galaxy in Aquarius
281	7727	23 39.9	−12 18	10.6	5.6×4.0	304	121	Round galaxy in Aquarius
38	7753	23 47.1	+29 20	12.0	3.2×1.7	89	45	Slightly elongated galaxy in Pegasus
276	7814	00 03.3	+16 09	10.6	6.0×2.5	170	81	Elongated galaxy in Pegasus
342	90	00 21.8	+22 25	13.7	2.2×0.8	126	63	Galaxy in Andromeda, in galaxy cluster
81	147	00 33.2	+48 30	9.5	15.0×9.4	60	30	Comet-like galaxy; satellite of M31
223	150	00 34.3	−27 48	11.3	3.4×1.6	306	141	Elongated galaxy in Sculptor
240	157	00 34.8	−08 24	10.4	4.0×2.4	261	121	Elongated "Amoeba Galaxy" in Cetus
239	247	00 47.1	−20 46	9.2	19.0×5.5	306	158	Very elongated galaxy in Cetus
56	270	00 50.6	−08 39	12.1	2.0×1.7	262	140	Galaxy in Cetus
64	404	01 09.4	+35 43	10.3	6.1×6.1	91	62	Round galaxy near β Andromedae
278	474	01 20.1	+03 25	11.5	10.0×9.2	217	120	Galaxy near NGC 470 in Pisces
34	488	01 21.8	+05 15	10.3	5.5×4.0	217	100	Elongated galaxy in Pisces
31	514	01 24.1	+12 55	11.7	3.9×2.9	173	100	Easily seen galaxy in Pisces
59	524	01 24.8	+09 32	10.2	3.5×3.5	173	100	Round galaxy in Pisces
238	578	01 30.5	−22 40	11.0	3.9×2.2	308	158	Elongated galaxy in Cetus
367	613	01 34.3	−29 25	10.0	5.2×2.6	352	158	Special galaxy in Sculptor
284	718	01 53.2	+04 12	11.7	2.4×2.0	218	119	Round galaxy in Pisces
341	755	01 56.4	−09 04	12.6	2.8×1.1	264	139	Elongated galaxy in Cetus
53	752	01 57.8	+37 41	5.7	50	92	61	Very large open cluster in Andromeda
62	898	02 23.3	+41 57	12.9	1.8×0.5	91	43	Elongated galaxy in Andromeda
99	949	02 30.8	+37 08	11.8	3.3×2.1	93	61	Very cometary galaxy in Triangulum
224	IC 1830	02 39.1	−27 27	11.9	1.9×1.5	310	157	Galaxy in Fornax
338	1042	02 40.4	−08 26	11.0	4.2×3.3	215	139	Galaxy in Cetus
340	1134	02 53.6	+13 00	12.1	2.3×0.8	175	99	Round galaxy in Aries
The Winter Sky								
44	1333	03 29.2	+31 25	5.6	6×3	94	60	A weird reflection nebula in Perseus
286	1360	03 33.3	−25 51	9.4	6.5	312	156	Beautiful planetary nebula in Fornax
324	Tom* 5	03 47.8	+59 03	8.4	14.0	28	39	Open cluster in Camelopardalis
50	1579	04 30.2	+35 16	—	12×8	96	60	Reflection nebula in Perseus
123	1600	04 31.7	−05 05	10.9	2.3×1.5	223	117	Round, diffuse galaxy in Eridanus
8	1624	04 40.4	+50 27	13.0	5×5	40	42	Cluster with nebulosity in Perseus
114	1637	04 41.5	−02 51	10.8	3.4×2.6	224	117	Comet-like round galaxy in Eridanus
273	1746	05 03.6	+23 49	6.1	42	134	77	Beautiful open cluster in Taurus
95	1999	05 36.5	−06 42	10.0	2×2	271	136	Diffuse nebula in Orion
125	2023	05 41.6	−02 14	—	10×10	226	116	Nebula near ζ Orionis
116	2158	06 07.5	+24 06	8.6	5	136	76	Compact cluster near M35 in Gemini
402	*2169*	06 08.4	+13 57	5.9	7	—	—	*"LE" cluster, after Lothar Epstein*
124	2174	06 09.7	+20 30	—	40×30	137	76	Large field of dust in Orion
161	2245	06 32.7	+10 10	—	5×4	182	95	Comet-like bright nebula in Mon
162	2252	06 35.0	+05 23	7.7	20	227	95	Open cluster like rope of stars, in Mon
160	2254	06 36.6	+07 40	9.1	4	182	95	Open cluster and star chain in Mon
159	2264	06 41.1	+09 53	3.9	20	183	95	"Christmas Tree Cluster" in Mon
296	2362	07 18.8	−24 57	4.1	8	319	153	Open cluster in Canis Major
158	IC2194/6/7	07 33.7	+31 19	(12.5)	—	(100)**	57	Three of the "Castor Cluster" galaxies
195	2419	07 38.1	+38 53	10.3	4.1	100	95	"Intergalactic Wanderer" in Lynx

* "Tom" refers to the catalog of 5 open clusters discovered by Clyde Tombaugh, better known as the discoverer of Pluto.

† This nebulosity forms the northern limit of the North America Nebula. ** Indicates combined magnitude.

DEEP-SKY GEMS (continued)

L#	NGC	RA (2000) h m	Dec ° ′	m_V	Size (′)	UI	UII	Remarks
The Winter Sky (continued)								
35	2420	07 38.5	+21 34	8.3	10	139	75	Open cluster in Gemini
384	Levy384	08 15.6	−13 58	—	2	(275)	(134)	Compact asterism in Puppis (special!)
256	IC2367	08 24.2	−18 46	12.5	2.3 × 0.5	321	153	Galaxy in Puppis
225	2613	08 33.4	−22 58	10.5	7.6 × 1.9	321	153	Edge-on galaxy in Pyxis
96	2681	08 53.5	+51 19	10.3	5.3 × 3.5	44	39	Galaxy in Ursa Major
The Spring Sky								
401		09 06.5	+38 30	—	—	—	—	Winston Churchill's "V" Signal
51	Arp321	09 38.9	−04 52	(12.5)	—	(233)	113	"Larry, Moe, & Curly" galaxies in Hya
131	2964	09 42.9	+31 51	11.3	3.2 × 1.8	103	56	Galaxy contains Mrk 404 in Leo
169	2986	09 44.3	−21 17	10.6	4.1 × 3.4	323	152	Round galaxy in Hydra
209	3049	09 54.8	+09 16	12.1	2.3 × 1.5	188	93	Comet-like galaxy in Leo
37	3055	09 55.3	+04 16	12.1	2.0 × 1.1	234	113	Comet-like galaxy in Sextans
133	3070	09 58.0	+10 22	12.3	1.6 × 1.6	189	93	Round galaxy near NGC 3069, in Leo
129	UGC5373	10 00.0	+05 20	11.3	5.5 × 3.7	234	113	Sextans B galaxy; Local Group member
337	0957 +561A/B	10 01.3	+55 54	15.5	—	45	25	Famous double quasar in Ursa Major (gravitational lens; distinct in 16″ scope)
130	3198	10 19.9	+45 33	10.3	9.2 × 3.5	72	39	Very elongated galaxy in Ursa Major
300	3226	10 23.4	+19 54	11.4	2.5 × 2.2	144	73	Galaxy in Leo
165	3245	10 27.3	+28 30	10.8	2.9 × 2.0	105	73	Elongated galaxy in Leo Minor
219	3309	10 36.6	−27 31	11	4.4 × 3.1	325	151	Hydra I galaxy cluster (five members)
	+ 3311	10 36.7	−27 32	10.9	4.0 × 3.6			
	+ 3312	10 37.0	−27 34	11.8	3.4 × 1.1			
	+ 3314	10 37.4	−27 41	12.8	1.5 × 0.8			(actually two spirals!!)
	+ 3316	10 37.6	−27 36	12.6	1.4 × 1.2			
167	3310	10 38.7	+53 30	10.8	3.5 × 3.2	46	25	Round galaxy in Ursa Major
331	3319	10 39.2	+41 41	11.1	6.9 × 4.0	72	38	Graceful spiral galaxy in Ursa Major
164	3486	11 00.4	+28 58	10.5	6.6 × 4.7	106	73	Round galaxy in Leo Minor
382	UGC6253	11 13.5	+22 10	12	15.0 x12.5	146	73	Galaxy in Leo
137	3718	11 32.6	+53 04	10.8	10.0x 4.7	47	24	Elongated galaxy in Ursa Major
136	3738	11 35.8	+54 31	11.7	3.2 × 2.8	47	24	Galaxy near M97 in Ursa Major
41	3810	11 41.0	+11 28	10.8	3.8 × 2.6	192	91	Round galaxy in Leo
201	3865	11 44.9	−09 14	12.0	2.0 × 1.6	282	131	Diffuse galaxy in Crater
181	3887	11 47.1	−16 51	10.6	3.5 × 2.4	292	131	Round galaxy in Crater
217	3923	11 51.0	−28 48	9.6	6.9 × 4.8	368	150	Elongated galaxy in Hydra
138	3953	11 53.8	+52 20	10.1	6.0 × 3.2	47	24	Very elongated galaxy in Ursa Major
193	4129	12 08.9	−09 02	12.5	2.3 × 0.7	283	131	Elongated galaxy in Virgo
135	4256	12 18.7	+65 54	11.9	4.1 × 0.8	25	13	Edge-on galaxy in Draco
134	4319	12 21.7	+75 19	11.9	2.8 × 2.1	9	5	Galaxy near 4291 & 4386 in Draco
42	4340	12 23.0	+16 43	11.2	3.7 × 3.1	193	91	Galaxy near NGC 4350 in Coma
171	4450	12 28.5	+17 05	10.1	5.0 × 3.4	148	72	Elongated galaxy in Coma
145	4473	12 29.8	+13 26	10.2	3.7 × 2.4	193	91	Very elongated galaxy in Coma
140	4485	12 30.5	+41 42	11.9	2.0 × 1.3	37	75	Elong. galaxy N of NGC 4490 in CVn
260	4519	12 33.5	+08 39	11.8	3.5 × 2.3	194	90	Galaxy in Virgo
192	4536	12 34.5	+02 11	10.6	6.4 × 2.6	239	110	Very elongated galaxy in Virgo
326	4570	12 36.9	+07 15	10.9	4.3 × 1.3	194	90	Comet-like elongated galaxy in Virgo
188	4591	12 39.3	+06 01	13.0	1.6 × 0.8	194	90	Elongated galaxy in Virgo
178	4596	12 39.9	+10 11	10.4	4.6 × 4.1	194	90	Elongated galaxy in Virgo
213	4623	12 42.2	+07 41	12.2	2.0 × 0.7	194	90	Very elongated galaxy in Virgo
182	4636	12 42.8	+02 41	9.5	7.1 × 5.2	239	110	Galaxy with bright core in Virgo
170	4651	12 43.7	+16 24	10.8	3.5 × 2.3	194	90	Round galaxy in Coma
210	4685	12 47.1	+19 28	12.6	1.5 × 0.9	149	71	"Winking Galaxy" in Coma
172	4689	12 47.8	+13 46	10.9	3.7 × 3.2	194	90	Elongated galaxy in Coma
215	4688	12 47.8	+04 20	11.9	4.0 × 4.0	239	110	Very large galaxy in Virgo
214	4713	12 50.0	+05 19	11.7	2.9 × 1.8	194	90	Elongated galaxy in Virgo
259	4722	12 51.5	−13 19	12.9	1.5 × 0.7	284	130	Round galaxy in Corvus

DEEP-SKY GEMS (continued)

L#	NGC	RA (2000) h m	Dec ° ′	m_V	Size (′)	UI	UII	Remarks
The Spring Sky (continued)								
191	4772	12 53.5	+02 10	11.0	2.7 × 1.3	239	110	Galaxy in Virgo
211	4779	12 53.8	+09 44	12.4	1.9 × 1.7	194	90	Round galaxy in Virgo
212	4795	12 55.0	+08 04	12.1	1.9 × 1.7	194	90	Round galaxy in Virgo
183	4818	12 56.8	−08 31	11.1	3.4 × 1.4	284	130	Very elongated galaxy in Virgo
257	4866	12 59.5	+14 10	11.2	5.5 × 1.2	194	90	Elongated galaxy in Virgo
190	4956	13 05.1	+35 11	12.4	1.5 × 1.5	109	53	Round galaxy in Canes Venatici
255	5016	13 12.1	+24 06	12.8	1.7 × 1.3	150	71	Round galaxy in Coma
187	5020	13 12.6	+12 36	11.7	3.0 × 2.6	195	90	Elongated galaxy in Virgo
232	5068	13 18.9	−21 02	9.6	7.1 × 6.6	330	149	Very large galaxy in Virgo
189	5127	13 23.8	+31 34	11.9	2.3 × 1.7	109	53	Round galaxy in Canes Venatici
184	5147	13 26.3	+02 06	11.8	1.6 × 1.5	240	110	Round galaxy in Virgo
315	5146	13 26.5	−12 19	12.3	1.8 × 1.2	285	130	Round galaxy in Virgo
185	5248	13 37.5	+08 53	10.3	6.2 × 4.6	196	90	Round galaxy in Boötes
267	5247	13 38.1	−17 53	10.1	5.2 × 3.2	331	130	Beautiful, diffuse spiral in Virgo
261	5350	13 53.4	+40 22	11.3	3.1 × 2.5	76	36	Galaxy in Canes Venatici
186	5371	13 55.7	+40 28	10.6	4.1 × 3.2	76	36	Round galaxy in Canes Venatici
231	5364	13 56.2	+05 01	10.5	6.6 × 5.1	196	89	Elongated galaxy in Virgo
27	5377	13 56.3	+47 14	11.3	4.1 × 2.3	76	36	Galaxy near Big Dipper's handle
202	5427	14 03.4	−06 02	11.4	2.6 × 1.8	286	129	Galaxy, interacting with 5426, in Vir
28	5473	14 04.7	+54 54	11.4	2.2 × 1.7	49	23	Comet-like galaxy near M101 in UMa
29	5474	14 05.0	+53 40	10.8	6.0 × 4.9	49	23	Galaxy near M101 in Ursa Major
82	5634	14 29.6	−05 59	9.4	4.9	287	109	Globular cluster in Virgo
83	5638	14 29.7	+03 14	11.2	2.3 × 2.1	242	109	Comet-like galaxy in Virgo
5	5676	14 32.8	+49 28	11.2	3.7 × 1.6	77	36	Small elliptical galaxy in Boötes
203	5668	14 33.4	+04 27	11.5	3.2 × 2.8	242	109	Comet-like galaxy in Virgo
268	5690	14 37.7	+02 17	11.8	3.3 × 1.0	242	109	Very elongated galaxy in Virgo
196	5694	14 39.6	−26 32	9.2	3.6	332	148	"Tombaugh's Cluster" in Hydra
317	5838	15 05.4	+02 06	10.9	3.5 × 1.6	242	108	Elongated galaxy in Virgo
121	5846	15 06.4	+01 36	10.0	3.0 × 3.0	243	108	Galaxy in Virgo
204	5850	15 07.1	+01 33	10.8	4.6 × 4.1	243	108	Comet-like galaxy in Virgo
266	5962	15 36.5	+16 37	11.3	2.6 × 1.8	199	88	Round galaxy in Serpens
The Summer Sky								
205	6106	16 18.8	+07 25	12.2	2.3 × 1.2	201	87	Galaxy in Hercules
236	6181	16 32.3	+19 50	11.9	2.3 × 0.9	156	69	Galaxy in Hercules
19	6207	16 43.1	+36 50	11.5	3.0 × 1.1	114	50	Spiral galaxy near M13 in Hercules
6	6229	16 47.0	+47 32	9.4	4.5	80	34	Compact globular cluster in Hercules
271	6287	17 05.2	−22 42	9.3	5	337	146	Globular cluster in Ophiuchus
334	6342	17 21.2	−19 35	9.8	3	338	146	Globular cluster near M9 in Ophiuchus
36	6364	17 24.5	+29 24	12.9	1.5 × 1.2	115	50	Comet-like galaxy in Hercules
207	6384	17 32.4	+07 04	10.4	6.4 × 4.3	203	86	Galaxy in Ophiuchus
208	6426	17 44.9	+03 00	11.1	3.2	248	106	Globular cluster in Ophiuchus
243	6440	17 48.9	−20 22	9.1	5.4	338	146	Globular cluster in Sagittarius
120	6451	17 50.7	−30 13	8.2	7.0	164	377	"Tom Thumb Cluster," OC in Scorpius
279	6522	18 03.6	−30 02	8.3	16.4	163	377	"Baade's Window," two faint GCs
	+6528	18 04.5	−30 03	10.6	8.3 × 8.3			(close to the galactic center in Sgr)
270	6535	18 03.8	−00 18	10.5	3.6	249	106	Globular cluster in Serpens
149	6553	18 09.3	−25 54	8.1	8.1	339	145	Faint globular cluster in Sagittarius
147	6638	18 30.9	−25 30	9.1	5	340	145	Globular cluster in Sagittarius
98	6709	18 51.5	+10 21	6.7	13	205	85	Open cluster in Aquila
110	6760	19 11.2	+01 02	9.1	6.6	251	105	Globular cluster in Aquila
262	6814	19 42.7	−10 19	11.2	3.0 × 3.0	297	125	Round galaxy in Aquila
220	6910	20 23.1	+40 47	7.4	7	84	32	Open cluster in Cygnus
156	6934	20 34.2	+07 24	8.7	5.9	208	84	Globular cluster in Delphinus

WIDE-FIELD WONDERS
BY CHRIS BECKETT

In recent years, wide-field eyepieces, short-tube refractors, fast (sub-*f*/4) reflectors, and large, imaged-stabilized binoculars have increased in popularity. Dark-Sky Preserves with transparent skies have become attractive observing destinations for amateur astronomers. Such equipment and sites lend themselves to viewing a host of wonderful wide-field deep-sky objects that exceed typical telescopic fields of view. Observing large objects such as star clouds, open clusters, diffuse nebulae, giant molecular clouds, and supernova remnants—often with multiple objects in the same field of view—allows the observer to gain an appreciation for the structure of our home galaxy, the Milky Way. Although many objects in the following list are visible under light-polluted skies, they are best observed from the darkest sites with the aid of a good selection of nebula filters. All you need to begin is a pair of handheld binoculars—try experimenting with a filter taped over one objective. Several objects are visible using this technique in a dark location—in fact, some become invisible once you move to large apertures or high power! In the following list, **RA** and **Dec** identify the brightest portions. Most object types are defined on p. 314; in addition, DN = dark nebula, GMC = giant molecular cloud, and Ast = asterism.

Object	Con	Type	RA (2000) h m	Dec ° ′	Size ′	Remarks
NGC 206	And	starcloud	00 41	+40 49	5	star cloud within dark lanes of M31
best seen in wide fields with M31 dust lanes to SW; use M32 and mag. 7 star to locate						
Collinder 463	Cas	OC	01 47	+71 52	57	Crescent Cluster
four dozen stars scattered in a crescent						
Stock 2	Cas	OC	02 16	+59 33	60	Mushroom Cluster
try to see the Double Cluster and Stock 2 in same field; note star chain leading to Stock 2						
IC 1805 & 1848	Cas	EN	02 34	+61 29	4.5°	Heart and Soul Nebulae
large complex of nebulae and star clusters; use filter; IC 1795 is brightest part of IC 1805						
Cosmic ? Mark	Cet	Ast	02 37	+06 56	2.5° × 1°	asterism known as the "Question Mark"
looks exactly like a large question mark, best seen in binoculars						
Melotte 20	Per	OC	03 25	+49 54	5°	Perseus OB3 Association
large cluster for small binoculars; look for a miniature "Draco" asterism, including 4 stars denoting the head						
Kemble's Cascade	Cam	Ast	03 59	+63 06	3°	asterism: colorful chain of 20+ stars
terminates at NGC 1502; named by Walter Scott Houston in honor of Father Lucian Kemble (1922–1999)						
Taurus Cloud	Tau	GMC	4h–5h	+16–31	25° × 15°	part of the Taurus Molecular Cloud
M45, NGC 1435, IC 353/349/1995; many dark nebulae; "haze" over background star field						
NGC 1499	Per	EN	04 02	+36 39	145 × 40	California Nebula
use magnification of 15× to 30× to detect wave detail and to train for fainter objects						
Sh2-245	Tau	EN	04 03	+03 06	15 × 90	Eridanus Arc
use Hβ filter; look for brightest section 3° S of ν Tau						
NGC 1647	Tau	OC	04 47	+19 10	40	large binocular cluster, 5° NE of Hyades
bright; often overlooked; telescope reveals many "double" stars; may be glimpsed without aid in a dark sky						
NGC 1746	Tau	OC	05 05	+23 50	42	NGC 1750 and NGC 1758 superimposed
15× binoculars show a nice cluster embedded in a chain of meandering stars						
IC 2118	Eri	RN	05 08	−07 12	3° × 1°	Witch Head Nebula
use low-power, wide-field binoculars or telescope on best nights.						
Collinder 65	Tau	OC	05 27	+16 43	6°	Giant Mushroom
binocular cluster, beautiful, but often not marked on charts; large mushroom-shaped arrow						
Orion GMC	Ori	GMC	05 35	−01 27	1° × 2°	Orion Molecular Cloud bright section
use low-power binoculars and filters; look for wave and gap SW of ε Orionis.						
Sh2-264	Ori	EN	05 36	+09 56	4.5° × 4°	Angelfish Nebula
use Hβ filter in vicinity of λ Ori to see this huge nebula						
Collinder 70	Ori	OC	05 36	−01 06	3°	Orion OB1 Association
3-D view of Ori belt stars over distant field; look for S-shaped star chain W of ε Ori						

Object	Con	Type	RA (2000) h m	Dec ° ′	Size ′	Remarks
Simeis 147	Tau	SNR	05 41	+28 06	3.5°	Taurus supernova remnant
look for "Skates Egg" knot, 10′ E of mag. 8 star SAO 77397						
Collinder 89	Gem	OC	06 19	+23 38	60	
large, loose cluster						
Collinder 132	CMa	OC	07 16	–30 42	80	large cluster
beautiful sprinkling of colorful stars visible even during full Moon						
MW 3	UMa	IFN	09 30	+70 11		Volcano Nebula
Mandel Wilson 3 Integrated Flux Nebula; use low power, dark sky, and luck						
Mel 111	Com	OC	12 26	+26 02	3°	Coma Star Cluster
best with very wide-field binoculars						
ρ Oph Complex	Sco		16 26	–23 27	60 × 25	star cloud with triple star and nebulae
IC 4604 surrounds ρ Oph (mag. 4.6); IC 4603 at HD147889 (mag. 7.9); IC 4605 at 22 Sco (mag. 4.8)						
Sh2-27	Oph	EN	16 33	–10 08	10° × 7°	very large emission nebula
use UHC filter and best sky possible; brightest section NW of M107; some uncertainty over classification						
LBN 1103	Sco	EN	16 34	–28 08	4° × 3°	SE of Antares
large sprawling nebula, 15 × binoculars give best view in dark sky						
Prancing Horse	Oph	DN	17 30	–24 00	10° × 7°	large, delicate, dark nebula
B59, B78, B77, B262, B63, B64, B268; observe dark rift in Cyg to Aql as warmup						
IC 4665	Oph	OC	17 47	+05 43	70	Summer Beehive
overlooked large star cluster; best in binoculars; fuzzy patch with the unaided eye						
NGC 6455	Sco		17 52	–35 20	2°	starcloud often mistaken as small OC
starcloud visible without optical aid; SW of M7, which is possibly superimposed						
Taurus Poniatovii	Oph	Ast	17 57	+05 10	10° × 5°	asterism: Poniatowski's Bull in NE Oph
main stars 72, 66, 67, 68, and 70 Oph; extends into Ser; Barnard's Star currently resides here; defunct const.						
NGC 6526	Sgr	EN	18 06	–23 41	40	nebula N of M8
large U-shaped nebula and star cloud N of a dark rift, look for NGC 6546 to NE						
IC 4685	Sgr	EN	18 10	–23 49	60	large complex
use nebular filters; look for: NGC 6559, CR 367, IC 1274/5						
IC 1284	Sgr	EN	18 18	–19 40	17 × 15	eye of M24
use Hβ filter; sweep SW of IC 1284 to detect 120′ × 30′ nebulous region						
Sh2-54	Ser	EN	18 19	–11 58	60 × 30	nebula & starcloud
large nebular haze N of M16; look for open cluster NGC 6604 & Simeis 3-132						
NGC 6633	Oph	OC	18 28	+06 31	27	Circular Cloud
large cluster sitting over top of apparent star cloud						
IC 4756	Ser	OC	18 40	+05 28	52	Graff's Cluster
visible without optical aid with NGC 6633 as "dueling clusters," discovered by Webb						
Basel 1	Sct	OC	18 49	–05 49	55	W of M11
small cluster in the bowl of a dipper-shaped asterism						
B111	Sct	DN	18 51	–04 56	2°	Half-Moon Nebula
large kidney-shaped dark nebula N of M11, superimposed on Scutum star cloud						
B138	Aql	DN	19 15	+0 52	140 × 20	Barnard's Black Lizard
huge dragon-shaped dark nebula below Altair; use binoculars						
NGC 6774	Sgr	OC	19 17	–16 18	60	Ram's Head
a "true cluster"; contains G2 stars; look for star chains running SE and SW						
Collinder 399	Vul	Ast	19 26	+20 15	89	Coathanger or Brocchi's Cluster
three dozen orange and blue stars in the pattern of a coathanger; look E for NGC 6802						
Stock 1	Vul	OC	19 36	+25 15	52	halfway between β Cyg and Coathanger
50 stars mag. 7 and brighter; best seen in binoculars						
Sh2-119	Cyg	EN	21 17	+43 46	2.5° × 2°	NE of North America Nebula complex
use large binoculars or RFT with nebular filter; sweep past 68 Cyg; visible if Pelican can be seen						
IC 1396	Cep	EN	21 40	+57 34	170 × 140	large emission nebula
locate μ Cep, then add nebular filter; attempt van den Bergh 142, Elephant Trunk Nebula						
Stock 12	Cas	OC	23 37	+52 36	40	
very large, loose, binocular cluster; look for star chain to SE						
Great Rift		DNs/GMCs			120°	overlapping dark nebulae and GMCs
huge naked-eye rift splitting the Milky Way from Cyg, through Aql, Oph, and Sco, to Cen						

SOUTHERN HEMISPHERE SPLENDORS

BY ALAN WHITMAN

Any serious deep-sky observer yearns to experience the far-southern sky, the home of the finest emission nebula (the Carina Nebula), the most obvious dark nebula (the Coalsack), arguably the best open cluster (NGC 3532), the most impressive globular cluster (47 Tucanae), the biggest and brightest globular cluster (Omega Centauri, although it is likely the core of a small galaxy absorbed by the Milky Way), the galaxy that offers amateur telescopes hundreds of targets within it (the Large Magellanic Cloud), and the closest naked-eye star in the night sky (α Centauri), just to name a few. Here is a checklist of "must-see" splendors, rated with one to three exclamation marks, plus 16 other significant objects. The author has observed all of these objects under fine, dark skies.

Dec −35° was chosen as the northern cutoff for this list. However, three slightly more northerly objects that greatly benefit from being viewed higher in the sky were included, notably M83, because it is one of the finest face-on spiral galaxies in the southern sky, but its three spiral arms are not well seen from northern states. Generous Australian amateurs provide dark-sky viewing with big Dobs for Northern Hemisphere amateurs. See **ozsky.org** for this non-profit observing. However, most objects on the list can be viewed from the southern Caribbean; many are visible from Hawaii or from the Florida Keys; some, including Omega Centauri and Centaurus A can be appreciated from the American Southwest. February through April are the preferred months for a southern observing run, since there are no far-southern splendors (those with exclamation marks) located between 20h and 0h of right ascension.

Data for open and globular clusters are from Archinal and Hynes's 2003 reference book *Star Clusters*, with the two noted exceptions. Data for other objects are mostly from Malin and Frew's highly recommended 1995 guidebook *Hartung's Astronomical Objects for Southern Telescopes*, 2nd ed. The dimensions of galaxies and nebulae and a few other numbers are mostly from various lists in the *Observer's Handbook* or from Sinnott's 1988 work, *NGC 2000.0*. Various sorces, including private communications, have provided some difficult-to-obtain data.

Notation used below is mostly as defined on p. 314; in addition, * = star or stars, CC = concentration class of a globular cluster (see p. 312), and DN = dark nebula. Numbers without a prefix in the **NGC** column are NGC numbers.

#	NGC	Con	Type	RA (2000) h m	Dec ° ′	m_V	Size″ ′	Remarks
1	55	Scl	G-SBm	0 14.9	−39 12	7.9	32 × 6	! in 100-mm scope: diffuse splinter
2	104	Tuc	GC	0 24.1	−72 05	4	50	!!! 47 Tuc; yellow core in 370-mm scope
3	β	Tuc	Dbl*	0 31.5	−62 58	4.3, 4.5	27″	! both blue-white
4	SMC	Tuc	G-SBm	0 52.7	−72 50	2.3	5°× 3°	!!! many NGCs included
5	362	Tuc	GC	1 3.2	−70 51	6.8	14	! Milky Way GC beside SMC; CC III
6	p	Eri	Dbl*	1 39.8	−56 12	5.8, 5.8	12″	! both yellow-orange dwarfs
7	1097	For	G-SBb	2 46.3	−30 17	9.3	13 × 8	! in 300-mm scope: bar and tough arms
8	θ	Eri	Dbl*	2 58.3	−40 18	3.2, 4.1	8.4″	! both white
9	1313	Ret	G-SBd	3 18.3	−66 30	8.9	9 × 7	in 370-mm scope: bar, one spiral arm
10		For	Gal Cl.	3 22.7	−37 12	—	—	position is for bright 1316, Fornax A
11	1365	For	G-SBc	3 33.6	−36 08	9.5	14 × 10	!! in 300-mm scope: bar with 2 spiral arms
12	f	Eri	Dbl*	3 48.6	−37 37	4.9, 5.4	8.1″	! yellowish stars
13	1566	Dor	G-Sc	4 20	−54 56	9.4	13 × 9	!! in 250-mm scope: two classic spiral arms
14	ι	Pic	Dbl*	4 50.9	−53 28	5.6, 6.5	12.5″	! very nice yellow pair
15	1851	Col	GC	5 14.1	−40 03	7.1	12	! brightest center of any GC; CC II
16	LMC	Dor	G-SBm	5 23.6	−69 45	0.1	11°× 9°	!!! many nights' work for large apertures
17	2070	Dor	EN/OC	5 38.7	−69 06	5.4	20	!!! Tarantula Nebula; "spider legs" easy
18	γ	Vol	Dbl*	7 8.7	−70 30	3.9, 5.4	14.4″	! gold and light-green pair
19	2451	Pup	OC	7 45.4	−37 57	2.8	50	! two OCs in radial line, 400 ly apart

SOUTHERN HEMISPHERE SPLENDORS (continued)

#	NGC	Con	Type	RA (2000) h m	Dec ° ′	m_v	Size ′	Remarks
20	2477	Pup	OC	7 52.2	−38 32	5.8	20	!! 300*; arcs of 12th-mag. –13th-mag. stars
21	2516	Car	OC	7 58	−60 45	3.8	22	!! 100*; resembles the Beehive but richer
22	γ	Vel	Dbl*	8 9.5	−47 20	1.8, 4.1	41″	! 4*; 1.8-mag. star is brightest Wolf–Rayet
23	2547	Vel	OC	8 10.2	−49 14	4.7	25	! The Heart Cluster (description by Dyer)
24	IC 2391	Vel	OC	8 40.3	−52 55	2.6	60	! o Vel Cluster; bright stars; fine in binocs
25	2736	Vel	SNR	9 0.4	−45 54	—	20×0.5	! Pencil Nebula, part of Vela SNR; use filter
26	2808	Car	GC	9 12	−64 52	6.2	14	! brightest CC I; like a pile of sand
27	3114	Car	OC	10 2.7	−60 06	4.2	35	! 120*; for arcs of stars in binocs
28	3132	Vel	PN	10 7.7	−40 26	9.2	0.8	Eight-Burst Nebula; colorless
29	3199	Car	EN	10 17.1	−57 55	9	22	! crescent formed by Wolf–Rayet star
30	3201	Vel	GC	10 17.6	−46 25	6.9	20	star chains right through core; CC X
31	3293	Car	OC	10 35.8	−58 14	4.7	5	!! Gem Cluster; EN/RN/DN involved
32	3324	Car	EN	10 37.3	−58 38	6.7	15	two-lobed nebula
33	IC 2602	Car	OC	10 43	−64 24	1.6	100	! θ Car Cluster, a.k.a. the Southern Pleiades
34	3372	Car	EN	10 45.1	−59 52	1.0	80	!!! Carina Nebula[A]
35	3532	Car	OC	11 5.5	−58 44	3	50	!!! Football Cluster; finest OC?; 55′ across
36	3699	Cen	PN	11 28	−59 57	11.3	1.1	dark rift visible in 200-mm scope
37	3766	Cen	OC	11 36.3	−61 37	5.3	15	! triangular; 60*; λ Cen Nebula nearby
38	3918	Cen	PN	11 50.3	−57 11	8.1	0.2	! the Blue Planetary; round
39	—	Mus	DN	12 25	−72	—	3°×12′	! the Dark Doodad; near 4372 and γ Mus
40	4372	Mus	GC	12 25.8	−72 39	7.2	19	! CC XII (size is from NGC 2000.0)
41	α	Cru	Dbl*	12 27.8	−63 13	1.3, 1.6	4.2″	! blue-white pair; 3rd star 4.9 mag. at 90″
42	DY	Cru	Red*	12 47.4	−59 42	9v	—	! Ruby Crucis; 3′ W of β Cru; B−V is 5.8
43	—	Cru	DN	12 51	−63	—	6°	!!! Coalsack; forms head of the Emu DN
44	4755	Cru	OC	12 53.6	−60 21	4.2	10	! Jewel Box; sparse in small apertures
45	4833	Mus	GC	12 59.6	−70 52	6.9	14	! CC VIII (magnitude is from W.E. Harris)
46	4945	Cen	G-SBcd	13 5.5	−49 28	8.4	20×4	! in 500-mm scope: dark lane on SW edge
47	5128	Cen	G-S0pec	13 25.5	−43 1	6.8	26×20	!! Cen A; merging spiral and elliptical[B]
48	5139	Cen	GC	13 26.8	−47 29	3.9	55	!!! Omega Cen; huge rich oval; CC VIII
49	5189	Mus	PN	13 33.5	−65 59	9.5	2.6	! the Spiral Planetary; use OIII filter
50	M83	Hya	G-SBc	13 37	−29 52	7.6	16×13	!! in 200-mm: bar, 1 arm; 370-mm: 3 arms
51	5286	Cen	GC	13 46.4	−51 22	7.4	11	! CC V; bluish PN 5307 nearby
52	5460	Cen	OC	14 7.6	−48 18	5.6	35	25 straggling*; trapezoidal asterism in S
53	α	Cen	Dbl*	14 41.1	−60 55	0.0, 1.3	4.4″	!! rapidly changing yellow pair: 22″–1.7″
54	5822	Lup	OC	15 4	−54 20	6.5	35	! triangular; stars are in discrete clumps
55	5927	Lup	GC	15 28	−50 40	8	6	CC VIII; pair with Nor GC 5946
56	B228	Lup	DN	15 45	−34	—	4°×20′	! an unknown wonder; opacity 6
57	5986	Lup	GC	15 46.1	−37 47	7.6	10	200-mm resolves large core; CC VII
58	6025	TrA	OC	16 3.6	−60 25	5.1	15	! triangular, in three clumps
59	6067	Nor	OC	16 13.2	−54 13	5.6	15	! 100*; many pairs
60	6087	Nor	OC	16 18.9	−57 54	5.4	15	! 40*; embedded in Norma Star Cloud
61	6124	Sco	OC	16 25.3	−40 40	5.8	40	100*; many trios around circumference
62	6231	Sco	OC	16 54.2	−41 50	2.6	14	!! ζ, 6231, and Tr 24 form the False Comet
63	6242	Sco	OC	16 55.5	−39 28	6.4	9	23*; good for small scopes
64	6259	Sco	OC	17 0.7	−44 39	8	15	like a fainter M11; 120*
65	6281	Sco	OC	17 4.8	−37 53	5.4	8	25*; shines in modest scopes
66	6302	Sco	PN	17 13.7	−37 06	9.6	1.5×0.5	Bug Nebula; bright core; knots at tips
67	IC 4651	Ara	OC	17 24.7	−49 55	6.9	10	! loops and chains of 70 equal-mag. stars
68	6388	Sco	GC	17 36.3	−44 44	6.8	10	450-mm scope resolves faint stars; CC III
69	6397	Ara	GC	17 40.7	−53 40	5.3	31	!! easily resolved 10th-mag. stars; CC IX
70	6541	CrA	GC	18 8	−43 42	6.3	15	! huge outer halo; CC III
71	6723	Sgr	GC	18 59.6	−36 38	6.8	13	! CC VII; part of fine complex below
72	6726–7	CrA	RN	19 1.7	−36 54	—	9×7	! 7th-mag. stars involved[C]
73	6752	Pav	GC	19 10.9	−59 59	5.3	29	!! easily resolved 11th-mag. stars; CC VI[D]
74	7582	Gru	G-SBb	23 18.4	−42 22	10.2	4×1	brightest member of Grus Quartet

[A] Chevron-shaped dark lane, many other DN involved, including Keyhole Nebula; tiny orange mag. 5 (variable) Homunculus Nebula at center; for OC involved

[B] Prominent broad dark lane; 370-mm scope reveals thin bright streak within the dark lane

[C] Part of !! complex with GC 6723, DN SL 40+41 (55′ long, opacity 6), variable RN 6729 (involved with R CrA), headlight Dbl* Brs 14 (mags. 6.6, 6.8 at 13″), and Dbl* γ CrA (both yellow-white, mags. 4.9, 5.0 at 1.3″ and widening)

[D] Curving star chains converge to a tiny central peak; very tight group of for 12th-mag. galaxies 1° SE

GALAXIES: BRIGHTEST AND NEAREST

BY BARRY F. MADORE AND IAN STEER

External galaxies are generally of such low surface brightness that they often prove disappointing objects for the amateur observer. However, it must be remembered that many of these galaxies were discovered with very small telescopes and that the enjoyment of their discovery can be recaptured. In addition, the central concentration of light varies from galaxy to galaxy, making a visual classification of the types possible at the telescope. Indeed, the *Hubble galaxy classification* (**Type**) given in Table 1 (facing page) is in part based on the fraction of light coming from the central bulge of the galaxy as compared to the contribution from a disk component. Disk galaxies with dominant bulges are classified as **Sa**; as the nuclear contribution declines, types of **Sb**, **Sc**, and **Sd** are assigned until the nucleus is absent at type **Sm**. Often the disks of these galaxies show spiral symmetry, the coherence and strength of which is denoted by Roman numerals **I** through **V**, smaller numbers indicating well-formed global spiral patterns. Those spirals with central bars are designated **SB**, while those with only a hint of a disk embedded in the bulge are called **S0**. A separate class of galaxies that possess no disk component are called ellipticals and can only be further classified numerically by their apparent flattening, with **E0** being apparently round and **E7** being the most flattened.

Environment appears to play an important role in determining the types of galaxies we see at the present epoch. Rich clusters of galaxies, such as the system in Coma, are dominated by ellipticals and gas-free S0 galaxies. The less-dense clusters and groups tend to be dominated by the spiral, disk galaxies. Remarkably, pairs of galaxies are much more frequently of the same Hubble type than random selection would predict. Encounters between disk galaxies may in some cases result in the instabilities necessary to form the spiral structure we often see. M51 (the Whirlpool) and its companion, NGC 5195, are an often-cited example of this type of interaction. In the past, when the Universe was much more densely packed, interactions and collisions may have been sufficiently frequent that entire galaxies merged to form a single large new system; it has been suggested that some elliptical galaxies formed in this way.

Table 1 on the facing page lists the 40 brightest galaxies taken from the *Revised Shapley–Ames Catalog*. As well as their designations, positions, and types, the table lists the total blue magnitudes, major and minor axis lengths (to the nearest minute of arc), the latest estimate of their distances in 10^6 ly, and their radial velocities corrected for the motion of our Sun about the galactic center. Although the Universe as a whole is in expansion, there are parts that are still bound together (or at the very least,

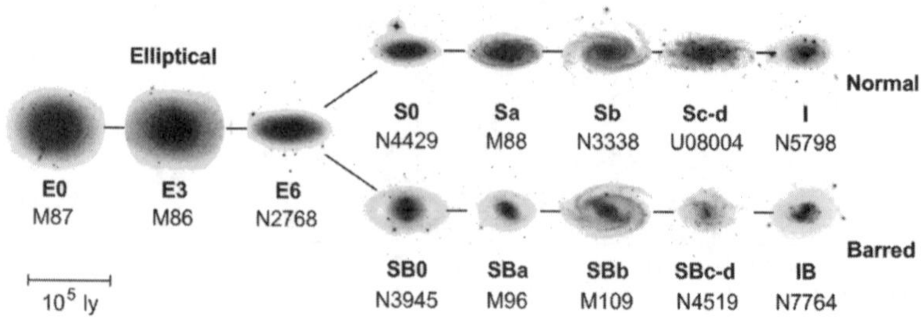

The Hubble "tuning fork" diagram of galaxy classification, using actual galaxy images, with the Messier, NGC (N), or UGC (U) number indicated below the type. (Diagram created by Ian Steer.)

held back in their expansion) by gravity. These groups and clusters are, in essence, representative of the largest material structures in the Universe. Recently, large-scale flows of material have been reported, far in excess of the velocities expected due to the perturbing presence of other galaxies and clusters of galaxies. Either there are exceedingly large concentrations of matter yet to be discovered just beyond our limited view of the world, or the Universe has had a much more interesting history than our present theories indicate. The brightest and nearest galaxies in Table 1 may be moving not only as a result of the universal expansion, but also through very complex interactions with distant parts as yet only postulated but not seen. A selection of nearest galaxies, listed on the following page in Table 2, form what is known as the Local Group of Galaxies. **(Data in Tables 1 and 2 have been updated for 2022.)**

TABLE 1—THE 40 OPTICALLY BRIGHTEST SHAPLEY-AMES GALAXIES

		RA (2000)	**Dec**		**Magnitude**	**Size**	**Distance**	**Rad. Vel.**
NGC	**Other**	h m	° ′	**Type**	B_T	′	10^6 ly	km/s
55		0 14.9	−39 11.8	SBm	8.84	32 × 6	6.48	131
205	M110	0 40.4	+41 41.1	E5 pec	8.92	22 × 11	2.67	−241
221	M32	0 42.7	+40 51.9	E2	9.03	9 × 7	2.54	−213
224	M31	0 42.7	+41 16.1	Sb I–II	4.36	190 × 60	2.50	−301
247		0 47.1	−20 45.6	SBd III–IV	9.86	21 × 7	12.0	156
253		0 47.6	−25 17.3	SBc	7.09	28 × 7	10.5	242
292	SMC	0 52.7	−72 49.7	SBm IV–V pec	2.70	320 × 185	0.195	158
300		0 54.9	−37 41.1	Sd III	8.95	22 × 16	6.58	144
598	M33	1 33.8	+30 39.6	Scd II–III	6.27	71 × 42	2.82	−180
628	M74	1 36.7	+15 47.0	Sc I	9.95	11 × 10	30.3	657
1068	M77	2 42.7	−00 00.8	Sb II	9.61	7 × 6	57.2	1137
1291		3 17.3	−41 06.5	SB0/a	9.39	10 × 8	25.0	839
1313		3 18.3	−66 29.9	SBd III–IV	9.20	9 × 7	14.3	470
1316	Fornax A	3 22.7	−37 12.5	S0 pec	9.40	12 × 9	57.7	1760
	LMC	5 23.6	−69 45.4	SBm III	0.90	645 × 550	0.163	278
2403		7 36.9	+65 36.2	SBcd III	8.11	22 × 12	10.9	133
2903		9 32.2	+21 30.1	SBbc I–III	9.68	13 × 6	28.4	550
3031	M81	9 55.6	+69 03.9	Sab I–II	7.89	27 × 14	11.8	−34
3034	M82	9 55.9	+69 40.8	I0	9.30	11 × 4	12.1	269
3521		11 05.8	−00 02.2	SBbc II–III	9.83	11 × 5	42.7	799
3627	M66	11 20.2	+12 59.5	SBb II	9.65	9 × 4	31.0	721
4258	M106	12 19.0	+47 18.2	SBbc II	9.29	19 × 7	24.2	448
4449		12 28.2	+44 05.6	IBm IV	9.99	6 × 4	12.3	207
4472	M49	12 29.8	+08 00.0	E2	9.37	10 × 8	52.5	981
4486	M87	12 30.8	+12 23.5	E0	9.59	8 × 7	54.0	1284
4594	M104	12 40.0	−11 37.4	Sa	8.98	9 × 4	33.7	1024
4631		12 42.1	+32 32.5	SBd	9.75	16 × 3	23.6	610
4649	M60	12 43.7	+11 33.2	E2	9.81	7 × 6	54.5	1110
4736	M94	12 50.9	+41 07.2	Sab	8.99	11 × 9	15.3	308
4826	M64	12 56.7	+21 41.0	Sab II	9.36	10 × 5	19.3	409
4945		13 05.5	−49 28.1	SBcd	9.30	20 × 4	11.8	563
5055	M63	13 15.8	+42 01.8	Sbc II–III	9.31	13 × 7	37.6	500
5128	Cen A	13 25.5	−43 01.1	S0 pec	7.84	26 × 20	11.9	547
5194	M51	13 29.9	+47 11.7	Sbc I–II pec	8.96	11 × 7	26.3	460
5236	M83	13 37.0	−29 51.9	SBc II	8.20	13 × 12	15.4	513
5457	M101	14 03.2	+54 20.9	SBcd I	8.31	29 × 27	22.6	241
6744		19 09.8	−63 51.5	SBbc II	9.14	20 × 13	25.8	841
6822		19 45.0	−14 48.2	IBm IV–V	9.31	16 × 14	1.68	−55
6946		20 34.9	+60 09.2	SBcd II	8.23	12 × 10	19.6	40
7793		23 57.8	−32 35.5	Sd IV	9.98	9 × 6	12.0	227

TABLE 2—THE NEAREST GALAXIES—OUR LOCAL GROUP

Name	RA (2000.0) h m	Dec ° ′	Type	Magnitude B_T	Distance 10^6 ly
Milky Way Galaxy			Sb/c		
IC 10	0 20.3	+59 18	IBm	11.80	2.47
NGC 147	0 33.2	+48 31	dE5 pec	10.47	2.47
And III	0 35.6	+36 30	dE	15.00	2.43
NGC 185	0 39	+48 20	dE3 pec	10.10	2.21
M110 = NGC 205	0 40.4	+41 41	E5 pec	8.92	2.67
M32 = NGC 221	0 42.7	+40 52	E2	9.03	2.54
M31 = NGC 224	0 42.7	+41 16	Sb I–II	4.36	2.50
And I	0 45.7	+38 02	dE3 pec	13.60	2.56
SMC	0 52.7	−72 50	SBm IV–V pec	2.70	0.195
Sculptor	1 0.2	−33 43	E7	8.78	0.268
Pisces 1 = LGS 3	1 3.9	+21 53	Irr	14.20	2.12
IC 1613	1 4.8	+02 07	IBm V	9.88	2.38
And II	1 16.5	+33 25	dE	13.50	2.10
M33 = NGC 598	1 33.8	+30 40	Scd II–III	6.27	2.82
Fornax	2 40	−34 27	dE4	9.28	0.462
LMC	5 23.6	−69 45	SBm III	0.90	0.163
Carina	6 41.6	−50 58	dE3	11.30	0.336
Antlia	10 4.1	−27 20	IBm	16.19	4.33
Leo I	10 8.5	+12 18	dE3	11.18	0.767
Sextans	10 13.1	−01 37	dE	10.40	0.285
Leo II	11 13.5	+22 09	dE0	12.60	0.710
Ursa Minor	15 9.1	+67 13	E	11.90	0.230
Draco	17 20.2	+57 55	E pec	10.90	0.262
Sagittarius	18 55.3	−30 33	dE	4.50	0.084
NGC 6822	19 45	−14 48	IBm IV–V	9.31	1.68

Editor's Notes:

(1) Aside from those famous companions of the Milky Way Galaxy, the Large Magellanic Cloud (LMC) and the Small Magellanic Cloud (SMC), there is only one galaxy beyond our own that is easily visible to unaided human eyes: M31, the Andromeda Galaxy (2.58 Mly distant). M33, the Triangulum Galaxy, can also be seen, but this is a difficult observation. To locate M31, see the NOVEMBER ALL-SKY MAP on p. 345, where the tiny cluster of six dots above the first "A" of "ANDROMEDA" indicates its location. With modest optical aid (e.g. binoculars) a dozen or more of the galaxies listed in Table 1 can be seen by experienced observers under dark skies. With a 250-mm telescope, the quasar 3C 273, at 1000 times the distance of M31, can elicit a noticeable signal in the visual cortex (see p. 323).

(2) An interesting article by G. Lake entitled "Cosmology of the Local Group" appears in *Sky & Telescope*, December 1992, p. 613.

(3) The National Aeronautics and Space Administration/Infrared Processing and Analysis Center (NASA/IPAC) Extragalactic Database (NED) is a comprehensive compilation of extragalactic data for 1.1 billion distinct extragalactic objects. The database includes most major catalogs and offers references to and abstracts of articles of extragalactic interest that have appeared in most major journals. Also online are 14.0 billion photometric measurements, 15.4 million redshifts, over 2.5 million images, and more than 500000 detailed classifications. It is possible to search the main NED database for objects selected by catalog prefix, position, type, or redshift. The database is available at ned.ipac.caltech.edu. See ned.ipac.caltech.edu/level5 for a knowledgebase of review articles and basic information.

GALAXIES WITH PROPER NAMES

BY BARRY F. MADORE

Below are the catalog designations and positions of galaxies known to have proper names, which usually honor the discoverer (e.g. McLeish's Object), identify the constellation in which the galaxy is found (e.g. Andromeda Galaxy), or describe the galaxy in some easily remembered way (e.g. Whirlpool Galaxy).

Galaxy Name	Other Names / Remarks	RA (2000) h m	Dec ° ′
Ambartsumian's Knot	NGC 3561, UGC 06224, ARP 105	11 11.2	+28 42
Andromeda Galaxy	M31, NGC 224, UGC 00454	0 42.7	+41 16
Andromeda I		0 45.7	+38 01
Andromeda II		1 16.5	+33 26
Andromeda III		0 35.3	+36 31
Antennae Galaxy	Ring Tail, NGC 4038/39, ARP 244	12 01.9	−18 52
Antlia Dwarf	AM 1001-270	10 04.0	−27 20
Aquarius Dwarf	DDO 210	20 46.9	−12 51
Arp's Galaxy		11 19.6	+51 30
Atoms For Peace	NGC 7252, ARP 226	22 20.8	−24 41
Baade's Galaxies A & B	MCG+07-02-018/19	0 49.9	+42 35
Barbon's Galaxy	Markarian 328, ZWG 497.042	23 37.7	+30 08
Barnard's Galaxy	NGC 6822, IC 4895, DDO 209	19 44.9	−14 48
Bear's Paw (Claw)	NGC 2537, UGC 04274, ARP 6	8 13.2	+46 00
BL Lacertae		22 02.7	+42 17
Black Eye Galaxy	M64, NGC 4826, UGC 08062	12 56.7	+21 41
Bode's Galaxies	M81/82, NGC 3031/4, UGC 05318/22	9 55.7	+69 23
Burbidge Chain	MCG-04-03-010 to 13	0 47.5	−20 26
BW Tauri	UGC 03087, MCG+01-12-009	4 33.2	+05 21
Carafe Galaxy	Cannon's Carafe, near NGC 1595/98	4 28.0	−47 54
Carina Dwarf		6 41.6	−50 58
Cartwheel Galaxy	Zwicky's Cartwheel, MCG-06-02-022a	0 37.4	−33 44
Centaurus A	NGC 5128, ARP 153	13 25.5	−43 01
Circinus Galaxy		14 13.2	−65 20
Coddington's Nebula	IC 2574, UGC 05666, DDO 81	10 28.4	+68 25
Copeland Septet	MCG+04-28-004/05/07 to 11, UGC 06597, UGC 06602, ARP 320, NGC 3745/46/48/50/51/53/54†	11 37.8	+21 59
Cygnus A	MCG+07-41-003	19 59.4	+40 43
Draco Dwarf	UGC 10822, DDO 208	17 20.2	+57 55
Exclamation Mark Galaxy		0 39.3	−43 06
The Eyes	NGC 4435/8, UGC 07574/5, ARP 120a/b	12 27.7	+13 03
Fath 703	NGC 5892	15 13.7	−15 29
Fornax A	NGC 1316, ARP 154	3 22.7	−37 12
Fornax Dwarf	MCG-06-07-001	2 39.9	−34 32
Fourcade–Figueroa	MCG-07-28-004	13 34.8	−45 33
The Garland	S of NGC 3077 = UGC 05398	10 04.2	+68 40
Grus Quartet	NGC 7552/82/90/99	23 17.8	−42 26
GR 8 (Gibson Reaves)	UGC 08091, DDO 155	12 58.7	+14 13
Hardcastle's Galaxy	MCG-05-31-039	13 13.0	−32 41
Helix Galaxy	NGC 2685, UGC 04666, ARP 336	8 55.6	+58 44
Hercules A	MCG+01-43-006	16 51.2	+04 59
Hoag's Object		15 17.2	+21 35

† Position errors caused these to be historically marked as nonexistent in the NGC and RNGC.

GALAXIES WITH PROPER NAMES (continued)

Galaxy Name	Other Names / Remarks	RA (2000) h m	Dec ° ′
Holmberg I	UGC 05139, DDO 63	9 40.5	+71 11
Holmberg II	UGC 04305, DDO 50, ARP 268	8 19.3	+70 43
Holmberg III	UGC 04841	9 14.6	+74 14
Holmberg IV	UGC 08837, DDO 185	13 54.7	+53 54
Holmberg V	UGC 08658	13 40.6	+54 20
Holmberg VI	NGC 1325a	3 24.9	−21 20
Holmberg VII	UGC 07739, DDO 137	12 34.7	+06 17
Holmberg VIII	UGC 08303, DDO 166	13 13.3	+36 12
Holmberg IX	UGC 05336, DDO 66	9 57.6	+69 03
Horologium Dwarf	Schuster's Spiral	3 59.2	−45 52
Hydra A	MCG-02-24-007	9 18.1	−12 06
Integral Sign Galaxy	UGC 03697, MCG+12-07-028	7 11.4	+71 50
Keenan's System	NGC 5216/16a/18, UGC 08528/9, ARP 104	13 32.2	+62 43
Kowal's Object		19 29.9	−17 41
Large Magellanic Cloud	Nubecula Major	5 23.6	−69 45
Leo I	Regulus Dwarf, UGC 05470, DDO 74, Harrington–Wilson #1	10 08.5	+12 18
Leo II	Leo B, UGC 06253, DDO 93, Harrington–Wilson #2	11 13.4	+22 10
Leo III	Leo A, UGC 05364, DDO 69	9 59.3	+30 45
Lindsay–Shapley Ring	Graham A	6 42.8	−74 15
Lost Galaxy	NGC 4535, UGC 07727	12 34.3	+08 11
McLeish's Object		20 09.7	−66 13
Maffei I	UGCA 34	2 36.3	+59 39
Maffei II	UGCA 39	2 42.0	+59 37
Malin 1		12 37.0	+14 20
Mayall's Object	MCG+07-23-019, ARP 148	11 03.9	+40 50
Mice	NGC 4676a/b, UGC 07938/9, IC 819/20, ARP 242	12 46.1	+30 44
Miniature Spiral	NGC 3928, UGC 06834	11 51.8	+48 41
Minkowski's Object	ARP 133 (NE of NGC 541)	1 25.8	−01 21
Pancake	NGC 2685, UGC 04666, ARP 336	8 55.6	+58 44
Papillon	IC 708, UGC 06549	11 33.9	+49 03
Pegasus Dwarf	UGC 12613, DDO 216	23 28.5	+14 44
Perseus A	NGC 1275/6, UGC 02669	3 19.8	+41 31
Phoenix Dwarf Irregular		1 51.1	−44 26
Pinwheel Galaxy	see also Triangulum Galaxy	1 33.9	+30 39
Pinwheel Galaxy	M99, NGC 4254, UGC 07345	12 18.8	+14 25
Pinwheel Galaxy	M101, NGC 5457, UGC 08981, ARP 26	14 03.3	+54 22
Pisces Cloud	NGC 379/80/82-85, UGC 00682/3/6-9, ARP 331	1 07.5	+32 25
Pisces Dwarf	LGS 3	0 03.8	+21 54
Polarissima Australis	NGC 2573	1 42.0‡	−89 20
Polarissima Borealis	NGC 3172, ZWG 370.002	11 50.3‡	+89 07
Reinmuth 80	NGC 4517a, UGC 07685	12 32.5	+00 23
Reticulum Dwarf	Sersic 040.03	4 36.2	−58 50
Sagittarius Dwarf		19 30.0	−17 41
Sculptor Dwarf	MCG-06-03-015	1 00.2	−33 42
Sculptor Dwarf Irregular		0 08.1	−34 34

‡The high declination of these objects makes the RA particularly uncertain.

GALAXIES WITH PROPER NAMES (continued)

Galaxy Name	Other Names / Remarks	RA (2000) h m	Dec ° ′
Seashell Galaxy	Companion to NGC 5291	13 47.4	−30 23
Sextans A	UGCA 205, MCG-01-26-030, DDO 75	10 11.0	−04 41
Sextans B	UGC 05373, DDO 70	10 00.0	+05 19
Sextans C	UGC 05439	10 05.6	+00 04
Sextans Dwarf		10 13.1	−01 37
Seyfert's Sextet	Serpens Sextet, NGC 6027/6027a-e, UGC 10116	15 59.2	+20 46
Shapley–Ames 1		1 05.1	−06 13
Shapley–Ames 2	NGC 4507	12 35.1	−39 55
Shapley–Ames 3	MCG-02-33-015	12 49.4	−10 07
Shapley–Ames 4	UGC 08041	12 55.2	+00 07
Shapley–Ames 5	MCG-07-42-001	20 24.0	−44 00
Shapley–Ames 6		21 23.2	+45 46
Siamese Twins	NGC 4567/4568	12 36.5	+11 15
Silver Coin	Sculptor Galaxy, NGC 253, UGCA 13	0 47.6	−25 18
Small Magellanic Cloud	Nubecula Minor	0 52.7	−72 50
Sombrero Galaxy	M104, NGC 4594	12 39.9	−11 37
Spider	UGC 05829, DDO 84	10 42.6	+34 27
Spindle Galaxy	NGC 3115	10 05.2	−07 42
Stephan's Quintet	NGC 7317-20, UGC 12099-102, ARP 319	22 36.0	+33 58
Sunflower Galaxy	M63, NGC 5055, UGC 08334	13 15.8	+42 02
Triangulum Galaxy	Pinwheel, M33, NGC 598, UGC 01117	1 33.9	+30 39
Ursa Minor Dwarf	UGC 09749, DDO 199	15 08.8	+67 12
Virgo A	M87, NGC 4486, UGC 07654, ARP 152	12 30.8	+12 23
Whirlpool Galaxy	Rosse's Galaxy, Question Mark Galaxy, M51, NGC 5194/5, UGC 08493/4, ARP 85	13 29.9	+47 12
Wild's Triplet	MCG-01-30-032 to 34, ARP 248	11 46.8	−03 49
Wolf–Lundmark–Melotte	MCG-03-01-015, DDO 221	0 02.0	−15 28
Zwicky #2	UGC 06955, DDO 105	11 58.4	+38 03
Zwicky's Triplet	UGC 10586, ARP 103	16 49.5	+45 30

Catalogs:

AM *Catalogue of Southern Peculiar Galaxies and Associations*, by H.C. Arp and B.F. Madore, Cambridge University Press (1987).

ARP *Atlas of Peculiar Galaxies*, H. Arp, *Ap. J. Suppl. 14*, 1 (1966).

DDO *David Dunlap Observatory Publ.*, S. van den Bergh, II, No. 5, 147 (1959).

IC *Index Catalogue*, J.L.E. Dreyer, *Mem. R.A.S.* (1895–1910).

MCG *Morphological Catalogue of Galaxies*, B.A. Vorontsov–Velyaminov et al., Moscow State University, Moscow (1961–1974).

NGC *New General Catalogue of Nebulae and Clusters of Stars*, J.L.E. Dreyer, *Mem. R.A.S.* (1888).

RNGC *The Revised New General Catalogue of Nonstellar Astronomical Objects*, J.W. Sulentic and W.G. Tifft, University of Arizona Press (1973).

UGC *Uppsala General Catalogue of Galaxies*, P. Nilson, *Nova Acta Regiae Societatis Scientiarum Upsaliensis*, Ser. V: A, Vol. 1, Uppsala, Sweden (1973).

UGCA *Catalogue of Selected Non-UGC Galaxies*, P. Nilson, Uppsala Astronomical Observatory (1974).

ZWG *Catalogue of Galaxies and Clusters of Galaxies*, F. Zwicky et al., Vol. 1–6, California Institute of Technology (1961–1968).

RADIO ASTRONOMY AND RADIO SOURCES

BY KEN TAPPING & HUGH PETT

Cosmic radio sources fall into two broad classes: "Continuum Sources," which emit over much of the radio spectrum and extend well beyond the frequency band used by any particular radio telescope, and "Spectral Sources," which emit radio spectral lines, such as the 1420.406 MHz (21-cm wavelength) spectral line from cosmic, neutral hydrogen. The continuum emissions are produced by high-energy electrons in magnetic fields, hot plasmas, or by plasma waves. These emissions are broadband but vary with frequency.

Frequency Bands Allocated for Radio Astronomical Use

The list below shows the frequency bands up to 31.5 GHz allocated by international treaty for use by radio observatories.

Band (MHz)	Primary Lines	Band (GHz)	Primary Lines
322.0–328.6	deuterium, D	4.8–5.0	formaldehyde, HCHO
406.1–410.0	continuum-only	10.6–10.7	continuum-only
608–614	continuum-only	14.47–14.50	formaldehyde, HCHO
1400–1427	hydrogen, H (21 cm)	15.35–15.40	continuum-only
1610.6–1613.8	hydroxyl, OH	22.21–22.50	water, H_20
1660–1670	hydroxyl, OH	23.6–24.0	ammonia, NH_3
2670–2700	continuum-only	31.3–31.5	continuum-only

Cosmic Radio Sources

The sources listed below are among those observable using small radio telescopes. Flux densities are given for 0.1, 0.5, 1, and 4 GHz (wavelengths of 3 m, 60 cm, 30 cm, and 7.5 cm, respectively) because equipment for these wavelengths is widely available.

Source	RA (2000) h m	Dec ° ′	Flux Densities (0.1, 0.5, 1, and 4 GHz) Jy	Remarks
Sun			20k/250k/450k/800k	"quiet" values; short, intense emissions from flares
Moon			2/50/210/3350	225 K thermal; plus near-surface emissions at <3 cm
Jupiter				Strong bursts at dekametre wavelengths
W3	2 25.4	+62 06	—/80/150/134	IC 1795; complex, bright HII region; OH emission
Taurus A	5 34.5	+22 01	1450/1250/1000/360	Crab Nebula; remnant of 1054 CE supernova
Orion A	5 35.3	−5 25	90/200/360/330	Orion Neb.; HII star-forming region; OH, IR source
IC 443	6 17.0	+22 34	350/140/80/20	Jellyfish Nebula; supernova remnant
Virgo A	12 30.8	+12 23	1950/150/300/120	M87; elliptical galaxy (E0) with jet; mag. +8.6
Centaurus A	13 25.4	−43 02	8500/5000/1900/200	NGC 5128; galaxy (S0 pec); mag. +6.8, $z = 0.002$
3C 295	14 11.4	+52 12	95/60/28/10	radio galaxy; mag. +20.5, $z = 0.461$
Galactic center	17 42.0	−28 50	4400/2900/1800/800	strong, diffuse emission from galactic center
Sagittarius A*	17 42.5	−28 55	100/250/200/336	compact source at gal. ctr.; assoc. with black hole?
Cygnus A	19 59.5	+40 44	15500/4000/2100/370	strong radio galaxy (E); mag. +16.2, $z = 0.056$
Cygnus X	20 22.6	+40 23	400/150/30/70	complex region
Cassiopeia A	23 23.4	+58 49	25000/4500/2800/810	supernova remnant

Technology is advancing too quickly for printed books to be very useful. However, for background radio-astronomy information, see *Radio Astronomy*, by J.D. Kraus (Cygnus-Quasar Books, Powell, Ohio, 1986). A number of small, simple radio telescopes and some projects to try are described in *Radio Astronomy Projects*, by William Lonc, Radio-Sky Publishing, 1997. Organizations focusing on amateur radio astronomy include the Society of Amateur Radio Astronomers (radio-astronomy.org) and the UK Amateur Radio Astronomy Network (ukaranet.org.uk). The RASC Okanagan Centre has an active radio-astronomy group led by Hugh Pett (hughirenep@gmail.com). He invites readers to look over the project images at rascoc.zenfolio.com/f339290108.

MAPS OF THE NIGHT SKY

BY ROY BISHOP

The maps on the following seven pages cover the entire sky. Stars are shown down to a magnitude of 4.5 or 5, that is, those that are readily apparent to the unaided eye on a reasonably dark night.

The first six maps are drawn for latitude 45°N but are useful for latitudes several degrees north or south of this. They show the hemisphere of sky visible at various times of year. Because the aspect of the night sky changes continuously with both longitude and time, while time zones change discontinuously with both longitude and time of year, it is not possible to state simply when a particular observer will find that his or her sky fits exactly one of the six maps. The month indicated above each map is the time of year when the map will match the ***late evening* sky**. On any particular night, successive maps will represent the sky as it appears every four hours later. For example, at 2:00 or 3:00 on a March morning, the May map should be used. Just after mealtime on a January night, the November map will be appropriate. The center of each map is the *zenith*, the point directly overhead; the circumference is the horizon. To identify the stars, hold the map in front of you so that the part of the horizon you are facing (west, for instance) is downward. (The four letters around the periphery of each map indicate compass directions.)

The southern-sky map is centered on the south celestial pole and extends to Dec 20°S at its periphery. Thus there is considerable overlap with the southern areas of the other maps. Note that the orientation of the various names is generally inverted compared to that on the first six maps, as most users of this Handbook will be residents of the Northern Hemisphere and will make use of the southern-sky map when they make trips to the tropics. Thus in "normal" use this map will be read in an area above its center, unlike the first six maps, which are normally read below their centers. The months indicated around the edge of the map may be used to orient it to each of the preceding six maps and have the same "late evening" significance as explained above. Tick marks around the edge of the map indicate hours of right ascension, with hours 0, 3, 6, etc., labeled. Starting at the center of the map, the series of small crosses along RA 0h indicates southern declinations 90°, 80°, 70°,…, 20°. With the aid of a drawing compass, an observer in the Northern Hemisphere can quickly locate a circle, centered on the south celestial pole, that represents the southern limit of his or her sky.

On all seven maps, stars forming the usual constellation patterns are linked by straight lines, constellation names being given in uppercase letters. Three constellations (Horologium, Mensa, and Microscopium) consist of faint stars; hence no patterns are indicated and the names are placed in parentheses. Small clusters of dots indicate the positions of bright star clusters, nebulae, or galaxies. The pair of wavy dotted lines indicates roughly the borders of the Milky Way. Small asterisks locate the directions of the galactic center (GC), the north galactic pole (NGP), and the south galactic pole (SGP). LMC, SMC, and CS signify, respectively, the Large Magellanic Cloud, the Small Magellanic Cloud, and the Coal Sack. Two dashed lines appear on each of the first six maps. The one with more dashes is the celestial equator. Tick marks along this indicate hours of right ascension, the odd hours being labeled. The line with fewer dashes is the ecliptic, the apparent annual path of the Sun across the heavens. Letters along this line indicate the approximate position of the Sun at the beginning of each month. Also located along the ecliptic are the Northern Hemisphere vernal equinox (VE), summer solstice (SS), autumnal equinox (AE), and winter solstice (WS).

The epoch of the maps is 1950.0. Because of the small scale of the maps, the effect of precession is not yet significant.

JANUARY ALL-SKY MAP

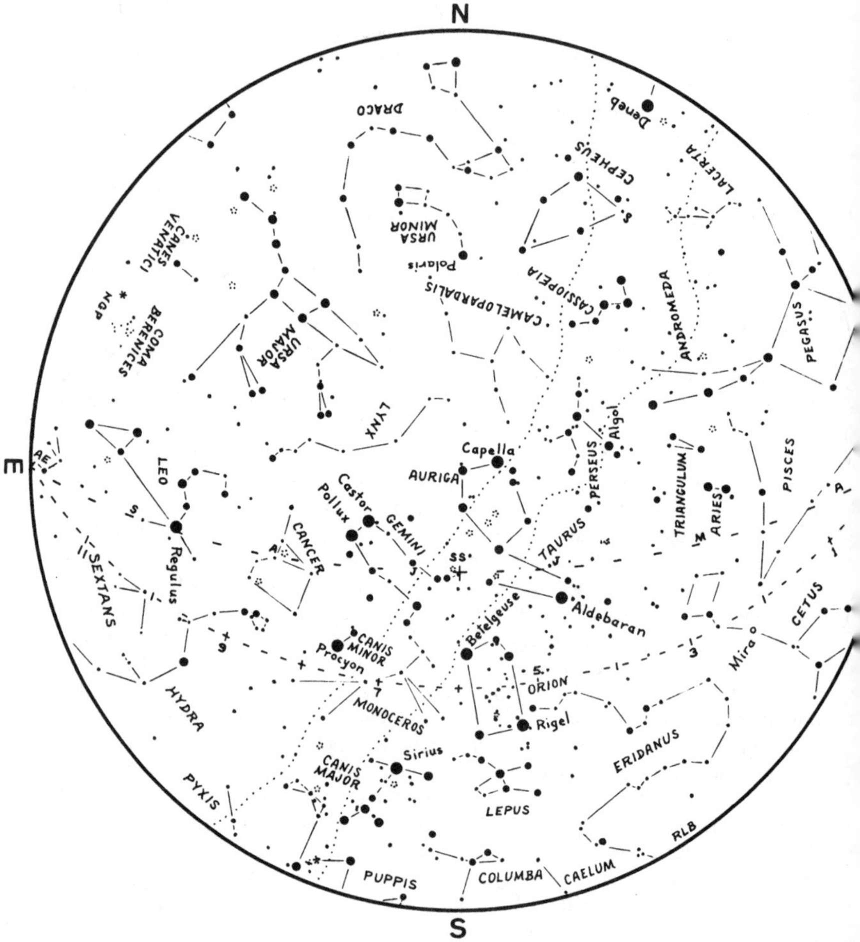

MARCH ALL-SKY MAP

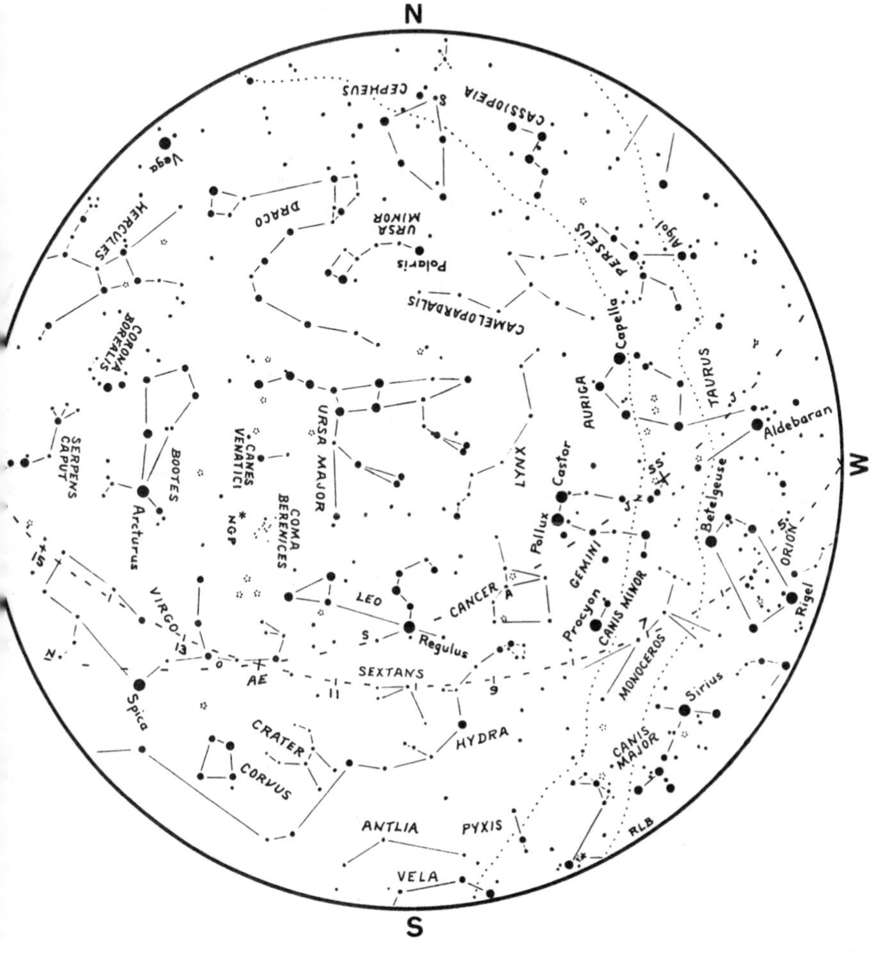

MAY ALL-SKY MAP

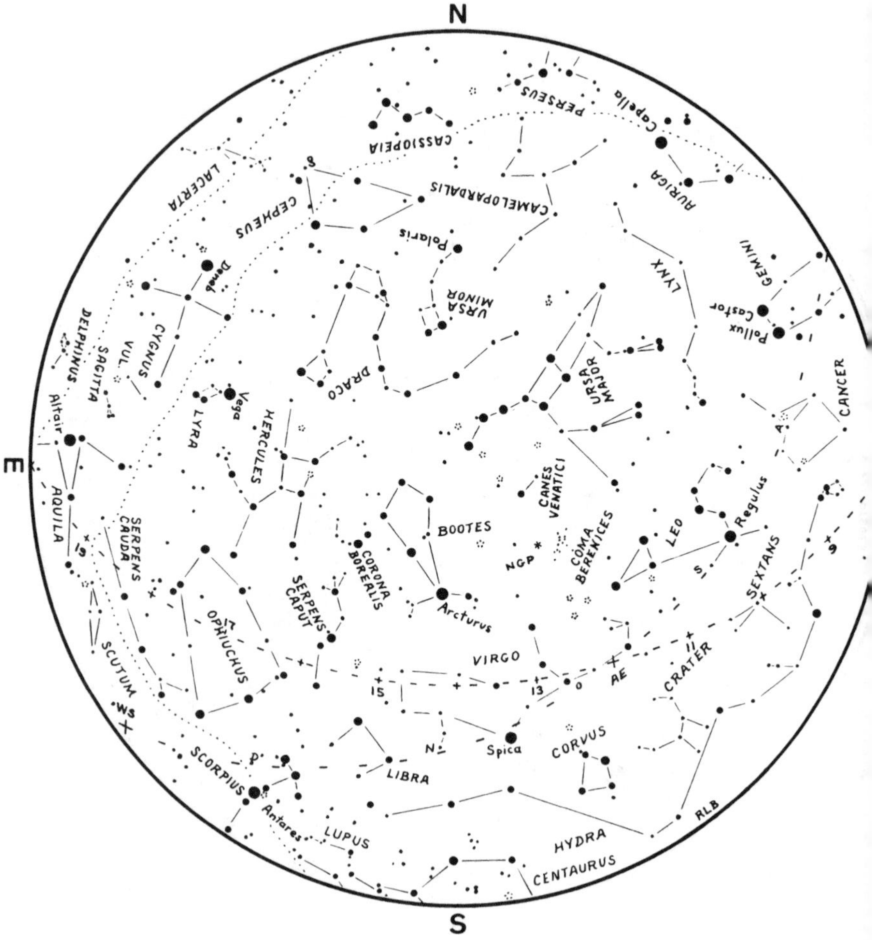

JULY ALL-SKY MAP

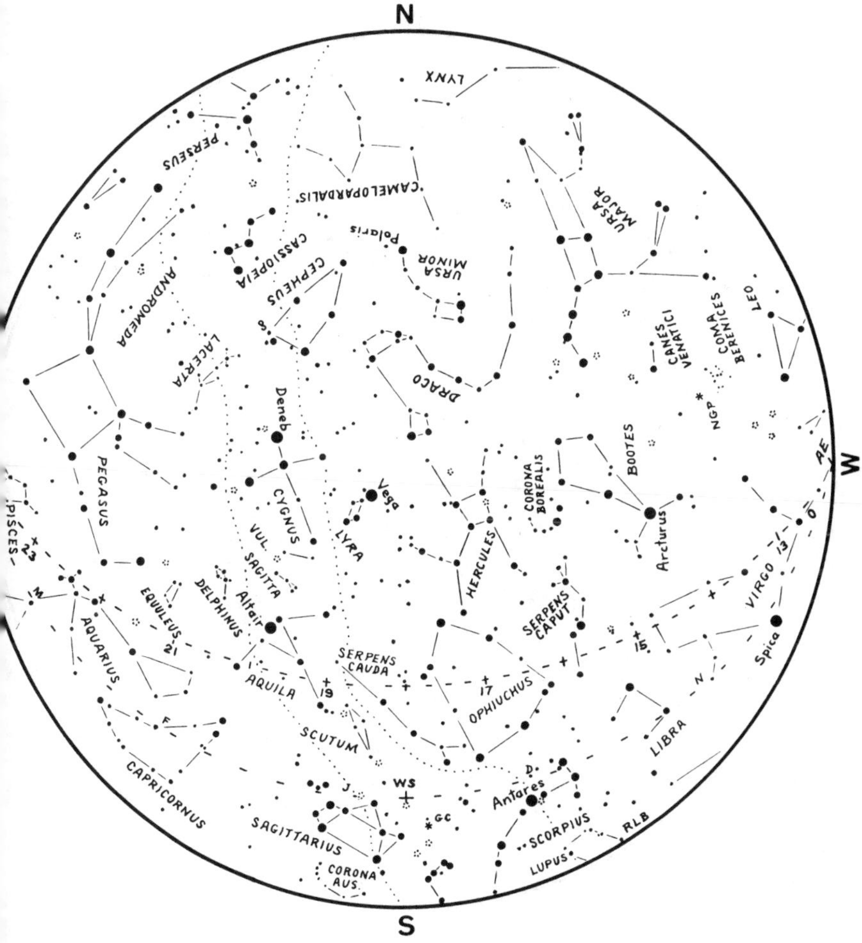

SEPTEMBER ALL-SKY MAP

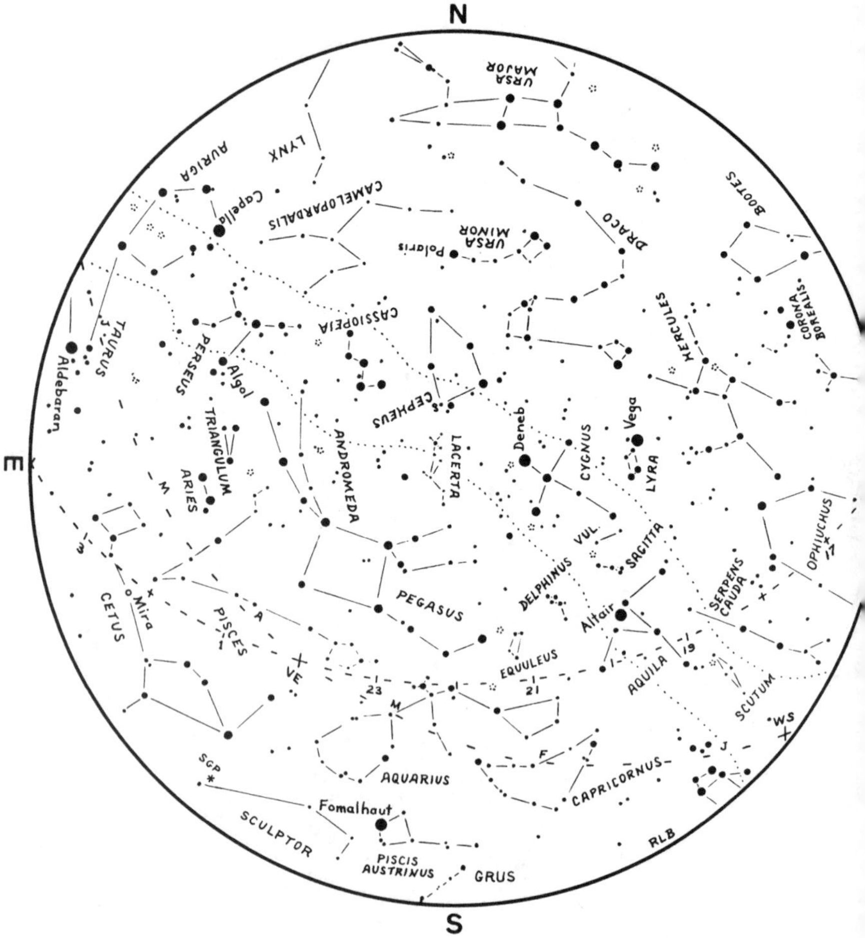

NOVEMBER ALL-SKY MAP

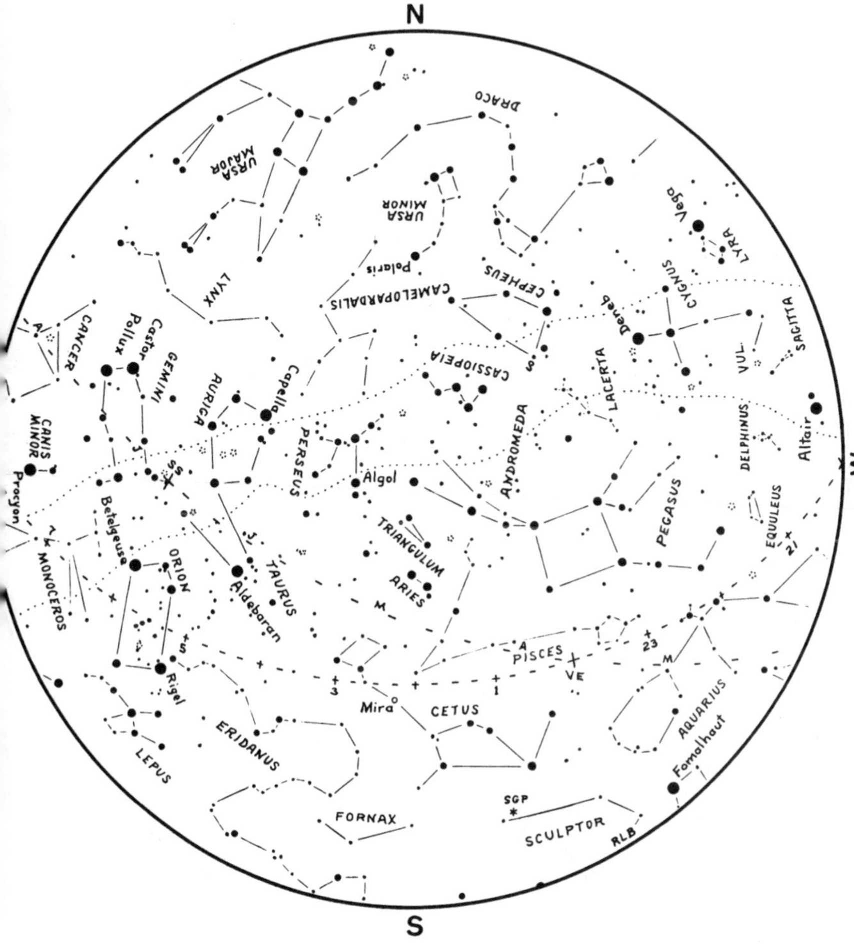

THE SOUTHERN SKY

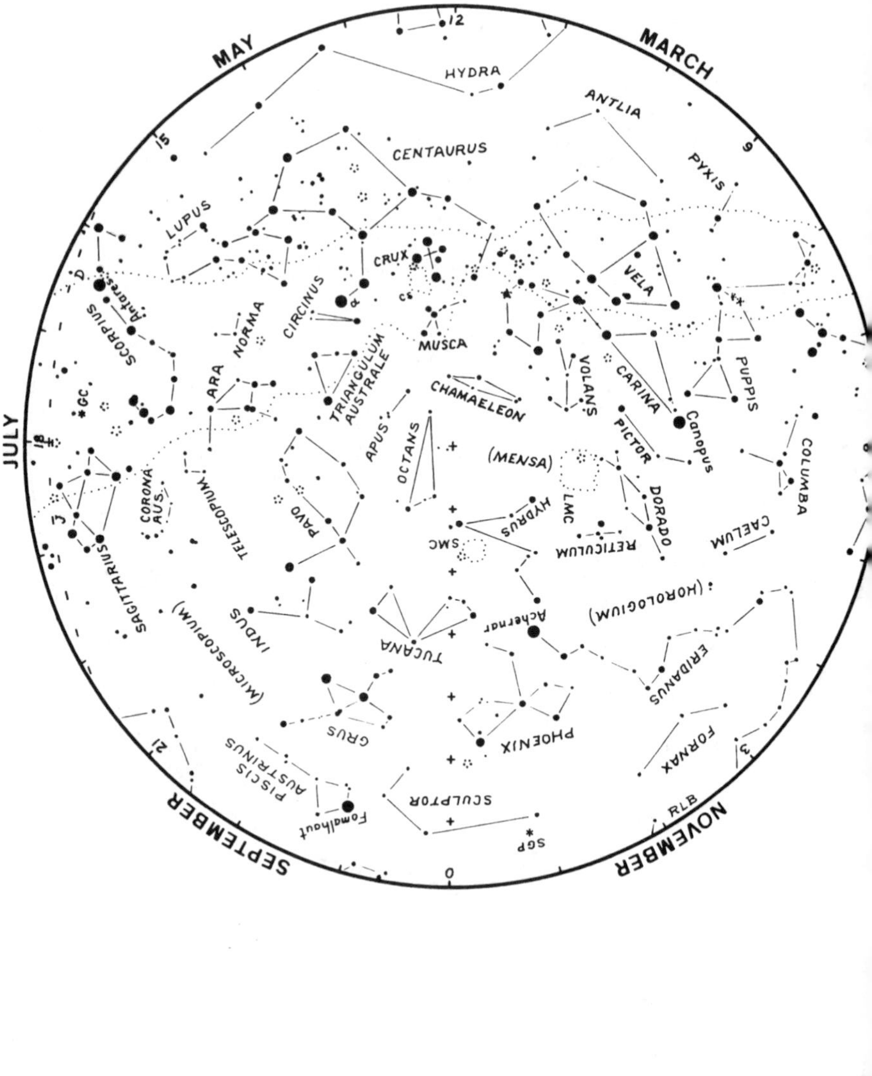

Editor's Note: A Glossary can be found online at rasc.ca/supplements.

INDEX

"MM" denotes the monthly pages of THE SKY MONTH BY MONTH starting on p. 98.

"MM" denotes the monthly pages of THE SKY MONTH BY MONTH starting on p. 98.

"MM" denotes the monthly pages of THE SKY MONTH BY MONTH starting on p. 98.

"MM" denotes the monthly pages of THE SKY MONTH BY MONTH starting on p. 98.

"MM" denotes the monthly pages of THE SKY MONTH BY MONTH starting on p. 98.

2022 HOLIDAYS AND SPECIAL DATES

New Year's Day	Sat. Jan. 1	
Martin Luther King Jr. Day (U.S.)	Mon. Jan. 17	
Winter Star Party, Florida Keys	Mon. Jan. 31	– Sun. Feb. 6
Chinese New Year (Year of the Tiger)	Tues. Feb. 1	
Washington's Birthday/Presidents' Day	Mon. Feb. 21	
Ash Wednesday (beginning of Lent)	Wed. Mar. 2	
Daylight Saving Time starts (see p. 45)	Sun. Mar. 13	
Naw-Rúz (Bahá'í New Year)*	Mon. Mar. 21	
First day of Ramadân*	Sun. Apr. 3	
Good Friday	Fri. Apr. 15	
First Day of Passover*	Sat. Apr. 16	
Easter Sunday	Sun. Apr. 17	
Earth Day	Fri. Apr. 22	
Midsouth Star Gaze, French Camp, Mississippi	Wed. Apr. 27	– Sat. Apr. 30
International Astronomy Week	Mon. May 2	– Sun. May 8
International Astronomy Day	Sat. May 7	
Memorial Day	Mon. May 30	
Cherry Springs Star Party, Harrisburg, Pennsylvania	Thu. Jun. 2	– Sun. Jun. 5
Apollo Rendezvous, Dayton, Ohio	TBA	
Golden State Star Party, Bieber, California (TBA)	TBA	
Juneteenth	Sun. Jun. 19	
RASC General Assembly, remotely	Fri. Jun. 24	– Mon. Jun. 27
Rocky Mountain Star Stare, Gardner, Colorado	Wed. Jun. 22	– Sun. Jun. 26
Green Bank Star Quest, Green Bank, West Virginia	Wed. Jun. 29	– Sat. Jul. 2
Independence Day	Mon. Jul. 4	
Oregon Star Party, Ochoco National Forest, Oregon	TBA	
Stellafane Convention, Springfield, Vermont	Thu. Jul. 28	– Sun. Jul. 31
Islamic New Year*	Sat. Jul. 30	
Labor Day (Canada and U.S.)	Mon. Sep. 5	
Rosh Hashanah (Jewish New Year)*	Mon. Sep. 26	
Illinois Dark Sky Star Party, Jim Edgar Panther Creek FWA	TBA	
Acadia Night Sky Festival, Bar Harbor, Maine	Wed. Sep. 21	– Sun. Sep. 25
Okie-Tex Star Party, Camp Billy Joe, Oklahoma	Fri. Sep. 23	– Sat. Oct. 1
Yom Kippur (Day of Atonement)*	Wed. Oct. 6	
Heart of America Star Party, Butler, Missouri	TBA	
Columbus Day	Mon. Oct. 10	
Diwali (Hindu Festival of Lights, main celebration Oct. 24)	Sat. Oct. 22	– Wed. Oct. 26
Staunton River Star Paty, Scottsburg, Virginia	Mon. Oct. 24	– Sun. Oct. 30
Halloween	Mon. Oct. 31	
Daylight Saving Time ends (see p. 45)	Sun. Nov. 6	
Veterans Day	Fri. Nov. 11	
Thanksgiving Day	Thu. Nov. 24	
Hanukkah	Mon. Dec. 19	
Christmas Day	Sun. Dec. 25	

*Begins at sunset the previous evening.

See p. 11 for websites and geographical coordinates for the listed *star parties*.